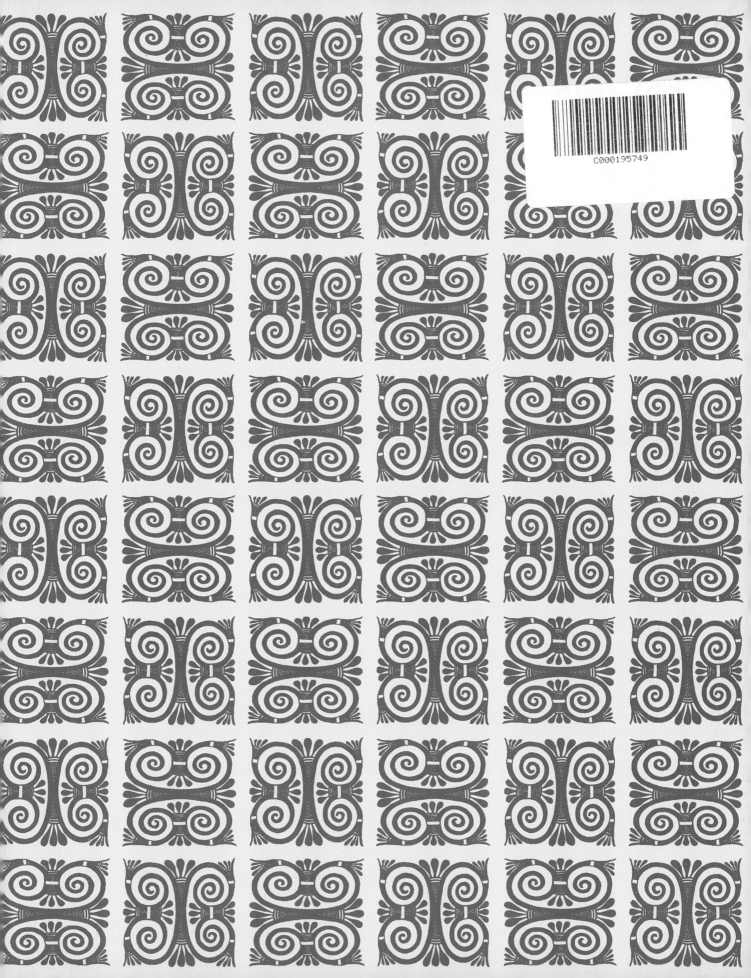

ORIGINS OF
CLASSICAL ARCHITECTURE

ORIGINS OF CLASSICAL ARCHITECTURE

TEMPLES, ORDERS AND GIFTS TO THE GODS
IN ANCIENT GREECE

MARK WILSON JONES

Mark Wilson Jones

YALE UNIVERSITY PRESS

NEW HAVEN AND LONDON

Designed by Gillian Malpass

Printed in China

Library of Congress Cataloging-in-Publication Data

Wilson Jones, Mark, 1956–
Origins of classical architecture : temples, orders and gifts to the gods in ancient Greece /
Mark Wilson Jones.
pages cm
Includes bibliographical references and index.
ISBN 978-0-300-18276-7 (cl : alk. paper)
1. Temples–Greece. 2. Architecture–Orders. 3. Symbolism in architecture–Greece. 4. Architecture and religion. I. Title.
NA275.W55 2013
720.938–dc23
2013017319

ENDPAPERS   Pattern of volute motifs (cf. Fig. 7.6).

PAGE i   Themis delivers a prophecy from her seat on the Delphic tripod to Aigeus, king of Athens.
Red-figure cup, Antikensammlung, Berlin (inv. 538).

PAGE ii   So-called temple of Concord, Agrigento, detail.

PAGES iv–v   Sanctuary of Asklepios at Epidauros, as reconstructed by Alphonse Defrasse,
detail of *envoi* of 1891–3, watercolour on Chinese ink base.

PAGE viii   Second temple of Hera (popularly known as the temple of Poseidon), Paestum, interior.

To my origins, my parents

In memory of Julia

CONTENTS

PREFACE

I make no apology for tackling the most intriguing field of research imaginable, to my mind: the question of how architectural form is created, specifically at that momentous time in ancient Greece that moulded the face of western civilization. But this choice of subject brings challenges – for the reader, too – on account of its complexity, its slipperiness and its significance.

FACING PAGE   Treasury of the Siphnians (formerly attributed to the Knidians), sanctuary of Apollo, Delphi, front elevation as reconstructed by Albert Tournaire. *Envoi* of 1894. Tournaire was one of the prize-winning French architects who were rewarded at the end of their Beaux-Arts training with a mission in Greece.

ABOVE   Louis Kahn, study of the temple of Apollo, Corinth, at sunset, 1951, 275 × 260 mm, pastel and charcoal on paper.

The issue of complexity stems from the multi-faceted nature of architecture. Its functional aspects make it more involved than products of the fine arts, just as its cultural premises make it more so than products of industry. The classical way of building is particularly rich and polyvalent, spanning as it does two millennia of contrasting historical conditions. Part of this richness consists of a certain quotient of contradiction and paradox that eludes simplicity of explication.

The origins of things are inherently elusive. As the novelist Ian McEwan remarks, there is no such thing as a beginning, for 'there are always antecedent causes'.[1] And for the formative period of Greek architecture, a time of transition from perishable to permanent materials, the evidence is often missing. Even where it

Stoa of Attalos II (ruler of Pergamon 159-138), Athens, created in the 1950s as a replica of the original. See also Fig. 3.11.

does survive it can be as fragile as text on a parchment so badly burnt as to crumble on contact.

The vacuum of evidence has sucked in conjecture and theory, along with their frequent companion, polemical bias. Further pressure comes from the allure of origins (witness continuing fascination with the origins of life), and the conviction that the first manifestations of phenomena hold special lessons for the here and now. Virtually every major architectural authority from 1750 to 1950 defended tenacious views on the genesis of the Greek temple and the Doric, Ionic and Corinthian orders. Besides objective facts, any fresh account has therefore to negotiate stances and theories that condition interpretation.

Our prime ancient source on architecture, Vitruvius's treatise, begins with the relation between theory and practice. Too dominant a concern for theory, he noted, leads to chasing after shadows and not reality. Yet he also seems to have understood a truth that Darwin expressed, namely that 'without speculation there can be no good and original observation'.[2] We need conceptual armatures so as to filter and use information. I seek to balance conjecture and evidence, aspiring too to keep an eye on the wider panorama of classical architecture and its general principles while paying due attention to the archaeological details that make up that picture. As with theory and practice each polarity seems incomplete, even pointless, without its complement.

Contrary to the popular view that the orders translate into stone habits of wooden construction shaped by lengthy evolution, formative developments were relatively sudden. They reflect particular historical circumstances along with the operation of choice, invention and happenstance. My own route into this field was, as it happens, entirely fortuitous. While aware of difficulties surrounding previous explanations, I had no inclination to pursue the subject until chancing to notice correspondences between the classical architectural vocabulary and forms encountered in other realms of material culture. Did one sphere contaminate the other? And if so, in which direction? The fact that the orders were first used for temples demanded reflection on the nature of these structures and their environment. Research led in unforeseen directions, and eventually to an appreciation of the consequences flowing from the Greeks' conception of temples as not just houses of the gods but also offerings to them. This affected size and cost as well as the dressing of temples with apposite columns and ornaments. As we shall see, classical architecture is cut from the same cloth as the art-offerings that populated sacred sanctuaries along with altars and temples. Despite copious speculation and scholarship, embracing repeatedly the tiniest details of the orders, this fundamental point had somehow got lost from view.

This book emerges out of a wish to develop these and other insights and so re-balance our understanding of

Greek architecture. The first duty of research is to carry the argument to specialists in relevant fields – archaeology, ancient history, classics, history of art and, to some extent, architecture. This last qualification reflects the architectural establishment's intent to spite itself by cutting off its roots in history, as if out of amnesia might spring a brave new environment. The column – above all the classical – has long been accorded a special, archetypal status, and it is this that explains the particular ardour with which it was repudiated in the twentieth century. Thus – despite an interest in antiquity that would lead to his famous decipherment of the Mycenaean script known as Linear B – the young architect Michael Ventris could declare in the wake of the apocalyptic war against the Nazis: 'The enemy has always been the classical . . . The columned building, antiquarian or monumental, insults its surroundings by its timeless irrelevance.'[3] Yet even while navigating away from the classical many a modern project still thrills to its siren call; Mies van der Rohe's experiments with a steel 'order' come to mind, as does the house Ludwig Wittgenstein helped design for his sister in Vienna, where there is a capital even in its negation (**Fig., this page**). Nor was Louis Kahn alone in paying homage to Doric temples in his travel sketches (**Fig., p. xi**). The mesmerizing abstraction of a Doric colonnade can, after all, look historic and modern at the same time (**Fig., facing page**).

As an architect with a foot in the discipline at large I value the design wisdom distilled in ancient archetypes. In symbolizing care and effort the Greeks' temples and orders offer perennial models of civilized building. Offering is not only an ancient concept; it has an almost universal anthropological basis.[4] Any work of art is in some sense a gift.[5] And it is no accident that we speak of a work of art, implicitly acknowledging the effort. Here is an ethical principle that John Ruskin celebrated as the 'lamp of sacrifice' glowing in medieval craftsmanship.[6] Ruskin portrayed this as a Christian sensibility, in antagonism to the pagan classical. But his prejudice blinded him to a vein of devotion running further back in time, just as it can run forward. Edwin Lutyens, one of the last great exponents of classical practice, hints at this in musing on his own experience of the Doric order:

Wittgenstein House, Vienna (1925–8), detail. The building was the result of a collaboration between Paul Engelmann and Ludwig Wittgenstein, commissioned by the latter's sister.

To be right you have to take and design it . . . You cannot copy: you find if you do you are caught, a mess remains. It means hard labour, hard thinking over every line in all three dimensions and in every joint; and no stone can be allowed to slide. If you tackle it in this way, the order belongs to you, and every stroke being mentally handled, must become endowed with such poetry and artistry as God has given you . . .[7]

Here is a disposition transcending limits of time and place and society. 'For art', the poet-rocker Patti Smith asserts – in line with Greek sentiment, Ruskin and Lutyens – 'sings of God, and ultimately belongs to him'.[9] It is not so much a question of religiosity that is at stake as a way of connecting production to higher things. And might an understanding of how care informs visual delight show us a way around present day ideological obstacles to beauty? Dedication has an ancient lineage and contemporary resonance, applicable to any fruit of human endeavour which aspires to transcend the contingent. The spirit of the gift may live in both the Parthenon and a minimalist shadow gap, or in any controlled union of precision with art.

The default format for a study such as this would be chronological–typological (proceeding by turn with the Doric temple and its components, then likewise for Ionic and Corinthian). This can bring advantages, and so has been adopted for sub-sections of the text. Yet it is not supple enough to handle wider considerations. A thematic structure promises greater traction, though raising the question of which themes to prioritize. As when the unity of daylight refracts into colours, so the orders may be seen through lenses of different tints. Construction, influence, appearance and meaning, being the recurrent concerns, each take its own chapters, ones loosely tied to the four main Greek column types: Doric, Aeolic, Ionic and Corinthian. There is also the conception of temples to be considered, their function, and their physical, social and religious setting. This and the cross-over between temple-offerings and art-offerings gives rise to further chapters, perforce adding further complexity to this project.

Adopting a thematic approach means that individual chapters have a partial or provisional character, just as a 'who done it?' detective story takes different suspects by turn. Not until the end of the book will the reader perceive the compound nature of the phenomena studied under the white light of the interpretative colours fused. It emerges that the amenability of classical architecture to contrasting readings is more than the product of centuries of use and speculation – this amenability was there right from the outset. The real task is neither to solve a puzzle, nor to choose between opposing positions, but rather to grasp the extent of simultaneous validity. Yet there is a simplicity about Greek architecture that belies all its layers and facets, a simplicity which invites a synthetic view in the final chapter (Ch. 10).

* * *

As is often the way, completion of this book was envisaged long ago. Despite today's target-driven climate, I regret none of the time spent changing emphasis, switching chapters and sections, selecting and de-selecting material and associated illustrations, manipulating notes and the seemingly endless rewriting and editing; all this is simply the price to be paid for the privilege of working on such a magnificently entangled topic. Where apology is needed, it is to family, friends and colleagues who have endured the prolongation of obsession. It proved impossible to take up some enticing projects (here Lisa Fentress's enthusiasm-with-forbearance comes especially to mind). Most of all I lament not finishing this project in time to show the book to my sister, Julia, before she died. Wise perhaps beyond her years, my teenage daughter, Georgia, ceased to inquire about progress at all.

Yet a lengthy gestation brings bonuses. Had this book been finished earlier it would not have been able to refer to an exceptional wooden base found at Olympia (thanks to a previously unnoticed article that Georg Herdt spotted). Nor would it have included Ditte Zink Kaasgaard Falb's confirmation of the relevance of Syrian temple plans, nor Manolis Korres's parallel between a libation bowl (*phiale*) and a Doric capital that added to the other examples I cherished, nor a newly unearthed early architectural model published by Anastasia Gadolou, nor news of ongoing excavations at Kalapodi supplied by Nils Hellner, nor certain insights of Clemente Marconi. The photographs of Maxim Atayants would not have graced these pages, nor reflections on the dynamics of art creativity by Sarah Walker.

ACNOWLEDGEMENTS

This book would be but a shadow of itself without diverse kinds of contribution and support. I owe an immense debt to institutions and individuals, so numerous and various that I fear the following tally must be incomplete.

In particular I express thanks and appreciation

– to those who have given invaluable comments and feedback on the text, be it single chapters, provisional drafts or more advanced versions: Judith Barringer, Antonio Corso, Ditte Zink Kaasgaard Falb, Caroline Goodson, Nils Hellner, Manolis Korres, Erik Østby, Paul Richens, Joseph Rykwert, David Scahill, Sarah Walker and Mantha Zarmakoupi, along with Robin Osborne and Clemente Marconi who in reviewing the project for publication improved it significantly;

– to funding bodies without the help of which this project could not have flourished: the British Academy, for supporting field trips relating to component aspects; the Graham Foundation, for sustaining early stages of development; the Arts and Humanities Research Council (AHRC, UK), for funding both a major grant enabling me to research the Ionic capital and a period of leave enabling me to concentrate on writing; the Canadian Centre for Architecture (CCA) in Montreal, for hosting a fellowship relating to modern reception of the subject, where Phyllis Lambert and Alexis Sornin made my stay both congenial and fruitful;

– to the foreign academies in Athens and Rome where I conducted indispensable research: the branches of the Deutschen Archäologischen Instituts in both cities; the American School of Classical Studies in Athens; the École française d'Athènes and the director of excavations on Delos, Jean-Charles Moretti, for hospitality there; the British School at Rome and the director, Christopher Smith; above all, the British School at Athens – fundamental as my base in Greece on repeated occasions – where I am most grateful to the director, Catherine Morgan, to Robert Pitt, to the librarians Penny Wilson and Sandra Pepelasis, as to Helen Clark and Vicky Tzavara for help with permits and administrative matters;

– to the Hellenic Ministry of Culture and Sports for permission to study material on archaeological sites and in museums, and in particular the 1st, 7th, 10th and 21st Ephorates of Prehistoric and Classical Antiquities as regards, respectively, Athens (1st Ephorate), Olympia (7th Ephorate), Delphi (10th Ephorate), and Delos, Paros and Naxos (21st Ephorate), along with the General Directorate of Antiquities for the National Archaeological Museum in Athens, where I have been kindly helped by Maria Salta and Anastasia Gadolou;

– to the libraries and staff of the Institute of Classical Studies in London, and to the British Museum, where I was made welcome by Ian Jenkins, Leslie Kurke and Susan Walker;

– to those who have assisted with research: Ida Leggio (during initial stages in Rome), Matthew Williams, Lian Chang (at the CCA), besides Georg Herdt, David Scahill and Mantha Zarmakoupi, each of whom went on to share the results of their own work as fellow researchers on a equal footing, while over the years from his vantage point at the American School in Athens David kept me up to speed with emerging developments social and scholarly, accompanying me on memorable expeditions;

– to all those who have created illustrations used here (see the list of credits), especially Georg Herdt and Maxim Atayants for their drawings and photographs respectively, many of which were created for this purpose;

– to experts in the field in Cyprus, Greece, Italy and Turkey, be these their own countries or their base at one time or another, for sharing their work, their understanding of texts and monuments, and their local knowledge: Meral Akurgal, Barbara Barletta, Antonio Corso, Nils Hellner, Manolis Korres, Dieter Mertens, Demetrios Michaelides, Margaret Miles, Elena Partida, Chris Pfaff, Philip Sapirstein, Tasos Tanoulas, Bonna Wescoat, Charles K. Williams and Nancy Winter;

– to scholars of antiquity with whom I have discussed related material, be it briefly or as part of a more extensive dialogue: Mary Beard, Malcolm Bell, Nancy Bookidis, Pieter Broucke, Amanda Claridge, Jim Coulton, Penelope Davies, Michael Djordjevitch (whose enthusiasm for my very first ideas encouraged me to go on to do more), Richard Ekonomakis, Gunnel Ekroth, Robert Hahn, Erik Hansen, Bruce Hitchner, Marie-Christine Hellmann, Thomas Howe, Jeffrey Hurwit, Jesper Jensen, Dorothy King, Ann Kuttner, Kenneth Lapatin, Eugenio La Rocca, Indra McEwen, Ian Morris, Sarah Morris, John Onians, Jim Packer, Jari Pakkanen, Nassos Papalexandrou, Jo Quinn, Brian Rose, Ingrid Rowland, Peter Schultz, Phoebe Segal, Andy Stewart and Gene Waddell, not forgetting some who are no longer with us, especially Gottfried Gruben;

– to friends and colleagues with whom I have enjoyed discussing ramifications for later theory and practice: Andrew Ballantyne, Howard Burns, Carmine Carapella, Joseph Connors, Maarten Delbeke, Caroline van Eck, Jutta Goetzmann, David Mayernik, Eric Parry, Demetri Porphyrios, Frank Salmon, Robert Tavernor, Marvin Trachtenberg, Bill Westfall, David Watkin;

– to those who have helpfully answered requests for information or have supplied me with information, leads, publications or drawings: Anton Bammer, Chrysanthos Kanellopoulos, Ulrike Muss, Werner Oechslin, Aenne Ohnesorg, Matthew Reeve, Robin Rhodes, Joseph Rykwert (who graciously gave me both advice and a trove of bibliography), Thomas Thieme and Carolyn Yerkes.

– to colleagues at the Department of Architecture and Civil Engineering at the University of Bath: Harry Charrington, Vaughan Hart, Fabrizio Nevola, Terry Robson, and especially Paul Richens, patient collaborator on the AHRC funded project and resourceful travel companion along with Paul Shepherd;

– to the impeccable London office of Yale University Press, to Gillian Malpass for being once again a model editor, indefatigable, involved right from the start and right to the end, to Hannah Jenner and to Eric Cambridge for copy-editing;

– and finally to my parents, to Donatella and to Georgia - long-suffering all!

This device of listing individuals by category for the sake of brevity is a blunt one, incapable of rendering the depth of debt owed to some. Special mention is owing to Georg Herdt for a role that has gone far beyond that of research assistant; without his unstinting efforts this book would be the weaker in terms of both form and content. Above all I am deeply grateful to Manolis Korres, my mentor and point of reference in Greece, ancient and modern.

NOTE TO THE READER

The default for dates cited is BC, save for those relating to commentary from the time of the Renaissance, when the period (AD) is implicit from the context. When ancient dates are AD this is specified. Overly precise periodizations (and possible regional variations) are avoided in favour of the following notional scheme (BC):

1700–1200	mid Bronze Age
1200–1000	late Bronze Age
1000–700	Geometric period
700–600	so-called Orientalizing period
700–c.490	Archaic period (down to the Persian wars)
490–c.323	Classical period (down to the death of Alexander the Great)
323–31	Hellenistic period (down to the Romans' complete control of the Mediterranean).

'Classical' with an upper-case 'C' refers to the period; 'classical' with a lower-case 'c' refers to the architectural tradition down to modern times.

Few of the standpoints expressed in this book hang on the finer points of dating, but attention to chronology is a necessary part of the enterprise. The dating of Greek architecture prior to the Classical period is less precise than is generally conveyed by phrases such as 'c.600', or 'around 575'. It is seldom possible to relate buildings to known historical events, and their dates are typically gauged on the basis of the style of any associated inscriptions or artworks (terracottas, statuary). But chronology in these areas is rarely as certain as is sometimes assumed. Even less reliable is the relative dating of architectural elements by means of proportional and stylistic comparison. Notwithstanding these observations, I provide guide dates as an aid for the reader in the tables that accompany some chapters, putting entries in the chronological sequence that seems to me the most likely in the light of current knowledge. These tables also serve as convenient places to collect bibliographical references for individual buildings.

Extensive as it is, the works cited in the bibliography remain but a selection from the complete spectrum. I have prioritized formative publications (often from the nineteenth century or earlier) and recent scholarship, especially where this provides a gateway to publications that have been omitted. As a courtesy to the non-specialist, the titles of publications in Greek have been rendered into English.

Scholarly works on ancient Greek material, even those with a linguistic or textual focus, frequently confess to 'the usual inconsistencies' in the deployment of Greek names and terms. In juggling correct usage on the one hand and convention on the other, I tend towards the latter where non-specialists might otherwise be thrown off piste. Thus Aigina and akroterion are preferable to Aegina and acroterion, but acropolis and Corinth are retained instead of akropolis and Korinthos. Where it seems helpful, Greek names are added in parentheses, e.g., when initially mentioning Paestum (Poseidonia), and more generally in captions to illustrations.

INTRODUCTION

The Greek temple and its orders set in train the architectural culture of the western world. The temple is the ultimate built statement of authority and of mystery beyond common experience. Though created for temples, the classical orders with their columns and ornaments went on to dress a spectrum of building types and so civilization itself. The orders are families of forms and yet so much more, implying as they do conditions of relationship, proportion, character and association. Yet rather than constraining creativity they possess an almost alchemical capacity to bring forth ideas and sensations out of materials won from the earth.

After successive renaissances and revivals the classical tradition finally foundered in the twentieth century. And yet the romance lingers: architects continue to find inspiration in its 'language' or individual achievements, while many underlying premises, despite appearances to the contrary, remain embedded in modern design

0.1 (FACING PAGE)   The Circus, Bath, by John Wood the Elder, completed by his son, John Wood the Younger (1754–68). A display of the three orders, Doric, Ionic and Corinthian, adapted to a residential context quite different to that for which they were originally created in ancient Greece.

0.2 (ABOVE)   Raphael and Gianfrancesco Penni, *Adoration of the Shepherds* (c.1515). The image presents also an abbreviated history of classical architecture, starting with the humble Biblical shelter, developing as a wooden 'proto-Doric' Greek structure, and culminating in a vaulted Roman monument with Corinthian half-columns.

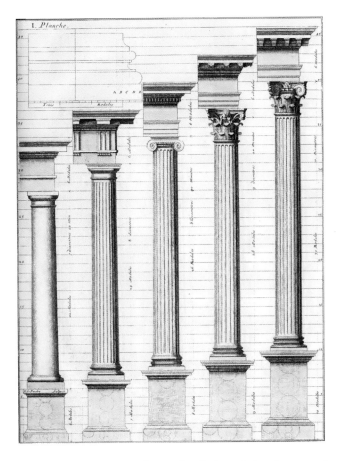

0.3   The five orders according to Claude Perrault (1683), arranged according to slenderness and elaboration; from left to right: Tuscan, Doric, Ionic, Corinthian and Composite.

principles.[1] There are also reasons to believe that the conceptual and technological advances associated with monumental temples influenced the development of early Greek philosophy, so without them European thought might have taken a different trajectory.[2]

Any simple definition of the Greek temple is problematic. A house of the god is as good a shorthand as any, but a temple could also accommodate multiple functions, some of which were as much social as religious, as we shall see in Chapter 1. Meanwhile the classical orders may be dryly defined as modes of construction based on distinct types of columns (the supports) and entablatures (the supported). The very term 'order' requires contextualization, however, being a

legacy of the Renaissance. A translation from the Italian *ordine*, this carries intimations of system and discipline that were absent from ancient practice, which embraced a range of playful hybrids sometimes called 'mixed orders'.[3] The sense of system is absent too from the lexicon of the Roman author-architect Vitruvius, and there is a looser quality about his usual choice of word, *genus*, or 'family'.[4] While I shall use *genus* and alternatives, such as 'mode' or 'style', the term 'order' is far too entrenched to be banished. (At the risk of grammatical indiscretion, the problem can also be sidestepped by making nouns out of the adjectives Doric, Ionic and so on.)

The conventional scheme of the five orders – Tuscan, Doric, Ionic, Corinthian and Composite – treats them as if of equivalent status on a sliding scale of slenderness and sophistication (**Fig. 0.3**). Another Renaissance contrivance, this misleadingly levels out extensive contrasts in their individual histories, while ignoring rival solutions such as the so-called Aeolic capital. Of the canonic five, Doric and Ionic were the earliest, with some of their elements appearing in stone at the end of the seventh century. In the fifth century arose Corinthian, limited at first to capitals inserted into otherwise Ionic-looking ensembles; it took until Roman times to earn its own entablature and to match its seniors in popularity, indeed to eclipse them. The capital we know as Composite was just an alternative for Corinthian that the Romans used, one swiftly dismissed by Vitruvius (IV,1.12) without being named.[5] He did mention Tuscan, but likewise its entablature knew no canon.[6] For these reasons Tuscan and Composite remain beyond the scope of this book.

Greek temple architecture, then, was – allowing for the inevitable exceptions – fundamentally a Doric and Ionic affair. After some experimentation the familiar patterns were established that would be refined to magnificent effect in the Parthenon, the Erechtheion and other landmarks of fifth-century Athens (**Figs 0.9, 1.3, 1.22, 9.1**). These same families of forms became employed for structures in sacred sanctuaries other than temples (free-standing columns, stoai, treasuries, gateways), then civic monuments, and on to the domestic realm. So the inquiring mind naturally wonders how Doric and Ionic came to be, and other questions besides. What made these two *genera* so very essential? What did they represent for the Greeks?

* * *

The quest to resolve such questions is hardly new – as a vast literature testifies. The origin of building lore figured in Vitruvius's treatise, the sole work of its kind to survive from antiquity and one that, despite being written in the final decades of the first century BC, provides glimpses of Hellenic ideas.[7] A wide range of Vitruvian notions were revisited in the Renaissance, though issues of origins were not at first accorded the importance they later acquired. For architects who had decided to shun medieval practice and revive classical models, the first question was *how* to use the orders, how to shape and distribute them. The question of *why* they were originally deployed received less attention; it was enough to be ancient to be right. The conditions for a more sustained debate followed the crisis of confidence in classical architecture that surfaced in the late seventeenth century, a crisis precipitated among other things by ideas about the subjective and 'arbitrary' dimension of its conventions, and its dependence on custom and taste.[8] While eighteenth-century engineers turned to calculation and functionality as the basis for design, architects working in the classical tradition now felt the burden of justifying it – otherwise the door would open to other styles (Gothic or Chinoiserie for example).[9] Legitimization was sought, and found, in origins. This made the topic a mandatory ingredient of architectural theory, while further pressure came from prevailing intellectual trends. As interest in the development of both the natural world and civilization intensified, the origins of law, art and science all came under scrutiny.[10]

From the middle of the eighteenth century onwards, origins preoccupied virtually every major architectural thinker, including Abbé Laugier, Carlo Lodoli and Quatremère de Quincy.[11] Laugier looked to cleanse architectural practice of illogical excesses by appealing

0.4 Charles-Dominique-Joseph Eisen, personification of Architecture in front of a 'primitive hut' formed from standing trees, frontispiece to the second edition (1755) of Laugier's *Essai*.

to the virtues of the Greek temple, these being underwritten in his eyes by the lessons inherent in the 'primitive hut' (**Fig. 0.4**). Speculations about primordial ways of building also took the form of projects or imaginary reconstructions, for example ones by William Chambers and John Soane (**Fig. 0.5**). The 'rediscovery' of Greece added further impetus. Though expeditions by intrepid western Europeans had taken place earlier, it was not until the publication of *Les Ruines des plus beaux Monuments de la Grèce* by Julien-David Le Roy (1758), along with the *Antiquities of Athens* by James Stuart and Nicholas Revett (1762–94), that the ruins of Greece could be studied with the aid of accurate drawings.[12] Attention then turned to Greek temples that could be

0.5 John Soane, perspective study for a dairy in imagined proto-Doric style at Hemel's Park. Soane Museum, London (inv. 13/7/10).

failed to dull the lustre of this architectural holy grail. Perhaps unexpectedly, debate reanimated in the late 1980s, since when five books in English have explored related fields of inquiry: John Onians's *Bearers of Meaning*, George Hersey's *Lost Meaning of Classical Architecture*, Indra McEwen's *Socrates' Ancestor*, Joseph Rykwert's *The Dancing Column* and Barbara Barletta's *The Origins of the Greek Architectural Orders*.[17] Discussion has also picked up in specialist literature,[18] as well as in synthetic works on Greek art or architecture.[19] There is, then, hardly a scholarly lacuna to fill – so why another book? The point is that in spite of such copious endeavour vital questions remain questions still; a satisfying account of the Greek temple and the *genera* represents a dual challenge that is yet to be met.

* * *

My own interest was triggered by correspondences between architecture and other branches of Hellenic design culture, correspondences usually passed over in silence. These present themselves in various ways, from the use of devices such as volutes to dramatic increases in size and cost affecting both statues and temples. Intuition suggests that an underlying connection lies in the domain of offering, a fundamental religious and social phenomenon. After all, most of the Greek artworks in today's museums were originally offerings that populated sacred sanctuaries along with the temples that themselves were offerings too. Did this affect the columns and ornaments that clothed them?

visited on Italian soil, most notably those at Paestum (**Fig., p. viii, Figs 3.1, 3.31**).[13] Travel to Egypt and the eastern Mediterranean together with nationalist sentiment in northern Europe fuelled the 'Battle of the Styles', which in turn stoked historical controversies. Nineteenth-century treatments of the rise of ancient architecture include Soane's didactic output and the writings of Heinrich Hübsch, Carl Bötticher, Gottfried Semper, Eugène Emmanuel Viollet-le-Duc, Charles Chipiez and Auguste Choisy. Figures such as Ruskin would intervene to score a polemical point or two, and even a philosopher like Hegel got drawn into the argument (Ch. 3, pp. 65–6).[14]

As archaeology blossomed in the decades before and after 1900 the study of ancient built culture shifted away from architects to become increasingly the province of specialists of antiquity.[15] Despite a certain loss of design insight, fresh discoveries and improvements in investigative methodologies went on to produce successive advances in understanding Greek architecture, including that of its early phases.[16] Many scholars distanced themselves from speculations that could not be proved, but nevertheless new explanations for the Greek temple and its orders continued to appear, to be criticized in their turn, perpetuating an often futile turnover that yet

Specialists of Greek religion have long known the temple to be on one level an offering, so why has this connection scarcely informed architectural research? Of course, temples were primarily houses of the gods, while the design of the *genera* responded to disparate factors, whether to do with construction, influences from earlier or foreign styles, visual effect or symbolism. These are all important – as we shall see – but the problem is that debate has tended to get stuck in the tramlines associated with each of these avenues, and in their enthusiasm for neat stories of origin many commentators have taken an overly partisan tack. Everyone filters the information they gather according to subjective bias. It is inevitable. Xenophanes famously quipped that if horses could paint a picture, a god would look like a horse (and likewise for oxen, lions and so on),[20] while modern philosophical developments have sensitized opinion to this problem.[21] When faced with historical and archaeological material everyone re-models the past from a personal point of view.[22]

We may agree with Darwin that speculation has a role to play in scientific inquiry (Preface, p. xii), yet it is an effective role only when there is evidence to be tested. The greater the gaps in the evidence the greater the scope for interpretation, and our knowledge of early Greek architecture is notoriously lacunose. The perishable materials used when Doric and Ionic developed have disappeared, so their original look is inherently hypothetical.[23] But this has not been cause to abandon the hunt for the grail – on the contrary, it has only added mystique. There is a prevalent conviction that the origins of a system are relevant for its later practice. A case in point is Jacques-Ignaz Hittorff's espousal in the nineteenth century of the – then radical – idea that Greek temples were coloured. One of the main players in publicizing discoveries which transformed learned perceptions of ancient architecture, he evidently felt it necessary to buttress the use of colour in his own projects by contending that this went back to when Greek temples were made of wood, though there is no evidence one way or the other.[24] The past intersects with the present and even the future in such thinking, which has its mirror in other creative pursuits. Writing of music Arnold Schönberg declared, 'One of the most noble tasks of theory is to reawaken love for the past, and at the same time to look to the future: in this way it [theory] can be historical, establishing links between that which has been, that which is, and that which presumably will be.'[25] Given this sense of mission, it is understandable that what evidence there is has been deployed selectively and that past explanations for the orders often depend on the agenda, covert or overt, of their authors.[26]

Doric has been particularly contested. The prominent frieze and its rhythmical run of triglyphs has been a frequent subject of debate; indeed the origin of the Doric frieze arguably represents architecture's oldest unsolved puzzle. It is hardly surprising that architects have favoured constructional explanations, given the solid, heavy and forceful character of many a Doric temple (**Figs 1.1, 1.24, 3.19, 3.31, 9.1**). In this they also follow both professional inclination and their 'father' Vitruvius. His account of a timber system in which the triglyphs masked the ends of beams has inspired all manner of 'proto-Doric' hypotheses down the centuries (**Figs 0.2, 3.2, 3.3**). Their popularity is further sustained by three enduring convictions: first, the applicability of evolutionary models of progress; second, the inherent 'honesty' of the primitive mind; third, the rational basis of Greek design (Ch. 3). These themes monopolized architectural discourse from the time when origins came to the fore in the eighteenth century, later to be propelled by Darwin's discoveries and then by technocratic mantras.[27] Thanks to its forthright appearance Doric has been held to epitomize such concerns, and the formation of this 'order of orders' was held to go right to the heart of the problem of how to create visually effective form.[28] All this explains why it was the last of the orders to be abandoned by the mainstream.[29]

By contrast archaeologists, classicists and art historians often find themselves bemused or impatient with what can seem to be an overplayed obsession. It was hardly necessary for the Greeks of the eighth to the sixth centuries to invent everything from first principles, for they had access to ideas, technologies and ornaments from other cultures. Obelisks transported to Rome by the emperors attracted curiosity in the Baroque period, and claims began to be made for the Egyptian origin of the orders in the mid-eighteenth century.[30] Napoleon's entry into Egypt ushered in a period of 'Egyptomania', and figures like the architect Charles Barry and the scholar Jean-François Champollion started a trend to refer to certain types of Egyptian column as 'proto-Doric' (Ch. 4, p. 95).[31] Cockerell's epic vision of European architectural history sees its masterpieces rising from an Egyptian platform (**Fig. 0.10**). The possibility that the Greeks learnt from cultures other than Egypt

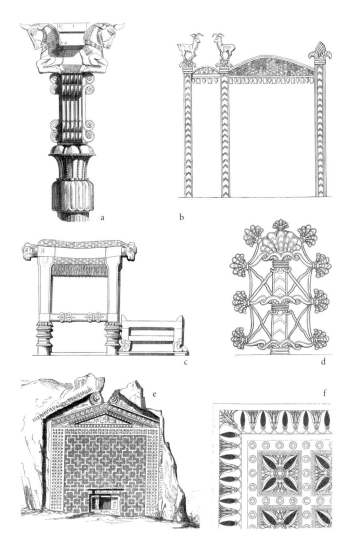

0.6 Illustrations from Gottfried Semper's *Der Stil* (1861–3). (a) Persian column capital from Persepolis; (b) Assyrian royal baldachin or pavilion as represented on a stone relief; (c) Assyrian chair and foot-stool on a stone relief; (d) Assyrian tree-of-life scheme on a stone relief; (e) So-called Midas monument, near Gordion, with relief patterns on the façade, perhaps inspired by textile designs; (f) Assyrian decorative scheme on a stone relief, inspired perhaps by carpet patterns.

such excavations as those of Austen Henry Layard in Assyria, where he and others noticed what they thought were Ionic capitals (Ch. 5, p. 126). Using publications like those of Layard, Semper's researches led him to compare Greek material with that from further east (**Fig. 0.6**). As for precursors on Greek soil, the occasional ruin such as the 'Treasury of Atreus' had already in antiquity been connected with a past age of heroes,[33] though it took Heinrich Schliemann's excavations at Troy and Mycenae to reveal extensive Bronze Age complexes.[34] Next it was the turn of Crete, where Sir Arthur Evans unearthed the civilization he baptized 'Minoan', with its own 'proto-Doric' columns. Interrelations between the Greeks and other cultures have been studied vigorously of late, as we shall see in Chapter 4.

Buildings are vehicles for imagery and aesthetic pleasure; the character and quality of spatial effects and visible surfaces are for most observers more significant than issues of construction or lineage. A keen observer of the phenomenon of diffusionism just mentioned, Alois Riegl, spearheaded a reaction to treating ornament as if it emanated from techniques such as woodworking or weaving. The urge for patterns had a more primal basis, he argued, the fruit of basic human impulses attested by prehistoric bone carvings and cave art, besides body painting practised in living cultures that do not use weaving (**Fig. 0.7**).[35] As for the ancient Greeks, their sensitivity to form and perfection has been a given of art appreciation ever since Roman times, and we might agree that for them 'beauty was like a sixth sense'.[36] In any event, the visual qualities of form were clearly of keen interest to ancient architects (Ch. 5).

Architecture can also be a vehicle for conveying power, with image and symbol deployed with communicative intent; this we know the Greeks to have done by the Classical period, when historical information becomes available – so why not before? Built patterns may also reflect social and religious patterns, and from such a standpoint architecture might be likened to frozen ritual (to adapt Goethe's famous dictum).[37] How, though, to interpret such patterns? Extending Villalpando and Prado's ideas, John Wood, the creator of Georgian Bath

goes back to around 1600, when the Iberian Jesuits Juan Bautista Villalpando and Jeronimo Prado speculated that the orders descended from Solomon's Temple in Jerusalem.[32] But it was not until the middle of the nineteenth century that colonial ambitions paved the way for

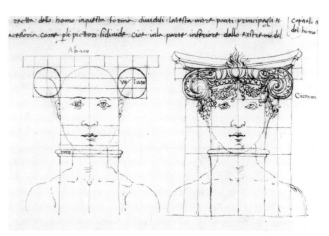

0.7   Illustrations from Alois Riegl's *Stilfragen* (1893), showing Maori face painting.

0.8   Francesco di Giorgio, anthropomorphic column studies (*c*.1490), Codex Magliabechiano, fol. 33v.

(**Fig. 0.1**), claimed a biblical authority for the orders that could be traced to the Levant, whence they descended via Solomon from Moses and ultimately God himself.[38] Another seam of architectural theory, going back to Vitruvius and beyond, likens columns to upright human bodies, while giving them gender. Evocative drawings by the likes of Francesco di Giorgio and John Shute represent just some of many such speculations (**Fig. 0.8**). Modern treatments of symbolism have a surer scholarly basis, as we shall see in Chapter 6; yet over-interpretation remains a danger.

Thus interpretations that privilege construction, influence, appearance and meaning vie for ascendancy. It is well to recall the Indian fable of the elephant and the blind (or blindfolded) men. By feeling just an ear, leg, tail, trunk or tusk, each conjures divergent visions of the same greater whole. Sadly we cannot simply materialize the Greek 'elephant', given that, at best, we know but the partially complete remains of its skeleton. Yet research that is receptive to multiple overlapping explanations has more potential to enhance our appreciation of ancient attitudes towards building.

The dearth of hard evidence from when we would need it most, that is to say the period leading up to the emergence of the orders, means that it is always easier for scholars to disprove than to prove theories of expla-

nation, rather as in political elections some people vote to keep out the parties they favour least. But understanding architecture is not like making a mark on a ballot paper. As Robert Venturi sustains, great buildings defy straightforward readings, often being poised between equally compelling different ones.[39] The dynamics of cultural phenomena cannot meaningfully be divided up along the lines of nineteenth-century thought and the tendency that Clifford Geertz identifies which would set in opposition symbolic to real, figurative to literal, aesthetic to practical, mystical to mundane, and decorative to substantial.[40] It is as with nature and nurture: there is in reality no sharp line between what, too often, are presented as opposites.[41] Artistic, religious, social and technical concerns overlap inextricably, and this is especially true of the ancient world. My own appreciation of this point is fuelled by experience as an architect, which teaches an awareness of the innumerable factors that bear on the production of buildings. Grand visions, fine details, theory, pleasure and practicalities may operate on different planes, yet they all intermesh in the designer's mind. In this arena the trivial and the profound are neither strangers nor antagonists.

An example may serve to connect the preceding observations to tangible material of the kind discussed in

0.9 Erechtheion, Athenian Acropolis; detail showing the columns of the east porch. Note the play of light and shadow that both fluting and mouldings promote.

this book. Fluting, that ubiquitous treatment for ancient column shafts of whatever denomination, epitomizes the multivalency inherent in classical form. By its crispness, fluting vaunts the exquisite precision of temple construction. There is a practical rationale too, for by their eye-catching verticality the concave channels

minimize the visual impact of any horizontal joints. Practicality also affected profiles; deeply cut Ionic fluting is characteristic of regions abundant in high quality marble (Ionia and the Cyclades), while the simpler and shallower Doric form that prevailed on mainland Greece was generally all that could be expected of lower grade indigenous stone, even where a finer appearance was obtained courtesy of a finishing coat of stucco.[42] The deep Ionic (and Corinthian) flute, often a semi-circle or nearly so, demanded a fillet simply because of the geometrical impossibility of doing without. At the same time, the Greeks of the Archaic period did not invent such responses: fluting was given to stone columns in both Bronze Age Greece and in Egypt, besides on furniture such as candelabra of eastern provenance (Ch. 4). Be this as it may, the Greeks' insistence on fluting betrays above all a deep aesthetic appreciation. It creates a play of light and shadow that helps to model columns, for a fluted shaft appears more definitely round, paradoxically, than one that is smoothly circular, as is clear when observing shafts that are part smooth, part fluted (**Fig., p. xii, Fig. 3.11**). (Where smooth shafts exist this is usually because they were not finished, as at Segesta (**Fig. 1.1**).) The progressive shadows cast by each arris give the eye geometrical proof of roundness (**Fig. 0.9**). Concave flutes are particularly effective because they capture gradations of shadow that straight facets cannot. Yet none of all this excludes investing fluting with further resonance. Some detect the legacy of trimming tree trunks with an adze. In sympathy with the gender theme, others see analogies of the kind that Vitruvius invites with the falling folds of a woman's dress (Ch. 6, p. 143). Classical form is promiscuous in its suggestive power.

In fluting, then, rival modes of explanation each make a contribution. As with any aspect of the classical tradition partial or partisan interpretations sell us short. Our preferred view does not exclude the views of others. Rigidity impoverishes. As Alvar Aalto was fond of saying in the early 1960s, 'we don't need to be so dogmatic'.[43] Perhaps the Greeks were not dogmatic either.

* * *

In various disciplines, origins have consistently been attributed fundamental importance. Émile Durkheim in effect reiterated a longstanding architects' conviction when he wrote in his seminal *Elementary Forms of Religious Life* (1912): 'Every time that we undertake to explain something human . . . – be it a religious belief, a moral precept, an aesthetic style or an economic system – it is necessary to commence by going back to its most primitive and simple form . . .'[44] Yet there are impediments in principle to so doing, as noted by McEwan (Preface, p. xi), as well as the practical limitations of history and archaeology. 'Beginnings ordinarily elude us' Jean-Pierre Vernant has remarked.[45] But in any case has everyone been going back too far? It is vain to seek the roots of the Greek temple in remote aboriginal shelters and rituals before making sense of it between the eighth and sixth centuries, the time it was effectively created. This is one of the primary aims of this book.

Some of my conclusions go against accepted wisdom on origins, an often self-satisfied wisdom deserving of irreverence. Provocation at the level of Gustave Courbet's *L'Origine du Monde* of 1866 – a slyly titled piece of pornography or eroticism at the height of Darwinian controversy – is not my intention. But we do well to guard against the seduction of grand trajectories traced from past to present, like water flowing from a mountain spring to the sea. Understanding history, says Michel Foucault, should teach us 'to laugh at the solemnities of the origin'. He invokes Friedrich Nietzsche's view of the origin as mirage, as nothing more than 'a metaphysical extension which arises from the belief that things are most precious and essential at the moment of birth'.[46] Both writers caution against projecting contemporary aspirations on the past; both promote a history that recognizes its ambiguities, its jolts, its conflicts.[47] Yet the Greeks themselves felt drawn to explain the world in terms of origins. Their myths are saturated with etiologies that root them to their land and their ancestors. There is a tension here that we cannot (and, perhaps, need not) resolve, for it dovetails, so it seems to me, with the multi-faceted nature of architectural design. If modernism has promoted functionalist principles over other concerns, which postmodernism has often trivialized, the present exploration appeals to sensibilities open to whatever complexities and surprises the study of the past happens to reveal.

⁂

So much for my approach; a final comment is needed on the nature of material invoked as evidence. Just as fluting illustrates, much can be learnt by observing surviving buildings, even if the better preserved of them all date to after the critical period for this investigation. But the need to concentrate on the period when Doric and Ionic emerged perforce directs us to excavation finds, be it architectural components, the negative imprints of vanished ones, or the mere outlines of foundations. Architectural models and representations of buildings on pottery and the like can be instructive (if approached with due caution). Given the paucity of architectural texts we cannot overlook *any* potentially relevant ancient textual testimony, whatever its date. This includes scraps of inscriptions and passages left by Greek writers such as Homer, Herodotus and Euripides, along with Vitruvius's treatise and Pausanias's 'guidebook', likewise formulated in Roman times. All such sources require interrogation, yet without artefacts to bridge the gap between theoretical and physical constructs even the most compelling thesis can falter. This study therefore gives more than usual weight to material culture outside the domain of architecture, in the light of shared attitudes that can be shown to unite the tectonic arts with the technical arts. So the reader should not be surprised to encounter such things as libation bowls, candelabra, thrones and tripods at intervals in the pages that follow.

This book does not systematically review the state of knowledge about early Greek architecture.[48] Though graphic presentation aims at consistency (many plans are shown at 1:1000), neither does it give the same weight to different aspects of temple design, nor equal coverage to each kind of column. Instead I concentrate on those subjects that seem to me to be the most illuminating, or the most requiring illumination. Since the orders need to be apprehended in the context of their parent temples, the main text starts with one chapter on their purpose and setting followed by a second on their early development. The next block of chapters takes up the recurrent modes of interpretation cited earlier. Chapter 3 concentrates on problems of construction, structure and material, and the *genus* usually portrayed in these terms, Doric. Chapter 4 turns to patterns of design that migrate across cultures, focusing on the Aeolic capital. Chapter 5 addresses the visual qualities of architectural form, and especially those of the Ionic *genus*. Chapter 6 then concludes this part by probing questions of symbolism and their manifestation in the Corinthian capital. (In reality, design is no respecter of this pairing of style and motivation, which is but a strategic device.) Chapters 7 and 8 change tack, picking up lines of argument about sanctuary environments initiated in Chapter 1 while exploring affinities between the architecture and the offerings that filled the sanctuaries. With the benefit of these new perspectives, Chapter 9 and Chapter 10 revisit the themes treated separately earlier. Different facets come together in the light of the notion that the Greeks conceived of their temples as gifts to the gods, an approach that had far-reaching consequences for the whole ethos of the classical way of building.

0.10   Charles Robert Cockerell, *The Professor's Dream* (1848), pencil, pen, grey ink and watercolour, with scratched highlights, 1122 × 1711 mm, Royal Academy, London (inv. 03/4195); detail. A graphic compendium of key monuments.

CHAPTER ONE

PURPOSE AND SETTING OF
THE GREEK TEMPLE

The orders can be properly understood only in the context of the temple, and likewise temples in the context of their religious function and physical setting. The question of function, or rather purpose (a word which speaks less narrowly of practical usage), clearly impacts on the character of buildings. Yet this has figured surprisingly little in the scholarship on Greek temples, given tendencies to divide components such as friezes, capitals, akroteria and roof tiles into sub-categories and study them in isolation with emphasis on chronology and typology.[1] The importance of setting might seem equally self-evident, and even today we can still enjoy some temples in a magical relation to the natural landscape (**Fig. 1.1**).[2] However the impression of glorious isolation is the product of loss and the demands of modern heritage management. In antiquity the surroundings of primary relevance were in fact the man-made sanctuary environments to which temples belonged.

The Greeks made contact with the divine chiefly via three overlapping activities: prayer, sacrifice and offering.[3] To some extent these could happen anywhere, according to circumstance or as the impulse arose, yet ritual and environment were strongly linked. The privileged locus for religious expression was the sacred space of a sanctuary, a place providing special access

1.1 (FACING PAGE)   Unfinished temple at Segesta, distant view (*c.* late fifth century).

1.2 (ABOVE)   Sanctuary at Metapontum, Puglia, as reconstructed in its mature state by Dieter Mertens and Margareta Schutzenberger.

to the gods. Here prayers were uttered, sacrifices made and offerings deposited, the better to attract the gods' attentions.[4]

SANCTUARIES

A sanctuary may be described as divine property created by and administered for the community.[5] As manifestations of collective will, sanctuaries became bound up with social and political developments linked to the *polis*, or city-state. In the ancient world this phenomenon was not unique to the Greeks, but what was unique were attitudes that made the *polis* also a citizen-state. Its formative phase saw the wresting of power from rulers and leaders to groups, be they just a few aristocrats or a larger body of landowning males. Later Greek historians were proud to say that the *polis* was not constituted physically, by buildings, walls and roads, but by men.[6] Such ideas set the conditions for experiments in democracy and government based on reasoned debate. The *polis* became central to life and culture, and with its strong social dimension Greek religion may be characterized as '*polis* religion'.[7] The shift of power from individuals to groups had a spatial correlate in the

transference of cult and ritual from private property to the collective sanctuary. Elected officials became responsible for aspects of ritual, although there was not the institutional hold over doctrine typical of later religions.[8] The *ethnos*, a federation of settlements with no distinct capital, was another kind of political structure connected with sanctuaries. That of Apollo at Thermon, for example, constituted the political as well as the sacred heart of the *ethnos* of Aetolia.[9] Tyrannies were another feature of the political landscape that put no lesser emphasis on sacred sites.[10] In all these political configurations the sanctuary was fundamental to defining group identity.

After the breakdown of Bronze Age society, sanctuaries grew from modest beginnings to acquire greater physical presence, especially from the mid-eighth century (Ch. 2).[11] They came in varying shapes and sizes and types of location. Allowing for inevitable exceptions, distinctions can be discerned between urban, rural and 'extra-urban' sanctuaries.[12] Urban sanctuaries served centres of population; they might occupy the social and commercial heart of the city – the *agora* – or a citadel stronghold – the *acropolis* (**Fig. 1.3**). By contrast, rural sanctuaries lay in out-of-the-way spots. These might be architecturally undeveloped, although this did not stop them enjoying an 'international' reputation, as in the case of Dodona. The four-yearly festivals at the great panhellenic sanctuaries of Olympia and Delphi were the prime occasions for the entire Hellenic world to come together, with different states competing not in war but in athletics and in the donation of art and buildings (**Figs 1.4, 10.1**).[13] Extra-urban sanctuaries were usually tied to a single *polis* and yet located in the countryside, perhaps where territorial limits intersected a major route. Hera's Argive sanctuary lay in just such a situation across the plain from the city of Argos (**Fig. 1.5**). Another example is the same goddess's sanctuary on the island of Samos, four or so miles from the city (**Fig. 1.11**).[14]

The ascendancy of sanctuaries is significant for the infancy of Greek architecture, when they constituted the main locus for building operations apart from fortifica-

1.3   Athenian acropolis; distant view from the north-west, as reconstructed by Manolis Korres.

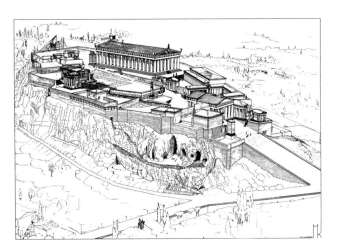

tions.[15] Much as temples were to become conspicuous they were not in fact central to religious practice. Instead the primary constituents of a sanctuary included a natural feature or focus, an altar or altars, offerings and a boundary.[16]

It was a hallowed natural feature – a cave, a spring, a rock, a tree or grove of trees – that may have determined the location of a sanctuary in the first place.[17] Contributory factors lay in the landscape, microclimate and numinous qualities that are as hard to define as they are undeniable (**Fig. 1.1**). The promontory of Poseidon's sanctuary at Sounion and the dramatic outcrops at Lindos and Athens exemplify sites with special natural advantages (**Fig. 1.3**). Might such places have drawn their power from their liminal status at the interface between earth and sky, earth and sea, above ground and below?[18]

The separation of sacred and profane required a boundary. The term *temenos*, indicating a space 'cut off' from the everyday world, underlined the sense of being special and set apart. Rites of purification kept contamination at bay, and at the entrance of a sanctuary (or temple) might be found a lustral basin-on-stand, or

1.4 (ABOVE) Sanctuary at Olympia as it appeared in the Roman period; reconstruction model.

1.5 (BELOW) Argive sanctuary of Hera; location map with inset showing its proximity to the remains of tombs of the Bronze Age.

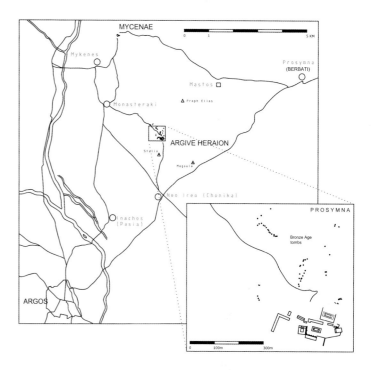

perirrhanterion.[19] The boundary could vary considerably; it could take the form of a fortification (as at the Athenian acropolis), a high protective wall in the later development of some sanctuaries (as at Delphi) or simply a virtual barrier marked by boundary stones, *horoi*.[20] Access sometimes became restricted to a few points of entrance; in richer sanctuaries these were celebrated by gateways or propylaia, or some other monumental device such as grandiose sculptures at the Samian Heraion.[21]

ALTARS AND SACRIFICE

Burnt sacrifice around the altar was the chief occasion for group worship. The difficulty of accommodating large numbers of people under a single roof, coupled with the need for smoke dispersal, favoured open-air altars communicating directly with those of the gods who inhabited the celestial sphere (**Fig. 1.2**). In effect altars were the seeds around which many a sanctuary developed. As they were renewed they grew in size and elaboration; by the sixth century Hera's altar at Samos had superseded several phases of expansion (**Figs 1.10, 1.11**).[22] Altars also multiplied in number. There were apparently as many as seventy at Olympia by the second century AD, when Pausanias mentioned twelve of Zeus besides his great ash altar, five of Artemis and so on, including one that had only recently been consecrated to Dionysos.[23]

There was need for space around the altar for the participants attendant on the sacrifice of a sizeable animal such as a pig, sheep or bull, or numbers of them. There was no prescribed formula, but amidst the flux common practices can be traced from the Bronze Age (**Fig. 1.6**), through the Classical period (**Figs 1.7, 1.8**) and down to Roman times (**Fig. 1.9**). Ceremonies often began at daybreak with a procession to chanting and music. Scenes on vase paintings show animals going to slaughter as if willingly, decked with fillets or ribbons and perhaps tips of gold leaf applied to their horns. After blood from the kill spattered the altar or was collected in special bowls

1.6   Processional presentation of offerings to a (?)divine statue by a shrine and altar-table to the right; note free-standing ceremonial or votive pillars carrying double axes on the left. Sarcophagus from Agia Triada, Crete, fourteenth century (Heraklion Museum, inv. 396).

and poured over it as a libation, the victim was then butchered (**Fig. 1.9**). Certain cuts might be ceremonially burnt on the altar so that the gods could savour the aroma: perhaps the tail or thigh-bones wrapped in fat or garnished with pieces of choice flesh.[24] But most of the animal was for human consumtion, typically at an ensuing banquet.[25]

Altars often faced east towards the rising sun. When a temple was present it tended to be aligned axially with the altar, facing east as well.[26] This occurred at Delphi despite sunrise being occluded by the nearby mountain (**Fig. 10.4**). The privileged position for worshippers was facing the altar, the temple at their backs. Temple interiors could also house small hearth-altars, especially on Crete in the Geometric period and seventh century (**Fig. 1.17**), or altar-tables for little gifts like fruit or cakes.[27]

For some time altars exhibited no great drive towards monumentality; many early ones were just partly worked outcrops of rock or rings of stones within which compacted ash piled up. At Olympia the great altar of Zeus remained so down to Roman times, 'the ash of the thighs of the victims' becoming a very substantial mound (Pausanias cites a height of 22 feet).[28] From the middle of the seventh century monumentality came into

1.7 (ABOVE LEFT) Red-figure *krater*, Archäologisches Museum, Frankfurt (inv. B413). Sacrificial scene at an altar smeared with blood in front of a statue of Apollo raised up on a column with a volute capital.

1.8 (ABOVE RIGHT) Black-figure *hydria* (so-called Ricci hydria) (*c.*530), Museo Nazionale Etrusco di Villa Giulia, Rome; detail. Preparation of a communal feast following a sacrifice.

1.9 (LEFT) Relief panel (second half of the second century AD) set up on the attic of the Arch of Constantine, Rome (*c.*315-16). Emperor Marcus Aurelius (whose head was re-cut in the likeness of Constantine) celebrates a *sauvretalia* sacrifice in front of the Roman army. The emperor sprinkles aromatic substances on a tripod-brazier, and assistants restrain the victims: an ox, a ram and a boar.

play; the stone altar at Isthmia attained a length of 100 feet. The early sixth-century altar at Samos was not so long, but it was wider and taller, with coursed squared stonework or ashlar and a triple-tier crowning moulding (**Fig. 1.10**).[29] As in other spheres, the Hellenistic period saw gigantism: the altar that Hiero built at Syracuse (Syrakusai) was fully 600 feet (195 metres) in length so as to accommodate a *hekatombe*, a sacrifice of no fewer than 100 bulls.[30]

Altars present a variety of types with recurrent characteristics (**Figs 1.7, 1.8**).[31] When decoration was used it

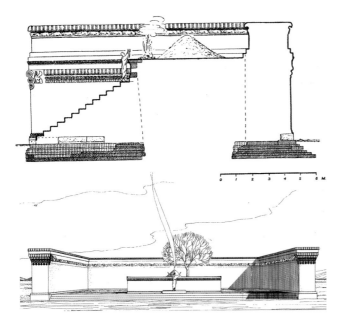

shared forms seen on temples. In and around the Aegean elements akin to the Ionic vocabulary were favoured (**Figs 1.10, 9.4**); the cornice of the mid-sixth-century altar of Poseidon at Cape Monodendri, for example, featured lobes, bead-and-reel, and up-turning volutes.[32] On the mainland and further west altars with Doric friezes were not uncommon (Ch. 3, pp. 71–2), while some vase

1.10 (LEFT)   Altar of Hera in her sanctuary on Samos; reconstruction of its appearance in the sixth century according to Hans Schleif (top) and Hans Walter (bottom). Monumental altars such as this often featured steps up to a sacrificial platform or table, with a parapet to protect the sacrificial fire from wind. See **Fig. 3.13**.

1.11 (BELOW)   Hera's sanctuary at Samos; plan showing the accumulation of the principal structures of varying dates, with inset showing the area around the altar in the seventh century.

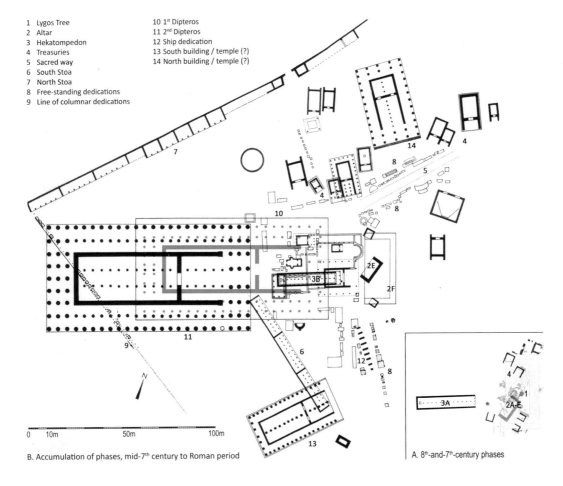

1 Lygos Tree
2 Altar
3 Hekatompedon
4 Treasuries
5 Sacred way
6 South Stoa
7 North Stoa
8 Free-standing dedications
9 Line of columnar dedications
10 1st Dipteros
11 2nd Dipteros
12 Ship dedication
13 South building / temple (?)
14 North building / temple (?)

0   10m   50m   100m

B. Accumulation of phases, mid-7th century to Roman period

A. 8th-and-7th-century phases

paintings show altars with both triglyphs and volutes, despite conventions that tended to keep them apart on architecture. In the Hellenistic period some major altars acquired a dressing of the orders (**Fig. 1.25**); that of Zeus at Pergamon was framed by a full-blown Ionic colonnade over a grandiose sculptural frieze and staircase.[33]

OFFERINGS

Whereas prayer asks favours of the divine, gift-offerings, like sacrifices, yield to the divine.[34] Since gore attracts even as it repels us, sacrifice features large in the popular image of Greek life – yet arguably it has been overstressed at the expense of offering. Both satisfy a basic need to engage supernatural powers with gifts, with the difference that offerings were not consumed, but became the permanent property of the gods.[35] Sacrifice and offering are frequently elided in text and art.[36]

Offerings participated in a two-way dynamic comparable with gift exchange between mortals.[37] There was the hope or expectation of future return. An inscription on an early seventh-century bronze Apollo from Thebes runs thus: 'Mantiklos has dedicated me to the far-shooting god with the silver bow, from the tenth of his profit; you, Phoibos, give pleasing return.'[38] The 'gods' 10%', the tithe from a successful trading or military operation, typically took the form of an offering set up in a sanctuary.[39] Potential donors would vow to 'repay' the god after favours received (a vow in Latin is *votum*, hence the English expression 'votive offering').[40] The attitude of offering was in itself significant, but whatever the offering, it was important to give up something of suitable worth; a recurrent anxiety for the rich was of incurring the gods' displeasure by not giving generously.[41]

There were myriad kinds of offering, humble or extravagant, encompassing almost the entire spectrum of Greek production: armour, baskets, chests, cloth, clothing, coins, crowns, figurines, furniture, ivories, jewels, paintings, plaques, seals, statues, vessels, weapons, and all manner of curiosities and trophies, even things as big as parts of ships; indeed on occasion entire ships

1.12 Monumental stone dedication of the Hellenistic period in the form of a statue surmounting the prow of a ship, Cyrene (Libya).

or ship-shaped creations in stone (**Fig. 1.12**).[42] Some classes of offering reflect the identity of the giver (brooches for women, armour for warriors), some were purpose-made to suit a particular divinity (figurines and statues), others mimicked aristocratic or Homeric gift-giving (cauldrons, tripods, foreign exotica). Varying dedicatory practices modulated significantly the worshipper's experience of individual sanctuaries.[43] Olympia and the Samian Heraion, for example, are noted for large bronze vessels with outward-facing monster heads or *protomes* bristling around the rim that were either of eastern Mediterranean provenance or made

1.13   Bronze cauldron on tripod-stand with monster-head protomes in Orientalizing style, Olympia (eighth century). Cauldrons with various kinds of stands, along with tripods and tripod-cauldrons (in which the three legs were fixed to the cauldron), were popular amongst the multitudinous offerings deposited at the site. For other finds from Olympia see **Figs 4.12, 4.13, 4.14**.

1.14   Clay statues and figurines from the sanctuary at Ayia Irini, Cyprus (*c.*700-550). These offerings, which may have numbered around two thousand, were excavated in situ positioned around the altar. Roughly half of the figurines are now in the Medelhavsmuseet, Stockholm, half in the Cyprus Museum, Nicosia.

locally in imitative 'orientalizing' style (**Fig. 1.13**).[44] The singularity of Ayia Irini on Cyprus lies in the accumulation of terracotta figures, tiny or massive according to budget (**Fig. 1.14**) – a phenomenon which still finds living parallels today in places as distant as Laos (**Fig. 1.26**).[45] In Greece dedicatory practices at sacred sites gathered pace particularly rapidly either side of 700, when, as Ian Morris puts it, 'the sanctuaries received offerings in quantities which leave excavators numb'.[46]

Smaller offerings were placed in niches and caves, arranged on shelves in buildings and hung from trees or raised up on bases and columns; every conceivable support could be put to use. Free-standing dedications – a

term for costly large offerings – were displayed prominently in and around temples, treasuries and the long porticoes known as stoai (**Fig., p. xii. Figs 1.4, 1.11**). The Greeks would have been accustomed to seeing architecture of note in the company of offerings of note (**Figs pp. iv–v, x, Figs 7.14, 10.1**). Display is in fact bound up with an ancient term for them, *anathemata* (singular *anathema*), literally 'things that are set up'.[47] Citizens could observe and evaluate each other's dedications, fuelling competitive ostentation as a means of accruing prestige and status, besides commemoration for posterity.[48] So as to be worthy of display objects had to be beautiful, which is inherent in another term, *agalma*. In

Homeric usage this can indicate a pleasing gift for both man and god, but over time it tended towards the latter. By the Classical period *agalma* had come to refer to votive statues or even statues in general, prime vehicles for visual delight in the ancient world.[49] Such delight was enhanced by high-value materials and technical/artistic bravura, to the point, ideally, of being singularly noteworthy or even objects of wonder. Herodotus and Pliny the Elder noted the extraordinarily fine workmanship of the Egyptian pharaoh Amasis's gift to the sanctuary at Lindos, his own corselet of embroidered linen, cotton and gold, each thread being spun from 360 strands.[50] To say that most Greek art is votive is not hyperbole: the indivisibility of beauty with dedications and sanctuaries explains why these places were in effect living art museums (Ch. 7, pp. 161–3).[51] Indeed, Pausanias's voluminous *Periegesis*, in one sense a travel and museum guide to Greece, devotes more text to votive material than anything else.[52]

TEMPLES

Today temples are often the most prominent remains at ancient sites, a situation that exaggerates their importance. As already mentioned, the temple was not such a prerequisite for Greek religion as were altars and offerings. Temples were born in the sanctuary, for the sanctuary, but they were not its raison d'être.[53] There were sanctuaries without temples, but no temples without sanctuaries. Altars appear earlier than temples, and not until the seventh century do the latter occur with any consistency.[54] Some sanctuaries long continued to have none, notably mountain-top shrines to Zeus.[55] His sanctuary at Dodona lacked a temple until the fourth century – and even then its small size belied the fame of the oracle.[56]

Since temples were not essential to cult practice, the motives for building them must have had social and political dimensions. A shelter for cult images and equipment was needed to protect them from the elements and from thieves, and a communal one recommended itself with the shift away from private control; with time such shrines acquired monumental form.[57] The new political order came to see in them a vector for collective identity and cohesion.[58] Temples went on to become one of the most potent symbols of Hellenic culture; indeed an ancient Greece without temples is as hard to imagine as an Egypt without pyramids or a medieval Europe without cathedrals.[59] Along with shared bloodlines, language and sacrifices, their own kind of temple formed part of what the Greeks thought made them Greek.[60]

What uses did temples fulfil? It is well to begin with negative statements so as to dispel any misconceptions. The Greek temple did not operate as do synagogues, churches and mosques in the Jewish, Christian and Islamic faiths. In ancient Greece congregations did not gather together under one roof for prayers, preaching, weddings or funerals. As we have seen, the chief locus for collective worship was the exterior altar. The situation at Eleusis, where the capacious Telesterion hosted large numbers of initiates to the mysteries, was unusual.[61] In most temples the main space was generally quite narrow, even in the Classical period (**Fig., p. viii, Fig. 2.25**).

THE TEMPLE AS A HOUSE FOR THE GOD

The temple was a multi-purpose structure serving various functions constellating around the terrestrial home for a divinity manifest in physical form, usually a statue (**Figs 1.15, 1.17, 1.21**).[62] Representations convey the notion of home by showing a god under a roof, or framed by a portal (**Figs 2.15, 4.21, 10.2**).[63] The house of god is a diffuse Indo-European concept, and *naos* or temple is related to *naiein*, to dwell. (*Naos* denoted only a divine home, while *oikos* and later *domos* could refer to those of both man and god.) Another name sometimes given to temples was *hekatompedon* (hundred-footer); this did not mean they had to be exactly 100 feet long; it registered that they were bigger and better than ordinary buildings.[64] Sanctuaries and/or temples were also often

1.15   Red-figure cup signed by Onesimos and Euphronios (early fifth century), Museo Nazionale Etrusco di Villa Giulia, Rome (formerly in the J. Paul Getty Museum, Los Angeles, inv. 83.AE.362). Rape of Kassandra. During the sack of Troy Aias (Ajax) seizes Kassandra, who in vain clings to the sacred statue of Athena for protection. Note the two large tripods in the background.

called after their deity, Artemision for one of Artemis, Heraion for one of Hera, and so on.[65]

The gods shuttled from Mount Olympus to their earthly houses (or ones they shared, as Athena and Erechtheus did the Erechtheion).[66] They might be manifest as cult statues that stood or sat on a throne, typically from a focal position on axis at the far end of the temple room, facing the entrance.[67] In early temples this was not often successfully achieved due to a conflict with the line of columns supporting the ridge of the roof. At some places this arrangement persisted into the second half of the sixth century (**Fig. 2.25**), although around 600 more ambitious architects worked out how to transfer load onto lateral files of columns, or tiers of columns (**Fig., p. viii, Figs 3.10, 7.22**). Thus the principal statues could dominate the axis.[68] Archaeology does not often allow an unerring distinction between the cult statue and attendant votive statues, reflecting a certain blurring for ancient minds.[69] In any event, as is still the practice in parts of India, the focal statues of temples received various attentions; practices of bathing, feeding and dressing them confirms their supposed animation.[70] The gods stared out through the great doorway beyond human measure that was also the main source of light; in this way they could observe the sacrifices around the altar and other rituals acted out in their honour.[71]

The altar, the temple and above all the god's image were 'hotspots' for attracting the god's attention. Physical contact offered the best claim to asylum – although not a sure-fire one, witness the fate of Priam's daughter Kassandra (**Fig. 1.15**). As the Greeks sacked Troy she fled to Athena's temple where she clung to the goddess's statue so very tightly that the 'lesser' Ajax (Aias) dragged it off with her to rape her.[72] Herodotus relates how a prisoner of war facing execution at Aigina escaped to Demeter's sanctuary in the hope of asylum. Intent no doubt on reaching her statue he only got as far as the temple door before being caught. That should have guaranteed his safety, but the pursuers carried him off all the same after severing his arms from his hands – which were left stuck to the door handles – an act condemned as sacrilegious and for which the perpetrators were exiled.[73]

TEMPLES AS PLACES FOR RITUAL DINING

Greek temples served a variety of purposes aside from sheltering the god's image, including as the place for oracles and ritual dining. The 'rulers' huts' of the Iron Age, which some regard as the antecedents of temples (Ch. 2), often provided the locus for banquets, though it can be hard to distinguish between meals for family and retinue as opposed to ones with a ritualistic character involving a wider public.[74] As already noted, Crete was home to a tradition of temples with interior altars, for example at Dreros (**Fig. 1.17**), Kommos and Prinias (**Fig. 2.8**).[75] At Dreros the spatial articulation of the building seems to reflect some differentiation between functions, including the storage of offerings, while ritual activities would also have taken place outside.[76] Yet Crete apart, the use of cult buildings for dining is relatively rare after the eighth century. The increasing provision of *hestiatoria*, rooms or buildings given over to banquets, suggests that this activity was no longer considered central to the temple institution.[77] The trend was to separate out distinct functions that had earlier cohabited.[78]

TEMPLES AS TREASURIES

The safe storage and display of offerings proved to be an enduring ingredient of temples. A passage from the *Odyssey* shows that this was an early and fundamental requirement; as atonement for the slaughter of cattle sacred to Helios, Eurylochus vowed that should he and his companions reach home they would 'at once construct a rich temple' for the god, 'and put into it many valuable show-pieces'.[79] The mention by Hesiod [*Theogony* 991] of a nightwatchman for a temple of Aphrodite implies that offerings deserving of protection were kept in temples by the late eighth century if not before. Indeed the very emergence of temples responded in part to the need to protect dedications from being stolen or damaged by natural causes.[80]

Treasuries (*thesauroi*) were erected at panhellenic and other major sanctuaries by city-states to protect their most valuable offerings, and indeed also as offerings in their own right.[81] The term *naos* could refer to treasuries as well as temples, evincing a certain common ground. Indeed, the safe-store-cum-display function was served by temples both before and after the emergence of treasuries. Treasuries did not need an altar, nor a peristyle like some temples, but otherwise they looked similar with their frontal orientation and pedimental roofs. The treasury of the Athenians at Delphi, for example, looks just like a little temple (**Figs 1.16, 7.14**).[82]

In urban sanctuaries the role of treasury storage fell in large part to temples, which made them, so some say, like 'reserve banks'.[83] The offerings kept safe on the Acropolis and in the Parthenon represented a major repository of the wealth of the Athenian state – indeed for a time the greatest concentration of wealth in the entire Hellenic world.[84]

1.16 Treasury of the Athenians (early fifth century), sanctuary of Apollo, Delphi.

Inside temples the most special or vulnerable dedications might be kept in a restricted chamber/area at the end of the cella, or in a rear room accessed separately. These rooms are often labelled *adyton* and *opisthodomos*, although in antiquity the terms were also applied in other ways.[85] The idea that an inner chamber/*adyton*, literally a 'place not to be entered', was a kind of holy-of-holies for secretive rites has been overstressed, reflecting assumptions that can be traced via Christian writers such as Isidore of Seville back to the biblical account of the Temple of Solomon.[86] In Greece such spaces could cater for oracles, cult equipment and cult statues, but the safe-keeping of particularly precious offerings was the most recurrent function.[87] A third-century text describing two women visiting a temple of Asklepios has them sacrificing a cock outside, entering and giving over a *pinax* (a painted panel or tablet), and then lingering to admire various statues in the main room of the temple before being admitted to a reserved area where the best works were kept. There they wonder at a statue seemingly 'chiselled by Athena herself', and are startled by a painting by Apelles, so lifelike were the figures depicted.[88] The separate rear room/opisthodomos, when present, was for unsupervised display. The typical layout, shallow and open between the flank walls, was designed for viewing art-offerings without entering the cella. Bronze grilles remind us that the risk of theft was an abiding preoccupation.[89] Yet only a fraction of offerings found a place inside temples or treasuries, and many clustered around, seemingly as near as they could get (**Figs, pp. iv–v, x, Fig. 7.14**). Temples, grand containers of offerings, doubled then as roofed museums within the open-air museum-complexes that were sanctuaries, an aspect to be explored further in Chapter 7.

TEMPLES AS DEDICATIONS

Temples were indivisible from the economics of giving in another way, for in a sense they too were dedications.[90] The early peripteral temple of Apollo at Syracuse bears a votive inscription on the top step of the stylobate. Whether the author of the inscription was the architect or patron is debated, but the point here is the dative phrasing, 'to Apollo', a standard formula for inscriptions on offerings.[91] Indeed temples (and treasuries) were on occasion called *anathemata* (offerings).[92] That the temple was the most sumptuous *anathema* a *polis* could donate is the key to a puzzle that Walter Burkert has highlighted, answering why the Greeks put so much investment into temples, or in other words into 'that which at first and second glance and on their own reflection they did not really need.'[93]

It is in political and dedicatory contexts that size mattered. Generally, a larger building is more impressive than a smaller one, while making for a superior offering simply by costing more. With no need to serve congregations the gigantism of some temples is certainly remarkable, and there can be a surreal quality about piles of fallen colossal blocks still to be found at sites like Agrigento and Selinunte (**Fig. 1.19**). In a few cases temples surpassed 100 metres long.

Table 1 Stylobate dimensions of selected temples in metres (width by length). For plans see **Figs 2.25, 2.26**.

Doric	
50.07 × 110.12	Selinunte (Selinus), Temple G
52.74 × 110.09	Agrigento (Akragas), Olympieion
30.88 × 69.50	Athens, Parthenon
Ionic	
55.10 × 115.14	Ephesos, Artemision (Archaic)
59.70 × 115.80	Samos, dipteros (estimated)
40.70 × 87.00 (approx.)	Didyma (Archaic)
51.13 × 109.34	Didyma (Hellenistic)
Corinthian	
41.11 × 107.89	Athens, Olympieion (Hellenistic–Roman)

The scale of statuary in relation to temples is also revealing. The size of a temple might be expected to be dictated by that of the cult statue it housed, but this was not so. Many early sacred images were wooden and called *xoana* (*xoanon* means 'woodcarving'), and most were small.[94] The three statuettes of hammered bronze recovered from Dreros give an idea of the sizes involved: the Apollo measures about 800 millimetres tall, his mother Leto and sister Artemis only half as much (**Figs 1.17, 1.18**).[95] Texts refer to cult statues being carried out of their temple-homes for processions and festivities, showing that they were readily portable.[96] Pliny reports that the hoary wooden Artemis at Ephesos was of 'very moderate' size.[97]

Some cult statues were made bigger in the sixth century, but truly colossal ones arrived only in the fifth century. The sculptor Pheidias made the two most

1.18 (ABOVE)   Bronze statuettes of Apollo (centre), Artemis and their mother, Leto, excavated from the temple of Apollo at Dreros.

1.17 (LEFT)   Temple at Dreros, Crete (second half of eighth century); reconstruction of interior by Andrew Stewart and Candace Smith.

1.19 (BELOW)   Ruins of temple 'G' at Selinunte (Selinus); a giant's playground of colossal stones.

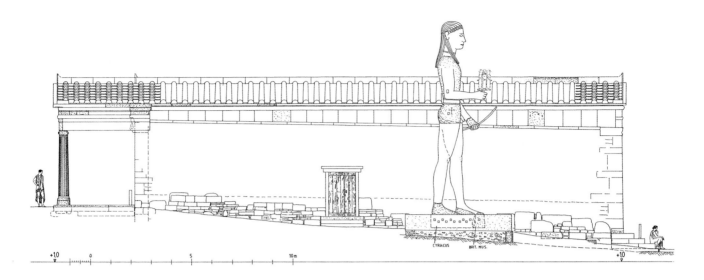

1.20 (ABOVE)   So-called Oikos of the Naxians on the island of Delos; reconstruction of the flank elevation with the adjacent monumental *kouros*.

famous examples, first the Athena Parthenos (**Fig. 1.21**) and then Zeus in his temple at Olympia (**Fig. 2.35**).[98] In emulation of eastern precedents, these were 'chryselephantine', made of gold and ivory and more besides.[99] An invisible timber skeleton was dressed with inlaid wood, ivory, gilding and precious stones, while realistic paint treatments were used for the face and other areas of exposed flesh. The effect was staggering. Pheidias's enthroned Zeus, at least 10 metres tall, attained the status of a world-wonder. For centuries the god struck awe into visitors before suffering dismantlement and re-erection in Constantinople in the fifth century AD, where not long after it was destroyed in a fire.[100]

Until the Classical period, then, grand buildings were not necessary for sheltering statues. When the 30 metre-long *hekatompedon* at Eretria was built in the late eighth century any cult image it contained would have occupied but a tiny portion of the space. At Ephesos the 'very moderate' wooden Artemis was not it seems replaced

1.21 (LEFT)   Interior of the Parthenon with Pheidias's chryselephantine statue of Athena Parthenos; reconstruction model created *c.*1971 for the Royal Ontario Museum, Toronto. The statue, probably about 12 m in height, holds in her outstretched hand a personification of Victory (Nike), supported by a column that may have had a Corinthian capital.

with a larger one despite the many re-buildings of her temple, which was already monumental by 600 and absolutely gigantic only a few decades later. Apollo's Hellenistic temple at Didyma provides another telling indication: its majestic open-air (*hypaethral*) court dwarfed the shrine or *naiskos* that presumably housed the cult statue (**Fig. 2.36**).[101] Where focal statues were colossal it is evident that they grew to fit the space available and not the other way around.[102]

Significantly, the increase in size of both temples and focal statues was anticipated in the votive arena. Having been substantially smaller, around the middle of the seventh century the occasional votive statue achieved life size.[103] Then rampant ostentation around 600 saw virile nudes or *kouroi* regularly exceed life-size. The *kouros* dedicated by one Ischys at the Samian Heraion reached 4.75 metres, and the colossos abandoned due to defects in the quarry at Apollonas on Naxos would have been over twice as tall.[104] Consider the situation at the sixth-century 'Oikos' of the Naxians on Delos. Inside there likely stood a cult statue of modest size. Outside stood the towering marble Apollo, about 9 metres tall and weighing around 30 tons and made of one piece, as boasted by the inscription on the equally heavy base (**Fig. 1.20**).[105] This was not a cult statue, but a dedication. The hugely costly Athena Parthenos (**Fig. 1.21**) may be interpreted as a votive as much as a cult statue; in any event the little Athena held to have fallen from the sky and kept in the Erechtheion remained the prime focus of the Athenians' religious attentions.[106]

There was thus no simple equation between size and sacrality. Nor was there a functional demand for large temples – so why such grandeur? It is in the context of political statement and offering that scale had intrinsic merit as a mark of 'conspicuous consumption'. Scale amplified cost, effort and effect, the more to impress mortals and immortals alike. The gigantism of Athena Parthenos was not 'necessary', yet it gave devotion impact. The famed frieze running around the cella of the Parthenon is open to a parallel interpretation; puzzlement may arise over the limited visibility of this exquisite sculptural programme, partly obscured as it was by

columns unless viewed at a steep angle from inside the peristyle.[107] As an art-offering this was not such an obstacle, for the gods could appreciate its worth and beauty. The dedicatory impulse – pious expenditure to the point of arousing wonder – lay behind the creation of such works, and indeed the spectacular dedication that was the Parthenon itself. As the prime offering of the Athenian state, the edifice transformed economic surplus into a permanent demonstration of piety and pride.

* * *

In summary, then, the temple was a house of the god but also more than that. As churches often did before relatively recent reforms, the temple fulfilled overlapping functional and symbolic purposes which varied from case to case and were not exclusively religious.[108] In itself an offering, it housed offerings besides the cult image and ritual equipment, thereby acting as safe-store and museum. There might be provision for oracles or ritual dining; the temple could receive visitors for prayer and processions during festivals. Individual projects could represent acts of atonement, thanksgiving or commemoration. Many a temple was financed from the proceeds of military successes.[109] The building of them was a focus for collective pride and identity, provoking inter-state competition. Multiple intentions converged in the temple institution; it was a nexus of religious, social and political life.

Sanctuaries embraced all of this, and as they evolved they acquired layers of elaboration and complexity. With time larger sanctuaries acquired not just altars, offerings, temples and treasuries, but also ancillary structures such as gateways, wells, fountains, dining facilities, stores, stoai, workshops for the fabrication of offerings and their repair, as well as tents erected for festivals. At some sites monumentality was enhanced by formal devices such as symmetry and axiality, culminating in orchestrated set pieces of the Hellenistic and Roman periods.[110]

From an architectural perspective it is notable that only rarely did programmatic concerns radically affect layout; indeed that of the Erechtheion is unique in the

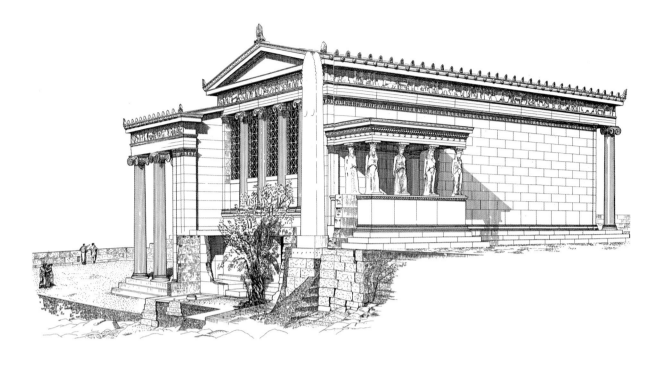

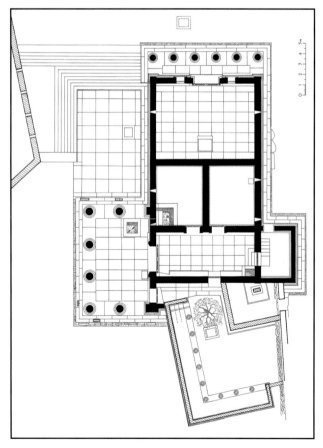

1.22 (ABOVE)   Erechtheion from the south west; perspective reconstruction by Manolis Korres.

1.23 (LEFT)   Erechtheion (421–407), Athenian Acropolis; plan.

extent to which it departed from archetypal formal models on this account (**Figs 1.22, 1.23**). The image of the temple predominated, while flexing to suit local needs. Key to this image, as to the visual impact of sanctuaries, were the Doric and Ionic *genera*, which appeared first on temples, votive columns and altars, then on other structures such as stoai and propylaia. Representative examples of the mature Doric *genus* include the fifth-century temples at Paestum (**Fig., p. viii, Fig. 1.24**) and Olympia (**Fig. 2.35**). Both have peripteral colonnades disposed on a plain rectangular platform or stylobate raised up on a three-step *krepis* or *krepidoma*. Their elevations present the canonic ingredients: tapering columns with robust fluted shafts and simple spreading capitals with a square abacus; a plain epistyle or architrave-beam capped by a simple *tainia* or fillet from which drop at intervals a little bar or *regula* with dowel-like *guttae*; a frieze of triglyphs and metopes; a crowning

1.24 Second temple of Hera, popularly attributed to Poseidon, Paestum (Poseidonia) (second quarter of the fifth century).

cornice or geison articulated by brackets or mutules, these also bearing *guttae*. The roofs terminate in pediments with akroteria, while along the flanks run antefixes and decorative spouts to throw off rainwater. Both these temples have the 'standard' six-column or hexastyle scheme, though others have fronts with four, five, seven, eight and nine columns.

Ionic practice is much more elastic than Doric (as we shall see in Chapter 5) to the point that a representative canon is an academic construct more than anything else. The Ephesian Artemision (in both its Archaic and Hel-

lenistic phases) and the Classical Erechtheion (**Fig. 1.22**) were highly influential, while Vitruvius drew his version from Hellenistic models such as Hermogenes's temple of Artemis at Magnesia (**Fig. 1.25**).[111] There may be no fixed Ionic regime, yet a familial unity of style is discernible in a preoccupation with graceful proportions, elegant enrichments and a taste for layering detail, as well as a recurrent though not mandatory vocabulary of curved mouldings, deep-cut flutes, runs of dentils and egg-and-dart, and above all the virtuoso capital with its hallmark paired volutes. Whereas it is possible to experience relatively well-preserved Doric temples at several sites (**Figs, pp. ii, viii, Figs 1.24, 3.31, 9.1, 9.13**), only the Erechtheion represents Ionic in the same way, with some help from Theophilus Hansen's nineteenth-century

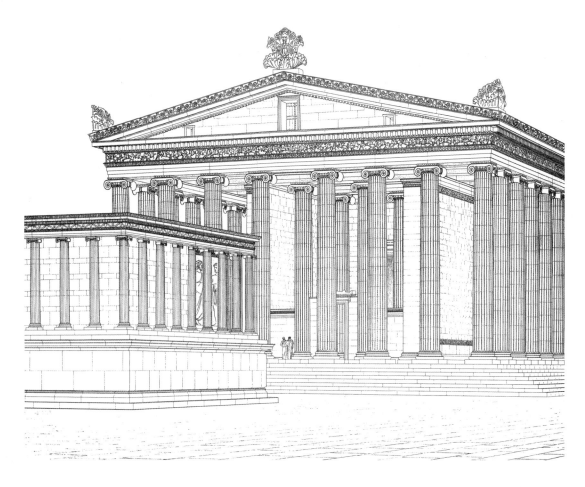

polychrome homage (**Figs 5.1, 5.26**). For the same reason, graphic reconstructions can facilitate visualizing how Ionic temples originally looked (**Fig. 1.25**).

Hellenic culture prized excellence in general, but it had particular relevance in sanctuaries. Everything offered to the gods that warranted preserving for them had to be expertly crafted. Did the spirit of dedication permeate not just the crafting of Doric and Ionic forms,

but the forms themselves? This is a question modern scholarship ignores, yet the suspicion reasonably arises that the look of temples responded to their nature. Before we can take up this point it is necessary to master other factors moulding the *genera* in Chapters 3–6. But the next task is to grasp the chronological trajectory culminating in the emergence of Doric and Ionic temples.

1.25 (ABOVE)   Temple of Artemis and her altar at Magnesia, Turkey, designed by Hermogenes (*c.*200), as reconstructed by Fritz Krischen.

1.26 (FACING PAGE)   Pak Ou cave, Laos, with its hundreds of statue offerings of the Buddha.

CHAPTER TWO
FORMATIVE DEVELOPMENTS

Greek monumental architecture had two beginnings. One starts with the first millennium, as Iron Age society slowly gathered momentum from a level that was as modest and unremarkable as it is obscure. The other

2.1 (FACING PAGE) Temple of Apollo, Delphi. The standing columns belong to the fourth century phase, while the blocks in the foreground, which were later re-assembled to make a fountain, were probably associated with the seventh- and/or sixth-century phases.

2.2 (ABOVE) Palace complex at Knossos; interior as reconstructed by Arthur Evans.

has its roots in the second millennium, when the Bronze Age civilizations that modern convention calls Minoan and Mycenaean intersected the heroic golden age of Homeric epic.[1]

Home of legendary King Minos and the Minotaur (hence the label 'Minoan'), the island of Crete for some centuries enjoyed blessed conditions, trading with Egypt and other foreign powers while safe, it seemed, from invasion, thanks to a wide intervening expanse of sea. Excavations have revealed gracefully decorated complexes at sites like Knossos (**Fig. 2.2**), Mallia and Phaistos. Building was employed for striking and expressive

Mykenae
Kyklopenmauer am Loewenthor

2.3   Lion Gate, Mycenae (Mykenai) (*c.*thirteenth century). The ram-
pant 'lions' honouring the sacred column may have been griffins.
Note characteristics of the capital akin to those that later typified
Doric style.

effect; architectural set pieces include grand courts, regular colonnades, processional flights of steps and interiors embellished with frescoes and coloured stones.
Ample storage facilities together with an organized
administration supported a high quality of life.

Characteristics of the architecture of Crete were
absorbed and translated to the Peloponnese, the home
of invaders who overran the island around the fourteenth century. These 'Myceneans', named so by Schliemann after his discovery of Mycenae (Mykenai), were
perhaps none other than the warlike and resourceful
Achaians who led against Troy the coalition of the

Greeks (or Hellenes, to use the name by which Greeks
later called themselves). Whatever we call the Myceneans, they were Greeks: Knossos, Mycenae, Pylos and
other sites on both Crete and the mainland have yielded
records kept in Linear B, an early syllabic form of Greek.
The palace-citadels of the Peloponnese had to cope with
a volatile environment, witness the thick defensive
megalithic walls of Mycenae (**Fig. 2.3**) and Tiryns (**Fig.
2.4**).[2] But elaborate spaces developed inside, focused
around a court onto which faced the megaron.[3] This the
main audience hall typically had a circular hearth and a
throne under a high ceiling held up by four fat columns.
Just outside Mycenae underground beehive-shaped or
'tholos' tombs bear witness to notable technological
capabilities. The so-called Treasury of Atreus spans
15 metres – a feat not matched till Roman times – and
incorporates a lintel block weighing more than 100

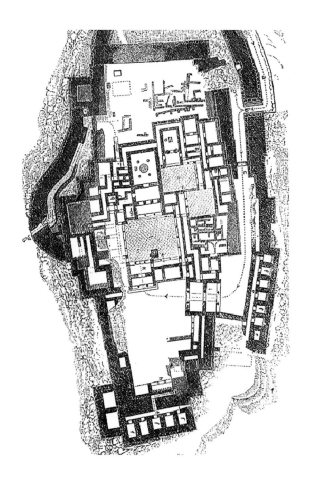

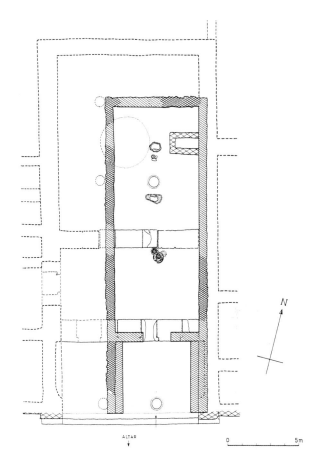

2.4 (ABOVE LEFT)   Mycenaean citadel complex at Tiryns; plan. The main megaron, with its circular hearth and four interior columns, is situated on the north side of the ceremonial courtyard, opposite the entrance side. For the outline (dashed) at a larger scale, see **Fig. 2.5**.

2.5 (ABOVE RIGHT)   Tiryns, plan of the 'megaron' (mid-eleventh century). The outline of the Bronze Age complex is shown in broken line. A flanks of the megaron was reutilized, while the lateral file of columns established the axis of the narrower new building.

tonnes.[4] The entrance façade was carefully composed of finely jointed stone-work, including decorative friezes over semi-columns treated with intricate zig-zag fluting (**Fig. 4.4**).[5] It cannot escape notice that the capitals, like those of the Lion Gate (**Fig. 2.3**), resemble later Doric ones (Ch. 4, p. 92).

It would have been natural for later Greeks to link Bronze Age ruins with the bygone age of heroes. Past

architectural splendours are evoked in the *Odyssey* and the *Iliad* (which Homer either consolidated from oral tradi-tion at the end of the eighth century or created during the seventh).[6] So we learn that Nestor's palace at Pylos boasted echoing porticoes, lofty doors and benches of smooth white marble.[7] On arriving at Menelaos's palace at Sparta on a quest to find news of Odysseus, his son Telemachos's eyes popped in wonder. It seemed that the great hall or megaron was 'lit by something of the sun's splendour or the moon's'. As Telemachos excitedly declared to his companion, 'The whole place gleams with copper and gold, amber and silver and ivory. What an amazing collection of treasures! I can't help thinking that the court of Zeus on Olympos must be like this inside.' [*Odyssey* IV,71–75]

Some see the Greek temple as a descendant of the Bronze Age megaron.[8] This is an appealing proposal, but there is a key typological difference in that the megaron is embedded within a complex while the temple is free-standing in a sanctuary. The severity and duration of the intervening rupture argues in any case against sophisticated architectural conventions surviving down to the Archaic period, though some habits will have persisted in some form.

A 'DARK AGE'?

The Mycenaean world went up in smoke, in some places quite literally, in waves of destruction from around 1200 that were ascribed to the 'Sea Peoples' by Egyptian texts, and by a current of modern scholarship to Dorian tribes wielding weapons of iron.[9] Social structures survived in modified form for some time, but then a general collapse set in; knowledge of writing was lost, populations shrank, and trade routes dried up as the eastern Mediterranean imploded into a 'Dark Age'.[10] Opinions differ as to whether the term is justified, and whether it should be suppressed in favour of the more neutral 'early Iron Age'. As is the case for the medieval 'Dark Ages', recent research in Greece reveals more activity in trade, craft and ritual than had previously been assumed.[11] Blood sacrifice at an open-air altar, a constant of later worship, could occur in the Bronze Age.[12] Stratigraphy has demonstrated continuity of cult practices on Crete, on Cyprus, on Naxos in the Cyclades, and also at mainland sites such as Kalapodi (Abai) and Eleusis.[13] The latter offers the tantalizing possibility of continuity stretching from a Bronze Age apsidal building down to the Telesterion which housed the famous mystery rites up until the Christian period.[14] Yet the fact remains that for many generations life was lived essentially on a local level.[15]

Attempts were made to recoup lost monumentality in some places, such as the acropolis at Tiryns. Not long after its destruction, around 1050, on top of the ruined megaron rose a new, narrower structure (**Fig. 2.5**).[16] In the changed world order only a scaled-down version was evidently thought viable. The new structure was possibly free-standing – like later temples – but did not survive for long the increasingly hostile environment.

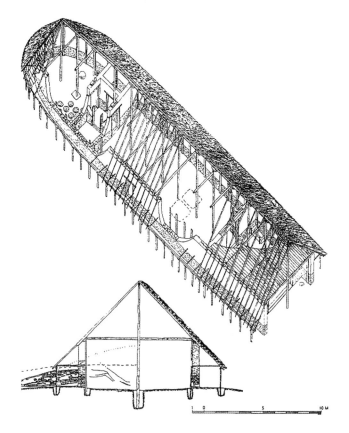

2.6   Apsidal building at Toumba, Lefkandi, on the island of Evvia (ancient Euboia), as restored by J. J. Coulton. Bottom: restored cross-section; top: axonometric projection. This is the grandest known building of its era, though whether it really had a 'veranda' around the perimeter is open to question. The burial shafts sunk into the floor in a later phase contain lavish material for the time, besides the skeletons of four horses.

Quite different in character is the singular structure located at the Toumba site near Lefkandi on the island of Euboia. Fully 45 metres long, this is by far the grandest building known from the early first millennium. It is particularly notable for its supposed 'veranda' – a term the excavators use so as to avoid the classical connotations of portico, colonnade or peristyle (**Figs 2.6, 2.8**), though this feature may have been a fence.[17] The function also defies categorization. Here it seems was the residence of a regional leader which became a memorial with dynastic pretensions once the building itself was destroyed, not long after it was erected, and interred within a tumulus.

HUTS AND TEMPLES

Although another exceptional discovery may yet surprise us again, excavations have turned up practically no other impressive structures dating from 1000 to 750. In keeping with neolithic patterns going back to the third millennium, single-cell buildings were made with little elaboration, huddling defensively together in small settlements. A minority of better-built structures stood apart; typically they have an entrance at one end, in front of which there might stand one or two posts. Some plans were more or less rectangular, but many had a curved end, or 'apse'. Widths being limited by feeble spanning capabilities, the desire for size found an outlet in length alone, hence U- or hairpin-shapes of varying elongation which compare with some long houses further north in Europe.[18] The plans of selected buildings from this period, along with many others mentioned in this chapter, are illustrated in **Fig. 2.8**. Key structures are also compiled in roughly chronological order in **Table 2**.

For much of the early Iron Age, hierarchies were perpetuated in depleted social structures centred on petty kings, local chiefs or 'big-men'.[19] They operated out of apsidal buildings of the kind just mentioned, for example those at Nichoria (**Fig. 2.8**).[20] Such structures have been called 'rulers' huts', a contradiction in terms that nicely registers the limited scale and the perishable materials employed. There are no signs of coherent architectural style.[21]

With their free-standing linear plan, entered from the front and covered with a pitched roof, 'rulers' huts' have claim to being antecedents of the Greek temple.[22] This is an attractive thesis, not least because the notion of temples as houses of the gods, found in many cultures, implies elision with ordinary houses.[23] A connection is also suggested by location, for apsidal buildings occur at sanctuaries where temples would later rise, for instance at Eretria (**Fig. 2.7**), Kalapodi, Tegea and Thermon (**Fig. 2.20**).[24] The sanctuary at Eretria has two apsidal structures (**Figs 2.7, 2.8**); the little one has been interpreted as a 'Daphnephorion', an echo of Apollo's legendary first Delphic temple built of laurel branches.[25] Over 30 metres long, the large one qualifies as a sacred *hekatompedon*

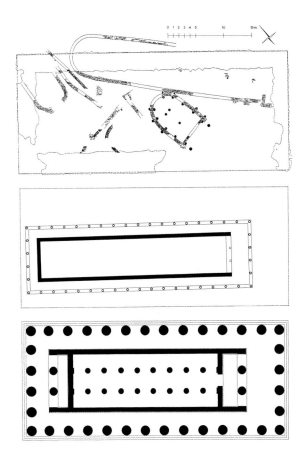

2.7 Sanctuary of Apollo, Eretria; main building phases as reconstructed by Paul Auberson. Top: eighth century, so-called Daphnephorion and Hekatompedon; centre: seventh century, rectangular temple with conjectural peristasis (for which there is no firm evidence); bottom: fifth century, stone temple (its outline is repeated as a reference for the preceding phases).

(Ch. 1, p. 21).[26] As befits a temple it faced an altar, while the interior has yielded noteworthy offerings, including bronzes of foreign provenance.[27]

A link between rulers' huts and temples need not imply a direct or sole line of descent. Ingredients of the Greek temple are perhaps to be found abroad (Ch. 4). And if there were a strong connection between the houses of gods and men, it seems curious that they diverged so markedly from around 700, when the courtyard started to be used for the latter.[28] The elongated buildings of the Iron Age constituted a multi-functional type that could be pressed into service for temples.

TABLE 2
KEY BUILDINGS FROM THE ELEVENTH TO THE SEVENTH CENTURIES
(EXCLUDING MAGNA GRAECIA)

The buildings listed in normal typeface can be reconstructed with varying degrees of certainty in plan. The buildings shown in italics cannot be reliably reconstructed. All pillars or columns, if present, have wooden shafts except where indicated to the contrary.

The nature of surviving architectural elements is denoted as follows:
b = base or bases   E = columns at front only   fr = frieze or friezes   g = geison or cornice   p = columns/posts all around
P = rectangular peristyle   r = roof-edging (e.g., antefixes)   t = tiled roof   wb = wall-blocks

fig. no.	site/building	external columns	use of terracotta	use of cut stone	guide date
2.5	Tiryns, Building T or 'megaron'[1]	E, 1			mid-11th c.
2.6	Toumba (Lefkandi)[2]				mid-10th c.
2.8	Nichoria, Unit IV–1[3]				10th–9th c.
	Nichoria, Unit IV–2[4]	E, 1			2nd half 9th c.
2.20	Thermon, so-called megaron B[5]				9th c.
	Kalapodi (Abai), apsidal building[6]	E, 4			
2.8	Kommos, Temple A[7]			b	first half 8th c.
2.7	Eretria, 'Daphnephorion'[8]	E, 2			mid-8th c.
2.7	Eretria, 'Hekatompedon'[9]	E?			last qu. 8th c.
2.8	Dreros, temple of Apollo[10]	E 2?		b, wb	2nd half 8th c.
2.8	Rakita (Ano Mazaraki), temple of Artemis?[11]	p (46)		b	late 8th c.
2.8	Emporion (Chios), 'megaron'[12]	E, 2		b?	c.700
2.8	Ephesos, temple of Artemis, I or B[13]	P, 4 by 8		b	c.700
2.17	Samos, 'Hekatompedon'[14]	E, 3?			
2.8, 13	Kalapodi, two side-by-side temples[15]	E, 2			1st half 7th c.
2.33	Yria, temple of Dionysos, III?[16]			b	1st half 7th c.
	Athens, Acropolis, temple (of Athena?)[17]				1st half 7th c.
2.7	Eretria, temple of Apollo[18]				2nd qu. 7th c.
	Delphi: temple of Apollo[19]		t		2nd qu. 7th c.
	Corinth: temple of Apollo[20]		t	wb, g	2nd qu. 7th c.
2.24, 25	Isthmia: temple of Poseidon[21]	P?	t	wb, g	c.650
2.25	Argive Heraion: temple of Hera[22]	P?	t	b	c.640
2.20, 25	Thermon, Temple C / of Apollo[23]	P?	fr, r, t		c.630
	Delphi, treasury of Kypselos[24]		t	shaft?	mid-2nd half 7th c.
2.16	Prinias, Temple A (Apollo?)[25]	E, 1		b, fr, r	mid-2nd half 7th c.
2.25	Tegea, temple of Artemis[26]	P		?	late 7th c.
2.23	*Mycenae (Mykenai), temple (of Athena?)[27]*		?	fr	late 7th c.
2.8	Eleusis, Telesterion I[28]			wb	late 7th c.
2.28, 5.22	Aigina, sanctuary of Apollo, sphinx column[29]		votive shaft	shaft	late 7th c.
	Kalydon, temple (of Artemis?)[30]		fr, r, t		c.600

NOTES TO TABLE 2

1 Maran 2000, 4–16; Mazarakis Ainian 1997, 159–61; LL&R 647.

2 Popham 1982; Popham *et al.* 1993 (including Coulton 1993); Antonaccio 1995; Pakkanen and Pakkanen 2000; Morris I. 2000, 218–25; LL&R 668.

3 The apse appears to have been added in a second phase, towards the end of the 9th century. McDonald et. al. 1983, 18–42, 316–29; Mazarakis Ainian 1988; idem 1997, 74–9; Fagerström 1988b; Hiller 1996; LL&R 673.

4 McDonald et. al. 1983, 47–53; LL&R 674.

5 Schmaltz 1980; Mallwitz 1981b; Wesenberg 1982; Antonetti 1990, 1–27; Kuhn 1993; Papapostolou 1994; idem 2006; idem 2010b; Hellmann 2006, 45–6; LL&R 505.

6 Felsch 1987; idem 1995; idem 2001; Mazarakis Ainian 1997, 137–40; Hellmann 2006, 54–5; LL&R 531–2; Niemeier 2007; Hellner 2010, 155–6, fig. 3–4; idem forthcoming.

7 Mazarakis Ainian 1997, 231–3; Shaw and Shaw 2000; Hellmann 2006, 64–6; LL&R 763.

8 Bérard 1971; Auberson 1968; idem 1974; Auberson and Schefold 1972, 113–21; Drerup 1986; Mazarakis Ainian 1997, 102–4, 243; Verdan 2000; Ducrey *et al.* 2004, 226–37; LL&R 684; Marconi 2009b, 10.

9 See n. 8.

10 Marinatos S. 1936; Drerup 1969, 5–7; Beyer 1976; Stewart 1990, 105, figs 16–17; Rykwert 1996, 191; Mazarakis Ainian 1997, 216–18; D'Acunto 2002–3. On the altar see Yavis 1949, 61–3.

11 Petropoulos 1990, idem 2002; Mazarakis Ainian 1997, 72–3; Barletta 2001, 33–4; Hellmann 2006, 48–9; LL&R 649.

12 Boardman 1967, 31–4; Fagerström 1988, 88; Mazarakis Ainian 1997, 197–8, 287–8; LL&R 732.

13 Bammer 1984; idem 1990; idem 1998; idem 2008a, b and c; Bammer and Muss 1996; Barletta 2001, 33; Muss 2001; LL&R 735–6. For the early excavations see Hogarth 1908; in favour of a 7th-century date see Weissl 2002, 321–9, and Bammer 2004 for defence of his mid 8th-century date and two separate phases of transformation in the 7th century.

14 The earlier literature, including Buschor 1930; Mallwitz 1981a, 624–33, is superseded by Kienast (1992; idem 1996; idem 2002a) who has discredited a peristyle, either for the first phase (*c.*700), or for a possible second phase (*c.*660). See also Gruben 1996a, 62–3 (in favour of a peristyle as a theoretical possibility); Barletta 2001, 32–3, 36; Hellmann 2006, 43–4; LL&R 744–5.

15 See n. 6.

16 Gruben 1987, 597–600; idem 1993; idem 1996a, 398–401; idem 1996b; idem 1997, 261–7; idem 2001, 375–8; Lambrinoudakis 1996, 57–60; LL&R 705–6. Bases or sub-bases made of stone point perhaps to two predecessors, a smaller phase I (early 8th c.), with a single central file of columns, and an enlarged phase II (late 8th c.), with three files, though the latter layout should be treated with caution.

17 Remains that might be speculatively linked to this hypothetical temple include a pair of rudimentary column bases (Hurwit 2000, 95), and a bronze openwork roundel with a standing gorgon currently on display in the National Museum, Athens (inv. 13050). This roundel, 770 mm in diameter, was probably either an acroterion or the focal decoration of a pediment: see Touloupa 1969, esp. 882, Hurwit 1999, 97, fig. 70.

18 See n. 8. The peristyle restored by Auberson is pure conjecture: see Mallwitz 1981b, 633–4.

19 Courby 1927, 171–84, 190–99; de la Coste-Messelière 1969; Hansen E. 1992, 135–9; Bommelaer and Laroche 1991, 183–4; Østby 2000, 242–5; LL&R 528. Tiles: Le Roy 1962, 19, 123; Winter 1993, 17, 150 n. 2.

20 Robinson 1976; Rhodes 1987; idem 2003; LL&R 610. Tiles: Sapirstein 2008.

21 Broneer 1971; Rhodes 1984; idem 1987; Gebhard 1993; Gebhard and Hemans 1992; Barletta 2001, 38, 50–51; Rhodes 2003; LL&R 625.

22 Waldstein 1902–5; Amandry 1952; Kalpaxis 1976, 42–7; Strøm 1988, 176 ff.; Pfaff 1990; Wright J. 1982; Antonaccio 1992; Billot 1997, 57 ff.; Østby 2006, 29–34; LL&R 637.

23 Kawerau and Soteriadis 1902–8; Mallwitz 1981b; Antonetti 1990, 14–20; Kuhn 1993; Winter 1993, 112–13 (on the tiles); Papapostolou 1994; idem 1995; idem 2010a; Mazarakis Ainian 1997, 125–35; Barletta 2001, 32, 67–8; LL&R 506. For the 'metopes' and terracotta roof edging see Soteriades 1900; Koch 1914; Payne 1925–6; Stucky 1988; Marconi 2007, 8–9. On the plan and metrology see Kalpaxis 1976, 47–50; De Waele 1995.

24 Courby 1927, 194–9; Le Roy 1967, 39; Bommelaer and Laroche 1991, 153–5; Winter 1993, 17; Østby 2000, 241–2; Partida 2000, 173–84; LL&R 524.

25 Pernier 1914; idem 1934; Beyer 1976; Stucchi 1974; Stewart 1990, 107, figs 29–32; D'Acunto 1995; Carter 1997, 87–95; Mazarakis Ainian 1997, 224–6; Watrous 1998–9; Palermo *et al.* 2004; Hellmann 2006, 66–8; Marconi 2007, 5–7. While most reconstructions follow Pernier in placing square pillars at the front, Gruben notes signs of a round base, perhaps indicating a round column (1957, 60). On the altar see Yavis 1949, 63–4.

26 Østby 1994; idem 2006b; Voyatzis 1990; eadem 1999, 131; Hellmann 2006, 51.

27 Wace 1923; Harl-Schaller 1975; Klein 1997; LL&R 644.

28 Noack 1927; Mylonas 1961; Clinton 1993; Cosmopoulos 2003b; Hellmann 2006, 240–41; Østby 2006, 12–16; LL&R 589–90.

29 Gruben 1965, 185–7; Walter-Karydi 1994, 125–8; Hoffelner 1996, 10–15; Bakker 1999, Col-8; Segal 2007, no.26. Given its faceted rather than fluted shaft this should be earlier than the votive column at the nearby Aphaia sanctuary, but Walter-Karydi's date of 620, based on a stylistic analysis of the sphinx, seems slightly early; Hoffelner (1996, 12), suggests nearer to 600 and the date of the adjacent Doric temple. The form of the capital, and so that of the column as a whole is unknown.

30 Dyggve 1948, 149–64, 236–9; Bookidis 1967, 157–65; Winter 1993, 125–8; Barletta 2001, 66–8, 72–4; Marconi 2007, 10–11.

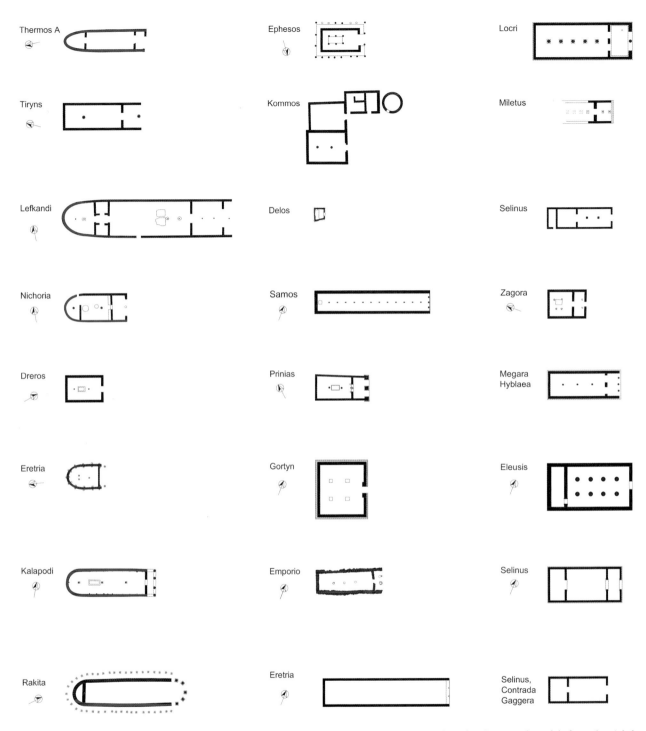

2.8   Plans of notable Greek buildings in the period from the eleventh to the seventh centuries, 1:1000.

2.9 (FACING PAGE)   Selected architectural models from the eighth to the fifth centuries: (1) Perachora (Athens, NM inv. 16684); (2) Argos (Athens, NM inv. 15131); (3) Samos (Vathy Museum inv. C 25); (4) Samos (Vathy Museum inv. C 8); (5) Sellada; (6) Sparta, fragment; (7) Nikoleika (?ancient Helike); (8) Sparta; (9) Medma.

1

2

3

4

5

6

7

8

9

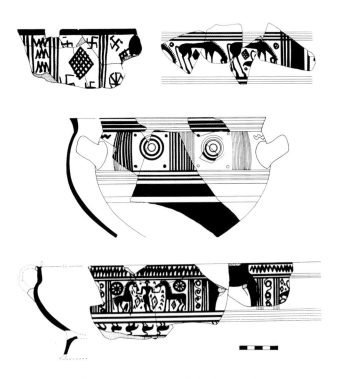

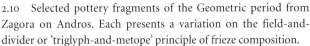

2.10   Selected pottery fragments of the Geometric period from Zagora on Andros. Each presents a variation on the field-and-divider or 'triglyph-and-metope' principle of frieze composition.

2.11   Temple of Aphrodite, Contrada Marasà, Locri (Locri Epizephiroi), Calabria (late seventh century); wall decoration consisting of terracotta revetment with a geometrical pattern.

Construction methods in the Iron Age typically featured perishable materials: walls of mud brick resting on socles of rubble stone, in conjunction with timber roof structures and coverings of reed or thatch.[29] To get a sense of how early Greek buildings looked we are obliged to turn to representations in the form of terracotta models (**Fig. 2.9**). Six examples from the eighth century or so are illustrated here: one each from Argos, Perachora and Sellada, two from Samos, plus another recently discovered at Nikoleika (?Helike).[30] Whether they represent homes or shrines is a matter of academic dispute; at this time it seems that function made little difference to appearance.[31] The Perachora model is particularly informative. Its curving and steeply pitched roof points to reed or thatch; its entrance porch is flanked by two pillars with square bases and capitals; instead of a pediment there was an opening for light and the egress of smoke, which was further facilitated by triangular perforations down the sides.[32] As on the models from Argos, Nikoleika and Sellada, the walls were decorated with geometrical patterns in tune with the art of this the 'Geometric' period (**Fig. 2.10**).[33] The sketchy quality and disproportionate size of the motifs can be attributed to the miniature scale of the models; real buildings like the *hekatompedon* at Eretria no doubt presented a more regular and composed display. Though destined to be eclipsed by figuration, geometrical ornament persisted later in some regions; neat patterns adorn the terracotta facing of a temple at Locri in southern Italy (**Fig. 2.11**).[34]

Social and economic conditions improved dramatically in the eighth century, a period sometimes called the 'Greek Renaissance'.[35] Significant increases occurred in population, in overseas trade, in the number and size of settlements and sanctuaries, and in the output of the technical arts including pottery, metalwork and weaponry. At first building activity lagged behind; it begins to impress only when these other trends had become established. But then imposing temples sprung up at many sanctuaries, competing for attention and prestige. The sudden nature of this phenomenon is remarkable, amounting to 'an explosion of temple-building around 700'.[36]

TEMPLE PLANS

Early temple-like structures exhibit disparate plans (**Fig. 2.8**). We have already encountered some: the horse-shoe plan (Eretria); the elongated apsidal building (Thermon, Eretria); the oval or double-apse plan (model from Samos). From the late eighth to the mid-sixth century the dominant type was a free-standing rectangular hall of varying length. The *hekatompedon* at Samos exemplifies the longer variety, with its linear roof, the predominance of wall construction and the entrance at one end (**Figs 2.8, 2.12**). Interior posts support the larger roofs, as here, and also at Kalapodi and Nikoleika (**Figs 2.13 and 2.14**) while one or more posts could confer a sense of importance on entrances.[37]

Some use the name megaron (for example the 'Megaron Hall' at Emporio on Chios), but it is best to avoid any implication of a Bronze Age lineage.[38] Meanwhile '*oikos*' has the disadvantage that ancient usage denoted residence, not layout.[39] Perhaps a better label is 'hall-temple', of which there were two main types. One has a flat front, perforated only by the entrance (it is this format which is sometimes called *oikos*); the other has an open-fronted porch framed by projecting side walls which Vitruvius called *antae*, hence the term 'anta-building'. Frontal columns became increasingly common, either in a 'prostyle' arrangement or 'in antis' as at Locri or Megara Hyblaia (**Fig. 2.8**). The two solutions are found side by side at Kalapodi, where the south temple is 'prostyle' and the north one 'in antis'.

Two of the better understood hall-temples erected between the late eighth and late seventh centuries are both found on Crete, the earlier at Dreros, the later at

2.12 Temple of Hera (or Hekatompedon), Samos; interior as reconstructed by Andrew Stewart and Candace Smith.

Prinias. A sacrificial hearth, or *eschara*, occupied the interior at Dreros, with posts supporting the roof, which no doubt had an opening for smoke. Around the interior ran a bench on which was displayed the statuettes of Apollo, Artemis and Leto mentioned in Chapter 1 (**Fig. 1.17**). A flat roof is suggested by the limited rainfall on Crete, as well as by models of varying date from both Crete and Samos (**Fig. 2.9**).

The form of Temple A at Prinias is equally uncertain; one school of thought advocates a flat roof, another a pitched one (**Fig. 2.16**). The real interest of the building lies in its friezes and other sculptural elements; indeed it

2.13   South temple at Kalapodi (mid-seventh century); interior as reconstructed by Nils Hellner.

2.14 (LEFT)   Temple at Nikoleika (ancient ?Helike); cut-away reconstruction by Erophile Kolia.

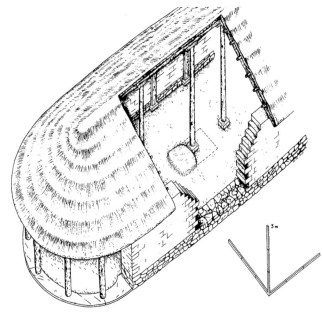

has a claim to be the earliest known Greek sculptural programme.[40] The desire for monumentality is epitomized by the lintel over the portal, this being designed to be seen not just from in front but also from below (**Fig. 2.16**). In addition there is a separate frieze of riders in procession that shares traits with eastern traditions; this probably went on the exterior, either at high or low level.[41] A single frieze-bearing limestone block from another Cretan site, Chania, is all that remains of a temple of comparable date (**Fig. 2.15**).[42] The position in elevation – high, low or middle? – is again uncertain, as, sadly, is generally the case for seventh-century friezes, including ones from Yria, Samos, Isthmia and Mycenae.[43] Nonetheless, friezes found their way to the top of buildings before long, as we shall see.

2.15 (?)Architectural frieze block from Chania, Crete (?mid-seventh century), limestone, height 390 mm. Pairs of archers resist enemy chariots attacking a sacred structure that is symbolized by the genre image of a goddess framed by a door.

2.16 (RIGHT) Temple A at Prinias, Crete. Top: reconstructed front elevation and plan; measuring more than 800 mm in height, the scale of the frieze calls into doubt the high-level position proposed by the excavator Luigi Pernier. Alternatively it sat on the ground in the manner of Hittite, Assyrian and Syrian orthostates. Bottom: architectural sculpture associated with the lintel over the door.

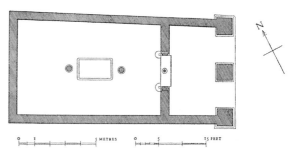

TRANSITION AND THE TILED ROOF

The seventh century was a time of technological transition. Construction generally employed perishable materials in the eighth century and permanent ones in the sixth, but there was no abrupt watershed. Always standard for roof structure, the use of timber for vertical supports is indicated by post-holes and stone bases without surviving shafts. The two side-by-side temples at Kalapodi had façades with four and two wooden posts/columns around 500 millimetres or so in diameter (**Fig. 2.8**). Inside the southern temple were roughly octagonal wooden pillars on axis and half-octagonal piers that reinforced the mud-brick walls, which were decorated by a cycle of paintings (**Fig. 2.13**). Though the stone bases are rather irregular, here is an incipient concern for visual effect that would later be satisfied by fluting.[44] By the side of one base, moreover, was found a tool possibly used for working it, which by its re-semblance to carpentry tools illustrates how builders adapted technology to emerging purposes.[45] Wooden columns were possibly used at the Heraion at

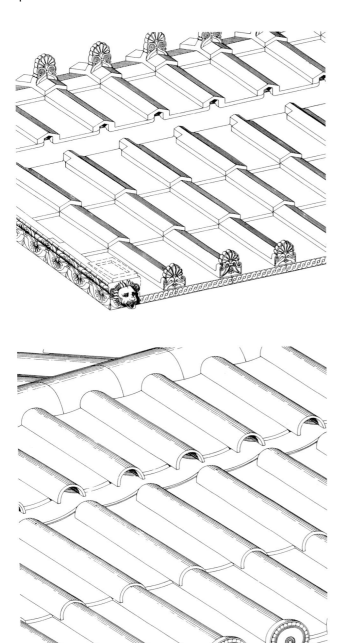

2.17 Two predominant types of tiled roof arrangements used in mainland Greece from the late seventh century, as reconstructed by Nancy Winter. Top: Corinthian system, typified by the second temple of Apollo, Corinth; bottom: Laconian system, typified by the Heraion, Olympia.

Olympia, later to be substituted by stone ones.[46] On rare occasions sixth-century stone capitals have sockets to receive timber shafts.[47] At Metropolis in Thessaly a mid-sixth-century Doric temple has been discovered that was ravaged by fire in the Hellenistic period.[48] The burnt-out remains were sealed by mud and luckily the site lay undisturbed until a few years ago, enabling excavation to proceed on the basis of modern stratigraphical techniques. Imprints of mud-brick and carbonized timber attest to internal wooden columns around a metre in diameter, nearly as large as the stone ones outside (**Fig. 2.25**). The use of columns occupying the central axis also illustrates the persistence of techniques that had become outdated elsewhere.

The most significant advance of the Archaic period was the temple-form roof: simple, linear, double-pitched. The critical catalyst, of inestimable importance, was the mould-made roof tile (**Fig. 2.17**). As early as the third millennium simple flat tiles had seen occasional use in Greece, cut irregularly with a knife out of a sheet of clay and then dried; in common with vernacular traditions elsewhere they required steep pitches, a large overlap and a thick bedding.[49] Tiles were used in some Mycenaean buildings, but they did not interlock.[50] The true mould-made system comprising a flat pan-tile and a narrower cover-tile, tapering so as to interlock with neighbours above and below, was a Greek invention of the first half of the seventh century, variations of which remain in widespread use today the world over.[51]

Apollo's temples at Corinth and Delphi and Poseidon's at Isthmia each had roofs of 'Proto-Corinthian' tiles. Quite quickly production over a wide area settled down into two main typologies, the Corinthian and the Laconian (**Fig. 2.17**).[52] Being vastly superior to coverings of thatch, mud or schist, tiles fast became imperative for temple building, thereby providing an impetus towards monumentality. One factor was sheer weight, for early tiles were thick and heavy, calling for robust supports. Walls of mud-brick had to become wider or be reinforced by timber framing and/or cut stone (**Fig. 2.18**). Vertical wooden supports had to thicken up, or be made of stone.

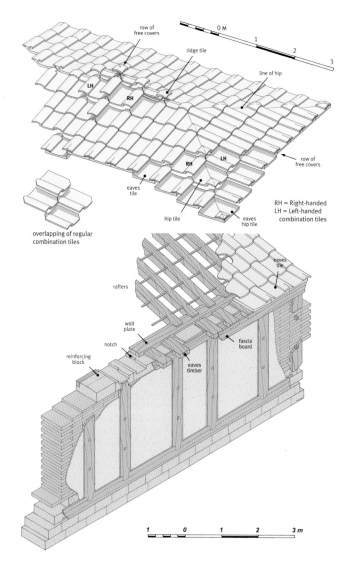

2.18 Temple of Apollo, Corinth; reconstruction of the seventh-century phase by Robin Rhodes and Philip Saperstein. Top: typical roof conditions at the ridge, hip and edge; bottom: wall construction and junction with the roof.

Modular production of tiles using moulds was key to minimizing trimming and one-off 'specials', and this called for orthogonal ground-plans, causing apsidal plans to fall out of use.[53] Since tiles were not normally nailed, the need to prevent slippage determined the low pitch of Greek roofs.[54] Another, fundamental, related ingredient of temples, the pediment, provided a solu-

tion for the ends. This was used first at the front, while at the rear hips provided continuity with superseded apsidal solutions before the pediment predominated here too. Its advantage lay in a combination of easier construction and the opportunities for display using reliefs or sculpture, while akroteria stood out dramatically at the apex and the edges.[55] As eye-catching display moved skywards, beholding the temple became an uplifting experience.[56] Improving technologies opened up possibilities for display; at the same time the desire for display was an inducement for technological development. Here is a chicken-and-egg relationship – it is impossible to say which came first.

The edging of roofs opened up further opportunities for ornamentation, including runs of terracotta upstands or antefixes that masked the bottom row of cover tiles. Around 630 these and other elements were contrived at Temple C at Thermon into a rich panoply of figuration. Female heads appear on the antefixes, rain spouts were fashioned as lion-heads, while a gorgon protected the end of the ridge beam. This same temple has famously yielded several impressive painted terracotta plaques (**Fig. 2.19**).[57] They did not necessarily form part of a Doric frieze, as is usually thought (Ch. 3, p. 82), yet these and other panels from Kalydon were probably situated at high level.[58] At Metapontum (Metapontion) and its environs in southern Italy terracotta decoration was designed to lap over the timberwork of the roof and so protect it from the elements (**Fig. 2.21**).[59]

Another material used for revetment was bronze. In Greece this was employed for doors, grilles and sculptural adornments such as akroteria, and more besides.[60] In Sparta the Archaic temple of Athena 'of the Bronze House' (*Chalkioikos*) was presumably called thus due to an unusually extensive metal carapace.[61] The tally of architectural metal from Olympia includes door furniture, decorated strips of revetment (mostly for door frames), a lobed collar for a capital or column necking (**Fig. 4.13**) and an Ionic volute (**Fig. 5.12**).[62] Of particular note are two large rectangular reliefs, possibly metopes, one showing a griffin suckling its young the other a kneeling archer (**Fig. 2.22**).[63] Most of this material dates

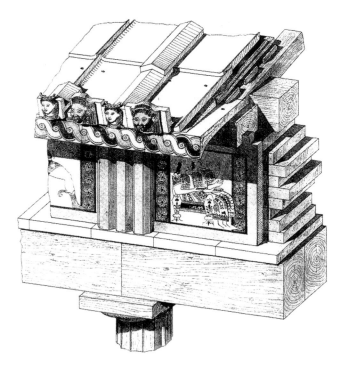

2.19 Temple of Apollo at Thermon; hypothetical reconstruction of the entablature, according to Kawerau and Soteriadis. The presence of triglyphs and their relation to the terracotta *pinakes* or metopes is conjectural (unlike the *pinakes*, not a single triglyph fragment survives). The supposed wooden triglyphs have in the past been seen as one of the main examples illustrating the theory of proto-Doric entablatures in this material.

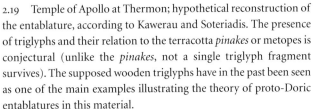

2.20 (RIGHT) Sanctuary of Apollo, Thermon; plan combining different phases, with annotations denoting: (A) an apsidal structure (second millennium); (B) a nearly rectangular 'megaron' (ninth century); (C) temple of Apollo (seventh century).

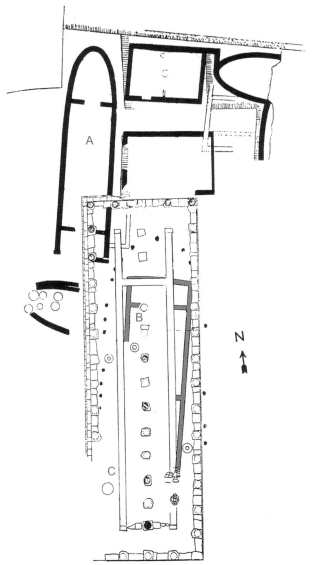

from before the monumental phase, suggesting that bronze revetment was relatively common in the seventh century.[64] Prone as it was to damage, decay and theft, bronze too was destined to be overtaken by stone. We have already observed stone friezes on Crete, and by the late seventh century figurative panels in this material appear on the mainland, notably on the temple of Athena at Mycenae (**Fig. 2.22 bottom**).[65]

* * *

EMERGENCE OF THE PERIPTERAL PLAN

In contrast to the buildings encountered so far, the dominant characteristic of the mature Greek temple is its open cage of columns, the peristasis, *pteron*, or peristyle (a Latin neologism). The earliest known possible precursor is the 'veranda' at Toumba (**Fig. 2.6**), but this differs in having closely spaced slim posts, if indeed posts they were, and not just supports for a fence. In any

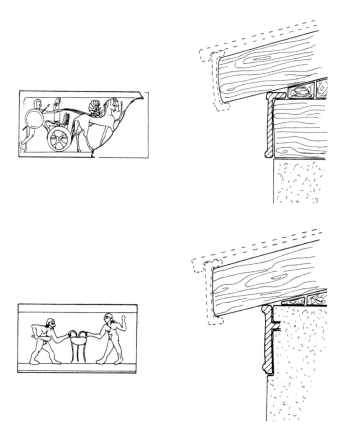

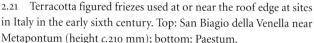

2.21 Terracotta figured friezes used at or near the roof edge at sites in Italy in the early sixth century. Top: San Biagio della Venella near Metapontum (height *c.*210 mm); bottom: Paestum.

event, the building had long been buried by the time the genuine peripteral temple appeared. Exterior colonnades perhaps appear around 700 at the temple of Artemis at Ephesos in Ionia, and at Rakita (Ano Mazaraki) in the north-western Peloponnese, where it seems stone bases carried wooden posts around the double-apsed *hekatompedon* (**Fig. 2.8**).[66] The Artemision is significant as the first of a succession of influential temples on the same spot while, being rectangular, the peristasis was more 'advanced' than at Rakita. But at this stage it was small, not much more than a large baldachin, and not particularly refined; the column bases are irregular, which argues against well-resolved capitals. On nearby Samos the Hekatompedon probably had

2.22 Early architectural panels, possibly metopes. Top: bronze relief with griffin and young from Olympia, height *c.*800 mm, now in the National Museum, Athens (inv. B104); middle: bronze relief panel with kneeling archer from Olympia, now in the National Museum, Athens (inv. 6443); bottom: architectural stone relief associated with the temple of Athena from Mycenae (Mykenai), now in the National Museum, Athens.

2.23 (ABOVE) Temple of Poseidon at Isthmia (mid-seventh century); hypothetical reconstruction according to Oscar Broneer. Geison blocks and fragments of painted mural decoration survive, but the Doric colonnade is entirely conjectural.

2.25 (FACING PAGE)   Plans of Doric and related temples, 1:1000.

2.24 (BELOW)   Blocks that belonged to the geison (cornice) of the Archaic temple at Isthmia. Note the absence of mutules and guttae.

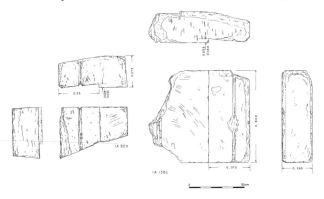

no exterior columns, or only at the front, and not a peristasis as used to be thought.[67]

The rectangular peristasis was possibly employed on the mainland around the middle of the seventh century, though the evidence is elusive here too. The signs are negative as regards the temples at both Delphi and Corinth (**Fig. 2.18**). One candidate is Poseidon's temple at Isthmia (**Figs 2.23**), a monumental structure from which survive numerous roof tiles and wall blocks (**Fig. 2.24**). Yet the evidence for a peristyle is tenuous; it can hardly have had fat proto-Doric columns like those the excavators visualized, and one may not have existed at all.[68] Another candidate is Hera's temple in her Argive sanctuary (**Fig. 1.5**). On top of the 'Old Temple Terrace' is a strip of stone blocks including alternate ones which supported timber columns up to 800 millimetres wide.[69] These probably belonged to a peristyle, though this is not certain (**Fig. 2.25**).[70] The situation is hardly any

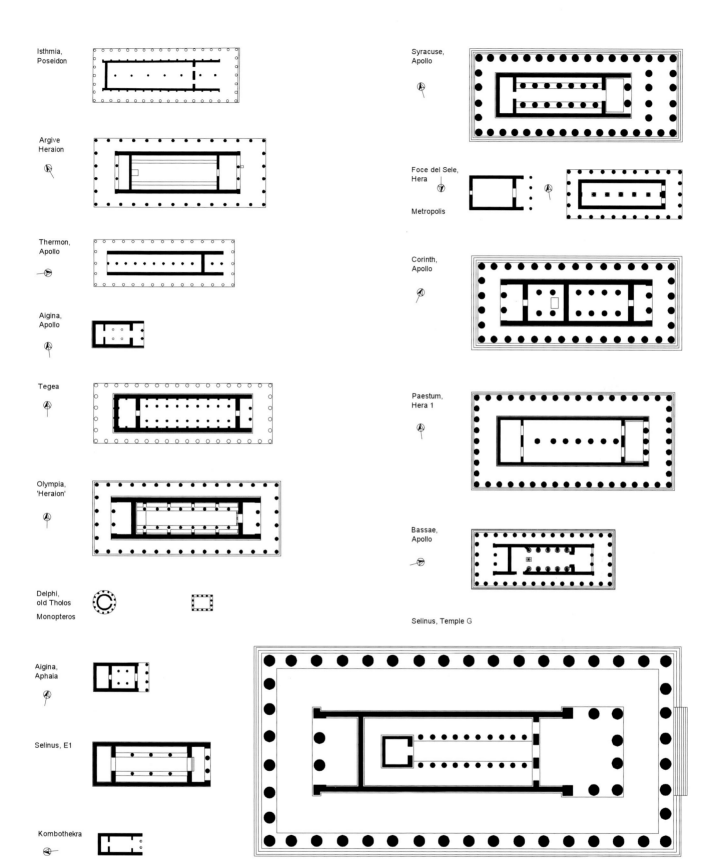

Isthmia, Poseidon

Argive Heraion

Thermon, Apollo

Aigina, Apollo

Tegea

Olympia, 'Heraion'

Delphi, old Tholos

Monopteros

Aigina, Aphaia

Selinus, E1

Kombothekra

Syracuse, Apollo

Foce del Sele, Hera

Metropolis

Corinth, Apollo

Paestum, Hera 1

Bassae, Apollo

Selinus, Temple G

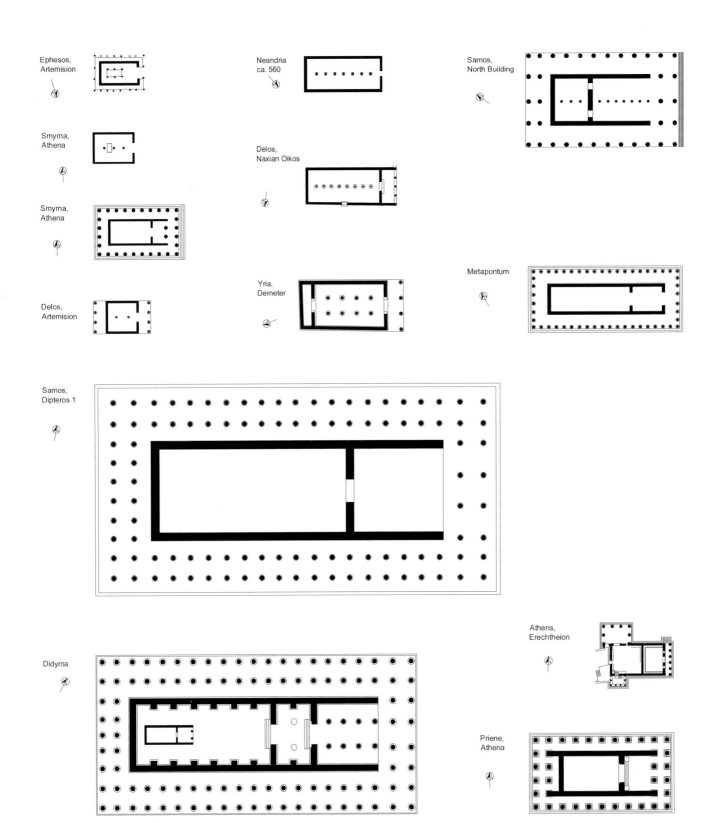

Ephesos,
Artemision

Smyrna,
Athena

Smyrna,
Athena

Delos,
Artemision

Neandria
ca. 560

Delos,
Naxian Oikos

Yria,
Demeter

Samos,
North Building

Metapontum

Samos,
Dipteros 1

Didyma

Athens,
Erechtheion

Priene,
Athena

clearer for Apollo's Temple C at Thermon. In theory a peristyle may have developed in stages in different buildings at the site, beginning with a late Bronze Age apsidal building (A) and then an almost rectangular structure (B) (**Figs 2.20, 2.25**).[71] But it now seems that Building B never had such a feature, while it is not even certain that Temple C had a peristyle before the Hellenistic period.[72] These and other difficulties seem insoluble, for the early and inadequately documented excavations frustrate stratigraphical analysis.[73] From this vexing picture we have to conclude that most seventh-century temples which had imposing exterior columns had them at the front alone.[74]

Sure signs of peristyles appear by the end of the seventh century. The outline of one can be surmised from the exiguous remains of a temple at Tegea (**Fig. 2.25**). Around the same time other aspects of temple layouts were improved, notably at the Heraion at Olympia, where the peristyle encloses a long tripartite cella-building comprising three parts: a porch or pronaos, the main cult room or naos, and a rear chamber. Here and perhaps at Tegea a further key advance was the provision of a central nave that allowed unimpeded viewing of the presiding god or gods courtesy of two lateral files of columns rather than a single axial file (Ch. 1, p. 22). Another development was a stepped krepis or substructure leading up to the stylobate that supported the columns; with time a peristasis on a krepis became a hallmark of the Greek temple, with three steps being particularly characteristic of Doric.

Vitruvius supplies two reasons behind the emergence of the peristyle (III,3.9), that the columns made for an imposing appearance while providing covered space to shelter from the rain. Both ring true but there were likely further motivations, differing perhaps in different places. Did Ionian builders have at the back of their minds Egyptian colonnades or eastern ceremonial baldachins, while on the mainland the impetus was more practical? An open roof gave protection for people, mud-brick walls and offerings alike.[75] The peristasis further enabled the visual bulk of a temple to grow impressively while avoiding a wide cella and the atten-

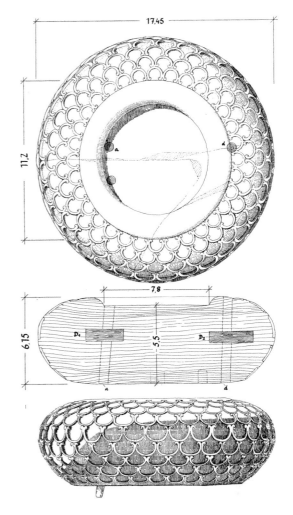

2.27 Wooden torus base found at Olympia. Note the socket in the upper surface to receive a wooden shaft, and the decorative array of so-called Cypriot crown motifs. The size points to a little shrine or baldachin, perhaps with two or four columns. The base was recovered from a well where it was dumped with material datable to around 600, suggesting an original use in the seventh century.

2.26 (FACING PAGE) Plans of Ionic and related temples, 1:1000.

dant problems of spanning it.[76] Above all, the temple was granted a splendid appearance from any viewpoint, which is important where the topography dictated that an east-facing temple was approached from the west, i.e., its rear.[77] This occurs at the Argive Heraion, at Assos and on the Athenian Acropolis.

The discussion of column layouts brings us to ask how the columns themselves looked. It is widely supposed that, before a shift to stone, Doric and Ionic forms were developed in wood (Ch. 3). Of considerable interest, then, has to be a wooden columnar element datable to before 600 that has been discovered at Olympia. This outstanding, albeit little discussed, find is a torus base recovered from a well (**Fig. 2.27**).[78] Only 175 mm in diameter, it formed part of a small column, perhaps one of a set of two or four supporting a shrine or baldachin not much taller than a man's height.[79] Vase painters depict similarly proportioned torus bases on structures which look old and/or made of timber.[80] The surface detail is singular: a quasi-fish-scale pattern based on a greater than semi-circular arc fashioned like a Phoenician or Cypriot crown, raising the question of whether the entire column/baldachin was donated from the eastern Mediterranean.[81] The very existence of this base makes one wonder how many different styles could be seen in Greek sanctuaries before Doric and Ionic came into the ascendant.

EMERGENCE OF THE DORIC *GENUS*

The lineage of the Doric family of forms is even harder to track than the peristasis because of the perishable materials used throughout the seventh century (see Table 3, p. 78). Even at the end of the century and in spite of its precocious plan, the Heraion at Olympia featured wooden columns and walls of mud-brick rising from stone orthostates and perhaps faced with timber boarding and/or bronze revetment.[82] Practically no traces of Doric survive from much before this time, despite the range of evidence potentially available, whether from models and representations, or from excavations (which can turn up elements from structures of which the outline or even the location may remain obscure).

There are at least indications as to the regions most likely to have been involved in the creation of Doric style. In contrast to the traditional emphasis on the Peloponnese, Attica and Ionia, in recent years greater

attention has been paid to regional developments.[83] Despite its relatively peripheral position, Aetolia played a pioneering role in figural applications of terracotta.[84] Crete put a formative stamp on aspects of decoration, especially friezes. The Cyclades hosted the earliest experiments with Ionic columns, a non-canonic Doric idiom, and buildings that fit neither category. Meanwhile Greek territories in southern Italy and Sicily, traditionally called 'Magna Graecia' and more recently 'West Greece', saw variant solutions throughout the sixth century, especially towards the junction with the roof where elaborate terracottas reigned.[85]

Nonetheless the north-eastern Peloponnese, the tract of land spreading from the isthmus and Isthmia southwards past Corinth to the Argive plain, remains a likely cradle of Doric architecture. Vitruvius specifically mentions Hera's temple at the Argive Heraion, built by Doros the progenitor of the Dorians, as the first to have employed Doric (IV,1.3). As we have seen, this building presents one of the better – though hardly watertight – claims for an early peristyle. In sympathy with hints by Pindar and Pliny the Elder, some recent scholars tend to look to Corinth and its hinterland.[86] The region was blessed with beds of clay suited to the production of pottery, terracotta and tiles, technologies in which it was a leading player.[87] Here too were easily accessible beds of an oolitic limestone that was both fine grained and easily cut, especially when still fresh, or 'wet'.[88] The city's early success in maritime trade not only generated the economic surplus to sustain euergetism but also testifies to prowess in shipbuilding, which calls for carpentry skills akin to those needed to construct large roofs.

From the late eighth century, construction in Corinthia was enhanced with cut stone for socles, corners, thresholds and jambs.[89] In the second quarter of the seventh century stone and tile came together for perhaps the first time in a monumental assemblage for Apollo's temple in Corinth itself (**Fig. 2.18**). As mentioned, there was no peristyle; walls were articulated by framing timbers and panels of render that were probably decoratively painted, as occurred earlier at Kalapodi, where the evidence suggests the painting faced internally (**Fig. 2.13**). At Corinth many of the tiles were designed for hips, showing that the temple was hipped, at least at the rear. Cuttings in the blocks capping the wall may suggest that the roof flattened out towards the eaves, in what has been called 'Chinese' fashion.[90] A broadly similar approach was echoed at Poseidon's slightly later temple at nearby Isthmia, to which can be attributed one incipient part of the Doric vocabulary. This is the course immediately below the roof, which brings to mind the later Doric geison or cornice (**Fig. 2.24, 3.26**).[91] There are no mutules, however, and the profile is a relatively generic solution that could have accompanied other styles. There is no evidence at all for the proto-Doric columns and frieze envisioned by Oscar Broneer (**Fig. 2.23**). As late as the mid seventh century, then, even in this technologically advanced region, there is no sure sign of Doric.[92] It remains possible that this style saw early use on another structure of which no trace survives, perhaps a predecessor of the so-called 'Great Temple' at Corinth.[93] Another candidate for the early adoption of Doric forms is the treasury that Kypselos, the tyrant of Corinth, built at Delphi.[94] An unusually slender column drum with 16 very shallow (almost flat) flutes may belong to this project.[95]

At Apollo's sanctuary on Aigina there is a lone drum, belonging not to a building but a free-standing column; it may tentatively be dated to the last two decades of the seventh century to judge from the style of the remains of a sphinx that it may have supported (**Fig. 2.28**).[96] The column was at least 1 metre in lower diameter, and so in all probability taller than any contemporary building, roof and all. But sadly both the height and the type of the column elude us in the absence of a capital. The strong taper of the drum suggests Doric, though the narrowness of the thirty-six facets is more akin to early Ionic.[97] This indeterminacy is just another of the frustrations that bedevil research into origins, yet this column is significant in alerting us to the possibility that the design of Doric and Ionic columns was resolved for sacred free-standing columns as well as buildings, an issue that will be further probed in Chapter 7.

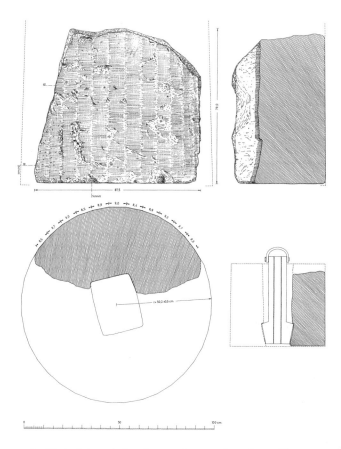

2.28 Part of drum belonging to a large votive column (?late seventh century); sanctuary of Apollo, Aigina. The style of the capital may have been Ionic or Doric, or indeed neither of these.

Turning to definite examples of the Doric vocabulary, their chronological sequence remains a matter of educated guesswork (see **Table 3**, p. 78). The current consensus holds the earliest to be the temple situated at the park of Mon Repos near the town of Corfu. Here have been found fragments of capitals and shafts (some of which might belong to votive columns), and numerous terracotta antefixes which suggest a date around 610. The same site has yielded a corner triglyph (**Fig. 3.25**), though this is not necessarily from the same building and it may have belonged to an altar.[98]

Finally, around 600, at the sanctuary of Apollo on Aigina, we have a temple which presents the virtually complete Doric repertoire in stone, including shaft, capital, epistyle (architrave) with tainia, triglyphs, and mutules elaborated with little cylindrical stubs or guttae (**Fig. 2.29**). The corner triglyph has just one upright on the flank, indicating a frontal disposition for

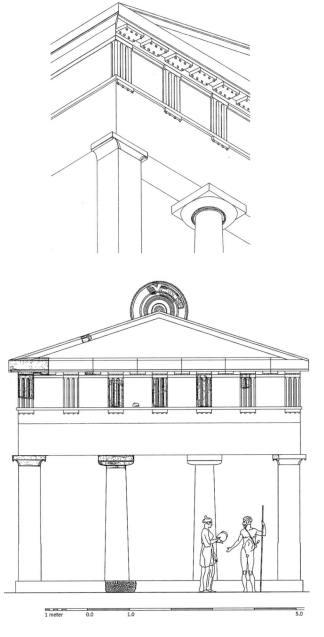

2.29 Temple of Apollo, Aigina; elevation and corner detail, as reconstructed by Klaus Hoffelner.

both the frieze and therefore also the columns, while the presence of a pediment is attested by a prominent akroterion. Recent excavations at Delphi show that the successor of the mid-seventh-century temple of Apollo, along with the precinct wall, its terrace and associated treasuries, all form part of a push towards monumentalization that began around 590 or so.[99] Tool markings on some surviving wall blocks suit equally well the earlier phase, but the later is perhaps suggested by an inscription on one of them, and stone column drums with cuttings for lifting with ropes. This material was recycled in the assemblage sometimes called the fountain of the muses on the south side of the temple (**Figs 2.1, 2.30**).[100] Possibly part of the same phase is a corner triglyph like the one from the Aigina, making a peristyle relatively unlikely here too.[101] It is often supposed that the *genera* were created for peripteral designs.[102] But this seems unlikely in the light of these front-facing triglyph friezes, together with the fact that Aeolic and early types of Ionic capital were similarly ill suited for turning the corner (Ch. 4, p.110, and Ch. 5, pp. 128–30). In any event, a fully Doric order set out on a peripteral layout soon made itself manifest for Apollo's temple at Syracuse and for that of his sister Artemis at Corfu (**Figs 2.25, 2.31**).[103] The complete scheme of the Doric temple was now well established, to be further honed into its canonic shape (Ch. 1, pp. 28–9).

As Coulton observes, 'early Doric architecture is not as consistent and rigid as it became later, but . . . the earliest surviving examples of each element are immediately recognizable for what they are'.[104] The triglyph from Mon Repos illustrates this point perfectly: it presents some curious features (notably the tapering sides and the ogee 'arches'), but there is nothing to suggest a primitive stage of development. It is quite simply a triglyph, even if a rather unusual one. The absence of partially developed traces of Doric style in the decades leading up to its definitive emergence brings the puzzle of its origins sharply into relief. Where did it all come from, and why?

* * *

2.30 Temple of Apollo, Delphi; Archaic blocks on the south side, including column drum with lifting holes. Later reassembled to make a fountain, these blocks belonged to either the mid-seventh- or early sixth-century temple. See also **Fig. 2.1**.

2.31 Temple of Artemis at Corfu (Kerkyra); façade as proposed by the excavators on the basis of numerous blocks belonging to the sculptures of the pediment and a smaller number of fragmentary architectural elements. Certain details and the overall width of the façade may be called into doubt; this was probably shorter, perhaps with fewer columns.

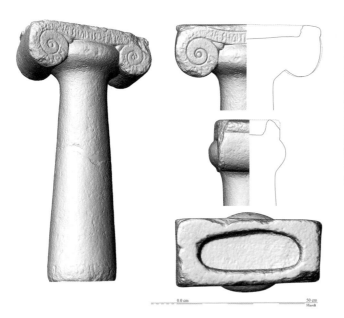

0.0 cm   50 cm
                                              Herdt

2.32   Votive column from Sangri on the island of Naxos, height
1.05 m, Naxos, Archaeological Museum. 3D digital facsimile by Georg
Herdt: plan, half sections and elevations, view. Note the dedicatory
inscription and the socket in the top surface to receive sculpture.

EMERGENCE OF THE IONIC *GENUS*

Vitruvius's testimony suggests that Ionic was created
after Doric, and this rings true in that the Ionic 'order'
took much longer to cohere (see **Table 5**, p. 120).[105] Some
elements that hint at later practice developed piecemeal
over the course of the seventh century in the Cycladic
islands and on Crete. Mouldings, scrolls and a figurative
frieze of uncertain positioning were used at Prinias (**Fig.
2.16**). Stone bases in the form of truncated cones were
used on Delos, possibly in the seventh century.[106] A little before 600 capitals appear with the hallmark Ionic
down-turning volutes, initially it seems as part of free-
standing votive columns. The stub column from Sangri
on Naxos is a modest little thing (**Fig. 2.32**), but the free-
standing column at the sanctuary of Apollo on Aigina,
seemingly just as early, was very substantial; since, as we
have seen (above, p. 55), Doric cannot be proved, it may
have been Ionic. In any event not long afterwards an
even more lofty votive column arose nearby at Aphaia's

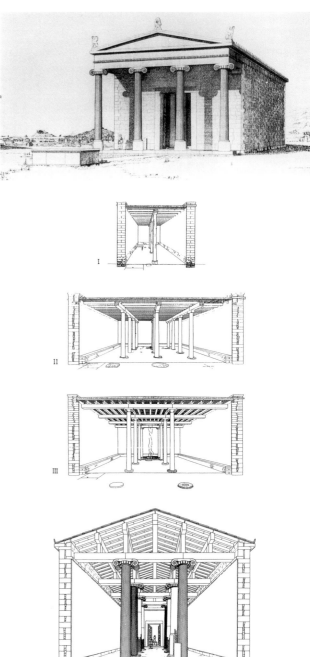

2.33   Temple of Dionysos at Yria on the island of Naxos. Top: perspective reconstruction of the exterior (see phase IV below) by
Manolis Korres; bottom: phased reconstruction by Gottfried Gruben
(I early eighth century; II second half of the eighth century; III early
seventh century; IV 580–50). Note the possible presence in the later
two phases of substantial cross-beams at the level of the frieze.

sanctuary on the same island, and this was definitely Ionic of sorts (**Figs 5.18, 5.22**). A couple of decades later the Naxians dedicated a more elegant successor at Delphi using marble brought from their island home (**Figs 5.18, 7.18**). In fact the exploitation of marble, initially in the Cyclades and then in Ionia and Attica, is almost a precondition for such exacting architectural style. By this time Ionic columns may have appeared as part of temples, although surviving definite examples are not known until that of Dionysos at Yria of *c.*580, once again on Naxos (**Fig. 2.33**).

Experimentation took contrasting directions in different regions. At Samos torus bases were enriched by

2.34 Temple of Artemis, Ephesos (mid-sixth century); perspective reconstruction by Fritz Krischen with emendations by Aenne Ohnesorg.

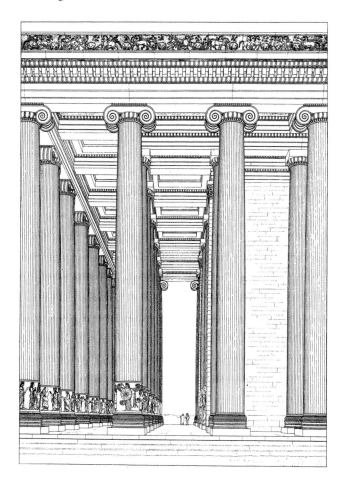

means of horizontal striations or fluting (**Figs 5.9, 5.10**).[107] The capitals of the first dipteros took a similar form, probably without volutes, though wooden ones (possibly sheathed in bronze) have been proposed.[108] Scotia mouldings were introduced into bases at Ephesos, where the magisterial Artemision was financed in part by the Lydian king Croesus (Kroisos) (**Fig. 2.34**).[109] Vitruvius (IV,1.7) cites this as the earliest manifestation of the Ionic *genus*, and it may well have been the first ensemble of column and entablature to be recognized as a model for later practice.[110] The formal language was pushed further in the temple of Apollo at Didyma near Miletos (**Fig. 2.36**), and then the second dipteros at Samos built by the tyrant Polykrates (**Figs 5.16, 5.22**).

The consolidation of Doric and Ionic peristyles coincides with a remarkable increase in size, witness the plans compiled here, all at 1:1000 (see also **Table 1**, p. 24). The scale of transformation was particularly pronounced in the Ionian megastructures; their colonnades were extraordinarily audacious and costly, on account of both their lofty height and their dipteral or doubled up layout. Whereas more than four modest columns was rare in the seventh century, these *dipteroi* each had a hundred or more giant ones.[111]

The situation at Samos is especially notable. Dozens of buildings the size of the earlier Hekatompedon could fit within the volume of the first dipteros. Many thousands of tiles were required. It is the substructure, though, that yields the most interesting conclusions. Recent examination shows that the second dipteros was not built due to the destruction of the first by fire, as used to be thought, for there are no traces of combustion. The problem lay in the groundworks. The first dipteros had a 'foundation' that was in reality just a large levelling course (about 1.5 m tall). This principle sufficed for smaller structures of mud-brick and timber, and also stone temples in Egypt, since they typically sat on bedrock. But it was woefully inadequate for putting such a huge stone edifice on a marshy (and earthquake-prone) site, and a sign of limited prior experience. The dipteros was, it seems, literally as well as metaphorically staggering; it shifted unevenly and either partly collapsed or threatened to do so, which is why it had to be dismantled and re-erected after less than forty years, this time with properly considered foundations.[112] The whole affair underlines the abruptness of advances affecting building technology and ambition, advances for which the builders themselves were not completely prepared.

* * *

Everything examined shows that early Greek architecture did not develop in a progressive evolutionary fashion, as is so often supposed. Instead there was a surprisingly rapid jump from unassuming shrines to grandiose stone peripteral display-temples. We have encountered some explanatory factors such as the technological innovation of the tiled roof and improved economic conditions. The preceding lack of architectural distinction between religious and domestic functions presumably became unsatisfactory, and Doric and Ionic stepped in to announce and celebrate the sacred. Architecture asserted pride in the state, temples became symbolic of the same, and *poleis* competed to build bigger and better ones. It was a race for splendour.[113]

But there seems to have been more to it. Might the new paradigms reflect changes in religious attitudes? No significant reorientation is known at this time that concerns ritual, but one of potentially striking relevance did affect the display of offerings. A case in point is the rise in the number, size, quality and worth of votive *kouroi* (Ch. 1, p. 27). The increased investment in sanctuaries this represented mirrored a decrease in the worth of grave goods from around 750; in other words there was a shift from private to public show.[114] What is more,

the ostentatious and competitive nature of the giving was amplified by a parallel shift from number to value: from swarms of small-scale votives to fewer large-scale dedications, including some donated by groups.[115] Temples represented *polis*-scale collective dedications, and it is the religious underpinning of offering (Ch. 1) that made them magnets for financial, social and political capital.

As state offerings temples had to be beautiful and impressive. To this end many things played a part: size and mass; symmetry and regularity; fine workmanship; prized and durable materials like bronze and stone. The so-called refinements – subtle effects that demanded extraordinary levels of precision (**Fig. 5.6**) – may be understood as a dedicatory phenomenon too. As already remarked for the Parthenon frieze (Ch. 1, p. 27), the greater the effort the better, whether or not the eye could make out the detail. But dedication of this kind could apply to buildings made in *any* style. So why then do Greek temples look as they do? Why did Doric and Ionic enjoy such runaway success? Was it simply because the Dorians tended to use the one, the Ionians the other, out of respect to lost precedents?[116] But this still leaves us wondering why these forms, and not others, were selected in the first place.

The signal importance of the orders for the history of architecture ensures no shortage of hypotheses. Might the *genera* be accounted for by constructional principles (Ch. 3)? Or by the influence of preceding traditions (Ch. 4)? Or by their visual impact (Ch. 5)? Or as symbolic manifestations of the value systems that created them (Ch. 6)? Clearly there is a great deal still to be explored.

2.35 (FACING PAGE TOP)   Temple of Zeus, Olympia; reconstructed section and polychrome interior elevation by Victor Laloux. *Envoi* of 1883, showing Pheidias's chryselephantine statue of Zeus, one of the Seven Wonders of the ancient world. The existence of akroteria in the form of tripods is also attested by literary sources.

2.36 (FACING PAGE BOTTOM)   Temple of Apollo, Didyma (Hellenistic phase); open-air court or adyton. View over the remains of the shrine (*naiskos*) looking towards the front, and the grand staircase leading to the great hall of the oracle. The configuration of the Archaic phase was similar, albeit slightly smaller.

OLYMPIE

RESTAVRATION DE L'ALTIS

TEMPLE DE JVPITER

CHAPTER THREE
QUESTIONS OF CONSTRUCTION AND THE DORIC *GENUS*

Enclosing space with structure distinguishes architecture from other realms of art and production. The intelligent deployment of materials and techniques to this end is one of the greatest sources of satisfaction for anyone involved in building. Early experiments with shelter must have had a primarily practical orientation, just as Vitruvius muses.[1] In remote times, he envisages, men lived like wild beasts, in woods and caves, and it was only after the discovery of fire that they began to commune, develop language and interact.[2] Blessed by manual dexterity thanks to their upright posture, they built using branches, reeds and mud, gradually improving by dint of learning from each other. Eventually progress led to peaceful civilization, and with expanding ideas born from the variety of their crafts, they produced houses rather than huts, on foundations, using brick or stone, and with roofs of wood covered with tiles (Vitruvius II,1.3–7). When discussing roofs in detail Vitruvius famously explained how aspects of timber construction were perpetuated in Doric temples:

3.1 (FACING PAGE)   Giovanbattista Piranesi, interior view of the second temple of Hera at Paestum (1778), Soane Museum, London (inv. P74).

3.2 (ABOVE)   John Soane, perspective study of a proto-Doric temple (after 1807), Soane Museum, London (inv. 23/4/8).

So it was that ancient carpenters, engaged in building somewhere or other, after laying the tie-beams so that they projected from the inside to the outside of the walls, closed up the space between the beams, and above them ornamented the coronae and gables with carpentry work of beauty greater than usual; then they cut off the projecting ends of the beams, bringing them into line and flush with the face of the walls; next, as this had an ugly look to them, they fastened boards, shaped as triglyphs are now made, on the ends of the beams, where they had been cut off in front, and painted them with blue wax so that the cutting off of the ends of the beams, being concealed, would not offend the eye. Hence it was in imitation of the arrangement of the tie-beams that men began to employ, in Doric buildings, the device of triglyphs and metopes between the beams. (IV,2.2)

The projecting brackets known as mutules in the crowning cornice or geison apparently arose in a similar manner:

> like the triglyphs from the arrangement of the tie-beams, the system of mutules under the coronae was devised from the projections of the principal rafters. Hence generally, in buildings of stone and marble, the mutules are carved with a downward slant, in imitation of the rafters. (IV,2.3)

Thus forms arise from construction and are copied from one medium to another, a principle sometimes known as skeuomorphism or, where stone is involved, petrification.[3] Vitruvius invoked such origins only for triglyphs, mutules and Ionic dentils (IV,2.5), but many a later commentator went further. Thus guttae (the little stubs projecting from mutules and regulae) represent wooden dowels; the concavity of flutes registers the fashioning of them using an adze; and so on. The literature on classical architecture contains scores of such speculations, often rendered graphically (**Figs 0.2, 3.2, 3.3**).[4] Doric has received most attention, although Tuscan 'dispositions' can be viewed in a similar light, and Ionic too.[5] The Florentine humanist Gherardo Spini, for

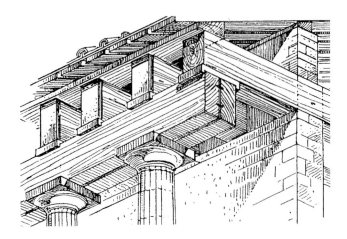

3.3   Vitruvius's derivation of the Doric entablature, as visualized by Josef Durm (1910).

example, visualized in egg-and-dart the effect of pebbles pushing through a bed of mortar under the weight of floor loading.[6]

Petrification offers a simple and compelling paradigm, though many are those who, like Spini, got carried away with remodelling the past to suit their viewpoint (Introduction, pp. 4–5). As debate over origins intensified in the eighteenth century visions of wooden prototypes proliferated – so much so that opponents talked disparagingly of *xylomania* (from the Greek for wood, *xylon*). The popularity of petrification persisited nevertheless, underpinned as it was by theorizing around three interrelated themes: the workings of Nature, the honesty of the 'primitive' mind, and the Greek capacity for reason.[7] Each combined an ancient pedigree with modern appeal.

THE NATURAL, PRIMITIVE AND RATIONAL

Aristotle saw parallels with man-made production aimed at utility, including building operations: 'if a house . . . was brought into being by nature, it would come into being . . . exactly as it now does by art.'[8] Later authorities espoused the natural order inherent in technological progress.[9] An incremental convergence on perfection was held to operate in the visual arts too, and in the second century BC Philo of Byzantium cited 'ancient buildings that are extremely unskilful', and explained how the orders and their refinements had subsequently been honed to perfection 'by trial and error . . . and by all sorts of experiment'.[10] In the Renaissance a vision of progressive evolutionary development including variants encompassing decline and fall appealed to artists like Raphael (**Fig. 0.2**), along with their biographer Giorgio Vasari, and then such influential writers as Winckelmann and Edward Gibbon.[11] Charles Darwin's concept of natural selection later inspired many to extend the model of biological evolution to the products of human culture, of which the architecture of ancient Greece has been held to be a paradigmatic example.[12]

Vitruvius's view of early construction presumes the ideal of simple bucolic life first sustained (in the west) by the Stoics and Cynics. In the eighteenth century the 'noble savage' acquired the status of an intellectual ideal for Jean-Jacques Rousseau and his sympathizers.[13] Abbé Laugier meanwhile, bent on ridding architecture of overblown Baroque excesses, extolled an imaginary para-Vitruvian 'primitive hut' as the embodiment of all the principles of building that it was necessary to know (**Fig. 0.4**).[14] It seems the modern mind finds comfort or inspiration in the notion of uncorrupted ancestors incapable of artifice and 'lies'. From the time of Laugier architects have retrojected the ideal of constructional honesty back to the Greeks just as they projected it onto future practice.[15]

The ideal of honesty to materials and processes has a rational component that is prefigured in Hellenic culture. Plutarch recounts an anecdote about the Spartan king Agesilaos, who, when dining in a mansion in Anatolia, contemplated the ceiling woodwork and then turned to ask his hosts in feigned surprise whether trees really grew square in their part of the world. 'And if they grew square' he added, 'would you want to make them round?'[16] Once again a notional watershed around 1750 is significant for the rise of rationalism as a mainstay of modern architectural theory, as exemplified in the mid-

nineteenth century by Viollet-le-Duc's lapidary analysis of the Greek temple.[17]

Vitruvius's explication of Doric finds thus sympathetic allies in the natural, primitive and rational currents of architectural thinking exemplified by Agesilaos's jibe. Appearances would seem to back this up; after all, Doric forms are robust and prismatic, at first sight very much the product of the saw, the adze and the chisel (**Figs 3.1, 9.1**).[18] Is not the 'order of orders' the celebration of structural stability and constructional technique?[19]

TECTONICS

The constructional origin of Doric finds further support in the notion of tectonic form – form that celebrates the poetics of structure. The term addresses the quality of what the builder or *tekton* fabricates and what the *architekton* designs or supervises (*archi-tekton* literally means chief-builder). The root *tek-* grew out of the vocabulary of carpentry and building and is found in Linear B in the word for carpenters, *te-ko-to-ne*. The related later term *techne*, denoting a craft, expertise or skill, by the Classical period generally implied an emphasis on measurement, exactitude and control that could be taught.[20]

The Greek temple has been upheld as a paradigm of the tectonic ever since the term entered the vocabulary of architectural criticism with Karl Bötticher's treatise *Die Tektonik der Hellenen* [1844].[21] Tectonics refers to the constructional 'presence' of building, like that of an actor.[22] A structure becomes tectonic when it declaims its logic and purposefulness via the handling of load-paths, materials, the design of components and of the junctions between them. This tectonic character is manifest in a number of ways: in the legibility of the structural system; in the visual distinction between members that play different constructional roles; in the refusal to use any element other than in its proper position; in the serial repetition of each class of element.[23] And whereas stone suggests arches and vaults, wood lends itself to post-and-beam architecture, as Hegel explained:

Without any need for extensive and difficult work-manship, the tree affords both stanchions and beams, because wood has already in itself a definite forma-tion; it consists of separate linear pieces . . . which can be directly put together at right, acute, or obtuse angles, and so provide corner-columns, supports, cross-beams, and a roof. On the other hand, stone does not have from the start such a firmly specific shape, but, compared with a tree, is a formless mass which, for the purpose must be split and worked before the separate stones can be brought together and piled on one another . . . Operations of many kinds are required before it can have the shape and utility that wood has in and by itself from the start.[24]

It is true that key architectural thinkers, including Jacques-Nicolas-Louis Durand, Bötticher and Semper, have warned against simplistic readings of the Greek temple as the descendant of the primitive hut,[25] but they proved to be protesting against the tide. The consensus at the end of the nineteenth century was summed up by Otto Wagner, a pivotal figure in the emergence of the modern movement:

> The first human building form was the roof, the pro-tective covering, surely as a substitute for the lack of the cave. The roof preceded the supports, the wall, even the hearth. . . . After an immeasurably long evo-lution, traditions together with art gradually elevated the basic forms of supports, walls and rafters to art-forms . . . Logical thinking must therefore convince us that the following tenet is unshakable: EVERY ARCHITECTURAL FORM HAS ARISEN IN CONSTRUCTION AND HAS SUCCESSIVELY BECOME AN ART-FORM.[26]

Wagner's use of the upper case leaves in no doubt the importance of the doctrine for designers of the modern era. Increasingly written by specialists other than archi-tects, twentieth-century treatments of Greek architec-ture tend not to be so preoccupied with construction, yet the fact remains that the majority of textbooks support the Vitruvian line.[27] While early editions of Banister Fletcher's *History of Architecture* balanced the orthodox explanation for Doric origins with counter-arguments, later editions carry just the following bald summary: 'Though at one time the question was debated, there is now no doubt that the Order had a timber origin.'[28] But can we really be so certain?

CONSTRUCTIONAL MIMESIS

With the theory behind us, now it is time to test the archaeological evidence for petrification, starting with generalities and progressively narrowing the focus. The perpetuation in permanent materials of forms created using degradable ones is a worldwide characteristic of vernacular building. The shift from timber, reed, fabrics, animal skins and unbaked clays to terracotta, brick and stone reflects technical advances, aspirations for pres-tige, and practical needs of defence against decay, insects, fire and military aggression.

In parts of Asia masonry details echo long-standing traditions of timber construction. The *duogong* brack-ets so typical of Chinese timber roofs have long been re-interpreted in stone, brick and tile friezes.[29] On the Indian subcontinent it is not uncommon to see timber columns and beams side by side with stone derivatives.[30] In ancient Egypt constructional mimesis can be deduced from representations on wall paintings and reliefs that show reed and papyrus woven to form walls or bundled to make columns; such techniques evidently inspired monumental solutions.[31] Numerous Lycian rock-cut tombs and free-standing sarcophagus-monuments have steep roofs redolent of thatch, while elevations seem to reproduce carpentry, complete with rafters, purlins and false mortise and tenon jointing, though not without contradictions (**Fig. 3.4**).[32] In Etruria and Phrygia rock-cut sepulchral chambers have ceilings carved as if con-structed of wood, and tombs near Gordion have gable fronts shaped as if roofing timbers crossed at the apex, a technique attested in the Far East and on Etruscan and Villanovan architectural models.[33] Semper's interpreta-tion of the Midas monument and surface patterns applied to stone in Assyrian palaces (**Fig. 0.6**) highlights

3.4 Viollet-le-Duc, perspective study of a Lycian stone sarcophagus fashioned in imitation of timber construction.

2, pp. 45–8). This is a context which renders petrification inherently plausible, while the mutating character of building finds poetic expression in the mythic history of Apollo's Delphic temple, with its successive manifestations made of first laurel branches, then wax (and/or feathers), then bronze, and finally stone.[36]

Architectural representations on Greek vases show structures that appear to be made of wood, with more slender and/or more widely spaced columns than would be the norm for stone (**Fig., p. i, Figs 3.6, 6.1, 9.2**).[37] Pausanias tells of old wooden structures surviving down to his day, the second century AD. These include a column inside the Heraion at Olympia [V,16.1]; the so-called pillar of Oinomaos at the same sanctuary

3.5 Aristocratic tomb at Tamassos, Cyprus (first half sixth century); detail of the entrance.

another kind of petrification, of patterns derived from textile arts.[34] A dromos tomb of the early sixth century at Tamassos on Cyprus presents a veritable essay on petrification (**Fig. 3.5**). Stone is made to ape wood details such as the ends of joists, closely butted ceiling members with a convex profile (rather like equivalents in traditional Scandinavian buildings), a barred door; there is even a pretend locking mechanism.[35]

In Greece of the seventh century construction experienced a shift towards permanent materials. Terracotta tiles replaced thatch and reed; dressed stone replaced mud brick; stone columns replaced wooden ones (Ch.

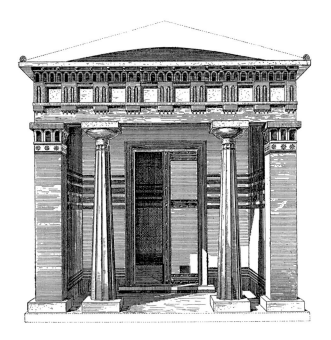

3.6   Doric temple or shrine on the François Vase (a large black-figure *krater* (*c.*570), Museo Archeologico, Florence). Note the slender column proportions and the presence of stone bases, both of which suggest shafts and perhaps capitals of wood.

3.7   City gate on the François Vase, graphic rendering (see **Fig. 3.6**). The braced construction points to timber (perhaps faced with metal). Timber dowels or metal fixings seem to be echoed on the crenellations (or mutules?) above.

[V,20.6–7]; a commemorative columnar monument at neighbouring Elis [VI,24.9]; the ruins of a temple sacred to Poseidon near Mantineia in Arcadia [VIII,10.2].[38] By implication these vestiges should pre-date the widespread use of stone, though this is hardly certain. Pausanias's testimony is also significant since the things he judged worthy of mention tended to be of a certain calibre. The temple at Metropolis, with its massive wooden interior columns about a metre wide, furnishes indirect confirmation of Pausanias's report of a timber column in the Heraion. In both temples the entablatures, being completely missing, must have been wooden. They may have been Doric too, though this we cannot know.[39]

Petrification clearly applied in the case of doors. The royal tombs at Vergina (Aigai) have stone doors articulated with frames and panels that make little sense in this material. In fact they recall doors made of wood (or of metal dressed onto a wooden armature), in line with representations on vases (**Figs 3.6, 3.7**).[40] Rare traces of actual wooden doors show that they did indeed exhibit the characteristics that stone and bronze versions imitated.[41] The marble coffered ceilings of Classical temples bring to mind wooden coverings made up of larger beams, smaller members and infill panels (**Figs 9.11, 9.12**).[42] The migration of forms across different materials affected other domains too. Thus the seventh-century terracotta *kalathos* illustrated in **Fig. 6.21** evokes wickerwork baskets.[43] Certain vase types arguably took their shape from prestigious metal vessels of which they were affordable copies.[44]

PROBLEMS WITH PETRIFICATION

In the Doric order petrification is clearly manifest in the mutules of the geison. Their inclination, size and spacing compare very well with timber rafters.[45] Not dissimilar projecting members occur on funerary structure in Lycia and the tombs from Tamassos mentioned earlier, and furthermore on early models from Samos (of a type of which one is illustrated in **Fig. 2.9**).[46] The canonic arrangement of three rows of six conical guttae per mutule seems too dense and mannered to mimic wooden dowels, but early formats with two rows of four cylindrical guttae are more convincing.[47]

So far, so good; Vitruvius's text, the teachings of theory, and archaeological evidence seem to march in step. However, Doric elements other than mutules are more resistant to constructional explanation. The spread of the capital reduces bending stresses in the beams, it is true. Yet, unlike bracket capitals in various traditions (including Ionic), the Doric echinus spreads radially and not just in line with the beam. For Viollet-le-Duc this disqualifies it as the product of carpentry, though actually it may simply show that structural redundancy was considered a price worth paying for four-way symmetry.[48]

The origin of the triglyph frieze is a much more contentious issue, and many an objection has been directed at Vitruvius's account.[49] In the abstract, linear roof structures feature primary members running front to back (ridge-beam, purlins and wall-plates) that support more closely spaced smaller rafters running cross-wise.[50] The typical Doric temple doubly negates this logic, in that first the triglyph-beams and mutule-rafters run round all four sides, and second they share the same rhythm. Interpreted literally this implies two superimposed grids of structure nonsensically notched into one another at every crossing, as visualized by the pro-Vitruvian Alois Hirt (**Fig. 3.8**).[51] It is also arguably illogical for two beam ends to meet at the corners.[52] As early as 1822 Hübsch demoted the role of timber to a memory, seeing the character of Doric as primarily a response to building with stone.[53] Viollet-le-Duc's critique went further: in his analysis the Doric temple (**Fig. 3.9**) was the rational product of using stone from the very outset.[54]

Temples with a clear central nave had to have the load from the ridge transferred via transverse beams, as may tentatively be reconstructed for the Heraion at Olympia (**Fig. 3.10a**). Such a solution chimes with Vitruvius's cross-beams, yet in well preserved peripteral temples the

3.8   The timber ancestor of the stone Doric temple according to Alois Hirt (1821).

3.9   Analytical cut-way of the structure of a Doric peristyle of the Classical period according to Viollet-le-Duc (1858).

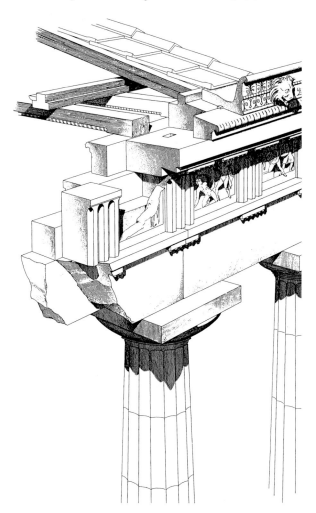

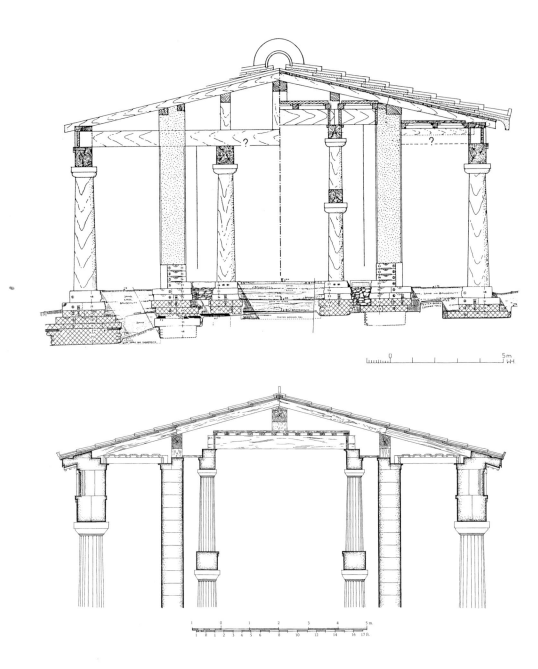

transverse members do not project into the peristasis, which was narrow enough to be spanned by rafters alone (**Figs 3.9, 3.10b**).[55] Indeed, beams as tall as triglyphs would have been enormously large and cumbersome given the spans involved.[56] Moreover, roof and ceiling structures typically lie above the triglyphs and not at the

3.10 Greek roof construction in the Archaic and Classical periods, cross-sections showing the principal roof timbers: (a) the Archaic Heraion at Olympia; (b) the Hephaisteion in Athens (mid-fifth century). The latter, which is well preserved, has T-shaped stone ceiling beams spanning at the level of the geison, as do beams in the Parthenon and other buildings (**Fig. 3.9**). The cross-section of the Heraion is open to two main possibilities, left and right.

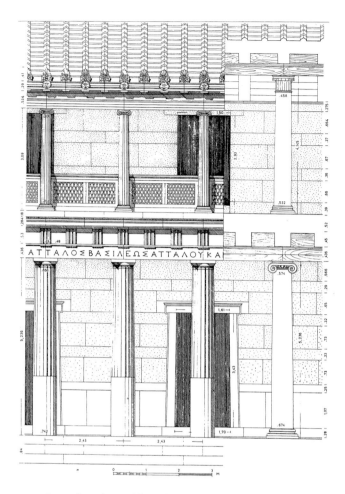

3.11   Stoa of Attalos II (the ruler of Pergamon 159–138), Athens; reconstructed elevation. Note the slenderness of the Doric columns and the relatively light entablature, with three triglyphs and metopes per bay. Inside the portico the ceiling beams sit at frieze level. See also **Fig., p. xii.**

3.12   Altar of Artemis at Kerkyra (Corfu) (early sixth century). This stood in front of, and was contemporary with her temple.

same level, as the petrification doctrine suggests.[57] Only wide spans, which normally did not apply to the peristyle, entailed beams low enough and large enough to bear comparison with triglyphs (**Fig. 9.11**).[58] Trusses did not take hold until the third century, however, by which time many buildings had not two triglyphs per bay but three or four, the smaller size of which made them more comparable with tie-beams (**Fig. 3.11**). Perhaps, then, Vitruvius's reading of Doric origins may mirror Hellenistic and Roman conditions.

To my mind an especially telling difficulty for the petrification doctrine stems from the presence of triglyph friezes on altars. Of all places, why should timber beams have to do with solid structures associated with fire?[59] This might be explained if triglyphs were first created (rationally?) for temples, and later copied (irrationally?) from temple to altar. There is no proven time lag, however. In the earliest *in situ* combination of a Doric temple and a triglyph altar, at Artemis's sanctuary on Corfu, these were contemporary (**Fig. 2.31, 3.12**).[60]

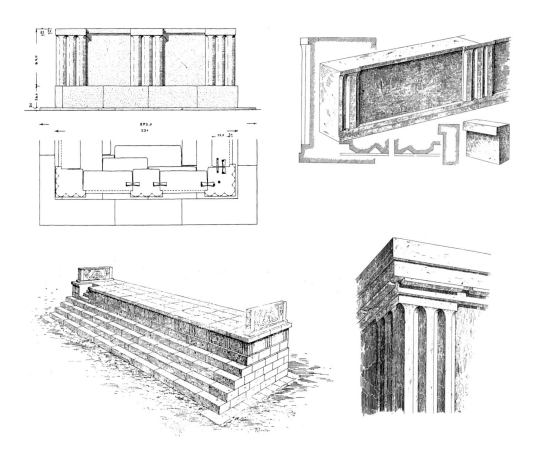

3.13 Selected triglyph friezes associated with altars. Top left: sanctuary of Artemis, Corfu; the remainder: sanctuary of Athena, Syracuse (top right: block with triglyph and metope belonging to larger altar; bottom left: reconstruction of larger altar; bottom right: detail from another frieze probably belonging to a smaller altar). Note the absence of guttae and the long metopes at Syracuse, where traces of red paint were found on some of the triglyphs.

Triglyph altars at Syracuse (**Fig. 3.13**) have unusual details and red pigmentation, which suggests an early date since triglyphs were generally painted blue by the mid-sixth century.[61] Who is to say that triglyphs did not appear on altars first, and from there were copied to temples? After all, as we saw in Chapter 1, altars were more fundamental to Greek religion than temples (Ch. 1, pp. 15, 21).[62]

Notwithstanding these various objections, we should not be dogmatic about the form of the first Doric structures to the point of concluding, as did Viollet-le-Duc,

that they were necessarily born in stone. Early wooden temples were no doubt lighter and more airy than their stone successors, as suggested by representations on vases. Pursuing this line of conjecture, the legacy of timber might explain the notorious 'corner problem' afflicting Doric design, and which gave rise to the narrowed or 'contracted' corner bays of many a temple (**Fig. 3.14**).[63] The problem occurs because epistyle-beams made of stone are much fatter than triglyphs, but arguably this would not have arisen in the case of timber superstructures.[64]

So as to explain the tectonic contradictions mentioned earlier 'proto-Doric' systems can be envisaged with triglyphs/beams only on the flanks, and with just one per bay; after all, the latter condition occurs at the so-called Monopteros at Delphi (**Fig. 3.19**). Or triglyphs occurred initially only at the front (**Fig. 0.2**), which is more likely in my view given the front-facing friezes of the early temples at Aigina (**Fig. 2.29**) and Delphi.[65] Presumably later architects decided to wrap the frieze all the way around simply because it looked better that way;[66] or, as Viollet-le-Duc put it, art intervened. Similar attitudes are reflected in the four-way symmetry of the Doric capital, as mentioned, as well as in the way that vernacular solutions for flat roofs and ceilings became 'civilized' in the fashioning of marble counterparts in temples. In this context genuinely structural members are readily integrated with 'false' ones for the sake of a symmetrical look (**Fig. 9.12**).[67] Evidently most Greek builders did not treat the principle of 'honesty' as narrowly as did King Agesilaos.

The possibility of reaching different conclusions from the same evidence depending on how you look at it also warns against dogmatism. Though removed from Doric practice, it is instructive to turn to the unusually well preserved temple of Demeter at Sangri on Naxos, this being due in part to having been made almost entirely of marble – including beams, rafters, tiles and all (**Figs 3.15, 3.16**).[68] On the one hand the superstructure is quite at odds with Vitruvian proto-Doric. Cross-beams are notable by their absence while, contrary to all convention, the columns rise and fall with the roof-pitch. Yet on the other hand the beams of the porch of this temple have a size and rhythm roughly compatible with a hypothetical frontal distribution of triglyphs, were such a building to have them (which it did not).[69] In sum, though the Doric frieze was by no means a mechanical representation of a logical structure, a loose association with beams cannot be ruled out.

It is quite another matter as regards the details of the triglyph. What explains the vertical elements? Why are there (almost) always three? Why are they chamfered? Why do they connect via arches at the top, with a capping piece above? Etymology yields little illumination; triglyph (*triglyphon*) suggests something with three glyphs, which can mean 'marks' or perhaps 'cuts', which most commentators identify with the recesses or channels. To make three, however, means counting the two whole recesses plus the two lateral half-recesses.[70] Vitruvius (IV,3.5) meanwhile says the Greeks used *meros*,

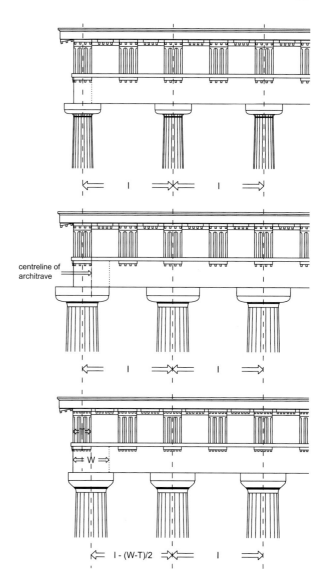

3.14 Doric design and the corner problem: (a) hypothetical configuration using timber; (b) conflict of axes and statics when using stone; (c) resolution of the conflict by means of corner contraction. Doric design privileged three design ideals: (i) regular spacing for the columns; (ii) regular spacing for the frieze; (iii) a whole triglyph terminating the frieze. These are combined hypothetically in (a). However, in stone temples it was typically impossible to reconcile all three ideals since the width of triglyph was substantially narrower than the epistyle-beam (b). One solution involved widening the metopes nearest the corner, while the more popular option involved shortening the column interval/s nearest the corner (c). The problem may be linked to the transition from timber to stone construction, for in a timber temple (a) arguably there would be no need for an epistyle-beam wider than the triglyph.

femur, to designate the legs or uprights, the three formal units comprising one frontal face and two chamfers.[71] There is no discernible technical need for treating
a beam-end with recesses or legs, and Vitruvius is silent
about such a possibility. Nonetheless others have stepped
in to supply the missing rationale. Winckelmann
wondered if channels were sunk into the wood to guide
and disguise any splitting that may occur.[72] Some detect
the legacy of tripartite beams, with the recesses perpetuating shadow gaps hiding the joints.[73] Surviving
cuttings for beams point however to squarish cross
sections, as do Greek carpentry specifications.[74] Meanwhile the terracotta plaques/covers protecting the
purlins of Etruscan temples – a close match to the func-

3.15 (ABOVE)   Temple of Demeter at Sangri on Naxos; interior
reconstruction by Manolis Korres.

3.16 (FACING PAGE TOP)   Temple of Demeter at Sangri on Naxos;
exterior reconstruction by Manolis Korres.

3.17 (FACING PAGE BOTTOM)   Etruscan protective terracotta cover
for a ridge beam, Acquarossa (Tuscany). Elements such as these
chime with Vitruvius's mention of covers for the *mutules* of Etruscan
roofs. The figurative treatment, however, contrasts with his account
of beam covers in the Doric context.

tion Vitruvius imputes to triglyphs – vary greatly in
appearance, from blank slabs to elaborate figural compositions (**Fig. 3.17**). Not one resembles triglyphs in any

way at all. In short, constructional readings have certain merits in terms of the general principle of the Doric frieze, yet they have nothing at all to offer as regards the detailed appearance of the triglyph.

TRIGLYPH OR METOPE AS APERTURE

The validity of the beam-end theory was evidently questioned by some Greek critics since Vitruvius mentions a rival explanation, namely that windows gave rise to triglyphs (IV,2.4). He found this ridiculous, given these lie 'at the corners and over the middle of columns – places where, from the nature of the case, there can be no windows at all'.[75] Vitruvius's very mention of the window hypothesis gives it some credibility, however. Perhaps he (or his source?) had got confused, for if anything apertures of some sort equate better to metopes. In his play *Iphigenia in Tauris*, Euripides tells how Artemis carried Iphigenia off across the Black Sea to be priestess at the grim sanctuary where stray Greeks were sacrificed. At one point her brother Orestes and his companion Pylades plot how to enter the temple undetected. 'Look', says the latter, 'there in the gaps in the frieze, where there is enough space for the body to pass through.'[76] The constructional and window hypotheses might be reconciled by imagining proto-Doric temples with openings in between beams or block supports, as suggested by Raphael (**Fig. 0.2**) and others.[77]

Despite Vitruvius's dismissal, some have conjectured that triglyphs really did descend from small windows with a central mullion of a kind known from Minoan house models, the occasional representation on vases, and Hellenistic houses on Delos.[78] Perhaps over a long period of mutation the jambs and the mullion fused together in response to the need for better security, or the greater weight of roof-tiles compared with thatch.[79] Or perhaps, as some have even suggested, triglyphs perpetuate the memory of an entire second storey.[80] The possibilities are evidently endless.

* * *

EVOLUTION AND TECTONICS REVIEWED

Many of the proposals just cited are frankly too fantastical to warrant comment, except that they attest to the lengths to which some have pushed the constructional cause. The conviction exemplified by Wagner's uppercase injunction (p. 66) is deep rooted, as is its reliance on two major planks of theoretical support already discussed: evolution and tectonics. Time and again proponents have posited a hypothetical constructional system along with a rationale for its mutation into the canonic Doric configuration. Some developmental change is indeed plausible – but is the evolutionary nature of Greek architecture overemphasized? The question needs addressing with reference to the evidence from surviving Doric structures (or elements), which are listed in rough chronological sequence in **Table 3** (pp. 78–9).

A linear evolution – which in the natural world usually involves a single distant progenitor and numbers of related but different descendants – sits ill with the sudden appearance of the *genera*, and the diversity of early temple layouts (Ch. 2, p. 43, **Figs 2.8, 2.25**). Heterogeneity characterizes well preserved early Doric buildings: the temple of Apollo on Aigina, the old tholos and the Monopteros at Delphi, the Artemision at Corfu, the Apollonion at Syracuse and the older temple of Aphaia on Aigina. Only the Artemision and the Apollonion have rectangular peristyles; the temples on Aigina have columns on the front alone (one prostyle, the other *in antis*); the structures at Delphi have unusual groundplans, one round and the other almost square (**Fig. 2.25**). The elevations are equally varied (**Fig. 3.19**).[81] Rather than the branches of an evolutionary tree there is much to be said for Rhys Carpenter's model: a trend from diversity to uniformity over time, from assorted solutions to the peripteral plan elevated with either Doric or Ionic.[82] Furthermore, design practice did not 'evolve' gradually, but advanced by sudden shifts of emphasis alternating with periods of relative stasis.[83]

We are accustomed to triglyphs and columns aligning with a sense of tectonic propriety, yet early Doric often behaved differently. In the Temple of Apollo at

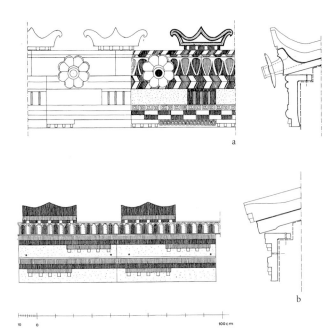

3.18 (ABOVE)   Archaic terracotta sheathing with 'horn' antefixes from southern Italy (mid-sixth century): (a) cult building at S. Anna, Crotone (Kroton, Calabria); (b) temple of Apollo, Cirò (Calabria).

3.19 (FACING PAGE)   Archaic Doric temples in elevation, with one from the Classical period for comparison, 1:250: Syracuse (Syrakusai), temple of Apollo, front (according to Orsi), and side (according to Mertens); Paestum, first temple of Hera; Aigina, temple of Apollo; Delphi, old tholos; Aigina, archaic temple of Aphaia; Delphi, so-called Monopteros; Sounion, temple of Poseidon (late fifth century).

Syracuse and the old tholos at Delphi, two of the earliest buildings that can be reliably reconstructed, triglyphs do not in fact align with column axes (**Fig. 3.19**). At the Apollonion this occurs but vaguely on the front, and only for some columns on the flanks.[84] As for the tholos, the *edges* of the triglyphs sit over the column centres. Meanwhile the main façade of the so-called Monopteros had triglyphs off-set slightly from the column axes, so as to allow a wider central bay (**Fig. 3.19**).[85] All this indicates a decorative handling of the frieze (Ch. 5, pp. 117–18). Thus the syncopated triglyphs and regulae on terracotta revetments like one from Crotone (**Fig. 3.18**) manifest not just individual caprice but genuine predilections of early designers.[86]

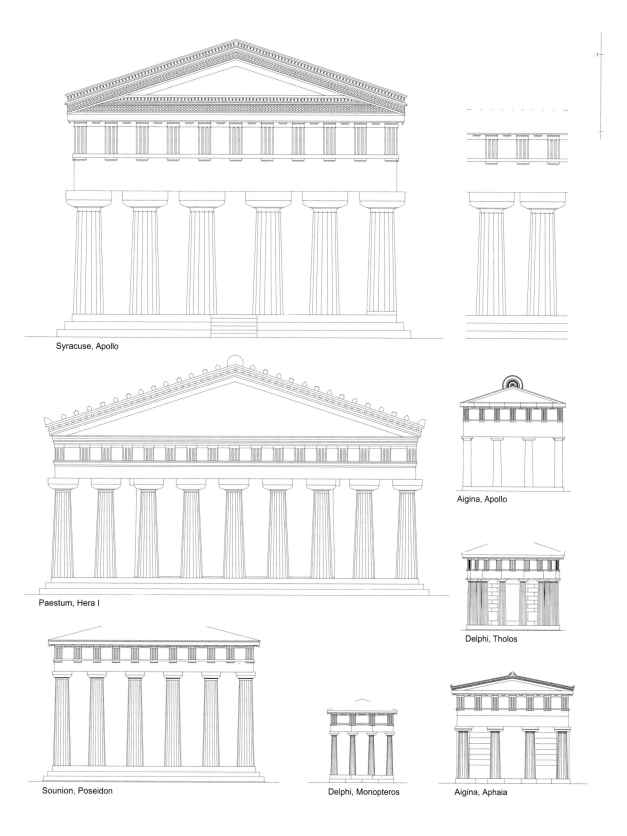

Syracuse, Apollo

Paestum, Hera I

Sounion, Poseidon

Aigina, Apollo

Delphi, Tholos

Delphi, Monopteros

Aigina, Aphaia

TABLE 3
BUILDINGS AND ARCHITECTURAL ELEMENTS ASSOCIATED WITH DORIC FORMS

E = entrance/front (*in antis* or prostyle)   P = peristyle   s = stone   w = wood

fig. no.	site/building	columnar context	comments	guide date
3.25	Corfu, Mon Repos, temple of Hera[1]		(lost) triglyph, roof edging	late 7th c.
2.25, 3.10a	Olympia, temple of Hera[2]	w/s P (6 by 16)	wood entablature?	c.600
2.25, 29, 3.25	Aigina, temple of Apollo[3]	E (4)	frieze faces front	c.600
3.20	Aigina, capital[4]	votive		early 6th c.
2.31, 3.25	Corfu (Kerkyra), temple of Artemis[5]	P (6 or 8 by 17)	sculpted metopes and pediment	c.580
3.20	Corfu, column of Xenvares[6]	funerary	shafts: 16 flutes; leaf necking	
3.21	Agrigento (Akragas), capital[7]	votive	deep abacus	after 580
2.25, 3.19, 21	Syracuse, temple of Apollo[8]	P (6 by 17)	non-alignment columns/frieze	580–570
3.21	Tiryns, capital[9]		16 flutes	
3.20	Delphi, temple of Athena (Pronaia)[10]	P?	slender shafts, 16 flutes	mid-1st half 6th c.
2.1, 30	Delphi, temple of Apollo[11]	E?	frieze faces front?	mid-1st half 6th c.
2.25, 3.19	Delphi, Old Tholos[12]	ring of 13	non-alignment columns/frieze	mid-1st half 6th c.
2.25, 3.24	Aigina, temple of Aphaia[13]	E (4)		mid-1st half 6th c.
7.15	Paestum (Poseidonia), free-standing column[14]	votive		
	Athens, Olympieion[15]	P (8 by 16?)		
2.25, 3.19	Delphi, Monopteros[16]	4 by 4	one triglyph per bay	2nd qu. 6th c.
	Athens, Temple H.[17]	P 6 by ?	slender shafts	565 onwards c.
	Eleusis, Telesterion II[18]	E (10?)		
3.21	Kalapodi, south temple[19]			
	Selinunte (Selinus), Temple Y[20]		sculpted metopes	c.560
2.25, 3.21, 25	Foce del Sele, temple of Hera[21]	P (8 by 16?)		
	Corinth, temple of Apollo[22]	P (6 by 15)		mid-6th c.
2.25	Selinunte, Temple E1[23]	E (2?)	'monoglyph'?	
4.9	Selinunte, Temple C[24]	P (6 by 17)		mid-6th c.
5.7	Assos, temple of Athena[25]	P (6 by 13)	frieze on epistyle	
3.20–3, 28, 30–1	Paestum, temple of Hera[26]	9 by 18	decorated capitals, no mutules	mid-6th c.
8.10	Metapontum, Temple A2[27]	8 by 18	triglyphs with ribs	3rd qu. 6th c.
7.11	Metropolis, temple[28]	w P (5 by 11)	wood entablature, decorated caps	3rd qu. 6th c.
3.20.5.22	Ugento, free-standing column[29]	votive		3rd qu. 6th c.
3.21	Tegea, temple of Artemis[30]	E (4)	leaf necking	
	Corinth, 'Great Temple'[31]	P		mid-2nd half 6th c.
viii, 1.24, 3.2, 27	Paestum, Hera II ('Poseidon')[32]	P (6 by 14)		2nd qu. 5th c.
1.3, 9.1	Athens, Parthenon[33]	P (8 by 17)		447–432
3.19, 25, 5.5	Sounion, temple of Poseidon[34]	P (6 by 13)		444 onwards

NOTES TO TABLE 3

1 Dontas 1968; idem 1976; Strøm 1988, 187–9 (suggesting a date of *c*.630); Mertens 1989, 434–5; Winter 2000, 251 ff.; Barletta 2001, 69–72; Marconi 2007, 10; Saperstein 2012.

2 Dörpfeld 1892; idem 1935, I, 161–85; Mallwitz 1966; Barletta 2001, 62–4, 77–80, 126–7; Sinn 2001; Donderer 2005; LL&R 655.

3 Hoffelner 1999, 15–45; Barletta 2001, 70, 83 (with a date of 580–570).

4 Wesenberg 1971, Abb. 108; Hoffelner 1996, 16–19; Barletta 2001, fig. 24; Segal 2007, no. 28. Part of a smaller capital of comparable date also survives; Hoeffelner (1996, 16) judges it to have supported a tripod (cf. Segal 2007, no. 27).

5 Rodenwaldt 1938; Schleif *et al.* 1940; Barletta 2001, 70, 83 (with a date of 580–570); Gruben 2001, 112–15; LL&R 775–6. Capitals: Wesenberg 1971, Abb. 96–7. Contemporary triglyph altar: Yavis 1949, 115. Rodenwaldt and Schleif restored the front with 8 columns, but this is doubtful: see Herdt *et al.* 2013.

6 Schleif *et al.* 1940, 76–8 (placing it earlier than the temple of Artemis); Hampe 1938, Abb. 2; Wesenberg 1971, Abb. 94–95; Jeffery 1990, 233, no. 13 (with a date, based on the script, of *c*.575–550); Barletta 2001, 60–62.

7 Wesenberg 1971, 51, Abb. 110; Alzinger 1982, 112–20; Barletta 2001, 60, fig. 30; Mertens 1993, Taf. 62; idem 2006, 103–4; Segal 2007, no. 3.

8 Cultrera 1951; Gullini 1974; Howe 1985, 360, 376–7; Wesenberg 1986, 145; Mertens 1996, 25–38; idem 2006, 104–9; Bartletta 2001, 70–1, 83; Marconi 2007, 38–50; LL&R, 839. Howe (1986) argued for an early date, while Barletta (2001, 83), gives 570–560.

9 Sulze 1936; Wesenberg 1971, Abb.104; Barletta 2001, 54–8, 60, 62, 173, fig. 25.

10 Demangel 1923; Bommelaer and Laroche 1991, 58; Bommelaer 1997; Barletta 2001, 57, 60–62; LL&R 519.

11 This phase burnt down *c*.548. See entry in Table 2 and Laroche 2001; Luce J.-M. 2008, esp. 98–108; Hansen 2009, 128–35.

12 Pomtow 1910; Courby 1911; de la Coste-Messelière 1936; Seiler 1986; Bommelaer and Laroche 1991, 120–21; Østby 2000, 248–52; Partida 2000, 82–93; LL&R 524.

13 Schwandner 1985; Gruben 2001, 121–3; LL&R 679–681.

14 Sestieri 1953; Doepner 2002, 226, no. 1003; Mertens 1993, 106, Taf. 56.3; idem 2006, fig. 391; Segal 2007, no. 60. Segal gives the lower diameter of the column, which stands on a stepped base with three tiers, at around one metre, and indicates that the remains of a base of an adjacent larger free-standing column is consistent with a diameter of around 1.5m.

15 Tölle-Kastenbein 1994; LL&R 580.

16 Pomtow 1910; Courby 1911, esp. 148; de la Coste-Messelière 1936, 452–3; Bommelaer and Laroche 1991, 121–3; Mertens-Horn 1996; Laroche and Nenna 1990; Partida 2000, 75–82; Østby 2000, 248–52; Marconi 2007, 16–17, 92–3; LL&R 523–4.

17 Wiegand 1904; Heberdey 1919; Korres 1997b; LL&R 554.

18 See Table 2.

19 See Table 2. Hellner forthcoming.

10 Mertens 1996, 32 ff.; idem 2006, 115–19. Metopes: Giuliani 1979, 37–66; Rizza 1996, 406 ff.; Marconi 2007, 84–5, 117–20.

21 This has been called by some the 'Thesauros'. Zancani Montuoro *et al.* 1954; Van Keuren 1989; Junker 1993; Conti 1994; de La Genière 1997, 177–9; Tocco 2000; Mertens 2006, 220–22; Marconi 2007, 27–8, 200–04 (with a date of 550–40); LL&R 798–9 (with a date of 570), while Barletta (2001, 83) gives 560–50.

22 Fowler and Stillwell 1932; Pfaff 2003; LL&R 610.

23 Gullini 1980; idem 1985; Mertens 2006, 104; Barletta 2001, 69, 174, n.4; LL&R 833–4 (with a suggested date of 580). The mid-century date suggested here reflects guidance kindly given by Dieter Mertens and Clemente Marconi.

24 Koldewey and Puchstein 1899, 95 ff.; Mertens 2006, 119–25; Marconi 2007, 127–33; LL&R 830–1.

25 Clarke, Bacon and Koldewey 1902–21; Dinsmoor 1975, 87–8; Wescoat 2012.

26 Krauss 1941; Mertens 1993; idem 2006, 140–48; Greco and Longo 2000; LL&R 796.

27 Mertens 1993, 131–3, Taf. 73; idem 2006, 149–52; LL&R 791–2. Note the contemporary triglyph altar (Mertens 1993, 132, Abb. 75; idem 2006, 155).

28 Intzesiloglou 2002; Hellmann 2006, 27–8; LL&R 509.

29 Displayed in the National Museum, Taranto, with its bronze statuette 730 mm tall, (inv. 1211327); Degrassi 1981; Stibbe 2000, 173–9; Segal 2007, no. 58.

30 Rhomaios 1952; Wesenberg 1971, Abb. 99; Østby 1991–2, 309–23; idem 2006b; LL&R 671.

31 Pfaff 2003.

32 Krauss 1941; Mertens 2006, 283–95; LL&R 797.

33 Dinsmoor 1975, 159 ff.; Korres 1994; idem 1995; idem 2002a; Gruben 2001, 173–90; Niels 2005; Hurwit 2005; LL& R 555–6; Marconi 2009a.

34 Dinsmoor 1975, 181–2; Gruben 2001, 229–32; Wilson Jones 2001, no. 4; LL&R 797.

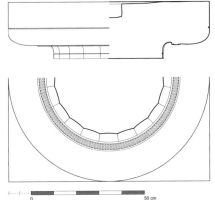

Aigina, votive column

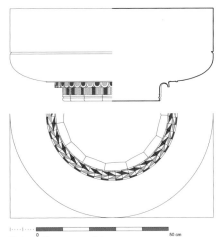

Kerkyra, Xenvares capital

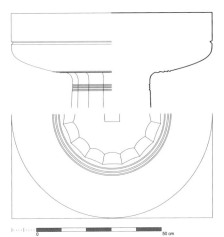

Delphi, sanctuary of Athena Pronaia

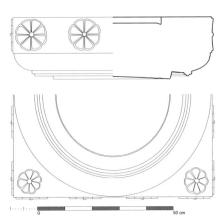

Ugento, votive column

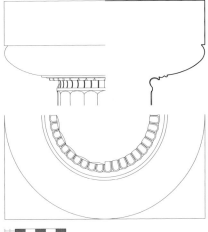

Paestum, Hera

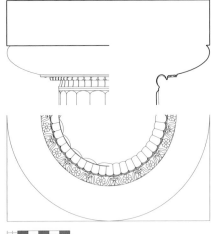

Paestum, Hera

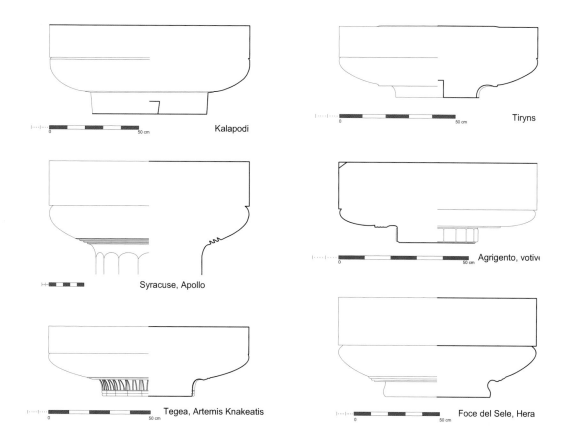

3.21 (ABOVE)   Selected Doric capitals of the Archaic period; half sections and elevations

3.20 (FACING PAGE)   Selected Doric capitals of the Archaic period; half sections, elevations and plans.

This suggests that the Doric elevation was 'tectonified' *after* the formal vocabulary had already existed. Again this does not exclude all connection with beam-ends but, together with the difficulties of explaining the look of triglyphs in such terms, it obliges us to downgrade the formative importance of constructional logic and to acknowledge that other factors must also have been in operation.

* * *

MATURATION OF DORIC VOCABULARY

This is a topic of interest in its own right, while offering a further commentary on the foregoing discussion. The drift from heterogeneity towards consensus is echoed in salient features of the Doric *genus*: fluting, capitals, mutules and triglyphs.

The Doric shaft did not acquire its canonic twenty scalloped flutes much before the middle of the sixth century. Earlier shafts could have flat facets or only slightly concave flutes.[87] Sixteen was as common a number as twenty, while the sanctuary of Artemis on Corfu has yielded Doric shafts with twenty-four, twenty-eight and possibly thirty-two flutes as well.[88]

Doric capitals display considerable variety, as visual comparison quickly demonstrates (**Figs 3.20, 3.21**). This variety can be gauged in three main respects: proportion (e.g., ratio of height to width), shape (principally the profile of the echinus) and detail (especially the junction between capital and shaft). Proportions become progressively more compact, but variation is encountered at any one time, especially up to the mid-sixth century.[89] The same is true of shape. One type of echinus presents an almost flat underside meeting a tight arc (e.g., Aigina). Another type is deeper, with a pronounced curvature (Kalapodi). The dominant profile however is a gradually accelerating curve. It is tempting to imagine a progressive smoothing culminating in the canonic profile of the Classical period, yet different solutions overlap chronologically. The treatment of the profile is also quite varied. Some early examples are completely smooth, but more usually the part near to the shaft, the necking, received rings in relief, or annulets, numbering two (Tiryns), three (Delphi) or four (the older temple of Aphaia).[90] The necking could also be fluted like the shaft, left smooth, or formed into a kind of 'overfall', which could be articulated with foliate relief or accompanied by a ring of chevrons (**Fig. 3.20, 3.22**).[91] In some of the capitals at Paestum lotus and palmette motifs were applied to the echinus (**Fig. 3.23**), while those from the temple at Metropolis present a comprehensive floral scheme (**Fig. 7.11**).[92] The abundance of solutions is at odds with a single canon.[93]

To understand triglyph development it is best first to clear out some unhelpful speculation. Triglyphs have repeatedly been imagined where not so much as a fragment exists, as in the case of Isthmia (**Fig. 2.23**).[94] The famous painted terracotta panels from Thermon are generally assumed to have been metopes that accompanied lost wooden proto-triglyphs (**Fig. 2.19**). But even if these 'metopes' did form part of a high-level frieze, which is not certain, and even if they were separated by dividers, these did not necessarily look like triglyphs.[95] A partly developed or 'proto-triglyph' has yet to be found.[96]

The earliest surviving triglyph belongs to the site of Mon Repos on Corfu, *c*.610 (**Fig. 3.25**).[97] This displays idiosyncratic touches that were later to be expunged, including tapering sides and ogee arches.[98] As with

3.22   Capital from the first temple of Hera at Paestum; detail. The overfall of the leaves may derive from Mycenaean precedents and/or ones made of bronze.

capitals, early triglyphs varied extensively (**Fig. 3.25**). Sometimes their proportions compare with later norms, sometimes they are more slender, as at Apollo's temple on Aigina. Triglyphs separated by unusually wide metopes appear on altars at Syracuse (**Fig. 3.13**).[99] Details vary, especially in the Greeks' western territories in southern Italy and Sicily. Triglyphs can have concave

3.23   Capitals from the first temple of Hera at Paestum; plans showing the decoration of the echinus.

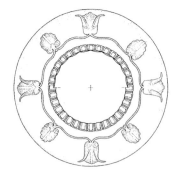
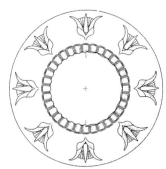

3.24 Temple of Aphaia at Aigina; detail. Perspective of corner as reconstructed by Ernst-Ludwig Schwandner.

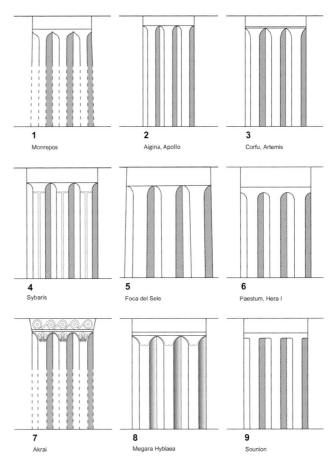

3.25 Selected triglyphs of the Archaic period; elevations, with one from the Classical period for comparison

rather than straight facets; the arches where the uprights meet can be semi-circular, pointed, or ogival; relief decoration can take the form of little ribs, running waves or palmettes.[100] And there is also the issue of colour: whereas later triglyphs were typically painted blue (**Fig., pp. iv–v, Fig. 7.14**), in line with Vitruvius's testimony (above, p. 64),[101] several early sets, including those from Syracuse, were painted blood-red. Other early examples were near-black, including ones from Aigina, Paestum, and the so-called H-architecture on the Athenian Acropolis.[102] Early practice admitted a range of options, and only in the second half of the sixth century did consensus settle on blue. There is no question of blue 'evolving' out of red or black; it was a matter of choice.

The earliest surviving geison belongs to the temple of Poseidon at Isthmia: a smooth slanting projection with no mutules (**Fig. 2.24**).[103] A Doric geison with mutules complete with guttae is not known until around fifty years later, at Aigina (**Fig. 2.29**). Like some other early sets, the guttae were disposed as two rows of four; later three rows of six became the norm. A step-by-step development might be postulated, from a smooth geison to one with plain mutules, to mutules with few guttae, and finally on to the elaborate canonic solution (**Figs 3.26, 3.27, 9.1**). The evidence, however, confounds a straightforward sequence.[104] Meanwhile, as already mentioned (Ch. 2, p. 54), altogether different kinds of cornices occur in western territories. With its colourful

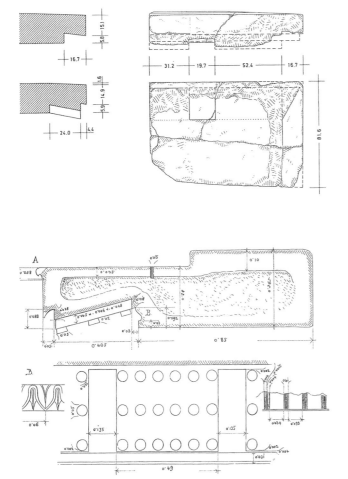

3.27   Second temple of Hera at Paestum (Classical period); detail of entablature. The guttae were made separately to the mutules of the geison – rather as dowels would be – and have since been lost.

3.26   Early and mature solutions for the geison. Top: Olympia, plan, elevations and sections of a corner geison from a treasury (?c.600) – note the absence of mutules along the side and the absence of guttae on the mutules on the front; bottom: Athens, Propylaia, an elaborate example of the Classical canon.

panoply of terracotta revetment, the temple of Hera I at Paestum offers a contrast to the usual Doric geison (**Fig. 3.30**). Archaic practice in Sicily and southern Italy is in fact often unorthodox in one way or other. From the middle of the sixth to the early fifth century Doric usage in the Cyclades deviated from mainland patterns, with unusually slender columns (sometimes without flutes and sometimes raised up on square base blocks), wider inter-columnations, low architraves, tall triglyphs and the frequent absence of a mutular geison.[105]

Finally, it is important to highlight the speed of developments. Roof-tiles came into service only in the first half of the seventh century (Ch. 2, p. 46), which is the earliest possible date for Doric style, since its heavy entablature presupposes a tiled roof. With few signs of tentative or preparatory stages, evidence for the Doric vocabulary materializes in the last quarter of the century. So at sometime around the third quarter of the seventh century was born a substantially new mode of building which swept precipitately over the Greek world.[106] The testimony of Vitruvius, the general operation of petrification in the seventh century, convictions as to the natural, 'honest' and rational character of pre-monumental construction, all this has put understandable pressure to accept a constructional genesis and a development analogous to natural evolution. Yet given the situation just summarized Doric may be less the fruit of evolutionary processes than of a sudden artistic revolution. As Manolis Korres affirms, 'the replacement of older wooden constructional and decorative forms

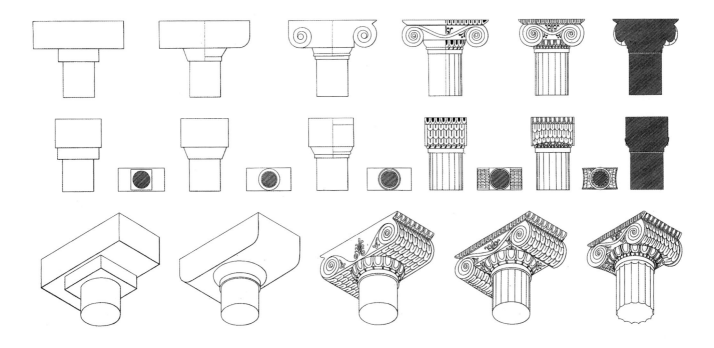

3.28 (ABOVE)   Development of the Ionic capital as the progressive elaboration of a constructional prototype, as visualized by Jacques-Ignaz Hittorff.

3.29 (RIGHT)   Hypothetical derivation of the Ionic capital from timber antecedents as visualized by Gottfried Gruben: (1) with poles for shaft and capital (impracticable); (2) with rectangular capital and rectangular shaft; (3) with rectangular capital and circular shaft; (4) same, with abacus and volutes (and a swelling at the top of the shaft!); (5) votive column from Sangri (end seventh century).

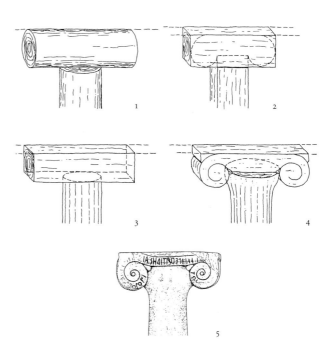

with equivalent ones in stone was not a simple, gradual development but a new eclectic creation, inspired only in part by the older wooden forms (which accounts for the problems inherent in modern attempts to reconstruct the wooden archetypes)'.[107] Precisely: only the mutules, guttae and regulae convince as artistically edited joinery, though how near or how remote to timber models it is impossible to say.[108] Triglyphs, the most stable and striking elements of this *genus*, convey a loose affinity with structure but their details completely elude this line of interpretation.

Ironically, a timber ancestry in some ways makes better sense for Ionic than for Doric. Unlike its Doric counter-part, the Ionic column has a base, the better to protect a timber shaft.[109] The shafts, being more slender, are more in tune with posts or tree-trunks. The lateral extension of volute capitals acts to reduce the span of the epistyle.[110] Comparable timber capitals with scrolled

brackets are known from ancient India to modern-day Turkey.[111] Thus some credence may be given to the hypothesis of wooden origins championed by Hittorff (**Fig. 3.28**) and more recently Gottfried Gruben (**Fig. 3.29**).

As for the entablature, dentils are plausible as the ends of timbers belonging to ceilings or flat roofs, in line with Vitruvius's testimony (IV, 2.5) and some architectural models (**Fig. 2.9**).[112] (The idea that the stepped fasciae of the epistyle represents overlapping planks or stacked beams is, however, a dubious modern idea.[113]) Finally, Ionic architecture in the Cyclades seems to have em-

ployed cross-beams at the level of the frieze, which was arguably a device for screening them (**Fig. 5.24**).[114]

The preceding observations cannot, however, prove a constructional origin for Ionic any more than for Doric. Though relevant, conceptualizations of the orders as responses to working with stone, wood and other materials have been overemphasized. Structure, construction and petrification are bound to have played a significant part in the creation of the orders, but only a part. Also at work were other factors, demanding a more multi-layered account. Architecture, after all, is about more than building in tune with technology.

3.30 (ABOVE) First temple of Hera, Paestum (Poseidonia), poly-chrome terracotta adornment, corner junction between the roof and the stone entablature at the corner.

3.31 (FACING PAGE) First temple of Hera, Paestum. Top: reconstruction by Dieter Mertens and Margareta Schutzenberger, viewed from the south west; bottom: the existing temple.

CHAPTER FOUR

QUESTIONS OF INFLUENCE AND THE AEOLIC CAPITAL

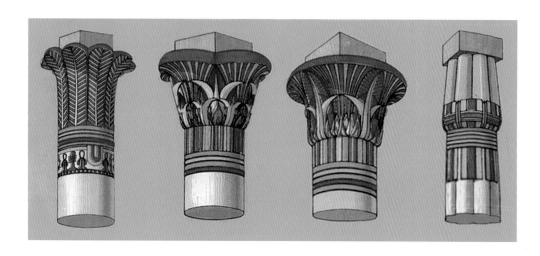

The shortcomings of explanations for the orders based on construction and evolutionary progress open the door to other models for the generation of architectural form. Might designs have been revived from earlier times, or borrowed and adapted in sympathy with the principle of diffusionism, whereby art, ideas and technology travel from more advanced to less advanced cultures?[1] Some ancient authors hint at this with their conviction that the arts arose in Egypt before progressing to Greece and then Rome.[2] Vitruvius is clear about the debt of his fellow Romans to the Greeks; however he gives little indication that they themselves borrowed.

In the modern era consideration of this possibility was for long hampered by a similar presumption of Greek superiority, along with simple lack of knowledge; published accounts by European travellers of lands to the east and south of Greece did not appear until the eighteenth century, and serious archaeological investigations were not undertaken until well into the nineteenth (Introduction, p. 6).[3] Only late in that century did the excavations of first Heinrich Schliemann and then Sir Arthur Evans bring the achievements of the Aegean Bronze Age into the public eye, and with it the cradle of Hellenic culture and design.

4.1 (FACING PAGE) Temple of Hathor, Dendera, Egypt (Ptolemaic period); hypostyle hall.

4.2 (ABOVE) Owen Jones, selected Egyptian capital types (1856). These typically derived from plants.

Identifying flows of influence calls for multiple lines of analysis, embracing formal comparison (though there is no standard methodology for ranking degrees of similarity), relative chronologies (based on evidence not presumption) and mechanisms of transmission.[4] Comparison should also take into account three and not just two dimensions. This point is made by the distinction between the palmette as it was first absorbed from the east as a surface ornament, and its later sculptural employment on stelai and akroteria (**Fig. 6.18**). This was a Greek innovation, made long after the motif had become thoroughly assimilated.[5]

Just as narratives of origin divide between those that privilege construction, influence, appearance or meaning, so there exist partisan views of influence in favour of Bronze Age Greece, Egypt and the eastern Mediterranean. But in the face of competing sources we should learn not to champion one at the expense of another. Rather we should seek to understand how different influences might operate alongside and reinforce one another. A case in point is that fabulous creation, the sphinx. For present purposes its ultimate roots in Egypt are less pertinent than its manifestations in Mycenaean, Assyrian, Syrian and Phoenician production from which the Greeks of the Archaic period may have learnt.[6] There were multiple potential pathways, in part the legacy of extensive cross-cultural interactions in the Bronze Age.[7] The Mycenaean enthusiasm for Egyptian style is exemplified by the reprise of running and interlocking spirals (**Fig. 4.3**), as well as the concave 'Doric flute' (**Fig. 4.6**).

The 'international' popularity of some architectural imagery is illustrated by the device of a sacred column

4.3 Egyptian and Mycenaean architectural spiral ornament. Top: faience wall or ceiling revetment with gold leaf highlighting the spirals and a border frieze on the field-and-divider principle, panel 987 mm × 737 mm, reconstructed from finds from the temple of Amun at Malqata, near Thebes, Egypt (c.1390–1352), now in the Metropolitan Museum of Art, New York. Centre: ceiling of the tomb known as the 'Treasury of Minyas', Orchomenos (c. thirteenth century). Bottom: comparison of Egyptian and Mycenaean schemes by Alois Reigl.

4.5 (ABOVE) Treasury of Atreus, Mycenae, split-rosette ornamental frieze band.

4.4 (LEFT) Treasury of Atreus, Mycenae (Mykenai) (*c.* thirteenth century); façade, as reconstructed by Durm (1881) (bottom half) and Wace (1923) (top half).

4.6 Egyptian and Mycenaean fluting compared. Right: Saqqara; left: Mycenae, tomb of Clytemnestra (Klytaimnestra). In both cases the flutes are shallower by comparison with mature Doric fluting, but some early Doric shafts had equally shallow flutes, while others had straight facets.

honoured by rampant beasts: its adoption in Greek art from the eighth century onwards could derive from examples such as that over the Lion Gate at Mycenae (**Fig. 2.3**), or from oriental precedents (**Figs 4.15, 4.16**).[8] The fact that the Lion Gate stood in the Peloponnese and not some distant land might seem decisive in its favour. But similar schemes appear on oriental bronzes that were put on display at Olympia between the eighth and sixth centuries.[9] Greek architects could have drawn inspiration from both spheres, and indeed from a much wider spectrum of sources – provided we admit the possibility of influence flowing from small scale to large scale, an issue to be discussed in Chapter 7.

Dogmatism is especially ill advised for any type of element for which only few specimens survive. Consider a foliate capital from Arkades on Crete that dates before the early sixth century, when it was re-used in a tomb (**Fig. 4.8**).[10] It recalls Pharaonic palm capitals, even if these are usually more vertical and have just eight segments/fronds (**Fig. 4.2**).[11] On the other hand Assyria and Syria produced a range of such designs, some of which have an overfall that compares well with that of the Arkades capital, although the lobes are relatively large and there is not usually a square abacus (**Fig. 4.28**).[12] This last particular, complete with a little rebate along the bottom, is instead found on Mycenaean ivory colonnettes (**Fig. 4.7**).[13] These, however, do not present such a prominent overfall, nor is the articulation of the echinus and the necking coordinated so as to suggest an array of leaves or fronds. In short each contender presents different merits – so how to choose between them? In fact there is no rationale that obliges us to do so. After all, similar motifs can be derived from different sources, as in the case of spirals and volutes inspired here by plants, there by shells.[14] To repeat, it is better to embrace the prospect of multiple overlapping inputs.[15]

MINOAN AND MYCENAEAN LEGACIES

The architectural culture of the Bronze Age in Crete and the Peloponnese held a limited but special place for columns (Ch. 2, pp. 34–5). The later Greek element that finds the clearest antecedents in this epoch is the Doric capital. Capitals with a circular neck, a square abacus and a bulbous transitional cushion or echinus are known from Minoan complexes (**Fig. 2.2**) and architectural representations from Knossos. More specific Doric traits are found at Mycenae on monuments such as the Lion Gate (**Fig. 2.3**) and the Treasury of Atreus, including a cavetto decorated with leaf points rising from the neck (**Fig. 4.4**).[16] A similar detail, albeit with a greater overfall, occurs on early Doric columns such as Xenvares's and ones at Paestum (**Fig. 3.21**). Acquaintance with Bronze Age styling may also have come via ivory

'proto-Doric' miniature columns, such as those that were deposited in the Archaic period as foundation offerings under the temple of Artemis on Delos (**Fig. 4.7 left**).[17] A Mycenaean component of the Doric capital thus seems incontestable.[18]

Minoan shafts taper in the reverse direction to their classical counterparts, but the fact they taper at all is arguably a common denominator. Mycenaean shafts tend to be more or less straight, though too few survive intact for clarity in this regard. Those of the Tomb of Clytemnestra (Klytaimnestra) have shallow concave flutes comparable to the Doric form (**Fig. 4.6 left**).[19] In addition, fluting appears on Mycenaean ivories like those just mentioned.

Varied production of the Minoan and Mycenaean periods featured a linear run of ornament known as the split-rosette frieze. This has with reason been claimed as the model for the Doric frieze on account of the tripartite motifs that split the rosettes.[20] The façade of the Treasury of Atreus originally displayed such a frieze made of decorative reddish stone (**Fig. 4.5**). Another example discovered by Schliemann and Wilhelm Dörpfeld at Tiryns employed alabaster and inlays of blue glass paste.[21] In contrast to triglyphs, however, the Bronze Age vertical dividers have horizontal bars top and bottom, and no chamfers on the uprights except very faint ones on an example in Nauplion.[22]

Despite these Minoan–Mycenaean foretastes little credence should be given to visions of the Doric order descending from Bronze Age prototypes as part of a more or less unbroken tradition, as Chipiez and others have proposed (**Fig. 4.9**). The disruption suffered in the early first millennium was too long and too deep for elaborate styles to have been transmitted (Ch. 2, p. 36). A more plausible explanation for the similarities observed is a reprise or revival.[23]

The Greeks were intensely concerned with their origins, with rooting themselves and their histories in their own land, and in tracing themselves back to their earliest ancestors. Besides bridging the realms of man and god, the heroes played a key role in this endeavour.[24] Epic tradition kept imagination alive of the legendary

4.8 (ABOVE) Limestone column capital from Arkades, Crete, found re-used in a sixth-century tomb.

4.7 (LEFT) Ivory colonnettes of the Mycenaean period from Delos (left) and Mycenae (right).

palaces of Menelaos and Nestor (p. 35), and it would have been natural for later Greeks to link such figures with ruins that still had an impact on the landscape. A similar desire for connection lives on today in the invented labels we continue to use (following Pausanias) for underground tombs like the 'Treasury of Atreus'. Ancient authors also tell us that tumuli rising conspicuously from the plains near Troy were attributed to Achilles, Patroklos and Aias (Ajax).[25] And though Bronze Age ruins may not have stood out so dramatically as did Roman monuments in medieval Italy, there was still enough to attract the Greeks, and so contribute to their own 'Renaissance' (Ch. 2, p. 42). Evidence of their attention lies in the offerings deposited and the sacrifices enacted at the entrances of Bronze Age tombs at various sites in the eighth and seventh centuries.[26] Particularly intriguing is the proximity of the tholos tombs at Prosymna to the Argive Heraion, while Mycenae and its monuments lay only three miles away (**Fig. 1.5**).[27] The Heraion, significantly, is the sanctuary which Vitruvius (IV,1.3) said was the locus of Doros's temple, the first of the style.

Some sanctuaries were sited over Bronze Age ruins because of the inherent defensive advantages, yet several Cretan 'ruin cults' were bound up with symbolic remembrance.[28] Both symbolic and defensive factors came together at the Athenian Acropolis, where parts of the walls as well as the shrines of Athena and Erechtheus sit over Mycenaean vestiges.[29] At the Argive Heraion image rather than defence was the main issue – presuming that the impressive temple terrace faced with 'pseudo-Cyclopean' masonry was newly built for this project. The huge blocks, some measuring 4 metres in length, resemble megalithic construction at Mycenae, Tiryns and elsewhere that were attributed to heroes or giants (cyclopes). The blocks look too big for builders of the early to mid-seventh century, yet on balance this is the most likely date.[30] Such gargantuan endeavour must have had an ideological purpose: the identification with ancestors and heroes to advance territorial claims and political capital.[31] The reprise of bygone architectural style delivered perhaps a similar message.

* * *

All too often Greece has been set apart on its own trajectory. But Greek culture cannot be meaningfully detached from the rest of the eastern Mediterranean.[32] By the middle of the nineteenth century Semper felt the need to move forward from 'antiquated scholarly theory . . . [that] saw Hellenic art as an indigenous growth on

Greek soil'. Rather it was for him 'the magnificent blossoming' of principles which had their roots 'deeply and widely planted' further afield.[33] Yet it can still be hard to overcome the traditional idealization of Greece as the unique origin of the west, and to look without bias beyond Europe and across the seas.[34]

AN EGYPTIAN CONNECTION?

Egypt was the home of a glorious architectural tradition, one that in the first millennium – unlike that of Mycenae – was still very much alive. Herodotus was much impressed and fascinated when he visited there in the fifth century, and earlier Greeks would have found the contrast with their own, as yet limited, achievements more startling.[35] As already noted, some ancient authors credited Egypt as the cradle of the arts, especially sculpture. Diodorus Siculus took it as a fact that 'the *rhythmos* of the ancient statues of Egypt is the same as that of the statues made by Daidalos among the Greeks'.[36] Egyptian influence was indeed significant for the emergence of free-standing Greek statuary in the second half of the seventh century – a roughly contemporary and similarly sudden blossoming as monumental architecture. Until this time sculptural figures consisted of small bronzes and wooden *xoana*, while the first almost life-size stone statues like Nikandre's plank-like dedication were relatively rudimentary. The jump in quality and size achieved with *kouroi* – some of which attained colossal dimensions by the early sixth century (Ch. 1, pp. 24–7) – cannot be explained only in terms of economic surplus and such like. It required knowledge of a more advanced artistic tradition, the most relevant of which was Pharaonic statuary in view of the shared stiff frontal pose, arms by the side and with one leg forward.[37] (It may be noted too that Greek metrological reliefs in anthropomorphic form appear to relate Greek foot-measures to the Egyptian royal cubit (**Fig. 5.4**)).[38]

Egypt is the ultimate fountainhead of much European ornament. This was Alois Riegl's view, whose illustrations comparing Egyptian and Mycenaean spiral

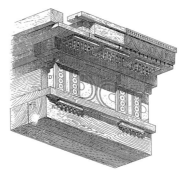

4.9   Derivation of the Doric entablature from Mycenaean precedents according to Charles Chipiez, as conveyed by comparison. Left: hypothetical arrangement inspired by remains from Tiryns; right: entablature of Temple C, Selinunte (Selinus), now in Palermo, Museo Archeologico Regionale.

schemes made obvious the debt (**Fig. 4.3**).[39] Riegl was anticipated slightly by William Goodyear's *The Grammar of the Lotus* (1891), while Flinders Petrie simultaneously reached similar conclusions. Referring to a range of European traditions he argued that 'it is very difficult, or almost impossible, to point out decoration which is proved to have originated independently, and not to have been copied from the Egyptian stock'.[40]

In recent decades the debate over Egyptian influence on Greek temple architecture has re-surfaced once more.[41] The Egyptians were the first to exploit the effect of monumentality in stone amplified by repetition, as exemplified by the 2 kilometres-long grand allée of around 700 'sphinxes' with rams' heads connecting the sanctuaries at Karnak and Luxor. It was this surely that inspired the shorter promenade of marble lions that the Naxians set up on Delos.[42] Whereas the Bronze Age Greeks used columns in a relatively limited capacity, the Egyptians not only understood the psychological force of column arrays but also commanded the means to build them (**Fig. 4.1**). It was they who invented the drama in stone of lines of columns playing shadows on sheer walls. The stupendous hypostyle halls of Egyptian temples find broad echoes in the Ionians' great double-colonnaded temples at Samos, Ephesos and Didyma (**Figs 2.26, 2.34**).[43] Plan typologies are in the main dif-

4.11 Beni Hasan, Luxor; tomb façade with prismatic columns. These have been called 'proto-Doric' but the capitals have no echinus.

ferent, however.[44] A columnar peristyle was not used in Egypt for a temple proper, with the notable exception of the one at Buhen which had colonnades on the front and flanks, though not at the back.[45]

Egyptian column types were inspired by plant forms, the most popular of which were derived from the papyrus and lotus plants, singly or bunched (**Figs 4.2, 4.10**). There also existed some unadorned columns exemplified by those of the tombs at Beni Hasan (**Fig. 4.11**).[46] Severe and stocky, such columns began to be called 'proto-Doric' in the nineteenth century.[47] Some Pharaonic shafts have sixteen facets – as did some early Doric shafts before twenty became the norm (Ch. 3, p. 81).[48] There are Egyptian antecedents too for the concave Doric flute, at Saqqara and Beni Hasan (**Figs 4.6, 4.11**). The capitals at the latter site have a square abacus, but without an echinus or equivalent device they do not much resemble classical counterparts. A bell-like, 'campaniform' Egyptian capital (**Fig. 4.2**) might be likened to the Corinthian *kalathos*, but again the similarity is notional.[50] Doric, Aeolic and Corinthian forms are vaguely presaged in the curious tiered columns now in Chicago from Ramesses III's fortified temple complex at Medinet Habu (**Fig. 4.10**). However these are not to be confused with actual prototypes. Egyptian palm

4.10 Limestone column with tiers of capitals inspired by plants, Ramesses III's fortified temple complex at Medinet Habu (*c.*1186–1155), now in the Oriental Institute of the University of Chicago. Doric, Corinthian and Aeolic forms are vaguely presaged in these capitals, though they cannot be considered prototypes.

capitals find more definite Greek echoes, but as we have seen for the example from Arkades these were not the only source. Egyptian trabeation is bipartite, without a frieze, while its cavetto cornice was little imitated in Greece. Nonetheless, the forthright plainness of the beam is comparable with the Greek epistyle, while bi-partite entablatures were quite often deployed over Ionic columns (Ch. 5, p. 136). Meanwhile decorative 'field and divider' friezes appear in Egyptian pictorial representations of architecture and small-scale applications (**Fig. 4.3**).[51]

Here then is a mixed picture. There are general parallels, yet specific Egyptian models were not copied in the *genera*.[52] There are no antecedents as striking as the Mycenaean capital and split-rosette frieze. The 'Doric' flute, despite its ultimate Pharaonic ancestry, probably came to the Greeks from Mycenae (**Figs 4.6, 4.7**). Egyptian influence convinces most for the 'feel' of the grander Ionian temples, and for details outside the Doric and Ionic canons, a case in point being the sculpted lintel of Temple A at Prinias (**Fig. 2.16**).[53]

The explanation lies on one level in the indirect operation of influence, both geographically (via Crete, Cyprus and Phoenicia) and chronologically. The incorporation of Egyptian style in Minoan and then Mycenaean column design lay dormant for centuries before being revived in the Archaic period.[54] This limited model of influence seems to fit the nature of contacts. After fluid 'international' exchange in the Bronze Age around the eastern end of the Mediterranean,[55] in the early first millennium Egyptians were wary of foreigners. Few Greeks penetrated beyond the seaboard before Ionian and Carian mercenaries were invited around 660 by Psamtik I (Psammetikhos in Greek) to help him rid Egypt of Assyrian dominance.[56] The monuments these men encountered must have set them dreaming of projects for their own gods and cities. By this time, however, the seed of the peripteral plan was already planted at Ephesos, Rakita and perhaps at Argos too, in which case Egypt's role was, as Coulton argues, 'to reinforce, and perhaps accelerate, an already active process'.[57] Exchanges with Egypt flourished again in the reign of Amasis II,

when the great Ionic temples at Samos, Ephesos and Didyma rose to the Egyptian challenge, though using a substantially non-Egyptian vocabulary.[58]

Other constraints on influence concern typology, for while the Hellenes built free-standing linear structures, Pharaonic architecture looked inwards, disposing courts and halls that were shielded from the desert by high walls. A further level of explanation might lie, paradoxically, in differences rather than similarities. As a rule the Greeks resisted anything too obviously Egyptian, shunning the profusion of Pharaonic motifs that permeated Phoenician art. Greek imaginations played with human-headed beasts such as centaurs, but – the Minotaur excepted – had less taste for the Egyptians' animal-headed bipeds.[59] Indeed, Herodotus observed that 'in most of their manners and customs the Egyptians exactly reverse the ordinary practices of mankind'.[60] As part of efforts to strengthen a sense of identity by contrasting themselves with the 'other',[61] did the Greeks consciously differentiate themselves from the Egyptians, and in so doing disguise the extent of influence? This would help explain why the most sustained impact of Pharaonic building lay in more abstract terms, the principle of columnar monumentality and edifices designed to last for ever. Other debts concerned the techniques needed to achieve this, for the rapid advances in Greek construction between 650 and 550 may reflect borrowings from Egypt ranging from clamps to ramps.[62]

AN ORIENTAL CONNECTION?

Peoples of lands around the eastern Mediterranean deferred to Egypt in terms of artistic originality, yet in combination they had a more direct impact on classical culture: Cyprus, Syria, Phoenicia, the Levant and, further inland, Assyria.[63] The case for eastern influence gained currency in the late nineteenth century, becoming quite fashionable for much of the early twentieth.[64] As scholarship matured, however, it grew wary of generalized if not naïve assessments; greater rigour has come to be expected along with the weighing of alter-

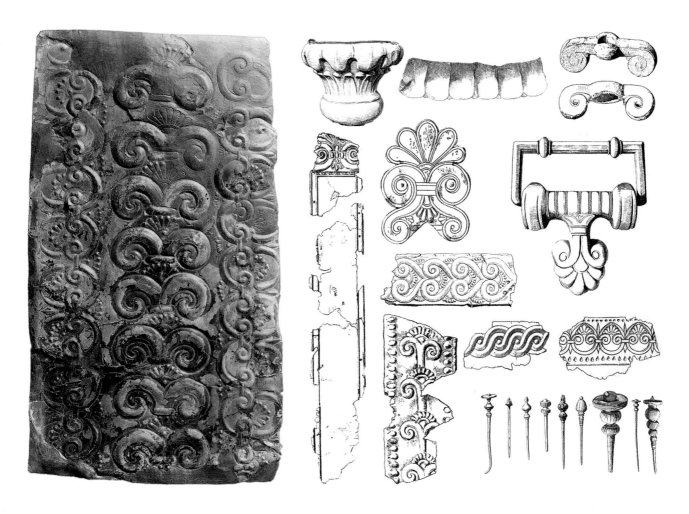

4.12 (ABOVE LEFT) Bronze relief with a pattern of repeating volutes and palmettes. Sheet of oriental, possibly Hittite, origin (ninth or eighth century), found in the sanctuary at Olympia (Archaeological Museum, inv. B 6183).

4.13 (ABOVE RIGHT) Miscellaneous small bronze finds from Olympia dating to the Geometric and Archaic periods. Compilation by Georg Herdt after Furtwängler (1890).

native interpretations. But by and large there remains good reason to characterize the seventh century as the 'orientalizing' period of Hellenic culture.[65] The imprint of the east made itself felt in the adoption of alphabetic writing (which the Greeks learnt from the Phoenicians), intellectual development, religion and the visual arts.[66]

Though many staple Greek ornaments may ultimately go back to Egypt, the eastern end of the Mediterranean was the source of direct models for palmettes, friezes or border patterns such as the guilloche and linked palmettes (**Figs 4.12, 4.13, 4.15**), along with imaginary creatures including gorgons, griffins and sirens. The field-and-divider principle, though not so common, also occurs in the east (**Fig. 4.15**).[67] This repertoire was injected into the Greek artistic bloodstream via assorted oriental material that ended up at major Greek sites, including Olympia (**Figs 4.12, 4.13, 4.14**).

Such things as ivories, jewellery and tableware, ceremonial vessels and stands made of bronze could, unlike buildings, travel; they travelled to the Greek world from the east as objects of trade, as booty and as gifts, whether

4.16 Ivory and gilded frieze from one of the royal tombs (no. 79) outside Salamis on Cyprus. The tomb likely dates to the late seventh century; the ivory, which decorates the back of a seat or throne, may be of earlier Phoenician manufacture.

4.14 Phoenician bronze bowl (eighth century) discovered at Olympia. Radial array of shrines with volute columns framing a standing divinity, in alternation with scenes of ritual activity.

4.15 Frieze of volute-trees flanked by rampant sphinxes and goats, with guilloche and triglyph-and-metope borders. Ivory relief, height 101 mm, from Nimrud, now in the British Museum.

personal or diplomatic.[68] Though now lost, prized textiles also came, transmitting ornamental patterns as they did so.[69] Foreign artefacts arrived at the major ports and sanctuaries of Ionia (Samos, Miletos), Aeolis (Smyrna, Mytilene on Lesbos), the Cyclades (Naxos, Paros, Delos), the western colonies in Italy and Sicily (Taranto (Taras), Syracuse), and central Greece (Corinth, Aigina, Athens, Euboia), going on to penetrate inland to sanctuaries including Delphi and Olympia.[70] The arrival of objects disassociated from their original context encouraged an eclectic approach to borrowing, all the more so since the Phoenicians, themselves highly eclectic, acted as intermediaries.[71]

Skills moved west with eastern craftsmen propelled by the prospect of profit or the threat of invasion by the likes of the Assyrians.[72] Greek counterparts returned home after sojourns overseas, perhaps at Al Mina, near the mouth of the Orontes.[73] Word of the magnificence of Assyrian palaces would have been spread by both élite guests and the itinerant labour employed in making them. The palaces of Menelaos and of Alkinoös, the mysterious king of the Phaecians (Phaiakians), are described in tantalizing terms in Homeric epic. With 'their' high-roofed halls, metal revetments, bands of blue (glazed tile?) ornament, animal statues and abundant gardens, these literary palaces echo not just Mycenaean complexes but also eastern palaces.[74] As a result of a reliance on mud-brick for the walls and timber for columns we have lost so much of the latter; yet there are plenty of clues that point to columns capped by volute and foliate capitals (**Figs 4.14, 4.15, 4.16, 4.17**).

4.17 Wall decoration made of polychrome glazed tiles from the throne room of Nebuchadnezzar II, Babylon, now in the Pergamon Museum, Berlin. The pilasters were originally restored with double-tier volute capitals, but triple-tiers, as shown here, are thought to be more likely.

The contribution of eastern Mediterranean territories to Greek architecture has often been played down, since their building traditions made relatively little use of stone.[75] But stoneworking techniques akin to those later exploited by the Greeks did exist: in the Hittite kingdom until its demise *c*.1000; in southern Anatolia and northern Syria, an area occupied by neo-Hittite principalities until they were overrun by the Assyrians; in the kingdom of Urartu around Lake Van before it too was conquered; in Phoenicia; in the Levant; and in certain parts of Assyria.[76] These techniques included the use of large fine-jointed stone slabs or orthostates at the base of walls,[77] and the drafting of smooth edge margins around facing blocks.[78] Stone bases with torus mouldings supported large wooden columns, notably in

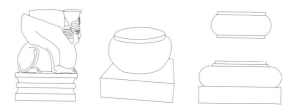

4.18 Selected stone column bases from Near Eastern sites between the ninth and seventh centuries: Nimrud, Assur, Tell Halaf and Nurkanli.

the vestibules of palace/temple complexes in Syria (**Fig. 4.18**).[79] Here and in Assyria and Urartu are found stone bases and capitals, as well as anthropomorphic pillars that presage Greek caryatids, just as much as do Egyptian Hathor columns (**Fig. 4.1**).[80]

Greek cult statues may ultimately look back to Egypt, but again these derive more directly from the eastern Mediterranean.[81] Practices of carrying cult images in procession, and of feeding, bathing and clothing them could have been acquired from the east around the eighth century.[82] Blood sacrifice 'shared' with the gods was a Semitic tradition, familiar from the Old Testament.[83] Indeed the very concept of the Greek temple and sanctuary is arguably anticipated in the east. As Walter Burkert observes:

The thesis can be upheld that Greek temple building, in its beginnings, is in fact a copy of Late Hittite, Aramaean and Phoenician temple building. It is not only the 'house' of the god, or rather of his or her statue, that is in question, but the whole organization of sanctuaries, the interrelation of temples with altars for burnt offering, banquet halls, and *anathemata* (votive dedications), and even sacrificial practice.'[84]

This claim is compelling, as long as the word 'copy' is not understood to embrace the specifics of configuration and structure. Precursors of sorts for the Greek temple survive in western Syria and northern Palestine.[85] Solidly constructed rectangular temples were located either adjacent to palaces or in a sacred precinct; they comprised a main hall or cella entered from one end, often via an entrance porch. Altars for burnt offerings stood right in front of the entrance, while symbols or images of the god(s) were placed near the rear wall, facing the entrance, and usually aligned with it. Luxurious offerings occupied both cella and porch.[86] Eastern temples do not have peristyles, but then Greek hall-temples did not have them either. Imposing eighth-century Syrian temples possessing a columnar porch include those at Ain Dara and Tell Tayinat (**Fig. 4.19**).[87]

4.19   Tell Tayinat; plan showing two free-standing temples (eighth and seventh centuries) in their context adjacent to a palace complex.

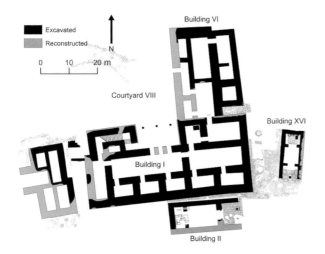

THE 'AEOLIC' CAPITAL

Of all Greek architectural elements the so-called Aeolic capital displays the greatest quotient of foreign influence, which helps explain its tangential relationship to the classical canon.[88] No claim in fact can be made for an Aeolic order. There was no such thing as an Aeolic entablature (though being typically made of wood, too little of this part has survived to be sure of its form). On Greek territory Aeolic columns were employed in the Cyclades, the peninsula of Halikarnassos, Attica, and most of all Aeolis, a region occupied by Aeolians that straddled the coast of modern Turkey and the nearby island of Lesbos. But by the fifth century Aeolic capitals seem no longer to have been used for monumental architecture anywhere in Greece, not even in Aeolis itself. All this accounts for Vitruvius's silence on the subject, and yet kindred capitals enjoyed a wide diffusion (notably in Cyprus, Etruria and Carthaginian territories), while in Greece they long remained popular for furniture and fittings. Vase paintings repeatedly show them on couches or thrones for gods and aristocrats (**Figs 6.1, 7.8**).[89] Another reason for embracing Aeolic capitals within this study is their affinity with Ionic counterparts (Chapter 5, pp. 124–5). There are in fact capitals, like that from Oropos (**Fig. 4.22**), which exhibit characteristics of both styles.

The term 'Aeolic' itself is a modern misnomer. Soon after the first Greek rising-volute capital was rediscovered at Neandria in the 1880s the name was advanced by scholars keen to match an architectural triad to Dorian, Ionian and Aeolian ethnic and linguistic divisions.[90] To give this capital a Greek name is unfortunate since comparable designs existed long before the Greeks took them on. Strictly speaking it would be better to call the volutes 'rising', 'vertical' or 'out-turning' in contradistinction to the horizontally linked down-turning Ionic kind.[91] Nonetheless 'Aeolic' is a convenient label worth maintaining for Greek examples.

Rising-volute capitals divide into two main tectonic categories: rectangular and circular, with the former including broad flat piers, door reveals and more or less square pillars. On Cyprus flat capitals were used in the

4.20 (ABOVE LEFT)   Stele capital with volutes and inward curling foliate crown from Cyprus (early fifth century), now in the Metropolitan Museum of Art, New York (inv. 74.51.2493).

4.21 (ABOVE RIGHT)   Black-figure Attic amphora (*c.*550), British Museum. Shrine framing a statue of a god, probably Apollo. The shrine is represented by two Aeolic columns spanned by an epistyle carrying a lion. Tripods stand either side, with birds on the ring-handles, in keeping with the popularity of little attachments such as those on actual tripods (**Fig. 8.4**).

4.22 (BELOW)   3D digital reconstruction of the volute capital of a votive column at Oropos.

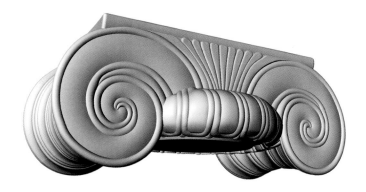

sixth and fifth centuries for tombs, funeral stelai, palaces and perhaps temples too. The volutes typically rise from a central triangle; prime examples still *in situ* belong to the tomb at Tamassos (**Fig. 3.5**).[92] Similarly schematic capitals accompany more slender rectangular or square pillars both on Cyprus and the Halikarnassos Peninsula.[93] At many Cypriot sites stelai were erected that belonged to a sister tradition, one which often terminated with inward-curling plant-inspired compositions sometimes called Cypriot or Phoenician crowns (**Fig. 4.20**).[94] Along with miscellaneous variations on the theme of the volute column, such devices were widespread in artistic output over an ample chronological and geographical range. Comparable representations appear on an ivory frieze from Nimrud (**Fig. 4.15**), for example, and another from one of the royal tombs outside Salamis on Cyprus dating to before the end of the seventh century (**Fig. 4.16**).[95] Were pillars or pilasters of this kind employed by this time in the sumptuous lost palaces of Salamis itself? We can turn now to Aeolic capitals and columns in the Greek world, the best preserved of which are listed in roughly chronological sequence in **Table 4.1** (pp. 102–3).

TABLE 4.1
AEOLIC CAPITALS AND THEIR PARENT STRUCTURES,
IN AND AROUND THE AEGEAN

fig. no.	provenance/findspot	columnar context	character of capital	guide date
4.23	Smyrna, temple of Athena[1]	peristyle	with 'mushroom' crown?	before 580
4.23	Smyrna, votive columns[2]	votive	with 'mushroom' crown?	before 580
4.26a	Delos[3]	votive?	flat, schematic	
	Larisa, free-standing column?[4]	votive?	flat front, sub-scrolls (with crown?)	1st qu. 6th c.
	Larisa, Old Palace[5]	porch	flat front, sheathed with bronze?	2nd qu. 6th c.
4.24, 26	Neandria, temple[6]	peristyle	including crowns?	2nd qu. 6th c.
	Delos[7]	votive	Ionic bolster, fish-scale torus	
4.22	Oropos, votive column[8]	votive	Ionic traits and bolster	mid 6th c.
4.26e	Athens, Acropolis[9]	shrine?	flat, schematic, painted	3rd qu. 6th c.
4.25	Klopedi, temple[10]	peristyle	convex canalis	2nd half 6th c.

NOTES TO TABLE 4.1

1   Smyrna, temple of Athena, several examples. It is a matter of dispute whether all or some belonged to the temple as opposed to votive columns, and whether they were combined with mushroom-shaped foliate crowns (see **Table 4.2**). Wesenberg 1971, Abb. 230; Betancourt 1977, 58–63, 138, no. 18, fig. 20; Kuhn 1986, 80; Cook and Nicholls 1998, 144, fig. 31; Bakker 1999, Aeol-1; Hellmann 2002, 167; Akurgal M. 2007, 129, fig 4; LL&R 751–2.

2   See preceding note.

3   Delos museum, schematic capital, possibly votive. P&C VII, pl. 53.1–2; Vallois 1944-78, II(1), 66, 163; Martin 1955–6, pl. 27.5; idem 1973, 373–4, no.1, figs 1–2; Betancourt 1977, 92, 140, no. 31, fig. 45; Kirchhoff 1988, 217, no. A6; Fraisse and Llinas 1995, no. 1, figs 340–42; Bakker 1999, Iver-3; Rocco 2003, fig. 18. This is a good example of a capital that is hard to date, given the combination of aspects that might seem early (the block shape and incised rather than plastic detail) with others that could be relatively late (the circular eyelets).

4   Larisa, capital for a free-standing column or building (Archeological Museum, Istanbul, inv. 1924). Boehlau and Schefold 1940, 142–3, pls 19a, 29, 40; Schefold 1938–9, 42 ff.; Wesenberg 1971, 78–9, Abb. 153, 154; Betancourt 1977, 74–6, 138, no. 20, fig. 34, pl. 42, 44; Kuhn 1986, 59; Bakker 1999, Aeol-3; Segal 2007, no. 21. It is a matter of dispute as to whether the capital was combined with a leaf crown: see **Table 4.2**.

5   Larisa, Old Palace (Archeological Museum, Istanbul). The presence of several fragments suggests a set of capitals. Fixing holes suggest they were sheathed with bronze. Schefold 1938–9, 42; Boehlau and Schefold 1940,

Wesenberg 1971, 78–9, Abb. 152, 155; Betancourt 1977, 138, no. 21, pl. 45–7; Bakker 1999, Aeol-4.

6   Neandria, more than one capital (Archeological Museum, Istanbul). Clarke 1886; Koldewey 1891; Schefold 1938–9; Martin 1955–6, 122–5; Wesenberg 1971, 77 ff., 132 ff., Abb. 158–64 (cf. 231, 275–6); Betancourt 1977, 63–73, 138, no. 19, figs 25, 26, 29, 32, pl. 41; Wiegartz 1994, esp. 125, 130–31; Bakker 1999, Aeol-2. Whether or not the volute capitals were combined with the multiple foliate crowns found is disputed: see **Table 4.2**.

7   Delos, votive column from the area of the Hypostyle stoa (museum, inv. 202). Vallois 1944-78, II(1), 66b, 165, no. 2; Kirchhoff 1988, 215, no. A2; Ohnesorg 1996, figs 4a, b; Fraisse and Llinas 1995, no. 3, figs 343–6; Bakker 1999, Iver-10.

8   Oropos (findspot at Sykaminon), capital of votive column (National Museum, Athens, inv. 4797). Betancourt 1977, 106, 141, no. 39, P. 67; Kirchhoff 1988, 215–16, no. A3; McGowan 1993, cat. 6; Shoe Meritt 1996, 122-4, pls 34–5; Bakker 1999, Iver-11. The canalis is convex on one side of the capital, concave on the other.

9   Athens, small shrine (Acropolis Museum inv. 9980). Borrmann 1888a, Taf. 18; idem, 1888b, 275–6; P&C VII, pl. 53; Betancourt 1977, 103–4, pls 56–9; Bakker 1999, Iver-9.

10   Klopedi, Lesbos, capital (Mytilene Arch. Museum). Koldewey 1890, 44 ff., Taf. 16.1–3; Betancourt 1977, 83–7; 139, no. 27, figs 41–2, pl. 49; Bakker 1999, Aeol-5.

TABLE 4.2

NON-STANDARD GREEK CROWNS OR CAPITALS, WITH RADIAL GEOMETRY, AND THEIR PARENT STRUCTURES

fig. no.	provenance/findspot	columnar context	character of capital	guide date
4.8	Archanes, re-used in tomb[1]	probable votive	foliate/palm + abacus	late 7th c.
4.27	Smyrna, varied examples[2]	votive or temple	'mushroom' (part of Aeolic?)	before 580
7.16	Samos, Heraion, tripod-on-column[3]	votive	smooth torus	mid 1st half 6th c.
5.22	Samos, Heraion III [1st dipteros][4]	dipteros (10 by 21)	striated torus (part of Ionic?)	575 onwards
4.27	Delos, free-standing column[5]	votive	lobed, with overfall	2nd qu. 6th c.
4.27	Larisa[6]	uncertain	foliate (part of Aeolic?)	2nd qu. 6th c.
4.24, 26	Neandria, varied examples[7]	votive or temple	foliate (part of Aeolic?)	2nd qu. 6th c.
7.12	Delphi, treasury of Knidos[8]	caryatids (2)	ribbed + abacus	3rd qu. 6th c.
4.27	Delphi, treasury of Massalia[9]	caryatids (2)	foliate/palm + abacus	3rd qu. 6th c.
4.27	Didyma, free-standing column[10]	votive	lobed + abacus	3rd qu. 6th c.
4.27	Samos, 2nd dipteros (of Polykrates)[11]	inner files?	lobed, with darts	530 onwards
9.5	Athens, Erechtheion, south porch[12]	caryatids (6)	lobed, with darts + abacus	421–407
4.27	Pergamon, stoa of Athena[13]	stoa	foliate/palm	early 2nd c.

NOTES TO TABLE 4.2

1 Arkades, capital. Levi 1927–9, 450–52; Wesenberg 1971, 45–9, Abb. 87; King 1997, 205–6, 213.

2 Smyrna, 'mushroom-shaped' capitals (several examples of differing size). It is a matter of dispute whether all or some belonged to the temple as opposed to votive columns, and whether they were combined with volute elements. For references see Table 4.1; for photographs see Wesenberg 1971, Abb. 230; Betancourt 1977, pl. 36.

3 Samos, Heraion, capital of votive column carrying a tripod. Kienast 1985, Abb. 16.

4 Samos, Heraion, first dipteros. General: Buschor 1930; Gruben 2001, 350–9; Kienast 1992, 174–80; Rocco 2003, 70–74. Bases: Johannes 1937; Hendrich 2007. Torus capitals: Kienast 1999; Bakker 1999, Tor-1; Hendrich 2007, esp. 38, Abb. 7, 14 where it is speculated that the torus capitals were combined with wooden volutes to constitute in effect Ionic capitals.

5 Delos, capital of votive column (museum, inv. 222). Martin 1973, 378–82, no. 4, figs 6–8; Kirchhoff 1988, 199-200, no. E4; Bakker 1999, Cym-4; Hellmann 2002, fig. 252.

6 Larisa, crown/capital. This was initially reconstructed as part of an Aeolic capital combined with volutes, but this is doubtful. For references see Table 4.1; for illustration see Wesenberg 1971, Abb. 277.

7 Neandria, varied crowns/capitals (some with more pointed leaves, others with more rounded ones); of debated collocation. For references see Table 4.1 and for illustrations see Wesenberg 1971, Abb. 158–62; Betancourt 1977, figs 27-9.

8 Delphi, sanctuary of Apollo, Treasury of Knidos. Durm 1910, 260; Dinsmoor 1913, fig. 3; de la Coste-Messelière 1943, 319-22, pls 55–7; Gruben 2001, 82-7, Abb. 61; Bakker 1999, Cym-13.

9 Delphi, sanctuary of Athena Pronaia, Treasury of Massalia. Dinsmoor 1913, 5 ff.; idem 1923; Daux 1923; de la Coste-Messelière 1957, 330, pls 214–17; Wesenberg 1971, Abb. 90-91; Bommelaer and Laroche 1991, 62–4; King 1997, 205–7, fig. 2; Bakker 1999, Cym-11; Hellmann 2002, fig. 253.

10 Didyma, capital of votive column (museum, inv. A 563). Tuchelt 2007, 403, Abb. 9.

11 Samos, 2nd dipteros, General: Reuther 1957; Gruben 2001, 359–65; Bases: Hellner 2009; lobed capitals: Buschor 1957, 16 ff.; Mace 1978, nos. 61–7; Kirchhoff 1988, 200, no. E5; Bakker 1999, Cym 5 and Cym 9.

12 See Table 5.

13 Pergamon, capital: Coulton 1976, 202, 275–6, fig. 31; King 1997, 205, 208, fig. 3.

4.24 (RIGHT) Capitals from Neandria, near Troy, as reconstructed by Robert Koldewey (1890). The volutes and each tier of crowns constitute separate blocks; they perhaps belonged to different columns (see Fig. 4.26).

4.26 (FACING PAGE) Aeolic capitals and related elements; three-dimensional studies by Perrot and Chipiez, with modifications by the author relating to those from Neandria. (a) Delos; (b) Neandria crown (see also Fig. 4.24); (c) Neandria volutes (see also Fig. 4.24); (d) Klopedi; (e) Athens; (f) Athens.

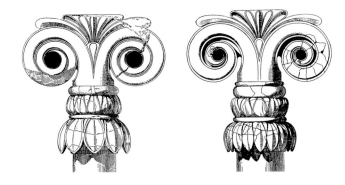

4.23 (BELOW) Columns belonging to the temple of Athena, Smyrna, alternative reconstructions according to Ekrem Akurgal.

4.25 (BELOW) Temple at Klopedi on Lesbos, the order as reconstructed by Philip Betancourt. The wooden entablature is conjectural.

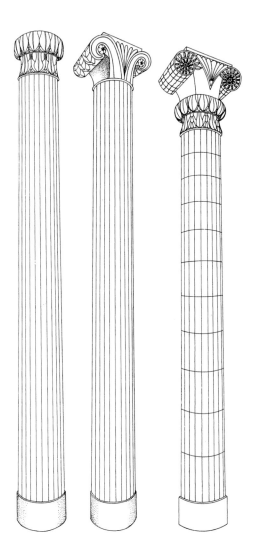

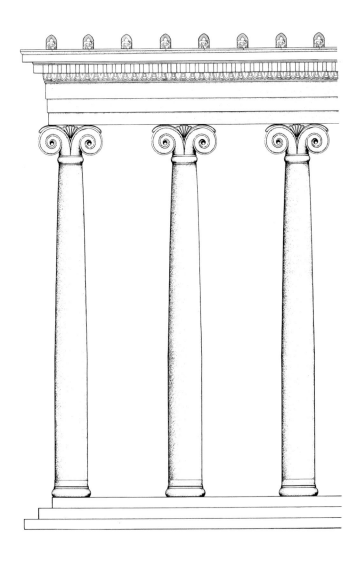

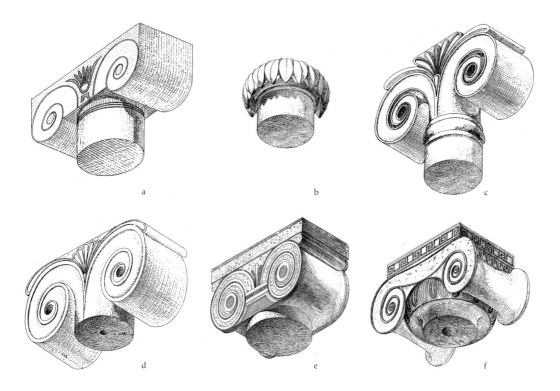

Our main concern is with circular columns, as suited to temples and free-standing dedications (i.e. votive columns). The foremost surviving ones with Aeolic capitals belong to Smyrna (**Fig. 4.23**) and Neandria (**Figs 4.24, 4.26c**) on the mainland, and Klopedi on Lesbos (**Figs 4.25, 4.26d**). Only the temples at Smyrna and Klopedi were truly monumental affairs, with stone columns in the region of 8 metres or more tall. At Smyrna the shafts were, unusually, not left smooth but treated with 32 facets.[96] The later temple at Klopedi presents a more balanced design.[97] When used in Attica, Aeolic columns were typically modest in size, and when illustrated on vases they often appear to be made of wood.[98] A representation of an Aeolic shrine shows it standing only marginally taller than the tripods on either side (**Fig. 4.21**).[99] The few stone capitals found suit either shrines or free-standing funerary or votive columns, like the one from Oropos (**Fig. 4.22**).[100]

The form of early Aeolic capitals is hard to pin down due to uncertainties surrounding the relationship between the volutes and the circular crowns. When used

in this context the latter helped effect the transition with the shaft.[101] The benefit can be appreciated by comparison with capitals that do not have an echinus/crown, for example one from Delos showing 'left-over' portions of the underside of the volute block (**Fig. 4.26a**). Capitals preserving the union of volute and crown, as does that from Oropos (**Fig. 4.22**), are unfortunately all too uncommon.[102] In fact when volutes and crowns are found belonging to separate blocks they should not simply be presumed to go together, since they could be employed separately. Volutes were used for stelai (**Fig. 4.20**), antae capitals, roof akroteria (**Fig. 2.16**) and altars (**Fig. 1.10**).[103] They also appeared in non-architectural contexts on large vessels, on lyres, staffs, mirrors and various kinds of luxury metalwork and furniture.

Crowns were used on their own for a comparable range of non-architectural production. Architectural examples, listed in **Table 4.2**, share no set pattern beyond a concentric array of elements abstracted from plant forms.[104] One group is characterized by an overfall recalling palms (**Figs 4.8, 4.27**), though Greek examples

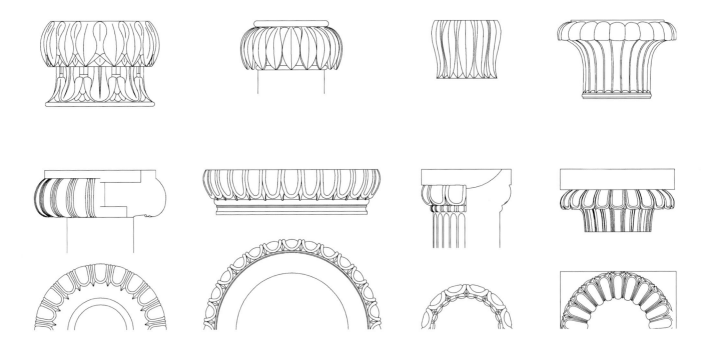

4.27   Miscellaneous Greek architectural foliate capitals or crowns from the sixth century, unless otherwise noted. Top, left to right: temple of Athena or votive column, Smyrna; temple or votive column, Neandria; temple or votive column, Larisa; stoa of Athena, Pergamon (*c*.190-180), bottom, left to right, with half-plans: votive column, Delos; second dipteros (temple of Hera), Samos; votive column, Didyma; Massalians' treasury, Delphi.

are less naturalistic than their Egyptian counterparts.[105] Other crowns have lobes that may derive from buds or petals. A further sub-group presents no overfall but rather a cup-like profile.[106] In some later capitals the lobes turn into the eggs of egg-and-dart, while, when a square abacus is present, the result also recalls Doric types (**Fig. 9.5**).[107]

The separate lineage of volutes and crowns suggests that the Aeolic capital was a composite configuration that fused two distinct traditions, rather as later the Composite capital would fuse Ionic and Corinthian elements. This helps explain why the union between the different parts was not always harmoniously resolved – at least to eyes accustomed to mature solutions. This is the case for the combinations restored for Smyrna

(**Fig. 4.23**) and Neandria.[108] The latter capitals did not have two tiers of crowns as originally reconstructed (**Fig. 4.24**). The ones with overhanging leaves probably constituted separate capitals in their own right (**Fig. 4.26b**).[109] The more compact elements (the upper tier in **Fig. 4.24**) have been interpreted as bases, which, independently of the merits of the case, underlines just how unsure this terrain is.[110]

ORIENTAL VOLUTES AND PETAL CROWNS

Volutes and crowns can be traced to the early second millennium in Egypt and the eastern Mediterranean. In Egypt volutes seem to derive from the lotus, lily or similar plants.[111] Eastern versions relate to the ubiquitous 'tree-of-life' and 'sacred tree' stylizations based primarily on the palm (**Fig. 0.6**).[112] The palm was clearly in the mind of the artist who around 700 fashioned a volute column on a relief at Tell Halaf, for it shows a man up a ladder harvesting its dates.[113] The elegant palms shown on a Minoan vase at Heraklion invite comparison with volutes and palmettes (**Fig. 6.3**).[114]

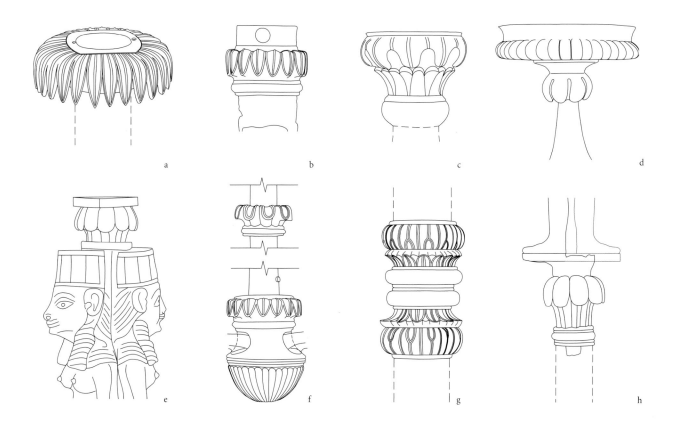

a   b   c   d

e   f   g   h

Rising-volute designs were popular for architecture all over the eastern Mediterranean, and there is space here to cite but a small selection. As already noted, flat-fronted capitals facing stone piers and doorways were common in tombs in Palestine between the tenth and sixth centuries.[115] With their prominent central triangle these were direct ancestors of the capitals at Tamassos (**Fig. 3.5**), but not of Greek columns in the round. Tall volute columns or pillars made of wood were evidently used in Assyria, as far as we can tell from the elaborate pilasters that adorned the polychrome throne room of Nebuchadnezzar II (**Fig. 4.17**).[116] Corroboration is provided by many a small-scale architectural representation such as the so-called Sun-disc relief from Sippar now in the British Museum.[117] The volute and palmette combination that went on to characterize Greek Aeolic abounds in the ivories recovered from Fort Shalmaneser at Nimrud that range from ceremonial fly-whisks to blinkers for the royal horses.[118]

4.28   Miscellaneous non-architectural foliate crowns originating from the eastern end of the Mediterranean and dating from the ninth to seventh centuries. (a) bronze palm crown furniture piece, Nimrud (British Museum, inv. N. 271); (b) Urartian bronze crown over winged bull with human upper torso and head, Toprakkale (British Museum, inv. ME 91247); (c) termination of a bronze stand, Olympia; (d) bronze incense burner with *phiale*-like brazier, Cerro del Peñon, Spain; (e) upper part of ivory double caryatid, Nimrud (British Museum); (f) Urartian bronze candelabrum, lower and middle sections (Museum für Kunst und Gewerbe, Hamburg, inv. 1960.61); (g) ivory colonnette, possibly belonging to a throne, Zincirli (Vorderasiatisches Museum, Berlin, inv. 5921); (h) ivory crown supporting a caryatid, Nimrud (British Museum).

Leaf or petal crowns abounded on disparate high status oriental furniture and ritualistic equipment: thrones and stools (**Fig. 4.28a, b, e, g**);[119] stands for vessels (**Fig. 4.28c**); candelabra (**Fig. 4.28f**); torch holders;[120] incense burners (*thymiateria*) and comparable objects (**Fig. 4.28d**).[121] North Syria and Assyria yield crown-

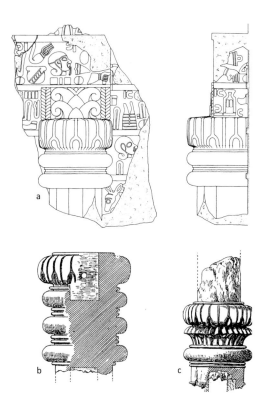

4.29 (ABOVE LEFT) Columnar elements on Syrian furniture. (a) Stone throne with relief decoration, Tell Tayinat; (b) and (c) ivories from Zincirli.

4.30 (ABOVE RIGHT) Balustrades incorporating stub columns with volute and crown capitals. Top: woman-at-the-window miniature ivory relief (British Museum, inv. 1848, 0720.13); bottom: limestone balusters from Ramat Rachel (now in the Israel Museum, Jerusalem).

capped colonnettes detached from their original assemblies, including ones made of stone.[122] Also informative are scenes in relief from Assyrian palaces. One depicting Ashurbanipal's 'Garden-party' (**Fig. 7.9**) shows various applications: on a throne, on an altar/table and on incense burners. Another shows a regal seat with petal crowns over torus mouldings (**Fig. 0.6c**).[123] Did comparable capitals adorn edifices such as the temples of Melqart at Tyre and of Solomon in Jerusalem?[124]

In the eastern Mediterranean volutes and crowns were generally employed separately, but also sometimes in combination. An example occurs on a stone throne fragment from Tell Tayinat (**Fig. 4.29**).[125] Other miniature forms include the balustrading of 'woman-at-the-window' ivories (**Fig. 4.30 top**).[126] Real balusters from Ramat Rachel present the same design (**Fig. 4.30 bottom**).[127] Did equivalents on some important monument or other provide the model for the capitals at Smyrna (**Fig. 4.23**)? Also of note is the miniature column of a portable altar shown on an Assyrian relief in the British Museum.[128] With its volute-and-collar capitals and unfluted shaft rising from a small flare over a torus base, this ensemble anticipates column design in Aeolis and in particular the solution adopted at Klopedi (**Fig. 4.25**). Greek artists and architects had sufficient exposure to such designs to be familiar with them. They may have borrowed volutes and crowns separately at first, and then combined them. Alternatively they could have known eastern antecedents in which the fusion had already taken place.

* * *

The oriental origin of the Aeolic capital might thus seem assured, but things are not so simple. It is to potential Minoan and Mycenaean sources that we now turn. These have curiously been overlooked, presumably because our image of the architecture of these periods has been so bound up with 'proto-Doric' columns ever since awareness of the monuments of Mycenae and of Sir Arthur Evans's reconstructions at Knossos (**Fig. 2.2**).[129] Yet small-scale volute designs feature in Minoan and Mycenaean luxury work and jewellery.[130] Frescoes on Akrotiri (Thera) depict ceremonial ships with little wooden 'stern cabins' that have rising-volute finals (**Fig. 4.34**). [131] These terminate with two kinds of central element, both of which were associated with volutes centuries later: fan-shaped palmettes became the norm for Aeolic capitals, just as did inwardly turning scrolls or 'Phoenician crowns' for Cypriot stelai (**Fig. 4.20**). A regal footstool or casket from Archanes features an architectural scheme of finely worked ivory pilasters, some terminating in double-discs, others in rising volutes (**Fig. 4.32**).[132] A pottery incense burner in the museum at Agios Nikolaos appears to illustrate a run of slender columns alternating with piers, a plan arrangement attested in the complexes of Bronze Age Crete (**Fig. 4.33**).

Ivories with volute devices from Mycenae are particularly pertinent in their details, including a concave

4.31 Ivory miniature volute ornaments excavated from Mycenae, Grave Circle A.

4.33 (ABOVE) Pottery incense burner painted with volute columns alternating with panels decorated with zig-zags (late Bronze Age), Archaeological Museum, Agios Nikolaos, Crete.

4.32 (BELOW) Mycenaean ivory (?)footstool from Archanes, Crete (museum at Heraklion), with pilasters, double-shield devices and rosettes. Some pilasters have capitals with paired discs, some, volutes.

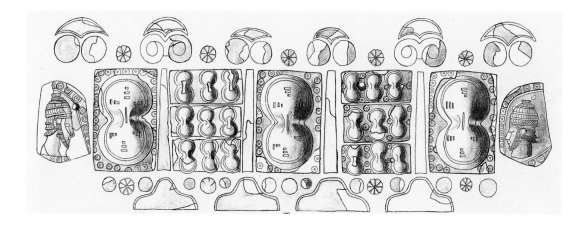

canalis spiralling into a round central boss or 'eye' (**Fig. 4.31**).[133] Both details characterize many later Aeolic and Ionic capitals, which is telling given that only a minority of these adopt the oriental flat or convex canalis (**Fig. 3.5**).

In line with observations made near the beginning of this chapter, the different potential influences on Aeolic design encountered here were not mutually exclusive. Volute capitals and foliate crowns were ubiquitous in virtually all the cultural contexts of any importance outside Greece before the seventh century.[134] The point is that Greek architects could hardly avoid them; they were almost bound to experiment with such forms.

LIMITATIONS OF THE AEOLIC CAPITAL

The adoption of rising volutes in parts of the Greek world is, then, hardly a surprise; but what explains why Aeolic capitals were dropped from monumental architecture as early as the fifth century? To be sure, there were historical factors at work. By the end of the sixth century Aeolis had been weakened economically and militarily in the face of the rise of Ionia. Then the Persians dominated the whole region, and once they were pushed back east the oriental flavour of rising volutes perhaps represented a liability. However, this is a matter of speculation, and a more tangible explanation for the demise of the Aeolic capital concerns its formal ·shortcomings.

These shortcomings are significant. First, the twinned configuration generates a flattish front suited to rectangular stelai and piers, but less so circular columns. In this context a dismayingly abrupt transition can occur (**Fig. 4.26a**). Greater continuity could be achieved by giving convexity to the canalis, as on the capitals at Neandria and Klopedi (**Fig. 4.26**). But this tied the hand of the designer (a concave canalis being out of the question),

while the need to flatten the volutes as they rose created a twisting that could be said to be anti-tectonic.

A second shortcoming concerns proportion. Aeolic column capitals typically have a narrow springing relative to their overall height and breadth.[135] This works well for slender columns, be they made of wood or freestanding. But a stone entablature called for thick columns, and the thicker the column the greater the height of the capital. The wish to avoid a top-heavy capital may explain the absence of stocky columns in this style.

A third difficulty concerns the corner condition, the importance of which in general terms is underlined by the notorious 'corner problem' affecting the Doric frieze (Ch. 3, pp. 72–3). Whereas the symmetry of Doric and Corinthian capitals meant that there was no need for a special corner type, Aeolic and Ionic capitals have fronts and backs that differ from the sides. This creates a conundrum for anyone wishing to build a peripteral temple. Should all the capitals face the same direction? Or should they face outwards on the flanks as well as on the fronts? And if so what happens at the corners? There is no easy answer. Theoretical solutions include L-shaped or heart-shaped piers, and cruciform capitals over square piers, as are known in Cypriot and Persian contexts (**Fig. 0.6**).[136] The Greek approach to tectonics demanded, however, a similar solution for each set of like elements, but this is impossible with sets of Aeolic columns that included ones at a corner.

Together with the Ionian political and economic hegemony, these shortcomings help explain why Greek architects left Aeolic to one side while pursuing Ionic alone. The Ionic capital effected a neater transition from circular to rectangular geometries, its more compact proportions were better suited to sturdy columns, and it could turn the corner of a peripteros. In so doing it paved the way for columns and temples that looked superior – naturally a matter of fundamental concern.

4.34 (FACING PAGE) So-called stern cabins from the *Flotilla of Ships* fresco painting in the West House at Akrotiri on the island of   Santorini (Thera) (*c.* sixteenth century). Top: volute finials, with palmette and in-turning crown motifs; bottom: pair of stern cabins.

CHAPTER FIVE

QUESTIONS OF APPEARANCE AND THE IONIC *GENUS*

That the orders were created to impress the eye should go without saying. The classical phenomenon is bound up with beauty, with the play of masses and details seductively modelled by light and shade. The migration of forms that has just been observed is predicated on their visual appeal. All major architectural traditions have striven to achieve effects that may variously be characterized as magnificent, severe, charming or novel, and strategies that would leave looks to look after themselves (as when elevating a functional plan), or override them

5.1 (FACING PAGE) Theophilus Hansen, Academy, Athens (1885); corner detail.

5.2 (ABOVE) Erechtheion, Athenian Acropolis; corner detail of the east porch.

with kill-joy ideologies, now seem peculiar to the twentieth century.[1] Already by the end of the nineteenth century the conviction that ornamentation is – or should be – an enhancement of the logic of fabrication (Ch. 3) had become dominant to the point of stifling research, in Riegl's view.[2] He laid the blame squarely on over-zealous followers of Darwin and Semper:[3]

> The theory of the technical, materialist origins of the earliest ornaments and art forms is usually attributed to Gottfried Semper . . . However, one must distinguish . . . between Semper and his followers as between Darwin and his adherents. Whereas Semper did suggest that material and technique play a role in the genesis of art forms, the Semperians jumped to the conclusion that all art forms were always the direct product of materials and techniques.[4]

In setting out broad principles of ornamental art, Riegl argued that these respond to a basic human impulse, since cave art and body painting pre-date craft techniques (Introduction, pp. 6–7).[5] There is pleasure to be found in forms abstracted from the natural world, just as are spirals and volutes from plants, horns and shells. In effect he contested the pejorative connotations behind phrases like 'mere decoration'. Today, as the link between 'Ornament and Crime' – the famous title of Adolf Loos's essay – is loosening in architectural circles, there should no longer be anything scandalous about the possibility that visual concerns moulded the orders. Scholars of ancient architectural sculpture are meanwhile in the process of rehabilitating surface decoration as more than empty formalism.[6]

* * *

So as to merit display in the gods' sanctuaries, temples, like the offerings all around them, had to be visually pleasing (Ch. 1, pp. 20–21). Visual delight was enhanced by high-value materials, artistic ingenuity and technical skill, but in seeking to understand more specifically architectural aspects of early Greek design we are hampered by ignorance of terminology from before the fifth century. As for English, the word 'beauty' brings with it

the presumption of approbation – though in some cases its opposite, just as 'pretty' can imply disdain. The modern concept of aesthetics may seem to offer a more objective foundation for analysis, but there are difficulties in mapping this onto ancient sensibilities. In short we have faint guidance as to the criteria by which early Greek architects would have preferred one appearance over another. In such circumstances we are obliged to treat considerations that seem to have been pertinent for the compelling aesthetic quality of later Greek architecture, which photographs in this book aim to capture. Such considerations include surface ornament, sculptural effect, tectonics, proportion, detailing and variety.

Ornaments such as guilloche and meander have already been encountered in discussing influences, and no further comment is necessary except to repeat that the stone carcasses of temples on view today, bereft as they are of terracotta, metal and practically all trace of polychromy, belie their original decorative aspect. Nonetheless there is a contrast between the *horror vacui* observable in early vase painting (**Figs 2.10, 7.2, 8.13**), and the restraint displayed in the treatment of temple walls. Apart from mouldings at the bottom and top, elaboration was the prime imperative of the orders, along with crowning pediments and akroteria.

When two-dimensional devices morph into three dimensions – as does the spiral in becoming a volute – sculptural effects and the agency of light and shade come into play. Appreciation of the modelling effect of shadow must have contributed to the insistence on fluting, for example (Introduction, p. 8). In this arena Greek architects were in their element, for they could be artists, sculptors and craftsmen too (Ch. 7, p. 160). A shared familiarity with materials and the tools used to work them was a prerequisite for resolving details such as mouldings and capitals.

Architectural design involves technical issues peculiar to the discipline, for stability requires stresses to be contained and loads to be transferred safely to the ground. This impinges on basic aspects of composition, including scale. Since stresses increase with size more than does the capacity of a material to resist them, a given design

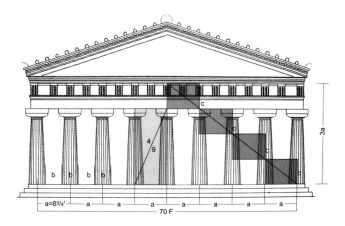

5.3   First temple of Hera, Paestum (Poseidonia); proportional analysis by Dieter Mertens.

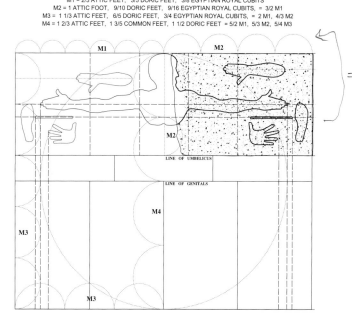

5.4   Metrological relief from Salamis (second half of fifth or early fourth century). Reconstruction of its original form by the author, assuming that the surviving block with anthropomorphic outlines and a foot rule (top right) was part of a symmetrical assembly, and that the height of the figure matched his width measured from finger tip to finger tip, 6 ft, in line with Vitruvius's stipulation for the proportions of the ideal male body and, perhaps, also the canon of Polykleitos. The length of the foot rule, *c.*327 mm or the 'Doric' foot, corresponds to $^1/_6$ of the arm span thus reconstructed.

cannot be scaled up with impunity; larger buildings tend to need stouter sections.[7] Along with a desire to impress, concern over spanning capabilities helps explain why the proportions of the temple of Apollo at Syracuse differ so markedly from those of smaller structures such as the Monopteros at Delphi (**Fig. 3.19**). Even though largely nineteenth-century in conception, the notion of tectonics offers useful insights into the aesthetics of statics. As we saw in Chapter 3, a tectonic design is one that displays a logical sense of structure. But it is not just a technical question; visual predilections were inherent to perceived success. For the Greeks this meant carefully handled junctions and clearly defined axes, column bays and other design units which suited the appreciation and manipulation of rhythm and proportion (**Fig. 5.3**).

In discussing the realm of design commonly designated by proportion we have access to theoretical concepts of the Classical period, thanks to a smattering of contemporary sources and Vitruvius's admittedly contorted later treatment of the subject. Its importance is stated insistently besides being implicit in his observation that credit goes to the patron for a sumptuous building (since he paid for it), and to the craftsman for one that is skilfully finished – 'but when it is well proportioned, the architect will have the glory' (VI,8.9). The quest for this glory was guided by two key principles, *symmetria* and *eurythmia*.

Symmetria, literally the coming together of measure(s), from *syn-* and *metron*, denotes mathematical harmony in terms of number, measure, ratio and shape – a primary goal for Greek and Roman architects.[8] Standard units of length set up on public view at least as early as Classical times bring the ideal of the human body – *the* point of reference for Vitruvius (III,1) – into a thoroughly practical domain (**Fig. 5.4**).[9] Indeed principle and practicality cannot be meaningfully disentangled. Although interpretations remain contested, by the early Classical period temple design aimed at coherent mathematical relationships (**Fig. 5.5**).[10] Back in the sixth century as yet unsolved difficulties, including those surrounding the irksome corner problem (Ch. 3,

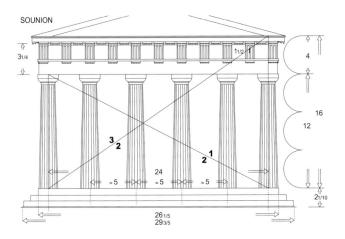

5.5   Temple of Poseidon, Sounion; analysis of the front elevation and its composition by the author, showing key ratios and modular values based on a module equivalent to the nominal width of the triglyph. This module equates to 25 digits of the so-called Doric foot of *c.*327 mm (see **Fig. 5.4**).

Needless to say different facets of visual pleasure can come together in a single design. Admire the bases from the Erechtheion, and multiple sources of delight: the deft spreading of the load from the shaft; the seductive cascade of mouldings swelling and contracting and swelling again; the supple modelling profile; the balanced proportions; the immaculate craftsmanship (**Fig. 0.9**). This reaches a sublime level in the capitals, though given the state of their preservation (**Fig. 5.2**), it is well also to contemplate Hansen's full-colour copies (**Fig. 5.1**).

5.6   Refinements of the Parthenon as visualized by means of exaggeration by Manolis Korres.

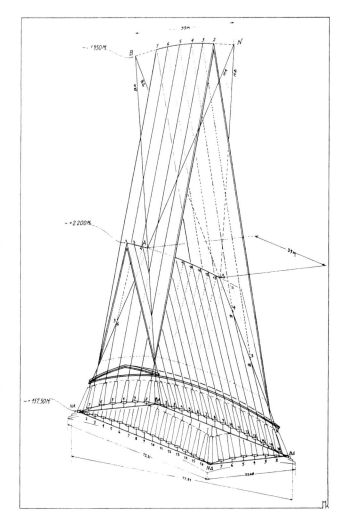

pp. 72–3), prevented the same level of coherence, yet a temple such as Hera's at Paestum was evidently designed with harmony in mind (**Fig. 5.3**).[11] There are signs of striving towards this goal as far back as we have monuments – structures designed to satisfy more than just practical needs – that are sufficiently intact to lend themselves to mathematical analysis.[12]

Eurythmia straddles both proportion and detailing. It equates to gracefulness, literally the quality of being well shaped, from *eu-*, well, and *rhythmos*, shape. *Eurythmia* informs aspects of architectural design as varied as the spacing of colonnades or the honing of the profile of a moulding. It also conveys a sense of fine workmanship, as with something well fitted and artfully made. Such appreciation is anticipated in the Homeric epics, with their many epithets for 'well finished', 'well fitted' and 'well built'.[13] One of the most fascinating aspects of temple design is the so-called refinements (chiefly columnar swelling or entasis, inward inclination of walls and columns, upward curvature in the stylobate).[14] Here is both sublimation of the principle of *eurythmia* as well as an invitation to wonder that accords perfectly with dedicatory impulses (**Fig. 5.6**).

A final principle is variety. Neoclassical academicism, a superficial reading of Vitruvius, and the use of the term 'orders' might suggest that they could be cloned on the basis of normative schemes. But an unwritten rule of ancient design prohibited plain copying. Be they variations on an established theme or more audacious ventures, new solutions were constantly emerging in the quest for emulation. Contrasting approaches and choices reflected differences in chronology, regional and local patterns, besides the specifics of individual commissions and the propensities of their designers. The will to 'play' with tradition is manifest in the unfettered variety of bases used for Ionic columns (see below, p. 123). It is not uncommon for different solutions to be brought together in the same building (a phenomenon which in some cases served to differentiate the identity of the aristocrats who donated separate columns). Yet at the same time Greek architects and their audience recognized perfection once they encountered it, after which there was less incentive for change. The result was a convergence towards consensus, as manifest in temple plans (Ch. 3, p. 76) and in the details of the Doric *genus* (Ch. 3, pp. 81–5). Even the Ionic base settled down into relatively predictable patterns by late Classical times. If an evolutionary metaphor must be engaged for Greek architecture, it is this: the *genera* represent the survival of the fittest-looking responses to the problem of building, which is to say the *survival of the finest*.[15]

DORIC ORNAMENT

Compared with Ionic and Corinthian, the Doric *genus* might seem to be a case apart. It is more severe and minimal – it had no base at all – while, after a phase of experimentation (Ch. 3, pp. 82–4), the entablature maintained a relatively stiff canon. The idea that Doric was a refined but ultimately 'no nonsense' representation of construction implies that aesthetic expression was limited to fine-tuning the system. But Doric temples embraced more decoration and variety than this view concedes, and this is not just because they could be

painted and decked out with sculpture and assorted metal fittings.

The Doric capital presents an interesting case, for it has never met with a satisfying constructional explanation aside from its success in mediating between a circular shaft and a square abacus (which is essentially a formal issue). It was not vernacular wood construction but elegant Bronze Age precedents that provided the starting point for later architects to emulate. The necking and even the echinus could be the locus for vegetal ornament.[16] Following the discovery of Greek architectural polychromy, some nineteenth-century architects restored Doric capitals with floral motifs painted on to the echinus (**Figs 2.35, 7.22**).[17] Examples survive that used relief, including those at Paestum and Metropolis (**Figs 3.23, 7.11**). A votive Doric capital from Phaistos presents an echinus which is completely covered by rings of overlapping leaf points.[18] Some non-canonic 'Doricizing' capitals display ornamental patterns comparable with the egg-and-dart of the Ionic capital (**Fig. 9.5**). Indeed there is a sense in which the Ionic and Doric echinus sit at opposite ends of a spectrum of ornamental variants.[19]

The existence of blank metopes (as on the flanks of the Hephaisteion in Athens) might encourage a constructional reading of the Doric frieze, but metopal decoration was part and parcel of early usage.[20] Sculpted metopes adorned the Artemision at Corfu, the so-called Thesauros at Foce del Sele and the Monopteros at Delphi.[21] Some later metopes such as ones from Megara Hyblaia are unashamedly ornamental.[22] It also seems significant that the Doric frieze occupies the middle course of the entablature, for in Ionic the equivalent zone was destined for figuration. (The presence of a figural frieze on the epistyle of the Doric temple of Athena at Assos is unique (**Fig. 5.7**).) This middle course was in fact just an option, not a structural necessity, for there are plenty of Ionic temples that have no frieze at all. Nor should it be forgotten that Vitruvius's account of the Doric frieze embraces visual concerns. Triglyphs were for him not beam-ends, but devices to mask them and create a superior look (Ch. 3, p. 64).

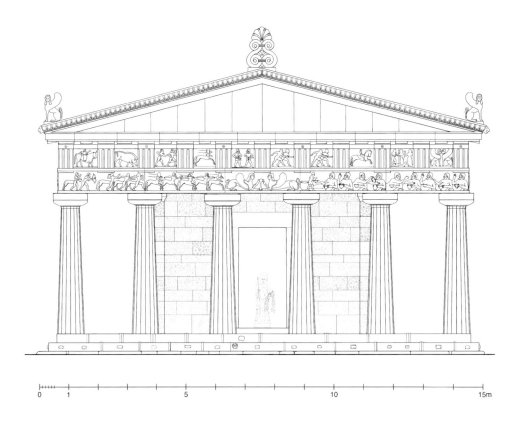

5.7   Temple of Athena, Assos; front elevation. Note the unconventional presence of a figural frieze on the epistyle (architrave).

The decorative character of the Doric frieze was recognized by Bötticher and Semper in the nineteenth century, though their specific interpretations need not detain us.[23] One line of scholarship sees it as a development of the genre of compartmentalized friezes that dominated early Greek art.[24] Between the ninth and seventh centuries vases and other products were often adorned with stripes and simple geometrical elements. A recurrent formula for friezes alternated more or less square fields with dividers in the form of groups of stripes – which pottery specialists often call 'metopes' and 'triglyphs' respectively. As with their built equivalents, such metopes were sometimes left bare, but normally they were adorned with geometrical designs or stylized plant motifs, giving way to mythological creatures, animals, warriors and riders (**Fig. 2.10**). On

pottery the number of stripes varies, but three is a quite common option.[25] By this token the occasional architectural occurrence in southern Italy and Sicily of 'tetraglyphs', and a single case of 'pentaglyphs', could be legacies from an earlier more fluid approach.[26] So it is possible that in the seventh century architects picked up on the field-and-divider genre when they came to elaborate their increasingly showy temples.[27] This could account for the insistence that the Doric frieze terminate with a whole triglyph/framing element, this being standard artistic practice for friezes in general.[28] A decorative origin sits well with the non-alignment of triglyphs and columns at the corners of temples, and indeed more generally in early practice (Ch. 3, pp. 76, 81). This approach to composition has been called 'paratactic', that is to say it is characterized by the serial distribution of discrete elements, as when stringing beads one by one to make a necklace. It is an approach that can produce local elements of dissonance in the process.[29]

This theory does not negate a revival of Bronze Age split-rosette friezes, since their traits also found their way on to Geometric vases.[30] Such conflation was possible because of the longevity of the underlying strategy; field-and-divider bands or friezes recur over a wide temporal range across Egypt, Crete, Cyprus (**Figs 1.6, 4.3, 4.5, 7.4, 7.7**) and Assyria as well (**Fig. 4.15**).[31] Different sources of inspiration could potentially reinforce each other, and this needs to be taken into account in formulating a more complete explanation for the Doric frieze.

THE IONIC *GENUS*

Elements of the vocabulary that would crystallize into the Ionic family evolved over a broader chronological span than for Doric. As we saw in Chapter 2 (pp. 58–9), the scope for experiment was greater, so much so that the very notion of an Ionic canon is questionable before Hellenistic times. It is certainly not applicable in the Archaic period, when two loose regional patterns of practice prevailed. One centred on the Cycladic islands, chiefly Naxos, Paros and Delos; the other centred on the eastern Aegean seaboard, especially Ionia and the island of Samos.[32] This regional division is manifest both in elevation and in plan (the peripteros is little known in the Cyclades). A relaxed approach is evident too in the willingness to use mouldings in locations other than the standard ones. Bead-and-reel, for example, an enrichment normally used at the top of the shaft, on capitals and on epistyles, found itself applied to the chunky base moulding wrapping around the Siphnian treasury at Delphi (**Fig., p. x**). As noted earlier, columns could be personalized to distinguish between the dedications of individual aristocratic patrons, as happened at the great Ionian temples of the Archaic period and can still be seen in the Hellenistic Didymaion (**Fig. 5.8**). For individual Ionic buildings and elements, listed chronologically, see **Table 5** (pp. 120–21).

5.8   Temple of Apollo, Didyma; detail of the east front. Note the varied treatment of bases (some of which are unfinished).

TABLE 5
BUILDINGS AND ARCHITECTURAL ELEMENTS, CAPITALS ESPECIALLY, ASSOCIATED WITH IONIC FORMS

D = dipteros   E = entrance/front (*in antis* or prostyle)   I = interior   P = peripteros

fig. no.	structure	columnar context	character of capital	guide date
2.28, 5.22	Aigina, sanctuary of Apollo, sphinx column[1]	votive	shaft only (may not be Ionic)	end 7th c.
2.32	Sangri, colonnette of Alexitides[2]	votive	schematic	c.600
5.12a,	Delos, capital found under colossos[3]	E pillar?	schematic	before 590
	Ephesos, Artemision III or C[4]			c.600
5.18a, 22	Aigina, sanctuary of Aphaia, sphinx column[5]	votive	domical 'echinus'	590–580
5.12b	Didyma, lost capital[6]		schematic	
5.12c	Delos, Naxian Oikos I[7]	I (8) + E (3)	schematic	c.580
5.12d	Delos, capital[8]	votive	schematic	
2.33, 5.18c, 22	Yria, temple of Dionysos IV[9]	I (2 by 8), E (4)?	Cycladic	580–570
5.18b, 22, 7.18	Delphi, sphinx column[10]	votive	Cycladic	580–570
5.22	Samos, Heraion III, 1st dipteros[11]	D (8/9 by 21)	torus only?	575 onwards
5.12e	Didyma, capital[12]	votive	striated echinus/torus	2nd qu. 6th c.
2.34, 5.18d, 22	Ephesos, Artemision IV or D[13]	D (8/9 by 20)		560 onwards
	Naukratis, temple of Apollo[14]			
	Delos, sphinx column[15]	votive	Cycladic, interrupted canalis	mid-6th c.
	Paros, column of Archilochos[16]	votive	Cycladic, interrupted canalis	
	Myus, temple of Dionysos[17]	P (6 by 10?)		mid-6th c.
5.23	Didyma, temple of Apollo II[18]	D (8/9 by 21)		550 onwards
5.22, 7.19	Cyrene, sphinx column[19]	votive	double tier of lobes	3rd qu. 6th c.
5.16	Samos, 2nd dipteros (of Polykrates)[20]	D (8/9 by 24)	decorated necking	530 onwards
5.19	Delos, Naxian Oikos, propylon II[21]	E (3)	corner capital	last qu. 6th c.
	Gela, capital[22]			last qu. 6th c.
4.26f	Athens, pair of votive columns[23]	votive	domical 'echinus', painted	last qu. 6th c.
7.20	Athens, column of Kallimachos[24]	votive		490
5.25	Metapontum (Metapontion), Temple D[25]	pseudoD (8 by 20)	decorated necking	first qu. 5th c.
5.20	Athens, Propylaia[26]	I (2 by 3)		437–431
5.2	Athens, Erechtheion[27]	two separate sets	decorated necking	421–407
5.22	Priene, temple of Athena[28]	P (6 by 11)		340–
1.25	Magnesia, temple of Artemis[29]	pseudoD (8 by 15)		late 3rd c.

NOTES TO TABLE 5

1   See **Table 2**.

2   Sangri, colonnette, Naxos (museum, inv. 8); Mace 1974, no.49; Kirchhoff 1988, 137; Gruben 1989, 161–5; McGowan 1993, cat.9; Bakker 1999, Ion-1; Barletta 2001, 103, 133–5; Herdt and Wilson Jones 2008; Segal 2007, no. 1.

3   Delos, roughly hewn capital found under the colossal statue of Apollo. Courby 1931, 237, fig. 5; Kirchhoff 1988, 176; Gruben 1996, 64, fig. 4; Bakker 1999, Preion-1; Barletta 2001, 101 and n. 31. The narrow space between the volute-blocks suggests the capital sat on a rectangular pillar, which Gruben (1996, 64) tentatively assigns to the Temple of Artemis.

4   Ephesos, Artemision III or 'C'. Bammer 1990; idem 1998; Bammer and Muss 1996; Weissl 2002. See also later entry.

5   Aigina, sanctuary of Aphaia, sphinx column. Wurz and Wurz 1925, fig. 242; Gruben 1965; Mace 1974, no. 1; Kirchhoff 1988, 20–22, no. 8; McGowan 1993, cat. 8; Bakker 1999, Ion-22, 70, no. Col-5; Barletta 2001, 101, 104, fig. 60; Segal 2007, no. 25.

6   Didyma, schematic capital (present location unknown). Wiegand 1941, pl. 213; Gruben 1963, 138–9, fig. 31; 1996, 63; Bakker 1999, Preion-2. Gruben (1963, 140) once judged it to be a roof acroterion and to date as late as 550, but subsequently (1996, 63) he visualized it on a rectangular timber post.

7   Delos, Naxian Oikos I. Opinion is divided as to whether this was Apollo's temple or not (e.g., Etienne 1992, 303–4, Gruben 1997, 301–47; idem 2001, 156–7, who emphasizes its singular typology). See also Rocco 2003, 63–9. Interior capital: Mace 1978, no. 22; Theodorescu 1980, no. 25; Kirchhoff 1988, no. 16; Ohnesorg 1996, 41–2, Abb. 1; Bakker 1999, Ion-24.

8   Delos, schematic capital. Vallois 1944–78, II(1), 170, no.6; Martin 1973, 374, no. 2; Kirchhoff 1988, 14, no. 2; Bakker 1999, Iver-4.

9   Yria, Temple of Dionysios IV. Lambrinoudakis and Gruben 1987, 569–608; Gruben 1996b, 67–70: idem 2001, 377–80; Lambrinoudakis 1991; idem 1996; Ohnesorg 1996, 41–3; Bakker 1999, Ion-7; Rocco 2003, 59–62; LL&R 706.

10 Delphi, sphinx column (museum, inv. 365). Amandry 1953; Jacob-Felsch 1969, 109–10; Mace 1974, no.33; Theodorescu 1980, no. 23; Kirchhoff 1988, 16–17, no. 4; Gruben 1993, 104; McGowan 1993, cat. 1; Bakker 1999, Ion-6, Col-7; Barletta 2001, 97–100; Segal 2007, no. 2.

11 Samian Heraion, first dipteros. See **Table 4.2**.

12 Didyma, capital of votive column, one of two similar examples. Tuchelt 1991; Ohnesorg 1996, Abb. 5; Bakker 1999, Ion-65. For a similar fragmentary capital found near Mykale see Büsing 2006.

13 Ephesos, Artemision IV or 'D'. Hogarth 1908; Lethaby 1917, 1–16; Krischen 1938, 19, pl. 33–34; Dinsmoor 1975, 127–32; Gruben 2001, 385–90; Schaber 1982, esp. 27–48 for reconstructions; Simon 1986, 27–53; Bammer 1991, 63–83; Weissl 2002; Rocco 2003, 75–83; Marconi 2007, 21–4; Ohnesorg 2007. Bases and columns: Boardman 1959, 201–5; Wesenberg 1971; Buxton 2002, 14–16, 55–61. Capitals: Mace 1978, nos. 39, 40; Kirchhoff 1988, nos. 48–9; Bakker 1999, Ion-16, 74–5; Ohnesorg 2001.

14 Naukratis, temple of Apollo. Petrie *et al.* 1896–8; Dinsmoor 1975, 125–6; Boardman 1999. Base: Wesenberg 1971, 122, 125. Capital: Petrie *et al.* 1896–

8, 11 ff., Pl. III; Mace 1974, no.47; Kirchhoff 1988, 188–9, E1; Bakker 1999, Cym-1; Barletta 2001, 87, 108, fig. 50; Koenigs 2007. The lobed crown/echinus was probably combined with volutes, but these no longer exist.

15 Delos, sphinx column (museum, inv. 583). Amandry 1953, 19–21; Martin 1973, no. 7–8, figs 14–17; Mace 1974, no. 19; Theodorescu 1980, no. 26; McGowan 1993, cat.2; Bakker 1999, Ion-18; Barletta 2001, 100.

16 Paros, capital of column of Archilochos (museum, inv. 733). Mace 1974, no. 53; Kirchhoff 1988, 26; McGowan 1993, cat.5; Ohnesorg 1993, 113; Bakker 1999, Ion-17; Rocco 2003, 50–51; Segal 2009, no. 15.

17 Weber, H. 1965; Bakker 1999, Ion-15; Weber B. 2002.

18 Didyma, Temple of Apollo II. Wiegand 1941; Gruben 1963; idem 2001, 396–400; Schattner 1996, 41; Marconi 2007, 25–6. Capitals: Mace 1974, no.35; Theodorescu 1980, no. 8; Kirchhoff 1988, nos. 51, 52; Tuchelt 1991; Bakker 1999, Ion-28.

19 Cyrene, votive sphinx column. White 1971; Mace 1974, no.12; Kirchhoff 1988, 256, no.11; McGowan 1993, cat.7; Bakker 1999, Ion-14; Segal 2007, no. 17.

20 Samos, second dipteros. For site references see **Table 4.2**. Bases: Hellner 2009. Capitals: Gruben, 1960; Bakker 1999, Ion-58; Rocco 2003, 88–93.

21 Delos, corner capital, possibly from the second propylon of the Naxian Oikos. Theodorescu 1980, no. 29; Gruben 1997, 356–72, figs 49–50; Bakker 1999, Ion-32; Herdt and Wilson Jones 2010.

22 Gela. Theodorescu 1974, no. 1; 1980, no. 75; Barletta 1983, 245–8; Bakker 1999, Ion-40a.

23 Athens, pair of votive columns; one is in the Acropolis Museum (inv. 135), the other in the National Museum (inv. 85). Borrmann 1888a, 15; 1888b, 277, fig. 18; Mace 1978, no.3; Theodorescu 1980, 163, no. 45; McGowan 1997, pl. 58; Bakker 1999, Ion-67.

24 Athens, column of Kallimachos, reconstructed from multiple fragments in the Acropolis Museum. Raubitschek 1949, 18–19, no. 13; Jacob-Felsch 1969, 35, 127; Theodorescu 1980, no. 48; Korres 1994, 174; Bakker 1999, Ion-62; Kissas 2000, 195–8; Segal 2007, no. 81.

25 Metapontum, Temple D. Mertens 1977; idem 2006, 296–302; Kirchhoff 1988, no. N4; Rocco 2003, 106–8; LL&R 792–3. Capitals: Mace 1974, no.42; Bakker 1999, Ion-46. Mertens's date of *c.*470 contrasts with Rocco's of the 3rd quarter of the 5th c.

26 Athens, Propylaia. Dinsmoor 1975, 199–205; Gruben 2001, 191–202; Hellmann 2006, 182–3; LL&R 548–50.

27 Athens, Erechtheion. While the two main orders (north porch and east porch) have friezes but no dentils, the caryatid porch has dentils but no frieze. Caskey *et al.* 1927; Dinsmoor 1975, 187–94; Gruben 2001, 209–22; Rocco 2003, 123–32; Hellmann 2006, 90–96; LL&R 558–9; Papanikolaou 2012.

28 Priene, temple of Athena. Wiegand 1904; Gruben 2001, 416–23; Rocco 2003, 149–56.

29 Magnesia, temple of Artemis. Humann 1904, 39–90; Dinsmoor 1975, 274–6; Gruben 2001, 426–31; Rocco 2003, 15–30.

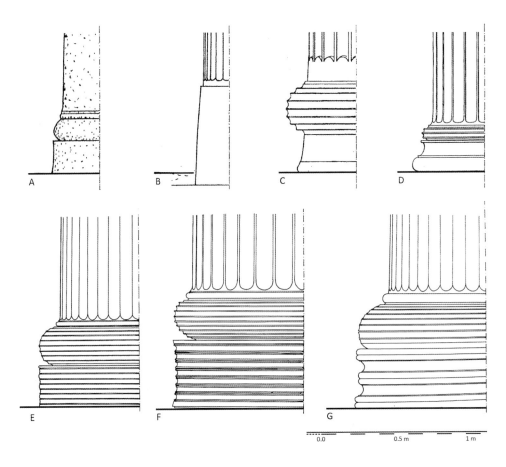

5.9 (ABOVE) Half elevations of selected Ionic bases. (A) exterior of the Oikos of the Naxians, Delos; (B) interior of the Oikos of the Naxians, Delos; (C) Temple D, Metapontum; (D) east porch, Erechtheion, Athens; (E) first dipteros, Samos; (F) second dipteros, Samos; (G) Artemesion, Ephesos.

This varied picture tells us that there can have been no single conceptual premise or authority on which the Ionic mode of building was based. There are characteristics that chime with constructive logic (Ch. 3, pp. 85–6), but not consistently; there are signs of frequent borrowing, though not of an even partially complete system. The variety of responses suggests an evolving research driven above all by aesthetic motives. It is in this sense that the more enduring solutions represent the survival of the finest. We can now observe this in more detail, starting with the base and concentrating on the capital.

* * *

5.10 (LEFT) Cylindrical lower half, sometimes known as a *spira* (or *speira*), of one of the giant Ionic bases from the second dipteros, Samos.

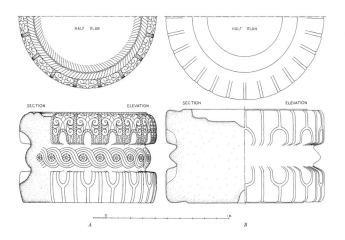

5.11   Decorated limestone bases from Zincirli, Syria (seventh century).

THE IONIC BASE

Bases might or might not incorporate the following elements: a square plinth; a slightly tapered cylinder or truncated cone; a flattish disc or cylinder (sometimes called spira/speira); a convex or tyre-shaped moulding (torus); a concave inversion (scotia); small ancillary fillets and astragals (**Fig. 5.9**). Some early bases maintained an elemental simplicity. The interior columns of the temple at Yria had just a flattish torus on a circular plinth partly set into the floor, while a simple cylindrical spira was adopted in the entrance porch (**Fig. 2.33**).[33] The bases inside the Oikos of the Naxians on Delos comprise two simple geometrical solids: tapering cylinders on top of flat discs (**Fig. 5.9**).[34] Those of the eastern porch, on the other hand, present a torus on a squatter spira, the faint concavity of which hints at the subtleties of later practice. A grander approach characterized the new style in Ionia, as well as a taste for virtuoso detailing; from around 570 an assortment of elaborate bases were created for the great temples at Samos, Ephesos and Didyma, elaborate in the number of elements, their geometry and in surface enrichments. The Samians pioneered horizontal concave striations for both torus and spira, with dozens of variations on the theme (**Figs 5.9, 5.10**).[35] The Ephesians gave the spira a more sculptural double scotia separated by one or more astragals,

sometimes with the addition of plant motifs in relief.[36] The so-called Attic base with a torus–scotia–torus sequence came to the fore in Attica in the fifth century, epitomized by the bases of the Erechtheion (**Fig. 0.9**); this went on to become the dominant solution when combined with a square plinth in the Hellenistic and Roman periods (**Fig. 1.25**).

There is a constructional aspect behind the origin of bases, in the sense that a stone one protects the bottom of a wooden shaft from rot (Ch. 3, p. 85). Yet at the same time many of the forms employed could have been borrowed from the east, the home of moulded bases of varied design.[37] The decorated wooden torus base discovered at Olympia testifies to a concern with visual form and delight (**Fig. 2.27**). Stone examples from palaces and temples in Syria also anticipate Greek usage, including ones combining a square plinth with a circular torus (**Fig. 4.18**). Equally striking are bases with stacked quasi-torus and scotia mouldings from Tell Tayinat and Zincirli (**Figs 4.29, 5.11**).[38] A similar vocabulary of fillets and convex and concave mouldings, astragals, torus and scotias is also characteristic of eastern furniture and ritual equipment (**Figs 0.6, 4.28, 4.29, 7.9**). Yet Greek solutions almost always differ in detail, while tending towards greater geometrical refinement. Given that the stone base is such a common constructional device, it is possible to imagine that the Greeks arrived independently at results not unlike those found elsewhere.[39] To do so, however, would be to fall under the sway of that old philhellenic bias.[40] It is illusory in any case to look for one kind of explanation, since different ones can fuse or operate in tandem. It is better to visualize the Greeks at times pursuing their own inventions, at times manipulating other solutions from different origins, not simply borrowing but testing and experimenting according to their own tastes and convictions.

Whether the ultimate origin of classical fluting lay in woodworking practices or the imitation of plant forms is not our concern, for the Greeks learnt it from their predecessors in the Mycenaean period and/or Egypt (Ch. 4, p. 96). Rather like Doric ones except with a tighter rhythm, early Ionic flutes meet simply at an arris.

Initially shallow, they progressively deepened, the better to catch shadow. The 'canonic' fillet-and-flute profile only took hold in the latter part of the sixth century, with the flutes going on to deepen further until becoming roughly semi-circular, the norm in mainstream Roman practice.[41] In the Archaic period shafts are known with 16, 28, 30, 32, 36, 40, 44, 48 and even 50 flutes, with 24 prevailing because this best suited a deeply cut flute with fillet (while also being easy to set out, like 16).[42] Some early Ionic shafts have no properly developed mouldings at the ends; the treatment given to the body of the shaft more or less stopped. This occurred at the Oikos of the Naxians and probably the first dipteros on Samos. Then the termination was registered by a little astragal, while a slight flare, the apophyge, was judged a superior transition, a solution prompted perhaps by the concave striations of Samian bases, perhaps by oriental precedents. A domical rounding to end the flutes made for a further effective detail. All these embellishments were brought together in the lavish Artemision and then the Didymaion, going on to become the rule at the top of the shaft as well.[43] In these temples a tier of drums sometimes provided the locus for banded figuration in relief (**Figs 2.34, 5.23**). In the Archaic period some columns had floral necking bands enhancing the junction of shaft and capital, as at Naukratis, Samos (**Fig. 5.16**) and Metapontum (**Fig. 5.25**).[44] The Erechtheion has the best known examples still *in situ* (**Fig. 5.2**).

AEOLIC AND IONIC CAPITALS COMPARED

Processes of construction and petrification played a role in the formation of Greek architecture, but they cannot by themselves create visually compelling form. The germ of a form had to have a prior existence in the designer's mind. Did the Ionic capital absorb a similar quotient of influences to those that affected the Aeolic? Aeolic and Ionic styles certainly share enough affinities to suggest a common inheritance. But is their relationship one of cousins, siblings or of parent and offspring?

Any attempt to chart the development of the Ionic capital runs up against considerable difficulties, both in terms of research but most of all in its presentation.[45] It is impossible to reconstruct a tidy family tree of volute capitals because no such thing existed; a better metaphor would be a lattice of criss-crossing stems and branches. Contrasts between Cycladic and Ionian approaches to capital design are too important to be glossed over, while the sheer variety of influences and solutions hampers clean-cut analysis.[46] Chronology is something of a minefield since so many early Ionic capitals are isolated, de-contextualized finds. Dating by style is fraught with dangers, notably the understandable tendency to place 'primitive' solutions before more sophisticated ones. But can we be sure that an unrefined design was not due to incidental factors? These might include those surrounding its commission, such as a limited budget, as well as the ability of the carver. The schematic capitals illustrated in **Fig. 5.12** do not necessarily represent initial steps of development, even if the one from Sangri is among the earliest Ionic capitals yet known (**Fig. 2.32**).[47] The earlier existence of sophisticated examples cannot be ruled out. A further complication lies in the fact that many early Ionic capitals belonged not to buildings but to free-standing votive columns.[48] In this context we may expect a greater proportional variation and decorative licence, a case in point being the double array of lobes on the echinus of the votive column at Cyrene (**Figs 5.22, 7.19**).[49]

Aware that fully disentangling this material is likely to tax the patience of some readers I will adopt a broad-brush approach, leaving greater detail for a separate publication. As long as detailed evidence is not contradicted, such an approach seeks to avoid the shortcoming of 'not seeing the wood for the trees'.

The commonality between Aeolic and Ionic capitals is extensive. Both are composites of volutes and collars / crowns, elements that had their own independent histories prior to being brought together (Ch. 4, pp. 105–8).[50] Aeolic and Ionic configurations both differentiate front / back versus the sides (whereas Doric and Corinthian do not); both have lateral volutes; both forms of

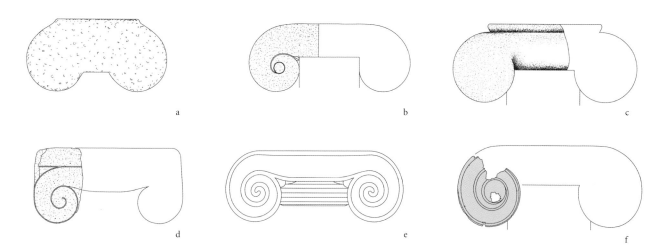

5.12   Schematic early Archaic volute capitals. (a) Delos, found under the colossus flanking the Oikos of the Naxians; (b) Didyma, lost capital; (c) Delos, Oikos of the Naxians, interior; (d) Delos, votive column; (e) Didyma, capital with striated torus; (f) Olympia, hypothetical capital reconstructed to suit surviving bronze volute (left).

echinus are normally articulated by lobed/foliate ornament. As for differences, the most significant concern the volutes. Ionic ones are linked horizontally by a continuous canalis; Aeolic ones rise as separate twins. The Ionic echinus differs in being prominent only front and back, while sitting in a higher position. Contrasts also affect the lateral connection between the volutes that is called the bolster (*pulvinus* in Vitruvian terminology). Aeolic bolsters are simply cylindrical; the Ionic bolster adopts a sensuous double curvature, flaring as does a trumpet or a pulley-wheel. As for details, the Aeolic canalis is usually flat or slightly convex, the Ionic is usually concave.[51] As they spiral inwards, Aeolic volutes typically perform around one and a half turns, Ionic volutes around two and a half. Further differences of detail are apparent when comparing individual examples from the two traditions.

Given the extent of common ground, Aeolic has sometimes been characterized as a kind of 'proto-' or 'ur-' Ionic.[52] This position was popular in the late nineteenth and early twentieth centuries, a time of rapidly increasing archaeological coverage of the eastern Mediterranean. However, Ionic capitals in the Cyclades are now known to date as early, if not earlier, than any surviving Aeolic ones (compare Tables 4.1 and 5). The last decade of the seventh century, more or less, is the date indicated by the inscription on the votive Ionic stub column from Sangri (**Fig. 2.32**). The Aeolic capitals from the temple of Athena at Old Smyrna may be just as early,

yet this is not at all certain. Since neither these nor any other known Aeolic capitals can be reliably dated before Ionic ones the current consensus denies the former precedence, seeing two parallel and roughly simultaneous lines of development.[53] It is also true that some Aeolic capitals betray signs of Ionic influence, a case in point being the capital from Oropos (**Fig. 4.22**).[54] Aeolic has even been called a variant of Ionic.[55]

This line of argumentation would be all very well if the only material of relevance were to be found in Greece but, as we saw in Chapter 4, this is not the case. Rising-volute capitals enjoyed international diffusion over a wide range of production, some knowledge of which must surely have percolated to Greek temple builders. This being so, is it really likely that Ionic and Aeolic capitals arose independently and just happened to share so many similarities? If the Aeolic capital were an offshoot of Ionic, is it not uncanny that it ended up looking so much like earlier designs? It is more probable that Greek architects took rising volutes as the point of departure, while improving on their shortcomings by adopting the horizontal format.

SOURCES FOR THE IONIC CAPITAL

Though completely outnumbered by rising volutes, precursors do exist for the horizontally linked configuration. Not dissimilar outline shapes occur on Hittite hieroglyphics,[56] and various spiral motifs and curlicues in Egyptian, Minoan and Mycenaean contexts. (**Figs 4.3, 4.5, 6.3**)[57] But the resemblance is never very close, while Near-eastern architectural parallels only tantalize and ultimately disappoint.[58] The most striking foretastes of the Ionic format terminate the supports of Cypriot tripod stands of the late Bronze Age (**Fig. 5.13**).[59] These are only schematic, two-dimensional devices, but the connection may be significant.[60] Further potential catalysts are 'ambiguous' volute motifs: out-turning volutes paired in such a way as to create linked configurations as by-products. Flourishes of this kind occur on miscellaneous artefacts, whether made from ceramic, ivory or metal, and are particularly frequent on thrones of oriental provenance or inspiration (**Figs 0.6, 7.9**).[61] In the seventh century the painters of Melian vases (**Fig. 7.6**) and Ionian craftsmen evidently enjoyed 'playing' with such forms, witness gold jewellery that has been recovered from the Artemision at Ephesos (**Fig. 7.1**).

Cypriot, Phoenician and Near Eastern volutes are typically more schematic than their Ionic equivalents which, in their greater plasticity, have more in common with Mycenaean antecedents.[62] The interlocking soffit of the tomb at Orchomenos has a concave channel (**Fig. 4.3**) as does the running spiral frieze of the Treasury of Atreus (**Fig. 4.5**). An ivory furniture-piece from Mycenae ends in delicately articulated volutes with a subtly concave canalis edged by a rounded bead (**Fig. 5.14**). As occurs on some Ionic examples, the canalis winds inwards to a round hub or 'eye'.[63] Another find from Mycenae, the alabaster vase illustrated in **Fig. 5.15**, has handles with virtuoso double curvature that in some ways presages the pulley-wheel shape of the mature Ionic bolster.[64]

There are partial antecedents too for the Ionic echinus. A Bronze Age ivory colonnette from Delos (**Fig. 4.7**) has twenty-four lobes on its echinus, the same number

5.13   Selected Cypriot bronze tripod stands (late Bronze Age).

as an Ionic capital from Gela, and broadly comparable with Cycladic examples. Metalwork from the eastern Mediterranean includes crowns with arrays of various numbers of lobes (**Fig. 4.28**). Some round altars and *phialai* have egg-shaped lobes not unlike the 'eggs' of egg-and-dart; more will be said on this subject in Chapters 7 and 9.

Thus aspects of the Ionic capital were prefigured in three main respects: rising-volute designs of a wide chronological and geographical spread; 'ambiguous' or linked configurations on small-scale material; a variety of partial antecedents for the echinus. Yet a properly resolved three-dimensional Ionic capital was a Greek invention. The genius of Greek architects of the Archaic period was to transform all they assimilated into a convincing architectural device of beauty and sophistication. From a later Eurocentric perspective – and indeed their own – the Greeks were capable of finer results than any people before them.[65]

CYCLADIC AND IONIAN CAPITALS

The key to understanding the development of the Ionic capital is the relationship between the Cycladic and Ionian variants, and the reasons why the latter eclipsed the former by the fifth century. The military and economic might of Ionia was an important factor, acting as it did as a brake on the fortunes of the Cyclades as well as Aeolis (Ch. 4, p. 110). And again as in the case of Aeolic style, issues of design constituted the other main factor.

Of these two regional types of capital the Ionian is far more familiar, since it led directly to mainstream Ionic design as codified by Hellenistic, Roman and Renaissance practice. Examples of the Archaic Ionian capital include those of the temple of Apollo at Didyma (**Fig. 5.23**), and the second dipteros at Samos built by its ruler Polykrates (**Fig. 5.16**). In the fifth century this model was further refined in Attica (**Figs 5.17b, 5.20**). The Cycladic type is exemplified by the capitals belonging to the temple of Dionysos at Yria on Naxos (**Fig. 2.33**) and the Naxians' sphinx column at Delphi (**Fig. 5.17a, 5.18b**).

Though perhaps not immediately obvious, the differences between these two types are significant (**Fig. 5.17**). Typically Cycladic capitals are more elongated than Ionian ones.[66] The greatest contrast, though, concerns the echinus; instead of the smaller and truncated Ionian form, the Cycladic echinus is larger and takes up a complete circle. Its profile combines a half-round or torus and an overfall in a manner of some leaf/petal crowns, besides recalling the overfalling rim of some lustral basins (*perirrhanteria*).[67] The Ionian echinus is more like a bowl or cup facing upwards, with no overfall, and later in Athenian practice its profile approximated to the quarter-ellipse known as an ovolo. Both the Cycladic and early Ionian echinus have flattish lobes, like curving leaf tongues, and the ribbed borders of adjacent lobes typically run parallel to each other. In the Ionian type a gap between the lobes then opens up to be filled by a leaf-point or dart. At the same time the radial geometry of the cup-shaped echinus acted in sympathy with a trend for the lobes to become egg-shaped, leading to egg-and-dart, a development that can also be observed

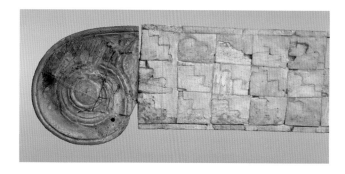

5.14 Cross-member of a piece of furniture, possibly a foot-stool, with ivory volutes and inlay, from Mycenae, National Museum, Athens.

5.15 Alabaster vase from Mycenae (Shaft Grave IV of Grave Circle A), height *c.*24 cm, National Museum, Athens.

on round altars (**Fig. 9.4**).[68] This appears towards the end of the sixth century in capitals on Delos (**Fig. 5.19**), going on to be further refined in Athens in the fifth. In addition the more plastic and dramatically flaring Ionian bolster contrasts with the Cycladic gently concave cylinder.

Several characteristics of Cycladic capitals show them to occupy a middle ground between the Aeolic and Ionian Ionic. First, Aeolic capitals present an elongated,

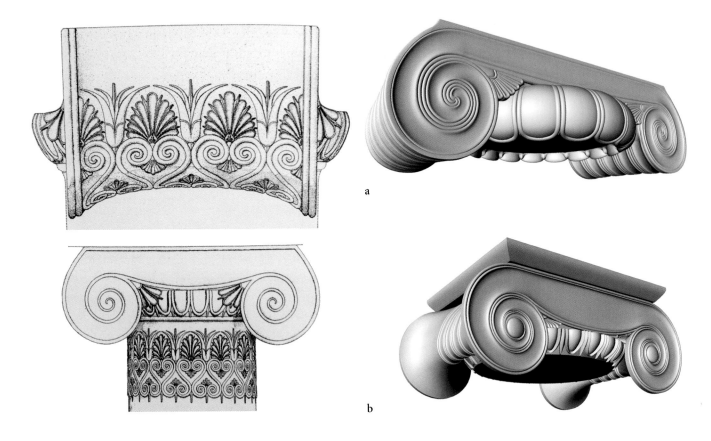

narrow, upper bearing surface, Cycladic ones less so, and Ionian ones still less so. Second, Cycladic capitals have a complete circular echinus, like some Aeolic capitals but unlike Ionian ones. Third, the overfall of the Cycladic echinus can occur on Aeolic examples but not on Ionian Ionic. Fourth, Aeolic volutes usually undergo around one-and-a-half turns as they wind inwards, Ionian Ionic volutes around two-and-a-half, while Cycladic capitals fall roughly in between.[69]

With respect to Aeolic capitals, which sit less well on circular columns, the Cycladic form represented an improvement. Its horizontal canalis made it look better as a support, whether for an entablature or a piece of sculpture, while its proportionately lower height suited more robust columns. Yet, in common with Aeolic counterparts, Cycladic ones, being elongated, do not lend themselves to corners. Any corner capital would have had to be either cruciform or very top-heavy. At any rate no known peripteral temple has Cycladic capitals.

5.16 (ABOVE LEFT)   Capital of the second dipteros at the sanctuary of Hera, Samos, as reconstructed by Gottfried Gruben on the basis of numerous small fragments.

5.17 (ABOVE RIGHT)   3D digital reconstructions of capitals representative of two major branches of Ionic design. (a) Naxian sphinx column, Delphi, exemplifying the Cycladic branch in the middle of the first half of the sixth century; (b) Propylaia, Athenian Acropolis, exemplifying the Attic development of the Ionian branch in the middle of the second half of the fifth century.

5.18 (FACING PAGE)   Selected Ionic capitals of the Archaic period shown in half-plan, elevation and section. (a) Aigina, sanctuary of Apollo, votive column; (b) Delphi, Naxian sphinx column (votive); (c) Yria on Naxos, temple of Dionysos; (d) Ephesos, Artemision.

The Ionian format, however, did succeed in turning the corner. The resolution of this conundrum produced some of the most sophisticated products of all Greek art. The trick was to create an external corner out of two

a

b

c

d

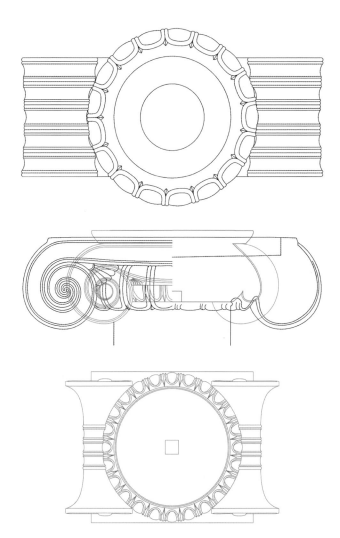

5.19 (FACING PAGE TOP) Ionic corner capital on Delos (probably from the prostyle porch of the Oikos of the Naxians), as reconstructed digitally by Georg Herdt. The surviving block is shown along with a semi-transparent overlay of its reconstructed original form.

5.20 (FACING PAGE BOTTOM) Ionic column of the interior of the Propylaia to the Athenian Acropolis (437–431). Re-erected as part of the comprehensive recent anastylosis under the direction of Tasos Tanoulas, the pale new marble pieces contrast with the darker weathered ancient material. The capital is a precision facsimile of the original design, based on several damaged examples.

5.21 (RIGHT) Cycladic and Ionian Ionic capitals compared: in grey, a Cycladic example of the Archaic period (see **Fig. 5.17b**); in red, a mature Classical example of the 'canonic' Ionian-Attic kind (see **Fig. 5.20**). The latter became more compact than the former owing to transformations affecting the bolster (which becomes flared) and the echinus (which becomes smaller and loses its overfall).

front faces, by allowing them to curve outwards to meet at 45 degrees (**Figs 5.1, 5.2, 5.19**). For this to be possible the front of a capital has to be not much wider than its side. With this in mind it is surely significant that the main differences between the Cycladic and Ionian types affected the front : side ratio. The elimination of the overfall of the echinus, the decrease in its size, the flattening of its profile and the introduction of pulley-wheel shaped bolsters all acted to reduce the effective total length (**Fig. 5.21**). Combined with further fine-tuning this produced a more compact design, thus facilitating the corner solution. It was this innovation that paved the way for Ionic peripteral temples.

Just possibly the puzzle had been resolved towards the middle of the sixth century for the renowned Ephesian Artemision. Its vast dipteral peristyle was capped by magnificent capitals, though sadly only fragments have come down to us. Some of these have been incorporated into two plaster reconstructions in the British Museum, but the rosettes that take the place of volutes in one of them may instead have been used for the internal angles of corner capitals.[70] The peripteral plan calls for a corner capital, but the solution for the external angle can only be guessed. A corner capital anticipating later solutions

may have been achieved in the Didymaion, but the actual remains make this a matter of guesswork too (**Fig. 5.23**).[71] The extraordinary virtuosity of the capitals of Polykrates's Heraion, along with their compact proportions, is also suggestive (**Fig. 5.16**). However we have to wait until the late sixth century for a well-preserved corner capital, that from Delos (**Fig. 5.19**). Thereafter the baton passed to Attica. The beautifully resolved capitals of the Erechtheion (**Fig. 5.2**) and the Propylaia remain the definitive models. The former, including a corner capital, can be appreciated in Hansen's reworking for the Academy, while the latter has recently been recreated with millimetric precision (**Fig. 5.20**).

Ionian Ionic was born, then, by improving the Cycladic type. Furthermore, the Cycladic configuration in certain respects occupies an intermediary position between Aeolic and Ionian solutions. This is consistent with an over-arching development from Aeolic to Cycladic to Ionian. And it is not entirely rhetorical to ask, if the more useful Ionic capital had already existed, why would an architect create and deploy the Aeolic form – a demonstrably retrograde step?

5.22 Archaic Ionic and related columns at a common scale, as reconstructed by Gottfried Gruben and supplemented by Georg Herdt. In practically all cases the heights proposed involve some degree of estimation. The final column (right), for comparative purposes, dates to the Hellenistic period.

We have also seen how the earliest Ionic capitals belonged to votive columns, Cycladic in style, as exemplified by the Naxians' great sphinx column at Delphi (**Fig. 5.22**). Ionic columns subsequently saw use along the front of temples (and inside), later to march all the way around peristyles once the corner problem was resolved. Taken together these developments tentatively suggest the following diagrammatic flow of inspiration and influence:

Diverse rising-volute designs →
  Archaic Aeolic →
   Cycladic Ionic (votive columns) →
    Cycladic Ionic (temple fronts) →
     Ionian Ionic (temple fronts and peristyles)

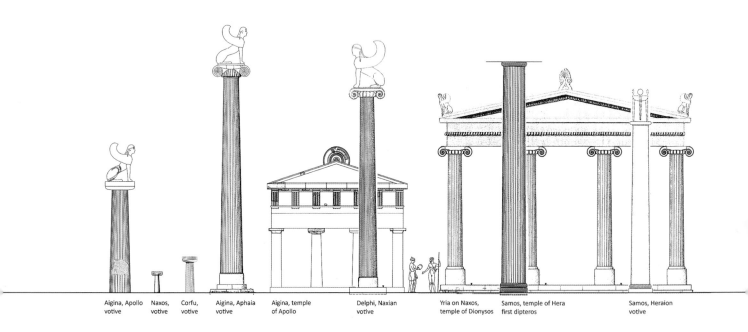

Aigina, Apollo votive   Naxos, votive   Corfu, votive   Aigina, Aphaia votive   Aigina, temple of Apollo   Delphi, Naxian votive   Yria on Naxos, temple of Dionysos   Samos, temple of Hera first dipteros   Samos, Heraion votive

This broad trend should not be mistaken for a progression which was in any sense inevitable. At any stage architects were simply seeking to produce the most attractive solution for a specific commission. There was ample experimentation, along with the production of variants that would turn out in the long run to be dead ends. For example, a few Ionic capitals have a horizontally striated torus/echinus of Samian inspiration, including a pair from Didyma (**Fig. 5.12**) and another recently discovered near Priene.[72] The early sphinx column at the sanctuary of Aphaia at Aigina employed a singular ribbed half-dome instead of an echinus (**Fig. 5.18a**). The slightly later sphinx column in Cyrene on the African coast had two rings of lobes (**Figs 5.22, 7.19**).

Ionicizing votive columns in Athens from the late sixth or early fifth century present further non-canonic solutions for the lower half of the capital. In short there is in every respect extensive variation, more or less successful. Right down to the Hellenistic period practically no two separate sets of capitals use the same design.[73] A range of approaches characterized the proportions of columns and so too of whole façades in the Archaic period, but little of certainty can be said on this subject. Reconstructing the height of all the columns illustrated in **Fig. 5.22** involves a greater or lesser degree of guesswork.

* * *

| Cyrene, votive | Ephesos, temple of Artemis | Ugento, votive | Athens, votive | Samos, temple of Hera second dipteros | Olympia, votive | Kalaureia, votive | Priene, temple of Athena |

0 m   10 m   15 m   20 m

THE IONIC ENTABLATURE

The Ionic entablature admitted just as much variety as the capital, and early developments were similarly conditioned by distinctions between Cycladic and Ionian practice.[74] As the sixth century advanced cross-fertilization between these and other regions produced various sequences of mouldings, though too few complete entablatures survive to be entirely confident about precise configurations.

The epistyle often presented a plain vertical surface or fascia capped by a moulding that, in Ionia, could feature runs of lobes or egg-and-dart and perhaps also bead-and-reel. In epistyles with plural fasciae, the upper one(s) step out slightly. The number of fasciae could be just one (as was often the case in the Cyclades), two (as at Metapontum) or three (the most common solution in Ionia). With time three fasciae became predominant for both Ionic and Corinthian practice. In the Archaic period differing numbers of fasciae could be used in a single building, as at Didyma, reflecting, perhaps, changing tastes over the lengthy construction period.[75]

It is impossible to gauge a reliable idea of arrangements above the epistyle, save for some general trends. Particularly obscure is the advent of dentils. Being uncommon in the Cyclades, an inception in Ionia might be presumed on account of projecting constructional elements on house models (**Fig. 2.9**), though Lycia represents an alternative potential source.[76] Dentil courses have often been restored for the Ephesian Artemision (**Fig. 2.34**) and the Didymaion (**Fig. 5.23**), but only on analogy with later practice. Scattered remains suggest that dentil courses were in use by the latter part of the sixth century,[77] although the first well-preserved examples of certain provenance appear in western colonies not before the fifth century, at Locri and Metapontum (**Fig. 5.25**). As for egg-and-dart, it has forebears both in runs of leaf-tongue and lobed ornament of ultimately oriental origin. Egg-and-dart may have been transferred to the entablature from the capital, or it may have had its own development as a linear ornament on the cornices of altars.

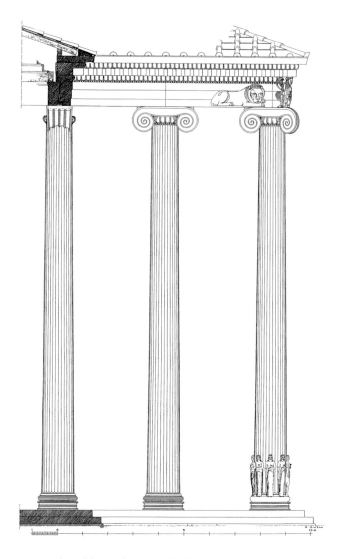

5.23   Order of the Archaic temple of Apollo at Didyma, as reconstructed by Gottfried Gruben.

The origin of the frieze entails two distinct aspects, one the decorative principle of bands of figural and vegetal composition, the other the architectural principle of a linear course between epistyle and cornice. In Hittite territory and Assyria sculpted stone friezes abounded in low-level positions, as a kind of dado or band of orthostates, while painted friezes were used at high level.[78] Bands of metal appliqué with figural decoration were common on monumental doors. The horse

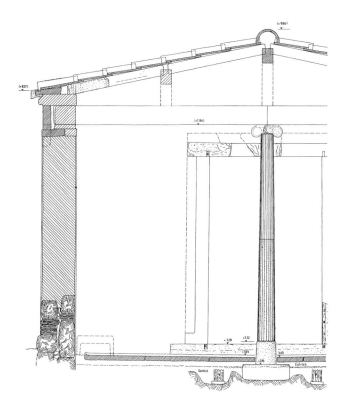

5.24 (ABOVE)   Oikos of the Naxians, Delos; half cross-section. Note the marked slenderness of the interior columns supporting the ridge, and the proposed cross-beams at the level of a blank frieze.

and rider frieze at Prinias (**Fig. 2.16**) signals the westward passage of eastern influence, though its collocation is uncertain – as is the case for most early friezes (Ch. 2, p. 44). Eastern influence also traversed the Anatolian land mass, spurring local innovations using terracotta revetment for roof edgings in both Phrygia and Lydia as well as Greece.[79] The word frieze may derive from a corruption of *opus phrygium*, while Vitruvius's *zophoros* was a latinized Greek term signifying 'that which bears animals'.[80] As already mentioned, the shafts of the great temples of Didyma and Ephesos could be the locus for sculptural figuration wrapping around like a looped frieze.

The Cyclades has the best claim to the frieze in the architectural sense of a course just below the cornice.[81] Along with bed mouldings and cornices that were likewise plain, early friezes are known from Yria on Naxos (**Fig. 2.33**) and on Delos. Here, at the Oikos of the Naxians (**Fig. 5.24**), there survive flat slabs consistent with a course at this level, one which, as mentioned at

5.25 (BELOW)   Temple D at Metapontum (Metapontion); capitals and entablature (first quarter fifth century), as reconstructed by Dieter Mertens.

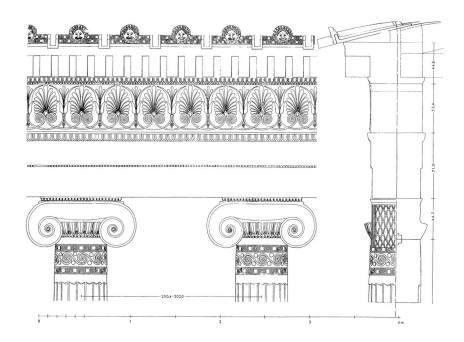

the end of Chapter 3, perhaps masked the ends of cross-beams. By contrast, in Ionia the cornice initially sat directly on the epistyle, without any intervening frieze (**Figs 2.34, 5.23**). There was no such feature at the Artemision, despite all the ornament lavished on it. It is as if designers and sculptors were searching for places to show off their skills, settling on the crowning cyma and the column shafts. The presence of a frieze at the Didymaion is disputed, since there is a case for placing figural reliefs on the epistyle instead, as happened in the roughly contemporary Doric temple at Assos (**Fig. 5.7**).[82] Thus the early use of a decorative band between architrave and cornice remains obscure, and all we can be sure of is that it became established in the fifth century with projects such as Temple D at Metapontum, the Erechtheion and the temple of Athena Nike. The frieze continued to be an option in the fourth century,[83] but it nonetheless remains one of the most captivating ingredients of many Ionic structures.

Aesthetic appeal was not the only motivation behind the frieze. It had a further dimension, animating as it did the Greeks' sanctuaries with commentaries in marble on their myths and achievements. Along with the pediment it made a good place to carry messages, reminding us of that other domain of architectural design that is the subject of the next chapter.

5.26 (FACING PAGE)   Theophilus Hansen, Academy, Athens (1885), front with one of the pair of flanking free-standing columns.

CHAPTER SIX

QUESTIONS OF MEANING AND
THE CORINTHIAN CAPITAL

Buildings of public importance cannot but be vehicles for meaning. The collective effort required to build them presupposes a culture, which in turn presupposes symbolic forms and conventions. Architecture distinguishes

6.1 (FACING PAGE)   Red-figure volute-*krater* (*c.*340), Museum of Fine Arts, Boston. Phoenix (left) and Achilles (right) in the latter's pavilion. Note the slender proportions of the timber columns, the small ceiling beams, and the trophies hanging from the superstructure.

6.2 (ABOVE)   Temple of Bacchus, Baalbek, Lebanon; Corinthian capitals and entablature of the Roman imperial period.

itself from mere building by virtue of the non-utilitarian ideas that go into its creation.[1] When available, historical documents time and again attest to architecture in the service of political and propagandistic ends. There can be no doubt, for example, that in Renaissance Italy allegory and allusion were embedded in projects for popes, cardinals and nobles. The capacity of the orders to bear meaning explains why the Puritans in Britain attacked, verbally and perhaps physically, classical columns identified with idolatry.[2] Revolutionary France produced '*architecture parlante*' or 'speaking architecture', and the notion of 'built ideas' is a commonplace of contemporary architectural criticism.[3]

All buildings hold some meanings for us, but understanding those that pertained in the past is not just a question of assembling historical evidence, it involves interpretation.[4] Over-interpretation is common, and this has engendered a reaction, with 'the search for "meanings"' being dismissed, not without reason, as a legacy of nineteenth-century Romanticism.[5] Indeed this is a domain in which there is even more latitude for subjectivity than for the material treated in previous chapters. Who can say, for example, which of the numerous rival explanations for the helical cupola of Francesco Borromini's S. Ivo in Rome best reflects his thinking?[6] Are the swollen appendages that deck the torso of the Artemis of Ephesos bulls' testicles, breasts, eggs, grapes or nuts? In the face of objections that can be levelled at each of these readings should we give up or continue the search?[7]

The search for meaning often entails the imposition of an all encompassing neatness. This is exemplified by the claim of John Wood and others that the orders flowed ultimately from God himself, a theory driven by the desire to legitimize what Christians might otherwise reject as pagan.[8] Another eighteenth-century figure, the shadowy *érudit libertin* Jean-Louis Viel de Saint-Maux, explained temples as 'poems to fecundity' participating in the primordial veneration of nature.[9] A certain sympathy with such ideas underlies the ritualist theory of Greek myth championed to wide acclaim by James Frazer and Jane Harrison in the early twentieth century.[10] It was also possible for Pugin to believe that Gothic construction was resolutely 'honest' and at the same time that 'every ornament, every detail has a mystical import'.[11]

To combat simplifications it is important to distinguish between connotations pertinent at the origin and those that later accrue, or dissipate, as Riegl explains:

Every religious symbol is destined, with time, if it has any artistic features at all, to become fundamentally . . . an ornamental motif. Its continued and widespread use, the outward form to which consecration imparts a stereotyped character, its execution in various materials, all this means that the symbol is made ever more familiar to man until it becomes almost a necessity for him to see it reproduced.[12]

As meanings tend to dilute it is tempting to imagine a time when their original potency was as yet undiminished. This constitutes the central idea of George Hersey's book *The Lost Meaning of Classical Architecture*. Origins and meanings are similarly entwined in the work of Joseph Rykwert, John Onians and Indra McEwen. In different ways they investigate the orders as vehicles for communication, engaging both scholarly and speculative modes of enquiry. Each operates at a different level from a Wood or a Viel de Saint-Maux, having benefited from intervening developments in archaeology, art history and hermeneutics.[13] It has become clear that meaning is a function of a specific context in time and place. It follows that signs do not have fixed meanings, and can be of plural valency, or polysemic.[14]

* * *

It is ironic that perhaps the clearest reading of meaning related to a Greek temple comes from its absence. By incorporating into the north wall of the Acropolis the debris of the 'pre-Parthenon' destroyed by the Persians, and for decades not building a replacement, the Athenians reminded themselves how close they had come to total disaster.[15] Nearby in the north porch of the Erechtheion a hole in the floor reveals the bedrock below, the spot, it seems, where Poseidon's trident struck the Acropolis to let issue forth a salt spring during the god's unsuccessful tussle with Athena for the city which took her name. Or perhaps this is where came to ground Zeus's thunderbolt, promptly putting an end to the argument. Indeed, there is a gap too in the ceiling, marking the imaginary path the trident (or thunderbolt) took (**Fig. 9.11**).[16] But in the main, temples spoke via the inscriptions they bore, the statuary they housed, and the sculpture they displayed on metopes, friezes, akroteria and pediments.[17] Through the work of playwrights like

Euripides we can glimpse modes of perception denied by modern categories, as his cast interacts with the heroes, gods and monsters sculpted on temples almost as if they were alive.[18]

It does not follow that ancient viewers were necessarily in the position, both physically and intellectually, to comprehend the details of architectural sculpture. We have already noted how difficult it would have been to make out the finer details of the Parthenon frieze (Ch. 1, p. 27).[19] Certain sculptural programmes (for example battles against giants, centaurs or Amazons) were popular across a range of contrasting commissions. It seems that there is a generic, ambient quality about much Greek architectural sculpture located at high level, remote from the viewer.[20] By virtue of their ubiquity, the Doric and Ionic *genera* had still broader connotations than the sculpture they framed. For Walter Burkert, whose insights into the religious basis of the Greek temple I cite repeatedly, this argues against the conveyance of any specific meanings. Writing in the same year that Hersey's and Onians's books on the meanings of the orders were published (1988), he affirms that it is not 'of much avail to look for special symbolic significance in the details of fluted columns, capitals, metopes, triglyphs and pediments. The architectural design used for temples was also used for other buildings such as halls, propylaia, and treasuries.'[21] Indeed; yet it is also important to register an inverse process to the progressive loss of meaning that Riegl studied. Architectural form could accrue significance by virtue of use in works of great prestige and by force of convention, as Cicero explains:

> It was certainly not the search for beauty, but necessity, that has fashioned the celebrated pediment of our Capitol and other religious edifices. But to tell the truth, once the principle had been established of collecting the water either side of the roof, dignity came to be added to the utility of the pediment, so much so that even if the Capitol were to be set up in the heavens, where it should not rain, it could hardly have any dignity without its double pitch roof.[22]

A not dissimilar trajectory applies to the cruciform plan of Christian churches; this evolved from that of Roman basilicas, and only later was the symbolic potential of the cross exploited. While Cicero equated the pediment first to utility and then dignity there was also an implicit divine dimension, as suggested by the deployment of the pediment in Greece primarily for religious architecture, rather as cupolas and steeples go with churches. For Semper the pediment combined with the peristyle to make a 'powerful monumental canopy (baldachin), the most ancient symbol of heavenly power and sovereignty'.[23] The Greek temple can also be understood as the symbolic expression of the *polis* (Ch. 2, p. 60). This sheds light on the cohesive social value of building temples but does not illumine the details of the *genera*. The simple fact that they were used on temples, altars and other structures of sacral character long before transferring over to civic and domestic architecture makes it likely that, initially at least, they conveyed appropriate religious overtones. When vase painters represented altars with volutes or triglyphs, sometimes combining them in ways which flout conventions that kept them apart on buildings, they maximized intimations of sacrality, precise or vague as they may be.

THE METAPHORICAL COLUMN

There are long-standing connections between columns and trees. Vitruvius sees the practical side when he cites early experiments in construction using tree-trunks and forked stakes, or when he recommends columns in upper storeys to be smaller than those below, following the manner of tree growth (V, 1.3).[24] But trees had sacral associations too; suffice it to mention the role of the palm in Egyptian religious culture, and the Mesopotamian–Assyrian tree-of-life tradition (Ch. 4, p. 106). Tree and pillar cults enjoyed a significant place in Minoan religious observances.[25] The elegant stylized palms that ring a vase in the museum at Heraklion bring to mind columns along with connections with the sacred that go beyond mere decorative effect (**Fig. 6.3**).

6.3   Minoan vase with stylized palm trees (mid-second millennium), museum at Heraklion. With their straight shaft, incipient volutes and the palmette configuration of the crown, these invite comparison with volute columns and related decorative applications.

Pliny commented that 'trees formed the first temples of the gods'.[26] Venerated trees were critical elements of many a Greek sanctuary.[27]

The column also had to do with the human body, the giver and the receiver of buildings.[28] Vitruvius refers to the body of architecture,[29] while engaging this theme in two main ways. One has to do with mathematical abstraction; in a celebrated passage (III,1.1) the *symmetria* of the well-shaped body is presented as the paradigm for a well-designed building (Ch. 5, p. 115). The other has to do with semantic possibilities:

> At the foot they [the Ionians] substituted the base in place of a shoe; in the capital they placed the volutes, hanging down at the right and left like curly ringlets, and ornamented its front with cymatia and with festoons[30] arranged in place of hair, while they brought

the flutes down the whole of the shaft, falling like the folds in the robes worn by matrons. (IV,1.7).

Scenarios such as this intrigued Vitruvianists in the Renaissance (**Fig. 0.8**), as did the sexing of columns: the adult male for Doric, the adult female for Ionic, and the virginal female for Corinthian. Some time after the first Doric temple was built for Hera near Argos by Doros, the Dorians' leader, Vitruvius says that a wave of emigration arrived in Ionia, where Ion built a Doric temple to Panionian Apollo (IV,1.3–5).[31] Its columns were made six diameters tall in imitation of a man whose height measures six times his foot: 'thus the Doric column, as used in buildings, began to exhibit the proportions, strength, and beauty of the body of a man' (IV,1.6). When the Ionians desired to construct a temple of Artemis (at Ephesos) in 'a new style of beauty', they chose columns eight diameters tall so as to give them womanly grace. Corinthian columns were later made like maidens, and so 'more slender on account of their tender years' (IV,1.7–8).

For Vitruvius gender could affect the very choice of *genus* (I,2.5). Doric was appropriate for temples of Ares/Mars, Herakles/Hercules and Athena/Minerva because of these gods' martial power; Corinthian suited temples of Aphrodite/Venus and other feminine deities; Ionic took the middle ground while leaning towards the femine side. This hardly finds echoes in practice. As we have just noted, Vitruvius himself tells that the first Doric temple was sacred to Hera. Early Doric temples were erected not only for her (Mon Repos, Paestum), but also for Artemis (Corfu) and Aphaia (Aigina). Much later, our writer's patron Augustus adopted 'virginal' Corinthian for his showpiece temple of Mars Ultor – Mars the Avenger, the divine embodiment of testosterone. Vitruvius's scheme thus offers no viable explanation for the distribution of column types; rather it reflects intellectual constructs of the late Classical and Hellenistic periods.[32]

There are earlier signs of gender association in Greek architecture all the same. Rather as Vitruvius suggests, early Ionic fluting bears comparison with the stylized

6.4 Statue of a young girl or *kore*, 1.92 m tall, part of a statuary group offered by Cheramyes, an Ionian aristocrat, to Hera at her sanctuary on Samos (*c.*570-60). The *kore* wears a veil (*epiblema*) over a cloak (*himation*) over a tunic (*chiton*), the falling pleats of which may be likened to architectural fluting. The almost cylindrical lower part and the way it flares to meet the plinth recalls a column. An inscription runs vertically along the edge of the *epiblema*: 'Cheramyes dedicated me to Hera as an offering'. Louvre, Paris, inv. Ma 686.

drapery of Cycladic and Ionian *korai* (**Fig. 6.4**).[33] The Corinthian capital, as we shall see, has for its core a *kalathos*, a kind of basket used for feminine activities such as woolworking.[34] (The artist Jean-Léon Gérôme,

with an eye to nineteenth-century appetites for classical erotica, made a quite different association, personifying Corinthe as one of the courtesans for which the city was legendary, and perching her naked save for her jewels on a gilded Corinthian capital.[35]) Various female statues carrying vessels on their heads which date from the Roman periods may have been inspired by Greek forerunners, and some of the vessels take the form of *kalathoi*.[36] As for anthropomorphic figures used as structural supports, male atlantes or telamons typically went with Doric forms (**Fig. 6.5**);[37] female caryatids with Ionic or Corinthian forms (**Fig. 6.6**).[38] Vitruvius links both kinds with stories about the submission of slaves or prisoners.[39] Yet this is to ignore eastern precedents of a quite different nature; the goddess Hathor, after all, could lend her image to columns in Egypt (**Fig. 4.1**).

The analogy between column and body, irrespective of gender, is more definite. Base can equate to foot in Greek and Roman terminology. In Greek, capitals were mostly called variants on *kranion*, cranium or skull, while the Latin *capitulum* was derived from *caput*, head.[40] In Greece (and further east) furniture supports frequently terminate in zoomorphic or anthropomorphic heads and feet (**Figs 0.6, 1.13, 5.13, 8.5**).[41] In Aeschylus's *Oresteia*, Clytemnestra treacherously beckons her doomed consort-king Agamemnon back home to the palace where he belongs, 'like the strong main post to the roof'.[42] As testimony to their special power, columns were reputed miraculously to have survived catastrophe, as spelt out on the bronze rubric set up in front of the column of Oinomaos at Olympia (Ch. 3, pp. 67–8):

Stranger, I am a remnant of a famous house,
I, who once was a pillar in the house of Oinomaos;
now by Cronus' son I lie with these bands upon me.[43]

In *Iphigenia in Tauris* Euripides's protagonist recounts a dream of an earthquake that razed her family home:

One single pillar (it seemed to me) was left
Of all my father's house. From the capital
Fair hair streamed, and then taking human voice
    it spoke . . .[44]

6.5   Temple of Zeus, Agrigento (Akragas); cork model reconstruction, Museo Archeologico Regionale. The location of the male figure-supports (telamons) is disputed.

For Iphigenia the columns of a house were also 'sons',[45] which by extension suggests that the columns of temples can be likened to the city's sons, its citizens.[46]

MILITARY METAPHORS?

Extending this notion, Onians compares the columns of temples to the warrior sons of the *polis*, its protectors in times of war. Thus the Doric peristyle becomes a metaphor for military cooperation, displaying the strength and disciplined regularity required of the hoplite phalanx.[47] Just as Homer likens the ranks of armed warriors to tightly fitted masonry, so Greek military commanders would have sought for the phalanx the immovable resistance of a temple.[48] Architects, reasons Onians, reciprocally created temples in the image of the phalanx: both are rectangular and are six or eight columns/men wide; the fluting of the shafts echoes the sharp edges of swords and spearheads.[49]

McEwen likewise explores the metaphorical world of men working in disciplined unison: but hers is a nautical symbolism suited to Ionia, which was settled by seafaring colonizers. The dipteral colonnades of the great Ionic temples at Ephesos, Samos and Didyma recall the double banks of oars that powered these cities' navies.[50] She notes the wordplay between *naus* signifying ship and *naos* signifying shrine.[51] The insistence on fine craftsmanship in temple building makes sense, she argues, as an echo of its essential, life-saving, role in shipbuilding.

* * *

6.6 Head of a marble caryatid from the propylon of Appius Claudius Pulcher, sanctuary of Demeter, Eleusis (mid-first century). She carries on her head a container used in the rites associated with the Eleusinian mysteries.

A SACRIFICIAL METAPHOR?

Temples and orders are for Hersey to be decoded as assemblages of sacrificial vestiges, noting aboriginal customs of hanging the victims from trees and shrines (**Fig. 6.7**).[52] The architectural display of sacrificial remains is in fact suggested in *Iphigenia in Tauris*: when Orestes and Pylades arrived in Tauris they saw in horror the skulls of Greeks hung as trophies on the walls.[53] Gore was no detraction from gifts to the gods: a warlike boast in Aeschylus' *Seven Against Thebes* vows to deck temples with 'spear-torn spoils' and crown them with the armour of the vanquished foes.[54] A vase painting of Achilles in a pavilion evokes just this kind of display (**Fig. 6.1**).

Since sacrifice normally involved animals, Hersey shifts the interpretation of terminology from human to animal anatomy. Thus a column base, *basis*, would be the foot of the victim, while the *speira* moulding would

6.7 Circular relief panel (*tondo*) dating from the 130s AD, set up on the Arch of Constantine, Rome (*c.* AD 315-16). Detail showing the Emperor Hadrian (whose head is re-cut in the likeness of Constantine), poised to sacrifice at a rural shrine sacred to Diana (Artemis). Note the boar's head hung from the tree.

take its name from the rope used to tie the animal, and so on.[55] But etymology is not a game to play lightly. In Greek and Vitruvian usage *basis* broadly denoted 'the bottom, or lower part, of a thing', and only rarely separate column bases. As we have just seen, Vitruvius links bases to *human* footwear. Indeed, thick-soled multi-layered Greek sandals may be said vaguely to resemble some striated Archaic bases (**Fig. 5.10**).[56] As for *speira* or *spira*, this usually indicated a whole base and only infrequently the convex moulding that Vitruvius called a torus.[57] Still, bases in the north porch of the Erechtheion do have an upper torus that is carved with guilloche, a pattern adapted from oriental ornament which, in three dimensions, recalls the weave of rope.[58] In the fifth century there were technological advances in the use of cranes, pulleys and rope; this, rather than sacrifice, was the likely context in which *speira* and/or rope imagery passed into architectural usage.[59]

Like so many before him, Hersey's thinking was also driven by visual prompts; the volutes of Ionic capitals resemble horns, 'those omnipresent sacrificial objects'.[60] Horns or horned skulls had long-standing sacral associations in the eastern Mediterranean, while in the Hellenistic and Roman periods bucrania, the skulls of oxen, were sculpted on altars, metopes and architectural friezes (**Fig. 6.25**).[61] Yet the lineage of spiral and volute motifs, as we saw in Chapters 4 and 5, suggests that they were derived primarily from plant forms. Indeed, there is little to be gained by pushing a reading beyond where it can reasonably go, as when, extending earlier ideas of guttae as stylized drops of rain, in Hersey's mind they become gouts of the victim's fluids draining from thigh-bones in the guise of triglyphs.[62] Moreover, on the basis of Vitruvius's noting that the Greeks used a word meaning 'thighs' to denote the uprights of triglyphs (Ch. 3, pp. 73–4), Hersey interprets these as thrice-cloven thigh-bones of sacrificial animals. Thigh-bones figure prominently in Homeric sacrifice, it is true.[63] This led the archaeologist Sandro Stucchi to see stylized bands of bunched thigh-bones in triglyph friezes on altars.[64] But can we really visualize triglyphs as thigh-bones, whether thrice-cloven or thrice-bunched? Definitely not! Man-made construction was instead the cue for another symbolic interpretation by Robert Demangel. Noting the window hypothesis discarded by Vitruvius (Ch. 3, p. 75), he saw Egyptian, Minoan and Oriental symbolic portals as 'cosmic hieroglyphs' that mutated into triglyphs.[65] A potential transitional step (which Demangel did not mention) might be the seventh-century frieze from Chania (**Fig. 2.15**). But this is just another game; yet again the triglyph eludes capture.

* * *

The ancient mind animated its environment with great imaginative richness, as Vitruvius and other writers show. I have no doubt that forms trigger associations that could impinge on the way the forms were later treated. Perhaps speculations like Hersey's led some Romans to fashion the dividers of lobed ornament into arrow-heads – hence the English term 'egg-and-dart' (**Fig. 6.25**).[66] But to explain how forms came into being in the first place is quite another matter. If spearheads, hoplite shields, horns and thigh-bones were relevant, would we not find more obvious traces of them in early Greek ornaments?[67] Without more tangible evidence to bridge the gap between theoretical and actual constructs the most compelling of readings founder.

THE CORINTHIAN CAPITAL

The Corinthian capital presents a model case for reading Greek architectural form for several reasons: the focus on the capital alone helps limit the scope of investigation; the role played by lost perishable materials is not critical; more is known about Greek architecture when Corinthian appeared in the fifth century compared to when Doric and Ionic arose; contemporary artistic representations and related artefacts contextualize ingredients of the new design. Vitruvius's passage on its origins also commands relative authority since his sources, mostly from the fourth to the second centuries, date not so long after the events in question.[68]

6.9 Temple of Apollo, Bassai; Corinthian capital that stood at the end of the cella, as reconstructed by Heinrich Bauer on the basis of surveys made before its disappearance by Charles Robert Cockerell and Haller von Hallerstein.

6.8 (ABOVE) Temple of Apollo, Bassai; interior, as reconstructed by Fritz Krischen.

6.10 (BELOW) Early Corinthianizing capitals with volutes in a lyre-shaped configuration. Left: Olympia, made of terracotta; right: Elis.

In Greece Corinthian capitals typically participated in arrangements that were otherwise Ionic. This was the case for the first known example, which once belonged to a single column standing at the head of Apollo's temple at Bassai, built in the last quarter of the fifth century (**Fig. 6.8**).[69] The capital itself has disappeared, but not before it was drawn and copied in the early nineteenth century, allowing its reconstruction (**Fig. 6.9**). This was not necessarily the first Corinthian capital ever; claims have been made for this a little earlier, inside

6.12 (ABOVE)   Corinthianizing capital from a funeral monument at Megara Hyblaia, Sicily (?early fifth century), now in the Museo Archeologico Regionale, Syracuse. Although acanthus is not present, this capital presents several parallels with later Corinthian capitals. Note the lyre-shaped configuration.

6.11 (LEFT)   Corinthian half-capital from the interior of the tholos in the sanctuary of Athena Pronaia (Marmaria), Delphi.

the Parthenon. One hypothesis sees the new invention terminating the four columns in the rear room,[70] another envisages a single prototype supporting the out-stretched arm of Athena Parthenos (**Fig. 1.21**).[71] These capitals did not necessarily have the same format as at Bassai; initially popular was a 'sofa' or lyre-shaped con-figuration of the volutes, one which is best not called Corinthian, but 'Corinthianizing'. Two examples, one made of terracotta, have been discovered at Olympia and neighbouring Elis (**Fig. 6.10**); these feature a short-hand foliate decoration at the bottom which is even less like acanthus than at Bassai.[72] A similar format is found on the interior half-columns of the marble tholos of

Athena Pronaia at Delphi, though this time the modest foliage is recognizably acanthus (**Fig. 6.11**).[73] All these capitals had a palmette on axis. The capitals of the (wooden?) columns of Achilles's pavilion were imagined with a lyre-like configuration (**Fig. 6.1**). This is also found outside the context of columns, as on a stele from Megara Hyblaia (**Fig. 6.12**).[74]

The supremely elegant capitals of the tholos of Epidauros set the tone for a great many later designs (**Figs 6.13, 6.14**). Here the acanthus takes up a greater share of the height than before, while the palmette is omitted and the helices rise up from behind the leaves and curl over in a relatively naturalistic fashion. Subse-

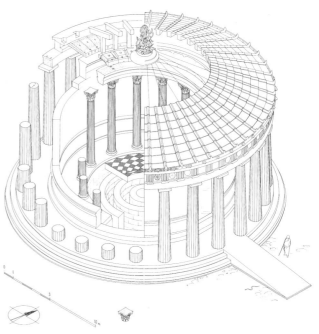

6.14 Tholos in the sanctuary of Asklepios, Epidauros; cut-away reconstruction by Chrysanthos Kanellopoulos.

6.13 Corinthian order of the interior of the tholos in the sanctuary of Asklepios, Epidauros, as reconstructed by Alphonse Defrasse. *Envoi* of 1891–3.

6.15 Monument of Lysikrates, street of tripods, Athens; detail of capitals and entablature. The monument was built by the *choregos* Lysikrates to commemorate the winning prize for a performance he sponsored in 335/334. The tripod prize originally crowned the three-cornered akroterion on the roof.

6.16   Kallimachos taking inspiration that would lead him to invent the Corinthian capital, as visualized by Roland Fréart de Chambray (1650) on the basis of Vitruvius's account.

quently, in the second half of the fourth century, a variant capital made its way onto the exterior of the Monument of Lysikrates (**Fig. 6.15**).[75] Only around the start of the second century were Corinthian columns chosen for the exterior of major temples (**Fig. 6.26**).[76] For long the entablature followed Ionic or even Doric models, just as Vitruvius allowed,[77] and it was not until the Augustan period that Corinthian emerged as a *genus* in its own right, with characteristic columnar proportions and a cornice incorporating brackets or modillions (**Fig. 6.24**).[78]

Writing in the Augustan age, in fact, Vitruvius visualized the birth of the Corinthian capital in the following terms (**Fig. 6.16**):

A Corinthian girl of good family, just old enough to think of marriage, fell ill and died. After the funeral her nurse gathered the pots and cups of which the girl had been very fond when she lived into a basket (*kalathos*) that she carried to the monument and laid on top of it. She covered the basket with a tile so that the things she put inside might survive that much longer than if it had been left open. As it happened, she had put that basket directly over an acanthus root which – being pressed by the weight – sprouted rather stunted shoots and leaves when the next spring came round. The shoots clung to the sides of the basket as they grew, and being forced outward by the weight of the tile, were bent into curls and volutes at the corners. Kallimachos (who for the elegance and refinement of his carving was called *katatechnos* by the Athenians) passed by the monument just then and noticed the basket and the tender leaves. Pleased with the whole thing and the novel shape, he made some columns for the Corinthians based on this model and fixed the rule of their proportion.[79]

Riegl set the tone for much later scholarship when he judged Vitruvius's story to be 'obviously fictitious, though admittedly charming'.[80] Rather than the fruit of a spontaneous invention, Riegl showed that early acanthus ornament was highly stylized, and at first grafted onto the palmette, then used in alternation, finally substituting it altogether. Naturalistic leaf treatments occurred relatively late.[81] The same point applies to the composition of the capital, the ingredients of which were slow to fall into the definitive Corinthian scheme. And while Vitruvius situates his account in a cemetery setting in Corinth, early instances of acanthus ornament occur on the terracotta anthemions of temple roofs in Attica (**Fig. 6.17**).[82] Experimentation led to the central akroterion of the Parthenon, an elaborate composition based on a palmette and a tracery of tendrils and helices

6.17 Terracotta roof edging (antefixes) from Brauron and Eleusis (first half of the fifth century). On two of these examples, leaf ornament – possibly acanthus – has been introduced at the bottom.

springing from a base of acanthus, a formula that was widely imitated or abbreviated (**Fig. 6.18**).[83] A little later hints of acanthus were woven into the floral ornamentation of the Erechtheion.[84]

A link between Vitruvius's account and historical perspectives exists in the person of his protagonist Kallimachos, a sculptor who was active on the Acropolis and in the Erechtheion in particular, for which he made a much admired gilded bronze 'lamp'.[85] Pausanias cites Kallimachos as the first to have conquered carving voids in marble,[86] a breakthrough that may have depended on his famed expertise in bronze-working.[87] Metal is indeed a suitable material for filigree detail and overturning leaves. 'It may be conjectured', wrote Dinsmoor, 'that he worked out the original design in bronze and then reproduced it in marble.'[88] Evidence of metallic details confirms Athens as an important locus for early developments.[89] Yet the importance of bronze for our subject returns us to Corinth too, by virtue of the city's renown for bronzeworking in general.[90] Interestingly enough, a *kalathos* capital has been discovered at Corinth that probably dates to the fourth century BC (**Fig. 6.19**).[91] Like Roman examples belonging to the temple of Bel at Palmyra, this stone core once bore a bronze carapace, presumably in the form of acanthus leaves, helices and possibly palmettes.[92] Thus it is pertinent to note formal affinities on early Classical metalwork ranging from armour to lampstands, mirror handles and tripods. In particular a rod-tripod discovered at Vulci in Etruria has colonnette capitals that prefigure Corinthian design

6.18 Marble akroterion incorporating half-palmettes, helices and acanthus foliage terminating a funeral stele (fourth century), National Museum, Athens.

in respect of lyre-shaped volutes rising from stems, an abacus, proportions and, once again, a central palmette (**Fig. 6.20**). The foliate treatment of the crown from a bronze stand illustrated in **Fig. 4.28** is also of note, since some of the leaves emerge from behind and between the main tier of leaves.

The alignment of Vitruvius's text with glimpses of historical context invites further consideration. Elements of Corinthian design may profitably be related to fifth-century burial customs, as Théophile Homolle argued in 1916 and as Rykwert has confirmed.[93] Acanthus, volutes and the basket-shaped core all played

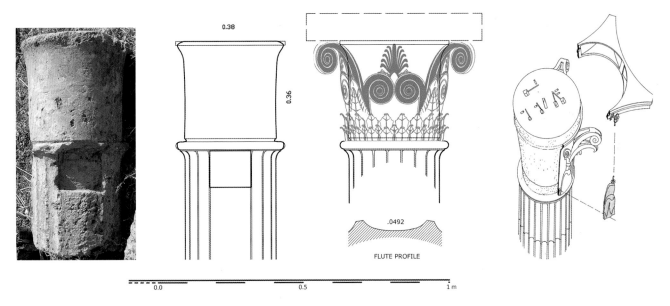

6.19   Corinthianizing capitals comprising a core in the form of a stone *kalathos*, to which were fixed bronze acanthus leaves and other decorative attachments: Corinth (fourth century) and (far right) Palmyra, Syria (Augustan period).

significant roles in this context. That the memory of a basket is inherent to the *kalathos* is suggested by an early terracotta example from Eleusis painted like wicker-work and illustrating the transference of ornament across media that Semper advocated as a general princi-ple (**Fig. 6.21**).[94] A small stone marker in the National Museum in Athens takes the form of a *kalathos* mounted on a plinth/casket (**Fig. 6.22**).[95] Both *kalathoi* and acan-thus feature prominently on scenes that show women visiting graves and honouring the dead.[96] So there are grounds for reading the new capital as an embellished funerary *kalathos* – but only up to a point, since early Corinthian capitals were not so *kalathos*-like as they later became.[97]

In representations of columnar tomb monuments acanthus is often shown at the bottom or top (**Fig. 6.23**).[98] The Greeks associated many plants with funeral rites, acanthus among them.[99] A palmette is frequently depicted on the top of grave monuments with acanthus, sometimes rising out of a lyre-like volute element. On stone stelai acanthus first appeared in tentative fashion, going on to become more prominent (**Fig. 6.18**).

The frequency of lyre configurations on representa-tions of funeral monuments is significant given their presence on early Corinthianizing capitals, as we saw earlier. Furthermore, lyre-shaped devices (often coupled with palmettes) were not uncommon in other domains, for example as decoration for the parapets of altars (**Fig. 3.13**).[100] Indirect influences on Corinthian design of small-scale work include volute capitals of eastern ori-gin,[101] but of more direct relevance is early Classical pro-duction, as we saw in the case of the tripod found at Vulci (**Fig. 6.20**).

Funeral stelai also contribute to Corinthian origins in other ways than those just discussed. An Athenian ex-ample from the early fifth century now in New York bears a cavetto capital which is broadly comparable with Corinthian capitals in its vertical emphasis.[102] To my mind the most significant precedent is the stele capital from Megara Hyblaia already mentioned (**Fig. 6.12**), which probably dates to the early fifth century.[103] In other words, long before the capitals of Bassai and Olympia, this exhibits a lyre-shaped Corinthianizing composition rendered plastically and not simply applied

6.20   Capital terminating a bracing rod of a bronze tripod-stand (*c.*500), discovered in a tomb at Vulci, Italy, and now in the British Museum.

6.22   Stone funerary monument in the form of a *kalathos* on a plinth (?fifth century), National Museum, Athens.

6.21 (BELOW)   Terracotta *kalathos* from Eleusis (probably seventh century), decorated with geometrical designs recalling basketwork.

superficially. The fact that this capital lacks acanthus hardly negates its relevance.[104] Indeed the obsession with acanthus, which Riegl called 'by far the most important vegetal ornament of all time',[105] has deflected attention from the other crucial components of the Corinthian capital: its vertical proportions; its moulded abacus; its volutes; and (in the early stages) the central palmette. Be it noted that acanthus plays a minor role at Bassai and Olympia – right at the bottom of these capitals. Indeed the leaves are not really acanthus, but generic foliate decoration. Only in the fourth century did the leaves start to resemble acanthus and to progressively climb, as it were, up the *kalathos*.[106]

In sum, the assembled evidence points to an extended development with differing strands, and the following tentative outline. Early in the fifth century influential

6.23   Selected scenes on white *lekythoi* from Attica (mainly late fifth century), showing tomb monuments decorated with fillets, volutes, palmettes and foliage with serrated leaves, possibly acanthus.

artistic centres (such as Corinth, Athens and Syracuse) spawned variants in the capitals of funeral stelai that prefigured the Corinthian solution in terms of morphology and proportions. Architects and sculptors learnt too from contemporary developments in luxury metalwork exemplified by the tripod from Vulci. Meanwhile acanthus crept onto temple roof ornaments and stone stelai. At some stage experiments began with column capitals, and with bronze attachments in the shape of stylized acanthus and palmettes. Kallimachos, consummately skilled with both stone and bronze, was perhaps involved. A core shaped like a *kalathos* was found to lend itself well to circular columns, while indirect catalysts may have included miscellaneous eastern foliate crowns and Egyptian campaniform capitals (**Fig.**

4.2).[107] Corinth hosted innovations using bronze, though the major advances also took place in Attica. Sub-sequently the foliage came to receive a more lifelike treatment, so the lyre-shaped configuration was abandoned in favour of the seductive fiction of natural growth sprouting from the shaft (**Fig. 6.13**). There was another reason too for discarding the lyre scheme, for it was better suited to frontal compositions of the kind used for stelai than to columns in the round.[108] Just as in the case of the Ionian and Cycladic branches of the Ionic capital, if we are to understand Greek architects' approach to design it is important to identify not just what they did but also what they chose to discard.

Making allowance for the ancient tendency to explain extended processes of development in terms of an artificially compressed moment, there may have been something behind the Vitruvian account after all. It would seem that the funerary allusions of Corinthian stood not for the triumph of death, but for the triumph over death, for regeneration. Perhaps such associations were seen to suit the rebirth of the Athenian Acropolis according to Perikles's vision, which would help explain the possible early deployment of the new design there.[109] With time meanings would have broadened. In the Monument of Lysikrates (**Fig. 6.15**), a structure which celebrated a victory in Athenian choregic performances, a triumphal symbolism may lie behind the adoption of Corinthian capitals and acanthus decoration for the crowning finial that originally held aloft the tripod prize.

The Romans loved Corinthian because it was the most magnificent, ornate and luxurious of the three *genera*, with a fluid design that presented no great problems at corners and so was better suited to articulated ground-plans.[110] Corinthian columns had been used to imposing effect in the gigantic (although for long unfinished) Olympieion in Athens (**Fig. 6.26**), but the runaway success of Corinthian – *the* Roman order – goes beyond strictly aesthetic and formal terms. A continuing awareness of its triumphal overtones would help explain why this capital was taken up in Rome by generals returning victorious from campaigns in Greece after Mummius sacked Corinth in 146.[111] The tholos by the

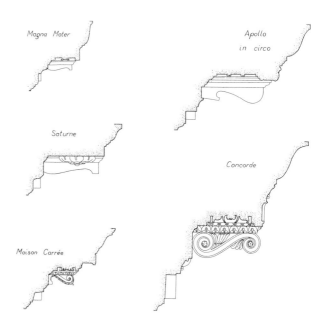

6.24   Selected Roman Corinthian cornices with modillions.

Tiber – possibly erected by the same general – was one of the first buildings in Rome to be made not only in the new style but also of solid Greek marble.[112] A century or so later the proto-emperor, Augustus, sponsored building projects tuned to a carefully orchestrated political programme, as exemplified by his temple of Mars Ultor. For his purposes Corinthian was ideal – a visually compelling model of Hellenic style that came without the ethnic associations of Doric or Ionic.[113] Acanthus spoke of victory, healing and regeneration – and Augustus promoted himself as the sole figure capable of healing the wounds of a world torn by civil war.[114] His endorsement went on to provide yet another layer of justification, and with time Corinthian columns became quite simply the default choice for imperial projects, the 'done thing'. The Augustan period also saw the consolidation of experiments in the design of the cornice, to which was added a course of bracket-like projections known as modillions that contributed a rhythmical cadence rather as did the mutules of the Doric geison. By contrast, modillions usually involved curvature in profile and sometimes a scroll-like configuration (**Fig. 6.24**). This development

6.25   Temple of Vespasian, Roman Forum (*c.* AD 90); cornice, now in the adjacent Antiquarium in the arches of the so-called Tabularium. The frieze presents bucrania along with ritual equipment related to sacrifice and offering.

is significant in that it gave Corinthian its own entablature, completing its maturation into a bona fide *genus* or order. Finally, in the first century AD, acanthus came to be applied as a decorative surcharge on the underside of the modillions (**Fig. 6.25**). Such a dynamic historical profile reflects not so much a simple progressive loss of meaning as a process of mutation and assimilation of new associations overlaid on a trend away from the singular and definite to the multiple and indefinite.

∗ ∗ ∗

Behind the make-believe, myths embrace real cultural phenomena to varying degrees, and this seems true of Vitruvius's tale of Corinthian origins. He may err in compressing developments that stretched over a lengthy period, and in passing over the role of Athens, yet some of his words align with undercurrents of meanings that can be historically validated. The success of Corinthian was founded on its visual appeal, but there was more to it than that; the capital was more than pretty decoration. Through their connections with the material culture of Greek life the very forms that brought delight to the eye resonated in the mind.

6.26 (FACING PAGE)   Temple of Zeus (Olympieion), Athens; standing Corinthian columns. Located on the site of a huge unfinished Archaic Doric predecessor, this temple was begun in the early second century and (almost) completed by the emperor Hadrian.

1

2

3

4

5

6

7

8a

8b

9

CHAPTER SEVEN

GIFTS TO THE GODS

The borderlines between architecture and other disciplines are more permeable than preconceptions tend to suggest. Some architectural theorists insist on theirs as an autonomous discipline, and it is often treated separately from other realms of visual culture in teaching, in publishing and on archaeological sites, where we see temples isolated from statues and small finds kept in museums. It is true that some museums do unite architecture and statuary in restituted pediments under the slopes of which the bodies of gods, heroes and monsters contrive to fit, but this is not the kind of interaction at issue here. The point is that temples were cut from the same cloth as everything else in the sanctuary. Similar forms danced back and forth between architecture, sculpture, furniture, ceramics, ivories, textiles and metalwork. Understanding how one sphere of

design could affect another is therefore of cardinal importance.

When comparing architecture and the 'minor' arts there reigns the presumption that influence flows from major to minor, from things that are large to things that are small, and from architecture to ancillary structures and portable objects. According to the first of Owen Jones's propositions on the grammar of ornament, 'The Decorative Arts arise from, and should properly be attendant upon, Architecture'.[1] This applies well to relatively recent movements such as Arts and Crafts and Art Nouveau, when architects like Rennie Mackintosh or Peter Behrens would turn their hand to chairs, lamps, tableware and so on. In the Gothic period similar strategies were employed for the design of architecture and the micro-architecture that is manifest in such things

7.1 (FACING PAGE)   Selected miniature offerings found at the sanctuary of Artemis at Ephesos, made of ivory, horn and gold (seventh century). These anticipate comparable motifs on architecture. Scale 5:4 (i.e., slightly larger than full size), except nos. 5 and 8, full size.

7.2 (ABOVE)   Sanctuary of Asklepios at Epidauros; panoramic elevation, as reconstructed by Alphonse Defrasse. *Envoi* of 1891–3, watercolour on Chinese ink base. For a detail from the right side, see **Fig., pp. iv–v.**

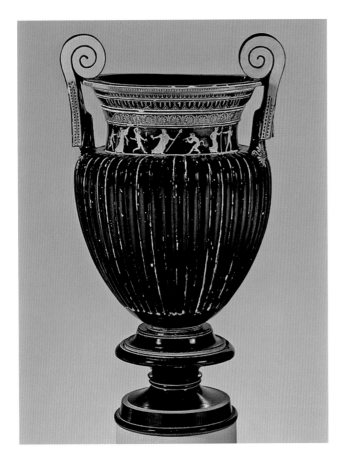

7.3 'Architectonic' red-figure Attic volute-*krater* with base (*c.*430), Metropolitan Museum of Art, New York. The moulded base, the vertical ribbing on the body, the figural frieze and the cornice-like ornament at the top combine with the volutes to give this vase a certain architectonic character.

a case in point being Assyrian and Phoenician 'woman-at-the-window' miniatures with balusters and capitals that mimic built equivalents (**Fig. 4.30**). The refined red-figure vase illustrated in **Fig. 7.3** has with good reason been labelled 'architectonic', given the mouldings, flutings and volutes that style it. When we encounter Doric and/or Ionic features on altars of the Classical period these no doubt were borrowed from architecture.[3] Yet the same direction of travel cannot safely be presumed at the time these forms emerged. In Greece in the eighth century there was no substantial indigenous tradition of building (Ch. 2, pp. 36–7). When, in the seventh century, the sight of Bronze Age ruins and reports of wonders overseas inspired the wish for monumentality, architects thirsty for guidance would have turned to prestigious portable material that they could see with their own eyes and touch with their own hands.

In Archaic Greece a career in architecture alone did not exist; the designers of buildings were artists and craftsmen too. Sources document various combinations of roles.[4] Theodoros, architect of the Samian dipteros along with Rhoikos, was famed as a sculptor, a miniaturist and a jeweller besides being said to be the first to make a self-portrait.[5] The same craftsmen could be involved in the production of ceramic vessels and architectural terracottas such as roof edging; at any rate similar moulds have been found for both applications.[6] Significantly, in his discussion of the rise of building (Ch. 2, pp. 63–4), Vitruvius envisaged early builders being inspired by ideas 'born from the variety of their crafts'.[7]

Reciprocity between architecture and other forms of production is manifest not just in overlapping decorative repertoires, but also in almost innate anthropomorphic responses to the articulation of supports – be they candelabra or columns – typically into three parts (a foot or base, a shaft or middle section, and a head or capital). Likewise there is a shared sensibility in the way the spread of load where a shaft or leg meets a base or the ground is poetically acknowledged by a flare or swelling.[8] In short, there are meaningful sympathies between the gods' '*immobili*' and their '*mobili*' (to use Italian, or '*immeubles*' and '*meubles*' in French).

as caskets, censers, lecterns, reliquaries, rood-screens, tabernacles and tombs. The predominant trend was for the large to influence the small, but from around the early fourteenth century AD the reverse could occur due in part to economic factors depressing major building projects, in part to the portability and shorter production times of the micro-architecture.[2]

As a general principle it would be unwise to insist on a flow from large to small or vice versa; the flow depends on circumstance, moving in different directions at different times. In antiquity as in the Gothic period influence from large to small was probably the general rule,

THE SANCTUARY ENVIRONMENT

Greek architecture, then, merits comparison with a wide range of productive arts. Some relevant artefacts had funerary associations. These include stelai and *kalathoi* that contributed to the formation of the Corinthian capital (Ch. 6, pp. 151–5), or amphoras which displayed geometric schemes that prefigured the rhythmical basis and severity of Doric style (**Figs 2.10, 7.4, 8.13**). The field-and-divider principle was also frequently used on the necks of large storage jars (*pithoi*) of Cretan manufacture. Attitudes to architectural composition perhaps grew out of the predilections of artists who produced such pottery for, after the Bronze Age, this was arguably the first technical art in which the Greeks achieved effects that were both grand and refined.[9] Yet the majority of objects that encapsulated lessons for architectural elaboration were high-calibre offerings displayed in sanctuaries. Temple-offerings and art-offerings shared common ground literally and conceptually (see Ch. 1), and the visitor always encountered the former in the company of the latter (**Figs, pp. iv–v, x, Figs 7.14, 10.1**).

The donation of offerings that was fundamental to Greek religious life accelerated over the eighth and seventh centuries, so much so that sanctuaries became awash with them. Whether shimmering under the bright Mediterranean sky or gleaming mysteriously in the dim depths of caves or temple interiors, whether small or large, whether hung from expedient supports (trees, pillars, walls) or proudly free-standing, offerings were at the heart of the Greeks' experience of a sanctuary. Inside temples and treasuries (*thesauroi*) bigger dedications stood on the floor, while smaller items were suspended from roof timbers, stacked on shelves, arranged on benches or tables, and deposited in offering boxes (also called *thesauroi*).[10] Add to this a continual turnover of festoons and the like, and it is almost as if the gods manifest as cult-images were suffocated by stuff.[11] Since only the best warranted continuing display, offerings periodically had to be culled. Metal ones would be melted down to make new dedications.[12] Others were consigned to pits inside the boundary (thus remaining divine property).[13]

While the most valuable and delicate dedications such as those made of gold and ivory (**Fig. 7.1**) were no doubt kept behind lock and key, others stood in the porches of temples, as attested at the Hellenistic Didymaion by cuttings for fixings in the floor. Offerings might also populate peristyles; cuttings pepper the stylobate of the early sixth-century Apollonion in Syracuse.[14] The colonnaded stoa likewise gave shelter for both offerings and their admirers. This was probably one of the main purposes behind the creation of this building type, before it was taken up for civic and commercial uses and gained an upper storey (**Fig. 3.11**).[15]

7.4 Large amphora from the Fortetsa cemetery, Knossos (eighth century), as restored by J. K. Brock. Note the field-and-divider treatment of different registers, and patterns created by repeating floral motifs.

The stock of offerings that survives today represents just crumbs of the original total. Marbles and ceramics dominate modern collections of antiquities essentially because such materials had the best chance of survival. Textiles and other perishables have mostly disappeared altogether, as has wood. Moreover, athough Greek art was profligate in its use of bronze, only a fraction survives that has not been corroded, robbed or melted down. The foremost sanctuaries were major repositories of wealth in the form of metal, including gold and silver as well as bronze.[16] Looting cities and sanctuaries for their treasures and their metal was a standard means of obtaining wealth, and numberless instances include the sack of Didyma by the Persians, of Akragas/Agrigento by the Carthaginians, and of scores of Greek sites by the Romans.[17]

A wide audience is by now aware that Greek architecture was not marble-white but polychrome, yet the purist vision of temples as essays in built geometry outlined against the landscape is deeply engrained.[18] Modern reconstructions usually show temples stripped of paraphernalia, if only out of understandable academic reluctance to publish the disprovable. Yet despite the fantastical nature of Hittorff's interior at Selinunte, his inclusion of so much 'stuff' hanging from the structure represents a welcome provocation (**Fig. 7.22**). Better still – they show free-standing offerings at floor level as well – are glorious colour restitutions by some of the great Beaux Arts-trained archaeologist-architects of the nineteenth century: Henri Labrouste (creator of the Bibliothèque Nationale and Bibliothèque Sainte-Geneviève in Paris), Charles Garnier (the Opéra), Victor Laloux (the Gare d'Orsay), Alphonse Defrasse and Albert Tournaire (**Figs, pp. iv–v, p. x, Figs 7.14, 10.1**).[19] Their *restaurations* may be flawed, yet, in their willingness to simulate sacred space, they serve us better – for the present argument at least – than sterilized views without the attendant artworks that cluttered the ground-plane and conditioned the experience of temples and sanctuaries.

* * *

SANCTUARIES AND TEMPLES AS MUSEUMS

In effect, sanctuaries and temples doubled as museums of art and history. The veneration of top-flight art by two women in a temple of Asklepios (Ch. 1, p. 24) was of a largely cultural-aesthetic kind, comparable with that of a modern art-lover visiting a church in Rome or Venice. Strabo characterized the Heraion at Samos as a picture gallery (*pinakotheke*), while Pausanias treated the Heraion at Olympia as a museum, with a particularly lengthy account of one of its main exhibits, the by then 700-year-old chest of Kypselos.[20]

The cultural agency of offerings on show in sanctuaries is eloquently attested by the Lindian Temple Chronicle, an inscription set up in 99 in honour of Athena. It supplemented the dedications then on view by commemorating treasures that had perished in an earlier fire.[21] Essentially a list of offerings, it promoted the community and its temple by recording items that attested to the attentions of heroes, kings and other notables. It tells of gifts contributed by the hero-founder Lindos, Minos, Menelaos, the Egyptian pharaoh Amasis, the Persian general Datis and Alexander the Great.[22]

The Greeks accorded great importance to their roots, constantly tracing themselves back to founder figures and heroes from the mythical past. At some sanctuaries efforts were made to preserve and valorize vestiges of ancient wooden structures, though we know neither their form nor their age (Ch. 3, pp. 67–8). Small-scale material constituted a complementary means by which past styles were transmitted; a singularly suggestive find is the stash of Mycenaean colonnettes recovered from a foundation deposit under a temple of the Archaic period on Delos (Ch. 4, p. 92). Having been originally copied from Bronze Age monuments these ivories acquired the potential to inspire new monuments. The venerable age of some dedications is noted in literary sources. Writing in the fifth century Herodotus cited three tripods at the sanctuary of Apollo Ismenion in Thebes which bore inscriptions in a script he judged to be very old.[23] The fact that Pausanias saw the same tripods nearly six centuries later underlines their longevity. On occasions archaeology can reveal the lapse between manufacture and deposit or display. By freakish luck ninth-century bronze pieces of horse armour carrying matching inscriptions of Syrian provenance have been recovered from eighth- or seventh-century contexts on Hellenic soil at different sanctuaries, Samos and Eretria.[24] A similar if not longer lapse applies to oriental bronzes discovered at Olympia that in some respects anticipated the design of Aeolic capitals (**Figs 4.12–14**).[25] A twelfth-century bronze Cypriot tripod-stand with 'Ionic' capitals has been found in an Athenian tomb dating at least four centuries later (**Fig. 5.13**).[26] Having served as aristocratic gifts, such objects were handed down the generations as heirlooms.[27]

It was customary for foreign rulers to make diplomatic dedications in Greek sanctuaries. Midas of the golden touch, king of Phrygia, gave his throne to Delphi around 700.[28] Herodotus also tells of gifts from the kings of Lydia, which in the seventh century became a leading power in Anatolia thanks to sources of gold that outstripped even those of Midas. Gyges sent to Delphi many offerings of silver and gold after his sovereignty had been ratified, including six golden bowls weighing 30 talents (approximately a tonne) that were the 'most worth remembering'.[29] These later stood in the treasury of the Corinthians along with benefactions of Gyges's great-great-grandson Croesus, who in the mid-sixth century showered on Delphi largesse on a scale that made Greek eyes pop.[30] He gave numbers of columns and golden oxen for the Ephesian Artemision, a golden tripod for the sanctuary of Ismenian Apollo at Thebes, and for Didyma a treasure apparently no less spectacular than that he gave to Delphi.[31] The recurrence of candelabra, cauldrons, incense burners, libation bowls, torch-holders and thrones amongst regal and diplomatic offerings stemmed from their original purpose in the eastern Mediterranean as high-status ritual objects and temple adornments with a votive aspect.[32] When artefacts of this kind arrived in Greek sanctuaries the associations were different, yet gifts to the gods they remained.

* * *

CROSSING OVER

Foreign offerings together with 'antiques' from Bronze Age times introduced to artists, craftsmen and the highest strata of Greek society design typologies that would be imitated in local production of the seventh and sixth centuries.[33] With the finds in mind from the Heraion at Samos – a site where, like Olympia, soil conditions have favoured survival rates – Helmut Kyrieleis contemplates the effect on artists in the pre-monumental period:

> The abundance and variety of splendid votives are all the more striking in such a modest setting. In these circumstances one comes to realize what the close proximity of such varied votives from widely different countries meant for the evolution of Greek art. The Greek sanctuaries were collecting points and meeting places for art works of all sorts. . . . Greek artists, above all, could go to such places for new stimuli and they evidently made rich use of their opportunities.[34]

The same point applies to the designers of the first monumental temples. Sacred buildings of the Iron Age, it may be remembered, were relatively rudimentary. Before stone temples were built in the seventh century, the most imposing and technically advanced sights in sanctuaries were dedications. Here were sources of inspiration for Greek temple builders who were keen to develop impressive architectural style.

Cross-fertilization between art and architecture manifests itself in various ways, most obviously in the shared ornamental repertoire of volutes, rosettes, palmettes, the guilloche, the meander, stylized leaf tongues, linked chains of lotus and/or palmette, and alternating 'triglyphs and metopes'. Working towards some of the thornier aspects of the *genera*, I will first illustrate the principle with an uncontroversial example, the case of fish-scale, a pattern that mimics the skin of fish, snakes and reptiles (as well as the plumage of some birds) by tiling semi-circles. This is found on a range of production going back to Minoan and Mycenaean times, and what follows is a diachronic selection from the first millennium, the first from Syria the rest found in Greece:

7.5 'Fish-scale' patterns from the seventh and early sixth centuries; selected examples. (a) Corinthian *lekythos* (*c.*650), Museum of Fine Arts, Boston, Mass. (inv. 08.281); (b) wings of a sphinx, sanctuary of Apollo, Aigina; (c) disc akroterion of the temple of Apollo, Aigina; (d) metope from Locri.

a late eighth-century Hittite bird-spirit or griffin from Tell Halaf; Orientalizing protomes of the late Geometric period (**Fig. 1.13**); mid-seventh-century pottery (**Fig. 7.5a**); late seventh-century sphinxes (**Fig. 7.5b**), early sixth-century akroteria and architectural terracotta panels (**Fig. 7.5c, d**); the echinus of an Aeolic capital on Delos (**Table 4.1**); the bolster of early fifth-century Ionic capitals at Metapontum (**Fig. 5.25**); door and window grilles from the fifth century onwards; balustrading from the fourth century onwards on buildings such as the stoa of Attalos (**Fig. 3.11**).[35] The overall trend is from non-architectural ornament to architectural surface ornament, and thence to three-dimensional building elements.

Fabulous monsters such as gorgons, griffins, sirens and sphinxes stared out from temples as they did from offerings. Detailed treatment depended on materials, technique and size, but the two populations are comparable. There are correspondences too in terms of positioning: the heads of such creatures (or lions) bristle around the rims of cauldrons (**Fig. 1.13**), and analogously around the roof edges of temples: on akroteria, antefixes and waterspouts (**Figs 2.17, 3.30, 5.1**). Beasts real or imaginary were also to be found on top of free-standing columns, whether in Greece or further east (**Fig. 0.6**).

Before Aeolic or Ionic capitals are known to appear in architectural contexts, volute compositions featured on both imported and locally made objects (Ch. 5, p. 126). Mid-seventh-century Melian amphoras present a riot of spiralling motifs (**Fig. 7.6**).[36] Similar devices abounded on armour, as reflected in the shield depicted on a black-figure plate from Rhodes, and indeed over most of the plate (**Fig. 7.7**).[37] Luxury artefacts of oriental provenance that anticipated aspects of Greek capitals range from a bronze vessel found at Olympia with a foliate crown (**Fig. 4.28c**) to ivory caryatids that have been recovered from Nimrud (their place of manufacture), as well as the destinations Crete and Rhodes (**Fig. 4.28h**). It is not just a question of components; representations of volute columns feature amongst the incoming material, including on ivories found at Salamis (**Fig. 4.16**), and on sheet bronzes found at Olympia (**Figs 4.12, 4.13**). The latter site has yielded a bronze bowl originally made in the region of Megiddo that presents a ring of shrines or baldachins each with a divinity framed by volute columns (**Fig. 4.14**). Objects such as this epitomize the linkage between columns and sacrality.[38]

The likelihood of designs passing from small-scale to large-scale is underscored by the recovery of gold jewellery and ivory knick-knacks from Artemis's renowned temple at Ephesos. At this important site for the development of the Ionic order – the prime site according to Vitruvius – we find craftsmen in the seventh century manipulating bead-and-reel, radial schemes of ribs or lobes, and linked volute devices in all kinds of combinations, with or without palmettes,

7.7   Pottery plate, made in Rhodes (late seventh century), British Museum. Menelaos and Hektor fight over the body of Euphorbos. Note the 'ambiguous' volutes in the shields and various kinds of ornament that find echoes on architecture: volutes with palmettes, guilloche, leaf tongue, and 'triglyphs and metopes' around the rim.

7.6   Patterns on so-called Melian vases (seventh century). Top: vase reconstructed by Alexander Conze as reproduced in Perrot and Chipiez; bottom: selected motifs from miscellaneous vases.

rosettes and the little 'drops' that in one way or other went on to find use in architectural capitals (**Fig. 7.1**).[39] Such work acted as a conduit by which the characteristics of Mycenaean spiral ornament could engage the

orbit of the designers of Aeolic and Ionic capitals around 600.[40] One curious object anticipates the pulley-wheel shaped bolsters of the Ionic capital.

Furniture is of special interest in the present context for it bridges small-scale decoration and structural form.[41] Thrones and stools are functional constructive assemblies that involve cross-pieces and uprights, often with bases and capitals (**Fig. 7.8**). As is evident from Midas's donation of his throne to Delphi, these were important regal and diplomatic gifts. Assyrian reliefs show such 'supreme symbols of power' repeatedly (**Fig. 7.9**), sometimes being borne as gifts, thereby declaring the far-reaching mobility of their rulers' dominion.[42] Devices perhaps introduced into Greece from eastern furniture include petal or leaf crowns, rising volutes and moulded bases. Out of what could be a much longer list, consider the following components of furniture: a miniature stone palm crown from Nimrud that pre-

7.8 (ABOVE LEFT) Poseidon seated on a throne with outstretched arm (to welcome Theseus). Detail of a red-figure volute-*krater* (*c*.470), Cabinet des Médailles, Bibliothèque nationale de France, Paris. Legs with volute capitals are recurrent characteristics of aristocratic thrones and couches.

7.9 (ABOVE RIGHT) 'Garden party' or 'banquet' relief from the North Palace of Ashurbanipal, Nineveh, Iraq (*c*.645), now in the British Museum, detail. Celebrating the triumphs of Ashurbanipal's reign (669–631), the relief as a whole shows the king and queen enjoying a banquet. The queen, who holds a ribbed *phiale*, is seated on a throne with moulded bases and 'ambiguous' volutes on the cross-members.

figures a column crown at Neandria; a wooden piece in Ankara that anticipates 'champagne-cork'-shaped capitals at Smyrna (**Fig. 4.23**); torus–scotia–torus sequences on eastern furniture (**Figs 0.6, 7.9**) that are echoed on Ionic bases. In common with ceramic objects, as noted earlier, thrones bear 'ambiguous' double-volute ornaments. Along with the capitals on Cypriot rod-tripods, such playful details could have catalysed the switch from rising to horizontally linked volutes, and so the Ionic configuration (Ch. 5, p. 126).

I do not claim actual connections between such-and-such an artefact and such-and-such a piece of architecture. The point is to observe the kind of opportunities that existed out of a panorama that was once far,

far more extensive than the sparse survivors might suggest. Once monumental building had taken hold in Greece, around 600, parallels like those observed could well reflect influence from architecture to art. Before this watershed, however, conditions were such that, on balance, architecture was more likely to be the recipient than the initiator of viral contagion propelling design creativity.

* * *

Many aspects of the previous discussion are played out in connection with two particular classes of object, *phialai* and tripods. The former are flat bowls or cups often made of metal which displayed various ornamental schemes derived more or less directly from plants; tripods will be discussed in detail in the next chapter. Both types of object enjoyed sacral connotations and featured amongst prestigious dedications; both were put on display in sanctuaries before the architectural features that they perhaps contributed to; both involve not just two-dimensional motifs, but fully plastic, three-dimensional forms.

THE ECHINUS AND *PHIALE*

The Doric echinus was sometimes decorated (Ch. 5, p. 107). In their reconstructions Laloux, Hittorff and others included capitals with ornamental schemes that would not be out of place on *phialai* (**Figs 2.35, 7.22**). It is unclear if such proposals had a basis in evidence, aside from the floral schemes known on the capitals of the Archaic temple of Hera at Paestum (**Fig. 3.23**). In any event, some of the recently discovered capitals from Metropolis display Egyptianizing lotus patterns used on *phialai* (**Fig. 7.10**). Examples with broadly similar devices are found over a wide geographical and chronological range (**Fig. 7.11**), while Korres has been able to pinpoint a kind with a particularly close correspondence in terms of date and form.[43] Two capitals from far away in eastern Kolchis, now in the Georgian State Art Museum in Tbilisi, bear in relief a variant lotus orna-

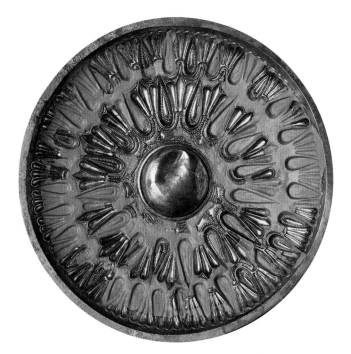

7.10 (TOP)   Silver *phiale* of Persian type with an array of lotus ornament (first half fourth century). From Ithaca (Ithake), Greece, now in the British Museum.

7.11 (ABOVE)   Capital from the temple at Metropolis, drawn by Manolis Korres so as to highlight correspondences with *phialai* comparable with the example in the preceding illustration (though others exist that are closer in both chronological and formal terms).

ment that was common on *phialai* in the Achaemenid empire either side of 500.[44] The caryatids of the Knidian treasury at Delphi likewise have capitals that resemble Doric in terms of their overall shape, while in this case the echinus is modelled with convex ribs or flutes (**Fig. 7.12**). In this respect they recall another kind of *phiale* treated in like fashion.[45] On such *phialai* the rhythm of radially organized ribs can vary extensively, from just a few bulbous ones to numerous more delicate ones.[46] A rhythm in the region of thirty-six, the

7.12 (LEFT)   Caryatid head and capital usually attributed to the Knidian Treasury, sanctuary of Apollo, Delphi, now in the Archaeological Museum.

7.13 (BELOW)   Selection of bronze and silver ribbed bowls, mostly of Urartian manufacture, of varying provenance and date (eighth to sixth centuries). (A) bronze, uncertain provenance (private collection); (B) bronze, from Karmin-Blur (Vorderasiatisches Museum, Berlin, inv. 796); (C) silver (Römisch-Germanisches Zentralmuseums, Mainz, inv. 39700); (D) silver, from Toprakkale (Adana Museum, inv. 637.1); (E) silver, uncertain provenance.

7.14 Treasury of the Athenians, sanctuary of Apollo, Delphi, flank elevation as reconstructed by Albert Tournaire. *Envoi* of 1894.

number of the ribs on the Knidian capitals, is not uncommon (**Fig. 7.13**). By some uncanny coincidence excavations only a few metres from the Knidian treasury have turned up an intact ribbed *phiale* akin to the scheme used for the caryatids.[47] This *phiale* was not *the* model for those capitals (it has too many ribs), but the find neatly reminds us of the possibilities for contagion. Meanwhile the curious ivory caryatid from Ephesos carries over its head twin *phialai* with thirty-two ribs (**Fig. 7.1**).

The famous caryatids of the Erechtheion represent another intriguing case; these very embodiments of the overlap between art and architecture carry on their heads a non-canonical kind of capital, Doricizing in form and Ionicizing in detail, with its ring of egg-and-dart decoration (**Fig. 9.5**).[48] Variations of egg-and-dart are once again anticipated by a branch of *phiale* design, sometimes with labia or rims around egg- or almond-shaped lobes, sometimes with leaf-points or 'darts' (**Fig. 9.6**). Being completely round, unlike the truncated Ionic echinus, that of the Erechtheion capitals betrays an unmistakeable affinity with a libation cup. (Understandably the 'darts' in the marble could be sharper than counterparts fashioned by beating metal sheet.[49]) Thus there are three types of treatment for the architectural echinus (lotus, ribbed and lobed), each of which compares with types of *phialai*. This congruity bears witness to 'conversations' between designers operating across

different media. The objects are more likely to have im-
pacted on the architecture than the other way around
since the former tend to be older, belonging as they do
to a long-standing sacred tradition. Relevant kinds of
phialai go back to the east at least as far back as the ninth
century. They were used as ritual bowls or cups for
collecting and pouring sacrificial libations, then
becoming also non-functional offerings; they were often
made of bronze, sometimes of silver or gold, and also
copied in ceramic.[50] The scene at Ashurbanipal's so-
called Garden-party or banquet shows a *phiale* associated with a gesture of offering (**Fig. 7.9**).[51] In Greece they
fell into parallel roles, as illustrated by vase paintings
(**Fig. 8.2**) and archaeological finds such as a golden

phiale dedicated at Olympia by a Greek aristocrat in the
late seventh century.[52] Deities and heroes were thought
to value such gifts; artists show them holding *phialai*, as
does Apollo in his temple at Delphi (**Fig. 10.2**). Themis,
personification of order and the will of the gods, might
hold one while pronouncing an oracle (**Fig., p. i**).

VOTIVE COLUMNS

Offerings and architecture intersect in the shape of
votive columns, these being both at the same time. The
roots of this type of monument in Greece are obscure,
though free-standing sacred pillars stood in Bronze Age

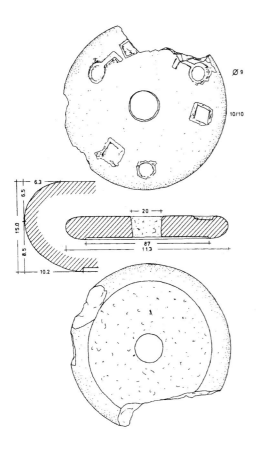

7.16 (ABOVE LEFT) Disc capital from a votive column, Heraion, Samos (?first half sixth century). The triangular arrangement of the cuttings on the top indicates that the column once bore a tripod.

7.17 (ABOVE RIGHT) Miniature limestone model of a votive column crowned by a vessel, Heraion, Samos (?first half sixth century). The same site has yielded numerous massive bronze vessels of comparable shape.

7.15 (FACING PAGE) Votive column at Paestum (Poseidonia), with the temple of Athena (formerly attributed to Demeter / Ceres) in the background. Note the remains of a base for a somewhat taller votive column on the left. The stepped bases of both columns recall the stepped krepis typical of Doric temples.

religious environments on Crete (**Fig. 1.6**), and are a recurrent feature of Mesopotamian, Assyrian, Syrian and Phoenician art (**Figs 4.14–17**). Of biblical fame are the columns of Jachin and Boaz next to Solomon's

temple.[53] Texts tell of other landmark pairs, including that which Herodotus says stood by Melqart's temple at Tyre, one column apparently made of gold (or gilded?), the other perhaps of malachite.[54] The Lion Gate presents at the entrance to Mycenae a column in relief laden with only a symbolic load (**Fig. 2.3**).

In sanctuaries from the Archaic period onwards various classes of offerings, among them cauldrons, sphinxes, statuary and tripods, were raised up on supports which themselves formed an integral part of the offering (**Figs 7.15–20**).[55] Many of these supports stand outside any canon, including ones that held *korai* on the Athenian Acropolis.[56] Some votive columns had capitals with petal or lobed ornament like those encountered in Chapter 4, while a torus (whether smooth or striated) was popular at Samos (**Fig. 7.16, 7.17**). The most majestic votive columns were Doric or Ionic, though only one monumental example of the former stands on site today,

7.18 (ABOVE LEFT)   Votive column with sphinx, from the sanctuary of Apollo, Delphi, now in the Archaeological Museum. The column was dedicated by the Naxians on the terrace to the south of
Apollo's temple.

7.19 (ABOVE RIGHT)   Votive column with sphinx, from Cyrene,
now in the Archaeological Museum. Note the unusal echinus that
combines arrays of down-turning and up-turning lobes.

where it was re-erected at Paestum (**Fig. 7.15**).[57] Archaeological remains show that the early Ionic examples at
Aigina and Delphi were extremely imposing for their
time, towering over temples that were as yet of modest
height (**Fig. 5.22**).[58] The largest Ionic capital known from
the mainland belonged to a free-standing column, one
erected around the end of the sixth century to mark the
reputed grave of Kekrops on the Athenian Acropolis.
The capital was nearly 2.5 m long, suggesting a column
height of somewhat more than 11 metres, perhaps even
14 metres or so, that is to say comfortably taller than
those of the later Parthenon and indeed the whole
Erechtheion.[59] The identification of sanctuaries with
free-standing columns was evidently deployed by artists
to denote sacred space or the realm of the gods (**Figs 1.6,
8.1, 8.6, 8.17**).[60] Today we are more accustomed to free-
standing columns and markers in an honorific context,
often isolated at the centre of a grand urban set piece,

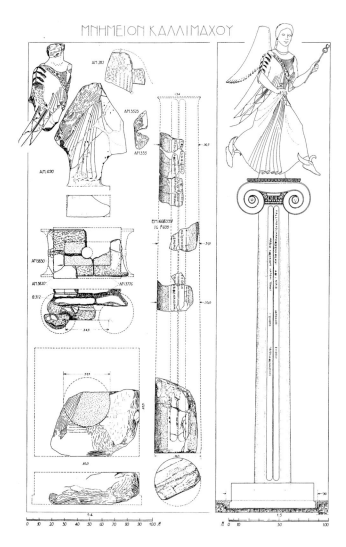

ΜΝΗΜΕΙΟΝ ΚΑΛΛΙΜΑΧΟΥ

7.20 Athenian Acropolis; votive column of Kallimachos, as reconstructed by Manolis Korres.

but Hansen's Academy reminds us of a more intimate connection between them and their cousins that played a structural role in buildings (**Fig. 5.26**).

Free-standing columns might be presumed to mimic counterparts belonging to buildings, though this is a presumption sustained by traditional ideas about origins that stress constructional aspects. It is true that the earliest known Doric capitals belong to structures rather than votive columns.[61] However, while the style of the

precocious monumental votive column at the sanctuary of Apollo on Aigina (**Fig. 2.28**) cannot be ascertained, a Doric capital cannot be ruled out (Ch. 2, p. 55). As regards Aeolic columns the primacy over built versus votive columns remains murky due to uncertainties as to which was which.[62] But turning to columns with foliate crowns and Ionic capitals, in both cases the antecedence of the votive over the architectural is reasonably clear. The earliest known Greek 'palm' capital, that from Arkades, probably belonged to a votive column (**Fig. 4.8**). The crown from Delos (**Fig. 4.27e**), certainly votive, anticipates by at least two decades comparable capitals in buildings: those of the second dipteros of Polykrates on Samos and the treasuries of Klazomenai and Massalia at Delphi (**Fig. 4.27f and h**).[63] The earliest Ionic column is thought to be the modest dedication found at Sangri on Naxos, datable to the end of the seventh century (**Fig. 2.32**).[64] The much larger column at Apollo's sanctuary on Aigina just mentioned may have been Ionic if not Doric, though this is unknowable. Soon after followed the sphinx column at Aphaia's sanctuary (**Fig. 5.22**). The Naxians' more famous version at Delphi was put up around the middle of the first half of the sixth century (**Figs 5.22, 7.18**), and only from about this time are temples also known to have had Ionic columns, though Ionic temples may have existed that are not known to us, for example the phase of the Ephesian Artemesion around 600. Furthermore, it seems that votive columns often provided the locus for experimentation in capital design (**Fig. 7.19**). In sum, there is a real possibility that aspects of the *genera* were created for votive columns. Of course, Doric and Ionic forms could have been pioneered earlier for wooden columns, but these did not necessarily belong exclusively to buildings. Free-standing columns may early have been erected in this material too, to judge from occasional heavy stone bases with deep sockets suited to receive lost timber shafts.[65]

Votive columns may also have played a part in the conception of 'forests' of columns in Ionian temples, reinforcing impetus from Egypt (Ch. 4, pp. 94–6). The first dipteros at the Samian Heraion launched this

wonder thus: did special sacred free-standing votive columns lead the process that saw refined monumental stone columns displace utilitarian posts of yesteryear?

There is, furthermore, a votive dimension to the very financing of some temples, for high status gifts could take the form of temple columns. Those of two important early temples, the Heraion at Olympia and the Apollonion at Syracuse, bear cuttings that once received donatory inscriptions.[67] As already mentioned, Croesus financed a large part of the Ephesian Artemision by giving columns. This form of patronage continued down to the Roman period, witness those of the temple of Zeus at Euromos that still bear votive plaques (**Fig. 7.21**). On different occasions the emperor Hadrian donated batches of 100 columns (or shafts).[68] Back in the Archaic period some *poleis* financed temple projects by subscription, by the collection of funds for offerings-cum-building components. The resulting temples were in a sense votive assemblies.[69] Peripteral temples had several virtues (Ch. 2, p. 53); yet perhaps their success was also due to them making superior gifts to the gods by multiplying both the cost and sacral associations of columns.

As Greek architecture emerged out of a rudimentary state in the late eighth and seventh centuries, designers tackled the problem of how to create temples and columns with a convincing appearance. Some gleaned clues from Mycenaean ruins or from Egyptian or eastern Mediterranean constructions that they had visited, or were told about. Critical seeds of inspiration, however, were on hand directly in the places where temples were to rise up, in the guise of high class offerings that were handed down as heirlooms or arrived from abroad, if not made by the most proficient local artists of the day. All such material constituted gifts to the gods, and so, dressed with kindred vocabularies befitting the dedication that went into them, temples radiated the same subliminal message.

tradition, and it may not be a coincidence that this site is notable for large numbers of grand bronze Orientalizing vessels, many of which stood on stone columns (**Fig. 7.16**). Soon after the start of the sixth century, perhaps *before the erection of the dipteros*, visitors to the sanctuary would have faced a striking array of votive columns.[66] These struck quite a contrast with the humble architectural achievements then on view: the long but narrow Hekatompedon, the mostly wooden South Stoa and some small shrines or *naiskoi* (**Fig. 1.11**), Given the various considerations raised it seems legitimate to

7.21 (ABOVE)   Temple of Zeus, Euromos, Turkey; detail of peristyle (second century AD). The columns bear plaques with dedicatory inscriptions that interrupt the fluting.

7.22 (FACING PAGE)   Jacques-Ignaz Hittorff, perspective reconstruction of the interior of Temple G at Selinunte (Selinus), extrapolating from texts and comparanda from other sites.

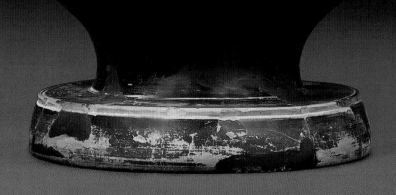

CHAPTER EIGHT
TRIGLYPHS AND TRIPODS

There could be no more fitting companion for a Greek temple than a tripod. Of all prestige offerings it was the most characteristic and universal, venerated from the era of epic down to Roman times. In major sanctuaries tripods stood in and around temples; sometimes they bestrode them, as akroteria, sometimes they stood on nearby free-standing columns. There has been cause to mention these sacred objects now and then in the course of this book, but here tripods are recruited to help illumine the age-old puzzle posed by the Doric frieze.

The most significant obstacle to understanding the Doric *genus* is indeed the frieze and its regular run of

8.1 (FACING PAGE)   Red-figure Attic bell-*krater* (440–30), Museo Archeologico Regionale, Agrigento. Sacrifice of a goat before an altar performed by a bearded priest and younger assistants, one of whom plays the pipes, in honour of Apollo (seated right). Apart from the altar, features of this sacred environment include a tree, a tripod dedication on a Doric column, and part of a temple.

8.2 (ABOVE)   Black-figure Attic neck amphora (*c.*520-10), Toledo Museum of Art, Ohio. The ransom of Hektor's corpse: King Priam of Troy entreats Achilles to accept the gifts of a tripod and libation bowls (*phialai*) carried by an aide, in exchange for Hektor's body, which is lying on the ground. That Achilles holds a *phiale* in his extended right hand alludes perhaps to his acceptance.

triglyphs. Their importance is evident on several counts. Their size made them the most prominent features of any of the orders apart from columns; they were the most stable single element of the classical vocabulary over time with the exception of fluting; the need for regularity in their disposition lay at the root of the notorious Doric corner problem; the width of the triglyph appears to have been the base unit of modular design methods that were developed during the fifth century.[1] Such things are hard to understand without understanding why triglyphs came into existence in the first place and, naturally enough, attempts at explanation have been numerous and varied, as encountered earlier in these pages. The stiff, forthright look of triglyphs gives credibility to Vitruvius's constructional explanation, yet this raises more problems than it solves (Ch. 3, pp. 68–75). Echoes of the Bronze Age split-rosette frieze reverberate in the Doric frieze, though triglyphs differ appreciably from the rosette-splitters (Ch. 4, p. 92). Another forerunner of sorts is the genre of 'triglyph and metope' friezes that were popular in the Geometric period, but correspondences remain rather vague (Ch. 5, pp. 117–18, and Ch. 7, p. 161). Each approach has its merits, but none of them adequately explains the size of triglyphs, nor details like the little arches or the capping band at the top (but not the bottom). As for proposals encountered in chapter 6, I find it hard to read triglyphs as stylized thigh-bones, whether thrice-cloven or thrice-bunched. In any case, the animal kingdom prefers two or four thighs/legs, not three.

Vitruvius's statement that the Greeks called the uprights of triglyphs thighs (*meroi*) begs for a simpler explanation. Here is probably nothing more than the prosaic naming of man-made objects after their maker. The Greeks used anatomical terms just as today we refer to the 'leg' of a table, the 'wing' of a country house, the 'nose' of a jet. Thigh, like leg, is tantamount to a support, so triglyphs are objects with three supports.[2] Tripods likewise are three-legged (literally three-footed) things. It seems strange that no one has dwelt on this parallelism in the past, all the more so given that tripods and triglyphs have a similar range of size and share

8.3 Medea and Jason: the elderly Jason, with white hair and a staff, commands the sorceress to return his youth to him, just as she was held to 'rejuvenate' a ram by cutting up and cooking the animal in a cauldron on a tripod stand, magically producing a lamb. Red-figured *hydria*, British Museum.

certain traits. Though I aim not to replace all previous theories, but rather to achieve a new synthesis in the next chapter, any proposed interpretative shift on a topic so long debated requires justification at a number of levels, taking each by turn.

What, then, were tripods? Their first function was practical, to find a stable purchase on uneven ground, an advantage that three legs have over four (which tend to rock). Metal tripods were used from the Bronze Age for cooking and for heating (**Fig. 8.3**). Homer's mention of tripods to heat water for bathing Hektor, Achilles, Odysseus, and Patroklos's corpse,[3] attunes with representations on vases.[4] Greek and Roman reliefs show sacrificial scenes with flames issuing from ceremonial tripods (**Fig. 1.9**). In such contexts versatile lightweight tripod-stands were used with a removable cauldron (**Figs 1.13, 5.13, 8.5**), rather as today we use modern equiv-

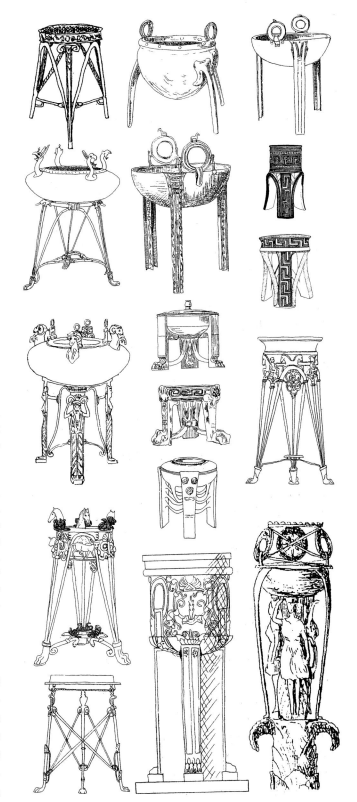

8.4 (ABOVE) Bronze tripod-cauldrons of the Geometric period at Olympia. Left: reconstruction of typical example; right: upper part of a massive tripod leg decorated with scene panels, including one showing two figures contesting a tripod.

8.5 (RIGHT) Various types of tripod from the Greek and Roman periods, including: bronze tripod cauldrons of the Geometric and Archaic periods from Olympia and other sites; mobile tripod stands with removable cauldrons or braziers (both Archaic and Roman); small late Archaic tripod kothons made of terracotta; late Classical and Roman marble monuments. One is the so-called Dancers' or Acanthus Column at Delphi, with lost bronze tripod restored; the other is a massive solid marble tripod from Miletos now in the Pergamon Museum, Berlin. Drawings are not to a consistent scale.

alents to support cameras, surveying equipment, easels and the like.[5] However the static fixed-leg so-called tripod-cauldron which transcended utilitarian purposes is our present focus (**Fig. 8.4**).[6] It is to this I refer by the term tripod on its own. The symbolic resonance of this object has all but disappeared from contemporary consciousness, though it was not so very long ago when, in tribute to the Greeks' contribution to democracy, tripods were used to flank the approach to Lincoln's Memorial and tripod-inspired lampstands to adorn US Government institutions in Washington's Federal Triangle.[7]

Mirroring developments for comparable three-legged objects as far away as China, in Greece the transition from practical to symbolic functions started in the late Bronze Age. There followed a great range of design and investment down to Roman times (**Fig. 8.5**).[8] Homer tells of tripods that were offered as prizes for athletic competitions in which protagonists in the Trojan wars act as donors or contestants.[9] Related imagery is common in the Geometric period.[10] With time action becomes progressively more dynamic, as when pairs of wrestlers or boxers are shown competing over tripods, a theme played out on a divine plane in the struggle between Herakles and Apollo (**Figs 8.6b, 8.11**).[11] Mirroring real events and practices, artists enlisted tripod prizes to stand not only for victory in foot, horse or chariot races (**Figs 8.6a, 8.15, 8.19**), but also competitive performances of poetry, theatre and music.[12]

In early Greece aristocrats practised gift exchange to commemorate hospitality and to seal friendships and ties. By contrast with cattle, horses, slave women and pieces of armour, tripods constituted the most important gift of primarily symbolic value.[13] They somehow encrypted wisdom and authority,[14] and from his temple at Delphi Apollo's pronouncements were delivered via Pythia or Themis, seated on the tripod (**Fig., p. i**), just as could the god himself in artists' imaginations (**Fig. 8.6c**).[15] Along with his bow, laurel and lyre, the tripod thus became one of the archer-god's principal symbols.[16]

Once the archetypal gift for mortal princes, the tripod became a gift for the gods. It was usual for the victors of contests held in sanctuaries to offer up their prizes to the host divinity. At Delphi and Olympia tripods were awarded as prizes, but there was more to it than that; there cannot have been enough victors to account for the copious quantities of them found, so it has been speculated that many were dedicated by visiting aristocrats or political entities concerned to vaunt

their piety before an 'international' audience.[17] With good reason scholars have called the tripod 'the most representative votive gift of Greek sanctuaries', the Greeks' dedication 'par excellence', 'the ultimate (dedicatory) gift', and simply '*the* gift'.[18] So representative were they of sanctuaries that vase painters employed tripods as shorthand symbols for sacred space, hence their presence in scenes such as the rape of Kassandra (**Fig. 1.15**), or a sacrifice rendered to Apollo (**Fig. 8.1**).

In short, the importance of the tripod for the Greeks is hardly in doubt. But there are methodological hurdles to overcome if the proposed connection with the triglyph is to improve on previous explanations. Without supporting evidence of the kind that bridges between the Corinthian capital and its *kalathos* core, this would remain yet another theory.

Let us begin with a point so banal it would be easy to overlook – size. There is a striking convergence in height between votive bronze tripods and triglyphs on temples. Both typically range between 600 and 1500 millimetres tall, with a few exceeding 2 or even 3 metres.[19] Tripods are frequently depicted in ways that show them to be at least of human height, if not more (**Figs 1.15, 8.6, 8.20**), and sometimes as tall as buildings (**Figs 4.21, 10.2**).[20] Then there is size relative to columns: in early Doric buildings triglyphs tend to be especially tall, as much as a quarter or a third of the column height (**Fig. 3.19**).

8.6 (FACING PAGE)   Selected scenes from Greek painted pottery involving representations of tripods. (a) Chariot race for tripod prizes at the funeral games for Pelias (volute-*krater*, the so-called Amphairaos Vase, formerly Antikensammlung, Berlin (F 1655), now lost); (b) struggle for the tripod between Apollo (right) and Herakles (left) (red-figure amphora, Museo Nazionale Etrusco, Tarquinia (inv. RC 6843)); (c) Apollo flying on a winged tripod from Delos to Delphi (red-figure hydria, Museo Gregoriano Etrusco, Vatican (inv. 16568)); (d) preparations for sacrificing a bull for the consecration of a tripod with a Nike or personification of victory (red-figure stamnos, Staatliche Antikensammlungen, Munich (inv. 2412)); (e) sacrificial scene at Delphi featuring parts of two tripod columns, one a Doric column (left), the other the Dancers' Column (right; see also **Fig. 8.5** (red-figure volute *krater*, National Museum, St Petersburg (inv. 33)).

Such a proportion cannot be justified in terms of the 'beam-end' theory. Monumentality is also foreign to the split-rosette frieze (that of the Treasury of Atreus is but a slim band of decoration, and one of many bands). Triglyph proportions are much more commensurate with the tripod-to-column ratio seen on free-standing monuments of this kind (**Figs 8.1, 8.6e, 8.17, 8.19**).[21]

The importance of tripods for religion and culture ensured that they featured commonly in art. In keeping with the abstract character of early Greek visual imagery, tripods were often rendered flat, almost as if in silhouette, with recurrent characteristics that share telling points in common with triglyphs:

— Tripods are shown symmetrically, but *not* so in the vertical sense. The cauldron can be abstracted as a more or less horizontal bar or band (**Fig. 8.7c, e, j and m**). As with triglyphs, there is no such element at the bottom.
— Tripod legs are typically shown straight and vertical,[22] though a minority are inclined (**Fig. 8.7b, f, g and k**), as on some early triglyphs (**Fig. 3.25 (5)**).[23]
— Tripod legs are frequently shown flaring out where they meet the rim of the cauldron (as on real bronze exemplars), but some artists combined the flares to create arches underneath (**Fig. 8.7l, m and o**). Archaic triglyphs display just such arches, be they semi-circular, pointed or ogival (**Fig. 3.25**).[24]

The artistic task of transposing the idea of tripods into two dimensions is potentially significant in explaining the elemental character of triglyphs. Painters and artists working in the medium of relief naturally find themselves editing and abstracting three-dimensional form. With their circular cauldron and triangular plan, tripods presented a particular challenge in this respect, arguably requiring a greater degree of abstraction than when creating a silhouette or side view of, say, a horse or chariot. Artists of the Mycenaean period faced similar issues when representing tripods (**Fig. 8.8**). The word *ti-ri-po-de* (and variants) is common on the Linear B tablets from Pylos, sometimes in connection with a simple three-legged pictogram (one of the few pic-

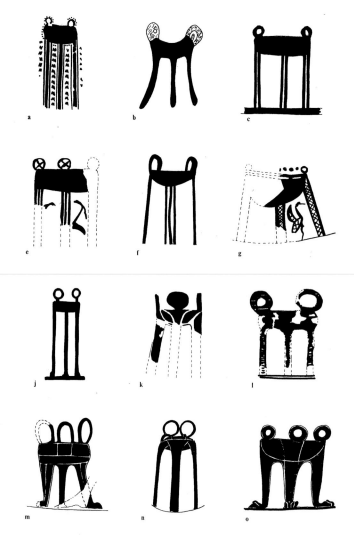

8.7 Selection of tripod silhouettes on painted pottery (eighth to sixth centuries), running in rough chronological order from left to right, and from top to bottom.

tograms used in what was otherwise a syllabic system). The necessarily abbreviated style of the pictogram may have paved the way for the abstraction that typified representations of tripods in this and later periods.

The uprights of triglyphs also share details with the legs of actual bronze tripods in the Archaic period. These often have a hexagonal cross section, which is to say that they present to the viewer a flat front and angled or chamfered sides (**Fig. 8.9**).[25] Triglyph-like, the tripod for which Apollo and Herakles struggle on the

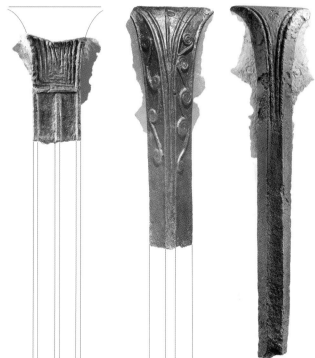

8.8 (ABOVE LEFT)   Hunting scene on a Mycenaean wall painting from Pylos: accompanied by large hunting dogs, two men carry tripods depicted in a simplified, abstract manner.

8.9 (ABOVE RIGHT)   Bronze tripod legs from Olympia (eighth and seventh centuries).

8.10 (RIGHT)   Triglyph from the so-called Tavole Palatine at Metapontum (Metapontion), Antiquarium.

Siphnian treasury has straight, chamfered legs of equal width (**Fig., p. x, Fig. 8.11**). The facets of bronze tripod legs are sometimes slightly concave, as are those of Archaic triglyphs from sites in southern Italy, including those from Metapontum (**Figs 3.25, 8.10**).[26] Further parallels include ribs running up their uprights, as on some tripod legs, and even little cross-ribs at the top.[27]

The affinity between the Doric frieze and 'field-and-divider' friezes on pottery discussed in Chapter 5 can be extended further, for there exists a sub-category in the form of tripod-and-metope friezes. Indeed, in the case of an architectural frieze of the Hellenistic period from

8.11 (ABOVE)   The struggle for the tripod as represented on the east pediment of the Siphnian treasury at Delphi (c.520), Archaeological Museum, Delphi. (See also **Fig., p. x**) Left: Herakles (right) tries to free the tripod from the grip of Apollo, while, in between them, Athena attempts to restrain the conflict; right: detail. Note the straight, parallel and chamfered legs of the tripod.

8.12 (RIGHT)   Part of a frieze from an unidentified building on Samos of the Hellenistic period (?third century). 'Triglyphs' in the form of stylized tripods alternate with metopes containing rosettes.

Samos it is hard to say whether its triglyph-tripods tend more towards the one or the other (**Fig. 8.12**).[28] The ring of stylized tripods interspersed between the capitals of Lysikrates's monument constitute a kind of frieze (**Fig. 6.15**). These examples are too late to have much bearing on the situation in the seventh century, but the genre of tripod friezes dates as far back as the eighth century on ceramics (**Fig. 8.13**).[29] As objects with heroic associations, tripods were initially, it seems, chosen for the 'metopes' in between the dividers formed by groups of stripes. Artists then turned to using the tripods themselves as dividers, as on a seventh-century cylindrical vessel from

Thasos (**Fig. 8.14**).[30] A terracotta votive slab from Kythnos with a tripod-and-metope composition would presumably have been fixed to a wall of a temple or shrine (**Fig. 8.15**).[31]

The sheer numbers of tripods ensured familiarity; in the eighth and seventh centuries tripods crowded major sanctuaries such as the Argive Heraion and those at Corinth, Delos, Delphi, Olympia, Samos and Thebes.[32] In Athens tripod monuments went on to become so numerous that they overflowed Dionysos's precinct, scaling the rock-face above the theatre and also creating the 'Street of Tripods' under the present Odos Tripodon.[33] When tripods were dedicated in groups they tended to be disposed in a line, a circle or some other positive ground-plan.[34] Though their original disposi-

8.15 (ABOVE)   Terracotta plaque from the island of Kythnos, repetitive frieze of tripods and horses with riders in the upper register (middle of the first half of the sixth century), Louvre, Paris.

8.13 (LEFT TOP)   Graphic reconstruction of a *krater* of the Geometric period (mid-eighth century), Musée Rodin, Paris. The frieze under the main register contained approximately forty tripods, usually but not always separated by narrow bands or stripes.

8.14 (LEFT BOTTOM)   Terracotta tripod kothon (second half of seventh century) discovered at Thasos, height 280 mm, now in the National Museum, Athens. The connection – here rather abstract – between such vessels and their bronze tripod models is made explicit by the tripod representations created by the addition of narrow legs between the principal supports. Below it is a graphic projection.

tion is not known, of note for their size, number, material, design and early date are a set of tripods from the Athenian Acropolis (**Fig. 8.16**). These were made of solid stone (in common with Assyrian examples), with decorative strips of bronze attached to timber inserts where bronze legs would normally be.[35] Standing at least 2 metres tall, they must have created quite a dramatic impression when they were set up in the seventh century, especially since any neighbouring buildings were much smaller than their sixth- and fifth-century suc-

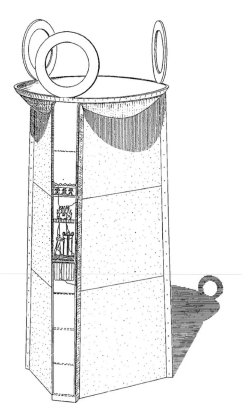

8.16   Monumental tripod, Athenian Acropolis (seventh century), as reconstructed by Manolis Korres and Evi Touloupa. Note the composite construction, of stone, wood and bronze, that evidently necessitated a transformation of the typical bronze form. This tripod belonged to a set of at least four.

cessors.[36] Even where collections of tripods accumulated over time an ordering principle could apply. On Mount Ptoon there are two sanctuaries, one of Apollo the other of the hero Ptoios, where the sacred way was lined by large bronze tripods of fairly uniform size and design, with stone central supports and bases (**Fig. 8.18**).[37] The original ensembles amounted to considerable architectonic features not unlike colonnades.[38] Thus the repetitive tripod friezes on vases and the like constitute the correlate of real spatial experience.[39]

   This experience finds echoes in the poetic imagination. A Homeric hymn tells that tripods stood 'all around the house' of the goddess Leto; might we visualize them distributed regularly, analogously to a peri-

style?[40] Tantalizing, too, are Hephaistos's tripods. The *Iliad* tells how after Patroklos lost his life to Hektor, and with it Achilles' armour, the hero's mother Thetis sped to Olympus intent on obtaining a replacement from the artisan-god: she found him sweating, whirling around the bellows, 'hard at work, for he was making twenty tripods, all to stand around the broad megaron, against the wall'.[41] Standing thus, did Hephaistos's tripods create something of the effect of a frieze or enfilade?[42]

   Tripods were also lifted into the air as akroteria, like those of the temple of Zeus at Olympia (**Fig. 2.35**).[43] The tripod scene painted on the roof of the late eighth-century temple model from Nikoleika in Achaia (**Fig. 2.9**) may mirror some such early instance of high-level display.[44] Apollo seated on a tripod occupied the centre of

8.17   Red-figure column-*krater* (*c*.410), Museo archeologico nazionale, Naples (inv. 81673); detail. Actors in the retinue of Dionysos around a tripod-on-column monument.

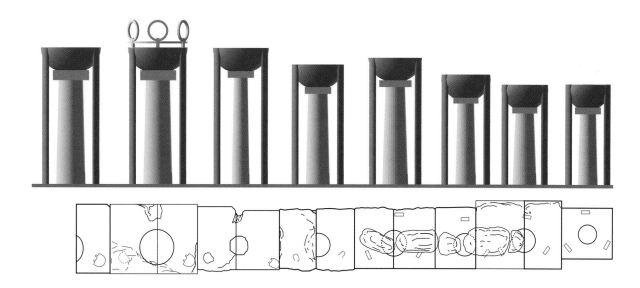

8.18 Enfilade of tripods lining the sacred way, Mount Ptoon. The tripods, typically around a metre and a half tall, were made of bronze, except for bases and central supports of stone.

the east pediment of the fourth-century iteration of his temple at Delphi,[45] and some such prominent tripod would not have been amiss on its predecessors. Lysikrates's monument and others lining the Street of Tripods were in essence glorified tripod supports. The most famous tripod-on-high of all was the Plataia dedication. Although its reconstruction is disputed, the golden tripod somehow surmounted this 30-foot tall helical twist of three gilded-bronze serpents. Tournaire's tour-de-force vision of Apollo's sanctuary in its mature state may indulge in fantasy, but the crowding around the temple of impressive dedications, many of them tripods and some of these lofty, is entirely plausible in its general effect (**Fig. 10.1**).[46]

Tripods on columns strike a particular chord, for they raise tripods up into the air at just the kind of elevation that the viewer might encounter friezes on buildings. Tripods-on-columns appear on several fifth- and fourth-century vase paintings (**Figs 8.1, 8.6e, 8.17**).[47] A fresco in the Roman villa at Oplontis shows a gilded bronze tripod on very tall legs on top of a pedestal (**Fig. 8.20**).

Archaeological corroboration is occasionally available, including for pairs of tripods-on-columns; two stood in Apollo's sanctuary on Delos,[48] while on the southern side of the Athenian Acropolis still stand a pair without their tripods but with appropriately triangular Corinthian capitals.[49] The beginnings of this tradition elude us, though the earliest known monumental example, in the Samian Heraion, may well have anticipated the first dipteral temple, indicating a date at least as early as 580. All that remains is a portion of the shaft and the stone torus capital that once received the tripod feet (**Fig. 7.16**); the size of both suggests a total height of between 6 and 10 metres.[50]

In short, the sacred and social significance of tripods, their aura of myth and epic, their prominence in sanctuaries, their size, their display in rows and at high level, - including on top of columns - all this creates a situation in which traits could potentially migrate to altars and temples. Design habits crossed over from architecture to tripods, as when big ones were given Doric-like columns as an additional central support for the cauldron (**Fig. 8.18**).[51] So why not in the other direction too? Large bronze tripods have in fact a certain architectural quality, a sense of stability and repose, standing like three-legged baldachins.[52] Some influence from tripods makes it possible to understand several features of

8.19   Red-figure Attic column-*krater*, Museo Archeologico, Arezzo. Chariot race for a tripod prize standing on a Doric column.

triglyphs that are otherwise baffling. It is the sympathy with tripods, as much if not more so than with beams, that could account for the marked height of the Doric frieze. While antecedent field-and-divider friezes of the Mycenaean and Geometric periods established the general principle of this type of frieze, I also contend that contamination from tripods explains specific details of the triglyph, the band only at the top and the little arches underneath. The chamfers of the uprights could perhaps be accounted for in other ways, but these too happen to find parallels on tripods and their representations.

Recalling the purpose of temples (Ch. 1) raises multiple parallels of a conceptual kind too. Tripods could be mementoes of victory and the god's share of war booty; temples likewise could be the fruit of military success. Tripod imagery would suit temples of Apollo, it being one of his symbols. In epic tradition tripods were valued by heroes and gods, who chose them to embellish their homes; such objects would hardly be out of place, then, on the gods' terrestrial homes. Tripod imagery would further advertise the museum-cum-treasury

function of sheltering costly dedications, not least because tripods were so often among them. And since temples were in themselves dedications, the tripod, *the* Greek dedication, bestowed appropriate overtones in this regard too. So multivalent and universal was the sacred charge of the tripod that it would indeed make a particularly fitting temple ornament.

While it is impossible to say exactly how the tripod connection arose, once it did arise it would have been compelling. The symbolic magnetism of the tripod gave the triglyph relative fixity, ending any search for potential alternative solutions for Doric friezes. The complex of associations thus evoked conveyed an authority that appealed, presumably, to those commissioning sacred temples and altars. The next generation of architects may well have understood the origins of the prototype as they further refined it, but how wide an audience would have appreciated its associations, and for how long, is unknowable. In line with patterns that Riegl observed (Ch. 6, p. 140), the abstract character of the Doric frieze combined with the dulling effect of familiarity meant that its original significance was inevitably destined to fade.[53] The relationship between form and meaning is nuanced and mutable.

The symbolic resonance of tripods explains why the design of triglyphs locked in tripod-like traits as opposed to others. Yet the triglyph is not a univalent symbol; it was *not* the architectural representation or equivalent of a tripod. If things were that simple the triglyph would no doubt have the ring handles that were so typical of tripod representations. The triglyph is first and foremost an architectural device, and as such it responds to multiple factors involved in the creation of architectural form. There were other antecedents for the compositional principles of the Doric frieze, a point noted earlier and to which we shall return in the next chapter. Design is far too slippery an enterprise to respond to one polarity of interpretation or another, and would rather negotiate somewhere in between.

8.20 (FACING PAGE)   Villa at Oplontis; Second-Style wall painting from Room 15 (second half of first century). At the centre of a peristyle seen through a screen of columns is a monumental golden (or gilded bronze) tripod set up on a pedestal.

CHAPTER NINE

CRUCIBLE

Design is a non-linear activity. It encompasses logic, yet is not wholly logical and nor is it susceptible to clean divides or polarities. The orders were not the result of an incremental evolution, and nor were they born in an instant, as when Athena sprung fully armed from the head of Zeus. They issued out of contrasting kinds of impetus, of revival, borrowing and invention. A period of testing and refinement followed, resulting in mature patterns of practice that differ from early manifestations. Though the peristyle is a hallmark of Greek temples, columns initially stood at the front alone (Ch. 2). The characteristic alignment of triglyphs with columns came after the Doric vocabulary was established, the product of a phase of 'tectonification' (Ch. 3). Details like the egg-and-dart of Ionic capitals could come to prosper though they were absent from formative stages (Ch. 5). Similarly, the Corinthian capital only gradually approximated to an acanthus-shrouded basket (Ch. 6).

9.1 (FACING PAGE) Parthenon, Athenian acropolis (447–432); detail of north-east corner.

9.2 (ABOVE) Black-figure *hydria* (*c.*520), Museum of Fine Arts, Boston (inv. 61.195); detail. Fountain house at which women fill their water jars (*hydriai*) from lion-headed (and one donkey-headed) spouts. Note the slenderness of the (?wooden) column shafts and the decoration of the vase itself, with motifs that would not be out of place on a building.

Experiment and insight contributed to shifts of direction that aimed at superior results. It follows that the shifts could have gone in different directions. Contagion between material culture and architecture also depended to some extent on chance; the choices that led some capitals to resemble libation bowls, for example, could have taken another trajectory in the hands of different designers or, for that matter, the same designers on another day. Yet the incorporation of attitudes and devices shared across a range of production gave a certain familiarity to the first generation of stone temples, tempering their novelty and making them belong. Only in this sense, rather than as the outcome of evolutionary processes, was there anything 'inevitable' about the orders.

This point is important since theorizing has often given a contrary impression. Indeed, modern architectural theory has hampered understanding of Greek temples and orders by retrojecting onto them preconceived notions about their development (Introduction, pp. 5–7; Ch. 3, pp. 64–6). Formulas such as 'form follows function' and 'honesty of construction' are too narrow to explain the generation of built form in the twentieth century, when these creeds were in vogue, let alone in earlier epochs. Nor is the myth of evolutionary progress and inevitability the province of architects alone; Rhys Carpenter, a specialist in Greek art, invoked an almost mystical teleology when describing developments in design leading to the Classical period as 'unhesitant as though the path were known and the goal sighted in advance'.[1] The idea is appealing, yet misleading. At any one stage designers sought to resolve specific issues, perhaps by focusing on them almost myopically; only later could the built decisions be effectively reviewed.[2] Happenstance and serendipity are vectors of cultural development that are too often ignored. Having little to do with post-rationalized neatness, design ideas may come out of the blue (or seemingly so), or be borrowed magpie fashion, triggering unpredictable lateral jumps in new directions. But once the process produces a form worthy of pursuing in earnest, any rigorous practice demands critical evaluation vis-à-vis convention, prac-

ticality and efficacy. Reflections on such dynamics come from figures as varied as Igor Stravinsky, writing on the tussle between inspiration and technique; Jacques Monod, on the workings of chance and necessity; and Richard Sennett, on the thinking inherent in making.[3] My own conclusions derive primarily from observing Greek architecture: its creation did not obey the same laws as those which later gave it such logic and clarity.

CONVERGENCE

The dynamics involved in the formation of Greek architectural conventions are epitomized by capital design and the specific case of the echinus. In Chapter 7 we saw that capitals from the temple at Metropolis recall a type of *phiale* with a lotus pattern, those of the Knidian Treasury a ribbed type, and those of the Erechtheion caraytid porch yet another type characterized by an array of lobes (**Figs 9.5, 9.6**). Yet it would be absurd to indulge visualizations of columns and caryatids as the petrified descendants of pillars or human figures carry-

9.3 François Blondel, evocation of the moment of artistic inspiration derived from ceremonial bowls set up on high. The affinities between capitals and vessels such as *phialai* respond, however, to more complex and nuanced factors.

L'Origine des Chapiteaux des Colonnes.

ing bowls and urns, as implied by François Blondel in the seventeenth century (**Fig. 9.3**). The parallelisms with *phialai* hardly usurp the Minoan–Mycenaean ancestry of a circular echinus capped by a square abacus (Ch. 4, p. 92). This type was re-established well before each of the capitals mentioned were contaminated by the agency of *phialai*.[4] The *phiale*-like characteristics thus represent at most a *secondary* and *partial* development. It is as when a new variety of apple tree that is valued for its fruit is grafted onto a hardier existing rootstock.

The prerequisite for this kind of grafting is formal convergence, which evidently could occur between two lines of development that initially were separate. When two objects charged with static electricity are brought close to one another, nothing noticeable happens - until the distance is sufficiently reduced, when all of a sudden a charge jumps across the gap. In our case the spark was one of recognition underpinned by a sense of semantic suitability in terms of prevailing cultural values.

Such a paradigm seems also to apply to the echinus of the Ionic capital with its canonic egg-and-dart. The first generation or so of Cycladic Ionic capitals typically had an echinus comparable to a petaled or foliate crown, usually with a down-turning overfall. It was not until the mid- to late sixth century that a more compact solution was introduced with the aim of solving the corner problem (Ch. 5, pp. 128–31). To achieve this goal the echinus acquired a quarter round or ovolo profile, thereby coming to resemble an up-turned bowl or cup as a by-product. Only after this occurred did someone happen to notice, and then exploit, the convergence with *phialai* and / or the crowning decoration of round altars (**Fig. 9.4**).[5] In fact in this latter context a parallel transformation of the foliate cyma that was also associated with linear runs of ornament was already under way. Having been characterized by almost rectangular leaves with rounded corners, and with space for only small points in between, the leaves or lobes tended to curve and contract, while the gaps in between them opened up and the points or darts became longer. In the process the scheme adapted itself better to curvature in plan; this encouraged greater plasticity. In the context of capitals,

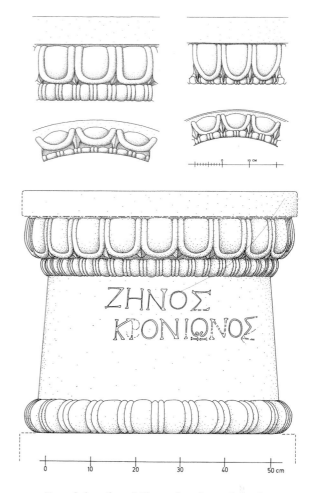

9.4   Round altars from Miletos; elevation and details.

the radius involved was tighter, hence an affinity with *phialai* and a receptiveness to the lessons offered by certain kinds of lobed examples. The lobes came to resemble eggs, as on such *phialai*, hence egg-and-dart. Yet in the earlier stages neither eggs nor *phialai* had anything to do with it. The fluid slippage of formal concerns is further illustrated by the later weakening of the connection between the echinus and the *phiale*. This is clear from the development of the Doric capital in the fifth century, when the echinus went on to acquire an almost conical shape. The celebrated geometrical severity of the Classical Doric capital is exemplified by those of the Parthenon (**Fig. 9.1**) and the so-called temple of Zeus at Cyrene (**Fig. 9.13**).

9.5 Caryatid of the south porch of the Erechtheion, Athenian Acropolis; detail.

9.6 Silver *phiale* of a lobed type known in Persia, Greece and elsewhere which descended from Assyrian prototypes, British Museum. An inscription in Old Persian Cuneiform around the inner rim (not visible here) names Artaxerxes I (464–424). The lobes – which in origin have little to do with eggs – appear to have developed from the negative shapes formed by an array of lotus decoration (cf. **Fig. 7.11**) going on to become in themselves motifs of decorative value.

Likewise the Doric frieze is not a representation, nor a petrification of a line of tripods. The widespread strategy of friezes punctuated by vertical dividers set down key parameters quite independently of tripods. Tripartite dividers evidently took hold, a development which led someone to notice a resemblance to representations of tripods. The agency of the tripod spurred a shift of emphasis, hence the capping band at the top of triglyphs and the little arches underneath. Again, the tripod-like characteristics of the Doric frieze represent a *secondary* and *partial* development. Grasping the dynamics of such processes helps explain the absence of consistency in terms of any single reading. Thus triglyphs do not resemble the dividers of the Minoan–Mycenaean split-rosette frieze as much as they might have done if the lower of the two horizontal bands had been omitted in favour of the tripod aspect. Similarly triglyphs do not resemble representations of tripods as much as they might have done if the ring-handles had not been omitted because they clashed with the linear principle of field-and-divider friezes.[6] The designer of the Samian frieze of tripod-triglyphs (**Figs 8.12, 9.9**) presumably omitted handles for similar reasons.

Acknowledging elements of hybridity, conflation and serendipity in design is crucial to appreciating how different theories of explanation can co-exist and intersect one another. The *genera* were the fruit of a creativity that was neither strictly logical nor predictable; chance and artistic inspiration played their part in producing a complex whole.

What is the nature of the cross-over and mutual inflections between different spheres of production? Did the entanglement between the *phiale* and the echinus, between the *kalathos* basket/vessel and the Corinthian capital, and between the tripod and the triglyph, arise unself-consciously or purposefully?

The extent of common ground between the tectonic and technical arts means that it is no surprise to encounter mutual echoes, like those between medieval reliquaries and cathedrals. The creator of the one does not necessarily have the other directly in mind. Artistic premises can become so embedded that they are deployed spontaneously. From this standpoint the universe of forms used in Greek artistic production could have simply rubbed off, as it were, on temple builders, silently conditioning and directing creative activity. The unpremeditated sharing of pleasing solutions between craftsmen working alongside each other on different projects in the same sanctuary is perhaps only to be expected. The fact that architects were often one and the same as the artists producing art-offerings makes it all the more likely that this contamination occurred in a casual, uncontrolled, viral fashion. This, rather than any considered intentions, explains how ornaments such as spirals and fish-scale could skip across different media as promiscuously as they did.

Yet none of this excludes the possibility that some temple builders privileged certain forms with the intent to impart a message, if not a suitable sacred tone, by virtue of their associations. Through their sacred purposes as libation bowls and offerings, the visual qualities of *phialai* lent an air of sacrality to cognate architectural forms. As already noted, the caryatids of the Erechtheion bear on their heads capitals which have an echinus not unlike certain kinds of *phiale* that were in vogue at the time (**Figs 9.5, 9.6**). By this token may we read the Erechtheion maidens as serene participants in ritual, frozen in marble?[7] After all, they seem to invite a connection of this sort - for they originally held *phialai* in their right hands (**Fig. 9.7**).[8] The sacred charge of the tripod made it too eminently fitting for a temple.

But beware oppositions such as that between the unselfconscious and purposeful. Different ancestries or motivations could produce the same results.[9] Objects like *phialai*, thrones and tripods resonated on both artistic and semantic levels. It is futile to try to drive a wedge

9.7 Caryatids, modelled on those of the Erechtheion, at the so-called Canopus, Hadrian's Villa, near Tivoli. Note the *phialai* they carry in their right hands.

between these domains, no less than between issues of nature and nurture (Introduction, p. 7); the most special and sacred classes of object were precisely those accorded the highest level of artistic investment.[10] Greek attitudes on this point are illustrated by the slippage of meaning involving the term *agalma*, which, having indicated a pleasing gift in Homeric times, eventually came to denote beautiful statuary (Ch. 1, pp. 20–21). The emphasis could shift from offering to beauty precisely because inherent to the concept of offering was giving to the gods something of value that pleased them.

* * *

INCLUSION AND EXCLUSION

The processes described evince an undogmatic, not to say eclectic, willingness to seize on the felicitous. In commenting on statues of late seventh-century date at the sanctuary of Apollo Ptoios, François de Polignac notes that, though mostly produced locally, 'they show a great stylistic diversity, some with markedly local features, others clearly inspired by Cycladic or Attic models, still others combining all these traditions and influences in various ways'.[11] Architectural design was no less open to foreign sources and precedents of Bronze Age vintage. To attach the word 'eclectic' to Greek design might seem heretical for, with regard to architecture, the term often implies the indiscriminate borrowing associated with the nineteenth century AD. But the Greeks discriminated as they borrowed: witness the language of Homeric epic, a wondrously unified amalgam of disparate dialectal forms.[12] Similarly Doric and Ionic represent far more than various ingredients thrown into the pot along with talent and judgement. As when metals are fused in a crucible, a gleaming new alloy can come forth that possesses a potential beyond all expectation.

Claude Lévi-Strauss has observed that for a culture to produce great things it must be convinced of its originality and superiority.[13] This certainly applied to the Greeks who, by their own judgement, were capable of finer results than any people before them.[14] In contrast to negative perceptions of the effect of modern western importations on traditional Japanese sensibilities,[15] for example, the Greek experience of appropriation was wholly positive. Instead of monuments and material acting on Greek artists and architects, they actively selected what appealed to them most.[16] To re-cast a quip that Stravinksy, Picasso and others were fond of, the Greeks did not so much borrow as steal; they took ownership and control.

The rapid coalescence of Doric style either side of 600 presumes a capacity for invention that went hand in hand with the Greeks' confidence.[17] In spite of their borrowings, architects of the Archaic and Classical periods can be credited with the invention of the stepped temple krepis, the pediment, the akroterion and the Corinthian capital. The peristyle and the Ionic capital were likewise fundamentally Greek, notwithstanding the respective lessons offered by Egyptian colonnades and miscellaneous antecedent volute capitals. Indeed, Greek architecture would hardly merit the attention it receives were it not the offspring of imagination, and without this the *genera* could not have emerged with such a sense of unity. This applies to other transformative moments in architectural history, as exemplified by Bramante's Tempietto in Rome, a new paradigm forged from plural contributory sources (ancient tholoi, the Pantheon, Roman Doric, medieval centralized buildings, *ad quadratura*, unbuilt schemes by both Francesco di Giorgio and Leonardo da Vinci). Bramante 'stole' liberally and yet the Tempietto exudes unity in its novelty. The original Doric scheme was perhaps no less the fruit of sudden flashes of genius like that which had Archimedes jumping from his bath shouting 'eureka!'

Design is also knowing what to leave out, what to exclude. The exclusion principle operated in the Italian Renaissance just as it did in the Modern Movement, the former purging anything Gothic, the latter anything historicist or 'arbitrary'.[18] Indeed, the exclusion of the arbitrary was for Bötticher a distinguishing feature of the work of Greek architects.[19] They spurned that which could not be justified on more than one level. They eliminated anything too foreign, hence the absence, despite their borrowings from the Phoenicians, of the Pharaonic styling that pervades Phoenician art. Above all, the Greeks excluded anything flawed in formal terms. Thus they discarded the Aeolic capital once they had the more successful Ionic. For similar reasons the Cycladic form of the Ionic capital lost out to the Ionian form (Ch. 5, p. 131). Likewise early Corinthian lyre-like schemes gave way to a complete ring of acanthus (Ch. 6, p. 155). It is as if designers inhaled all manner of things, drawing in that which was of use, while exhaling that which was not. As when an athlete's breathing become finer and more controlled after a period of exertion, so it was with design and successive iterations of trial and evaluation.

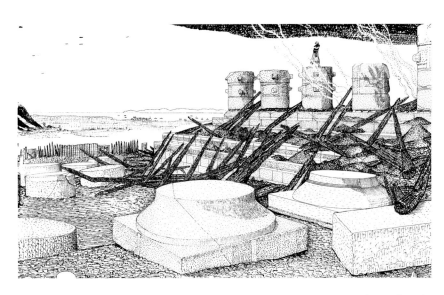

9.8   So-called pre-Parthenon after it was torched by the Persians in 480, when still under construction, as visualized by Manolis Korres.

Progress was fuelled by love of competition, a central characteristic of Hellenic culture that is manifest in sport and the performative arts, not forgetting state-level contests for prominent sculptural commissions and building projects. In the major sanctuaries inter-state rivalries found an outlet in institutionalized events such as the Olympic games, and also in the setting up of dedications.[20] Individual *poleis* vied for prestige by erecting treasuries, and by investing in temples back home. Agreed standards for contests in athletics, drama and music facilitated comparison of like with like, so that the best could be readily identified.[21] In architecture the restricted designers' palette served similar purposes. Widespread adherence to the Doric and Ionic *genera* allowed other variables to be evaluated: size, cost, materials, precision and quality of execution. The collective nature of temple projects no doubt stimulated group discussion over such things as well as questions of character and decorum (*prepon*), and symbolic resonance.[22] As in the political arena, many of the Greeks' achievements relied on the conviction that by debate and demonstration it was possible to identify the best (*ariston*): the best strategy, the best course of action, the best work of art, the best architectural form.

The funding of temples also had implications. In the earlier part of the sixth century many a temple was financed, wholly or in part, by the donations of rulers and aristocrats (Ch. 7, p. 174). At Didyma such practices continued in to the Hellenistic period, witness the personalized ornamentation of columns, or groups of columns, to signal their sponsors' contribution (**Fig. 5.8**). Work started perhaps from one end of the building site and progressed as funds became available. On the mainland it became more usual by the fifth century for projects to be managed as state enterprises subject to majority committee vote. Temples were put up faster and systematically in demonstrations of democratic unity.[23] Considering its extensive sculptural programme and exacting refinements the Parthenon was put up remarkably quickly, the bulk of it in under ten years, starting in 447. The vestiges of the partly built Pre-Parthenon torched by the Persians are also eloquent. Many column drums survive from the first two courses, several from the third course and few beyond that (**Fig. 9.8**). Evidently at the time of destruction the works had reached a fairly uniform level across the site, testimony to rationalized procedures.[24] Standardization and the suppression of detail played their part in this endeavour.

UNITY IN MULTIPLICITY

The bias that often accompanies theory, exacerbated by adversarial tendencies at the heart of dialectical method and modern political debate, favours exclusive lines of argumentation, whereby if one explanation seems valid alternatives are deemed invalid. Those who see the orders in terms of construction often find it necessary to dismiss meaning, for example. Or if debts to preceding epochs are discussed, the Egyptian and Mycenaean traditions can find themselves cast as rivals and pitted one against the other. The creation of architectural form evades such reasoning; different justifications overlap and reinforce each other, and even coexist with an element of paradox and contradiction.[25] Continuity with indigenous tradition, borrowing or revival, and fresh invention may run in parallel.[26] The concept of 'unity in multiplicity', which has been applied to the poetry of Greek epic, is also pertinent to visual culture.[27] While I take the multi-faceted nature of architecture to be axiomatic (Introduction, p. 7), the *genera* teach the same point. Only rarely do they answer to just one or two kinds of explanation. Perhaps this was the case for mutules, guttae and dentils, appearing as they do to be artistically edited evocations of timber joinery. Normally issues of construction, influence, appearance and meaning all played some part.

Different modes of explanation come together in the invention of the peristyle (Ch. 2, p. 53), the fluting of column shafts (Introduction, p. 8), and in the main kinds of Greek capital. The Doric capital effects the transition from a circular column to a linear beam, while the spread of the abacus reduces structural spans. The principle of mediating a square abacus and a circular shaft with an echinus was pioneered in Minoan–Mycenaean precursors, by way of which Egyptian models with only an abacus exerted indirect influence (Ch. 4, pp. 92–6). Decorative concerns are evident in various details applied to the necking and the echinus (Ch. 5, p. 117). The components of Bronze Age ancestry arguably gave the capital, and so too the column as a whole, heroic intimations, which contributed perhaps to later theorizing about Doric's masculine character that would find echoes in Vitruvius's gender scheme (Ch. 6, p. 142).

In common with bracket capitals of vernacular traditions, the lateral spread of Aeolic and Ionic capitals in line with the beam reduces spans in a more rational manner than for Doric. (Actually this often only *seems* to be so, for the top surface of the volutes was often cut down so as not to bear the load of the beam and to avoid the attendant risk of fracture.) To differing extents both volute configurations absorbed disparate influences from Bronze Age Greece as well as more recent eastern Mediterranean cultures.[28] Ionic trumped Aeolic in terms of its visual resolution, looking stronger, more elegant and more confident with its virtuoso double curvature. Moreover it adapted better to circular columns, especially to sturdy ones, as well as to the corner condition imposed by peripteral plans (Ch. 5, pp. 128–31). In tune with the traditions from which they were borrowed, volutes carried sacral and regal overtones imbued with fertility, hence no doubt the feminine qualities of which Vitruvius tells.

As for Corinthian, this luxuriant invention subsumed multiple sources: funeral monuments and the *kalathos*, metalwork, indirect echoes of foliate capitals from Egypt and elsewhere. With time the acanthus became a vehicle for naturalism and a profusion of enchanting detail, while conveying subtle intimations of the triumph over death and the regenerative cycle of life. There arose no formal difficulties at the corner as in the case of the Ionic capital, and, being less stiff than Doric, the Corinthian was well suited to articulated ground-plans. The verticality of the capital created a fluid union with the shaft, and as the Romans would come to appreciate, curving and over-turning forms made a happy prelude to vaulting. Considerations of proportion and standardization further explain the centrality of Corinthian to the imperial Roman building machine.[29] Structural and constructional aspects are less in evidence than for the older *genera*, yet the younger capital and its parent column was nonetheless solid enough to support the grandest temples. Yet again there is unity in multiplicity.

Arriving towards the end of this study it is apposite to return to the beginning in a sense, to architecture's oldest puzzle, the Doric frieze. Here again is a hybrid design that synthesized multiple kinds of input. The compositional principle echoes diverse field-and-divider antecedents, principally those from Egypt, Mycenae and Geometric Greece. This point is illustrated by a selection of friezes from disparate contexts, which, in one way or another, could have come into the ambit of designers in the seventh century (**Fig. 9.9**). There is no methodological reason to choose one source to the complete exclusion of the others, and the possibility must be left open of multiple contributions. Proto-triglyphs could perhaps have arisen out of the melding of striped frieze dividers of the Geometric period with Bronze Age rosette-splitters; indeed, a melding of this kind did occur on some seventh-century vases. One from Zagora (**Fig. 9.9e**), for example, presents dividers with running spirals of probable Bronze Age inspiration. Perhaps tripod traits came to be overlaid on an archi-tectural framework of this kind, rather as tripod-and-metope friezes were created in other media. The last example illustrated, the Hellenistic frieze from Samos (**Fig. 9.9h**), reminds us too of the ambiguity just dis-cussed: are the triglyph-tripods tripodified triglyphs or triglyphied tripods? As for symbolism, the outcome spoke to the princely traditions of ancestors and heroes just as it resonated with prestige, piety and the virtue of offering.

Where does this leave constructional readings in tune with the authority of Vitruvius? There are serious short-comings surrounding mechanical readings of the Doric frieze in terms of the beam-end theory (Ch. 3, pp. 68–

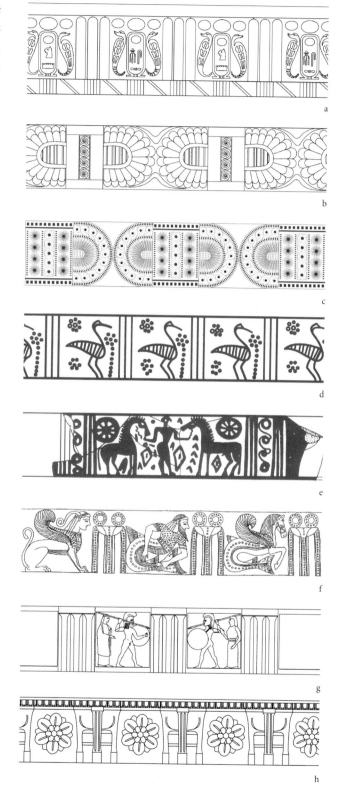

9.9 Potential influences bearing on the formation of the Doric frieze. (a) Egyptian cornice (after Durm); (b) split-rosette frieze from Mycenae (see **Fig. 4.5**); (c) split-rosette inlaid frieze from Tiryns; (d) frieze from a pot from Zagora (see **Fig. 2.10**); (e) frieze from a pot from Zagora (see **Fig. 2.10**); (f) frieze from a seventh-century tripod kothon from Thasos (see **Fig. 8.14**); (g) Doric frieze from the temple of Artemis at Corfu; (h) Doricizing third-century architec-tural frieze from Samos (see **Fig. 8.12**).

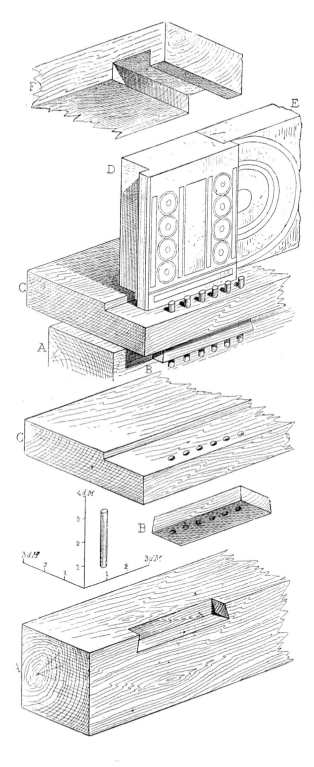

9.10   Hypothetical Mycenaean split-rosette frieze made out of wood, as visualized by Charles Chipiez (1876).

75). Yet this does not mean that construction had no relevance at all. It is interesting to observe how Greek artists could represent Doric architecture in ways that are both decorative and constructional (**Fig. 9.2**). Could the genesis of the Doric frieze have had a constructional aspect at the same time as being decorative and symbolic? In the late nineteenth century Charles Chipiez proposed just such a synthesis, a rendering of Mycenaean frieze traditions adapted to timber detailing (**Fig. 9.10**). The problem here, as with so many past proposals, is its literalness; no great work of art is so mechanically literal. In any case, such explanations fail to account for the details of the triglyph (Ch. 3, pp. 73–5). The key to resolving this impasse is in fact supplied by Vitruvius himself, for he did *not* say triglyphs *were* beam-ends. Since raw construction would have been ugly, he explained, early Greek builders concealed the beams with covers of a superior appearance (Ch. 3, p. 64). In other words this was not merely a utilitarian solution. Once construction is put in its proper place as an important factor, but not the sole determining factor, it becomes possible to reconcile aspects of Vitruvius's testimony with the preceding discussion. Triglyphs could have arisen as 'tripodified' dividers of Mycenaean–Geometric ancestry, and yet still have served as beam-covers, or had a loose association with structure.

Given that the Doric entablature was not primarily driven by construction, and nor by evolutionary progression, it is scarcely possible to visualize the specific logic by which a prototype (or prototypes) would have emerged. Nonetheless it is worth framing its creation in terms of the typological and constructional parameters operating in the eighth and seventh centuries, bearing in mind discussion in Chapters 2 and 3, and in particular the following points: temples and kindred structures tended to have long and narrow plans, with an entrance at one end; the use of exterior columns was predominantly associated with the entrance; the elements of Doric style that best attune with the legacy of carpentry are confined to the epistyle (a beam or wall-plate?) and the geison with its mutules (the ends of rafters?).

9.11   North porch of the Erechtheion; view of superstructure that responded to a relatively wide span, illustrating an arrangement in which ceiling beams running front to back sit on top of the epistyle-beams and at the level of the frieze.

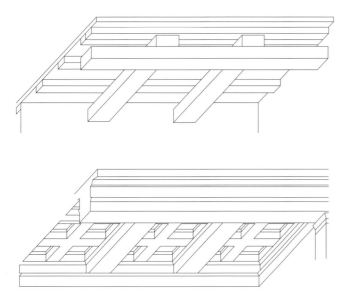

9.12   Arrangement of ceiling beams of a typical Greek temple (bottom) compared with likely vernacular patterns of construction on which it was based (top).

On the basis of these observations, a regional preference or tradition may be intuited, one that seems especially likely in the western Peloponnese. This could have developed in the context of linear structures comprising mainly walls, some columns and a timber superstructure supporting a tiled roof. I tentatively visualize a bi-partite wooden entablature comprising an almost plain epistyle and a geison punctuated by (or as if by) the ends of wooden rafters. To repeat, there was no need for a frieze.

Two scenarios could have led to the introduction of a frieze. In one scenario we may imagine that, for some project or other, a desire arose for an unusually impressive and deep column-fronted porch. Perhaps it was spanned by a layer of beams running longitudinally and resting on top of the epistyle beams, and so at the level of what would become the frieze. Such an arrangement would have become necessary since wide spans call for relatively large beams compared with the columns on which they sit (this is true whether the material is wood or stone). There would not have been much room to seat substantial internal beams at the same level as the

epistyle, and this, furthermore, would have had to be notched to accommodate such beams. The solution, evidently, was to create an extra layer of construction, with the internal beams resting on top of the epistyle, as occurred in the mid-sixth century at Sangri (**Fig. 3.16**), and later still on the Athenian acropolis, in both the Propylaea and the north porch of the Erechtheion (**Fig. 9.11**). Back in the seventh century tie-beams running cross-wise (as implied by Vitruvius) seem unlikely, while in early temples the fronts were typically the most important locus for monumental expression, as noted.[30] The new strategy would in effect have created an additional element of the elevation, that is to say the frieze. For this the chosen dressing was inspired firstly by the field-and-divider principle, and secondly by a connection with tripods. In short this scenario reconciles a variant of the Vitruvian model with a new explanation for the specific look of triglyphs.

In a second scenario the frieze would have arisen primarily for artistic and/or symbolic reasons. Rather as seen on some architectural models (**Fig. 2.9**), field-and-divider friezes may have been located near the tops of walls by the seventh century. Then traits associated with Mycenaean usage and tripods came into play. The wish for a grander façade for some temple or other – one that had columns – then led to the addition of the resultant frieze over them as a way of gaining height and a sense of gravity. Owing to the size of the triglyphs, as befitted the tripod connection, they generated strong vertical accents that could hardly be ignored in compositional terms. This encouraged the process of 'tectonification' that would later find them aligned with columns (Ch. 3, p. 81). Hence the correlation between triglyphs and structure on which Vitruvius would later dwell.

Of course, other scenarios may be envisaged, but whatever the niceties of events, structure and construction surely played a part, even if a looser and less deterministic part than is often envisaged. We have to accept that relationships between structure and its visual expression were not always strictly 'honest'. Be it noted that when designing ceilings Greek architects in later periods felt themselves at liberty to combine genuinely structural members with 'false' ones for the sake of a symmetry and aesthetic effect (**Fig. 9.12**).[31] Though the frieze may initially have been used only on the fronts of temples, architects presumably decided to wrap one all around simply because it looked better that way, especially when a peristyle was involved.[32] In effect, aesthetic judgement trumped constructional rigour. The outcome may not be entirely logical, but it is effective, beautiful and at the same redolent of structure.

At this point we may avail ourselves of ideas of those nineteenth-century luminaries Bötticher and Semper, who both worked more or less simultaneously on design theory and Greek style. Both men saw affinities between the tectonic and technical arts. Semper's name has come up in most of the preceding chapters, despite their varying emphasis, since for him understanding a historic style meant embracing '*all* the preconditions and circumstances of its becoming'.[33] Even if his writings have long been superseded archaeologically, his attitude remains instructive for its embrace of complex and contradictory considerations, unafraid of paradox and nuance. He could reject the primitive hut as the ancestor of temples, but yet see it as their mystical-poetic kernel.[34] He could link ornamental motifs to techniques like knotting and weaving, but resist constructional readings of the Doric frieze.[35] Semper also appreciated the Greek column both as a free-standing entity and as a member of a peristasis.[36]

Bötticher used the Doric temple to advance his concept of the connection between a building's structural core-form (*Kernform*) and its exterior art-form (*Kunstform*).[37] This came later to be condensed into the more mechanistic binary of the 'bones' of a building and its 'skin', but Semper's concept of 'dressing' (*Bekleidung*) is more supple.[38] The theory of dressing holds that technique and functional criteria such as comfort, fit and performance are all significant yet not deciding factors in the creation of form. Appearance (*apparel*) also responds to tradition, status, identity and individual taste. Along with other ingredients of the classical canon, the Doric frieze may profitably be seen as an architec-

tural dressing. It embraces a sense of structure and construction tempered by aesthetic and symbolic sensibilities; at the same time it suited the purpose of the religious structures it adorned and associated customs. From this standpoint, the dressing of the Greek temple is not so different from other manifestations of culture. A tattoo can be both decorative and a mark of status and clan (**Fig. 0.7**). A rapid closing of the eye performs a biological function, yet a blink can also be a wink, a knowing sign of complicity.[39] Hats keep off the rain while reflecting in their form the materials and techniques employed to make them; designs register status and flex with fashion, saying something about the wearer and at times being used for communication – should one be lifted or removed, whether with a gesture of respect, cordiality or even mockery.[40] The Greek architectural *genera* were hardly less inclusive and layered in scope and depth, nor filtered any less by personal interpretation.[41]

In short, both Bötticher and Semper proffer a corrective to subsequent scholarship which in its concern for detail can miss the forest for the trees. Intuitions and connections that once flowed freely through nineteenth-century inquiries have been sacrificed on the altar of specialism. Where old theories are flawed or outdated they should naturally be put to one side, but beware casting out ideas that may still hold value.[42] Let us aspire to the big picture while yet holding on to minutiae that should be accounted for with forensic scrutiny.

* * *

Looking beyond polarized interpretations reveals the cultural resonance of Greek architectural form and its dependence on construction, influence, appearance and meaning, all inextricably entangled. There is no simple litmus test to establish which was dominant, nor to what extent acts of design were unselfconscious or purposeful. It is up to individual readers to judge. It is as when some see a sculpture by Barbara Hepworth and enjoy the abstract play of an oval hole in an organically sinuous stone, while others see the form of a belly and are reminded of the lost pregnancy she suffered. Recovering the intention of the artist herself is another step, perhaps unknowable. Looking so much further back in the past any specificity of interpretation must elude us; indeed this is just as it should be. As Robert Venturi muses, great art and architecture resist clear interpretation. Being poised ambiguously between different readings is part of the greatness.[43] The longevity of the classical tradition rests precisely on its capacity for multiple reinterpretation.

Ambiguity and ambivalence may strike contemporary chords – think of Heisenberg's uncertainty principle, fuzzy-set theory and quantum computing – but they have a long ancestry. Greek commentators such as Herodotus repeatedly set out different explanations for the same phenomenon.[44] The ideal of obtaining the most effect with the least means goes hand in hand with a delight in the ambiguous and the contradictory. Greek thought displayed a willingness to embrace alternative and even dissonant conceptions of the divine world, perceiving them as complementary rather than mutually exclusive.[45] This disposition finds perhaps its most characteristic expression in laconic oracular pronouncements and diplomatic responses, as typified by the reply issued by Delphi to King Croesus's question: should he invade Persian territory? The oracle foretold a great power would fall, and so it did, but Croesus made the mistake of presuming this to be his enemy, not his own Lydia.[46] In myth and tragedy, as later played out in Shakespeare's *Macbeth*, it is the human propensity for wrong interpretation that often lies at the heart of a plot. Is this not a comfort when we err as we try to grasp the long shadow of Greek creativity?

Yet in architecture rarely is it a simple case of right or wrong. For sure, certain explanations are more plausible than others, and distinguishing between them is rightly a goal of scholarship. But even so the historical implausibility of an idea (say that volutes derive from horns) does not mean it should be banished entirely from the field of creative speculation. The ability of the classical vocabulary to provoke contrasting readings, the source of so much contention and appreciation from Vitruvius to Venturi, was right there from the start. It was enjoyed and indeed promoted by the Greeks themselves. So it is that diverse ingredients and intentions could fuse into coherent designs of such enigmatic intensity.

9.13   Temple of Zeus at Cyrene, Libya; detail of the peristasis.

CHAPTER TEN
QUESTIONS ANSWERED AND UNANSWERED

The multivalency embedded in the orders, the number and complexity of the factors informing their design, the gaps in the evidence relating to their emergence, all this conspires against a concise summary of their origins. Yet the delivery of this book by thematic chapters, addressing parts of the picture by turn, invites (or even demands) a concluding overview of the whole. And when all is said and done the Greek temple presents us with such a simple, archetypal and unified image that we might reasonably be sceptical of any exposition of its architecture that cannot itself be simply expressed. This final section therefore sets down my understanding of the origins of temples and orders that reconciles the present research with a wider body of scholarship. The

format is a series of summary statements, nuances being left behind in the main text for the sake of brevity. If as a consequence the style tends towards the categorical, the intention is not to be categorical in substance, but the better to confront the fundamental issues.[1] Some questions can be answered more or less straightforwardly; others, discussed towards the end, remain unanswerable, yet are too compelling to pass over. Here analysis and argumentation find an ally in intuition, and a fresh but imperfect idea acquires value if it might lead to a better idea in future. In this spirit the progressive shift from affirmation of fact to open-ended conjecture represents an invitation for further exploration beyond the limits of these pages.

10.1 (FACING PAGE)   Sanctuary of Apollo at Delphi as it would have appeared in Roman times, as reconstructed by Albert Tournaire. *Envoi* of 1894, watercolour on Chinese ink base; detail. The Plataia tripod (cf. **Fig. 10.2**) is shown on the far right of the temple terrace.

10.2 (ABOVE)   Red-figure calyx-*krater* fragment (*c.*390), Allard Peirson Museum, Amsterdam. Apollo's temple at Delphi with the god standing in the doorway, holding his bow and a *phiale*. The monumental bronze tripod on the left may denote the Plataia tripod.

The Greek temple made its appearance relatively suddenly; it was not the culmination of a gradual development. The temple was not a progressively bigger and better version of a hoary primitive hut, nor a direct descendant of a Bronze Age megaron, nor yet an elaboration of 'rulers' huts' of the Iron Age (though it continued some of their traits). The monumental temple rose up in Greek sanctuaries in the seventh century. Substantially unannounced in their turn, Doric and Ionic forms appeared in stone towards the end of that century, and were consolidated during the sixth. The possibility that they were pioneered earlier in perishable materials can be neither proved nor disproved, but anything of comparable solidity and sophistication seems unlikely before the advent of the tiled roof in the early to mid-seventh century. It is as much a case of revolution as evolution (Ch. 2).

The form of the Greek temple and its orders is not the result of a linear or logical development. It is common to project the coherence of mature Doric and Ionic temples back to their inception, a tendency encouraged by theorizing about nature and evolution, the 'honesty' of the primitive mind, and the Greeks' innate rationality (Ch. 3, pp. 64–5). But we should not confuse consistency of result with consistency of causation.[2] There was extensive early variety in early temple layouts and constructional techniques, followed by a trend from heterogeneity to conformity. The same is apparent in the convergence of Doric and Ionic forms on relatively predictable canons. Thus there was little that was 'inevitable' about the appearance of the Greek temple; rather it reflected the exercise of choice. Indeed Doros, the legendary progenitor of the Dorians, 'chanced' to build a temple in the style that came to be known as Doric, according to Vitruvius (IV,1,3). There was also a fortuitous element to the account he gives of Kallimachos's creation of the Corinthian capital. Ideas and connections come to the writer while writing, the composer while playing, and so they come, unpredictably, to artists and designers in the course of their work.

The Greek temple does not closely reflect functional needs; it represents cultural imperatives and an act of collective will. The temple was not so essential to Greek worship as was the altar. There was no need to cater for congregational worship, and while the temple was fundamentally a house of the god it did not have to be big for this purpose (statues in Geometric and Archaic times were typically small). Temples might accommodate other functions such as oracles or ritual dining; they also served as a safe-store or treasury for valuable offerings, this being perhaps the most widespread utilitarian requirement for covered shelter (Ch. 1, pp. 23–4). Since none of these needs initially made heavy demands on space (it took time to amass quantities of votives), it follows that monumentality had a political and symbolic dimension: the temple prominently displayed piety and collective ambition.

Greek temples were houses of the gods and also offerings to them. Aside from its utilitarian functions the temple constituted a gift to its god. This provided conceptual justification for monumental structures, for the greater their worth in terms of cost and effort the more the gods would appreciate them. Offerings were made to be displayed in sanctuaries and had to be artfully crafted to merit the honour; the same applied to temples. Just as social pressures fuelled ostentation in private dedications, the competitive dimension of public gift-giving stimulated inter-state rivalries in temple building. Size, quality of workmanship and materials, the impressiveness of technical feats, even such details as the refinements, all these enhanced not just the visual effect of temples, but also their value from this perspective (Ch. 1, pp. 24–7; Ch. 2, p. 60).

The peristasis was primarily a Greek invention. Early buildings occasionally had circuits of columns, but the dominant type in the late Geometric period was a simple hall with posts or columns at the front. No direct model for the peristyle existed outside Greece, though Egyptian colonnades and shrines proved the worth of column displays and gave an impetus towards the construction of colossal sixth-century temples (Ch. 4, pp. 92–4). On the mainland experimentation may have had roots of a more practical nature, including shelter. The success of the peripteral format is explained by its effectiveness in terms of display: it made a temple look good when approached or viewed from any angle; it allowed size and visual impact to be increased without increasing structural spans; it multiplied the number and impressiveness of columns and so too the connotations of the sacred (Ch. 2, p. 53). It also meant that a temple could no longer be confused with a domestic structure.

Key Doric and Ionic components sustained the votive theme. The triglyph did this for Doric via its appropriation of qualities proper to tripods, the Greeks' offerings par excellence. The Ionic capital did this in two ways: firstly by its absorption of forms such as volutes and arrays of lobes that were used on prestigious offerings ranging from thrones to libation bowls; and secondly by association of usage, given that Ionic capitals appeared on votive columns before they did on temples – a trend that seemingly affected other types of column as well (Ch. 7, pp. 173). Meanwhile smaller scale ornaments, along with fabulous monsters, crossed over from offerings to architecture. Temples, treasuries and altars were cut from the same cloth as the votive material all around them, partaking of a shared ethos.

The character of the temple and the orders cannot be reduced to any single interpretative key. Mono-causal interpretations sell us short whatever their focus, by simplifying complex phenomena and cherry-picking from the surviving evidence. Explanations to do with construction, influence, appearance and meaning have too often been treated in partisan fashion, or to the exclusion of the others. Yet each came into the picture to varying degrees.

Constructional principles shaped the orders, but rather less than has often been assumed. Soundness of construction is an ever present concern of those who commission and erect buildings. Many features of early Greek temples make sense from this viewpoint; the diminution of column shafts combats tendencies towards toppling, for example. The shift from perishable to durable materials characterizes constructional developments in the seventh century, and the invention of the terracotta roof tile was fundamental for the overall form of the temple, its rectangular plan and linear

pedimented roof. Yet, at the detailed level, Vitruvius's account of petrification only works well for mutules, guttae and dentils, though they probably evoked carpentry prototypes rather than literally reproducing them (Ch. 3, pp. 84–5). Other components of the *genera* resist mechanical explanations of this kind, though their distribution favours loose associations with structure and a pervasive if vague sense of tectonic balance.

Varied influences from earlier traditions seeded concepts fundamental to the scheme of temples as well as forms subsumed into the orders. Essential aspects of the Greek temple, including its conception as a house of a god and its links with altars and votives, were anticipated in the eastern Mediterranean, as was the typology of the hall-temple with its frontal disposition and cult statue at the rear facing an imposing doorway and porch (Ch. 4, p. 100). Whether by the movement of people, ideas or artefacts, this part of the world also furnished the Greeks with varied surface ornaments besides volutes and foliate crowns. In combining these forms in ways used in the east, the Aeolic capital might be called the most exotic of the Greek columnar forms. Thanks to surviving ruins like the Treasury of Atreus and objects of antiquarian appeal, Mycenaean approaches to design could be revived in the detailing of Aeolic and Ionic capitals, as well as to that of the Doric column and its frieze. Influences from the east were felt most in the Cyclades and the eastern Aegean, whereas Minoan and Mycenaean legacies were felt most in central Greece.[3] Filtered indirectly via both Cretan and Phoenician intermediaries, Egyptian influence is limited as regards typology and surface detail but is present nonetheless in extremely important ways: in the new-found ambition of the Greek temple, in the ideal of durable monumentality and the belief in the efficacy of the column. All this is exemplified by the imposing dipteroi of sixth-century Ionia (Ch. 2, pp. 59–60). Irrespective of their provenance, and wheresoever their formal antecedents may once have originated, another source of influence resided in the foreign art-offerings in bronze, ivory and ceramic that found their way to the Greeks' own sanctuaries (Ch. 7, pp. 161–3).

The quest for visually effective form moulded the orders and their handling. There is no question of the Greeks merely imitating; their assimilation of external influences is characterized by revaluation, experiment and transformation. This process was driven by the desire to impress the eye, a multi-faceted enterprise that embraced surface ornament, sculptural effect, tectonics, proportion and detailing. Once shaped according to these pressures, mere replication was shunned, as illustrated by the variety of options for Ionic bases and capitals, and indeed the very invention of the Corinthian type. With time and repeated experimentation, consensus coalesced around the solutions that were felt to be the finest, and the most coherent – and which thus acquired the authority of a canon.

Meaning could lie behind architectural form or be acquired by association, but not in ways that were universal, consistent or static. Greek temples gave visible expression to collective identity and piety. Aspects of the *genera* echo the dedicatory nature of the temple, yet this is only one of a number of complementary readings. Columns had diffuse and long-standing connotations to do with the special and the sacred. By virtue of a partial descent from Bronze Age ruins which the Greeks linked to the protagonists of Homeric epic, the Doric capital and frieze bear overtones at once ancestral, aristocratic and heroic (Ch. 4, pp. 92–3; Ch. 9, p. 198). Tinged with an exotic and regal air, volute capitals evoked fertility and perpetuity. The acanthus of the Corinthian capital compounded this with further intimations of rebirth (Ch. 6, p. 155). At the same time, project-specific messages could be imparted via figural sculpture that looked down on the viewer from pediments, akroteria, antefixes and friezes. (For more functional members such as epistyle-beams, however, any symbolic component is likely to be absent or much reduced.) Readings and associations provoked by architectural form ebb, flow and expire, and it is unwise to extrapolate from a later period to an earlier. If the egg-and-dart on the echinus of mature Ionic capitals brings to mind libation cups, and hence sacrifice and offering, this had little to do with the early development of the echinus (Ch. 5, pp.

127–31; Ch. 9, p. 193). Similarly, Roman initiatives that fashioned the darts of egg-and-dart like arrow heads tell us nothing about their original vegetal derivation. With time the replication of the orders inevitably became in part a matter of convention, of 'doing the right thing'. Earlier readings were diluted or lost, while new forms and new readings grew up.

Contrasting justifications for Greek architectural form overlap and reinforce each other, and coexist with an element of contradiction. The multivalent character of the *genera* needs underlining given the historic dominance of exclusive modes of argument (whereby if one explanation seems valid alternatives are deemed invalid). With the chief exception of Gottfried Semper, it is unusual for commentators to fully embrace this multivalency. Only a minority of Greek building components answers primarily to one or two kinds of explanation, for example in the way that mutules, guttae and dentils appear to be artistically edited evocations of timber assemblies. Issues of construction, influence, appearance and meaning could all play a role, fluting being one case in point, so too the capitals of each of the Greek *genera*, Doric, Ionic and Corinthian (Ch. 9, p. 198), the Doric frieze yet another (Ch. 9, pp. 199–202). The relative weight of different factors is a matter of interpretation, and the endurance of the classical tradition depends precisely on its capacity to mean different things to different people. The laconic principle of obtaining the most with the least is a Greek cultural trait with deep architectural resonance. The capacity of the orders to accommodate the multi-faceted intentions that went into them has been the source of tensions and ambiguities which, by never being fully resolved, have provoked perpetual renewal and reinterpretation.

Components of the genera are heterogeneous in origin, character and design modality. Distinct ingredients can fuse inextricably, as if in a crucible, as Doric, Ionic and Corinthian capitals each demonstrate. This is not a universal rule, however, and components of disparate origins can find themselves simply juxtaposed in the entablature. The Doric presents functional and constructional concerns in its epistyle (a straightforward beam) and the mutular geison (a device for keeping off rain and terminating the rafters), but – even if Vitruvius's account of triglyphs as aesthetically pleasing beam-covers cannot be ruled out – the frieze combines decorative traditions and symbolic resonances. The more fluid Ionic entablature was dominated by ornamentation, though the dentils provided a solitary constructive allusion. At the same time different modalities or approaches to design are in evidence: aspects of temples exhibit continuity with autochthonous patterns of building descending from the Iron Age; others revive Bronze Age practices that had been substantially lost, or betray foreign borrowings; still others result from spontaneous invention.[4] Early Greek archi-

tects operated different strategies as they drew from all manner of sources; theirs was an undogmatic and eclectic creativity.

The initial eclectic character of Greek temples and orders contrasts with the coherence they gained with maturity. As in other fields of cultural endeavour the Greeks discriminated as they borrowed, testing and then adapting what they acquired in the search for satisfying solutions. That which failed the test, or which seemed too arbitrary or foreign, was discarded. The motor powering this process was above all the desire for an impressive experience and visual impact. The convergence on a limited repertoire of forms facilitated comparison of like with like and so fuelled the Greeks' propensity for competitive rivalry (Ch. 9, p. 197). These forces in combination explain how it was possible for the coherence of mature temples and orders to arise out of such heterogeneous beginnings.

10.3   François Blondel, evocation of architectural invention catalysed by objects of significance, detail of **Fig. 9.3**.

The preceding summary sets out the state of play as regards those questions of origin and early development that seem capable of resolution. Details contained in the body of this book qualify these conclusions, and no doubt future advances will call for some of them to be revised. Yet the edifice as a whole, I hope, is sufficiently robust to stand. Now we may turn to questions that, for want of evidence, only provoke further questions in place of answers. Ever since Vitruvius's fictional visualization of how the Corinthian capital came into being, courtesy of Kallimachos (**Fig. 6.16**), enquiries into the origins of classical architecture have necessarily involved speculation. In the seventeenth century Blondel continued this tradition when he transposed a similar scenario to embrace things set up on columns (**Fig. 10.3**). This is hardly a vision that can be endorsed today in the literal sense. With the benefit of archaeology and scientific method we are in a better position to get nearer the truth. Yet the gaps in our knowledge remain such that speculation can still be useful in seeking to complete the picture, if only hypothetically.

What can be said of the creation of the Doric genus *in temporal terms?* Following the invention of the roof tile there arose around the middle of the seventh century a 'pioneer generation' of temples that deserve to be called monumental on account of their size, regularity and solidity of construction: notably those at Corinth, Isthmia, the Argive Heraion and, a little later, Thermon.[5] No Doric elements survive for any of these buildings, though there has been plenty of speculation in this regard (Ch. 2, pp. 50–54; Ch. 3, pp. 81–2). The earliest known instances belong to the site of Mon Repos on Corfu (*c*.610), but there is nothing to suggest that the style was born there. The advent of Doric thus occurred in the preceding decades, or perhaps during an earlier pioneer generation using perishable materials of which no traces survive. It is theoretically possible that the entire Doric *genus* was created or assembled in the course of a single project, even by a single 'hero-architect'.[6] Perhaps more likely is a short but intense bout of activity involving two or more nearly contemporary projects.[7]

What can be said of the creation of the Doric genus *in geographical terms?* Scholarly research has for some time focused on the north-east Peloponnese.[8] The Corinthians have in their favour the command, if not leadership, of key technologies: tile production, stoneworking, bronzeworking and carpentry (Ch. 2, pp. 54–5, Ch. 6, p. 151). Many early Doric temples were built either in Corinthian colonies (Corfu, Syracuse), in places under the sway of Corinth (Thermon, Delphi), or simply nearby (Aigina).[9] Mud-brick walls, timber columns and framing elements prevailed for longer in Argive territory, but there are other arguments in its favour. The Argive Heraion was an important sanctuary, and Vitruvius identifies Hera's temple there as the first of this kind. The close proximity of Bronze Age tombs could have provoked a revival of Mycenaean-inspired forms which contributed to Doric style (Ch. 4, pp. 92–3).

Mention, too, should be made of the central and western Peloponnese, including Spartan territory, though only occasionally is this region linked to the development of Doric style.[10] The Spartans continued to employ timber after it had been largely superseded by stone elsewhere, and we know of regulations restricting the use of ornament. Lycurgos, the founder of their laws, decreed that citizens could use no other tools but axes to make the roofs of their houses, and saws to make the doors.[11] One aim was to avoid luxurious display that could be a divisive source of envy, and for similar reasons Spartan girls were forbidden cosmetics. Whatever social attitudes these laws were supposed to promote (be it self-sufficiency or straightforwardness), they probably fostered details that were extrapolated from a basis in construction – in short an approach not completely unlike the ideal of Otto Wagner and others in the modern period (Ch. 3, p. 66). After all, the later Spartan King Agesilaos in effect advocated that buildings should exhibit logic and 'constructional honesty' (Ch. 3, p. 65). It may not be just a coincidence that the efforts Pausanias reports to preserve venerated wooden structures all happen to be located in the western or central Peloponnese (Olympia, Elis and Mantineia). Did builders in these regions employ a bi-partite wooden entablature comprising an epistyle-beam plus a geison or cornice articulated by projecting rafters, all bound together with dowels? Perhaps an extra layer of beams and frieze was added at some point for a project with an unusually deep porch (Ch. 9, p. 202). Does such a context lie behind Vitruvius's account of petrification?

In the Peloponnese of the seventh century, in any event, at least three distinct traditions coexisted. At the risk of over-simplifying, we may imagine the following: the Corinthians pioneering massive constructions using a higher proportion of stone; the Argives reviving a local Mycenaean heritage including friezes and capitals while relying on mud-brick, timber and limited amounts of stone; and builders in the central and western Peloponnese pursuing a construction-based language primarily using timber. Some styles and techniques would have crossed state boundaries; painted friezes typical of Geometric art along with bronze dressings were probably more common than we can guess from the meagre surviving traces. Meanwhile Aetolia made significant contributions to the development of figural ornamentation using terracotta on or near the roof (antefixes, akroteria, covers for ridge-beams, metopes or metope-like plaques).[12]

What gave Doric its panhellenic character? The possibility that Doric resulted from a lengthy trans-regional evolutionary development seems improbable given not only the absence of 'proto-Doric' stages, but also the eclectic character of the entablature, with its decorative/symbolic frieze sandwiched between a workmanlike epistyle and geison. On the other hand the hypothesis that the Doric temple was invented in a single moment implies a dominant locality, and this runs contrary to the political rivalry endemic between Greek states. Is it likely that the Corinthians would embrace a system entirely created by the Argives, or vice versa? This is not impossible, it must be admitted; wheresoever they were instigated the conventions that sculptors used for *kouroi* enjoyed widespread diffusion. Yet there is relatively clear regional differentiation in pottery styles (in spite of their geographical proximity, this is true of Attica, Aigina and Corinth, for example). It would be unwise to presume

one model or the other, and instead it is important to reflect on conditions that could have fostered diffusion. I intuit the imprimatur of some neutral superior authority in the shape of one of the great panhellenic sanctuaries, Olympia or Delphi. Both were relatively independent of any single state; both were chock-a-block with impressive dedications of the kind that influenced architectural detailing; both drew the élite from all over the Greek world. A landmark temple built at either site had access to an influential audience, perhaps to inspire them to commission something similar on returning home.

Olympia has claim to primacy by virtue of the Olympic games held there four-yearly since 776 (according to tradition), one of the greatest manifestations of Greek cultural solidarity, or 'Greekness'. Symbolic of this is the suspension of military hostilities for the duration of the games. There were clay beds for tile-making in the locality, and the site harnessed advanced capabilities in the production of architectural terracottas, bronzes and all manner of dedications. Though we know not the look of the wooden entablature of the 'Heraion' (more likely Zeus's temple), its plan is the earliest that has the canonic peripteral format.[13] Did the entablature partake of the same tradition as the wooden relics Pausanias reported (Ch. 3, pp. 67–8), whence the emergence of features like guttae?

Delphi was just as likely a cradle for the Doric temple. There could be no better place from which a ripple effect could emanate than the reputed epicentre or 'navel' of the Greek world, specifically Apollo's Delphic temple and the omphalos it sheltered.[14] This accords with Delphi's importance as the hub of Greek cultural expansion, as expressed in the practice of seeking oracular sanction for the founding of colonies, and with them new temples.[15] It happens that Apollo had more temples built to him than any other divinity in the seventh and sixth centuries, and his Delphic home would have made a fitting model for the others.[16] Despite its location up on the slopes of Mount Parnassos, Delphi had access to the latest thinking on art and building due to close relations with nearby Corinth.

It is pertinent to recall the mythical phases of the Delphic temple, said to evolve from versions made of laurel branches, then wax (or feathers), then bronze, and finally stone (Ch. 3, p. 67). This is usually interpreted as a poetic encapsulation of technological progress, or alternatively as an allusion to myths and rites associated with Delphi and Apollo (hence laurel), and modes of divination based on observing bees or birds (hence wax or feathers). A recent hypothesis sees in the penultimate bronze phase of the temple an allusion to Apollo's bronze tripod and the copious tripod dedications set up in the sanctuary.[17] Might we imagine this temple with a tripod frieze, or with a single prominent tripod in the pediment?

In any event, one version of this myth credits the design of the bronze phase to the divine crafting of Hephaistos and Athena, while another credits Hephaistos alone. The linkage between this material and divinity is intriguing since it was not only used to dress temples in the seventh century but was also the prime ingredient of so many prestigious offerings. No doubt characteristics were more prone to cross between artefacts and architecture when the medium was the same. The prestige and cost of metal vessels ensured that they were reproduced in more affordable media such as ceramic,[18] and as temple builders strove for permanence, the vulnerability of bronze revetment arguably made it too a candidate for mutation into stone. Indeed the placing of the bronze phase just before the stone one in this myth seems to give a key role to metal in the crystallization of architectural style.

Names are also given to the architects of the stone temple that followed: Trophonios and Agamedes.[19] It so happens that this pair of legendary figures is mentioned in a separate tradition involving divine and then heroic agency in the lead up to the man-made phases: first Apollo himself laid the foundations and then Trophonios and Agamedes built the first stone temple.[20] Pausanias also attributed to them a temple at Mantineia – one of the wooden structures, significantly, the remains of which were deliberately preserved. Indeed, he refers to the two architects as those 'who worked oak logs and

fitted them together'.[21] Thus their names are bound up with two critical aspects for the genesis of Doric, the petrification of perishable materials on the one hand and woodworking skills on the other. It is instructive too to note a common theme operating at another level in all these accounts: the passing on of divine architectural authority from gods to heroes to men, that is to say a mechanism for sanctioning the typology and formal resolution of the (presumably Doric) temple.[22]

The absence of established building traditions at either Olympia or Delphi (these being sanctuaries and not major centres of population) seems to fit the eclectic origination of Doric style.[23] Was the entablature of the first Doric temple created at one of these sites by taking a bipartite timber system native to the west or central Peloponnese, and adding a course of beams and/or frieze composed in a style favoured by the Argives? Was heavy stone construction capped by a tiled pedimented roof the Corinthians' contribution? Was the overlay of tripod imagery the spontaneous invention of Trophonios and/or Agamedes?

Not everything had to be determined for one project, as already noted. The initial step could have been taken at the Argive Heraion to be followed by resolution at Olympia, or vice versa; alternatively Corinth and Delphi were involved.[24] We can do no more than contemplate such combinations. In any event, further honing and abstraction then occurred in the next wave of stone temples built around 600.

What can be said of the creation of the Ionic genus *in temporal and geographical terms?* By comparison with Doric, Ionic took longer to coalesce and embraced more variety and greater regional distinctions. Over the course of the seventh century experimentation began with moulded bases, friezes and volutes in Crete, the Cyclades and Ionia. Inspired by the traditions of nearby Phoenicia and Syria, soon after the mid-century rising-volute capitals were probably introduced into Cyprus at the royal palace at Salamis (Ch. 4, p. 101). By the last quarter of the century it may be assumed that rising volutes were adapted to Greek tastes in the Cyclades or Aeolis. Aeolic capitals then went on to be used intermittently before fading from use by the end of the sixth century. Their eclipse can be attributed to the invention of the Ionic solution in the Cyclades a little before 600, which improved on the shortcomings of the Aeolic configuration. At first Ionic capitals were used on free-standing votive columns and then for temple fronts. In the second quarter of the sixth century there emerged an Ionian type that succeeded, unlike the Cycladic kind, in turning the corner and so satisfying the desire for peripteral projects (Ch. 5, p. 131). This breakthrough initiated a rich vein of formal research, which, among other things, led to the introduction of egg-and-dart and the definitive fifth-century Athenian capital. Differing regional emphases can also be traced in the entablature, the design of which remained fluid down to the Hellenistic period (Ch. 5, pp. 134–5).

From this is it clear that Ionic never represented such a coherent system as Doric. To the limited extent that it may be characterized as such, this perhaps occurred as a reaction to Doric. Awareness of the new mainland style would have spread quickly thanks to visitors to the principal sanctuaries. But whereas Doric was taken up in Dorian territories as far afield as Sicily, it was not so favourably received in spheres of Ionian predominance. There operated perhaps the perception of an ethnic divide, although this can be over-stressed; to people whose tastes had begun to be accustomed to elegant, ornamental forms, Doric may have appeared cumbersome and alien. But its power made an impact, prompting the Ionians to strive for something no less impressive.

Once again major sanctuaries were the centres of building enterprise and investment, besides being places for the concentration of votive material from which architects could learn. Given the number of early volute capitals found in the Cyclades, including Delos, it seems possible that this sacred island – the spiritual hub of the Aegean – played a comparable role for Ionic to that which Delphi or Olympia played for Doric.[25] The neighbouring Naxians, pioneers in monumental applications of marble, were as active at Delos as the Corinthians were at Delphi. Over on the Ionian coast, the peripteral plan had already been created in miniature for Artemis's temple at Ephesos, and then around 570 the first dipteros as the Samian Heraion rendered it on a colossal scale. (Here the capitals may not have been Ionic, however.) The re-building of the Ephesian Artemision went further in magnificence, becoming the model for much later practice, and in this sense justifying Vitruvius's statement that Ionic saw its first use at this site (Ch. 6, p. 142).

Saving one of the most elusive questions for last: *what explains the predominance of Doric and Ionic to the exclusion of other solutions?* The usage of columns in ancient and traditional cultures is often characterized by stylistic discipline: witness the prevalence of capitals with papyrus and lotus in Egypt. Especially dominant modes of building tend to accompany centralized state power or be imposed by conquest. Neither condition pertained in the fragmented Greek political context, yet once Doric and Ionic appeared they quickly carried all before them.

Various facets of explanation for this may be intuited, including the rapidity of the Greeks' success around 700, engendering a desire for monumentality for which the local traditions were inadequate and so ripe for total overhaul. In this context the notion of a 'Greek Renaissance' throws up useful (if necessarily limited) parallels with Italy of the fifteenth century AD, where medieval patterns of building were displaced by a completely different style. The classical manner based on the orders was taken up for civic, religious and princely commissions in places as varied as Florence, Milan, Rome and Urbino before spreading over much of Europe. The workings of fashion are only a small part of the equation compared with the values associated with the new movement. The humanist 'project' aimed at nothing less than the reconciliation of pagan and Christian cultures, while the revival of ancient Roman forms gave the enterprise a sense of mission that could be grasped by the élite and the general population alike.

In the seventh century in Greece a renaissance of sorts found its architectural complement in the revival of ancient forms conferring identity. Greeks of Dorian descent took ownership of the incipient Doric *genus*, it seems, because they believed it to emulate the style of their ancestors. As some may have argued at the time – presumably persuasively – the column recalled precedents of heroic vintage from Mycenae and its environs, the epistyle and geison perpetuated old woodworking customs, while the frieze burnished time-honoured modes of composition with the lustre of venerable tripods. A greater quotient of foreign influence qualified any intimations of nationhood that Ionic sustained; nonetheless Ionians may have felt that volutes and the like descended from Bronze Age Greeks (which, in part, they did). Here a lesser degree of conviction goes hand in hand with the greater fluidity of solutions, especially as regards the entablature.

Panhellenic endorsements emanating from Olympia, Delphi and Delos helped the Doric and Ionic architectural styles to function as kinds of cultural glue, reinforcing the more fundamental bonds of shared language and religious practices that the Greeks understood, despite their differences, to keep them distinct from the barbarian 'other'.[26] The convergence on standard conventions facilitated their competitive urges and the acting out of inter-state rivalries by means of temple building.

This is to explain Doric and Ionic temples on the social and political plane, highlighting qualities and associations that made them belong, that made the Greeks identify with them and feel they owned them. On a religious plane, meanwhile, an inverse principle was no less fundamental: that of reaching out to the numinous by the act of giving, of yielding up. The houses of the gods were also offerings to them, and this book shows that key characteristics of Greek temples spoke to this theme. Their size, cost and excellence of materials proclaimed the splendour of the gift, while the details of the orders resonated in tune with the offerings constellating the sanctuaries.

The gift operates at a deeper level too, symbolizing sentiment. Gift giving defines humanity, connecting child and parent, man and god. Any building requires dedication, a great one particularly so. In architecture as in anything else, you give in the hope of a return, uncertain, intangible or miraculous as it may be.

10.4   View of Delphi and the temple of Apollo, May 2013.

ABBREVIATIONS

Note: References to Vitruvius's treatise are generally given in the text, in round brackets, e.g., (III, 1, 5). With the exception of Vitruvius, the style of abbreviations used for ancient sources conforms to those used in *The Oxford Classical Dictionary.*

GENERAL

AA.VV.	*auctores varii* (various authors)
BM	British Museum, London
c.	century
c.	*circa*
cat.	catalogue of exhibition
con.	congress, conference, colloquium, symposium and other like terms in any language.
DAI	Deutschen Archäologischen Instituts
diss.	dissertation/thesis
ed.	edition/edited by
eds	editors
EFA	École Française d'Athènes
ENSBA	École nationale supérieure des Beaux-Arts
et al.	*et alii* (and others)
rev.	revision/revised
supp.	supplement
s.v.	*sub voce* (under the heading of)
trans.	translation/translated by

BIBLIOGRAPHICAL

AA	*Archäologischer Anzeiger*
AAA	*Αρχαιολογικά ανάλεκτα εξ Αθηνών* (*Athens Annals of Archaeology*)
ActaArch	*Acta Archaeologica* (Copenhagen)
ActaAArtH	*Acta ad Archaeologiam et Artium Historiam Pertinentia*
AJA	*American Journal of Archaeology*
AM	*Mitteilungen des Deutschen Archäologischen Instituts, Athenische Abteilung*
AnnASAtene	*Annuario della Scuola Archeologica Italiana di Atene*
AntDenk	Antike Denkmäler
AntK	*Antike Kunst*
ArchCl	*Archeologia Classica*
ArchEph	*Αρχαιολογική εφημερίς* (*Archaeological Journal*)
BABesch	*Bulletin Antieke Beschaving*
BAR	British Archaeological Reports International Series
BASOR	*Bulletin of the American Schools of Oriental Research*
BCH	*Bulletin de Correspondance Hellénique*
BEFAR	Bibliothèque des Écoles Françaises d'Athénes et de Rome
Boreas	*Boreas: Münstersche Beiträge zur Archäologie*
BSA	*Annual of the British School at Athens*
CID	Corpus des Inscriptions de Delphes
CRAI	*Comptes rendus des séances de l'Académie des Inscriptions et Belles-lettres, Paris.*
CSMG	Atti del Convegno di studi sulla Magna Grecia, Taranto
CVA	Corpus Vasorum Antiquorum
EAA	*Enciclopedia dell'Arte Antica*
EurHss	Europäische Hochschulschriften
ExpDélos	Exploration Archéologique de Délos
FdDelphes	Fouilles de Delphes, École Française d'Athènes
FiE	Forschungen in Ephesos
FRGV	Adolph Furtwängler and Karl W. Reinhold, *Griechische Vasenmalerei* (3 vols, Munich 1904–32)

GRBS	*Greek, Rome and Byzantine Studies*	OlForsch	Olympische Forschungen (Berlin)
Hephaistos	*Hephaistos. Kritische Zeitschrift zur Theorie und Praxis der Archäologie und angrenzendes Wissenschaften*	*OpAth*	*Opuscula Atheniensia. Annual of the Swedish Institute in Athens*
Hesperia	*Hesperia: The Journal of the American School of Classical Studies at Athens*	P&C	Georges Perrot and Charles J., Chipiez, *Histoire de l'Art dans l'Antiquité*, (10 vols, Paris 1882–1914)
HfMedd	*Historisk-filosofiske Meddelelser (Royal Danish Academy of Sciences and Letters)*	*Praktika*	*Πρακτικά της εν Αθήναις Αρχαιολογικής Εταιρείας (Proceedings of the Archaeological Society at Athens)*
HN	*Historia Naturalis*	*Qedem*	*Qedem: Monographs of the Institute of Archaeology, Hebrew University of Jerusalem*
IstMitt	*Istanbuler Mitteilungen* (Deutschen Archäologischen Instituts)		
IG	Inscriptiones Graecae (Berlin 1873–)	*QuadTic*	*Quaderni Ticinesi di Numismatica e Antichità classica*
JdI	*Jahrbuch des Deutschen Archäologischen Instituts*	*RA*	*Revue Archéologique*
JHS	*Journal of Hellenic Studies*	*RDAC*	*Report of the Department of Antiquities, Cyprus*
JMA	*Journal of Mediterranean Archaeology*	*RE*	*Paulys Real-Encyclopädie der classischen Altertumswissenschaft (= 'Pauly-Wissowa')*
Kerameikos	*Kerameikos. Ergebnisse der Ausgrabungen* (Munich)		
Ktema	*Ktema. Civilizations de l'Orient, de la Grèce et de Rome antiques*	*RendPontAcc*	*Atti della Pontificia Accademia romana di Archeologia*
LIMC	*Lexicon iconographicum Mythologiae classicae* (Zurich and Munich 1981–)	*RES*	*Anthropology and Aesthetics*
LL&R	Enzo Lippolis, Monica Livadiotti and Giorgio Rocco, *Architettura greca: storia e monumenti del mondo della polis dalle origini al V secolo* (Milan 2007)	*RM*	*Mitteilungen des Deutschen Archäologischen Instituts, Römische Abteilung*
		SIMA	Studies in Mediterranean Archaeology
MarburgWP	Marburger Winckelmann-Programm	*SkrAth*	*Skrifter utgivna av Svenska Institutet i Athen, 8th series*
MonAnt	*Monumenti antichi*	*ThesCRA*	*Thesaurus Cultus et Rituum Antiquorum. Lexikon antiker Kulte und Riten* (Los Angeles 2004–)
MüJb	*Münchner Jahrbuch der bildenden Kunst*		
ÖJh	*Jahreshefte des Österreichen Archäologischen Institutes in Wein*	*Xenia*	*Xenia: Konstanzer Althistorische Vorträge und Forschungen*
OlBericht	Bericht über die Ausgrabungen in Olympia		

NOTES TO THE TEXT

PREFACE

1 Ian McEwan, *Enduring Love* (London 2006, 17), adding that 'A beginning is an artifice, and what recommends one over another is how much sense it makes of what follows.' The novel concerns stalking (De Clérambault's syndrome).

2 Charles Darwin, letter to Alfred Russel Wallace, 22 December 1857 (*The Life and Letters of Charles Darwin*, ed. Francis Darwin (3 vols, London 1885), II, 108).

3 At the time he wrote this, Ventris was a student at the iconoclastic Architectural Association in London, and since the age of fourteen he lived in Berthold Lubetkin's Highpoint apartment complex, perhaps the most progressive of all British experiments with the theories of Le Corbusier. Mauss 1990 [1950]; Sahlins 1972; Godelier 1996.

4 Hyde 1979.

5 Ruskin 1849, ch. 1.

6 Lutyens, letter to Herbert Baker dated 29 June 1911; cf. Christopher Hussey, *The Life of Sir Edwin Lutyens* (Country Life ed., London 1950 (facsimile 1984)), 133.

7 Patti Smith, *Just Kids* (New York 2010), ix.

INTRODUCTION

1 The interpretation of architecture using linguistic analogies has its roots in Renaissance Italy (Payne 2000, 150). The metaphor was extended in the eighteenth century by figures such as Germain Boffrand and Quatremère de Quincy (Lavin 1992), becoming commonplace in twentieth-century architectural history and criticism, to cite just two books out of many, John Summerson's *The Classical Language of Architecture* (1963) and Charles Jencks's *The Language of Post-Modern Architecture* (London 1977). The parallel goes beyond classical forms, as illustrated by a quotation of Mies van der Rohe: 'I'm working on architecture as a language, and I think you have to have a grammar in order to have a language. You can use it, you know, for normal purposes, and you speak in prose. And if you are good at that, you speak a wonderful prose. And if you are really good, you can be a poet.' See Whyte 2006 for related notions including 'reading' and 'translating'.

2 McEwen 1993, 123–30; Hahn 2001; idem 2010.

3 Hellström 1988; idem 1994; Wilson Jones 2000a, ch. 6. See also Raubitschek, I, 1950; Ortolani 1997.

4 *Genus* was used in fifteenth-century Italy, along with *costume, maniera, modus, sorte* and *specie*. It was Raphael, or a collaborator, who first adopted *ordine*, which became translated as 'order': see Rowland 1994; Rykwert 1996, 4; Wilson Jones 2000a, 109. See also Forssman 1961; Bruschi 1992; and other essays in AA.VV. 1992f.

5 The Composite capital, a fusion of Corinthian with Ionic, was initially created in the late Hellenistic period: see Strong 1960; Pauwels 1989; Corso and Romano 1997, I, 440–41, n. 80. In antiquity it never commanded its own entablature, in contrast to efforts to assign one to it in the sixteenth century, when Sebastiano Serlio adopted the term 'Composite'.

6 Vitruvius referred to Tuscan as a *genus* only once, otherwise using 'manner', 'dispositions' and 'work', see III, 3.5 (*tuscanico more*); IV, 6.6 (*tuscanicis dispositionibus*); IV, 8.5 (*tuscanicis generibus* and *tuscanicorum . . . operum*). For commentary see Morolli 1985a, esp. 50; idem 1985b; Corso and Romano 1997, I, 493, n. 230.

7 For introductions to Vitruvius and associated scholarship see Pollitt 1974, 66–70; Romano 1987; Germann 1991; Howe and Rowland 1996; Gros 1997; idem 2006; Corso and Romano 1997; Wilson Jones 2000a, ch. 2; McEwen 2003; Gordon Smith 2003; Schofield and Tavernor 2009.

8 In his famous *Ordonnance* of 1683 Claude Perrault distinguished between 'positive' or objective properties (such as the quality of materials) and 'arbitrary' ones such as proportions. See Herrmann 1973; Rykwert 1980, ch. 2; Perez-Gomez 1984, 18ff.; Picon 1992, 39–41, 54–61, 96–8. Perrault's analysis of Roman columns caused him to reject their proportional basis, which eluded him, see Wilson Jones 2000a, 2–6, ch. 7.

9 Picon 1992: on legitimacy 256–60, on functionality 135–9, 146–9, 312–16.

10 Condillac, Hume, Locke and Rousseau are the best known protagonists of this debate; note too the title of Goguet's *De l'Origine des Loix, des Arts, et des Sciences; et de leurs Progrès chez les anciens Peuples* (Paris 1758). For architectural consequences see Watkin 1996, 114–15, 159–64; Lavin 1992, ch. 1.

11 Lodoli did not publish, but his ideas were divulgated by the writings of Francesco Algarotti (1756) and Andrea Memmo (1786). Other publications of note include those by the Comte de Caylus (1756), William Chambers (1759),

Giovanbattista Piranesi (1765), Jacques-François Blondel (1771–7), Francesco Milizia (1781) and Viel de Saint-Maux (1787).

12 Wiebenson 1969, chs 1 and 2; Tsigakou 1981; Hellmann *et al.* 1983; Middleton and Watkin 1987, 65–9; Etienne and Etienne 1992; Raspi-Serra 1998; Le Roy 2004 [1770]; Susan Weber Soros, *James 'Athenian Stuart', 1713–1788: The Rediscovery of Antiquity* (New Haven and London 2006); Georgopoulou *et al.* 2007; Christopher D. Armstrong, *Julien-David Leroy and the Making of Architectural History* (London 2011).

13 Raspi-Serra 1986; de Jong 2010.

14 Other significant publications include those by Alois Hirt (1821; 1823), Joseph Gwilt (1825), Jean-François Champollion (1833), Augustus Welby Pugin (1841), J. A. S. Fergusson (1849; 1855 and later), F. von Reber (1866; 1898), Jacques-Ignaz Hittorff (1851; Hittorff and Zanth 1870), Joseph Bühlmann (1872–7). For commentary see Weickenmeier 1985, ch. 3.

15 Gruben 2007, 32–65; Barletta 2011, 615–19.

16 Note various works by Coulton, Gruben, Korres, Martin, Mertens and Wesenberg. For a balanced review of 'The Problem of Beginning' see Coulton 1977, ch. 2. Perhaps the most important advance with respect to earlier accounts of the orders has been the discovery of the Cycladic branch of Ionic design (Ch. 5).

17 Onians 1988a (with a reprise, idem 1999, 26–47); Hersey 1988; Rykwert 1996; McEwen 1993; Barletta 2001. In the 1980s two important dissertations also appeared: Thomas Howe's on the origins of Doric (Howe 1985) and Norbert Weickenmeier's on that of its frieze alone (Weickenmeier 1985). See also Mazarakis Ainian 1997 on developments in Iron Age Greece.

18 Hölbl 1984; Ditlefsen 1985; Schwandner 1985; Mertens 1993; Holmes 1995; Fehr 1996; Mussche 1997; Hoffelner 1999; AA.VV. 2001a; Laroche 2001; Kienast 2002a; Wilson Jones 2002a; Rhodes 2003; Østby 2006; Kyrieleis 2008; Wesenberg 2008; Barletta 2009.

19 Recent architectural manuals include Hellmann 2002; eadem 2006; Mertens 2006; Spawforth 2006; Lippolis *et al.* 2007.

20 Xenophanes, frag. 15; cf. Dodds 1964, the chapter 'Rationalism and Reaction in the Classical Age', esp. p. 181.

21 In this the ideas of Friedrich Nietzsche, Bertrand Russell and Karl Popper seem particularly significant: see B. Russell, *An Outline of Philosophy* (London 1927), ch. 3; Alexander Nehamas, *Nietzsche: Life as Literature* (Cambridge, Mass., 1985), 1–2 and ch. 2 (42–73) on Nietzsche's 'perspectivism'; Sourvinou-Inwood 1991, 4, 10.

22 Giedion 1941, 5; cf. Wilson Jones 2000a, 1–6. For debate see *Rethinking History* 4, no. 3 (December 2000), including Hayden White's 'An Old Question Raised Again: Is Historiography Art or Science?', 391–406.

23 Howe 1985, 5–7.

24 The observation of polychromy on Greek architecture goes back to Stuart and Revett (Korres 1999, 173–4). Yet it was only after Quatremère de Quincy's work on sculpture that systematic treatments of architecture followed, most notably by Hittorff (1851; Hittorff and Zanth 1870) and by Semper (1989, 2–16, 45–73, 75–101). For recent appraisals and discoveries see Summitt 2000; Hellmann 2002, ch. 11; Tiverios and Tsiaphake 2002; Brinkmann and Wünsche 2004; Jenkins 2006, 34–44; Marconi 2006.

25 'Eine der vornehmsten Aufgaben der Lehre ist es, den Sinn für die Vergangenheit zu wecken und gleichzeitig den Ausblick auf die Zukunft zu öffnen. Auf diese Art darf sie historisch sein: da sie die Verbindungen herstellt zwischen dem, was gewesen ist, dem, was ist, und dem, was mutmaßlich sein wird.' (Arnold Schönberg, *Harmonielehre* (Vienna 1922), 31; author's translation.)

26 Howe 1985, 1–11, 29–50; Weickenmeier 1985; Forster 1996.

27 Such ideas used generally to go unchallenged, but not so in recent times. For example, the architect David Chipperfield (*Theoretical Practice* (London 1994, 22)) notes how 'Creeds such as "form follows function", "truth to materials" and "clarity of structure" became the mumbled justifications of ill-considered decisions.' See also Watkin 2001 [1977].

28 In the eighteenth and nineteenth centuries Doric was frequently held to be more significant or essential than the other orders. As Quatremère de Quincy put it, 'to deal with the origin of this order is to go back to the very birth of art' (1832 s.v. 'Doric', trans. Younés 1999, 146). Rykwert (1996, 9–11) shows that critics such as Jacob Burckhardt held Doric to be the 'order of orders', a sentiment shared by Perrot and Chipiez (P&C VII, ch. 5). As Barletta (2001, 2) notes, there is some justification for this position in Vitruvius's text.

29 Howe 1985, iv, 1–2; Forster 1996. See also Rykwert 1996, 16–24, 27; Watkin 2001 [1977].

30 The Comte de Caylus broached the idea in general terms (1756, esp. 308), while hints by Memmo suggest that Lodoli thought along similar lines. Further suggestion came from Blondel (1771–7, I, 193) and a letter by Antonio Paoli to Carlo Fea published in Fea's edition of Winckelmann in 1784 (Rykwert 1972, 50–51; Barletta 2001, 162, n. 84). Paoli and other Italians, including Piranesi (2002 [1765]), convinced themselves that Egyptian influence came to Rome via the Etruscans. Quatremère de Quincy (1803, part 3, 263–6) admitted a relatively limited influence.

31 In an excursus in his edition of Chambers's treatise, Joseph Gwilt (1825, 37–40) included a text by Barry that takes the columns at 'Benihassan' and other features to 'clearly point to Egypt as the source of both Greek and Roman Architecture'. The term proto-Doric is accredited to Champollion (1833, 28, 42, 75; cf. Barletta 2001 (n. 85 on 162).

32 Villalpando and Prado 1596–1604. Some of the ideas may

have come from Juan de Herrera, architect of the Escorial in Madrid; see Rykwert 1972, 121–37; idem 1996, 27–9; Morolli 1985b, 92ff.; Ramirez 1991. In the eighteenth century curiosity was whetted by Johann Bernhard Fischer von Erlach's inclusion of Asiatic buildings (fantastical as they may be) in his *Entwurff einer historischen Architektur* (Leipzig 1725), and Richard Pococke's digest of his voyages in the years 1737–42 (Pockocke 1743–5).

33 Pausanias II, 16.5–7; Boardman 2002, 47–52, T.218. For an example of such labels in use before the time of Schliemann see Gwilt 1825, 20.

34 Schliemann 1878; Dörpfeld 1886; Wace 1949. See also Trail 1995.

35 For Riegl [1893], viii (Quintavalle 1981, 16) 'there is nothing to make us suppose *a priori* that the oldest geometric decorations are linked to particular techniques, and especially those of the art of weaving . . . In fact, the need to adorn the body . . . [is] far more primary than the need to protect it with woven products. Decorations which serve no other purpose than that of fulfilling the desire for ornament, including linear and geometric forms, appear long before the art of weaving originates.' In this Riegl was to some extent prefigured by Owen Jones (1856, 13–14).

36 Nancy Etcoff, *Survival of the Prettiest. The Science of Beauty* (New York and London 1999), 9.

37 Though the notion of architecture as frozen music is generally attributed to Goethe, Hegel gave credit for it to Friedrich von Schlegl, while Madame de Staël claimed it as hers: see Rykwert 2008, 135.

38 Wood 1741.

39 Venturi 1966.

40 C. Geertz, *Negara: The Theater State in Nineteenth-century Bali* (Princeton, N.J., 1980), 135–6 (cf. Morris, I. 1993, 27). See also Geertz 1973.

41 Evelyn Fox Keller, *The Mirage of a Space between Nature and Nurture* (Durham, N.C., 2010).

42 Some early Doric shafts have 16 facets rather than the 20 flutes that became canonic, and 16 can reappear later when relatively poor stones were used. For further practical considerations see Claridge 1983; Wilson Jones 2000a, 7, 11; Barletta 2001, 62; Pfaff 2003, 96.

43 Harry Charrington and Vezio Neva, *Alvar Aalto: The Mark of the Hand* (Helsinki 2011), 236. This was Aalto's rebuff to an implied criticism of his proposals to use columns in a non-structural capacity.

44 Durkheim 1915, 15; see also Dominick LaCapra, *Émile Durkheim: Sociologist and Philosopher* (Chicago 1985).

45 Vernant 1982, 102.

46 Foucault 1984, 79, quoting Nietzsche, *The Wanderer and his Shadow* (1880), 3. See above, n. 21.

47 Foucault 1984, 80.

48 For a survey of recent research into Greek architecture see Barletta 2011.

CHAPTER ONE

1 Tomlinson 1976, 16–17; Marconi 2004, 212; idem 2007, 2; Barletta 2011, esp. 621–6. Osborne (2009, 2) traces the decontextualization of Greek art to Roman times, when so much of it was removed from sanctuaries. In the nineteenth century a more contextual approach came naturally to Hittorff and Semper (1851, 29).

2 Vincent Scully (1969) popularized the idea that temples were sited in sympathy with views to/from natural landmarks; this is usually dismissed by specialists, but for a more sympathetic reception see Whitley 2001, 147–8.

3 Van Baal 1976; AA.VV. 1981a; Jameson 1988; Bremmer 1996; on prayer in particular see Graf 1991; Pulleyn 1997. For introductions to Greek religion see Dietrich 1974; AA.VV. 1985; Ferguson 1989; Burkert 1985; Bruit Zaidman and Schmitt Pantel 1992; Bremmer 1994; Garland 1994; Price 1999; Mikalson 2005; Ogden 2007.

4 In domestic contexts the slaughtering of an animal and its consumption could be accompanied by informal ritualistic actions and prayers, as on the occasion of Eumaeus's sacrifice [*Odyssey* XIV, 414–56].

5 General studies of Greek sanctuaries: Berve and Gruben 1963; Bergquist 1967; Tomlinson 1976; Langdon 1993; de Polignac 1995a; Graf 1996; Whitley 2001, chs 7, 9 and 12; Emerson 2007. Collected essays: AA.VV. 1991b; AA.VV. 1992d; AA.VV. 1993; AA.VV. 1994. For further bibliography see Østby 1993, and on Roman sanctuaries see Stambaugh 1978, 568–74.

6 Thucydides VII, 77.7; cf. Plutarch *Apophthegmata Laconica*, 210e. In her *The Human Condition* (Chicago, Ill., 1958, 198) Hannah Arendt observed, 'The *polis*, properly speaking, is not the city-state in its physical location; it is the organization of the people . . . and its true space lies between people living together for this purpose, no matter where they happen to be.' See also Murray 1988; idem 1990 (esp. p. 1, from where this quotation was taken). On the other hand, Hansen (M. H. 1993, 7) observes that the citizen-state concept 'does not do justice to polis in the sense of an urban community'. For literature on the *polis* see the publications of the Copenhagen Polis Centre (AA.VV. 1993f; AA. VV. 1995a; Hansen, M. H. 1995; idem 2006), and also Starr 1986; Sakellariou, M. 1989; AA.VV. 1993d; AA.VV. 1996c; AA.VV. 1997a.

7 Sourvinou-Inwood 1990; Burkert 1992b, 533; idem 1995, 202–3; Klindt 2009 (with caveats). See also Burkert 1985; Bruit Zaidman and Schmitt Pantel 1992; Bremmer 1994.

8 The terms 'priest' and 'priestess' can only approximately be transposed to the Greek context, and there was no equivalent of the Bible or Koran. See Beard and North 1990; Pirenne-Delforge 2005; Connolly 2007. On sacred laws and regulations see Lupu 2005.

9 Morgan 1997, 2003; Freitag *et al.* 2006. See also Hall 2002.

10 Mossé 1969; Andrewes 1974; Young 1980; Shapiro 1989; McGlew 1993; Mieth 1993; AA.VV. 2009c, ch. 6.

11 Snodgrass 1971, esp. 419–22; Coldstream 1977, 317–22; Morgan 1990; Osborne 1996, 88–98; Whitley 2001, 134–50.

12 de Polignac 1995a; Pedley 2005, esp. ch. 4. For qualification see Langdon, M. 1997, 122–3; Whitley 2001, 150. See also AA.VV. 1992d.

13 On Panhellenism see Rolley 1983; Morgan 1990; eadem 1993; Bruit Zaidman and Schmitt Pantel 1992, ch. 11; Yalouris 1995. On athletics and the Olympic games see AA.VV. 1988c; AA.VV. 1989; AA.VV. 1992b; AA. VV. 1997c; Miller, Stephen 2004; König 2010. On the buildings of Olympia see Adler 1892. On Delphi see Price 1985; Parke and Wormell 1956; Malkin 1987; idem 2000; Maass 1993, and for the games there Fontenrose 1988a. Isthmia and Nemea came later to acquire panhellenic status: for Isthmia see Gebhard 1993; for Nemea see Miller, Stella 1988; Miller, Stephen 1990. In the Aegean the sacred island of Delos had an almost comparable status. On festivals see Simon 1961; Pickard-Cambridge 1968; Osborne 1993; de Polignac 2009.

14 Argos: Hall 1995; de Polignac 1994; idem 1995a, 33–41. Samos: Pedley 2005, ch. 10.

15 The monumentalization of the agora did not occur until the sixth century, see Morgan and Coulton 1997.

16 Martienssen 1956, 63–4; Tomlinson 1976, 16–17.

17 On sacred groves and gardens in sanctuaries see Cazenove 1993; Birge 1994; Bonnechere 2007; Carroll 2007.

18 For contrasting approaches to location see Doxiadis 1972; Scully 1969; Schachter in AA.VV. 1992d; Martienssen 1956, s.6; de Polignac 1995a; Marconi 2007, 28.

19 Dinsmoor Jr. 1980, 31–4; Gebhard 1993, 160. On *perirrhanteria* see Ducat 1964; Boardman 1978, 25–6; Herrmann K. 1994; Pimpl 1997; Kerschner 1996. On purification see Parker 1983.

20 Bergquist 1967, 5; Goldstein 1978, 296–9.

21 Kienast 2002a, 324–5. See also Tomlinson 1976, 39–40.

22 Buschor and Schleif 1933; Schleif 1933. A tenth-century date has been proposed for the earliest altar at Samos, but for doubts see Rupp 1983, 102, 107.

23 Pausanias V, 13–15. Evidence of cult and craft activity at Olympia goes back to the tenth century, see Heilmeyer 1969; idem 1979; Morgan 1993, 20–27; Himmelmann 2002; Kyrieleis 2006.

24 Van Straten 1988; idem 1995; Mylonopoulos 2006, 72, 77–8. See also Ch. 6, n. 63.

25 There was no single 'correct' procedure, rather numerous local variations. For an extended description of sacrificial rite see *Odyssey* III, 436–63. For recent scholarship see Burkert 1966; idem 1983 (esp. 3–7); idem 1985, 55–7; AA.VV. 1981b; Jameson 1983; Durand, J.-L. 1986, esp. ch. 4; idem 1987; AA.VV. 1988b; Detienne and Vernant 1989; Durand and Schnapp 1989; AA.VV. 1991c; Étienne 1992; Bowie 1995; van Straten 1995; Ekroth 2005. On regulations governing the apportionment of the parts of the animal between the gods, officials and celebrants see Petropoulou 1984.

26 There are plenty of exceptions, as indicated by the north arrows accompanying plans in Chapter 2; see also Bergquist 1967, 72–80, 112–14. On the Athenian Acropolis the non-alignment of Athena's altar with the Erechtheion and the Parthenon is explained by the prior existence of the temple of Athena Polias in between.

27 Yavis 1949, 75–7, 86, 224–6; Roux 1984, 165; Kaminski 1991; Hollinshead 1999, 200–02, 204.

28 Pausanias V, 3.8–11; Schleif 1934; Yavis 1949, 208–13; Rupp 1983, 101–2; Étienne 1992, 292–7; Rykwert 1996, 147; Whitley 2001, 134 and fig. 7.1; Hellmann 2006, 127–8. The form as well as the location of Zeus's ash altar remains unverified.

29 Schleif 1933; Yavis 1949, 96–8, 118–20; Kienast 1991. Part of the cornice moulding survives in the Roman re-building.

30 Yavis 1949, 189.

31 Yavis 1949 (who divides twenty-five variants into eight classes which can partly overlap, see p. 55); Şahin 1972; Rupp 1974; idem 1983; Mertens 1991; Étienne 1992. For representations on vases see Rupp 1991; Aktseli 1996.

32 Wiegand 1915; Yavis 1949, 102–3. See also Ohnesorg 2005.

33 Yavis 1949, 197–9; Şahin 1972, ch. 6; Hoepfner 1989.

34 Van Baal 1976; Burkert 1985, 66, 68–9; idem 1988, 36; AA.VV. 1981a. In the introduction to the latter volume Versnel (p. xi) views offerings and sacrifices as connecting with the gods by the way of action, in contradistinction to the way of the word that is prayer and oracular consultation. See also Bremmer 1996.

35 van Baal 1976, 161, cf. 178; Burkert 1987; idem 1996b, 149–52; Linders 1987, 119–20; Patera 2012.

36 A passage in the *Iliad* recounts how, as the Greeks were on the verge of taking Troy, Hekabe and her attendants sought to move Athena to save the city and its children by a visit to her temple and the gift of the queen's most treasured robe with the promise to sacrifice twelve sleek heifers [*Iliad* VI, 86–96, 269–311].

37 Mauss 1990 [1950], ch. 1, section 4; Finley 1956, 68–70, 106–8; Sahlins 1972, chapter entitled 'The Spirit of the Gift'; van Baal 1976, esp. 161, 178; Hyde 1979; Gordon 1979, 18; van Straten 1981; Coldstream 1983; essays by Burkert, Langdon and Linders in AA.VV. 1987; Burkert 1996b, esp. 149–52; Bremmer 1996. Whitley (2001, 140) notes that the nature of the exchange was more subtle than that implied by the formula *do ut des* ('I give so that you may give'); likewise Mikalson 2005, 26–7; Patera 2012, 57–70. See also Satlow 2013.

38 Boston, Museum of Fine Art, inv. 03.997; van Straten 1981, 73; Burkert 1996b, 129. See also Pulleyn 1997, 41. The statuette may originally have decorated the rim of a tripod, see Papalexandrou 2005, 81, 84–6.

39 Kendrick-Pritchett 1971, 93–100.

40 Burkert 1985, 69; Keesling 1995, 413–15; eadem 2003, 4–6.

Inscriptions often make vows explicit, but in their absence it is better to use the more general terms 'offering' and 'dedication' (Brulotte 1994, 9–14, esp. 10). I reserve the latter for larger, free-standing offerings but for convenience use votive as an adjective.

41   On affordability see Keesling 1995, ch. 7.

42   Rouse 1902 (yet to be superseded as a general study); van Straten 1981; idem 1992; Brommer 1985 (lists of offerings attested by written sources); Burkert 1985, 68–70, 92–5; idem 1987; Linders 1987; Aleshire 1992; Harris 1995; Osborne 1996, 92–8, 207–11; Hollinshead 1999; Hamilton 2000; Whitley 2001, 140–46; *ThesCRA* I (2004), s.2; AA.VV. 2009d. For armour see Jackson 1991; for ship dedications see Herodotus III, 59; VIII, 121; Rouse 1902, 105; Blackman 2001; Wescoat 2005. Rich hoards can be found from even relatively modest temples; the small rear room of an Archaic temple on Kythnos has recently yielded more than a thousand items, including figurines, beads, corals, ostrich eggs, seals, ivories, bronze ornaments, jewels and seashells: see Mazarakis Ainian 2005.

43   AA.VV. 1987; Ampolo 1989–90; Snodgrass 1989–90; AA.VV. 1992e; Whitley 2001, 141–6.

44   Olympia: Furtwängler 1890; Willemsen 1955; Herrmann H. V. 1972; idem 1972b; Maass 1978; Borell and Rittig 1998; Himmelmann 2002; Guralnick 2004. Samos: Jantzen 1972; Walter 1976; Kyrieleis 1979; Brize 1997.

45   Gjerstad 1948; Karageorghis 2002, 183–7.

46   Morris 2000, 273. Totals of tens of thousands can be estimated for some small classes of item. For changing numbers over time see Snodgrass 1980, 52–4; Osborne 1996, 92–5.

47   Burkert 1985, 92–3; van Straten 1992, 248; Keesling 2003, 3, 11.

48   Snodgrass 1989–90; Marconi 2004, 218. Mylonopoulos (2006, 87–9) speaks of a 'war of monuments' between competing states.

49   Philipp 1968, 103–8; Lazzarini 1976, 95–8; Donohue 1988, 25–7; Keesling 2003, 10; Stieber 2004, 21–3.

50   Herodotus III, 47; Pliny the Elder, *HN*, XIX, 2 (who cites 365 strands); Shaya 2005, 431, 432, 435.

51   Tomlinson 1976, 20; Whitley 2001, 136; Shaya 2005.

52   On Pausanias's enterprise see Arafat 1996; Alcock 2002; Georgopoulou *et al.* 2007. The term *theoria* could mean both going to a sanctuary and beholding, see Marconi 2004, 224.

53   'L'architecture grecque est née dans les sanctuaires et pour les sanctuaires' (Roux 1984, 153). For introductions to the Greek temple and its functions see Berve and Gruben 1963; Coldstream 1985; Burkert 1988; Mazarakis-Ainian 1988; Gruben 1996; idem 2001; Spawforth 2006; Hellmann 2006, 18ff.

54   For early appreciation of this point see Gwilt 1825, 22–3. For recent scholarship see Holloway 1973, 53; Burkert 1985, 85–

8; idem 1992b, 535; Sourvinou-Inwood 1993, 10–11; Mazarakis Ainian 1997, 383; Svenson-Evers 1997, 136; Whitley 2001, 134; de Polignac 2009, 427. The priority of the altar over the temple is also manifest in patterns of re-building. Successive altars typically maintain orientation on the same spot, rooted by its sanctity (Yavis 1949, 57). Temples had more latitude for relocation.

55   Langdon, M. K., 1976. Zeus's temple at Olympia dates to the fifth century, but it is likely that the earlier 'Heraion' was sacred to Zeus or perhaps to both Zeus and Hera (Moustaka 2002, esp. 204).

56   Carapanos 1878; Cook A. 1902, 5–28; James 1966, 28–9; Treadwell 1970; Dakaris 1971; Gartziou-Tatti 1990; Vokotopoulou 1995; Dieterle 2007. Sanctuaries of Aphrodite typically had neither temples nor large cult-statues until Hellenistic times.

57   Svenson-Evers 1997; Mazarakis Ainian 1997, 340–49, 384.

58   Snodgrass 1980, 33–4, 58–64; Hurwit 1985, 77; Murray 1988, esp. 443–6; Burkert 1988, 39–42; idem 1992b, 538–9; idem 1995, 205–7; Morgan 1996; Fehr 1996; Höcker 1996. But for a caveat against too literal an equation of temple and *polis* see Morgan and Coulton 1997, 110. It has been said, metaphorically, that temples replaced the palace-complexes of the Bronze Age, or as Victor Ehrenberg (1965, 19) put it, the god became the monarch.

59   Burkert 1988, 27; idem 1992b, 536.

60   Herodotus VIII, 144.

61   On the Telesterion see Table 2 and Burkert 1985, 285–90. It is not certain it was a temple.

62   As with most generalizations about Greek religion and architecture there are inevitable exceptions. Not all temples are certain to have had a cult or focal statue, with some being 'empty' in these terms, see Miller J. 1996; Ridgway 2005, 112.

63   For a mid-sixth-century marble model from Sardis showing a goddess framed in the door of her shrine/temple see Hanfmann 1975, 12, figs 23–6; Boardman 1999, figs 61, 109. For a Protogeometric round model from Archanes framing a (?)god see Sakellarakis and Sapouna-Sakellaraki 1997, 566–7, though this may have represented a tholos tomb and not a temple.

64   For ancient use of *hekatompedon* or *hekatompedos* see Tölle-Kastenbein 1993, 43. Kalpaxis (1976, esp. 32) equates buildings in the region of 30 m long with *hekatompeda* on the basis that, in later periods, Greek foot measures ranged between 290 and 350 mm. Units of *c.*294 and 327 mm are the most common, see Wilson Jones 2000b.

65   A further term, *hieron* ('something sacred'), could refer to an offering or a cult instrument or indeed an entire sanctuary.

66   *Iliad*, II, 546–51. For the possibility that the 'Heraion' at Olympia was shared by Zeus and Hera see n. 55 above.

67   The designation *hedos*, literally 'that which is made to sit',

implies the taking up of residence, see Burkert 1988, 32 (cf. idem 1985, 89), and Nagy 1998. Texts and images can give different signals. The story of Hekabe's supplication to Athena (see n. 36 above) suggests that her statue, the famous Palladion, was seated, given that a robe could be laid on the knees. But in vase paintings the statue is often shown standing (**Fig. 1.15**).

68 The wide stone base at the end of the nave of the Heraion at Olympia perhaps lodged both a seated Hera and a standing Zeus, see Pausanias V, 17.1. Axial files of columns persisted somewhat later at some sites, e.g., Metropolis.

69 Burkert 1988, 33, 43; Miller, J. 1995, 205–16, esp. 216; Donohue 1997, esp. 31–4, 37, 43; Nick 2002, 79–88, 158–76; Keesling 2003, 14; Ridgway 2005, 111–12; Prost 2009; Mylonopoulos 2010. For the Roman period see Stewart 2003.

70 Romano, I. 1980, 411–19; eadem 1988; Mansfield 1985, ch. 7 (438–587). For representations of cult images see De Cesare 1997; Oenbrink 1997; Nick 2002; *ThesCRA* II (2004), s.5. As with Christian images that supposedly weep tears or blood there was a gamut of responses and beliefs. There is also a literary topos of the statues of mortals 'coming alive': see Gordon 1979; Marconi 2009b, 8–9, 12–13.

71 Graf 1996b; Broder 2008. Notable in the Roman context are temple-theatre complexes (Gabii, Palestrina, the Theatre of Pompey in Rome), and temples lining processional routes.

72 For depictions on vase paintings see *LIMC s.v.* Ilioupersis; Oenbrink 1997, cat. A3–A9, A12, A14–A24 (Taf. 1–6); Nick 2002, Taf. 1–2. See also Connelly 1993.

73 Herodotus VI, 91. On asylum and the related concept of supplication (*hiketeia*) see Sinn 1993.

74 A building on a fortified summit near Smari on Crete could have been either a ruler's residence or a temple, or some conflation of the two. The only certainty is that before its destruction in the seventh century there was communal dining, given animal bone deposits, a central hearth and a bench around the interior. See Mazarakis Ainian 1988, 109; idem 1997, 220–22.

75 For references see **Table 2**, pp. 38–9.

76 D'Acunto 2002–3.

77 *Hestiatoria* could be numerous; by the end of the sixth century at the sanctuary of Demeter and Kore at Corinth there were some 14 dining rooms accommodating 100 people or more, see Bookidis 1993; Mylonopoulos 2006, 80–84. On the architecture of dining see Goldstein 1978; Börker 1983; Schmitt Pantel 1992; Leypold 2008, esp. 202–6 in relation to early temples.

78 Assessing the evidence can be problematic. The unusually elongated seventh-century 'temple of Apollo' (27.30 × 4.46 m) at Halieis (modern Porto Cheli) on the Argolid coast has been interpreted as a temple with three compartments, one for the cult statue, one for dining (the findspot of copious goat horns and pig bones), one for storing offerings (including thousands of miniature cups): see Maza-

rakis Ainian 1988, 118; idem 1997, 162–4. But Bergquist (1990) argues that only in the fourth century was a temple function added to the original dining function.

79 *Odyssey* 12.345–7.

80 Mazarakis Ainian 1997, 383. Apart from excavation, our knowledge of the offerings held in temples comes from inventories and from texts by writers such as Herodotus, Cicero and Pausanias (see Ch. 8).

81 On treasuries see Dinsmoor 1913; Couch 1929; Rups 1986; Behrens-du Maire 1993; Laroche and Nenna 1993; Partida 2000 (who stresses the non-utilitarian, dedicatory aspect); Hölscher 2001; Marconi 2006 (who underlines the dual role as votive container and votive *per se*, esp. 159). For individual treasuries at Delphi see Audiat 1933; Michaud 1973; Daux and Hansen 1987. On the relationship between temples and treasuries see Roux 1984, 154–9.

82 Büsing 1994. Contrariwise the early fifth-century temple of Artemis at Delion on Paros, with its distyle-in-antis plan and modest dimensions, looked just like a treasury (Schuller 1991). It is chiefly the presence of the altar in front that marks it as a temple. Some see the Parthenon as a treasury as much as a temple: Preisshofen 1984; Roux 1984, 159–62; Hurwit 2000, 27; Nick 2002, 119–32.

83 Bogaert 1968, 279–304. See also Ampolo 1989–90; Linders 1989–90; eadem 1987 (with qualification, for votives were of course also demonstrations of piety and status); eadem 1992; Bremmer 1994, 32.

84 Perikles cited 'gold and silver in private and public dedications', and even the gold on Athena Parthenos, that could in an emergency be 'borrowed', to be returned once it had passed (Thucydides, 2.13.5).

85 *Adyton* was the name given to the open-air court of the Didymaion. Both this label and *opisthodomos*, literally a place behind a house or temple, sometimes applied to non-temple structures. On terminology see Casevitz 1984; Hollinshead 1999. For *adyton* see Thalmann 1976, 2–20; Hollinshead 1999, 190–95, esp. 193 on Didyma; for *opisthodomos* see *ibid.* 210–13.

86 I Kings 6–8; II Chronicles 2–4; Isidore of Seville, *Etymologiae (Origines)* XV 4.3–5. Hollinshead examines modifications of temple interiors subsequent to their original construction (1999, 202–4), concluding that such works were typically aimed at improving safe storage rather than cultic activity. Her research points to 'a larger economic role for many temples and less secret ritual than has been assumed' (189).

87 Thalmann 1976, 2–3, 179–82; Hollinshead 1999, esp. 190–94. For a rear room evidently chock-full of votives see n. 42. above. On settings for oracles see Friese 2010.

88 Herodas, *Mime* 4; Manakidou 1993, 18–40; Hollinshead 1999, 207.

89 Hollinshead 1999, 209–10; Mylonopoulos 2011. On the grilles of the Hephaisteion in Athens see Stevens 1950.

90 Burkert 1988, 43–4; idem 1992b, 540; idem 1996, esp. 24–5. Kähler (1949, 10) sees the triple-stepped stylobate as holding up the temple 'wie ein Weihgeschenk'. See also Tomlinson 1976, 18; Stewart 1990, 46, who writes of temples as 'quasi-votives'; *ThesCRA* I (2004), s.2, 271 on the nuanced implication of gift. On the economics of temple building see Burford 1965; eadem 1969.

91 Guarducci 1949; eadem 1987; Mertens 2006, 104–9. Some columns also displayed dedicatory inscriptions. On votive formulas in general see Lazzarini 1976; eadem 1989–90.

92 Roux 1984, 154–5; Rups 1986, 6; Partida 2000, 291. The Parthenon and indeed the whole Acropolis was called an *anathema*, see Demosthenes, *Oration* 22.76; Plutarch, *Pericles* 12.1, 14.1; Burkert 1988, 43–4; idem 1992b, 540.

93 Burkert 1988, 27, 43–4; idem 1996. See also Coldstream 1985; Svenson-Evers 1997, 132.

94 On *xoana* and early cult images see Romano, I. 1980; eadem 1988; Boardman 1978, 16–17; Donohue 1988; Stewart 1990, 44–6, 104–5; Papadopoulos, J., *s.v.* Xoanon, in *EAA*, 2nd supplement V (1997): 1094–5; Bettinetti 2001, ch. 3. Not all early cult statues were small: at the cave sanctuary of Anemospilia on Crete there survive two near life-size clay feet that possibly belonged to a cult statue (Sakellarakis and Sapouna-Sakellaraki 1997, 236, 530–39). On occasions Pausanias cites huge wooden statues (VII, 5.9), including one he says was old (VII, 26.6).

95 Stewart 1990, 12, 105, fig. 17; Dimopoulou-Rethymiotaki 2005, 373. The stone 'lady of Auxerre' in the Louvre (inv. Ma 3098) that dates to around the third quarter of the seventh century measures only 650 mm tall, see Stewart 1990, 107, figs 27–8; Donohue 2005, 131–43, ch. 4.

96 Miller, J. 1996, 94, 202; Svenson-Evers 1997, 140; Bettinetti 2001, ch. 6; Broder 2008. For related Near Eastern practices see Ringgren 1973, 77. The story of Kassandra's rape suggests Athena's statue could be moved (by a hero). Statues portrayed on vases typically look smaller than life size, see for example one of Apollo on a fifth-century vase in Vienna (Kunsthistorisches Museum, inv. IV 741; *LIMC s.v.* Apollon 6; De Cesare 1997, cat. 185, fig. 42; Nick 2002, Taf. 2, 5).

97 Pliny the Elder, *HN* XVI, 79.

98 Leipen 1971; Nick 2002; Hurwit 2005.

99 Lapatin 2001, and 44–60 for influence from the East.

100 Pausanias V, 11.1–11. Some thought the god too big for his home, for were he to stand up he would have struck the ceiling (Strabo VIII, 3.30; Lapatin 2001, 80, 189). For later recycling of this story see Wilson Jones 2000a, 23–4. Substantial fragments of a smaller sixth-century chryselephantine statue survive at Delphi (Lapatin 2001, 57–60, cat. no. 33).

101 The function of the *naiskos* is, however, uncertain: see Miller J. 1996, 195.

102 Svenson-Evers 1997, 135.

103 A case in point is the pillar-like 1.65 m-tall stone *kore*, or girl, dedicated on Delos by one Nikandre (unless this was a cult statue, according to some): see Richter 1968, 23–6; Hurwit 1985, 186–91; Stewart 1990, 108, figs 34–5; Donohue 2005, 26–34.

104 Richter 1960; Hurwit 1985, 194–202; Stewart 1990, 109–10, fig. 43; Kyrieleis 1996 (for Samos). The beginnings of large-scale terracotta statuary on Cyprus, and at Ayia Irini in particular, have been dated to around 650: see Gjerstad 1948, 355.

105 Hermary 1993; Gruben 1997, 267–87; Giuliani 2005. The monument in reality comprises two pieces, base and statue proper; the inscription might mean they both came from the same block, or alternatively from the same quarry (on Naxos).

106 Herington 1955; Romano I. 1980, 42–57; Prost 2009, 247. Athena Parthenos did not have her own altar and priestess, and she was known as an *anathema*, just as were other famed temple statues including the Olympian Zeus and the Cnidian Aphrodite. The dividing lines between cult and votive statues were more blurred than modern categorization suggests, see n. 69 above.

107 Marconi 2009, esp. 164ff.; Hölscher 2009, 54–5.

108 For this point in the Roman context see Stambaugh 1978.

109 'Without wars, few of the temples and other sacred buildings of Greece would have been built' (Kendrick-Pritchett 1971, 100). See also Stambaugh 1978, 583–5; Aberson 1994.

110 Ito 2002. The layout of many a Greek sanctuary may appear haphazard, but the cumulative effect of many interventions can mask considered design at the time each was made. Views to and from the sanctuary, processional routes, the hierarchical separation of space and the relationship between temple and altar were all factors to be taken into account. For contrasting assessments see Bergquist 1967, 1–2; Tomlinson 1976, 47–8; Hölscher 2002.

111 For references see **Table 5**.

CHAPTER TWO

1 As David Watkin puts it: 'To begin at the beginning means that we must look far beyond the serene composure and shining intellectual achievements of the Parthenon to a mistier world of primeval romance which the ancient Greeks could not forget, though its details were even to them mysterious' (Watkin 2000, 19).

2 Iakovidis 1983 (Tiryns 3–20; Mycenae 23–72; Athens, 73–90); idem 1999. For studies of Minoan and Mycenaean architecture, considered separately or together, see Dinsmoor 1975, ch. 1; Lawrence 1983, part 1; Küpper 1996; Preziosi and Hitchcock 1999; Eichinger 2004; Palyvou 2005; Poursat 2008, ch. 20. See also AA.VV. 2005a; Castleden 2005.

3 Greek in origin, the term was adopted for this specific de-

notation in the nineteenth century (e.g., Jebb 1886; P&C VII, 80). In Homeric usage it could apply to less important structures, see Hellmann 2006, 36–43, esp. 37.

4   Wace 1949, ch. 6; Coulton 1974.

5   Plommer (1977, 75, 78) highlights aspects of Bronze Age architecture that were never surpassed even in the Classical period, for example the ceremonial doors of Minoan palaces, ingeniously designed to fold back into the recesses formed by H-shaped jambs. See also Lippolis *et al.* 2007, 9–10.

6   See Ulf 2009 for a review of this debate; West (2011) favours the creation of the *Iliad* by Homer *c.*680–640, and that of the *Odyssey* by another, slightly younger, poet. Here I use 'Homeric' as a convenient shorthand for both epics.

7   *Odyssey* III, 388–407. See Plommer 1977 contra the thesis of Drerup (1969) and others, that the architecture of Homer's own day was the basis for his descriptions. See also Lorimer 1950; Luce 1975, 49–53; AA.VV. 1997g.

8   P&C VII, 350–51, 654; Gardner 1901, 303–4; Durm 1910, 363; Hiller 1986; idem 1991, 129–31. For scepticism see Holland 1939; Picard 1948, 283–4; Roux 1984, 153. For recent appraisals see Hellmann 2006, 36–43; Østby 2006a, 10–19.

9   Desborough 1964; Chadwick 1976; Sandars 1978; Kilian 1991 and other essays in AA.VV. 1991c; Dickinson 1994; Cartledge 2000, chs 6, 7; Morgan 2009.

10 Snodgrass 1971; idem 1977; Desborough 1972; Starr 1977; idem 1991; Hiller 1991; Whitley 1991a. For rejection of the 'Dark Age' concept see Papadopoulos 1993, 194–7; for recent syntheses Osborne 1996, 19–32; Whitley 2001, ch. 5; Morris, I. 2000, ch. 3; idem 2009; Lemos 2002.

11 For debate over continuity versus discontinuity see Murray 1980, 16–20; Marinatos 1988; Matthäus 1988; Hiller 1986; idem 1991; AA.VV. 1991c; Dietrich 1991; Antonaccio 1994, 86–9; Whitley 2001, 137–8; Rolley 2002. De Polignac (1995a, 29, echoed in idem 2009, 428) makes the point that 'What needs to be done is not to decide once for all whether there was a general "break" or a general "continuity" . . . but rather to try and see what part was played by both breaks and continuity in the history of each sanctuary and each cult, and to understand their implications . . .'.

12 Open-air altars have been discovered at Tiryns and Mycenae, and on Cyprus (Dietrich 1986, ch. 4; idem 1991). The ritual depicted on the sarcophagus from Agia Triada (**Fig. 1.7**) anticipates later Greek sacrifice, as does Bronze Age cave cult activity, see Dietrich 1991, 142, 145. See also Mylonas 1977.

13 For Crete in general see Prent 2005a; eadem 2005b. Key sites include the Idaian cave (Sakellarakis 1998), Kato Syme (Mazarakis Ainian 1997, 222–3; Bergquist 1988, 23–7) and Kommos (Shaw and Shaw 2000). An example on Cyprus is Paphos (Maier and Karageorghis 1984). As Burkert (1988, 28; idem 1992b, 535) notes, however, neither the Cypriot nor Cretan sites can be said to be typically Greek. For Yria on

Naxos and Kalapodi (which used to be identified as ancient Hyampolis) see **Table 2**.

14 Pro continuity: Mylonas 1961, 33–49; Cosmopoulos 2003b; Østby 2006a, 12–16. Contra: Darcque 1981; Clinton 1993, 114; Whittaker 1997, 14–16. See also Mazarakis Ainian 1997, 147–50; Travlos 1988, 91ff.

15 Osborne (1996, 19, 32), who uses the metaphor of 'a slate rubbed clean'.

16 For references for this and other buildings mentioned see **Table 2**.

17 Georg Herdt has a study of this problem in preparation.

18 Sinos 1971; Hägg and Konsola 1986; Werner K. 1993, chs 1, 2. For a long house in Moravia, see Bouzek 1997, 64 and fig. 1.

19 Ruby 1999. Some local leaders had the title *basileus*, a term which carried regal associations going back to Linear B, see Drews 1983; Carlier 1996; de Polignac 1995a, 6–7.

20 'Unit IV-1' and 'Unit IV-5' (see **Table 2**). Local leaders presumably presided over cult activity and communal dining as suggested in Unit IV-1 by benches, a hearth and a round paved area. The structure at Smari that served for dining (Ch. 1, n. 74) could likewise have doubled as a ruler's residence and/or a shrine.

21 Coulton 1977, 30. In similar vein, Plommer writes: 'If I were asked for my own view of ninth- and eighth-century trends in architecture, I should reply that I saw none. Architecture, as I should hope to define it, did not then exist. No one was consciously applying a well-reasoned aesthetic . . . There was everywhere a series of hits and misses . . .' (1977, 83).

22 Mazarakis Ainian 1988, 113–19; idem 1997, esp. 375–96. For qualification see Lang 1996, 68–70; Svenson-Evers 1997, 134; Whitley 2001, 138–9.

23 Raglan 1964.

24 Mazarakis Ainian 1988, 109–13; idem 1997; Hiller 1996. At Tegea the apsidal shrines either side of 700 were tiny: see Østby 1994; idem 2006b.

25 For references see **Table 2**. The post-holes revealed by excavation have been seen as consistent with pairs of poles tied to a wattle-and-daub armature for the wall, but mudbrick would have been more normal. For the Delphic myth see Ch. 3, p. 67.

26 Imposing ground-plans cannot prove temple function. A case in point is the so-called Megaron Hall at Emporio on Chios. This was a substantial construction (18.25 by *c.*6.60 m, with blocks up to 1 m long and stone bases for posts *c.*500 mm in diameter). Yet the absence of offerings or a nearby altar points to a ruler's residence.

27 Mazarakis Ainian 1997, 62–3. The finds include horse armour from north Syria, see here Ch.7, p. 163.

28 At some sites dwellings share a common yard, while single courtyard houses appear at Zagora on Andros, see Cambitoglou *et al.* 1988, esp. fig. 4; Mazarakis Ainian 2001, 151–2. See also Lang 1996; Pesando 1987; Cahill 2002. The

29 Drerup 1969; Coulton 1977; Fagerström 1988; Mazarakis Ainian 1988; idem 1997; idem 2001; Barletta 2001, 25–7. Rubble stonework tended to be used more extensively on Crete and the Cyclades compared with the mainland.

30 On architectural models generally, see Markman 1951; Drerup 1969, 69–76; AA.VV. 1997h; Muller 2001; Barletta 2001, 40–46; and especially Schattner 1990.

31 Since such models were offerings some deduce that they represented temples (see Staccioli 1989–90 on Italic models). However, many come from sanctuaries sacred to Hera, where they may have honoured her role as goddess of the domestic sphere, and so should represent houses (Schattner 1990, ch. 4; Hellmann 2006, 41–2). On the other hand later models with tiled roofs and triglyphs more likely represent temples.

32 The model has been linked to the temple of Hera Akraia at Perachora (Payne 1940, 27–77; Salmon 1972; Mazarakis Ainian 1997, 63–4). But the interpretation of a nearby structure as an apsidal predecessor, the hypothetical subject of the model, is flawed: see Menadier 1995, 77–8.

33 Schweitzer 1971; Snodgrass 1971; idem 1977; Coldstream 1977; Hurwit 1985; Boardman 1998.

34 De Franciscis 1979; Mertens 1993, 117–19; idem 2006, 95–6.

35 AA.VV. 1983; AA.VV. 1999c, ch. 2; Whitley 2001, 98–101; Boardman 2002, 45–79. For the concept of an eighth-century revolution see Starr 1991, 99; Snodgrass 1980, 15–84; I. Morris in AA.VV. 2009c, ch. 4.

36 Morris, I. 2000, 274; de Polignac (2009, 427) calls the Archaic period the 'age of sanctuaries', noting that 'No other phase of Greek history saw so many new sacred spaces appear . . .'.

37 Drerup 1969, 91–2; Schwandner 1985, 111; Lambrinoudakis 1991, 184–5; Gruben 1996a, 401.

38 Werner K. 1993, 3–5; *contra* Darcque 1990; Hellmann 2006, 36–43.

39 An inscription dating to the first half of the sixth century from Aphaia's sanctuary at Aigina refers to her house/temple as an *oikos*: see Williams, D. 1982, 60. See also Barletta 2001, 30; Hellmann 2006, 51–5.

40 Watrous 1998–9, 75. For further references see **Table 2**.

41 Pernier envisaged the frieze as being 800 mm in height and at a high level. Alternatively it sat on the ground in the manner of Hittite, Assyrian and Syrian orthostate friezes (Marconi 2007, 5).

42 Beyer 1976, Taf. 44.2; Felten 1984, 19, no.1, Taf. 1.1; Felten 1984, 133, n. 60; Andreadaki-Blasaki 1997, fig. 36; Boardman 1999, fig. 60; Marconi 2007, 3.

43 For a review of figural ornament at these sites see Marconi 2007, 3–6.

44 I thank Nils Hellner for informing me of developments at Kalapodi in advance of publication. For the evidence of paintings, see Niemeyer 2007, 76–7. On octagonal supports (and Egyptian precedents) see Hellner 2011. Wooden posts were also used to reinforce the walls at a recently discovered temple at Nikoleika, see Kolia and Gadolou 2011.

45 On stone bases for wooden shafts see Hellner 2004; idem 2010; Herdt 2013.

46 The extensive variation in the stone columns of the Heraion peristyle is often attributed to a gradual substitution of supposed wooden predecessors, while Barletta (2001, 126–7) posits piecemeal donation or procurement. Donderer (2005) emphasizes the practical difficulties of substituting columns and visualizes an alternative process, whereby the stone columns were dedicated as free-standing votives until enough were assembled for a complete re-build of the temple. See also Ch. 3, pp. 67–8.

47 For an Aeolic example from Delos with a torus decorated with fish-scale see **Table 4.1**. For a leaf crown from Paros with a socket which perhaps received a wooden tenon see Donos 2008, K55 (Taf. 15c).

48 See **Table 3**.

49 As documented at the so-called House of Tiles at Lerna, see Wiencke 2000, figs 102a, 104b; Sapirstein 2008, 37–8.

50 Both flat and curved tiles have been excavated from Mycenaean buildings. Despite arguments in favour of their use on pitched roofs (Iakovidis 1990; Küpper 1996, 105–10, Abb. 210–17), the numbers of curved tiles are much fewer, so they probably served for drainage runs and the like (Blegen 1945; Sapirstein 2008, 38–54).

51 AA.VV. 1990a; Winter 1993; Billot 2000; Hellmann 2002, ch. 14; Aversa 2002; Sapirstein 2009; idem 2011.

52 The tiles at Corinth and Delphi are very large (*c.*600–700 mm square and 30 kg in weight), while fusing pan and cover into a single 'combination tile'. This points to a pioneering phase using separate pans and covers, see Robinson 1984; Coulton 1977, 35; Gruben 1996, 406; Schwandner 1990; Sapirstein 2008. However Wikander (1990; idem 1992) points out that new technologies can also develop from elaborate beginnings to more efficient and cheaper solutions. For the tiles at Isthmia see Hemans 1989. Tiles were also in early use at Olympia, see Heiden 1990; idem 1995.

53 Coulton 1977, 35. Accurately orthogonal plans with strong walls are a possible indication of the use of tiles, though at Kalapodi the two temples with parallel walls were roofed by thatch, not tile.

54 In addition, the lower the pitch the shorter the slope, the fewer the tiles and the less the weight.

55 Goldberg 1982; Danner 1989; idem 1997. Some early disc akroteria can appear disproportionately large by comparison with later norms.

56 Marconi 2004, 214; idem 2007, 8ff.

57 The style of these and other terracottas guides the dating of the temple: see Mertens-Horn 1978, esp. 36–40. For further references see **Table 2**.

58 For those at Kalydon, see Dyggve 1948, 149–64, 236–9. For comparative discussion see Bookidis 1967, 157–65; Barletta 2001, 67–8 (with other examples cited in n. 36). The find at Thermon of a (sixth-century?) terracotta element combining a triglyph with a metope (Demangel 1947–8, fig. 5) may suggest that earlier plaques were indeed metopes. For a fragmentary painted terracotta panel of *c*.600 or later from the Athenian Acropolis see Glowacki 1998, 82, fig. 8.1.

59 Mertens-Horn 1992; Greco 2000; Hellmann 2002, 311; Mertens 2006, 93–4; Marconi 2007, 15–16.

60 Verzone 1951; Drerup 1952; Martin 1965, 155–62; Normann 1966; Hellmann 2002, 242–3; Marconi 2007, 7–8.

61 Pausanias X, 5.9ff., esp. 11. Elsewhere (VI, 19.2–4) he described the Treasury of the Sikyonians at Olympia and its two bronze chambers (*thalamoi*), one supposedly Doric the other Ionic. The smaller of them weighed 500 talents or about 18 tonnes. See Dörpfeld 1883, 67ff.; Rykwert 1996, 268–9.

62 Furtwängler 1890; for the volute (inv. B 201) see Herrmann, K. 1996; for the lobed collar see Hampe 1938, and for one from Samos, see Kyrieleis 1988a, Abb. 1–2. Another find from Olympia is a piece of heavy gauge bronze with an overfall that probably surmounted a (votive?) column or pier, see Daux 1965.

63 At about 800 mm tall and roughly square, the griffin relief (Olympia, inv. B104) is plausible as a metope, but this remains only one possibility. See Hampe and Jantzen 1937, esp. 90–92, Taf. 34–5; Verzone 1951, 272–94, fig.2; Philipp 1994, 489–98. Bookidis (1967, 251–3) judges it to be a door panel. In its complete form the archer panel probably had more vertical proportions, and is less suitable for a metope.

64 Marconi 2007, 7–8.

65 The thinness and the rebated edge detail is consistent with employment as metopes, see Klein 1997.

66 The bases are consistent with the Geometric period in not belonging to a unified stylobate, but they conform to later practice in roughly combining a square plinth/bottom and a round bearing surface. Some take the supposed 'peristyles' at Toumba and Rakita to point to wider usage, for example Hellmann 2006, 35, 48–9; Lippolis *et al.* 2007, 46, 63, but this is debatable. The stratigraphy at Rakita does not allow for precise dating of the peristyle (Gadolou 2002). The recently discovered temple at Nikoleika, not far from Rakita and of similar date, also has an entrance at a curved end, but there is no peristasis. See Kolia 2011.

67 Kienast 1996, 20–24; Hellmann 2006, 43. For further references and chronology see **Table 2**. With Lefkandi, Rakita and Ephesos in mind Gruben (1996b, 62–3) proposed rectangular wooden posts for the South Stoa at Samos (idem 1957), but this too is doubtful (Kienast, personal communication).

68 Despite the lack of stone bases or a stylobate, a peristyle was proposed by Broneer (1971) and defended by Gebhard

1993; Gebhard and Hemans 1992. But as Rhodes (1984; idem 1987) and Barletta (2001, 38, 50–51) point out, the 'geison' blocks most likely crowned walls, not a peristasis. There are technical similarities with the temple at Corinth, which had no peristasis (Rhodes 2003, esp. 92).

69 The remains may be attributed to the old temple that Vitruvius (IV, 1.3) mentioned, and which stood until a fire in the fifth century (Pausanias II, 17.7; Thucydides IV, 133).

70 In the muddle following the excavations of the 1890s there is little hope of using small finds for dating purposes. The rudimentary 'stylobate' points to the third quarter of the seventh century (so Barletta 2001, 35 and n. 47); yet Weickert (1929, 43) prefers early in the seventh century and Bergquist (1967, 19–20) as late as the mid-sixth. On the terrace see Ch. 4, n. 30.

71 A step towards a peristyle was seen to be the addition to Building B in the eighth century of a circuit of timber posts. This was doubted (Antonetti 1990, 8–9; Mazarakis Ainian 1997, 125–35; Hellmann 2006, 45–6) and is now ruled out: see Papapostolou 2010b. For alternative proposals see Mallwitz 1981b, 621–4 (open-air enclosure); Wesenberg 1982, 154–7 (separate apsidal building); Kuhn 1993, 40–47 (paved area).

72 The case for a seventh-century peristyle is set out by Kuhn 1993. For doubts see Schmaltz 1980, esp. 331; Mazarakis Ainian 1997, 134; Barletta 2001, 38–9.

73 For reviews of the excavations see Antonetti 1990, 3; Papapostolou 1994; idem 1995; idem 2010a; Morris, I. 2000, 225–7.

74 Mallwitz 1981b, esp. 624–33; Barletta 2001, 32–9, esp. 35–9; Hellner forthcoming. For the situation in Magna Graecia see Romeo 1989. A tiled roof does not imply a peristyle; the first temples to have had large tiles, those at Corinth and Delphi, were not peripteral.

75 Østby (2006a, 29) judges this especially relevant at Rakita given the exposed conditions dictated by the altitude 1150 m above sea level. See also Hellmann 2006, 48–9.

76 Coulton 1977, 74–7.

77 Østby 2006a, 29. See also Kuhn 1985.

78 Mallwitz 1982. This find was discarded into the well around the end of the seventh century, so it must have belonged to an earlier structure.

79 The socket in the upper surface seems too shallow for a single free-standing column without risk of wobbling. The shaft probably extended to the edge of the plain band, suggesting a diameter of *c*.110 mm.

80 Herdt 2013.

81 Mallwitz 1982, 266–7. This torus has a smaller radius towards the top, in common with those of the Classical period. While the origin of such profiles in the eastern Mediterranean cannot be ruled out, this detail may suggest Greek workmanship.

82 Dörpfeld 1935, I, 172–5, 190–97. There is an element of over-

interpretation, however, on which see Riorden 2009, 202. For further references see **Table 3**.

83 Regional variation is one of the main threads running through Barletta's publications; the catalogue of sites in Lippolis *et al.* 2007 has a welcome geographical range.

84 Marconi 2007, 8–12.

85 Barletta 2001; Mertens 2006; Lippolis *et al.* 2007; Marconi 2007.

86 Pindar, *Olympian Odes*, XIII, 21–22 seems to credit Corinth with the invention of the pediment; Cook, R. 1951; idem 1970; Coulton 1977, 39; Rykwert 1996, 208; Rhodes 1987; idem 2003. Howe is of the opinion (1985, 367, 370) that 'The Doric temple could just as well have been built in the West', i.e., Sicily or southern Italy, 'so long as it was in one of the wealthier cities on the trade routes that passed through Corinth'. However, regarding monumentality in Sicily, Marconi (2007, 36–7) confirms its lag behind the mainland. Korres (2002b, 6) gives preference to Argos.

87 Pliny the Elder (*HN* XXXV, 151–2 [43]) associates Corinth with pioneering developments in painted and figural terracotta work. For commentary see Corso *et al.* 1988, 473; Winter 2000; Williams and Bookidis 2003. On the early history and success of Corinth see Dunbabin 1948; Salmon 1984; Morgan 1988. The city was also famous for bronze-working (Ch. 6, p. 151).

88 Brookes 1981; Hayward 2003, 32; Rhodes 2003, 85. The recent discovery in ninth-century contexts of monolithic stone sarcophagi, one of which, weighing over 2 tonnes, demonstrates the precocious exploitation of this resource, see Pfaff 2007, esp. 472, 503–4. I thank Guy Sanders for bringing the issue of weight to my attention.

89 Holmes 1995; Rhodes 2003, 86.

90 Goldberg 1983; Rhodes 2003, 91.

91 Klein 1991; Barletta 2001, 71–5.

92 Rhodes 2003, esp. 92; idem 2011.

93 The late sixth-century 'Great Temple' was substantially larger than the impressive mid-century temple of Apollo, part of which still stands (Pfaff 2003, 112–19). Whatever its identity (a temple of Zeus or another of Apollo?) the 'Great Temple' must have been very important for the Corinthians, and so too, presumably, its predecessor.

94 This was by all accounts a sumptuous affair, though a foundation and some blocks are all that survive, see Partida 2000, ch. 10.

95 Østby 2000, 242, fig. 2.

96 For references see **Table 2**.

97 The degree of taper is between 50 and 60 mm per metre. Though this seems too strong for an Ionic (or Aeolic) column, this is not impossible if the drum were the bottommost and it flared (as occurs on some Archaic shafts such as those at Sangri). Doric style could be suggested by the location, for this sanctuary was home to one of the earliest temples of this genus, though the sphinx-carrying column

at Aphaia's nearby sanctuary was Ionic. Alternatively neither style was present.

98 For references, see **Table 3**. In favour of an altar is the lack of finds from other parts of a Doric entablature (e.g., guttae or regulae); I thank Phil Sapirstein for sharing the initial findings of ongoing investigations.

99 This phase follows the so-called *maison noire* and other domestic buildings dated by small finds, since they were demolished for the purpose: see Luce, J.-M. 2008, esp. 98–108.

100 See Courby 1927, 171–84, 190–99; Østby 2000, 243–5, fig. 3. The block with the inscription is inv. 5102, see Daux 1937, 57–60; Hansen E. 1992, 135–9. It is also possible that some of this material belonged to the seventh-century phase.

101 Delphi, inv. N284, see Laroche 2001. Luce (J.-M. 2008, 103), however, judges this phase of the Delphic temple to have been peripteral. Perhaps plural phases were involved.

102 Thus, for example, Semper 2004 [1861], 765; Howe 1985, 278–9.

103 I am sceptical, however, of the accepted restoration of the temple of Artemis with eight columns on the front and a 'pseudo-dipteral' layout. See Herdt *et al.* 2013.

104 Coulton 1977, 38.

105 Vitruvius IV, 1.3–8. See Ch. 6, p. 142.

106 The Heraion on Delos had several such bases in white limestone contrasting with the green-grey schist used for most of the structure. For chronologies which range from *c.*700 to the middle of the sixth century see Bruneau and Ducat 1983, 230–31; Barletta 2001, 35; Hellmann 2002, 146.

107 Hendrich 2007; this strategy went on to be refined in the bases of the second dipteros, see Hellner 2009.

108 Kienast 1999; idem 2002a, 321; Hendrich 2007, esp. 38, Abb. 14 (see also Buschor 1930, 87; Gruben 2001, 357; Hellmann 2002, 164). A striated torus was used later as an echinus on Ionic capitals from Didyma (**Fig. 5.13**). The roughness of the upper surfaces of the Samian torus elements suggests contact with wood; however this could have been the architrave. After all, votive columns at Samos terminated with just a torus (**Fig. 7.15, 7.16**). Furthermore Vitruvius (VII, Pref., 12) mentioned 'the Doric temple of Juno which is in Samos'; though this may be an error (so Corso and Romano 1997, II, 1069, n. 34), the term 'Doric' is more understandable if volutes were not present.

109 For references, see **Table 5**. It is impossible to know the extent to which the look of the Archaic temple (phase IV or D) was anticipated in the *c.*600 phase. Perhaps this already had Ionic characteristics, so Corso and Romano 1997, I, 416–19, n. 36. For the phasing see Weissl 2002, esp. Abb. 11, 14.

110 See also Pliny the Elder (*HN* XVI, 213–16 [79]; XXXVI, 95–7 [21]). Vitruvius (VII, Pref., 16) places the (Hellenistic) Artemision first in his list of four 'all time greats', see Corso and Romano 1997, I, 213–14, n. 144; (cf. Vitruvius, II, 9.13,

III, 2.7, VII, Pref., 12). However the mention of the architect Chersiphron suggests the *c.*560 phase. Pliny mentions seven phases, though only four major phases are documented archaeologically (i. eighth/seventh century, ii. *c.*600, iii. *c.*560, iv. Hellenistic).

111 The plans in **Fig. 2.26** show 104 columns for the first dipteros at Samos, 104 at Ephesos and 110 at Didyma. Perhaps the first of these was initially intended to have 100 columns, but the rear colonnade was modified to avoid the huge spans necessitated by an octastyle front.

112 Kienast 1991; idem 1998, 119–124; idem 2002a, 321; Gruben 2001, 359. I am grateful to Hermann Kienast for his cordial on-the-spot explication. For inexperience at the site of the Apollonion in Syracuse see Marconi 2007, 42.

113 Howe 1985, 211–15.

114 Snodgrass 1980, 52–4; idem 1989–90; de Polignac 1995a, 14–15; Morris, I. 1987, esp. 25–8; idem 2000, 276–9. See also Seaford 1994, 195; Strøm 1995, 51–2; Osborne 1996, 78–102, esp. 101; Whitley 2001, 144.

115 Snodgrass 1989–90, esp. 292–4.

116 According to a tradition that Vitruvius embraced (IV, 1, 3–8), Doric architecture belonged to the Dorian tribes, Ionic to the Ionian tribes. There is a broad correspondence, but this was not consistent. Dorian cities could adopt Ionic style and vice versa, while Athens would come to use both, or hybrid modes (Korres 1994). In myth Hellen was the ancestor of all Greeks (Hellenes), whose sons were Doros, Xouthos and Aiolos, of whom it was Xouthos's stepson Ion who gave his name to the Ionians (see Will 1956; Alty 1982; Hall 1997). See Hall 1997 (esp. 111–42) and idem 2002 for caution as regards mapping artistic and ethnic patterns; see also Musti 1985; Hall 2002; Rose 2008. For commentary on the Vitruvian text see Corso and Romano 1997, I, 354–5, 408–14.

CHAPTER THREE

1 For introductory literature on Vitruvius see Ch. 1, n. 7. He treats questions of origins unsystematically in a series of passages, chiefly:
   I, 1.5–6 on the origins of anthropomorphic supports;
   II, 1 on the origin of building;
   IV, 1.3–8 on historical background, founder figures (Doros, Ion), the first Doric and Ionic temples and the proportions of their columns;
   IV, 1.9–10 on the origins of the Corinthian capital;
   IV, 2.2–4 on the origins of the Doric entablature;
   IV, 2.5 on the origins of dentils.

2 For an extended poetic rendering of this theme see Lucretius, *De Rerum Natura* 5.1011 ff.

3 Petrifaction is also occasionally used. As Rykwert (1996, 124) notes, the Greek term *mimesis* does not imply literal imitation so much as doing something after the fashion of the model. On skeuomorphism with particular regard to metal vessels see Vickers and Gill 1994; Vickers 1999.

4 Soane (Watkin 1996, ch. 3); Aikin 1810; Hirt 1821; idem 1823; Hittorff 1870, 313–366; Choisy 1899, I, 279–88 (esp. 288, fig. 2), 299–301; Bühlmann 1921–2; von Gerkan 1947–8. For historiography see Weickenmeier 1985; for a synthetic review see Rocco 1994a, 52–6; for recent criticism see Kienast 2002a; Wilson Jones 2002a; Barletta 2009; Riorden 2009. But see also Wesenberg 2008.

5 For Italian opinion around the eighteenth century to the effect that Tuscan was older than Doric see Morolli 1985a, ch. 5; idem 1985b.

6 This imagined origin disqualified egg-and-dart from use at eaves or cornice level for Spini (1980, 158–9, pl. 24); Payne 2000, 153. Alberti had already made the link between egg-and-dart and stones in mortar (Alberti 1988, 212 ([1485], VII, 9)).

7 Spini 1568–9; Wilson Jones 2014. Though mindful of the advisability of using quotation marks, as in 'primitive' (Lévi-Strauss 2005, 12; cf. idem 1966), I have chosen not to do this systematically since the problematic aspects of the term are by now commonly understood.

8 Aristotle, *Physics* II 8 (199a); cf. Rykwert 1996, 125, n. 31. Numerous modern echoes include Quatremère de Quincy's entry for Doric (s.2) in his *Dictionnaire* (1832), which states that the emulation of wood construction 'introduced into architecture the same spirit and procedure that Nature follows in all her works'; cf. Younés 1999, 147.

9 Edelstein 1967; Dodds 1973, 1–25. Lucretius, Pliny and other writers as well as Vitruvius expanded on the theme, see Lucretius, *De Rerum Natura* 5.1011ff., 5.1436ff.; Pliny the Elder, *HN* XXXV, 15–17 [5–6], on painting; XXXV, 151–3 [43], on modelling using clay. See also Lovejoy and Boas 1935; Panofsky 1939, ch. 2; Howe 1985, 121–6.

10 Philo, *Belopoeica*, 50–51 (trans. Marsden 1971, 106–9). See also Howe 1985, 123, and on the visual arts Quintillian, *Institutio Oratoria* 12, 10.3–9; Pollitt 1974, 81–4; idem 1990, 5.

11 Winckelmann (2006, 71; [1764, ix–x]) declared that 'The history of art should tell us the origin, the growth, the alteration, and the fall of art . . .', with much further elaboration (e.g., 2006, 20–23, 71, 227); Potts 1994, 50–54; Donohue 1995, 329–38 (who demonstrates Winckelmann's debt to Vasari and ancient authors); Morris, I. 2000, 42–4; Barletta 2001, 12–17; cf. Vidler 1987, 175–87.

12 William Bell Dinsmoor's influential handbook (1975) is not alone in structuring the text with chapters titled so as to advertise a progression from 'Rise' to 'Culmination' before the onset of 'Decadence'; the template was already provided by Anderson and Spiers 1902, which Dinsmoor revised.

13 On the architectural echoes of Rousseau's ideas see Vidler 1987, 3–4, 14–18; Watkin 1996, 114–15, 159–64.

14 Laugier 1753, 2ff. The 'primitive hut' became an important theme in architectural theory: see Herrmann, W. 1962; Rykwert 1972; Howe 1985, 14–50; Vidler 1987, 7–21, 149–51; Watkin 1996, 115–29. The ideal also exerted an appeal that reached beyond strictly architectural circles; for recent echoes see Michael Pollan, *A Place of My Own* (London 1997); Odgers *et al.* 2006.

15 Following Pugin, Owen Jones (1856, 5) states that 'Decoration should never be purposely constructed. That which is beautiful is true; that which is true must be beautiful.' Truth to function and materials became a central tenet of modernist design principles. On this in relation to ancient Doric see Forster 1996 and Wilson Jones 2014.

16 Plutarch, *Apophthegmata Laconica* ['Sayings of the Spartans] 210d–e. See also 227c for another version of the first question.

17 Viollet-le-Duc (1990, 50, 57, 59) repeatedly stressed the ational essence of Greek design: 'the Greek architect thinks, and with reason …'; 'the Greek is above all a logician'; 'the Greeks, the inventors of logic …'.

18 For qualifications however see Barletta 2009, 156–9.

19 For the term 'order of orders' see Introduction, n. 28.

20 For etymology: Chantraine 1968, IV, 1100, 1112). For discussion: Pollitt 1974, 32–7; Angier 2010, 3, 5, 7, 22. Cf. Hellmann 1992, *s.v.* τέκτων; eadem 2002, 33–4.

21 Bötticher 1874–81, I. The germ of this concept arguably goes back to the sixteenth century: see Payne 2000, 154.

22 As Kenneth Frampton (1995, 2) puts it, the concern is not for 'the mere revelation of constructional technique but rather its expressive potential'.

23 Bötticher (1874–81, I, 24–5) believed the Doric temple to exemplify his distinction between *Kernform* and *Kunstform*, the core-form structure being expressed as art-form triglyphs and mutules. For the notion of 'tectonic form' see Carpenter 1962, ch. 4 (with no mention of Bötticher); Howe 1985, ch. 3. On its importance for modern design theory see Frampton 1995, 4, 81–4.

24 Excerpt from Porphyrios 2006, 135–6.

25 Laugier's theory amounted to an impoverished fable for Durand (1819, 9; Rykwert 1996, 11–12), while Gwilt (1825, 30) said the same only more gently. Semper ridiculed scholars 'who tired themselves out in making ingenious deductions to prove that Chinese architecture had derived from the tent' or 'Greek architecture from the hut' (see Herrmann, W. 1984, 165–6). Quatremère de Quincy (1832, *s.v.* 'Doric', s.1) distinguished between the rustic 'cabane' and Doric forms that he associated with advanced timber construction, an opinion which Gwilt (1825, 36) shared.

26 Wagner 1988 [1901], 92. Wagner depended most on Semper along with Quatremère de Quincy (1832 *s.v.* Doric, s.1, trans. Younés 1999, 147), who portrayed Greek lithic architecture as the fruit of an 'imperceptible progression of toil and taste [that] modified the supports, the roofs, the porches, the ceiling and all the elements of [the original] wood construction'.

27 Support for variations of Vitruvius's account in English publications include: Dinsmoor 1975, 56–7; Summerson 1980, 13; Lawrence 1983, 111–12 (but see 123ff. for the observation that the Doric entablature was 'as much decorative as structural'); Porphyrios 2006, 49; Curl 1992, 17–18; Watkin 2000, 25; Tadgell 2007, 381–3; Wightman 2007, 436, 440. Of general surveys Janson (1977, 115–17) balances most successfully petrification with Egyptian and Mycenaean influences. As regards in-depth studies Rykwert's position is curious, since, despite his concern for the non-material dimension of architecture, he affirms (p. 182) that 'All that belongs to and happens above the Doric columns, together with the whole cornice or entablature they carry, is a confused and confusing representation of a wooden roof structure.'

28 Fletcher 1961, 108. The first edition dates to 1896 and the text was later revised by R. A. Cordingley.

29 On the *duogong* see Qinghua Guo, *The Structure of Chinese Timber Architecture* (Gothenburg 1995), 41–7. For masonry examples see L. G. Liu, *Chinese Architecture* (New York and London 1989), 54, 59–63.

30 A case in point is the palace at Padmanbhapuram in Kerala (*c.*1600–1750), see Heston 1996, esp. fig. 12.

31 Lloyd and Müller (1986, 75) endorse a body of opinion descending from ancient authors and later William Chambers (1825, 109–10), Quatremère de Quincy (1803), and others in the twentieth century: see Andrae 1930; idem 1933; Frankfort 1941; Arnold 1991, 14–15; Rykwert 1996, 160.

32 Note the problematic implied intersection at the corners of a vertical post and two crossing members (Barletta 2009, 161). See Mühlbauer 2007, and also Borchhardt 1975, esp. 95–149 for the tombs of Myra; Rykwert 1996, 285–9; Strathmann 2002.

33 A stone volute akroterion from a Phrygian 'megaron' may be interpreted as corroboration, see Young, R. S. 1956, 261–2, pl. 93, fig. 41. See also Young 1962; Liebhart 1988, 111–12; Haspels 1971, pls 8, 189, 513–15, 523; Berndt-Ersöz 2006.

34 Semper 2004, 369–70 [1861–3, I, 429–30].

35 Ohnefalsch-Richter 1913, 16–19; Masson 1964, 221–3 (with extract of text in English by Ohnefalsch-Richter); Buchholz 1966, 38–41, pl. 42.

36 Pindar, *Pythian Ode*, VIII, 58–99; Pausanias X, 5.9–13. For contrasting or partial versions see *Homeric Hymn to Apollo*, 295–9; Strabo IX, 421. For discussion see Sourvinou-Inwood 1979; eadem 1991, 192–216; Rutherford 2001, 216–32; Marconi 2009b, 9–12. See also Ch. 10, pp. 213–14.

37 Some representations show wood grain and other details that evoke timber construction. See Hittorff and Zanth 1870, 254–66, pl. 81; Eckhart 1953; Oliver-Smith 1969, 20–24. For canopies and pavilions of light-weight construction see Weber, M. 1990, Taf. 33–5. Perhaps the oldest known repre-

sentation of a Doric column survives on pottery fragments from Perachora dating after the middle of the seventh century, see Dunbabin 1962, pl. 22, no. 420; Oliver-Smith 1969, 40, 75, no. 1, fig. 31; Wesenberg 1971, 59–61, Abb. 112; Howe 1985, 267, fig. 139; Barletta 2001, 128, fig. 75. A wooden shaft on a stone base is shown on a late seventh-century skyphos-krater (National Museum, Athens, inv. 16384), see Eckhart 1953, 60; Oliver-Smith 1969, 75, no. 6, fig. 8; Howe 1985, 267, fig. 140; Hurwit 2000, 97, fig. 69. On question marks over the fidelity of such representations see Eckhart 1953; Oliver-Smith 1969, 2–3; Barletta 2001, 129. Some representations show implausibly slim poles, especially when combined with roofs of shallow pitch (and as such presumably tiled). Perhaps artists wished to gain space for figural depictions.

38 Pausanias relates that the pillar of Oinomaos was a vestige of this legendary figure's house. Alternatively the pillar could have been the turning post of the stadium at Olympia before it was moved eastwards: see Brulotte 1994a.

39 Korres reasonably restores a timber triglyph frieze at Metropolis (see Intzesiloglou 2002), since by this time Doric predominated. We cannot be so confident about the look of the earlier Heraion at Olympia (see Kienast 2002b, including discussion of Adler's reconstruction, Abb. 2).

40 The advantage of rail and panel lies in the practicalities of jointing, savings in material, and restraining warping. For Vergina see Andronicos 1984, 31–37, figs 36, 57, 160; Lawrence 1983, 274–5. For comparanda see Dyggve *et al.* 1934, Abb. 43, 44; Hellmann 2002, fig. 337. Representations of wooden doors or gates appear on vases, see for example a Campanian neck amphora (*Masterpieces of the J. Paul Getty Museum. Antiquities* (Los Angeles 1997), p. 86, inv. 92.AE.86). The grandest surviving ancient bronze examples belong to the Pantheon (Gruben and Gruben 1997). On Greek doors see Büsing-Kolbe 1978; Hellmann 2002, 242–3; cf. Büsing 1988.

41 Hoepfner and Schwander 1986, 65–6.

42 Korres and Bouras 1983, 23. In some cases, such as the north porch of the Erechtheion (**Fig. 9.9**), there is a clear distinction between the main beams and the infill. See also Hoepfner 1991.

43 For a comparable example, see Connor 1973.

44 Vickers and Gill 1994; Vickers 1999.

45 This is commonly accepted, see for example Rhodes 1984, 144–5, *pace* the insubstantial objections of Demangel (1931b). For Viollet-le-Duc (see below) the presence of mutules on both front and flanks of temples represents a lapse of constructional logic; however, this cannot be said of hipped roofs, which were present on some early temples, e.g., at Corinth and Isthmia.

46 Schattner 1990, cat. nos. 19, 24, 26, 32. The mutules of the old tholos at Delphi do not follow the radial geometry of the plan, but are rectangular, as would be the ends of

rafters. Significantly, Vitruvius (IV, 7.5) used the term mutule for the ends of Etruscan timber purlins.

47 The mutules represented on the so-called Olive-Tree pediment from the Athenian Acropolis have just one row of three guttae, although this may reflect difficulties of making them at such a small scale. See Heberdey 1919, 21–25, Abb. 13; Kiilerich 1989. For objections to timber guttae in terms of the practicality of woodworking see Holland 1917, 141; Demangel 1931b, 8–9, who reads the guttae as the heads of metal nails or rivets.

48 Contrary to King Agesilaos, Viollet-le-Duc thought timber columns/posts should be square, presuming the use of the saw. Columns in stone he saw to be naturally circular, the better to be rolled from quarry to site. In fact, timber posts in Geometric buildings could be both square and circular (Coulton 1977; idem 1993, 41), while column shafts were not usually transported by rolling (Korres 1995).

49 Wilson Jones 2002a; Kienast 2002b; Barletta 2009. For reviews of earlier debate see Howe 1985; Weickenmeier 1985; cf. Riorden 2009.

50 On Greek roofs see Hodge 1960; Coulton 1977, 74–86, 155–60; Hellmann 2002, ch. 13; cf. Mühlbauer 2007.

51 What constructional explanation can there be, asks Viollet-le-Duc (1990, 59, cf. 46–9) for 'triglyph-beams underneath the pediments, so far from the roof?' The typical Lycian tomb 'exhibits no such absurdity', he says, 'the purlins are plainly indicated on the gable ends, and the joists of the ceiling that supports the roof are not returned along the fronts of these gables'.

52 Gwilt 1825, 38–9.

53 Hübsch (1822) observed that, since stone and wood were used at the same time, it is difficult to say which influenced which. He was contested by Hirt (1823), to whom he responded in 1824. Hübsch's convictions about the Greek temple also inform his influential *In welchem Style sollen wir bauen?* of 1828.

54 Later support for Viollet-le-Duc is exemplified by Warren (1919, 192), who declared that 'the Doric column in its earliest period is so distinctly and characteristically a stone form, is so absolutely expressive of that material, that it is difficult to imagine that it can have had its direct origin in any other'.

55 The section can be reconstructed with confidence at the late Archaic Temple of Aphaia on Aigina: see Bankel 1989; idem 1993, Abb. 75–78. Cf. Coulton 1977, 74ff., figs 26 and 47. The Arsenal at Piraeus also had cross-beams only over the central nave, with rafters spanning the lateral spaces, see Jeppeson 1957.

56 At the Tholos at Delphi the slots in the frieze blocks for housing timbers show them to have only one-eighth of the cross-sectional area of its triglyphs. As is also the case for the Monopteros, spans are trivial, and timber sections commensurate with the much smaller mutules would suffice.

The painted plaques from Thermon and the possible bronze metope from Olympia measure 915 mm and 840 mm respectively, implying heights for triglyphs/beams far too great for the likely spans. The problem of triglyph size has long been noted, see Holland 1917, esp. 142–6.

57   Cuttings for timbers are typically housed in the geison and not in the frieze, save for the odd exception such as the Thebans' treasury at Delphi: see Michaud 1973. However there may also be a regional aspect involved, since temples with high ceilings were more typical in and around Attica than further west.

58   The first steps towards the truss might go back to the mid-sixth century, either in Etruria (Turfa and Steinmeyer 1996, esp. 8–18) or Sicily (Klein 1998).

59   It is also of note that triglyph altars are not normally accompanied by guttae or other echoes of timber detailing until the Classical period (see Durm 1910, fig. 35; Schleif *et al.* 1940, 66–8 for examples). On triglyph altars see also Demangel 1937, 431–6; Payne, H. 1940, 89–91; Yavis 1949, 138–9; Roux 1953a, 117–23; Rupp 1974, 274, 308–9; Mertens 1991, 190–91; Aktseli 1996, 59–60; Hardwick 1999, 181–91; Hellmann 2006, 141–4.

60   Schleif *et al.* 1940, 63–9; Yavis 1949, 115.

61   The altars at Syracuse may have been at least as early as the Archaic temples nearby: see Orsi 1919, esp. 687–715; Yavis 1949, 129–30 (though this is a confused summary). Excavations suggest that the frieze blocks of the small altar were re-used from an earlier structure. This is likely to have been an altar given that the epistyle has a pair of fascias instead of a tainia. The parapet decorated with a lyre-shaped composition that has been restored on one of the altars seems to date from the mid-sixth century or later, however. Perhaps different phases were involved.

62   The distribution of triglyph altars may indicate a Corinthian origin after 600, following on from the use of triglyphs on buildings (Yavis 1949, 139; Hardwick 1999). However the earliest triglyph yet known, the corner one from Mon Repos, may have been part of an altar (Ch. 2, p. 55).

63   Vitruvius (IV, 3.1–2) says that such solutions were flawed to the extent that leading Hellenistic authorities argued against using Doric for temples. See Tomlinson 1963; Coulton 1977, 60–64; Wilson Jones 2001, 677; Osthues 2005.

64   Rocco 1994a, 50.

65   Several temples and treasuries have a Doric frieze only on the front, but none has triglyphs only on the flanks.

66   This was the position of Bötticher (1874–81, I); see also Durm 1910, 253ff.; Rocco 1994a, 52–6.

67   Korres 1983, 23.

68   Lambrinoudakis and Gruben 1987; Gruben 1996b, 70–74; idem 1997.

69   For the rationale in certain situations for beams running longitudinally at the level of the frieze see Ch. 9, p. 202.

70   Ferri 1948, 407; Hellmann 1992, 263. Expressions involving the term triglyph have also been interpreted to designate the Doric frieze as a whole, but this seems unlikely to have been the primary meaning: see Corso and Romano 1997, I, 449, n. 102.

71   This led Silvio Ferri to wonder why triglyphs were not called *trimeroi*, things with three thighs or legs/uprights. See Ferri 1960, 149–50, see also idem 1948, 407, 412–13.

72   Winckelmann 1762, 23. He was one of the first to have commented on the topic having seen Greek temples at first hand, those at Paestum, for which see Raspi-Serra 1986; Mertens 1990; Greco and Longo 2000; de Jong 2010.

73   Such reconstructions appeal to Vitruvius's mention of Etruscan *trabes compactiles*, beams separated by a gap for air to circulate and so reduce rotting (IV, 7.4): see Rodenwalt 1938, *Korkyra*, I, 75; De Angelis D'Ossat 1941–2. Stucchi (1974) believed the 'bi-glyph' on a fifth-century temple model from Himera to point to bipartite ridge-beams. However there is already a ridge-beam over the 'bi-glyph', and in this the model from Medma is similar (**Fig. 2.9**). Other proposals include unlikely assemblies of small constructive elements, e.g., Choisy 1899, I, 288, fig. 2; cf. von Reber 1883, 195–6. No such proposal gets near to explaining the arches of triglyphs.

74   A square is the orthogonal shape that can be converted from tree-trunks with minimal loss of heartwood. For cuttings and complementary evidence, see Hodge 1960; Coulton 1977, 147. While it is true that epistyle beams in the Parthenon are made up of separate members, this (sophisticated and relatively late) solution served to reduce the weight of *stone*. Wooden planks would have been difficult to produce without using the plane, a tool that is unlikely to have seen use much before the fifth century, see Holland 1917, 147; Barletta 2009, 155–6, 159. This undermines a constructional interpretation for the tainia, the fillet at the top of the epistyle.

75   Vitruvius, IV, 2.4; Ferri 1960, 155ff. Vitruvius defended his own position with the observation that the Greeks named the nests or seatings of beams *opai*. Hence *met-ope* means 'space between the beam-nests', which allies the latter with triglyphs, see Wesenberg 1986; Hellmann 1992, 262–4; Rykwert 1996, 185–6; Corso and Romano 1997, II, 453–6, n. 110. Washburn (1918; idem 1919) tried in vain to argue that metopes correspond to beam-ends. In my view the early presence of triglyphs on altars weakens window theories just as it does beam-end theories.

76   *Iphigenia in Tauris*, 112–13. Orestes's later escape by the same route is suggested in *Orestes*, 1371–2.

77   Soane wrote of a structure in which 'the metopes were left open': see Watkin 1996, 505; cf. Viollet-le-Duc 1990, 60; von Reber 1883, 195–6; Guadet 1909, fig. 242; von Gerkan 1948–9; Gullini 1974. Since windows are superfluous in a peristyle, it may be supposed that Euripides had in mind a

building without one. Such buildings could have been illuminated by high level openings like those on a model from Sellada (**Fig. 2.9**), and one of Italic provenance in the Villa Giulia Museum, Rome. Large rectangular openings feature in the hypostyle hall at Karnak, in this case to reconcile two different column heights, see Vandier 1955, fig. 434.

78 Parallels have been proposed from ancient Egypt and modern Portugal, see Roux 1992, esp. 159; Peschken 1988; idem 1990. The fifth-century temple-model from Medma has triglyph-like features which might recall slitted windows, an idea helped by the way the model has been drawn. As Ferri (1948, esp. 404) observes, in reality these look more like elements applied to the surface (**Fig. 2.9**). See also Demangel 1931a; idem 1946; idem 1949 (whose theories are mentioned in Ch. 6).

79 Zancani Montuoro 1940; cf. Beyer 1972; *contra* Cook 1970, 17.

80 Richard 1970; Peschken 1988; idem 1990.

81 There is great variation in columnar slenderness; the columns of the temple of Apollo at Syracuse and of Athena Pronaia at Delphi have slenderness ratios of about 1 : 4 and 1 : 6.5 respectively.

82 Carpenter 1962, 213–14; Korres 2002a, 366.

83 If parallels must be drawn with evolution in nature, one might be its episodic character, alternating sudden advances with periods of stasis, as championed by Stephen Jay Gould (1980; idem 1993); cf. Howe 1985, 124–6.

84 Howe 1985, 360, 377; Wesenberg 1986, 145; Barletta 2001, 70–71; Mertens 1996, 25–38; idem 2006, 104–9; Osthues 2005, 58. The situation on the flanks can be deduced by some surviving blocks; no such blocks survive for the front, but the wide central bay probably prevented consistent axial coordination (Howe 1985, 360).

85 Blocks from the Monopteros, like those from the tholos, were found where they had been recycled in the foundations of the Sicyonians' treasury: see Laroche and Nenna 1990; Partida 2000, 75–82. For doubts over Pomtow's reconstruction, see Courby 1911, esp. 148. On the column spacing see de la Coste-Messelière 1936, 452–3; Østby 2000, 248–52. My elevation rectifies the likely relationship of architrave to column.

86 Mertens 1993, 123–9; idem 2006, 106; Aversa 1996; idem 2002. Note also architectural models with triglyphs disposed irregularly, as in the case of one from Sparta (**Fig. 2.9**); cf. Barletta 2001, 44. Like triglyph altars, such models show that triglyphs did not have to accompany columns, as Wesenberg (1986, 145–6) notes. For Demangel (1947–8) the existence of terracotta triglyphs argues against a constructional derivation, but they suit Vitruvius's reading of them as devices to mask the beams, while also comparing with Etruscan terracotta beam protectors.

87 Hoffelner 1996, 14; Østby 2000, 242; Pfaff 2003, 96.

88 This is suggested by variations in the necking of the capitals: see Schleif *et al.* 1940, 87; Barletta 2001, 63. Sixteen facets/flutes may have been the initial preference, for it is an easy number to execute (Coulton 1977, 39), by bisecting quadrants and bisecting again. Barletta (2001, 62) and Pfaff (2003, 96–7) argue that size was a factor too, since sixteen flutes are relatively common on smaller columns. (Some temples had external columns with twenty flutes and smaller internal columns with sixteen.)

89 Proportions: Coulton 1979, esp. 103; Barletta 2001, 60. Details: Schleif *et al.* 1940, 80–86; Wesenberg 1971, 49–62; Herrmann, K. 1983; Howe 1985, 325–6; Barletta 1990, 45–52. See also Williams 1984.

90 There is a long term trend towards four annulets, but it is not a progressive one. The shape and number of the annulets reflect 'factors such as the geographical location, architectural placement, and the size of the capital' (Barletta 2001, 60). According to the model of linear development supposedly 'primitive' pieces, such as capital 'C' from the Argive Heraion should be early but, as Pfaff (2005) argues, tool-marks may indicate Roman workmanship!

91 For a photograph of Xenvares's capital see Hampe 1938, Abb. 2.

92 For Paestum see Mertens 1993, 18–28, 67–72. A votive Doric capital from Phaistos is completely covered with overlapping registers of leaves, see La Rosa 1974; Segal 2007, cat. 18.

93 Barletta 2001, 60–62.

94 Broneer 1971, esp. 34–8, figs 54, 64. For the problem of its peristyle see Ch. 2, p. 50.

95 Terracotta triglyphs have been found at Thermon, though not for Temple C: see Demangel 1947–8, 364–5, fig. 5. Metope-like terracotta plaques from Thermon, Kalydon and the Athenian Acropolis (Ch. 2, n. 58) could just as well have alternated with simple framing blocks or strips. Schwandner (1996, 51–4) cites an early sixth-century panel from Spathari with a capping band suggesting an intermediate stage between Thermon and full-blooded Doric. However I would not be as confident as Schwandner or Marconi (2007, 9) that this is proof of wooden triglyphs.

96 The only find from any site that might be likened to a proto-triglyph is a smooth, tapering 'mono-glyph' from Temple E1 at Selinunte. Yet this building was built after Doric style had already been invented (not earlier as the excavators originally proposed: see Gullini 1980; idem 1981, 104–12; idem 1985, 422–35); in which case the 'mono-glyph' could represent a shorthand for conventional triglyphs.

97 The date of 630 proposed by Strøm (1988, 187–9) seems slightly early. For further references see **Table 3**.

98 A recent laser scan of the surviving lower half does not, however, back up the bowing flare that Schleif showed, see Sapirstein 2012. The triglyphs from the so-called Thesauros at Foce del Sele (**Fig. 3.24**) are also tapered. This could make

sense in terms of construction but only when using stone, by making any intervening elements/metopes have a reverse taper and so, like the voussoirs of a flat arch, less prone to slipping.

99 Orsi 1919, 689, 699.

100 For assembled photographs and drawings see Mertens 1993; for recent discussion see Marconi 2007, ch. 2. Only on occasions can such details be found on the mainland, for example ogee arches at Tegea, see Rhomaios 1952, figs 8, 10; Barletta 1990, 64, fig. 19; Mertens 1993, Taf. 75, 5.

101 For well-preserved blue triglyphs at Vergina see Andronicos 1984, fig. 57.

102 At Paestum the temple of Hera I probably had charcoal-black triglyphs, to judge by traces of pigment on the mutules, which normally were coloured like the triglyphs. My thanks to Dieter Mertens for this observation.

103 Broneer 1971, figs 41, 42.

104 The simpler forms appear as late as 500, long after the appearance of the canonic solution: see Herrmann, K. 1976, 323; Amandry 1952, 252–3. Some early treasuries at Olympia have mutules with guttae at the front and smooth mutules along the flanks.

105 Cycladic buildings between the mid-sixth and early fifth centuries which shun the mutular geison include the Heraion on Delos (Schuller 1985, 340–47; idem 1991, 96–9), the temple of Artemis at Delion on Paros (Schuller 1991), that of Apollo Pythios at Kartheia on Kea (Papanikolaou 1998), and the propylon on the upper temple terrace of the same site (Kanellopoulos 2003, 218–25). More generally see Gruben 1972; idem 1993; idem 1997; Barletta 2001, 81–91, 101–6, 114–15; Kanellopoulos 2003.

106 As Howe (1985, 370) put it, development was 'not like a draught of hemlock that produced a slow petrification working from the ground up; it was more like the flash of the Gorgon's mask'. See also Korres 1994, 21; idem 2002b, 6.

107 Korres 1994, 21.

108 Carpentry formed the Doric order as much by analogy and abstraction as by strictly imitative procedures. Though a minority position, there is a long tradition of appreciation along these lines: see Quatremère de Quincy (1832, *s.v.* Doric, s.2). Carpenter (1962, 218–19) has argued that 'its apparent timber form was not a direct conversion to a wooden structure in stone, but a purely visual metaphor'. See also Coulton 1977, 41; and Kostof 1985, 123, for whom Doric '*expressed* some of the effects of wood detailing rather than trying to petrify them exactly'.

109 There are rare exceptions to this general division; at Metropolis some of the exterior wooden columns had stone bases.

110 For opinion in this vein see Dinsmoor 1975, 58–9 (though this is not his only line of interpretation); Martin 1967, 85; Bingöl 1990; Gruben 1957 (hypothetical bracket capitals for

the south stoa at Samos); idem 1996b, 65; Barletta 2001, 133–7; Hellmann 2002, 164; Rocco 2003, 39. But for qualification see here Ch. 9, p. 198.

111 Shiloh (1979, 43–4) cites a capital from north-east India dated to the second to fourth centuries AD, now in the British Museum (inv. 1928, 10–22, 11). For a bracket capital in Turkey see Müller-Wiener 1988, Abb. 52.

112 Choisy 1899, I, 336–40, 352–3; Durm 1910, 329, fig. 315; Von Gerkan 1946–7, 17, 24; Dinsmoor 1950, 64; Vallois 1944–78, II(1), 66, 266–7; Lambrinoudakis 1996; Wesenberg 1996, 13–14. For Lycian comparanda see Mühlbauer 2007 (e.g., Abb. 62). For dentils on models see Schattner 1990, cat. nos. 19, 24, 26, 32, pp. 172–3; Barletta 2001, 119–20, 137. Earlier dentils tend to be relatively large (as at the temple at Metapontum (**Fig. 5.25**)), which suits a constructional hypothesis. However the earliest known Ionic entablatures do not have dentils, suggesting these represent a second stage invention inspired by wooden construction, but not actually derived from it.

113 P&C VII, 641–645; Warren 1919, 287; von Gerkan 1946–7, 17; Kähler 1949, 25; cf. Boardman 1959, 214, n. 2, and for recent scepticism see Barletta 2009, 159. Early architraves tended to be plain, and it seems that fasciae were added for aesthetic effect; see Gruben 1972, n. 86; Barletta 2001, 136. Stepped fasciae are a standard feature of the Assyrian 'woman-at-the-window' genre (**Fig. 4.29**), and were probably employed for temples as well as tombs comparable with the one at Tamassos (**Fig. 3.5**).

114 Gruben 2001, 157. Gruben (1963, 149–50) argues that to stack dentils/joists over a frieze, and so the beam it notionally masks, would constitute a constructional solecism, thus explaining why this combination was at first avoided.

CHAPTER FOUR

1 This stands in opposition to the notion that the 'natural' logic of 'primitive' peoples gives rise independently to similar customs in different parts of the world (see for example Raglan 1964, 195–9).

2 Diodorus Siculus I, 97.5–6 (Pollitt 1990, 15). See also I, 61ff., I, 98, 5–9, where he tells that Daidalos, the hero-founder of the arts in Greece, learnt to sculpt in Egypt and had worked there as an architect. For Daidalos, see Morris, S. 1992.

3 Semper [1861–3] was one of the first to take account of the publication of eastern material (e.g., Layard 1850; idem 1853), which Owen Jones (1856) had already sampled. Chipiez (1876) considered foreign influences extensively in his collaboration with Georges Perrot (P&C I–VIII (1882–9)), on which see Rykwert 1996, 6–7.

4 Boardman 1959, 212–18. Relative chronology is important in order to discount any 'return traffic', by which motifs of oriental descent were taken up by the Greeks and carried

back east again, for example to Pasargadae and Persepolis; see Nylander 1970. See also Cook J. 1962; Rowland B. 1935.

5 On the palmette see Rykwert 1994; Albend 2005, 108–11.

6 D'Albiac 1995, esp. 72.

7 On the transmission of motifs see Crowley 1989. See also n. 55 below.

8 Oppenheim 1931, Taf. 24b; Danthine 1937, fig. 218, with comparanda pls 32–5; Opitz and Moortgat 1955, Taf. 86, with comparanda Taf. 70–78.

9 Borell and Rittig 1998; Guralnick 2004.

10 Levi 1927–9, 450–52; Wesenberg 1971, 45–9; King 1997, 205–6, 213; Shaw 2001.

11 Boardman 1999, 143; Watrous 1998–1999, 75. King (1997, 219) supplies a list of Egyptian palm capitals; Egyptian influence is clearest on Hellenistic examples such as those of the Mausoleum at Belevi.

12 For signs on Crete of north Syrian immigrants see Boardman 1999, 58, and of Phoenicians, see Hoffmann 1997, 172–6.

13 Wurz 1913, 23; Wesenberg 1971, 146. The running spiral on the abacus also recalls an abacus or plinth from Mycenae (Wesenberg 1971, Abb. 8).

14 Persson 1942, 131. See also Krischen 1956, 52–3.

15 Sarah Morris (1992, 161) makes the point that 'Oriental inspiration' and 'Egyptianizing style' are not mutually exclusive.

16 Mycenaean influence on the Doric capital was first suggested by Thiersch (1879), Middleton (1886, 163) and Puchstein: see Wesenberg 1971 (49–50, nn. 240–43 for references), with discussion 3–23, 49–62; Abb. 4–6, 9–17.

17 Gallet de Santerre and Tréheux 1947–8, 193–7, pl. 34; Drerup 1969, 115; Wesenberg 1971, 62. Numerous ivory 'proto-Doric' colonnettes have been recovered from Mycenae: see Poursat 1977, pls VIII (71/7429 and 72/7430, both with a foliate necking and a lobed echinus), XIII, XXII, XXVII.

18 As Østby remarks (2006a, 19), this theory 'seems so generally accepted that it is not now considered necessary to argue for it'. See also Berve and Gruben 1963, 407–8; Coulton 1977, 39; Hölbl 1984, 6–9; Barletta 1990, 45–52; eadem 2001, 54–63, 138–41; Wesenberg 1996, 6; Hellmann 2006, 40.

19 Dinsmoor 1975, pl. XIII; Coulton 1977, 39 (n.41); Østby 2006a, fig. 6. A column at Pylos has 'flutes' with a very tight rhythm, see Rykwert 1996, 175, fig. on p. 177. On Mycenaean columns see Meurer 1914; Küpper 1996, 94–104; Eichinger 2004.

20 For late nineteenth-century opinion see P&C VI, ch. 8 and Weickenmeier 1985. Von Reber (1898) revised his earlier pro-Vitruvian views (1866) after Dörpfeld's report, imagining a proto-Doric Bronze Age temple. Dörpfeld himself (1886, 286–7) initially noted resemblances while rejecting the proto-Doric tag, but following advocacy by others (e.g., Holland 1917), he gave this more weight (Dörpfeld 1935, I,

198–200). For recent support see also Ditlefsen 1985; Østby 2006a; Kyrieleis 2008.

21 Dörpfeld 1886, 284–92, pl. IV; Durm 1910, 40–41, Taf. II, top. See also Schliemann 1878; von Filseck 1986.

22 Nauplion, archaeological museum, inv. no. 13578. The bolder treatment of the triglyph could result from transposing it into wood, so Østby (2006a, 23) following Holland (1917, 149–50). Tripartite motifs from the Throne Room at Knossos make for less convincing precedents, *pace* Bowen (1950, 119–25); cf. (Barletta 2001, 141 and fig. 84).

23 Østby (2006a) makes the point that the relationship between Bronze Age and later Greek architecture could operate differently for function/plans and decoration/elevations, similarities being explained by *continuatio* for the former and *renovatio* for the latter. See also Kyrieleis 2008.

24 Luce 1975; Kearns 1992; Boardman 2002; Albersmeier 2009.

25 Strabo XIII, 1.32; Aslan 2011. For recent excavations at Troy pending full publication see Rose 2000.

26 At Sparta Bronze Age structures were associated with cults of Menelaos and Helen (Tomlinson 1992; Antonaccio 1994, 96–9; eadem 1995, 155–66). The 'Treasury of Minyas' at Orchomenos, which Pausanias (IX, 38.2) judged 'a wonder second to none' had become a heroön by the Hellenistic period: see Alcock 1991, 462–3; Antonaccio 1995, 127–30. Ritual at such tombs c.700 (Morris, I., 1988) may have had to do with hero cults (Coldstream 1976; Abramson 1978; Boehringer 2002) or ancestor cults (Snodgrass 1980, 37–40; idem 1987, 160–64; Antonaccio 1995), if not both, a debate reviewed in Whitley 2001, 152–3. See also de Polignac 1995, 128–40; AA.VV. 1999a.

27 Blegen 1937; Antonaccio 1992; eadem 1994, 93–6; eadem 1995, 53–65; Mazarakis Ainian 1999, 33–6; Boardman 2002, 52–7; Boehringer 2002, 144–60.

28 Prent 2003, esp. 82; eadem 2005a, 508–54; eadem 2005b. For mainland Bronze Age sites see Iakovidis 1983; idem 1999.

29 Nilsson 1950, ch. 14; Hurwit 2000, ch.4 (67–84); Iakovidis 2006. At Mycenae the temple of Athena sat directly over the Bronze Age megaron, probably not by chance (Klein 1997).

30 There has been justifiable scholarly anxiety over the slim pottery evidence behind the dating, see Wright 1982, esp. 192; Antonaccio 1992, 91–8; eadem 1994, 95; Billot 1997, 23, 70; Whitley 2001, 151; Østby 2006a, 29–34. See Blegen 1937, 19–20 for the initial account and dating of the pottery. The blocks used, some exceeding 20 tonnes, tend to surpass Bronze Age sizes, but at the Heraion the builders benefited from being able to detach and drag stones from a quarry just above the site. At Tiryns and Mycenae builders of the Bronze Age were capable of raising and accurately dressing stone members transported from much greater distances. Particularly notable are jambs and lintels belonging to the entrances to citadels and tholos tombs; the lintel of the Treasury of Atreus weighs over 100 tonnes (Ch. 2, pp. 34–5).

Only towards the middle of the sixth century did later Greeks handle blocks of more than 30 tonnes, see Coulton 1974.

31 Snodgrass 1980, 39.

32 For the Greeks' external relations, see AA.VV. 1988e; AA.VV. 1992c; Morris, S. 1992; eadem 1997; AA.VV. 1997f; Bouzek 1997; AA.VV. 1999b; Boardman 1999.

33 Semper 2004, 242 [1861, 218]. Earlier, Hübsch (1824, 5) guessed Ionic to be substantially derived from the east.

34 Morris, I. 1994, 43; idem 2000, ch. 2; see also Astour 1967; Morris, S. 1992; AA.VV. 1997f; Burkert 2003, Introduction. Catalysts for a reaction to the traditional Greek-centred view include Edward Said's *Orientalism* (Said 1978), and Martin Bernal's *Black Athena* (Bernal 1987; idem 1991; idem 2001). For repercussions see Lefkowitz and Rogers 1996; Berlinerblau 1999.

35 Herodotus II. See also Lloyd, A. 2004.

36 Diodorus Siculus I.97.5–6, trans. Pollitt 1990, 15.

37 Richter 1960, 2–3, 27–8; Boardman 1978, 18; idem 1999, 144 (with qualifications); Howe 1985, 314–18; Stewart 1990, 34, 108. *Contra* Cook 1967, esp. 25–7, and for emphasis on Near Eastern influence, see Nagy 1998, 187–190, n. 30. Some *kouroi* perhaps adapted or corrupted Egyptian modular canons. For metrical correspondences see Guralnick 1996; cf. eadem 1978; eadem 1981; eadem 1997; Kyrieleis 1996, 30–37, 68, 108, though these are now contested, see Carter and Steinberg 2010. For the Egyptian systems see Iversen, E. 1975.

38 Wilson Jones 2000b. The Egyptian and Samian cubits were equivalent for Herodotus (II, 168); cf. Wilson Jones 2001, Appendix, no. 1. The use of a system of measures gives credibility to the story of two brothers from Samos who made halves of a statue in different quarries, bringing them together to fit perfectly (Diodorus Siculus I, 98.5–9; Pollitt 1990, 28; Rykwert 1996, 162, n. 66). However, the unlikely nature of the vertical join suggests that this tale was embroidered.

39 Riegl 1992, 6–10 [1893, ix–xv]. On the floral derivation of a range of geometrical motifs see Himmelmann 2005, esp. 12–26. Wurz and Wurz (1925) over-emphasized tracing everything back to the Egyptian palm.

40 Petrie 1895, 5; idem 1930; Goodyear 1891. For context see Gombrich 1979, 180–89 and, on Riegl's debt to Goodyear, see Iversen, M. 1993, 50–60.

41 See the Introduction, p. 5. for early opinion. For recent positions see Coulton 1977, 24, 32–3, 39, 42–3; Howe 1985, ch. 6; Hölbl 1984; Höcker 1996; AA.VV. 2001a; Tanner 2003.

42 Costantini 1999; cf. Boardman 1999, 144.

43 There are also Egyptian precursors for the wider bays towards the central axis and sculpted portions of column shafts used at Ephesos and Didyma.

44 Small barque shrines or 'kiosks' provided possible inspiration for the Greek peristyle, though these typically had square pillars before the Ptolemaic period. However, structures with round columns did exist earlier: see Vandier 1955, part 6, ch. 1, for 'les temples a déambulatoire'; Coulton 1977, 33. The kiosk of Taharqa in the first court of Amun at Karnak (Kushite period, 716–664) has round columns down both flanks, see Arnold 1999, 51–3. Note also columnar entrance porches: see Vandier 1955, 857–60; Arnold 1999, fig. 243.

45 The temple at Buhen also differs from the Greek temple in being contained within a high blind wall. The opinion compiled in AA.VV. 2001a relating to Egyptian influence on the Greek temple remains on balance circumspect. The case is taken up again in Bammer 2008b, 245; cf. idem 2008c, Abb. 210.

46 Newberry and Fraser 1893–1900; Phillips 2002, 233–7.

47 For Champollion and Barry, see Introduction, p. 5. See also Coulton 1977, 33; Howe 1985, 313–20, 327; Rykwert 1996, 158–60; Phillips 2002, 69, who highlights the porticoes at Deir el-Bahri.

48 Coulton 1977, 39.

49 Beni Hasan, tomb 2, see Newberry and Fraser 1893–1900, I, 9ff., pls III–IV. See also Jéquier 1924, 179–82; Phillips 2002, figs 73–4, 132, 142, 257. Some of the pillars are octagonal; for octagonal supports in Greece see Hellner 2011.

50 Borchardt 1920, Abb. 65–6.

51 Comparable friezes occur in Egyptian sarcophagus ornamentation, see Montet 1952, fig. 24; cf. Coulton 1977, 41 and n. 49 (p. 168). Chipiez (1876, 35–6) alludes to architraves decorated on a similar principle.

52 Mixed opinion was already present in nineteenth-century debate. Gwilt (1891 [1842], 57–62) melded Egyptian influence with Vitruvian and evolutionary explanations. Fergusson (1855, 226, cf. 262–3) stated that Doric was derived from the prototype at Beni-Hassan to the point of being 'indubitably copied', though in a later work (idem 1893, I, 252) these last words are omitted. On the other hand Perrot and Chipiez (P&C VII, 655) distanced themselves from '*prétendu* proto-dorique'.

53 Watrous 1998–9.

54 Hölbl 1984, 6–9.

55 Demargne 1947; Smith, W. 1965; AA.VV. 1988e; Dietrich 1991, 143–4; AA.VV. 1992c; Hoffmann 1997. Herodotus (II, 113–120) supplies an alternative to the epic account, according to which Helen never went to Troy at all but to Egypt, from where Menelaos retrieved her after the war.

56 In the wake of this venture coastal trading settlements were established, of which Naukratis was the most important: see Herodotus II, 152–4; Boardman 1999, 118–33; Coulton 1977, 32; AA.VV. 2006. From around this time Egyptian curiosities arrived at Samos (Kyrieleis 1993, 138, 145–6), and at Cretan sites (Boardman 1999, 112–13; Watrous 1998–9, 75).

57 Coulton 1977, 49. See also Chipiez 1876, 239–40; Hurwit 1985, 179–86; Boardman 1999, 143; Østby 2001. Hellmann

(2006, 43) uses the same evidence to argue for limited Egyptian influence.

58 During his long reign Amasis II (570–526) contributed to the re-building of Apollo's temple at Delphi after the fire of 548 and forged alliances with Croesus of Lydia and Polykrates of Samos: see Herodotus II, 180; Cook, R. 1937; Austin 1970; Guralnick 1997; Pernigotti 1999.

59 On the 'human animal' see Padgett 2003.

60 Herodotus II, 35.

61 Gruen 2011. See also AA.VV. 2005b.

62 Coulton 1977, 45–50; cf. idem 1974; Howe 1985, 320–27; for qualifications see Ratté 1993. On Egyptian building technique see Clarke and Engelbach 1930; Arnold 1991.

63 On Cyprus see Karageorghis 2002; AA.VV. 2003; AA.VV. 2009a. Of all these regions Syria is the most elusive, not least because this was a name that some Greeks, including Herodotus (I, 105; II, 116; III, 5, 91), used to refer to the entire coast between modern Turkey and Egypt, with no indication of an eastern boundary: see Bunnens 2000; Akkermans and Schwartz 2003, esp. ch. 11.

64 Layard 1850, II, 469; idem 1853, 444; von Sybel 1888; von Lichtenberg 1907; Puchstein 1907; Poulsen 1912; Warren 1919, 274ff.; Kunze 1931; Payne, H. 1931; Demangel 1932; Krischen 1956; Dunbabin 1957; Akurgal 1968. See also Barnett 1956, with 212–13 for further citations.

65 Boardman 1999, esp. chs 2–3 and Epilogue; Murray 1980, ch. 6; Morris, S. 1992, esp. ch. 5; eadem 1997; Osborne 1996, 167–8; idem 1998, ch. 3; Whitley 2001, ch. 6. See also AA.VV. 1988e; AA.VV. 1992c; AA.VV. 1997f; AA.VV. 2005b.

66 Hence the title of Walter Burkert's book *The Orientalizing Revolution* (1992a); see also West 1971; idem 1997; Dietrich 1974, ch. 2; AA.VV. 2001c; Beekes 2003; Noegel 2007. On the Phoenician component of the Greek alphabet see Osborne 1996, 107–12, and on the Phoenicians as intermediaries see Dunbabin 1957, ch. 3; Moscati 1988; Aubet 1993; Markoe 1996; AA.VV. 2003. Homer, Hesiod, Archilochos and others adapted myths of eastern origin, see West 1997; Burkert 2003, esp. ch. 2, 66, 72–3, 100; Louden 2011. See also Astour 1967; Penglase 1994; Bremmer 2008.

67 On the gorgon see Goldman 1961; on siren cauldron attachments see Muscarella 1962. As regards the field-and-divider principle, an example of particular note occurs on a recently discovered tenth-century stone model of a shrine from Tel (Khirbet) Qeiyafa in Israel. This brings to mind the Doric frieze in two respects, first in its position near the top of the shrine, and second in the treatment of the tripartite elements, which might suggest brackets or constructive elements of some sort.

68 Barnett 1956; Boardman 1999; Helm 1980; Kilian-Dirlmeier 1985; AA.VV. 1988e; AA.VV. 1992c; Burkert 1992a, esp. 14–25; Muscarella 1992; Bouzek 1997; AA.VV. 1999b; AA.VV. 2003; Stampolidis 2003; Gunter 2009. Fantalkin (2006) stresses the variability of contacts according to period.

69 Hekabe's most treasured robe (Ch. 1, n. 36) came from Sidon. Oriental influence can also be deduced from the garments on statuary, see Nagy 1998, 186–7.

70 Stampolidis 2003. Metal cauldron attachments shaped as giffins, sirens or bulls' heads had their first home in the east: see Muscarella 1962; idem 1992; Herrmann, H.-V. 1966; Cross 1974; Hoffmann 1997; Markoe 2003.

71 As Osborne (1996, 40) observes: 'The fact that the Phoenicians not infrequently borrowed motifs, without borrowing the setting from the donor culture, meant that those motifs were made particularly readily available for re-use in a new context, and so encouraged the eclectic use of an already eclectic art.'

72 Muscarella 1992, 44–5. Project-related international migration can be traced from the time of Solomon's temple in Jerusalem down to multiple ventures of Darius (522–486).

73 There was a Greek presence at Al Mina by the late eighth century, see Boardman 1999, esp. 38–54. Al Mina is often regarded as a Greek colony or emporion, but for the view that it was 'a typical north Syrian settlement' which specialized in trading with Greeks and Cypriots: see Luke 2003, 1–3, 20–23, 60. See also Markoe 1996; idem 2000; Niemeyer 2004.

74 *Odyssey* VII, 81–102; cf. Cook, E. 2004, esp. 52–3; see also Helm 1980, ch. 7 and on Menelaos's palace see Ch. 2, p. 35. For eastern palaces see Nielsen 2001.

75 Coulton (1977, 32), for example, treats the question briskly by contrast with the consideration he gives to Egyptian influence.

76 For general coverage of building in these regions see Naumann 1971; Frankfort 1954; Liebhart 1988; Werner, P. 1994; Wright 2000; Wightman 2007. For Urartu see Herrmann, H.-V. 1966; Vanden Berghe and De Meyer 1982; Forbes 1983; Pecorella P., *s.v.* Urartea, in *EAA*, 2nd supplement (1994): 889–94; and the bibliography in Zimansky 1998, esp. 178–85.

77 The employment of stone orthostates can be seen in Assyria, Syria and Hittite territory, see Frankfort 1954; Akurgal 1968, 79; Naumann 1971; Wright 2000, 75, who also notes precursors for Greek anathyrosis (the smooth contact band around the edge of individual stones).

78 Edge margins are known in the Levant from the Bronze Age, and later in a few Assyrian and Urartian buildings (Hult 1983, 80–83; Sandars 1986; Sharon 1987; Ratté 2011, 54–5). While earlier forms have been termed 'functional' (Shiloh 1979, 60–70; Jacobson 2000, 139), drafting came to take on a decorative aspect, as when it appears in Lydia: see Coulton 1977, 47, 49; Ratté 1989, 39–42; idem 1993; idem 2011, esp. 34–7, ch. 4.

79 Frankfort 1954; Haines 1971; Naumann 1971, 131–49.

80 On oriental and Egyptian precursors for anthropomorphic supports see Schmidt-Colinet 1977, 10–18. For the caryatid porch at Tell Halaf see Oppenheim 1931, frontispiece, Taf. 13,

fig. on p.114; Rykwert 1996, fig. on p. 140; Schmidt 1982, esp. 33–48; Vonderstein 2000. For a caryatid that is intermediate geographically and chronologically between those of Tell Halaf and Greek examples see Laroche-Traurecker 1993, 17.

81 Dinsmoor 1975, 41; Stewart, A. 1990, 104; Nagy 1998; Lapatin 2001, ch. 4.

82 Romano 1988, 133; Miller J. 1995, 16–27, with a note of caution (215–17). For eastern cult practice see Ringgren 1973, including p. 77 on processions.

83 Genesis 8.21; Leviticus 26.31; I Kings 8.5. See also Brown 1979; Dietrich 1991, 146.

84 Burkert 1992b, 545. See also Dietrich 1991, 142.

85 Most Mesopotamian and Assyrian temples contrast from Greek practice in being located in high-walled courts and attached to palaces. But in Syria temples could be free-standing, see Kaasgaard Falb 2006.

86 Ottosson 1980, 115–18; Biran 1981; Kaasgaard Falb 2006; Wightman 2007, 159–62, 193–7, 432.

87 Ottosson 1980, 54. The key temple at Tell Tayinat measures 11.75 by 25.35m, see Haines 1971, 53–5, pls 80–81, while another has recently been discovered nearby (**Fig. 4.18**), see Harrison and Osborne 2012. For the even larger neo-Hittite temple (21 by 32m) at Ain Dara see Abou Assaf 1990; Wightman 2007, 193–6. For Syrian temple building from the third millennium (e.g., Tell Chuera) see Wright G. 2000; Kaasgaard Falb 2006; Wightman 2007. Greek pottery has been found at Tell Tayinat, indicating either trade or visits by Greeks (Luke 2003, 20–21). Haines (1971, 53) sees the plan of the temple at Tell Tayinat as evidence of a 'western [i.e. Greek] origin or inspiration', a thesis contradicted by Syrian antecedents. It is also possible that this type arose fortuitously in different places (so Frankfort 1954, 175).

88 The main study of the Aeolic capital is Betancourt 1977. See also Newcomb 1921; Wurz and Wurz 1925, 73–85; Schefold 1938–9; Wesenberg 1971, 74–86. For kindred volute capitals in Palestine and Syria see Ciasca 1962, 13–19 and Shiloh 1979; for Etruria see Ciasca 1962; Rykwert 1996, 294–7; for Carthage see Shiloh 1979, 39–41.

89 For furniture, *klinai* and thrones see Ransom 1905; Richter 1966; Kyrieleis 1969; for images of such on vase paintings, see Oliver-Smith 1964; Betancourt 1977, appendix B. On the furniture from Gordion see Simpson 2010.

90 Betancourt 1977, 4, 58, 63ff. It was Koldewey (1890), the discoverer of the capitals from Neandria, who coined the term 'Aeolic' (other proposals include 'proto-Ionic' and, in German, 'Aeolisch-Ionisch'). A three-way ethnic/linguistic division is debatable: see Buck 1955; Hall 2002; and above, Ch. 2, n. 116.

91 Martin 1955–6, 121; idem 1973, 373–8; Hellmann 2002, 165.

92 Masson 1964; Buchholz 1966; Betancourt 1977, 47–8.

93 Examples from Cyprus are currently in storage facilities at Palaiopaphos and the museum at Paphos. For those from Alâzeytin on the Halikarnassos peninsula see Betancourt 1977, ch. 3.

94 Karageorghis 2000, no. 347. On Cypriot rising-volute capitals see Shiloh 1979, 35–9; Shefton 1989; Hermary 1996; Rykwert 1996, 290–92, 297. See also P&C III, fig. 51–53, 152 and Betancourt 1977, fig. 9 for a capital in the Louvre. In-turning volutes feature on building models from Palestine of the early first millennium: see Muller, B. 2002; Miroschedji 2001, 72–5.

95 Tomb 79. Karageorghis 1973–4, pls LXVII, LXIX (nos. 298, 301, 302, 316–18). This frieze could have been made in Phoenicia decades before the tomb deposit, see pp. 94–97. For other pillars with volute capitals see pl. LXVIII. See also Karageorghis 2002, 164–7.

96 The monumental phase of the temple of Athena was either created before the city of Smyrna was razed by the Lydians around 590, or rebuilt soon after. See for contrasting positions Akurgal 1983, 88–97; Cook and Nicholls 1998, 134; Nicholls 1991, 159.

97 Betancourt 1977, 82–7.

98 Betancourt 1977, ch. 5, appendix B; Oliver-Smith 1964.

99 Weber, Marga, 1990, cat. B 106, Taf. XXIII, 88; De Cesare 1997, fig. 33 (cat. 413); Wilson Jones 2002a, cat. 52.

100 For references see **Table 4.1**. For a votive stone capital in the Athenian Agora, see Betancourt 1977, 100, fig. 47. Another capital found to the north-east of the Erechtheion may have been architectural since the upper surface has no cutting to accept the tenon of a sculpture (Acropolis inv. 9980, Borrmann 1888b, 269ff.; Betancourt 1977, 103–4). However not all free-standing columns necessarily carried sculpture.

101 The reconciliation of circular and orthogonal geometries on an early capital from Larisa was achieved courtesy of a lower tier of scrolls. The original setting of this 1.3 m wide capital is unknown; the excavators (Boehlau and Schefold 1940, pl. 69) envisaged a free-standing votive column.

102 This is also the case for the capital from Delos with a fish-scale on the echinus, see **Table 4.1**.

103 According to Weickert (1929, 59) the scrolls at Prinias may have belonged to capitals and not to roof akroteria. In any event volute akroteria are known at the Archaic temple ('H') of the Athenian Acropolis.

104 For the source of Egyptian designs (palm or bunched ostrich feathers?) see Phillips 2002, 16–18, esp. figs 34 a and b.

105 After use in the mid-sixth century for the Delphic treasuries of Massalia and Klazomenai there followed a decline until a Pergamonese revival in the Hellenistic period: see Börker 1965; Wesenberg 1971, ch. 3; King 1997; Liljenstolpe 1999; Hellmann 2002, 177–9.

106 On Samos lobed capitals were used on both the second dipteros (see **Table 4.2**) and the North Building (*Nordbau*), for which see Furtwängler and Kienast 1989, 52.

107 Apart from the Erechtheion, doricizing capitals enriched

with egg-and-dart were used in the Hellenistic period (in the Bouleuterion at Miletos, see Wilson Jones 2000a, fig. 6.3), and later in the Roman period, for example on the Parthian Arch of Augustus in Rome. Some Greek examples had a round abacus, as on votive examples from Didyma, Delphi (Durm 1910, Abb. 341; Wurz 1914, Abb. 192; Wurz and Wurz 1925, Abb. 206b), and Keos (Ohnesorg 1996, Abb. 6).

108 Crowns from the temple terrace at Smyrna vary appreciably in size, suggesting different sets of columns, some of which may have been free-standing: Morris, S. 1985, 178; Akurgal, M. 2007, esp. 131. For doubts, see Cook and Nicholls 1998, 143, and for further references see **Table 4.1**.

109 There are dowel holes in the lower surfaces of the volute elements at Neandria, yet no matching holes on the larger crowns. Perhaps the latter capped the interior columns while the volutes capped the exterior columns, possibly with the smaller crowns/collars. The backs of the volute blocks are roughly carved, indicating they were seen from the front, which is consistent with use on the exterior.

110 See Wesenberg 1971, 77–9, 111–14, 132ff., fig. 164. He interprets similarly a crown from Thasos (*contra* Betancourt 1977, 70–71; *pro* Wiegartz 1994), as well as the 'mushroom' or 'champagne-cork'-shaped crowns from Smyrna, and puts them upside down. Kuhn (1986, 39–46) accepted these as bases, but the usual way up. To the objections of Nicholls (1991, 161–2; Cook and Nicholls 1998, 138–45) and of Akurgal, M. (2007, 130–31), it can be added that champagne-cork elements, the usual way up, are prefigured on balusters at Ramat Rachel (Betancourt 1977, 60), and an Urartian candelabra now in Hamburg (**Fig. 4.28**), see Barnett 1950, fig. 14, pl. 19; Işik 1986, Abb. 4, 7, Taf. 9, 13. Furthermore a comparable wooden furniture piece from Altintepe now in the museum at Ankara has an attached animal hoof which makes the usual orientation certain.

111 Riegl 1992, ch. 3; Betancourt 1977, 19–20; Shiloh 1979, 26, 35, 42–3.

112 On the tree-of-life tradition see Danthine 1937; Perrot 1937; James 1966; Betancourt 1977, 18–19; Kepenski 1982; Rykwert 1996, 155–6, 290, 302. For sacred tree compositions involving volutes see also Barnett 1982, pls 18b, 31d, 47b, 47d; Herrmann, G. 1986, nos. 119–20, pls **22–5**. Stylized pomegranates could also be involved, as on a frieze from the palace of Tukuklti-Ninurta I (1243–1207), see Di Pasquale and Paolucci 2007, 190–91, cat. no. 1.4 (Berlin, Vorderasiatisches Museum, Ass. 981.37).

113 Akurgal 2001, 243, fig. 151b; cf. Przyluski 1936, 10–11.

114 For echoes of the tree-of-life tradition on Crete see Kourou 2001.

115 Boardman 1959, 215; Betancourt 1977, ch. 2; Shiloh 1979. Some mid-span supports of ceremonial doorways were carved to be seen on all four sides, as at Hazor, see Betancourt 1977, pl. 6.

116 Andrae 1933, Taf. 7; Krischen 1956, 53, Taf. 14.

117 The ninth-century sun-disc relief (BM 91000–91002) shows volutes in three locations, including as the capital of a circular column-cum-palm tree. See Puchstein 1907, Abb. 33; von Lichtenberg 1907, Abb. 41; von Luschan 1912, Abb. 32; Wurz 1914, Abb. 111; Andrae 1930, Abb. 30; Wesenberg 1971, Abb. 140; Betancourt 1977, pl. 2; Shiloh 1979, fig. 67; Weber, Marga, 1990, cat. 48, Taf. XI, 40; Rykwert 1996, 301, fig. on p. 297.

118 For blinkers see Orchard 1967, nos. 36–7, 108, 122–4, 149–87. The volutes do not generally spiral in on themselves, but some do, e.g., nos. 162–4 (pl. XXXV). For a fly-whisk datable to c.800 see Mallowan 1966, I, 144–5. Volutes and palmettes were also a staple of oriental tableware and jewellery: see Shefton 1989; Merhav 1991, 190–94.

119 Assyrian traditions had a strong influence on Urartian furniture, which made use of bronze crowns as connecting pieces for wooden members. See Barnett 1950; Özgüç 1969; Işik 1986; Merhav 1991, 246–61; Seidl 1996.

120 Cypriot bronze torch holders found their way to the Samian Heraion and other sites further west: see for example Jantzen 1972, e.g., B 468 (no. 43), Taf. 41; Franz 1998–9, fig. 4; Stampolidis 2003, cat. no. 879, and for further examples nos. 878, 880–83. For a non-functional ivory version found at Salamis on Cyprus see Karagheoghis 1973–4, nos. 33–5, pl. LIV; see also pl. LV, 117 and Stampolidis 2003, cat. 1050, p. 77.

121 On *thymiateria* see Wigand 1912; Franz 1998–9; Zaccagnini Cristiana 1998b; *ThesCRA* V 2 b IV (pp. 212–29). For stone examples such as one from Megiddo, see Krischen 1956, 55, Abb. 20; Franz 1998–9, fig. 11; Miroschedji 2001, 47–51.

122 Kyrieleis 1969, Taf.10.4, 11.4, 12.1, 13.1–4; for the last, see also Betancourt 1977, pl. 24. For a colonnette from Zincirli made of serpentine stone, see Andrae 1943, Taf. 12g; Akurgal, E. 1968, fig. 53; Wesenberg 1971, Abb. 77–8.

123 BM 124564–6 (the date is c.883). See Barnett 1960, pl. 28; Kyrieleis 1969, 7, no.1, Taf.1; Merhav 1991, 250 (no. 3.1). For this type of royal seat see Barker 1966; Kyrieleis 1969; Mallowan and Herrmann 1974; Curtis 1996. See also Roaf 1996.

124 Franz 1998–9, 92–6, 104–5. Alternatively these temples had volute capitals (Shiloh 1979, 82–3, 90–91), or composite designs. Biblical descriptions mention 'bowl-shaped capitals' (II Chronicles 4.12) and capitals 'shaped like lilies' (I Kings 7.20). For the idea that Solomon's temple influenced the Greek temple see Mazar 1992, 184; for the Jerusalem temple see I Kings 6–7; II Chronicles 2–4; Busink 1970–80; Wright 1985, 254–67. See also Zwickel 1999.

125 Haines 1971, pl. 118; Betancourt 1977, pl. 24. The collar co-exists with a central triangle, showing them not to be mutually exclusive.

126 Barnett 1957, 145–51, pl. IV; Boardman 1959, 215–16; Betancourt 1977, Appendix A, pl. 23; Herrmann, G. 1986, nos. 102–11 (pls 18–20).

127 Betancourt 1977, pl. 26; Shiloh 1979, pl. 14, 3 (cf. pp. 8–10). For ones from Arslan-Tash see Thureau-Dangin 1931, pl. XLIV. For similar ivory 'balusters' that likely belonged to thrones or footstools see Herrmann, G. 1986, pl. 43, a-b.

128 Layard (1853, 444) believed the capital to be Ionic. For his pencil visualization see Barnett *et al.* 1998, no. 422, pl. 321. Today the relief is too badly worn to be sure, but the column most likely had rising volutes. I thank Dominique Collon for helping to locate this piece, and for supporting observations.

129 On Evans's reconstructions see Klynne 1998. Betancourt (1977, 18, 21) passes over possible Minoan or Mycenaean precedents rapidly, in just two sentences. A recent study of the Minoan and Mycenaean columns (Eichinger 2004) neglects volutes, yet the tree-of-life featured in Minoan and Mycenaean traditions, see Kourou 2001. Interestingly Lethaby speculated that 'There is some evidence which suggests that even the Ionic order may have been developed by the Hittites before it was adopted by the Greeks, although I think it probable that it was known in the Minoan age.' (Lethaby 1917, 14).

130 For a pair of miniature volute ornaments from Archanes see Sakellarakis and Sapouna-Sakellaraki 1997, fig. 644; Dimopoulou-Rethymiotaki 2005, 319. For examples from Mycenae see Sakellariou 1985, pls 18, 41, 47, 48, 94, 100, 114, 117, 119. Fimmen (1921, 202) links such volute motifs to Egyptian lily ornaments.

131 For the paintings with the pavilions (in room 4), see Doumas 1992, 50–62, and for the frieze with flotilla (room 5), see figs 35, 37. Cf. Morgan, L. 1988, and Palyvou 2005, 46–53 on the West House.

132 Sakellarakis 1996, 108, pl. 27b; Sakellarakis and Sapouna-Sakellaraki 1997, 721–9; Dimopoulou-Rethymiotaki 2005, 332. For comparable material from Mycenae, see Poursat 1977, pls IX, XV, XXII.

133 National Museum, Athens, 3214; Sakellariou 1985, E 3214 (9), 248, pl. 120; Poursat 1977, pl. XXXIII, 315/3214 (cf. pl. I, 44/3024). I am indebted to Manolis Korres for directing me towards these pieces. For further examples see Persson 1942, 131.

134 P&C VII, 658.

135 By contrast, the capital from Oropos does achieve a more than usually compact design, by learning it seems from the Ionic configuration (**Fig. 5.20c**).

136 Votive pillars on Cyprus in the Archaic period (e.g., at Palaiopaphos) have capitals comprising four out-turning pointed horns or stylized palm fronds; for a representation in Ankara, see Rykwert 1996, 295. The pavilion of Assurnassipal that Semper illustrates (**Fig. 0.6b**) is taken from a relief in the British Museum (inv. 124548). See Semper 2004, 294 [1861, 308]; Puchstein 1907, Abb. 34; Wurz 1914, Abb. 127; Wesenberg 1971, Abb. 141; Weber Marga, 1990, cat. 49, Taf. XI, 41–2).

CHAPTER FIVE

1 Once so denigrated, surface ornament is becoming rehabilitated in architectural discourse: see Brent C. Brolin, *Architectural Ornament: Banishment and Return* (New York 2000 [1st ed. 1985]); James Trilling, *Ornament: A Modern Perspective* (Seattle, Wash., 2003); Rob Gregory, 'The Trouble with Ornament', *Architectural Review* 222, no. 1329 (Nov. 2007), 30–35. Note the recent work by practices such as Herzog & de Meuron, Caruso St John, and Hild und K.

2 Riegl 1992, 4 [1893, vi].

3 Despite his brilliance as a practitioner, Otto Wagner exemplifies the 'over-zealous' follower Riegl, a fellow Viennese, had in mind. For one of Wagner's pronouncements, see Ch. 3, p. 66; for background, see Iversen, M. 1993, 25–30.

4 Riegl 1992, 4 [1893, vi–vii].

5 Riegl's work brought a theoretical rigour that went beyond Owen Jones's pioneering *Grammar of Ornament* (Jones 1856). On Riegl's approach see Quintavalle 1981 and Castriota's introduction in Riegl 1992. See also Gombrich 1979.

6 Marconi 2007; AA.VV. 2009b, with essays by Osborne and Hölscher, who is not the first to point out (2009, 62) that the term decoration is derived from the Latin *decor* (*prepon* in Greek), a concept that embraced the appropriateness of form in social terms (Wilson Jones 2000a, 43–4). See also Peponi 2012.

7 Stresses increase in ratio to the cube of linear distances, while resistance increases in ratio to their square. For consequences for Greek design see Coulton 1977, ch. 4.

8 For the roots of *symmetria* in mathematics and philosophy, see Pollitt 1974, esp. 15; Knell 1985; Gros 1989; Wilson Jones 2000a, 10, 40–43.

9 Vitruvian man belongs to a Greek tradition epitomized by the canon of Polykleitos on the one hand and metrological reliefs on the other. See Rykwert 1996, 97–115; Wilson Jones 2000b; McEwen 2003, 156–62.

10 Wilson Jones 2001; idem 2006.

11 For principles of ancient design and proportion see Coulton 1975; idem 1977, esp. ch. 3; Wilson Jones 2001; idem 2006.

12 Plommer (1977, 77–8) points out that while Mycenaean architects gave attention to proportion, it is unlikely to have been of such concern in the Geometric period. See Kalpaxis 1976 for metrical analysis, though most early structures are too poorly preserved to merit such study.

13 The bed-chamber which Odysseus built for Penelope and himself [*Odyssey* XXIII, 184–99] possessed these qualities along with defensive walls and military formations [e.g., *Iliad*, XVI, 212–16].

14 Haselberger 1999; Zambas 2002.

15 I owe this wordplay – along with much else of more substance in this chapter – to Paul Richens.

16 Wesenberg 1971; Herrmann, K. 1983; Mertens 1993.

17 Hittorff 1851; Hittorff and Zanth 1870; Hellmann *et al.* 1983; Herrmann, K. 1983, 12.

18 La Rosa 1974; Segal 2007, no.18.

19 Egg-and-dart was later applied to a doricizing type that found favour in Hellenistic Pergamon and Rome.

20 Of relevance are the painted terracotta plaques from Thermon (**Fig. 2.18**), though they did not necessarily belong to a Doric ensemble.

21 For references see **Table 3**.

22 Barletta 1990, fig. 17; Mertens 1993, Taf. 85, 4. For decorative aspects of Doric in later periods see Rumscheid 1994; King 2000.

23 Bötticher [1844–52] judged only the frontal triglyphs of temples to have a constructional aspect, those on the flanks being there for visual effect. Semper wondered whether triglyphs might be traced back to edging devices employed for textiles (2004, 125). He also declared (2004, 769 [1863, 416]) that 'The triglyph . . . neither supports the cornice nor does it transfer its load to the centre of the column; rather it is an *attached dressing* (angeheftete Bekleidung).' Durm (1910, 261) later agreed that it has little to do with construction.

24 Laum 1912, part I; Cook, R. 1951; idem 1970. See also Holloway 1973, 52–3 (for whom guttae 'are not structural but have been added to the Doric temple as decoration'); Lawrence 1983, 123; Weickenmeier 1985, 132–9; Coulton 1977, 41; Barletta 2001, 146–50. See Ch. 3, p. 85 above.

25 An example from a medium other than pottery is an electrum band of the late Geometric period, see Sapouna-Sakellaraki 1997.

26 Examples of 'tetraglyphs' include terracotta ones from Crotone (Mertens 1993, Abb. 74); an anta in the temple of Hera (E) at Selinunte; ones on the exterior of the Roman theatre at Arles (Wilson Jones 2000a, fig. 6.4). 'Pentaglyphs' are known from the temple at the Casa Marafioti site at Locri Epizephiroi, see Costamagna and Sabbione 1990, fig. 230. Ferri (1948, 407–8) explains tetraglyphs as arising from the belief (by some) that triglyphs should have three whole glyphs/channels, as the name suggests, and therefore four uprights.

27 Although triglyphs were normally painted blue by the Classical period, early ones were black or red (Ch. 3, p. 83), colours used for painting clay. Perhaps the germs of triglyphs were painted on terracotta revetment, a connection suggested by patterns in red paint on an Archaic temple model from Sparta (**Fig. 2.9**).

28 Cook 1970, 18. Once the idiom had taken hold, triglyphs could have received a more plastic treatment so as to exploit the effects of shadow, rather as dividers were rendered in relief on Cretan terracotta *pithoi*, for which see Anderson 1975. On connections between workshops producing archi-tectural terracottas and ceramics such as *pithoi*, see Simantoni-Bournias 1990.

29 The term 'paratactic' has been applied to literature (e.g., Perry 1937; Bakker, P. 1997; Versnel 2011, 213–15, 226–9). For use as regards art and architecture see Howe 1985, 87, 102, who notes (89–90) the absence of vertical coordination between the components of different registers on Geometric pottery.

30 Some painted pottery 'triglyphs' of the Geometric period have a middle section treated with running spirals reminiscent of split-rosette precursors (**Fig. 2.10**). See Coldstream 1968 for further examples, including pls 5f, 8f, 10k, 13a. For Bronze Age frieze-dividers with running spirals see P&C VI, figs 228, 277; Dimopoulou-Rethymiotaki 2005, 35.

31 For a field-and-divider frieze on a terracotta model of a wheeled cart from Palaikastro dating to the Minoan prepalatial period (*c.*2000–1800), see Dimopoulou-Rethymiotaki 2005, 75.

32 Barletta 2001, 84, 95, 153–5; Hellmann 2002, 146–52. Awareness of Cycladic practice, on which Vitruvius was silent, has gained steadily since the late nineteenth century.

33 For a review of base designs see Barletta 2001, 85–95.

34 The Archegesion on Delos also had bases of this kind, but here the shafts were possibly wooden as opposed to stone in the Oikos. See Daux 1963, 862–5; Barletta 2001, 85. The Heraion may have had conical bases as early as the seventh century, but this is not certain; see Ch. 2, n. 106.

35 Johannes 1937; Hendrich 2007; Hellner 2009.

36 Hogarth 1908; Ohnesorg 2007, 42–53. See also Wesenberg 1971, 116–30; Barletta 2001, 91–5; Rocco 2003, 77–8.

37 Von Luschan 1912, 11–13; Naumann 1971, 131–50; Akurgal, E. 1968, 80–87; Wesenberg 1971, 87–104, Abb. 179–213.

38 Jacoby and von Luschan 1911, 11–13; Wurz and Wurz 1925, Abb. 54–5; Akurgal, E. 1968; Haines 1971, 46, pl. 75, 116.

39 It was in part signs of incremental development discovered at Yria that led Wesenberg (1996, 8) to give more weight to the possibility of indigenous as opposed to eastern origins he had sustained earlier (idem 1971, 87ff., 129). Cf. Barletta 2001, 90.

40 Marchand 1996. See Ch. 4, n. 24.

41 For the rationale behind semi-circular flutes see Wilson Jones 2000a, 11.

42 Dinsmoor 1975, 125, 130; Barletta 2001, 98. The numbers of flutes could vary within the same building; the Ephesian Artemision has shafts with 40, 44 and 48 flutes. For a votive column from Delos with just 16 fillet-and-flutes see Fraisse and Linas 1995, fig. 241; Hellmann 2002, fig. 193.

43 Some bases of the Artemision incorporate the apophyge and/or astragal within the same block, a technique sometimes used later. Nonetheless the general trend makes it clear that these belonged conceptually to the shaft.

44 Baran 2007. Such necking, sometimes incorporated into the same block as the capital, recurs intermittently down to the Hellenistic period.

45 On the general development of the Ionic capital see Mace

1974; Theodorescu 1980; Bakker, K. 1999; Barletta 2001, ch. 4; Rocco 2003; Hellmann 2002, 146–65. For specific aspects see Martin 1955–6; idem 1973; Gruben 1963; idem 1965; idem 1989; Kirchhoff 1988; McGowan 1993; Korres 1996; idem 1997a; Ohnesorg 1993; eadem 1996; eadem 2002.

46   For a valiant graphic portrayal of the relationships between volute capitals see Theodorescu 1980, pl. 3.

47   Capitals that have been attributed early dates include three from Delos. An unfinished one for a pillar was discovered under the colossal Naxian Apollo (see **Table 5**) which does make an early date certain. For the other two see Martin 1973, 382–91, nos. 5 and 6 (who dates them to the second quarter of the sixth century); Fraisse and Llinas 1995, figs 340–60; Ohnesorg 1996, 39–40 (who argues for the late seventh century).

48   McGowan 1993; Ohnesorg 1996; Barletta 2001, 101, 134.

49   White 1971; Segal 2007, no. 17.

50   Martin 1955–6; Hellmann 2002, 147, 164.

51   Some Ionic capitals like one from Paros have a concave canalis on one side and a convex one on the other. The same is true of the Aeolic capital from Oropos.

52   Clarke 1886; Dinsmoor 1975, e.g., 59; Drerup 1952, 7ff.; Akurgal, E. 1960; Boardman *et al.* 1967, 17. Perrot and Chipiez (P&C VII, 630) regarded the 'chapiteau à volutes adossés' as 'la forme primitive du chapiteau ionique'. See also Persson 1942, 130; Martin 1955–6, 121.

53   Koldewey 1891, 33ff.; Schefold 1938–9; Martin 1955–6, 127; Betancourt 1977, 128–30; Barletta 2001, 100–01; Hellmann 2002, 168.

54   This influence is manifest in the concave canalis (on one side, the other is convex), the relatively high position of the echinus, and in the concavity of the bolster.

55   Rocco (2003, 44) speaks of a 'variante locale dello ionico asiatico'.

56   Hieroglyphics meaning 'great king' took the shape of pillar-like triangles capped by horizontally linking curling outlines: see von Sybel 1888, fig. 63; von Luschan 1912, Abb. 37; Wurz, R. 1914, Abb. 210; more recently Rykwert 1996, 278–9; Akurgal, E. 2001, esp. 105–6, 126–9.

57   Von Luschan 1912; Wurz, R. 1914; Wurz and Wurz 1925, 11, Abb. 18, 19, 21, 23; Krischen 1956, 50–61; Rykwert 1996, 290–315.

58   Inspection of 'Ionic' volutes claimed for Near Eastern sites reveals them to be wishful thinking, as in the case of a relief from Khorsabad (P&C II, 221, fig. 77). See also Chipiez 1876, 75–8; von Sybel 1888, fig. 64; Wurz, R. 1914, Abb. 132; Wesenberg 1971, Abb. 148–9. The same is true for an Assyrian colonnette in relief, which Layard thought was Ionic (above, Ch. 4, p. 108, and n. 128).

59   Catling, H. 1964, 190–223; idem 1984, 69–91; Matthäus 1985; idem 1988; Karageorghis 2002, figs 198–204. Of particular note are tripods found in eighth- or seventh-century contexts, such as a tomb in Athens (National Museum, inv.

X 7940; Wurz and Wurz 1925, Abb. 231; Catling, H. 1964, 194, no. 6, pl. 28a). Such objects were evidently prized heirlooms. See also a fragment found at Samos (Catling, H. 1964, 198, no. 16, pl. 30d; Jantzen 1972, B. 964, 40–42, pl. 37; Stampolidis *et al.* 2003, cat. 731). An elaborate Cypriot four-legged wheeled stand from Kition(?) displays 'Ionic' colonnettes flanked by antithetical sphinxes (Altes Museum, Berlin, inv. 8947); Wurz and Wurz 1925, 88–9, Abb. 227; Catling, H. 1964, 207–8, no. 35, pl. 36a; Matthäus 1985, no. 708 (318–19).

60   Chipiez 1876, fig. 83; Wurz and Wurz 1925, 86–91; Berve and Gruben 1963, Abb. 104. The fact that Cypriot stands mix 'Aeolic' with 'Ionic' configurations may have led designers around 600 to regard them as in some respects interchangeable.

61   'Ambiguous volutes' appear in relief on shields and other objects from Crete, including some of seventh-century date, see Kunze 1931, 118–23, who uses the term 'Gepaarte Doppelvoluten'. For such motifs on Assyrian and Urartian thrones like those illustrated here see von Luschan 1912, Abb. 6; Wurz and Wurz 1925, 24–6; Krischen 1956, Abb. 14, 18; Kyrieleis 1969. Also of note are ivories such as a blinker from Nimrud, and painted schemes on Melian amphoras, see Papastamos 1970, esp. 94–97.

62   I am indebted to Manolis Korres for encouraging me to search out the connections observed in this paragraph.

63   Wace 1932, 84, no. 54, fig. 30; Persson 1942, 129–32; Poursat 1977, pl. XXXIV, 322/6443.

64   This vessel probably dates to the middle of the second millennium: see Hampe and Simon 1981, 130, figs 119–20.

65   *Epinomis* (traditionally attributed to Plato) 987d–988a.

66   This division between Cycladic and Ionian complements, though it is not the same as that which Theodorescu (1980) makes between large volute and small volute capitals.

67   One in the museum at Delphi is a case in point; for *perirrhanteria* see Ch. 1, n. 19.

68   Berti and Masturzo 2000, 223. See also Berges 1996; Koenigs 1996.

69   Here, too, I am indebted to Manolis Korres.

70   Ohnesorg, 2001; eadem 2007, 74.

71   Gruben 1963.

72   Tuchelt 1991; Büsing 2006. For speculation that similar designs incorporating wooden volutes were used for the first dipteros at Samos see Ch. 2, p. 59.

73   An exception to this rule is the identical design used for the volutes of capitals from the Asklepieion and the Illissos temple in Athens, see Korres 1996, 97.

74   Barletta 2001, 115–20; Hellmann 2002, 148–53; Rocco 2003, 43, 58.

75   Marconi 2007, 26–7. A similar range of mouldings and enrichments were used for architraves framing doors.

76   Lycian influence may manifest itself in the incorporation of dentils in the tomb at Tamassos (**Fig. 3.5**).

77 The cornice of the dipteros at Samos is lost, but fragments of Archaic dentil courses are known from Samos and other sites: Bingöl 1990, 101–8; Barletta 2001, 119; Hellmann 2002, 152–3.

78 For examples at Nimrud, Khorsabad and Tell Barsip, see Albend 2005, esp. 130. For one at Arslan-Tash see Thureau-Dangin 1931, pl. XVII.

79 Demangel 1932, 130ff.; Ridgway 1966; Ratté 1989; Barletta 2001, 117–19; Hellmann 2002, 164, 309. For developments further west see Mertens-Horn 1992.

80 Rykwert 1996, 182; Corso and Romano 1997, I, 344–5, n. 193.

81 Gruben 2001, 157 (writing of the Oikos of the Naxians).

82 Gruben (1963, 142–7; idem 2001, 404) attributes two corner blocks with gorgons (one of which bears part of a reclining lion) to the architrave, whereas Schattner (1996) sees the gorgons stacked above one another on both architrave and frieze (the latter having the lion). The problem is not easy to resolve, not least because the gorgons are different in height; in addition, one block is smooth and the other has fasciae. Marconi (2007, 25–6, n. 116) favours the architrave.

83 A case in point is the temple of Athena at Priene, see Koenigs and Philipp 1996 for this and other examples.

CHAPTER SIX

1 'As the pigments are but the vehicle of painting, so is building but the vehicle of architecture, which is the thought behind form, embodied and realised for the purpose of its manifestation and transmission. Architecture, then, inter-penetrates building, not for satisfaction of the simple needs of the body, but for the complex ones of the intellect.' So William Lethaby (1891, 'Introductory'). On culture and the communication of ideas and attitudes, see Geertz 1973, esp. 89.

2 Vaughan Hart, *Inigo Jones: The Architect of Kings* (New Haven and London 2011).

3 On the metaphor of language see Introduction, n. 1.

4 As Juan Pablo Bonta observes in *Architecture and Its Interpretation* (London 1979), 22: 'efforts to construct a meaning-proof architecture have always been *de facto* unsuccessful . . . An architecture designed to be meaningless . . . would *mean* the desire to be meaningless, and thus could not actually *be* meaningless.' Seminal twentieth-century studies on meaning in the visual arts include Erwin Panofsky's volume with that title (1955) and Michael Baxandall's *Patterns of Intention: On the Historical Explanation of Pictures* (New Haven and London 1985). See also Whyte 2006 (esp. 158), who notes that the 'reading' or 'translating' of meanings in architecture is rendered more complex than for art or text on account of its functional and non-representational aspects.

5 Branko Mitrovic, *Learning from Palladio* (London and New York 2004), 9.

6 For a new twist to the 'huge literature on the spiral' see Louise Rice, 'The Pentecostal Meaning of Borromini's Sant' Ivo alla Sapienza', in *Francesco Borromini: Atti del Convegno internazionale*, con. (Milan 2000), 259–70.

7 Dissatisfaction with preceding theories led Sarah Morris (2001) to a new intuition, that the appendages represent a type of goatskin pouch, a *kursa* (hence *borsa* and purse in European languages), which can be traced back to Hittite ritual.

8 Wood 1741. See here Introduction, pp. 6–7.

9 Viel de Saint-Maux 1787, ix; cf. vii, 16. Viel took pleasure in veiling his identity and in a certain subversive mischievousness, while the ironic tone of his letters makes it hard to know how much his polemic represents conviction as opposed to provocation. See Benaissa 2007, and Pérouse de Montclos 1966 on the identities of the author and the better known Charles-François Viel.

10 Frazer's *The Golden Bough* first appeared in two volumes in 1890, with further volumes and editions. For contextualization see Fontenrose 1966; Morris, I. 1993, 16–24; Segal, R. 1999, esp. ch. 3.

11 Pugin 1841, 2.

12 Riegl 1992 [1893], 43–4 (Quintavalle 1981, 16). Myth arguably supplies meanings for phenomena that have become obscure, or as William Robertson Smith (Smith 1889, 19) put it, 'an explanation as could not have arisen had the original sense of the usage not more or less fallen in to oblivion'.

13 Hermeneutics (from the Greek *hermeneuein*, to interpret) grew up out of the desire to go beyond biblical exegesis by establishing a more rigorous grounding for decoding texts: cf. Bill Thompson, 'Hermeneutics for Architects?', *Journal of Architecture* 12 (2007), 183–91.

14 Sourvinou-Inwood 1991, 5, 11, 122.

15 This was perhaps done in accordance with an oath apparently made before the battle of Plataia in 479, see Diodorus Siculus II, 29.3; Hurwit 2000, 141.

16 Hurwit 2000, 203–4; Marx 2011, esp. 33–4. This legend was also represented on the west pediment of the Parthenon.

17 For avenues into an ample bibliography see Knell 1990; Stewart 1990; Jenkins 2006; Marconi 2007, idem 2009b; Scott 2007; AA. VV. 2009b. For approach and method see Hölscher 2004.

18 Euripides, *Ion*, 185–231. On the perceived animation of statuary see here Ch. 1, p. 22.

19 There is an evident contradiction, equally apparent in other examples, between what Hölscher (2009, 54–6, 66) has called 'high meaning' and 'low communication'.

20 Hölscher 2009, 56–7, 63. High-level architectural sculpture arguably sustained a sacred atmospheric background against which the cult statue and prestigious votives stood

out as the star performers, dominating the attention of observers such as Pausanias.

21   Burkert 1988, 34.

22   *De Oratore* 3, 180. On the concept of *decor*, see Ch. 5, n. 6.

23   Semper 2004, 764–5, similarly 623 and an unpublished manuscript (Herrmann, W. 1984, 171, n. 42). For echoes see Durm 1910, 363–4; Drerup 1962. Other symbolic interpretations of the peristasis include: as a way of emphasizing the exterior once sacrifices were moved outside (Martini 1986); as a manifestation of communal identity (Höcker 1996); and as a symbol of divine protection of the *polis* (Fehr 1996, 181–8).

24   Occasional Roman monolithic column shafts such as ones left behind in the quarries at Proconnesos are knobbled and knotted like tree-trunks (a device used by Bramante at S. Ambrogio in Milan). Other manifestations of this theme include medieval rib vaulting shaped like entwined boughs (Rykwert 1972, 80–101) and Laugier's primitive hut (**Fig. 0.4**). For Soane's derivation of the Gothic cathedral from a grove of trees see Watkin 1996, 179, pl. VII.

25   Evans 1901; Nilsson 1950, chs 7 and 8. For Minoan crypts see Rutkowski 1986, 21–45; Marinatos 1993, 95–8. For interpretations of the Lion Gate relief and its column see Åström and Blomé 1964; Shaw, M. 1986; Rykwert 1996, 156–7. See also Kourou 2001.

26   Pliny the Elder, *HN* XII, 2. On the linkage between trees, columns and temples see Bötticher 1856, esp. 9; Wurz and Wurz 1925; Allsopp 1965, 9; Rykwert 1972; idem 1996, 122; Birge 1994.

27   For the sacred oak of Zeus at Dodona see James 1966, 28–9; on the evidence of Pausanias see Birge 1994, 236–45.

28   A popular Renaissance theme, this is evident in such diverse texts as those Francesco di Giorgio, John Shute and Jacques-François Blondel. For critical exploration, see Rykwert's work, esp. 1996, chs 2–5; Dodds and Tavernor 2002.

29   McEwen (2003, 5–13, esp. 9) notes that Vitruvius was possibly the first to use the word *corpus* to characterize a body of work in the sense still used today.

30   'Festoons of fruit', 'runs of fruit', and 'festoons' are popular translations of the Latin *encarpis*. However, Gros (1992, 6, 69) points out, while opting for '*festons*' (festoons), that the term *encarpis* is a Vitruvian hapax (or 'one-off'), perhaps suggesting some sort of container.

31   On the Dorian invasion and Ionic migration see Snodgrass 1971, 296–323 and 373–8 respectively, and for background here Ch. 2, n. 116. Ancient tradition on this is arguably largely an invention of the Archaic period: see Osborne 1996, 35–7. For the theory that Ion's temple was an unidentified precursor of the Hellenistic Doric temple of Apollo at Claros see Gros 1993; Corso and Romano 1997, I, 414, n. 32.

32   Gros 1988; idem 1995. On Vitruvius's sources see Romano, E. 1987, 66–76, 101–8; Gros 1997, lxiii–lxxii.

33   Plommer 1970, 185; Gros 1992, 70–71; Ridgway 1977, 85–119;

Coulton 2007, 206, fig. 5, who notes that in some cases the drapery flares out at the bottom like the apophyge at the foot of column shafts. For *korai* see Richter 1968; Karakasi 2003.

34   Lissarrague 1995, 95; cf. cat. 46. A fifth-century vase painting shows one placed on top of a tomb decorated with strips or fillets (*tainia*) probably of woven wool: Vienna, Kunsthistorisches Museum 3736; Kurtz 1975, fig. 33.2 (cf. p. 212); Oakley 2004, figs 134–5; cf. fig. 15. For related examples see Nakayama 1982, A-N-17, B-II-1, D-III-11; Oakley 2004, col. fig. Ia, figs 106, 133, 152.

35   Cuzin 2000, 180–81, no. 34; Édouard Papet, 'Autour de la *Corinthe* de Jean-Léon Gérôme', *Revue des Musées de France. Revue du Louvre* 4 (October 2009): 73–84.

36   Schmidt-Colinet 1977, W 18 (Rome, featuring basket-weave: see Gordon Smith 2003, fig. 210.), W 22, W 51 (Istanbul).

37   Schmidt-Colinet 1977; Rykwert 1996, 129–132. For those belonging to the gigantic Olympieion at Agrigento, see Broucke 1996; Marconi 1997; Vonderstein 2000.

38   On caryatids see Vitruvius I, 1.5; Gwilt 1825, 53–9; Homolle 1917; Schmidt-Colinet 1977; Plommer 1979; Schmidt, E. 1982; Rykwert 1996, 133–8; Hellmann 2002, 201–11.

39   Vitruvius (I, 1.5–6) mentions a Spartan portico with Persian slaves in place of columns, while explaining how caryatids were named after women from Carya who were enslaved following the defeat of the Persians, with whom this small town in the Peloponnese had sided. Alternatively the region of Carya neighbouring Ionia was involved. See Rykwert 1996, 129–38; Hellmann 2002, 204–6.

40   The name 'hypotrachelion' for the band of rings closing the Doric echinus evokes a kind of necking (*trachelos*); however there are caryatids that carry on *top* of their heads *kalathoi* and *phialai*, vessels that may themselves be linked to capitals.

41   The reverse taper of Minoan columns might follow anthropomorphic reasoning. As Rykwert (1996, 156) observes, with their feet close together and broad shoulders, telamons and caryatids expand towards the top.

42   Aeschylus, *Agamemnon*, 895–900. See also Allsopp (1965, 7), for whom the column became the conceptual support for the family, attracting 'certain significances or even active magical properties'. Rykwert goes into more depth (1996, esp. 119–23, 128–9, 151–7), musing on 'the primal post' and asking (153) 'are not columns in some sense always the holiest part of a building?'

43   Pausanias V, 20.7. See also Brulotte 1994b; Rykwert 1996, 206–7. The bands were presumably made of metal and used to restrict splitting of the wood.

44   *Iphigenia in Tauris*, 50–52, trans. Rykwert 1996, 129.

45   *Iphigenia in Tauris*, 57.

46   Compare McEwen's interpretation (1993, 110–13, 119–20) with that of Fehr (1996) and Höcker (1996); see n. 23, above.

47   Onians 1989, 57–8; idem 1999; cf. Jackson 1991.

48 'As when a man knits together the wall of his lofty house with close-fitting stones, keeping out the force of the hot winds, so did the helmets and bossed shields fit together, shield against shield, helmet against helmet, man against man': *Iliad* XVI, 211–15. See Onians 1989, 43; idem 1999, 10–12, and also *Iliad* XII, 105; XV, 618. For a remark by King Agesilaos to the effect that the walls of Sparta were its armed citizens see Plutarch, *Apophthegmata Laconica*, 210e.

49 Onians 1989; idem 1999, 28. The logic of the phalanx was predicated on seventh-century developments in arms and armour that demanded compact formation, discipline and solidarity, see Murray 1980, 120–31. Studies on Greek warfare include Jackson 1991; AA.VV. 2001b.

50 McEwen 1993, 51, 118–19.

51 McEwen 1993, 101–2, and 109 on analogies between building and weaving crafts.

52 Offerings were sometimes suspended from trees inside sanctuary precincts, see Bötticher 1856 (Hersey's prime source); de Cazenove 1993; Brulotte 1994a, 315–19. Hersey (1988, 3) takes care, however, to avoid claiming that this explains 'how the orders really did come about' – which leaves the question up in the air.

53 Euripides, *Iphigenia in Tauris*, 67–75. The altar too dripped with the Hellenes' blood.

54 Aeschylus, *Seven Against Thebes*, 265–78a, trans. G. Hutchinson, from Jackson 1991, 239.

55 Hersey 1988, 21.

56 Coulton 2007, esp. 203–5.

57 Coulton 2007, 201–2. See also Wesenberg 1971, 127–9.

58 Compare the neck of a vase in the Louvre, Walter 1968, no. 592 (Taf. 116).

59 Meanwhile the concave scotia shares the name *trochilos* with the pulley-wheel channels through which ropes pass. I thank Manolis Korres for his reflections while on a visit to the Erechtheion.

60 Hersey 1988, 30. Volutes and rams' horns have been frequently compared, see Rykwert 1996, 271, 303–7, who judiciously concludes (p. 315) that by not being tied too closely to any one theme the capital maintained connections with all of them: sacrificial horns, oriental sacred trees, Egyptian Hathor-wigs and more.

61 Rumscheid 1994, 276–7.

62 The term *guttae* is Latin, meaning drops; the Greek term for these details is not known. Wood (1741, 204–6) likened the vertical recesses of triglyphs to stylized drainage channels, and believed the Doric frieze as a whole was 'derived from the embroider'd Curtains of the [Holy] *Tabernacle*, when they were drawn up'. For commentary see Rykwert 1996, 27–9. For nineteenth-century interpretation of guttae see Hittorff and Zanth 1870, 349; Chipiez 1876, 246–7; Weickenmeier 1985, esp. 76.

63 Hersey 1988, 31, 40, 42. Note the following appeal to Apollo by his priest Chryse, whom Agamemnon humiliated in front of the whole Greek army: 'if it ever pleased your heart that I built your temple, / if it ever pleased you that I burnt all the rich thigh pieces / of bulls, of goats, then bring to pass this wish I pray for: / let your arrows make the Danaans pay for my tears shed' (*Iliad* I, 36–42, trans. Lattimore). For other Homeric mentions of thigh-bones, see *Iliad* I, 459–64, II, 422–9, XV, 372–3, XXII, 170–71 and *Odyssey* III, 9, 178, 273–74, 457–62, IV, 764, IX, 553; XII, 360, XIII, 26, XXI, 267. For comment: Burkert 1966, 104–5; idem 1983, 6; idem 1985, 57; Jameson 1988, 970–71; van Straten 1988; idem 1995, 122–7, 141–4; Zaccagnini, Carlo 1988; Le Guen-Pollet 1991, 17–19; Pulleyn 1997, 16.

64 Stucchi 1974, 115, n. 150. Stucchi's thinking (not cited by Hersey) is curiously selective, for he pursued a structural/evolutionary reading in the case of the triglyphs on temples.

65 Demangel 1931; idem 1937; idem 1946; idem 1949. For oriental parallels see Amiet 1980, pls 11, 23, 24, 46–8, 48 bis, 52, 61, 118 (of these fig. 659 on pl. 46 is the most striking). For symbolic portals in Doricizing friezes from Alexandria, see Pensabene 1993, Tav. 100 and 136.

66 Hellenistic examples are rare, see Rumscheid 1994, 257.

67 Temples of the Classical period are known to have been hung with votive shields commemorating victories (for example the bastion of the Nike temple on the Athenian Acropolis, see Lippman *et al.* 2006). See also Hittorff and Zanth 1870, 141, 154, 185–6 for more speculative proposals. However stone friezes involving shield motifs only appear relatively late, and not on temples but on commemorative monuments (for one such see Markle 1999).

68 Vitruvius (VII, Pref. 12) specifically cited *De symmetriis corinthiis*, a work probably of the fourth century by a certain Arcesius (also mentioned IV, 3.1). See Corso and Romano 1997, I, 426, n. 49, 459–60, n. 119.

69 For the date see Cooper 1996, 305–24. For the capital see Bauer 1973, 14–65; Haller von Hallerstein 1976, esp. pls 56–7; Cooper 1996, vol. IV (folio), pls 49–50. See also Hauglid 1947, 98; Wotschnitsky 1948, 53ff.; Roux 1953b; Bankel 1986, 122–4. Some past reconstructions have envisaged three Corinthian columns rather than just one, but one is more likely.

70 Pedersen 1989. This is an appealing if unprovable theory.

71 The chief evidence is the miniature copy known as the Varvakeion Athena in the National Museum at Athens. It is possible that the original had leaf ornament which could not be rendered this small. See Leipen 1971; Stewart 1990, 157–9, figs 361–3. For doubts that the column formed part of Pheidias's original conception, see Lapatin 2001, 86–8.

72 For the Olympia capital and a comparable one from Elis dating probably to the second half of the fourth century see Mallwitz 1981b; Hellmann 2002, 170–71.

73 These capitals, one of which is on display in the museum, have been dated either side of 400, see Charbonneaux and

Gottlob 1925, 20–22, pls 23–6; Bauer 1973, 84–7, 136–9; Seiler 1986, 65–7.

74   Orsi and Cavallari 1890, Tav. II bis; Mertens 1993, 115, Taf. 76.1. The exact date is unknown, but it must precede 483, when the neighbouring Syracusans ravaged the city. An Amazon-cum-caryatid of Roman date with a 'sofa' Corinthianizing capital stands in the National Museum in Athens (inv. 705), see Schmidt-Colinet 1977, W 23.

75   Stuart and Revett 1762–94, I, ch. 4; Le Roy 2004 [1770], 349–53, pls 33–5; Riemann 1956b; Travlos 1971, 348–51; Bauer 1977; Amandry 1997, 463–70; Alemdar 2000; Wilson 2000, 219–26.

76   The two most notable Corinthian temples from this period were dedicated to Zeus, the one at Athens the other at Diocaesarea in Cilicia, see Wilson Jones 2000a, 135, 238, n. 4.

77   Vitruvius IV, 1.2; Wilson Jones 2000, 111–13.

78   On the Roman 'normalkapitell' see Heilmeyer 1970. On the entablature see von Hesberg 1980. For the Romans' methods for designing Corinthian columns see Wilson Jones 2000, ch. 7.

79   Vitruvius (IV, 1, 9–10), as translated in Rykwert 1996, 317. See also Gros 1993b; and the translations in Gros 1992 and Corso and Romano 1997, I, along with the relevant notes.

80   Riegl 1992, 191, cf. 13, 205 [1893, 212–213, cf. xv, 231]. Castriota's note 'x' to the text on p. 207 summarizes later appreciation of Riegl's case. See also Gros 1993b, 29 and works cited in Rykwert 1996, 495, n. 7.

81   Riegl 1992, 191, 199 (Castriota's notes 'b' and 'n'). Riegl (1992, 195 [1893, 218]) went so far as to declare that 'the acanthus ornament was originally nothing more than a palmette'.

82   Billot 1993.

83   On this and other akroteria see Gropengießer 1961; Delivorrias 1974; Goldberg 1982; Danner 1989; idem 1997.

84   Riegl 1992, 99, fig. 116; Caskey et al. 1927, pl. 29.

85   Kallimachos may have also made the bronze palm which reached the roof, see Pausanias I, 26.6–7; Dinsmoor 1975, 157, n. 6; Palagia 1984. The Erechtheion accounts (IG 3, 476, I.259–65) cite wax models for making bronze rosettes and acanthus for the coffering. Kallimachos's lamp, made c. 420, dates some years after the Parthenon akroterion.

86   Pausanias I, 26.7.

87   Pliny the Elder, HN, XXXIV, 92 [19].

88   Dinsmoor 1975, 157, n. 6.

89   For holes for fixing lost metal flourishes on Athenian Ionic capitals see Scahill 2009, 44–5, likewise a capital set up near the Stoa of the Athenians at Delphi, see Rykwert 1996, fig. on p. 244. The delicacy of the Parthenon marble akroterion suggests it followed openwork precedents in bronze. For a fourth-century bronze palmette akroterion incorporating acanthus from the Athenian Agora (inv. B 1386a, b, c, and B 1636) see Houser 1987, 255, 261–2. I thank David Scahill for showing me this piece.

90   On Corinthian bronze see Jacobson and Weitzman 1992.

Hellenistic use of the term korinthiourges ('of Corinthian workmanship') in some cases denotes bronze. It has been proposed that Kallixenos of Rhodes, writing probably in the early second century (De Alex. frag. 1, as reported in the Roman period by Athenaeus [Deipnosophistae, 5.205c]), called the capitals of Ptolemy IV's state barge 'of Corinthian work' because they were made of bronze (or both made of bronze and Corinthian in form). Although Pliny mentioned Corinthian capitals made of bronze (see n. 92, below), Roman usage of the term 'Corinthian' does not otherwise imply anything about this material: see Roux 1961, 361–2; Corso and Romano 1997, I, 399–400, n. 8.

91   Scahill 2009, 45–50. For the role of metal in Corinthian design see Chipiez 1876, 306–21, figs 149, 150; Choisy 1899, I, 371, fig. 2; Vallois 1944–78, I, 308–10; Dinsmoor 1975, 157, n. 6; Roux 1961, 359–62; Martin 1965, 156–7 (who like Roux sees a limited role); Bauer 1973, 11–12; Onians 1988a, 19; Normann 1996, 113–20.

92   Amy, Seyrig and Will 1975, fig. 42. Pliny the Elder (HN, XXXIV, 13 [7]) reported bronze Corinthian capitals in Rome belonging to Agrippa's Pantheon and the porticus of Octavia. A magnificent pair of bronze Corinthian capitals, probably of early imperial date, is incorporated into columns of the transept of the Lateran basilica in Rome.

93   Homolle 1916 (anticipated to some degree by Meurer 1896; idem 1909); Rykwert 1996, 320–27. See also Roux 1961, 190; Onians 1988, 19; Giuliano 1994; Wesenberg 1996, 4–5 (with qualification); Hellmann 2002, 170; Scahill 2009.

94   Small kalathoi were offered in the Geometric period in sanctuaries of female divinities, see Pemberton 1989, 19–25.

95   National Museum, Athens, 1052; Brümmer 1985, 66, fig. 38a; Lissarrague 1995, 96, fig. 7, cf. p. 72, fig. 21 in same volume; Wesenberg 1996, 4–5, Abb. 6. Recent excavations have turned up a fine kalathos from the ancient necropolis near the Evangelismos metro station.

96   Such scenes are particularly common on white-ground lekythoi, vessels with little receptacles for oil hidden within the main body which were popular as grave offerings in Attica in the fifth century, see Beazley 1938; Kurtz 1975; Kunze-Götte 1984; Oakley 2004. For background see Osborne 1998, ch. 10.

97   In some imperial Roman capitals such as those of the temple of Vespasian in Rome (Wilson Jones 2000a, fig. 7.20b) the upper rim of the core spread outwards with a pronounced overfall, it would seem pointedly recalling kalathoi.

98   Riegl 1992, 203; Homolle 1916; Nakayama 1982, group E, Taf. 21–6; Rykwert 1996, 323; Oakley 2004, 195–9.

99   Besides the vine and the olive, Rykwert (1996, 321) includes selinon, a plant with fluted stalks comparable with those sometimes used in acanthus ornament (e.g., on akroteria), as well as the cauliculus from which spring the helices of some capitals.

100 For altar parapets decorated with volute flourishes, sometimes in the form of sinuous lyre-shaped compositions, see Koenigs 1989; Aktseli 1996, Abb. 7–18; Barletta 2000, 204–5; Ohnesorg 2005, e.g., Taf. 13, 23, 31. For an example in vase painting see Walter 1968, no. 592 (detail Taf. 117).

101 The indirect nature of any connection needs stressing. Boardman illustrates his warning against the dangers of making spurious connections as follows: 'palm leaves between volutes on an ivory fly-whisk from Nimrud may, in some way, anticipate the Corinthian capitals of 300 years later, but there can be no causal relationship between what was an isolated motif in North Syria in the eighth century, and an architectural member whose origins with the development of Greek decorative design are clear' (Boardman 1959, 213, n. 2).

102 Stewart 1990, pl. 60. The incised ornament involves a stylized leaf and palmette device emerging out of a rising-volute motif. Simpler schemes occur on the anta capitals of Doric temples as far back as the early temple of Apollo at Aigina (**Fig. 2.28**). For examples in Italy see Mertens 1993, 63–5, 111–16.

103 See n. 74 above.

104 Although not infrequently reproduced (for example Wurz and Wurz 1925, Abb. 213), only occasionally has this piece been related to the development of the Corinthian capital (Poulsen 1913, 75; Hauglid 1947, 99, 101).

105 Riegl 1992, 10 [1893, xv].

106 Similarly, acanthus only gradually assumed prominence on funeral monuments. Large tombs with finials in the form of Corinthian capitals occur in the Hellenistic and Roman periods, for example the Lion tomb at Knidos, and that of the Curii at Aquileia (Wilson Jones 2000a, fig. 4.19).

107 A substantial Egyptian component is, however, untenable, as pointed out by Dinsmoor (1975, 157, n. 6).

108 A hypothetical capital with a lyre scheme would have four places on the diagonal axes where the bottom scrolls had to meet those of the adjacent set of scrolls, junctions that would conflict with the sense of circularity of the shaft and lower half of the capital.

109 Intimations of healing may have invited the use of Corinthian in both Apollo's temple at Bassai and Asklepios's tholos at Epidauros. But healing aspects of the cult at Bassai have arguably been overplayed, since Apollo was manifest there as the protector of mercenaries.

110 A concern to eliminate the corner problem affecting Ionic may have been a factor in using Corinthian at Bassai, for the canted form of the Ionic capital was also introduced there: see Lauter 1986, 237ff.; Knell 1980, 8ff.; Mallwitz 1981a. This argument works best if there were three Corinthian capitals (and therefore two at internal corners), however only the central one is certain.

111 Gros 1995, 27.

112 Wilson Jones 2000a, 138. If, as seems possible, this was one of Mummius's projects, his choice of Corinthian may in part have been prompted by the commemoration of his deeds inherent in the name of the city he sacked.

113 McEwen (2003, 215–20, esp. 218) sees a further layer of meaning to the Vitruvian story in the re-founding of Corinth by Augustus's adoptive father Julius Caesar. She also argues that Vitruvius invented the story he gives for its origin.

114 Note the prominence given to acanthus on Augustus's symbolically charged Ara Pacis. McEwen 2003, 285.

CHAPTER SEVEN

1 Jones 1856, 5. Edward Lucie-Smith (*Furniture: A Concise History* (Oxford 1979), 14) states that 'Furniture . . . has constantly been influenced by architecture. Ornament on furniture is, more often than not, borrowed from this source.' But see Roaf 1996.

2 François Bucher, 'Micro-architecture as the "Idea" of Gothic Theory and Style', *Gesta* 15 (1976): 71–89. Ethan Matt Kavaler, 'Renaissance Gothic in the Netherlands: The Uses of Ornament', *Art Bulletin* 88 (2000): 226–51.

3 A systematic comparison between the decoration of early temples and altars is overdue, but beyond the scope of this study. Suffice it to note early triglyphs on both altars and buildings (Ch. 3, pp. 71–2) and the possibility that the earliest triglyph yet known, from Mon Repos, may have belonged to an altar (Ch. 2, p. 55).

4 Bötticher 1874 [1844], 4. Coulton (1977, 23 and n. 51) mentions 'numerous instances of men practising as both architects and sculptors'; see also Svenson-Evers 1996. A parallel may be drawn with the Italian Renaissance, a time when architects tended to be artists or craftsmen first (e.g., Francesco di Giorgio, Raphael, Michelangelo, Palladio).

5 Vitruvius VII, Pref. 12 (who mentions only Theodorus in connection with the Samian temple); Diodorus Siculus I, 98.5–9; Diogenes Laertius II, 103; Herodotus I, 51 (the huge silver bowl Croesus had dedicated at Delphi), III, 41 (the golden ring made for Polykrates); Pausanias III, 12, 10; VIII, 14.8; X, 38.6; Pliny the Elder, *HN* XXXIV, 83 [*19*]; XXXVI, 90 [*19*]. For translations and references see Stewart 1990, 244–6. The varied output of the hero-architect Daidalos is a mythic expression of this reality, see Morris, S. 1992. On distinguishing the contributions of Rhoikos and Theodoros see Kienast 2002a. See also Ch. 10, n. 24 below.

6 As Simantoni-Bournias (1990, 194) reports, pots and architectural revetment on Chios were made of clay from a common source, with ornaments 'made in matrices obviously carved by the same hand, a fact which perhaps implies they were both worked in the same establishment'.

7 Vitruvius II, 1.7: 'ex varietate artium natis'.

8 There has been surprisingly little discussion of such sensi-

bilities since the writings of Bötticher and Semper in the nineteenth century.

9 Coulton 1977, 41; Howe 1985, 79–97.

10 Hittorff and Zanth 1870, 141, 153, 186–7. Brulotte (1994a, 263ff.) usefully collects evidence by category. On offering boxes see Kaminski 1991.

11 'Suffocated' may sound melodramatic, but there were real dangers; the old wooden temple at the Argive Heraion burnt down in the fifth century, apparently after an aged priestess of Hera fell asleep, allowing garlands to catch light from the flames of a lamp: Pausanias II.17.7; Thucydides 4.133. Van Straten 1981, 78, writes 'it was only with the greatest difficulty that the believer made his way (to the cult statue) past the votive offerings standing all over the place'. See also idem 1992.

12 Meiggs and Lewis 1988, 72, 78–9; Linders 1989–90; Snodgrass 1989–90; Aleshire 1992, 97–8; Harris 1995, 28–9, 31–8; Vickers and Gill 1994, 56.

13 Thanks to such culls many of the finest known Archaic Athenian statues have been excavated from where they were buried on the Acropolis in the aftermath of the Persian sack, see Keesling 2003. Further information comes from writings by the likes of Herodotus, Cicero and Pausanias, along with inventories compiled in the Classical and later periods, for which see Harris 1995; Hamilton 2000; Higbie 2003; Shaya 2005. Some third-century treatises dealt exclusively with dedications, such as the lost works by Alketas of Rhodes and Polemon of Ilium.

14 Mertens 2006, 108, speaks of 'innumerevoli doni votivi'.

15 Kuhn 1985, 306ff.; Karakasi 2003, 22–3. For the development of the stoa see Coulton 1976, ch. 2 (whose analysis shows it to be an autochthonous Greek invention); Hellmann 2006, 212–17.

16 The principle behind some dedications was monetary. For Delphi Croesus had a 'vast quantity' of silver and gold melted down and made into ingots, along with a solid gold lion weighing ten talents. See Herodotus I, 50–51; cf. I, 92; Parke 1984; Vickers and Gill 1994, ch. 3, esp. 55–6, 60.

17 Vickers and Gill 1994, esp. 57–63. Not only metal objects were taken, of course. On the theme of 'art as plunder', and in particular the notorious despoliations of Gaius Verres, the Roman governor of Sicily, see Miles 2008.

18 For polychromy see the Introduction, n. 24.

19 Hellmann et al. 1983.

20 Pausanias V, 17.5–19.10; for the Heraion V, 17.1–20.3. See also Brümmer 1985, 85–9. Eckstein (1969, 97), writes of the Heraion at Olympia as a 'monumental container of dedications'; cf. Arafat 1995.

21 Higbie 2003; Shaya 2005.

22 Some gifts were rich in monetary terms, but of no lesser value was the rich history they conveyed: Menelaos's offering was just a leather helmet, but not any old helmet, for apparently he had won it from Paris outside the walls of Troy. The most famous of Amasis's dedications was his wondrous corselet (Ch. 1, p. 21), but he also gave to the Lindian sanctuary two statues and ten *phialai*. The compilers of the Chronicle were assiduous in supplying evidence in support of each entry; sometimes the bibliography took up more lines of text than the description of the object and its history. See Shaya 2005, 427, 432.

23 Herodotus V, 59–61. One tripod was a prize set up by a certain Skaios, the victor of a boxing contest, another was a 'political' gift donated as a visible act of piety by the earlier ruler Laodamas. The oldest of the three was apparently given by Amphitryon, a legendary figure, who according to Pausanias (IX, 10.4) offered it in memory of Herakles's participation in the local *daphnephoria* festival, where it became the custom for a young aristocrat to dedicate a tripod. See Papalexandrou 2008, 256–9.

24 Their inscriptions in Aramaic link them to the late ninth-century court of King Hazael of Damascus. See Kyrieleis and Röllig 1988; Burkert 1992a, 16, fig. 2, cf. 159–60, n. 15; Kyrieleis 1993, 146–8; Osborne 1996, fig. 76; Gunter 2009, 124ff.

25 Many imports would have been displayed unaltered, but sheet material was often incorporated into new compositions. See Borell and Rittig 1998; Guralnick 2004.

26 See Ch. 5, n. 59. For tripods of the Geometric period that were found amongst much later material see also Brize 1997, 126.

27 Catling, H. 1984; Matthäus 1988. For a tripod-stand won by a Macedonian prince that remained in his family for two or three generations before deposition in the tomb of a descendant, see Andronicos 1984, 164–6.

28 Herodotus I, 14. Midas may be identified with the King Mita who is mentioned in Assyrian records c.738–696, see Lorimer 1950, 450; Jacquemin 1999, 72, n. 288; Buxton 2002, 27–8 (with further references).

29 Herodotus I, 14; Buxton 2002, 3. Such gifts were underpinned by diplomatic practices that were widespread. The Lydian kings, for example, treated not just with the Greeks but also with Egypt, Assyria and other powers. See Buxton 2002, 23–24, and Muscarella (1992, 41) for oriental cauldrons that arrived at Gordion as part of a transaction sealing a royal alliance between Phrygia and Karkemish in the late eighth century.

30 Herodotus, I, 49–51. See Buxton 2002, 7 for a full list, which includes a pile of gold and electrum ingots, a lion and a statue of solid gold, two massive kraters, one gold, one silver (the latter had a capacity equivalent to 600 wine amphoras), lustral basins (*perirrhanteria*), cauldrons and *pithoi*.

31 Herodotus I.92; Hanfmann 1975, 11.

32 Curtis 1996, 177. For example, an impressive bronze candelabra with tiers of petal crowns now in the Israel Museum in Jerusalem carries a dedicatory inscription of the ruler

Menua (810–786) to the god Haldi, see Merhav 1991, 47–8, 263–71. The bronze work, the weight of which was 'beyond all reckoning', that Hiram made for Solomon's temple was votive in nature, and when the building was finished the king had the 'sacred treasures of his father David . . . deposited in the storehouses of the house of the Lord' (I Kings 7.47–51). For incense burners in biblical contexts see Franz 1998–9, 103.

33 Oriental influence is particularly evident in the Greeks' own versions of *phialai*, thrones and aristocratic couches (*klinai*), for which see Kyrieleis 1969.

34 Kyrieleis 1993, 148; cf. idem 1996, 101. Of 32 bronze *thymiateria* (incense burners) that Franz (1998–9, 100) notes as having been imported into Greek sanctuaries, 29 of them were found at Samos.

35 For the bird-spirit from Tell Halaf see Akurgal 2001, fig. 147; for the serpent and gorgon wings on the pediment of the temple of Artemis, Corfu, see Rodenwaldt 1938, Abb. 4, Taf. 3, 4, 6. Also of note, with its 'Cypriot crown' variant, is the wooden torus base from Olympia (**Fig. 2.26**). Fish-scale was widely used in the Roman period, for example over the portal of the Pantheon and the windows of numerous early Christian churches. I thank Georg Herdt for bringing much of this material to my attention.

36 Papastamos 1970. For spirals and volutes in varied contexts see Riegl 1992 [1893]; Puchstein 1907; Newcomb 1921; Wurz and Wurz 1925; Alzinger 1978; Shiloh 1979; Himmelmann 2005.

37 British Museum 1860, 0404.1 (A 749); Walter 1968, no. 623. For shield decoration see Kunze 1931.

38 The bowl is now in the National Museum, Athens (inv. 7941), see Markoe 1985, G3, 156, 204–5, 316–17. For one in the British Museum exhibiting shrines and volute columns see P&C II, fig. 399.

39 The miniature ornaments from the Ephesian Artemision illustrated in **Fig. 7.1** include:
1 gold appliqué with three rotating linked volute devices (AA.VV. 2008b, cat. 69);
2 gold brooch with bead-and-reel (AA.VV. 2008b, cat. 62; Pülz 2009, cat. 47);
3 gold appliqué with six rotating linked volute devices (AA.VV. 2008b, cat. 70);
4 and 6 gold appliqués with four linked volute devices in a square (AA.VV. 2008b, cats 72–74; Pülz 2009, 329);
5 ivory lid of a pyxis decorated with quadrants with volute and palmette motifs facing inwards (AA.VV. 2008b, cat. 130);
7 gold and bronze appliqué disc with rosette (AA.VV. 2008b, cat. 80; Pülz 2009, cat. 378);
8 ivory caryatid with two ribbed *phialai* (AA.VV. 2008b, cat. 113);
9 ivory astragal shaped (AA.VV. 2008b, cat. 157–9).
I thank Ulrike Muss for supplying all the photographs.

40 For background, see Riegl 1992, 106–45, esp. 117, 144.

41 Roaf 1996, esp. 22. See also Schmidt-Colinet 1977, 12–18.

42 Muscarella 1992, 42. Cf. Gunter 2009. Pausanias (V, 12.5) cites a throne he saw in the pronaos of the temple of Zeus at Olympia that was apparently given by Arimnestus the legendary king of Etruria.

43 I thank Manolis Korres for the drawing reproduced here in advance of his own forthcoming publication.

44 Shefton 2000.

45 Drerup 1952, 27–8. For the building and comparison with other treasuries see Dinsmoor 1913; Gruben 1972, with n. 46 for further references; Partida 2000, 221–4.

46 The golden *phiale* now in Boston (see below, n. 52) has just nine divisions; the bowl on the bronze stand found at Cerro del Peñon has around forty (**Fig. 4.26**). There was also plenty of variation in the profiles of ribbed *phialai* from which an architect could learn. See Luschey 1939, esp. 78–83; Howes Smith 1984; Stampolidis 2003; Klebinder-Gauß 2007, 134–40; Hasserodt 2009, Taf. 2–4.

47 Luce 2008, II, pl. 55.

48 For comparable capitals of later date, see Ch. 4, n. 108.

49 For note of the metallic quality of these capitals see Drerup 1952, 28–30.

50 Luschey 1939, esp. 78–83; Howes Smith 1984; Hasserodt 2009, Taf. 2–4; *ThesCRA* I (Dedications).

51 BM 124920; Barnett 1960, pl. 105; Kyrieleis 1969, Taf. 6.

52 Luschey 1939, 133–5; *ThesCRA* I (Dedications), 2 d 158 (p. 306, pl. 78), Boston Museum of Fine Arts, inv. no. 21.1843. The inscription near the rim reads: 'The Kypselidai dedicated (this) from Herakleia'.

53 I Kings 7, 15–22; II Chronicles 3, 15–17. See also Busink 1970–80 (esp. I, 299–320 for the twin columns); Rykwert 1996, 294 and n. 121, with commentary and further bibliography.

54 Herodotus II.44. Malachite seems more likely than the emerald that appears in some translations. Another pair of bronze columns was reported as far afield as Cadiz by Strabo (III. 170). On the development of the votive column see Herdt 2013.

55 Sphinxes were particularly favoured for early Ionic votive columns, see Moret 1984.

56 Raubitschek, A. 1943; idem 1949; Kissas 2000; Keesling 2003.

57 Sestieri 1953; Doepner 2001, 226; Segal 2007, no. 60.

58 On this issue of relative scale see Herdt 2013.

59 Korres 1997a; Segal 2007, no. 33; Herdt 2013.

60 For a range of images see Moret 1984; Oenbrink 1997; Nick 2002; Segal 2007; Herdt 2013.

61 See **Table 3**. Difficulties with dating isolated finds are exemplified by the case of a votive capital from Agrigento which, with its wide echinus and heavy abacus (**Fig. 3.26**), might be thought to convey a 'primitive' air. However the narrowness of the shaft that helps create this impression may reflect the slight load-bearing function, while the deep abacus could also have been judged appropriate for a

statue support. In any event, the capital is unlikely to date before the foundation of the city, c.580; see Mertens 2006, 103, fig. 151–2 (also fig. 153 for a votive capital from Selinunte). The style of the inscription on Xenvares's column (for the capital see **Fig. 3.21**) may place it slightly earlier, but perhaps not before Apollo's Doric temple on Aigina.

62 For the suggestion that the 'peristyle' of the temple at Neandria was really lines of votive columns see Morris, S. 1985, 178. However some capitals are roughly worked (on the backs?), which is understandable if used for a narrow, shaded, space. See Ch. 4, p. 106.

63 Barletta 2001, 106. See also Dinsmoor 1923.

64 Having argued the precedence of votive columns over architectural ones in the Aegean, Kirchhoff (1988) went too far in imagining that volute capitals were copied from the stands of votive bronze vessels, as Barletta (2001, 106) points out. Ohnesorg (1996, 39) maintains the primacy of architectural columns, limiting the input from votive columns to decorative aspects.

65 For the possibility that small bases previously attributed to a peristyle at the Hekatompedon at Samos could have been for free-standing stelai or votive supports, see Kienast 1996, 20–24; Hellmann 2006, 43. See Herdt 2013 on the question of wooden votive columns.

66 Kyrieleis 1993, 149–51; Kienast 2002.

67 Rumscheid 1999; Weber, B. 2002; Donderer 2005. See also Herrmann, K. 1984.

68 Fant 1993.

69 Fehr 1996; Davies 2001; Donderer 2005 (cf. above, Ch. 2, n. 46). A fourth-century inscription from Delphi lists various states that contributed to the construction of the temple of Apollo (CID ii: 31, 2). For a comparable list from Stratos see IG IX, 446.

CHAPTER EIGHT

1 Wilson Jones 2001a.

2 Not without reason did Ferri wonder why triglyphs were not called *trimeroi* (Ch. 3, n. 71).

3 *Iliad* XXII, 443 (Hektor); XXIII, 40 (Achilles); *Odyssey* VIII, 434–7, X, 359–61 (Odysseus); *Iliad* XVIII, 344–8 (Patroklos).

4 For representations of tripods as cooking vessels see *LIMC s.v.* Peliades and Pelias; Sakowski 1997, 325–7. The collective stew that followed animal sacrifice was sometimes cooked in large bodied tripod-cauldrons (**Fig. 1.9**). Stone tripod mortars were early used in the preparation of spices, perfumes and dyes, see Yavis 1949, 10–13. In the Near East examples go as far back as the third millennium (Buchholz 1963).

5 For early metal tripod stands see Ch. 5, p. 126; for Archaic and Classical examples found in Etruria see Riis 1998; Stibbe 2000, 78–88.

6 Furtwängler 1890, 75–93; Schwendemann 1921; Benton 1934–5a; Riemann 1956a; Willemsen 1957; Schweitzer 1971, 164–85; Weber, Martha 1971, 13–30; Rolley 1977; Maass 1977; idem 1978; idem 1981; Strøm 1995; Sakowski 1997; Papalexandrou 2005; idem 2008; Kiderlen 2010.

7 For modern (eighteenth and nineteenth century) tripods inspired by ancient models see Cuzin 2000, 336–53.

8 Ancient Chinese bronze tripods are known as *Li*, of which the Museum of Fine Arts at Boston has a large collection dating from the eighteenth to the twelfth centuries BC. Sumerian three-legged stands could be inlaid with precious materials such as lapis lazuli (Louvre, inv. Sb 2737, early second millennium).

9 'For by pillage may cattle and sheep be had', observed Achilles, 'and by winning, tripods and tawny horses', *Iliad* IX, 406–7. See also *Iliad* IX, 407; XI, 700; XXIII, 259–64, 485, 513, 702–18; Sakowski 1997, 43–5, 243–51.

10 In Geometric art the idea of prize is rendered by a heraldic composition of a tripod flanked by horses: see Rombos 1988; Sakowski 1997, 65–72; Wilson Jones 2002a, cat. nos. 9, 13, 19.

11 Wilson Jones 2002a, cat. nos. 5, 68, 59; cf. nos. 56, 97, 99. For discussion see von Bothmer 1977; Schefold 1992, 153–8; Sakowski 1997, 113–58.

12 Wilson 2000, ch. 5; see also Osborne 1993. Tripods are also shown in connection with the outcome of competitions, as when victors and/or their stewards are shown carrying off prizes, see Wilson Jones 2002a, cat. nos. 39, 43, 50, 55, 58.

13 Finley 1956, esp. 64–6; Hägg 1987; Seaford 1994 (including 195–6 on tripods); Burkert 1996b, ch. 6; Sakowski 1997, 22–4. For the anthropological context see Mauss 1990; Burkert 1987; Godelier 1996. Odysseus had thirteen tripods as parting gifts from the Phaeacian nobility for him to take back to Ithaca: *Odyssey* XIII, 13. Quite remarkably thirteen tripods have been discovered at the Polis cave on Ithaca (Ithake), where Odysseus supposedly left them: *Odyssey* XIII, 362–72. These may be Hellenistic 'fakes', however. See Benton 1934–5b, 56–73; Raubitschek 1992; Malkin 1998, 95–119; Papalexandrou 2005, 22–3.

14 In a story about the Seven Sages, a tripod was given in turn by each recipient to him whom he judged wiser until it was eventually dedicated to Apollo, see Diogenes 1.27–33; Plutarch, *Sol.*, 4; Diodorus Siculus IX, 3, 13.2, Schwendemann 1921, 158–9; Parke and Wormell 1956, I, 388–90, II, nos. 247–8; Papalexandrou 2005, 47–8.

15 Texts cite tripods that 'spoke' and mediums in trance making utterings that came 'as if from a tripod', while Aristophanes, in mocking vein, had the god 'shout from the (Delphic) adyton amid priceless tripods' (*Knights* 1016).

16 See Wilson Jones 2002a, cat. nos. 52, 53, 71, 79, 90, 91, 93; for further examples see *LIMC s.v.* Apollon.

17 Inter-state rivalries found an outlet in formalized athletic

competitions while competitive energies were also channelled into prestigious dedications. See Langdon 1987; Morgan 1990, esp. 46; eadem 1993, 24; eadem 1999, 406; de Polignac 1996. Many tripods were fabricated at sanctuaries expressly for the purpose of dedication (Snodgrass 1989–90, 292).

18 Burkert 1985, 93; Maass 1981, 19; Morris, I. 1997, 37; idem 2000, 278. See also Kyrieleis 1996, 102. For a distribution map of sanctuaries with tripods see Kiderlen 2010, who stresses the élite character of this form of dedication.

19 The largest known bronze tripod from the Geometric and Archaic periods stood on the Athenian Acropolis; one of its ring handles originally had a diameter of about 700 mm, suggesting a total height of about 3.5 m (Touloupa 1972, 61; Papalexandrou 2005, 155). On tripod size see also Benton 1934–5a, 94; Guillon 1943, 2, 43–57; Willemsen 1957; Maass 1978; Papalexandrou 2008, 278–9. The largest triglyphs are those of the Olympieion at Akragas, with a height of 3.1 m.

20 Wilson Jones 2002a, cat. nos. 30 (fig. 14), 31 (fig. 9), 36, 61, 64, 66, 70 (fig. 9), 91. Sixth-century vase paintings also show tripod prizes being borne off by powerfully muscled victors who stagger visibly under the strain, see ibid., cat. nos. 50, 55; Wilson Jones 2002b.

21 Tripods on columns seem to range from about a fifth to two-fifths of the column height (to judge from archaeological remains such as those at Samos on the one hand and artistic representations on the other).

22 Whereas later lifelike treatments differentiate between the central leg and the side legs, early tripod representations often have legs of equal width (**Fig. 8.7 a, c, e, f, h**). Prior to the second quarter of the sixth century tripod legs are typically shown without the lion-paw feet that later became the norm. See Wilson Jones 2002a, 368–70.

23 Tapering triglyphs occur at Mon Repos and Foce del Sele (see **Table 3**); for further examples see Barletta 1990, 63–4.

24 For round arches see Mertens 1993, Taf. 47, 1; 72, 6; 74, 7; 75, 2. Apart from the triglyph at Mon Repos, the most pronounced ogive arches are found on the temple of Artemis Knakeatis at Tegea (Rhomaios 1952; Barletta 1990, fig. 19; Mertens 1993, Taf. 75, 5).

25 For profiles from Delphi, Olympia and other sites see Benton 1934–5a, fig. 7; Rolley 1977; Maass 1977, 37; idem 1978; idem 1981. On dating and stylistic analysis see Rolley 1975; idem 1986, 60; Strøm 1995, esp. 49–50.

26 For examples from Metapontum, Paestum, Foce del Sele and Megara Hyblaia see Barletta 1990, 63; Mertens 1993, 116ff., Taf. 72–5. For ones at Syracuse see Orsi 1919, 699.

27 Wilson Jones 2002a, 371. For comparable details on tripods from Olympia see Furtwängler 1890, Taf. 34, a and e.

28 Tölle-Kastenbein 1974, Abb. 75–6; Rumscheid 1994, Taf. 55. Tripods also appear in positions usually associated with triglyphs on the early imperial temple of Augustus and Roma at Mylasa. It had Corinthian columns, but this did

not exclude a Doric (or Doricizing) entablature, as Vitruvius allows (IV, 1, 2).

29 Sakowski 1997, PR-1; Wilson Jones 2002a, cat. 1.

30 Ceramic vessels with three legs are known as tripod kothons, for which see Scheibler 1964, 72–108; for their derivation from tripods see Catling 1964, 213–17; Kilinski 1990, 56; Langdon 1993, 163–4. For the example from Thasos see Haspels 1946; Wilson Jones 2002a, cat. 28.

31 Wilson Jones 2002a, cat. 32, and for another example on a Cretan *pithos* see cat. 23.

32 For distribution, see Kiderlen 2010, esp. 103. For tripods of the Geometric and early Archaic periods at Olympia and Delphi, see Morgan 1990, 30–47, 137–46; for the Argive Heraion, see Strøm 1995; eadem 1998; for Athens, see Touloupa 1972; eadem 1991; Hurwit 2000, 91–2; Keesling 2003, 3, n. 4; for Samos, see Brize 1997; for Thebes, see Papalexandrou 2008. In effect, 'bronze tripods bridge the two worlds of Homeric poetry and archaeological reality', so Langdon 1987, 108–9. Although at Olympia the rate of new tripods declined after the seventh century, their popularity endured in Attica, Boiotia and the Peloponnese down to the Hellenistic period and beyond, see Amandry and Ducat 1973; Amandry 1987.

33 For the Street of Tripods see Travlos 1971, 566–8; Choremi-Spetsieri 1994; Miller, Stephen G. 1995, 211; Schnurr 1995; Robertson, N. 1998, 287; Wilson 2000, 209–13. For those above the *cavea* of the theatre, including Thrasyllos's Monument, a double-bay façade fronting a cave which carried three tripods, see IG II, 3056, 3083; Pausanias I, 21.3; Stuart and Revett 1762–94, I, ch. 4; Welter 1938; Travlos 1971, 562–5; Dinsmoor 1975, 239; Amandry 1997, 446–63; Wilson 2000, 229–35. See also Amandry 1976.

34 At Dodona the sacred oak of Zeus was encircled by a ring of tripods, at least from the Hellenistic period if not before (see Ch. 1, n. 56. for references).

35 Stevens 1951; Touloupa 1991, 242–54; Keesling 1995, 241–42. The amalgam of these and other materials was characteristic of seventh-century temples. For Assyrian antecedents see Layard 1850, II, 469–70; Nassouhi 1925.

36 Touloupa 1993, esp. 242. Although a solution with two blocks cannot be ruled out (Stevens 1951, fig. 3c), these tripods probably comprised three blocks. Since the tallest block measures around 770 mm and others around 550 mm, the likely total height exceeded 2 m. My thanks to Tasos Tanoulas for showing me half a dozen blocks in 2007.

37 The sanctuary of Ptoios, founded after Apollo's in the sixth century and located some 2 km east of the city of Akraiphia (modern Akraiphnion), has yielded the most numerous surviving tripods. Nine have been found on the north side and nineteen on the south side of the sacred way, see Guillon 1943, I, 28–43; Ducat 1971; Papalexandrou 2008, 262–6, 271–6; de Polignac 2009, 430–34. Lines of tripods were set up in the Hellenistic period at Orchomenos, some of which

38 For graphic reconstructions see Guillon 1943, I, fig. 3; Papalexandrou 2008, figs 14–15, and p. 273 for evidence suggesting that the avenue of tripods extended about 125 m, perhaps more.

39 Apart from tripod-and-metope friezes, also of note are vase paintings showing multiple or serial tripods; a case in point is a *loutrophon* from Kerameikos with two rings of ten tripod-carriers: see Scheibler 1988; Wilson Jones 2002b, fig. 6; 2002a, cat. no. 40 and also p. 263 for other examples. This phenomenon may have echoes in the putative Delphic oracle which foretold that victory in the First Messenian War (*c.*700) would go to the side who first dedicated a hundred tripods to Zeus around the altar at his sanctuary on Mount Ithome: Pausanias IV, 12.7–10. The beleaguered Messenians apparently made their tripods of wood, but the Spartans chose clay and got theirs finished sooner. The story was most likely an invention of the fourth century (Papalexandrou 2014), yet it nonetheless implies the memory of tripods as space definers.

40 *Hymni Homerici in Mercurium*, 61.

41 *Iliad* XVIII, 372–7; Morris, S. 1992, 9.

42 The text adds that Hephaistos's tripods were wheeled, recalling ten wheeled bronze stands made by Hiram for Solomon's Temple, see I Kings 7.27–37; Zwickel 1986; Morris, S. 1992, 9–10. Wheeled examples feature amongst actual Cypriot stands (Ch. 5, n. 59).

43 A tripod is one of the possible solutions for the crowning akroteria of the temple of Athena Nike on the Acropolis, see Schultz 2001, 24–6. The Monument of Nikias in Athens had a single tripod crowning the pediment. See Dinsmoor 1910; Travlos 1971, 357–360; Wilson 2000, 226–9. For a perspective reconstruction see Korres 2002b, fig. 36.

44 Gadolou 2011.

45 Croissant 2003, pl. 2–9, 86; Amandry and Hansen 2010, esp. fig. 18.1.

46 The same point is made by the line drawing by Didier Laroche published by Rolley (1994, fig. 30). Up the slope from the Plataia monument stood the late Classical so-called Dancers' or Acanthus Column, which carried a bronze tripod on top of three dancer-caryatids, see Homolle 1908; Chamoux 1970; Rykwert 1996, 327–9; Martinez 1997.

47 Wilson Jones 2002a, cat. nos. 71, 75, 83; see also *LIMC s.v.* Apollon 303, Apollon 769 (foliate), Apollon 1040, Asklepios 1 (Ionic), Oreias 1.

48 Bruneau and Fraisse 2002, 42–4, fig. 33.

49 Travlos 1971, 562–3; Amandry 1997, 446–63.

50 Kienast 1985, 383–5; I thank Hermann Kienast for sharing his understanding of the monument on site.

51 Papalexandrou 2008. One of the shafts of these central supports bears a dedicatory inscription running up the fluting, just as on a votive column from the Acropolis of similar design (see Whitley 2001, fig. 7.3).

52 For appreciation of this point see Maass 1978, 77.

53 The use of tetraglyphs and pentaglyphs at some southern Italian sites in the second half of the sixth century (Ch. 5, p. 118) suggests that the point behind three uprights had already become forgotten.

CHAPTER NINE

1 Carpenter 1959, 114; the same theme appears in idem 1962. See also above, Ch. 3, p. 76.

2 For related observations concerning practice in fourteenth- to fifteenth-century AD Italy see Marvin Trachtenberg, *Building-in-Time: From Giotto to Alberti and Modern Oblivion* (New Haven and London 2010), 134ff.

3 I. Stravinsky, *Poetics of Music in the Form of Six Lessons* (Cambridge, Mass. 1942); J. Monod, *Chance and Necessity: An Essay on the Natural Philosophy of Modern Biology* (New York 1971); R. Sennett, *The Craftsman* (New Haven and London 2008).

4 On the concept of agency see Tanner and Osborne 2007.

5 For round altars see Berges 1996; Koenigs 1996. On the difficulties of distinguishing between the cyma mouldings of Ionic capitals and round capitals see Berti and Masturzo 2000, 233. See also Altekamp 1991.

6 Further supplementary factors may have argued against ring-handles. Architects may have regarded them as visually unsuited to the task of carrying cornice and roof. It is significant that ring-handles were typically omitted from tripods made of clay or stone, presumably due to their fragility. Only exceptionally do terracotta tripod-stands have ring-handles (e.g., Benton 1934–5a, fig. 1B; *Kerameikos* 1, 95, Taf. 63). Tripod-kothons occasionally have handles folded down on top of the vessel, but usually there are none at all (**Fig. 8.5**), see Wilson Jones 2002a. The same can be observed for non-Greek examples; for a small handle-less stone tripod from Tell Halaf in the British Museum see Oppenheim 1931, Taf. 48a.

7 As noted in Ch. 6 (p. 143), Vitruvius saw in caryatids figures of the conquered and attempted to link the name to a particular historical circumstance and geographical place. But interpreted as pious participants in ritual the Erechtheion caryatids compare with the *kanephorai*, bearers of ritual baskets, that served as caryatids in the late first-century propylon at Eleusis (**Fig. 6.6**). See Lauter 1976; Scholl 1995; Rykwert (1996, 135), who notes that the Greek verb *karyatizein* meant to 'to dance in a stately way'. However neither Rykwert, Scholl, nor Hersey - who could have used the point to further his sacrificial reading - remarked on these *phiale*-like elements.

8 See Schmidt-Colinet 1977, 25; Pensabene 2010, esp. 383–7,

409–12. Also of note are *phialai*-bearers sculpted on the east frieze of the Parthenon: see Barringer 2008, 93, fig. 74.

9   Persson 1942, 131.

10   Riegl 1992, esp. 50–51.

11   De Polignac 2009, 432. On eclecticism in the Hellenistic period see Quinn 2013.

12   Luce 1975, 49–69; Cartledge 2002, 288; West 2011. Osborne (1996, 40) underlines the role of the Phoenicians in favouring eclectic tendencies in the borrowing of artistic motifs. In the realm of architecture Coulton (1977, 50) is unusual in noting the eclectic nature of the Greeks' assimilation of Egyptian influences, likewise Korres (1994, 21; see above, Ch. 3, pp. 84–5) when speaking of 'a new eclectic creation'.

13   Lévi-Strauss 2005, 15.

14   'Plato', *Epinomis* 987d–988a.

15   Jun'ichirō Tanizaki, *In Praise of Shadows* (New York 1977 [1st ed. 1933–4]).

16   For parallel reflections see Michael Baxandall, *Patterns of Intention: On the Historical Explanation of Pictures* (New Haven and London 1985), 58–62; Stewart and Korres 2004, 97–8; Quinn 2013.

17   Many of the Greek treatises that Vitruvius (VII, Preface) mentions were concerned with advances or inventions made in the context of specific projects. *On Inventions* ('Peri Eurematon') was the title of a lost fourth-century treatise by Skamon of Mytilene: see *RE s.v.* Skamon; Donohue 1988, 197–8.

18   For Brunelleschi's position and contemporary perceptions of the alien nature of Gothic style see Onians 1988a, 132–3. In his turn Alberti banned features that Brunelleschi used, including arches over columns [VII, 15], see above, n. 2; Trachtenberg 2010, 370–73. Adolf Loos's essay 'Ornament and Crime' (1908) is a seminal modern text on the principle of exclusion. See also Alina Payne, *From Ornament to Object: Genealogies of Architectural Modernism* (New Haven and London 2012).

19   Oechslin 2002, esp. 49, 192, 196.

20   Langdon 1987; Morgan 1990, esp. 46; eadem 1993, 24; eadem 1999, 406; de Polignac 1996.

21   Hesiod, in the opening section of *Works and Days* [12–26], discusses two kinds of strife, one destructive, the other, peer-to-peer competition, beneficial. See also Onians 1988b.

22   Among the Archaic inscriptions compiled by Meiggs and Lewis (1988) many concern offerings donated collectively or by states (sometimes ruled by tyrants); see nos. 11, 16, 19, 22, 25, 27, 28, 36 and 42B.

23   Korres 2002a, 366.

24   I thank Manolis Korres for these observations. See Korres 1995 and further references in **Table 3**.

25   Chipiez and Semper are notable for their understanding in this respect, see below. For more recent appreciation of plural readings see, for example, Morris, S. 1992, 161; Rykwert 1996, 315. Writing of the Ionic order Dinsmoor (1975,

58) states that 'Few, if any, architectural features can be attributed to one cause alone; practically all can be traced back to a combination of impulses.' However when treating Doric (56–7) his endorsement of the Vitruvian model inflects only slightly to accommodate decorative concerns and possible Mycenaean antecedents for the capital.

26   Østby 2006a.

27   Austin 1975, 81–107; Padel 1992, 45–8; Bakker, P. 1997; Versnel 2011.

28   For similar conclusions in relation to palm capitals, see Ch. 4, p. 92.

29   By the Augustan period architects had developed a coherent design methodology based on certain key proportions conceived to accommodate shafts with standardized lengths (20, 25, 30 and 40 Roman feet being the most common larger sizes): see Wilson Jones 2000a, 143–56.

30   The possibility that the Doric frieze was initially developed for temple fronts is consistent with the front-facing friezes of the early temples at Aigina and Delphi.

31   Korres and Bouras 1983, 23. See also Hoepfner 1991.

32   In other words art intervened, as Viollet-le-Duc put it. See also Durm 1910, 253ff.; Rocco 1994a, 52–6.

33   Semper, *On Architectural Styles* (Ueber Baustil), 1989 [1869], 269; the emphasis is my own. For translation and discussion see Mallgrave, introduction to Semper 2004, 53.

34   For Semper the primitive hut was the mystical-poetic and artistic *motiv* of the temple, but '*not* its material model' (2004, 665 [1863, 275], his emphasis); see also 623).

35   Semper (2004, 769 [1863, 416]) called the triglyph an attached dressing ('angeheftete Bekleidung').

36   With his usual capacity for paradox Semper (2004, 768) regards the Doric capital with its four-way symmetry as so perfectly suited to use in a peristasis that it seems destined for it, 'though it undoubtedly existed long before as a valid art-form … as the head of an entirely free-standing isolated stele, a support for the sacred crown' (this last, 'geweihten Aufsatzes', may perhaps best be rendered as 'the sacred thing on top'). See also Riegl 1992 [1893], 62.

37   See Ch. 3, n. 23. On the relationship between Semper and Bötticher see Herrmann, W. 1984, ch. 3; Oechslin 2002, 44–61; Mallgrave 1996, 219–22; Wilson Jones 2014.

38   Semper (2004 [1863] esp. ch. 3 and ch. 4, ß, the section on 'The Principle of Dressing … in Architecture').

39   Geertz 1973; see also above, Introduction, p. 7.

40   I doff my metaphorical hat to the opening section of Erwin Panofsky's seminal *Studies in Iconology* (1939).

41   Mylonopoulos (2006, 92) makes a similar point about the perception of dedications: 'No votive offering contained just one message, nor had just one purpose; depending upon the level of education and interest and upon the origins of the visitor, the communicative exchange between votive offering and observer was altered too.'

42   A parallel complaint relating to early twentieth-century

scholarship on Greek poetry is voiced by Versnel: 'Now why', he asks, 'do we or some or most of us, modern readers, feel embarrassed by these discoveries of a former generation to such a degree that appreciative references to them – as I found out – may disqualify a scholar as a scholar? . . . The simplest – and decisive – answer of course would be that they have been proven wrong. It is obvious that in the flush of their discoveries scholars may have overplayed their hand in some respects . . .'. (Versnel 2011, 215).

43 Venturi 1966. At the background of his thinking lies, it seems, William Empson's *Seven Types of Ambiguity* of 1930.

44 See for example Herodotus VI, 84 for contrasting explanations of the madness of the Spartan king Kleomenes.

45 Versnel 2011, esp. 10. See also Padel 1992.

46 Herodotus I, 53. On oracles and Delphi's role see Amandry 1950; Parke and Wormell 1956; Parke 1967; Fontenrose 1978; Morgan 1990; Maass 1993.

CHAPTER TEN

1 Despite this choice of format I remain conscious of Coulton's warning: 'it would obviously be misguided to be too categorical about what in fact inspired the invention [of Doric], for we are dealing with the psychology of men dead for two and a half thousand years' (Coulton 1977, 39).

2 As Nietzsche (1967, 77) states: 'the "evolution" of a thing, a custom, an organ is . . . by no means (only) its *progressus* towards a goal', still less is it a logical 'progressus'.

3 Krischen 1956, 55.

4 Østby (2006a) distinguishes between three contrasting paradigms of *continuatio, renovatio* and *innovatio* at work in the creation of the Doric temple. To this *imitatio* might be added to stand for the imitation and assimilation of foreign influences.

5 For the concept of a 'pioneer generation' see Howe 1985, 268–79. The presence of very large early roof tiles at Delphi points to a significant temple there in the second quarter of the seventh century, but in the absence of stonework its wall construction must have relied on perishable materials.

6 Cook 1951; idem 1970; Howe 1985, esp. 372–4.

7 It should be borne in mind that we know of only a portion of the number of temples that existed. There are plenty of sites where early temples can be presumed to have once stood, but of which we have no trace. The urban centres of Argos and Megara come to mind, for example. At Corinth a possibility might be an earlier incarnation of the so-called Great Temple, see Ch. 2, p. 55.

8 Cook 1951; idem 1970; Coulton 1977, 39; Barletta 2001, 48, 146–7, 154 (with qualification).

9 Østby 1997.

10 Williams (1984, 67–8) notes the preponderance in areas of Spartan domination of Doric capitals with leaf necking of

Mycenaean flavour and the disk akroterion, two characteristic features of early Doric temples.

11 Plutarch, *Apophthegmata Laconica*, 227b.

12 Marconi 2007, 8–12.

13 The exisiting 'Heraion' at Olympia may not, however, have been the first instance of Doric if the accepted date of *c.*600 is correct, since this could be after the temple at Mon Repos. For Doric to have been invented at Olympia this must have happened in connection with some earlier structure, a theoretical possibility given the presence of roof tiles dating to around the middle of the seventh century.

14 The term *naos*, the most common designation for temples, found early use to denote Apollo's Delphic temple, and its model status seems to be suggested by the epithet *Pronaia* applied to Athena's sanctuary just below (or 'in front of') Apollo's sanctuary. As Roux (1984, 155) has put it, out of all the Greek sanctuaries, Delphi 'is the only truly panhellenic one in the full sense of the term' ('le seul vraiment panhellénique au sens plein du terme, face à Olympie, plutôt pan-dorienne, et à Delos, plutôt pan-cycladique').

15 That it was usual for temples to be built (or land for them to be allocated) when colonies were founded is implied by a passage in the *Odyssey* [VI, 7–10] which presumably reflected attitudes in Homer's own time: cf. Sourvinou-Inwood 1993, 5.

16 Miller, J. 1996, 207. This survey of temples and cult-statues shows that temples to Artemis were the next most common after her brother Apollo's. Perhaps his Delphic temple would have made a suitable model for her temples as well, e.g., the Artemision at Corfu.

17 Papalexandrou 2005, 151–8.

18 Vickers and Gill 1994; Vickers 1999.

19 Pindar, *Paean* VIII, 58–99; Pausanias X, 10, 5, 13; Sourvinou-Inwood 1979, 240–42; eadem 1991; Marconi 2009b, 9–12. One tradition held Trophonios and Agamedes to be brothers, which suggests they operated as a pair. But in other respects they seem to fall into different categories. Trophonios was credited in some sources as being a son of Apollo, and his oracle in Boiotia was important if not nearly so famous as his father's; these other-worldly traits set him apart from Agamedes. On the fate of the pair see Parke and Wormell 1956, I, 368, 380, II, no. 140.

20 *Homeric Hymn to Apollo*, 294–299.

21 Pausanias VIII, 10.2.

22 Sourvinou-Inwood 1991, 204–8.

23 Following the lead of Cook, R. (1951; idem 1970), Coulton (1977, 39) locates the creation of Doric in the north-east Peloponnese, while yet noting that 'We need not believe that all their inspiration came from a single source . . .'.

24 A possible Delphic contribution may have involved the germ of the tripodic element of the future Doric frieze in a high-level tripod representation, either in the pediment or at frieze level and possibly made of bronze. As regards

location there are three main candidates: one is on the mid-seventh-century temple that had a tiled roof but otherwise may be presumed to have been made mainly of mud-brick, wood and perhaps bronze. The second would be the trea-sury of Kypselos, tyrant of Corinth, a structure notionally datable to *c.*630 that seemingly had stone columns and which, hypothetically at least, can be restored as Doric. The third would be the stone Doric temple attributable to the period after 590 (Ch. 2, pp. 56). In any two-stage scenario Trophonios could be the author of the first, Agamedes of the second. The naming of Theodoros and Rhoikos as the architects of the Samian Heraion may conflate two chronologically distinct phases. Some sources cite Rhoikos as the father of Theodorus (Corso 2012, 23), so one may have designed the *c.*570 temple and the other, the *c.*530 temple (see Kienast 1998, 127–31; idem 2002a). On the other hand pairs of architects are securely attested

in later periods, usually with a distinction between overall and supervisory responsibilities, see Coulton 1977, 28.

25 See n. 14 above. Apollo's sister Artemis was central to the early cultic identity of Delos. Together with the importance Vitruvius gives to her Ephesian temple, and the fact that the number of early temples sacred to her were second only to those of her brother Apollo (see n. 15. above), this points, perhaps, to a sibling involvement with the origins of the orders. Though the nature of this remains obscure, echoes of it may have given rise to the gender polarity of which Vitruvius tells (Ch. 6, p. 142). See also AA.VV. 1997f.

26 Gruen 2011; cf. Hall 2002. The process of self-fashioning, by which a people defines its national character, did not, in the Greek case, strike a crude oppositional contrast vis-à-vis foreign peoples. Rather, as Gruen emphasizes (p. 352), this involved 'links with, adaption to, and even incorporation of the alien'.

BIBLIOGRAPHY

NOTE TO THE READER

Where reference is made to an edition other than the one generally used, its date of publication is given in the text and the Bibliography in square brackets.

AA.VV. 1981a   *Faith, Hope and Worship: Aspects of Religious Mentality in the Ancient World*, ed. H. S. Versnel, Leiden.

AA.VV. 1981b   *Le Sacrifice dans l'antiquité* (Fondations Hardt pour l'étude de l'antiquité classique: Entretiens 27), con., Vandoeuvres-Geneva, 1980, ed. Jean Rudhart, Geneva.

AA.VV. 1983   *The Greek Renaissance of the Eighth Century BC: Tradition and Innovation*, con., Athens, 1981, ed. Robin Hägg, Stockholm.

AA.VV. 1985   *Greek Religion and Society*, ed. P. E. Easterling and J. V. Muir, Cambridge.

AA.VV. 1987   *Gifts to the Gods* (*Boreas* 15), con., Uppsala, 1985, ed. Tullia Linders and Gullög Nordquist.

AA.VV. 1988a   *Early Greek Cult Practice* (*Proceedings of the 5th Int. Symposium at the Swedish Institute in Athens*), con., Athens, 1986, ed. Robin Hägg, Nanno Marinatos and Gullög Nordquist, Stockholm and Göteborg.

AA.VV. 1988b   *Sacrificio e società nel mondo antico*, ed. Cristiano Grottanelli and Nicola Parisi, Rome.

AA.VV. 1988c   *The Archaeology of the Olympics: The Olympics and Other Festivals in Antiquity*, ed. Wendy J. Raschke, Madison, Wis.

AA.VV. 1988d   *Acts of the 12th International Congress of Classical Archaeology*, con., Athens, 1983.

AA.VV. 1988e   *East and West: Cultural Relations in the Ancient World* (*Acta Hyperborea* 1), con., Copenhagen, 1987, ed. Tobias Fischer-Hansen.

AA.VV. 1989   *Mind and Body: Athletic Contests in Ancient Greece*, cat., Athens.

AA.VV. 1990a   *Proceedings of the First International Conference on Archaic Greek Architectural Terracottas* (*Hesperia* 59), con., Athens, 1988, ed. Nancy Winter.

AA.VV. 1990b   *L'Habitat égéen préhistorique*, con., Athens, 1987, ed. Pascal Darque and René Treuill, Paris and Athens.

AA.VV. 1991a   *New Perspectives in Early Greek Art* (Studies in the History of Art 32), con., Washington, 1988, ed. Diane Buitron-Oliver, Hanover and London.

AA.VV. 1991b   *L'Espace sacrificiel dans les civilizations méditerranéenes de l'antiquité*, con., Lyon, 1988, ed. Roland Étienne and Marie-Thérèse Le Dinahet, Paris.

AA.VV. 1991c   *La transizione dal Miceneo all'Alto Arcaismo: dal palazzo alla città*, con., Rome, 1988, ed. Domenico Musti *et al.*, Rome.

AA.VV. 1992a   *The Iconography of Greek Cult in the Archaic and Classical periods* (*Kernos*, supp. 1), con., Delphi, 1990, ed. Robin Hägg, Athens.

AA.VV. 1992b   *Proceedings of an International Symposium on the Olympic Games*, con., Athens, 1988, ed. William D. E. Coulson and Helmut K. Kyrieleis, Athens.

AA.VV. 1992c   *Greece between East and West: 10th-8th Centuries BC*, con., New York, 1990, ed. Günther Kopcke and Isabelle Tokumaru, Mainz.

AA.VV. 1992d   *Le Sanctuaire grec* (Foundations Hardt pour l'étude de l'Antiquité classique. Entretiens 37), con., Vandoeuvres-Geneva, 1990, ed. Albert Schachter, Geneva.

AA.VV. 1992e   *Economics of Cult in the Ancient Greek World* (*Boreas* 21), con., Uppsala, 1990, ed. Tullia Linders and Brita Alroth.

AA.VV. 1992f   *L'Emploi des ordres dans l'architecture de la renaissance*, con., Tours, 1986, ed. Jean Guillaume, Paris.

AA.VV. 1992g   *Delphes: Centenaire de la 'Grande Fouille' réalisée par l'École Française d'Athènes (1892–1903)*, con., Strasbourg, 1991, ed. Jean-François Bommelaer, Leiden.

AA.VV. 1993a   *Greek Sanctuaries: New Approaches*, ed. Nanno Marinatos and Robin Hägg, London.

AA.VV. 1993b   *From Pasture to Polis: Art in the Age of Homer*, ed. Susan Langdon, cat. Museum of Art and Archaeology, University of Missouri, Columbia, Mo.

AA.VV. 1993c   *Les Grands Ateliers d'architecture dans le monde égéen du VIᵉ Siècle av. J.-C.* (Varia Anatolica III), con., Istanbul, 1991, ed. Jacques des Courtils and Jean-Charles Moretti.

AA.VV. 1993d   *Die griechische Polis: Architektur und Politik*, ed. Wolfram Hoepfner and Gerhard Zimmer, Tübingen.

AA.VV. 1993e   *Acanthe: l'acanthe dans la sculpture monu-men-tale de l'antiquité à la renaissance* (Mémoires de la section d'Ar-chéologie et d'histoire de l'Art 4), con., Paris, 1990, Paris.

AA.VV. 1993f   *The Ancient Greek City-state* (*HfMedd* 67), con., Copenhagen, 1992, ed. Mogens Herman Hansen.

AA.VV. 1993g   *Cultural Poetics in Archaic Greece: Cult, Perfor-mance, Politics*, con., Wellesley, 1990, ed. Carol Dougherty and Leslie Kurke, New York.

AA.VV. 1994   *Placing the Gods: Sanctuaries and Sacred Space in Ancient Greece*, ed. Susan E. Alcock and Robin Osborne, Oxford.

AA.VV. 1995a   *Studies in the Ancient Greek Polis* (*Historia, Ein-zelschriften* 95), ed. Mogens Herman-Hansen and Kurt Raa-flaub, Stuttgart.

AA.VV. 1995b   *La Magna Grecia e i grandi santuari della Ma-drepatria* (CSMG 31), con., Taranto, 1991, Taranto.

AA.VV. 1996a   *Religion and Power in the Ancient Greek World* (*Boreas* 24), con., Uppsala, 1993, ed. Pontus Hellström and Brita Alroth.

AA.VV. 1996b   *Säule und Gebälk, zu Struktur und Wand-lungsprozeß griechisch-römischer Architektur*, ed. Ernst-Ludwig Schwandner, Mainz.

AA.VV. 1996c   *The Role of Religion in the Early Greek Polis* (*SkrAth* 14), con., Athens, 1992, ed. Robin Hägg, Stockholm.

AA.VV. 1996d   *The Furniture of Western Asia: Ancient and Traditional*, con., London, 1993, ed. Georgina Herrmann, Mainz.

AA.VV. 1997a   *The Development of the Polis in Archaic Greece*, ed. Lynette Mitchell and Peter J. Rhodes, London.

AA.VV. 1997b   *Kult und Kultbauten auf der Akropolis*, con., Berlin, 1995, ed. Wolfram Hoepfner, Berlin.

AA.VV. 1997c   *Olympia – Sport und Spektakel: Die Olympischen Spiele im Altertum und ihre Rezeption im modernen Olymp-ismus* (*Nikephoros: Zeitschrift für Sport und Kultur in Altertum* 10), con., Graz, 1996, ed. Ingomar Weiler.

AA.VV. 1997d   *Héra: Images, Espaces, Cultes* (Collection du Centre Jean Bérard 15), con., Lille, 1993, ed. Juliette de La Ge-nière, Naples.

AA.VV. 1997e   *New Light on a Dark Age: Exploring the Culture of Geometric Greece*, con., Columbia, 1993, ed. Susan Langdon, Columbia, Mo.

AA.VV. 1997f   *Greeks and Barbarians: Essays on the Interactions between Greeks and Non-Greeks in Antiquity and the Conse-quences for Eurocentrism*, ed. John E. Coleman and Clark A. Walz, Bethseda, Md.

AA.VV. 1997g   *A New Companion to Homer* (*Mnemosyne*, supp. 163)*, ed. Ian Morris and Barry Powell.

AA.VV. 1997h   *Las Casas del Alma: Maquetas arquitectónicas de la Antigüedad*, cat., Barcelona.

AA.VV. 1998a   *Ancient Greek Cult Practice from the Archaeo-logical Evidence* (*SkrAth* 15), con., Athens, 1993, ed. Robin Hägg, Stockholm.

AA.VV. 1998b   *ΣΤΕΦΑΝΟΣ: Studies in Honor of Brunilde Sismondo Ridgway*, ed. Kim J. Hartswick and Mary C. Sturgeon, Philadelphia, Pa.

AA.VV. 1999a   *Ancient Greek Hero Cult* (*SkrAth* 16), con., Göte-borg, 1995, ed. Robin Hägg, Stockholm.

AA.VV. 1999b   *Ancient Greeks, West and East* (*Mnemosyne*, supp. 196)*, ed. Gocha R. Tsetskhladze.

AA.VV. 1999c   *Ancient Greece: A Political, Social and Cultural History*, ed. Sarah B. Pomeroy *et al.*, Oxford.

AA.VV. 2000a   *Delphes: cent ans après la Grande Fouille. Essai de bilan* (*BCH*, supp. 36), con., Athens–Delphi, 1992, ed. Anne Jacquemin.

AA.VV. 2000b   *Die Ägäis und das westliche Mittelmeer: Beziehungen und Wechselwirkungen 8. bis 5. Jh. v. Chr.* con., Vienna, 1999, ed. Friedrich Krinzinger, Vienna.

AA.VV. 2001a   *Archaische griechische Tempel und Altägypten*, ed. Manfred Bietak, Vienna.

AA.VV. 2001b   *War as a Cultural and Social Force: Essays on Warfare in Antiquity* (*Historisk-filosofiske Skrifter* 20), con., Co-penhagen, 1998, ed. Tønnes Bekker-Nielson and Lise Hanne-stad.

AA.VV. 2001c   *La questione delle influenze vicino-orientali sulla religione greca*, con., Rome 1999, ed. Sergio Ribichini *et al.*, Rome.

AA.VV. 2002   *Excavating Classical Culture: Recent Archaeolog-ical Discoveries in Greece*, ed. Maria Stamatopolou and Marina Yeroulanou, Oxford.

AA.VV. 2003   *ΠΛΟΕΣ: Sea routes. Interconnections in the Mediterranean 16th–6th c. BC*, con., Rethymnon, 2002, ed. Nicholas C. Stampolidis and Vassos Karageorghis, Athens.

AA.VV. 2005a   *Knossos: Palace, City, State* (*BSA Studies* 12), con., Heraklion, 2000, ed. Gerald Cadogan, Eleni Hatzaki and Adonis Vasilakis.

AA.VV. 2005b   *Cultural Borrowings and Ethnic Appropriations in Antiquity* (Oriens et Occidens: Studien zu antiken Kul-turkontakten und ihrem Nachleben 8), ed. Erich S. Gruen, Stuttgart.

AA.VV. 2005c   *Periklean Athens and its Legacy*, ed. Judith M. Barringer and Jeffrey M. Hurwit, Austin, Tex.

AA.VV. 2006   *Naukratis: Greek Diversity in Egypt*, ed. Alesan-dra Villing and Udo Schlotzhauer, London.

AA.VV. 2008a   *Original und Kopie: Formen und Konzepte der Nachahmung in der antiken Kunst*, con., Berlin, 2005, ed. Klaus Junker and Adrian Stähli, Wiesbaden.

AA.VV. 2008b   *Das Artemision von Ephesos: Heiliger Platz einer Göttin*, cat. Istanbul, ed. Wilfried Seipel, Vienna.

AA.VV. 2009a   *Cyprus and the East Aegean: Intercultural Contacts from 3000 to 500 BC*, con., Samos, 2008, ed. Vassos Karageorghis and Ourania Kouka, Nicosia.

AA.VV. 2009b   *Structure, Image, Ornament: Architectural Sculpture in the Greek World*, ed. Peter Schultz and Ralf von den Hoff, Oxford and Oakville, Conn.

AA.VV. 2009c   *A Companion to Archaic Greece*, ed. Kurt A. Raaflaub and Hans van Wees, Oxford.

AA.VV. 2009d   *Le Donateur, l'offrande et la déesse: systèmes votifs dans les sanctuaires de déesses du monde grec* (*Kernos*, supp. 23), con., Lille, 2007, ed. Clarisse Prêtre, Liège.

Aberson, Michel 1994   *Temples votifs et butin de guerre dans la Rome republicaine* (Bibliotheca Helvetica Romana 26), Rome.

Abramson, Herbert 1978   'Greek Hero-Shrines' (diss., University of California, Berkeley).

Abou Assaf, Ali 1990   *Der Tempel von Ain Dara*, Mainz.

Adler, Friedrich *et al.* 1892–6   *Olympia II* (Die Baudenkmäler von Olympia), 2 vols, Berlin.

Aikin, Edmund 1810   *An Essay on the Doric Order of Architecture*, London.

Akkermans, Peter M. M. G., and Glenn M. Schwartz, 2003   *The Archaeology of Syria*, Cambridge.

Aktseli, Dimitra 1996   *Altäre in der archaischen und klassischen Kunst: Untersuchungen zur Typologie und Ikonographie* (Internationale Archäologie 28), Eselkamp.

Akurgal, Ekrem 1960   'Vom äolischen zum ionischen Kapitell', *Anatolia* 5: 1–7.

—— 1968   *The Birth of Greek Art: The Mediterranean and the Near East*, London [1st (German) ed. 1966].

—— 1981   'Frükharchaische Kapitelle vom Tempel der Athena in Alt-Smyrna', *AnnASAtene* 59: 127–32.

—— 1983   *Alt-Smyrna*, I: *Wohnschichten und Athenatempel*, Ankara.

—— 1988   'L'Art classique en Asie Mineure', in AA.VV. 1988d: 12–19.

—— 2001   *The Hattian and Hittite Civilizations*, Ankara.

Akurgal, Meral 2007   'Hellenic Architecture in Smyrna 650–546 B.C.' (Milesische Forschungen 5), con., Güzelçamli, 1999, ed. Justus Cobet *et. al.*, Mainz: 125–36.

Albend, Pauline 2005   *Ornamental Wall Painting in the Art of the Assyrian Empire*, Leiden and Boston, Mass.

Albersmeier, Sabine, ed. 2009   *Heroes: Mortals and Myths in Ancient Greece*, cat., Baltimore, Md.

Alberti, Leon Battista 1988   *On the Art of Building in Ten Books*, trans. Joseph Rykwert, Robert Tavernor and Neil Leach [1st ed., *De Re Aedificatoria*, Florence, 1485].

Alcock, Susan E. 1991   'Tomb Cult and the Post-classical Polis', *AJA* 95: 447–67.

—— 2002   *Archaeologies of the Greek Past*, Cambridge.

——, John Cherry and Jaś Elsner, eds, 2001   *Pausanias: Travel and Memory in Roman Greece*, Oxford.

Alemdar, S. 2000   'Le Monument de Lysicrate et son trépied', *Ktema* 25: 199–206.

Aleshire, Susan 1992   'The Economics of Dedication at the Athenian Asklepieon', in AA.VV. 1992e: 85–99.

Algarotti, Francesco 1756   *Saggio del Conte Algarotti sull' architettura e sulla pittura*, Milan.

Allsopp, Bruce 1965   *A History of Classical Architecture: From its Origins to the Emergence of Hellenesque and Romanesque Architecture*, London.

Altekamp, Stefan 1991   *Zu griechischer Architekturornamentik im sechsten und fünften Jahrhundert v. Chr.* (*EurHss* 37), Frankfurt.

Alty, John 1982   'Dorians and Ionians', *JHS* 102: 1–14.

Alzinger, Wilhelm 1978   'Wandernde Künstler und ionische Spiralen in früharchaischer Zeit', in *Classica et Provincialia: Festschrift Erna Diez*, ed. Gerda Schwarz and Erwin Pochmarski, Graz: 17–32.

—— 1982   'Tuscanicae dispositiones und griechische Tektonik', *Pro Arte Antiqua: Festschrift für Hedwig Kenner*, Vienna: 23–7.

Amandry, Pierre 1950   *La Mantique apollinienne à Delphes: essai sur la fonctionnement de l'oracle* (BEFAR 170), Paris.

—— 1952   'Observations sur les monuments de l'Heraion d'Argos', *Hesperia* 21: 222–74.

—— 1953   *La Colonne des Naxiens et le portique des Athéniens*, (FdDelphes II), Paris.

—— 1976   'Trépieds d'Athènes, 1: Dionysies', *BCH* 100: 15–93.

—— 1987   'Trépieds de Delphes et du Péloponnèse', *BCH* 111: 79–131.

—— 1997   'Monuments chorégiques d'Athènes', *BCH* 121: 445–87.

——, and Jean Ducat 1973   'Trépieds déliens', *Études Déliens* (*BCH*, supp. 1): 17–64.

——, and Erik Hansen 2010   *Le Temple d'Apollon du IVᵉ siècle* (FdDelphes II, 14), Paris.

Amiet, Pierre 1980   *La Glyptique mesopotamien archaïque*, Paris [1st ed. 1961].

Ampolo, Carmine 1989–90   'Fra economia, religione e politica: tesori e offerte nei santuari greci', *Scienze dell'Antichità* 3–4: 271–9.

Amy, R., H. Seyrig and E. Will 1975   *Le Temple du Bel à Palmyre*, Paris.

Anderson, Linda H. 1975   'Relief Pithoi from the Archaic Period of Greek Art' (diss., University of Colorado).

Anderson, W. J., and R. Phené Spiers 1902   *The Architecture of Greece and Rome: A Sketch of its Historic Development*, London.

Andrae, Walter 1930   *Das Gotteshaus und die Urformen des Bauens im alten Orient*, Berlin.

—— 1933   *Die ionische Säule: Bauform oder Symbol?* (Studien zur Bauforschung 5), Berlin.

—— 1943   *Die Kleinfunde von Sendschirli* (Ausgrabungen in Sendschirli V), Berlin.

Andreadaki-Blasaki, Maria 1997   *The County of Khania through its Monuments*, Athens.

Andrewes, A. 1974   *The Greek Tyrants*, London [1st ed. 1956].

Andronicos, Manolis 1984   *Vergina: The Royal Tombs and the Ancient City*, Athens.

Angier, Tom 2010   *Techne in Aristotle's Ethics: Crafting the Moral Life*, London and New York.

Antonaccio, Carla M. 1992   'Terraces, Tombs, and the Early Argive Heraion', *Hesperia* 61: 85–105.

—— 1994   'Placing the Past: The Bronze Age in the Cultic Topography of Early Greece', in AA.VV. 1994: 79–104.

—— 1995   *An Archaeology of Ancestors: Tomb Cult and Hero Cult in Early Greece*, Lanham, Md., and London.

Antonetti, Claudia 1990   'Il santuario apollineo di Termo in Etolia', *Mélanges Pierre Lévêque* 4, Paris and Besançon.

Arafat, K. W. 1995   'Pausanias and the Temple of Hera at Olympia', *BSA* 90: 461–73.

—— 1996   *Pausanias' Greece: Ancient Artists and Roman Rulers*, Cambridge.

Arnold, Dieter 1991   *Building in Egypt: Pharaonic Stone Masonry*, New York.

—— 1999   *Temples of the Last Pharaohs*, Oxford and New York.

Aslan, Carolyn Chabot 2011   'A Place of Burning: Hero or Ancestor Cult at Troy', *Hesperia* 80: 381–429.

Astour, Michael C. 1967   *Hellenosemitica: An Ethnic and Cultural Study in West Semitic Impact on Mycenaean Greece*, Leiden.

Åström. P., and B. Blomé 1964   'A Reconstruction of the Lion Gate Relief at Mycenae', *OpAth* 5: 159–91

Auberson, Paul 1968   *Le Temple d'Apollon Daphnéphoros* (Eretria 1), Berne.

—— 1974   'La Reconstitution du Daphnéphoréion d'Érétrie', *AntK* 17: 60–8.

——, and Karl Schefold 1972   *Führer durch Eretria*, Berne.

Aubet, María E. 1993   *The Phoenicians and the West: Politics, Colonies and Trade*, Cambridge [1st (Spanish) ed. 1987].

Audiat, J. 1933   *Le Trésor des Athéniens* (FdDelphes II), Paris.

Austin, Michel M. 1970   *Greece and Egypt in the Archaic Age* (Proceedings of the Cambridge Philological Society, supp. 2).

Austin, Norman 1975   *Archery at the Dark of the Moon: Poetic Problems in Homer's Odyssey*, Berkeley, Calif., and London.

Aversa, Gregorio 1996   'Tetti con elementi della trabeazione dorica', *Sanctuari della Magna Grecia in Calabria*, ed. E. Lattanzi *et al.*, Naples: 259–60.

—— 2002   'Decorazioni architettoniche fittili di età arcaica tra Grecia propria e Occidente coloniale: realtà a confronto', *AnnASAtene* 80: 231–79.

Azarpay, Guitty 1968   *Urartian Art and Artifacts: A Chronological Study*, Berkeley, Calif.

Bakker, Karel A. 1999   'A Corpus of Early Ionic Capitals' (diss., University of Pretoria).

Bakker, P. E. J. 1997   *Poetry in Speech: Orality and Homeric Discourse*, Ithaca, N.Y.

Bammer, Anton 1972   *Die Architektur des jüngeren Artemision von Ephesos*, Wiesbaden.

—— 1984   *Das Heiligtum der Artemis von Ephesos*, Vienna.

—— 1990   'A *Peripteros* of the Geometric Period in the Artemision of Ephesus', *Anatolian Studies* 40: 137–60.

—— 1991   'Les Sanctuaires de VIIIᵉ et VIIᵉ siècles à l'Artémesion d'Éphèse', *RA*: 63–84.

—— 1998   'Sanctuaries in the Artemision of Ephesus', in AA.VV. 1998a: 27–47.

—— 2004   'Mykene und der ephesische Peripteros', *Studi di archeologia in onore di Gustavo Traversari*, ed. Manuela Fano Santi, Rome: 29–45.

—— 2008a   'Vom Peripteros zum Dipteros', in AA.VV. 2008b: 75–91.

—— 2008b   'Der Peripteros und sein Vorgänger', in Muss 2008: 243–9.

—— 2008c   'Der sogenannte Hekatompedos und Tempel C', in Muss 2008: 251–4.

——, and Ulrike Muss 1996   *Das Artemision von Ephesos: Das Weltwunder ioniens in archaischer und klassischer Zeit*, Mainz.

Bankel, Hansgeorg ed. 1986   *Carl Haller von Hallerstein in Griechenland 1810–1817: Architekt, Zeichner, Bauforscher*, Berlin.

—— 1989   'Aus Holz und Stein: Ein spätarchaischer griechischer Dachstuhl', *IstMitt* 39: 65–72.

—— 1993   *Der spätarchaische Tempel der Aphaia auf Aegina* (Denkmäler Antiker Architektur 19), Berlin.

Baran, Abdulkadir 2007   'The Column-necks in Antiquity', in *Patronvs: Festschrift für Coşkun Özgünel zum 65. Geburtstag*, ed. E. Öztepe and M. Kadıoğlu, Istanbul: 73–85.

Barker, Hollis S. 1966   *Furniture in the Ancient World: Origins and Evolution*, London.

Barletta, Barbara A. 1983   *Ionic Influence in Archaic Sicily: The Monumental Art* (SIMA 23), Gothenburg.

—— 1990   'An "Ionian Sea" Style in Archaic Doric Architecture', *AJA* 94: 45–72.

—— 2000   'Ionic Influence in Western Greek Architecture: Towards a Definition and Explanation', in AA.VV. 2000b: 203–16.

—— 2001   *The Origins of the Greek Architectural Orders*, Cambridge and New York.

—— 2009   'The Greek Entablature and Wooden Antecedents', in *Koine: Mediterranean Studies in Honor of R. Ross Holloway*, ed. Derek B. Counts and Anthony S. Tuck, Oxford: 153–65.

—— 2011   'Greek Architecture', *AJA* 115: 611–40.

Barnett, Richard D. 1950   'The Excavations of the British Museum at Toprak Kale near Van', *Iraq* 12: 1–43.

—— 1956   'Ancient Oriental Influences on Archaic Greece', in *The Aegean and the Near East. Studies Presented to Hetty Goldman on the Occasion of her Seventy-fifth Birthday*, ed. Saul S. Weinberg, Locust Valley, N.Y.: 212–38.

—— 1957   *A Catalogue of the Nimrud Ivories*, London.

—— 1960   *Assyrian Palace Reliefs and their Influence on the Sculptures of Babylonia and Persia*, London.

—— 1982   *Ancient Ivories in the Middle East and Adjacent Countries* (*Qedem* 14), Jerusalem.

——, Erika Bleibtreu and Geoffrey Turner 1998   *Sculptures from the Southwest Palace of Sennacherib at Ninevah*, 2 vols, London.

Barringer, Judith M. 2008   *Art, Myth and Ritual in Classical Greece*, Cambridge.

Bauer, Heinrich 1973   *Korinthische Kapitelle des 4. und 3. Jahrhunderts v. Chr.* (*AM* Beiheft 3), Berlin.

—— 1977   'Lysikratesdenkmal, Baubestand und Rekonstruktion', *AM* 92: 117–227.

Beard, Mary, and John North, ed. 1990   *Pagan Priests: Religion and Power in the Ancient World*, London.

Beazley, John D. 1938   *Attic White Ground Lekythoi*, Oxford.

Beekes, Robert S. P. 2003   'The Origin of Apollo', *Journal of Near Eastern Religions* 3: 1–21.

Behrens-du Maire, Arne 1993   'Zur Bedeutung griechischer Schatzhäuser', in AA.VV. 1993d: 76–81.

Benaissa, Ramla 2007   'Erudite Laughter: The Persiflage of Viel de Saint Maux', in *Chora: Intervals in the Philosophy of Architecture* (Montreal) 5: 51–80.

Benton, Sylvia 1934–5a   'The Evolution of the Tripod-Lebes', *BSA* 35: 74–130.

—— 1934–5b   'Excavations in Ithaka III', *BSA* 35: 45–73.

Bérard, Claude 1971   'Architecture érétrienne et mythologie delphique: le Daphnéphoréion', *AntK* 14: 59–73.

Berges, Dietrich 1996   *Rundaltäre aus Kos und Rhodos*, Berlin.

Bergquist, Birgitta 1967   *The Archaic Greek Temenos: A Study of Structure and Function*, Lund.

—— 1990   'Primary or Secondary Temple Function: The Case of Halieis', *OpAth* 18: 23–37.

Berlinerblau, Jacques 1999   *Heresy in the University: The* Black Athena *Controversy and the Responsibilities of American Intellectuals*, New Brunswick, N.J.

Bernal, Martin 1987   *Black Athena: The Afroasiatic Roots of Classical Civilization*, I: *The Fabrication of Ancient Greece 1785–1985*, New Brunswick, N.J., and London.

—— 1991   *Black Athena: The Afroasiatic Roots of Classical Civilization*, II: *The Archaeological and Documentary Evidence*, New Brunswick, N.J., and London.

—— 2001   *Black Athena writes Back: Martin Bernal responds to his Critics*, Durham, N.C., and London.

Berndt-Ersöz, Susanne 2006   *Phrygian Rock-Cut Shrines: Structure, Function and Cult Practice*, Leiden and Boston, Mass.

Berti, Fede, and Masturzo, Nicolò 2000   'Aree di culto ed elementi architettonici di periodo arcaico a Iasos (Caria)', in AA.VV. 2000b: 217–29.

Berve, Helmut, and Gottfried Gruben 1963   *Greek Temples, Theatres and Shrines*, London, 2 vols [1st (German) ed. 1961].

Betancourt, Philip 1977   *The Aeolic Style in Architecture: A Survey of its Development in Palestine, the Halicarnassos Peninsula, and Greece*, Princeton, N.J.

Bettinetti, Simona 2001   *La statua di culto nella pratica rituale greca*, Bari.

Beyer, Immo 1972   'Der Triglyphenfries von Thermos C. Ein Konstruktionsvorschlag', *AA*: 197–226.

—— 1976   *Die Tempel von Dreros und Prinias A und die Chronologie der kretischen Kunst des 8.und 7. Jhs. v. Chr.*, 2 vols, Freiburg.

—— 1980   *Der minoisch-mykenische Palasttempel und seine Wirkung auf den dorischen Tempel*, Freiburg.

Billot, Marie-Françoise 1990   'Terres cuites architecturales d'Argos et d'Épidaure: Notes de typologie et d'histoire', in AA.VV. 1990a: 95–139.

—— 1993   'L'Apparition de l'acanthe dans le décor des toits du monde grec', in AA.VV. 1993e: 39–74.

—— 1997   'Recherches archéologiques récentes à l'Héraion d'Argos avec une annexe: propositions pour une restitution du temple archaïque', in AA.VV. 1997d: 11–82.

——1997–8   'Sanctuaire et cultes d'Athéna à Argos', *OpAth* 22–3: 7–52.

—— 2000   'Centres de production et diffusion des tuiles dans le monde grec', in *L'Artisanat en Grèce ancienne: les productions, les diffusions*, con., Lyon, 1998, Lille: 193–240.

Bingöl, Orhan 1990   'Überlegungen zum ionischen Gebälk', *IstMitt* 40: 101–8.

Biran, Avraham ed. 1981   *Temples and High Places in Biblical Times*, con., Jerusalem, 1977, Jerusalem.

Birge, Darice 1994   'Trees in the Landscape of Pausanias' *Periegesis*', in AA.VV. 1994: 231–45.

Blackman, David J. 2001   'Ship Dedications in Sanctuaries', in Böhm and von Eickstedt 2001: 207–12.

Blegen, Carl William 1937   *Prosymna*, Cambridge.

—— 1945 'The Roof of the Mycenaean Megaron', *AJA* 49: 35–44.

Blondel, Jacques-François 1771–7 *Cours d'architecture ou traité de la décoration, distribution et construction des bâtiments*, ed. P. Patte, 6 vols, Paris.

Boardman, John 1959 'Chian and Early Ionic Architecture', *Antiquaries Journal* 39: 170–218.

—— 1967 *Excavations in Chios, 1952–1955: Greek Emporio* (*BSA*, supp. 6).

—— 1978 *Greek Sculpture: The Archaic Period: A Handbook*, London.

—— 1998 *Early Greek Vase Painting: 11th–6th Centuries BC: A Handbook*, London.

—— 1999 *The Greeks Overseas: Their Early Colonies and Trade*, London [1st ed. 1964].

—— 2002 *The Archaeology of Nostalgia: How the Greeks Re-created their Mythical Past*, London.

——, et al. 1967 *The Art and Architecture of Ancient Greece*, London.

Boehringer, David 2002 *Heroenkulte in Griechenland von der geometrischen bis zur klassischen Zeit. Attika, Argolis, Messenien* (*Klio*, Beihefte, Neue Folge 3), Berlin.

Boehlau, J., and Karl Schefold 1940 *Larisa am Hermos*, I, Berlin.

Böhm, Stephaine, and Laus-Valtin von Eickstedt, eds 2001 *ΙΘΑΚΗ: Festschrift für Jörg Schäfer zum 75. Geburstag*, Würzburg.

Börker, Christoph 1965 *Blattkelchkapitelle, Untersuchungen zur kaiserzeitlichen Architekturornamentik in Griechenland*, Berlin.

—— 1983 *Festbankett und griechische Architektur* (*Xenia* 4), Konstanz.

Bötticher, Karl 1856 *Der Baumkultus der Hellenen nach den gottesdienstlichen Gebraüchen und den überlieferten Bildwerken*, Berlin.

—— 1874–81 *Die Tektonik der Hellenen*, I: *Die Lehre der tektonischen Kunstformen: Dorische, ionische und korinthische Bauweise* (1874), II: *Der Tempel in seiner räumlichen Anordnung und Ausstattung* (1881), Berlin [1st ed. 1844–52].

Bogaert, Raymond 1968 *Banques et banquiers dans les cités grecques*, Leiden.

Bommelaer, Jean-François 1997 *Marmaria: Le Sanctuaire d'Athéna à Delphes* (EFA, Sites et Monuments 16), Paris.

——, and Didier Laroche 1991 *Guide de Delphes: Le Site* (EFA, Sites et Monuments 7), Paris.

Bonnechere, Pierre 2007 'The Example of the *Alsos* of Trophonios at Lebadeia (Boeotia)', *Sacred Gardens and Landscapes: Ritual and Agency*, ed. Michel Conan, Washington, D.C.: 17–41.

Bookidis, Nancy 1967 'A Study of the Use and Geographical Distribution of Architectural Sculpture in the Archaic Period' (diss., Bryn Mawr College).

1993 'Ritual Dining at Corinth', in AA.VV. 1993a: 45–61.

Borchardt, Ludwig 1920 *Die aegyptische Pflanzensäule*, Berlin.

Borchhardt, Jürgen, ed. 1975 *Myra: Eine lykische Metropole in antiker und byzantinischer Zeit* (Istanbuler Forschungen 30), Berlin.

Borell, Brigitte, and Dessa Rittig 1998 *Orientalische und griechische Bronzereliefs aus Olympia* (OlForsch 26), Berlin.

Borrmann, Richard 1888a 'Altionische Kapitelle', *AntDenk* 1: 15–16.

—— 1888b 'Stele für Weihgeschenke auf der Akropolis zu Athen', *JdI* 3: 269–85.

Bothmer, Dietrich von 1977 'The Struggle for the Tripod', in *Festschrift für Frank Brommer*, ed. Ursula Höckmann and Antje Krug, Mainz: 51–63.

Bouzek, Jan 1997 *Greece, Anatolia and Europe: Cultural Interrelations during the Early Iron Age* (SIMA 122), Jonsered.

Bowen, M. L. 1950 'Some Observations on the Origin of Triglyphs', *BSA* 45: 113–25.

Bowie, A.M. 1995 'Greek Sacrifice: Forms and Functions in *The Greek World*', ed. Anton Powell, London and New York: 463–82.

Braun-Vogelstein, Julie 1920 *Die ionische Säule*, *JdI* 35: 1–48.

Bremmer, Jan N. 1994 *Greek Religion*, Oxford.

—— 1996 'Modi di comunicazione con il divino: la preghiera, la divinazione e il sacrificio nella civiltà greca', Settis 1996, 1: 239–83.

—— 2008 *Greek Religion and Culture, the Bible and the Ancient Near East*, Leiden and Boston, Mass.

Brinkmann, Vinzenz, and Raimund Wünsche, eds 2004, *Bunte Götter: Die Farbigkeit anitker Skulptur*, Munich.

Brize, Philip 1997 'Offrandes de l'époque géométrique et archaïque a l'Héraion de Samos', in AA.VV. 1997d, 123–39.

Brock, J. K. 1957 *Fortetsa: Early Greek Tombs near Knossos*, Cambridge.

Brockmann, Anna D. 1968 *Die griechische Ante: Eine typologische Untersuchung*, Marburg.

Broder, Philippe-Alexandre 2008 'La Manipulation des images dans les processions en Grèce ancienne', in *Image et religion*, con., Rome, 2003, Naples: 121–35.

Brommer, Frank 1985 *Griechische Weihegaben und Opfer (in Listen)*, Berlin.

Broneer, Oscar 1971 *Temple of Poseidon: Isthmia I*, Princeton, N.J.

Brookes, Alan C. 1981 'Stoneworking in the Geometric Period at Corinth', *Hesperia* 50: 285–90.

Broucke, Pieter 1996 'The Temple of Olympian Zeus at Agrigento' (diss., Yale University).

Brown, J. P. 1979   'The Sacrifical Cult and its Critique in Greek and Hebrew', *Journal of Semitic Studies* 24: 159–73.

Bruit Zaidman, Louise, and Pauline Schmitt Pantel 1992   *Religion in the Ancient Greek City,* Cambridge [1st (French) ed. 1989].

Brulotte, Eric L. 1994a   'The Placement of Votive Offerings and Dedications in the Peloponnesian Sanctuaries of Artemis' (diss., University of Minnesota).

—— 1994b   'The "Pillar of Oinomaos" and the location of Stadium I at Olympia', *AJA* 98: 53–64.

Brümmer, Elfriede 1985   'Griechische Truhenbehälter', *JdI* 100: 1–168.

Bruneau, Philippe, and Jean Ducat 1983   *Guide de Délos* (ECF, Sites et Monuments 1), Paris [1st ed. 1965].

Bruneau, Philippe, and Philippe Fraisse 2002   *Le Monument à abside et la question de l'autel de cornes* (ExpDélos 40).

Bruschi, Arnaldo 1992   'L'Antico e il processo di identificazione degli ordini nella seconda metà del Quattrocento', in AA.VV. 1992f: 11–57.

Buchholz, Hans-Günther 1963   'Steinerne Dreifusschalen des ägäischen Kulturkreises und ihre Beziehungen zum Osten', *JdI* 78: 1–77.

—— 1966   *Tamassos: Ein antikes Königreich auf Zypern* (SIMA 136), Jonsered.

Buck, C. D. 1955   *The Greek Dialects*, Chicago, Ill.

Bühlmann, Josef 1872–7   *Die Architektur des klassischen Altertums und der Renaissance*, 3 vols, Stuttgart.

Bühlmann, M. B. 1921–2   'Vorstufen dorischer Architektur', *MüJb* 12: 165–9.

Büsing, Hermann H. 1988   'Dorische Türrahmen', in *Bathron: Beiträge zur Architektur und verwandten Künsten für Heinrich Drerup*, ed. Hermann Büsing and Friedrich Hiller, Saarbrücken 1988: 107–14.

—— 1994   *Das Athener Schatzhaus in Delphi: Neue Untersuchungen zur Architektur und Bemalung* (MarburgWP, 1992), Marburg.

—— 2006   'Ionische Kapitelle aus dem archaischen Panionion', in *Maiandros: Festschrift für Volkmar von Graeve*, ed. Ralf Biering *et al.*, Munich: 55–9.

Büsing-Kolbe, Andrea 1978   'Frühe griechische Türen', *JdI* 93: 66–174.

Bunnens, Guy 2000   'Syria in the Iron Age: Problems of Definition', *Ancient Near Eastern Studies*, supp. 7: 3–19.

Burford, Alison M. 1965   'The Economics of Greek Temple Building', *Proceedings of the Cambridge Philological Society* 191: 21–34.

—— 1969   *The Greek Temple Builders at Epidauros: A Social and Economic Study of Building in the Asklepian Sanctuary, during the Fourth and the Early Third Centuries B.C.*, Liverpool.

Burkert, Walter 1966   'Greek Tragedy and Sacrificial Ritual', *GRBS* 7: 87–121.

—— 1983   *Homo Necans: The Anthropology of Ancient Greek Sacrificial Ritual and Myth*, Berkeley, Calif. [1st (German) ed. 1972].

—— 1985   *Greek Religion: Archaic and Classical*, Oxford [1st (German) ed. 1977].

—— 1987   'Offerings in Perspective: Surrender, Distribution, Exchange', in AA.VV. 1987: 43–50.

—— 1988   'The Meaning and Function of the Temple in Classical Greece', in *Temple in Society*, ed. Michael V. Fox, Winona Lake, Ind.

—— 1992a   *The Orientalizing Revolution: Near Eastern Influence on Greek Culture in the Early Archaic Age,* Cambridge, Mass. [1st (German) ed. 1984].

—— 1992b   *The Formation of Greek Religions at the Close of the Dark Ages* (*Studi Italiani di filologia classica* 10): 533–51.

—— 1995   'Greek Poleis and Civic Cults: Some Further Thoughts', in AA.VV. 1995a: 201–10.

—— 1996a   'Greek Temple-builders: Who, Where and Why?', in AA.VV. 1996c: 21–9.

—— 1996b   *Creation of the Sacred*, Cambridge, Mass.

—— 2003   *Die Griechen und der Orient*, Munich.

Buschor, Ernst 1930   'Heraion von Samos: Frühe Bauten', *AM* 55: 1–99.

—— 1952   'Ein frühdädalidischer Ringhallentempel', *Festschrift Andreas Rumpf*, ed. Tobias Dohrn, Krefeld: 32–7.

    1957   'Altsamischer Bauschmuck', *AM* 72: 1–34.

——, and Schleif, Hans 1933   'Heraion von Samos: der Altarplatz der Frühzeit', *AM* 58: 146–73.

Busink, Th. A. 1970–80   *Der Tempel von Jerusalem*, 2 vols, Leiden.

Buxton, Angela H. 2002   'Lydian Royal Dedications in Greek Sanctuaries' (diss., University of California, Berkeley).

Cahill, Nicholas 2002   *Household and City Organization at Olynthus*, New Haven and London.

Cambitoglou A. *et al.* 1988   *Zagora 2: Excavation of a Geometric Town on the Island of Andros*, Athens.

Carapanos, Constantin 1878   *Dodone et ses ruines*, 2 vols, Paris.

Carlier, P. 1996   'Les *basileis* homérique sont-ils des rois?', *Ktema* 21: 5–22.

Carpenter, Rhys 1959   *The Esthetic Basis of Greek Art*, Bloomington, Ind. [1st ed. 1921].

—— 1962   *Greek Art: A Study of the Formal Evolution of Style*, Philadelphia, Pa.

Caroll, Maureen 2007   'Boschetti sacri e giardini dei templi nella Grecia antica', in Di Pasquale and Paolucci 2007: 44–9.

Carter, Jane B., and Laura J. Steinberg 2010   'Kouroi and Statistics', *AJA* 114: 103–28.

Cartledge, Paul 2002   *Sparta and Lakonia: A Regional History 1300–362 BC*, London [1st ed. 1979].

Casevitz, M. 1984   'Temples et sanctuaires: ce qu'apprend l'étude léxicologique', in *Temples et sanctuaires: Séminaire de recherche 1981–1983*, ed. Georges Roux, Lyon: 81–95.

Caskey, Lacey D., Gorham P. Stevens *et. al.* 1927   *The Erechtheum*, Cambridge, Mass.

Castleden, Rodney 2005   *Mycenaeans*, London and New York.

Catling, Hector W. 1964   *Cypriot Bronzework in the Mycenaean World*, Oxford.

—— 1984   'Workshop and Heirloom: Prehistoric Bronze Stands in the East Mediterranean', *RDAC*: 69–91.

Catling, R. W. V. 1994   'A Fragment of an Archaic Temple Model from Artemis Orthia, Sparta', *BSA* 89: 269–75.

Caylus, Comte de [Anne-Claude-Philippe de Tubières] 1756   'De l'Architecture ancienne', *Histoire de l'Académie Royale des Inscriptions et Belles-Lettres* 23, Paris: 286–319.

Cazenove, Olivier de 1993   'Suspension d'ex-voto dans les bois sacrés', *Les Bois sacrés: Collection du Centre Jean Bérard* 10, con., Naples, 1989: 111–26.

Cesnola, Luigi Palma di 1914   *Cyprus: Its Ancient Cities, Tombs and Temples*, New York [1st ed. 1877].

Chadwick, J. 1976   'Who were the Dorians?', *Parola del Passato* 31: 103–17.

Chambers, William 1759   *A Treatise on the Decorative Part of Civil Architecture*, London.

—— 1825   *A Treatise on the Decorative Part of Civil Architecture, with Illustrations, Notes and an Examination of Grecian Architecture by Joseph Gwilt*, London.

Chamoux, François 1970   'Trépieds votifs a caryatides', *BCH* 94: 320–26.

Champollion, Jean-François 1833   *Lettres écrites d'Egypte et de Nubie en 1828 et 1829*, Paris [reprinted 1973].

Chantraine, P. 1968–80   *Dictionnaire étymologique de la langue grecque: Histoire des mots*, 4 vols, Paris.

Charbonneaux, Jean, and Karl Gottlob 1925   *Le Sanctuaire d'Athena Pronaïa: La tholos* (FdDelphes II), 2 vols, Paris

Chipiez, Charles 1876   *Histoire critique des origines et de la formation des ordres grecs*, Paris.

Choisy, Auguste 1899   *Histoire de L'architecture*, 2 vols, Paris.

Choremi-Spetsieri, A. 1994   'The Street of Tripods and the Choregic Monuments of Ancient Athens' (trans. from Greek), in *The Archaeology of Athens and Attica under the Democracy*, con., Athens, 1992, ed. William D. E. Coulson *et al.*, Oxford: 31–42.

Ciasca, Antonia 1962   *Il Capitello detto eolico in Etruria*, Florence.

Claridge, Amanda 1983   'Roman Methods of Fluting Columns and Pilasters', in *Città e architettura nella Roma imperiale (Analecta Romana Istituti Danici*, supp.): 119–28.

Clarke, Joseph T. 1886   'A Proto-Ionic Capital from the Site of Neandria', *AJA* 2: 1–20.

——, Francis H. Bacon and Robert Koldewey 1902–21   *Investigations at Assos*, 2 vols, London.

Clarke, Somers, and Reginald Engelbach 1930   *Ancient Egyptian Masonry: The Building Craft*, Oxford.

Clinton, Kevin 1993   'The Sanctuary of Demeter and Kore at Eleusis', in AA.VV. 1993a: 110–24.

Coldstream, J. Nicholas 1968   *Greek Geometric Pottery: A Survey of Ten Local Styles and their Chronology*, London.

—— 1976   'Hero-cults in the Age of Homer', *JHS* 96: 8–17.

—— 1977   *Geometric Greece*, New York.

—— 1983   'Gift Exchange in the Eighth Century BC', in AA.VV. 1983: 201–7.

—— 1985   'Greek Temples: Why and Where?', in AA.VV. 1985: 67–97.

Connelly, J. B. 2007   *Portrait of a Priestess. Women and Ritual in Ancient Greece*, Princeton, N.J.

Connor, Peter J. 1973   'A Late Geometric Kalathos in Melbourne', *AA*: 58–67.

Conti, Maria Clara 1994   *Il più antico fregio dallo Heraion del Sele*, Florence.

Cook, Arthur B. 1902   'The Gong at Dodona', *JHS* 22: 5–28.

Cook, Erwin 2004   'Near Eastern Sources for the Palace of Alkinoos', *AJA* 108: 43–77.

Cook, John M. 1962   *The Greeks in Ionia and the East*, London.

——, and Richard N. Nicholls 1998   *Old Smyrna Excavations: The Temples of Athena (BSA, supp. 30)*.

Cook, R. M. 1937   'Amasis and the Greeks in Egypt', *JHS* 57: 227–37.

—— 1951   'A Note on the Origin of the Triglyph', *BSA* 46: 50–52.

—— 1967   'The Origins of Greek Sculpture', *JHS* 87: 1967: 24–32.

—— 1970   'The Archetypal Doric Temple', *BSA* 65: 17–19.

—— 1989   'The Francis-Vickers Chronology', *JHS* 109: 164–70.

Cooper, Frederick A. 1992–6   *The Temple of Apollo Bassitas*, I: *The Architecture*, IV [volume of folio drawings], Athens and Princeton, N.J.

Corso, Antonio 2012   'The Education of Artists in Ancient Greece', *Hyperboreus: Studia Classica* 18: 21–53.

Corso, Antonio, Rossana Mugellesi and Gianpiero Rosati 1988   *Gaio Plinio Secondo, Storia naturale V, Mineralogia e storia dell'arte, Libri 33–37* (trans. of Pliny the Elder's *Natural History* Book 5 with commentary), Turin.

Corso, Antonio, and Elisa Romano 1997   *Vitruvio: De Architectura* (trans. with commentary), 2 vols, Turin.

Cosmopoulos, Michael B., ed. 2003a   *Greek Mysteries: The Archaeology and Ritual of Ancient Greek Secret Cults*, London.

—— 2003b   'Mycenaean Religion at Eleusis: The Architecture and Stratigraphy of Megaron B', in Cosmopoulos 2003a: 1–24.

Costamagna, Liliana, and Claudio Sabbione 1990   *Una città in Magna Grecia: Locri Epizefiri. Guida archeologica*, Reggio Calabria.

Costantini, Alessandra 1999   'Riflessioni sulla scultura di scuola nassia a Delos: La colossale statua di Apollo e la terrazza dei leoni', *QuadTic* 28: 39–81.

Couch, Herbert N. 1929   *The Treasuries of the Greeks and the Romans*, Menasha, Wis.

Coulton, James J. 1974   'Lifting in Early Greek Architecture', *JHS* 94: 1–19.

—— 1976   *The Architectural Development of the Greek Stoa*, Oxford.

—— 1977   *Ancient Greek Architects at Work. Problems of Structure and Design*, Oxford.

—— 1979   'Doric Capitals: A Proportional Analysis', *BSA* 74: 81–153.

—— 1988   'Post Holes and Post Bases in Early Greek Architecture', *Mediterranean Archaeology* 1: 58–65.

—— 1993   'The Toumba Building: Its Architecture', in Popham *et al.*: 33–70.

—— 2007   '"A Base for a Shoe": Women and Columns in Vitruvius 4.1.7', Αμύμονα έργα: τιμητικός τόμος για τον καθηγητή Βασίλη Κ. Λαμπρινουδάκη ('Noble works: essays in honour of professor Vassilis K. Lambrinoudakis'), Athens: 201–10.

Courbin, Paul, 1973   *Le Colosse naxien et le palmier de Nicias* (*BCH*, supp. 1), Paris.

—— 1980   *L'Oikos des naxiens* (ExpDélos 33), Paris.

Courby, Fernand 1911   'La Tholos du trésor de Sicyone à Delphes', *BCH* 35: 132–48.

—— 1927   *Le Sanctuaire d'Apollon: La Terrasse du temple* (FdDelphes II), Paris.

—— 1931   *Les Temples d'Apollon* (ExpDélos 12), Paris.

Croissant, Francis 2003   *Les Frontons du temple du IVe siècle* (FdDelphes IV, 7), Paris.

Cross, Toni M. 1974   'Bronze Tripods and Related Stands in the Eastern Mediterranean from the Twelfth through the Seventh Centuries B.C.' (diss., University of North Carolina).

Crowley, Janice L. 1989   *The Aegean and the East: An Investigation into the Transference of Artistic Motifs between the Aegean, Egypt and the Near East in the Bronze Age* (SIMA 51), Jonsered.

Cultrera, Giuseppe 1951   'L'Apollonion-Artemision di Ortigia in Siracusa', *MonAnt* 41: 701–859.

Curl, James S. 1992   *Classical Architecture*, London.

Curtis, John 1996   'Assyrian Furniture: The Archaeological Evidence', in AA.VV. 1996d: 167–80.

Cuzin, Jean-Pierre, *et al.* eds 2000   *D'après l'antique*, cat. Louvre, Paris.

D'Acunto, Matteo 1995   'I cavalieri di Priniàs ed il tempio A', *Annali di archeologia e storia antica* 2: 15–55.

—— 2002–3   'Il tempio di Apollo a Dreros: il culto e la 'cucina del sacrificio', *Annali di archeologia e storia antica* 9–10: 9–62.

Dakaris, Sotiris I. 1971   *Archaeological Guide to Dodona*, Ioannina.

—— 1988   'The Triglyphs at the Doric Temple' (trans. from Greek), *Acts of the 12th International Congress of Classical Archaeology*, 4, Athens: 41–8.

D'Albiac, Carole 1995   'The "Diagnostic" Wings of Monsters', in *Klados: Essays in Honour of J. N. Coldstream*, ed. Christine Morris (*Bulletin of the Institute of Classical Studies*, supp. 63), London: 63–72.

Danner, Peter 1989   *Griechische Akrotere der archaischen und klassischen Zeit* (*Rivista di Archeologia*, supp. 5), Rome.

—— 1997   *Westgriechische Akrotere*, Mainz.

Danthine, Hélène 1937   *Le Palmier-dattier et les arbres sacrés dans l'iconographie de l'Asie occidentale ancienne*, 2 vols, Paris.

Darcque, Pascal 1981   'Les Vestiges mycéniens découverts sous le telestérion d'Eleusis', *BCH* 105: 593–605.

—— 1990   'Pour l'abandon du terme "mégaron"', in AA.VV. 1990b: 21–31.

Darwin, Charles 1859   *On the Origin of Species by Means of Natural Selection or the Preservation of Favoured Races in the Struggle for Life*, London.

Daux, Georges 1923   'Les deux trésors', *Le sanctuaire d'Athéna Pronaia* (FdDelphes II), Paris.

—— 1937   'Inscriptions et monuments archaïques de Delphes', *BCH* 61: 57–78.

—— 1963   'Chronique des fouilles et découvertes archéologiques en Grèce en 1962', *BCH* 87: 689–879.

—— 1965   'Chronique des fouilles et découvertes archéologiques en Grèce en 1964', *BCH* 89: 683–1008.

——, and Erik Hansen 1987   *Le Trésor de Siphnos* (FdDelphes II), Paris.

Davies, John K. 2001   'Rebuilding a Temple: The Economic Effects of Piety', *Economies Beyond Agriculture in the Classical World*, ed. D. J. Mattingly and J. Salomon, London and New York: 195–208.

De Angelis D'Ossat, Guglielmo 1941–2   'L'origine del triglifo', *RendPontAcc* 18: 117–33.

De Cesare, Monica 1997   *Le statue in immagine: studi sulle raffigurazioni di statue nella pittura vascolare greca*, Rome.

De Franciscis, Alfonso 1979   *Il santuario di Marasà in Locri Epizefiri*, I: *Il tempio arcaico*, Naples.

Degrassi, Nevio 1981   *Lo Zeus stilita di Ugento*, Rome.

de Jong, Sigrid 2010   'Redisovering Architecture: Paestum in Eighteenth-Century Architectural Experience and Theory' (diss., University of Leiden).

de la Bandera Romero, Maria Luisa 1994   El timiaterio orientalizante de Villagarcía de la Torre (Badajoz), *Archivo español de Arqueología* 67: 41–58.

de la Coste-Messelière, Pierre 1936   *Au musée de Delphes. Recherches sur quelques monuments archaïques et leur décor sculpté*, Paris.

—— 1943   *Delphes (photographies de Georges de Miré)*, Paris.

—— 1963   'Chapiteaux doriques du haut archaïsme', *BCH* 87: 639–52.

—— 1969   'Topographie delphique', *BCH* 93: 730–58.

Delivorrias, Angelos 1974   *Attische Giebelskulpturen und Akrotere des fünften Jahrhunderts*, Tübingen.

—— 2009   'The Throne of Apollo at the Amyklaion: Old Proposals, New Perspectives', in *Sparta and Laconia: From Prehistory to Pre-modern*, con., Athens, 2005, ed. W. G. Cavanagh *et al.*, London: 133–5.

Demangel, Robert 1923   *Sanctuaire d'Athéna Pronaia: Les Temples de tuf* (FdDelphes II), Paris.

—— 1931a   'Fenestrarum Imagines', *BCH* 55: 117–63.

—— 1931b   'Sur l'origine des mutules doriques', *RA* 34: 1–10.

—— 1932   *La Frise Ionique* (BEFAR 136), Paris.

—— 1937   'Triglyphes bas', *BCH* 61: 421–38.

—— 1946   'Fenestrarum Imagines, bis', *BCH* 70: 132–47.

—— 1947–8   'Anecdota dorica, II: Triglyphes en terre cuite', *BCH* 71–2: 359–68.

—— 1949   'Retour offensif des théories vitruviennes sur la frise dorique', *BCH* 73: 476–82.

Demargne, Pierre, ed. 1947   *La Crète Dédalique: Études sur les origines d'une renaissance* (BEFAR 164), Paris.

de Polignac, François 1994   'Mediation, Competition, and Sovereignty: The Evolution of Rural Sanctuaries in Geometric Greece', in AA.VV. 1994: 3–18.

—— 1995a   *Cults, Territory, and the Origins of the Greek City-State*, Chicago, Ill. [1st (French) ed. 1984].

—— 1995b   'Repenser la 'cité'? Rituels et société en Grèce archaïque', in AA.VV. 1995a: 7–19.

—— 1996   'Offrandes, mémoire et compétition ritualisée dans les sanctuaires grecs à l'époque géometrique', in AA.VV. 1996: 59–66.

—— 2009   'Sanctuaries and Festivals', in AA.VV. 2009c: 427–43.

Desborough, V. R. d'Arba 1964   *The Last Mycenaeans and their Successors: An Archaeological Survey c. 1200–1000 B.C.*, Oxford.

—— 1972   *The Greek Dark Ages*, London.

Detienne, Marcel, and Jean-Pierre Vernant 1989   *The Cuisine of Sacrifice among the Greeks*, Chicago, Ill. [1st (French) ed. 1979].

De Waele, Jos A. K. E. 1995   'Der Apollontempel (C) von Thermos und sein Vorgänger (B): Disposition und Entwurf', *ArchEph*: 85–98.

Dickinson, Oliver 1994   *The Aegean Bronze Age*, Cambridge.

Dieterle, Martina 2007   *Dodona: Religionsgeschichtliche und historische Untersuchungen zur Entstehung und Entwicklung des Zeus-Heiligtums*, Hildesheim.

Dietrich, Bernard C. 1974   *The Origins of Greek Religion*, Berlin and New York.

—— 1986   *Tradition in Greek Religion*, Berlin.

—— 1985–6   'Divine Concept and Iconography', *Grazer Beiträge* 12–13: 171–92.

—— 1991   'Aegean Sanctuaries: Forms and Function', in AA.VV. 1991a: 141–49.

Dimopoulou-Rethemiotaki, Nota 2005   *The Archaeological Museum of Heraklion*, Athens.

Dinsmoor, William Bell 1910   'The Choragic Monument of Nicias', *AJA* 14: 459–84.

—— 1913   'Four Ionic Treasuries at Delphi', *BCH*: 4–82.

—— 1923   'The Aeolic Capitals of Delphi', *AJA* 27: 164–73.

—— 1975   *The Architecture of Ancient Greece. An Account of its Historic Development*, New York.

Dinsmoor, William Bell Jr. 1973   'The Kardaki Temple Re-Examined', *AM* 88: 165–174.

—— 1980   *The Propylaia to the Athenian Akropolis*, I: *The Predecessors*, Princeton, N.J.

Ditlefsen, Finn 1985   'Gedanken zum Ursprung des dorischen Frieses', *ActaAArtH* 5: 1–24.

Di Pasquale, Giovanni, and Fabrizio Paolucci, eds 2007   *Il giardino antico da Babilonia a Roma*, cat. Florence, 2007, Livorno.

Di Vita, Antonio 1998   'I Fenici a Creta: Kommos, i "troni di Astarte" a Phalasarna e la rotta "delle isole"', *AnnASAtene* 70–71: 175–203.

Dodds, Eric R. 1951   *The Greeks and the Irrational*, Berkeley, Calif.

—— 1973   *The Ancient Concept of Progress and other Essays on Greek Literature and Belief*, Oxford.

Dodds, George, and Robert Tavernor 2002   *Body and Building: Essays on the Changing Relation of Body and Architecture*, Cambridge, Mass., and London.

Doepner, Daphni 2002   *Steine und Pfeiler für die Götter: Weihgeschenkgattungen in westgriechischen Stadtheiligtümern* (Palilia 10), Wiesbaden.

Dörpfeld, Wilhelm 1883   'Über das Schatzhaus der Sikyonier in Olympia', *AM* 8: 67–70.

—— 1886   'The Buildings of Tiryns', in *Tiryns: The Prehistoric Palace of the Kings of Tiryns*, London: 177–308.

—— 1892   'Das Heraion', *Die Baudenkmäler von Olympia*, Berlin: 27–36.

—— 1935   *Alt-Olympia: Untersuchungen und Ausgrabungen zur Geschichte des ältesten Heiligtums von Olympia und der älteren griechischen Kunst*, 2 vols, Berlin.

Donderer, Michael 2005   'Das Heraion in Olympia und sein Säulenkranz', *BABesch* 80: 7–20.

Donohue, Alice A. 1988   *Xoana and the Origins of Greek Sculpture*, Atlanta, Ga.

—— 1995   'Winckelmann's History of Art and Polyclitus', in *Polykleitos, the Doryphoros, and Tradition*, ed. Warren G. Moon, Madison, Wis.: 327–53.

—— 1997   'The Greek Images of the Gods: Considerations on Terminology and Methodology', *Hephaistos* 15: 31–45.

—— 2005   *Greek Sculpture and the Problem of Description*, Cambridge and New York.

Donos, Dimosthenis 2008   *Studien zu Säulen und Pfeilermonumenten der archaischen Zeit*, Hamburg.

Dontas, Georgios 1968   'Le Grand Sanctuaire de Mon Repos à Corfou', *AAA* 1: 66–9.

—— 1976   'Denkmäler und Geschichte eines kerkyräischen Heiligtums', in Jantzen 1976: 121–33.

Doumas, Christos 1992   *The Wall-paintings of Thera*, Athens.

Doxiadis, C. 1972   *Architectural Space in Ancient Greece*, Cambridge, Mass.

Drerup, Heinrich 1952   'Architektur und Toreutik in der griechischen Frühzeit', *Mitteilungen des Deutschen Archäologischen Instituts* 5: 7–38.

—— 1962   'Zur Entstehung der griechischen Tempelringhalle', in *Festschrift für Friedrich Matz*, ed. Nikolaus Himmelmann-Wildschütz and Hagen Biesantz, Mainz: 32–8.

—— 1969   *Griechische Baukunst in geometrischer Zeit* (Archaeologica Homerica 2), Göttingen.

—— 1986   'Das Sogenannte Daphnephoreion in Eretria', *Studien zur klassischen Archäologie: F. Hiller zu seinem 60. Geburtstag*, Saarbrücken: 3–21.

Drews, Robert 1983   *Basileus: The Evidence for Kingship in Geometric Greece*, New Haven and London.

Ducat, Jean 1964   Périrrhantèria, *BCH* 88: 577–606.

—— 1971   *Les Kouroi du Ptoion: Le Sanctuaire d'Apollon Ptoieus à l'époque archaïque* (BEFAR 219), Paris.

Ducrey, P., et al. 2004   *Eretria: A Guide to the Ancient City*, Athens.

Dunbabin, Thomas J. 1948   'The Early History of Corinth', *JHS* 68: 59–69.

—— 1957   *The Greeks and their Eastern Neighbours*, London.

—— 1962   *Perachora II. The Sanctuaries of Hera Akraia and Limenia: the Pottery, Ivories, Scarabs and other Objects from the votive Deposit of Hera Limenia*, Oxford.

Durand, Jean-Louis 1986   *Sacrifice et labour en Grèce ancienne. Essai d'anthropolgie religieuse*, Paris and Rome.

—— 1987   'Le Boeuf à la ficelle', in *Images et société en Grèce ancienne: L'Iconographie comme méthode d'analyse*, con., Lau-sanne, 1984 (Cahiers d'archéologie Romande 36), Lau-sanne: 227–41.

——, and Alain Schnapp 1989   *Sacrificial Slaughter and Initiatory Hunt: A City of Images. Iconography and Society in Ancient Greece*, Princeton, N.J. [1st (French) ed. 1984]: 53–70.

Durkheim, Émile 1915   *The Elementary Forms of Religious Life*, trans. J. W. Swain, London [1st (French) ed. 1912].

Durm, Josef 1881   *Die Baustile: Historische und technische Entwicklung. Handbuch der Architektur*, I: *Die Baukunst der Griechen*, Darmstadt.

—— 1910   *Die Baukunst der Griechen*, Leipzig 1910 [3rd (revised) ed. of Durm 1881].

Dyggve, Ejnar 1948   *Das Laphrion, der Tempelbezirk von Kalydon*, Copenhagen.

——, Frederick Poulsen and Konstantinos Rhomaios 1934   *Das Heroon von Kalydon*, Copenhagen.

Eckhart, Lothar 1953   'Bemerkungen zu dorischen Säulen auf archaischen griechischen Vasen', *ÖJh* 40: 60–72.

Eckstein, Felix 1969   *Anathemata. Studien zu den Weihgeschenken strengen Stils im Heiligtum von Olympia*, Berlin.

Edelstein, Ludwig 1967   *The Idea of Progress in Classical Antiquity*, Baltimore, Md.

Ehrenberg, Victor 1965   *Der Staat der Griechen*, Zurich.

Eichinger, Wolfgang 2004   *Die minoisch-mykenische Säule. Form und Verwendung eines Bauglieds der ägäischen Bronzezeit*, Hamburg.

Ekroth, Gunnel 2005   'Blood on the Altars? On the Treatment of Blood at Greek Sacrifices and the Iconographical Evidence', *AntK* 48: 9–29.

Emerson, Mary 2007   *Greek Sanctuaries: An Introduction*, Bristol.

Étienne, Roland 1992   'Autels et sacrifices', in AA.VV. 1992d: 291–319.

——, and Françoise Étienne 1992   *The Search for Ancient Greece*, London and New York [1st (French) ed. 1990].

Evans, Arthur J. 1901   'The Mycenaean Tree and Pillar Cult and its Mediterranean Relations', *JHS* 21: 99–204.

—— 1921–36   *The Palace of Minos at Knossos*, 4 vols, London.

Fagerström, Kåre 1988a   *Greek Iron Age Architecture: Developments through Changing Times* (SIMA 81), Göteborg.

—— 1988b   'Finds, Function and Plan: Iron Age Nichoria', *OpAth* 17: 33–50.

Fant, J. Clayton 1993   'Ideology, Gift and Trade: A Distribution Model for the Roman Imperial Marbles', in *The Inscribed Economy* (JRA, supp. 6): 145–70.

Fantalkin, Alexander 2006   'Identity in the Making: Greeks in the Eastern Mediterranean during the Iron Age', in AA.VV. 2006: 199–208.

Faustoferri, Amalia 1996 *Il trono di Amyklai e Sparta. Bathykles al servizio del potere*, Naples.

Fehr, Burkhard 1996 'The Greek Temple in the Early Archaic Period: Meaning, Use and Social Context', *Hephaistos* 14: 165–91.

Felsch, Rainer 1987 'Bericht über die Grabungen der Artemis Elaphebolos und des Apollon von Hyampolis 1978–1982', *AA*: 1–99.

—— 1995 *s.v.* Kalapodi, in *EAA*, 2nd supplement, III: 159–61.

—— 2001 'Drei frühe Phasen des dorischen Tempels: Delphi – Kalapodi – Mykene', *JdI* 116: 1–15.

Felten, Florens 1984 *Griechische tektonische Friese archaischer und klassischer Zeit*, Waldsassen.

Ferguson, John 1989 *Among the Gods: An Archaeological Exploration of Ancient Greek Religion*, London and New York.

Fergusson, James A. S. 1849 *An Historical Enquiry into the True Principles of Beauty in Art, more especially with Reference to Architecture*, London.

—— 1855 *The Illustrated Handbook of Architecture*, 2 vols, London [based on Fergusson 1849].

—— 1893 *A History of Architecture in All Countries from the Earliest Times to the Present Day*, London [1st ed. 1865].

Ferri, Silvio 1948 'I tempietti di Medma e l'origine del triglifo', *RendPontAcc*, series 8/3: 402–13.

—— 1960 *Vitruvio: De Archtectura dai libri I–VII*, Rome.

Filseck, Moser K. von 1986 'Der Alabasterfries von Tiryns', *AA*: 1–32.

Fimmen, Diedrich 1921 *Die kretisch–mykenische Kultur* (Leipzig and Berlin).

Finley, Moses I. 1956 *The World of Odysseus*, London [1st ed. 1954].

Fletcher, Banister 1961 *A History of Architecture on the Comparative Method*, London [1st ed. 1896], London.

Fontenrose, Joseph 1966 *The Ritual Theory of Myth*, Berkeley, Calif.

—— 1978 *The Delphic Oracle: Its Responses and Operations with a Catalogue of Responses*, Berkeley, Calif.

—— 1988a 'The Cult of Apollo and the Games at Delphi', in AA.VV. 1988c: 121–40.

—— 1988b *Didyma: Apollo's Oracle, Cult and Companions*, Berkeley, Calif.

Forbes, Thomas 1983 *Urartian Architecture* (*BAR* 170), Oxford.

Forssman, Erik 1961 *Dorisch, Ionisch, Korintisch: Studien über den Gebrauch der Säulenordnungen in der Architektur des 16.–18. Jahrhunderts*, Stockholm [reprinted Braunschweig 1984].

Forster, Kurt W. 1996 'L'ordine dorico come diapason dell'architettura moderna', in Settis 1996, 1: 665–706.

Foucault, Michel 1984 'Nietzsche, Genealogy and History', in *The Foucault Reader*, ed. Paul Rabinow, New York: 76–100.

Fowler, Howard, and Richard Stillwell 1932 *Corinth, I: Introduction, Topography, Architecture*, Cambridge, Mass.

Fraisse, Philippe, and Christian Llinas 1995 *Documents d'architecture hellénique et hellénistique* (ExpDélos 36), Paris.

Frampton, Kenneth 1995 *Studies in Tectonic Culture: The Poetics of Construction in Nineteenth and Twentieth Century Architecture*, Cambridge, Mass.

Frankfort, Henri 1941 'The Origin of Monumental Architecture in Egypt', *The American Journal of Semitic Languages and Literatures* 58: 329–58.

—— 1954 *The Art and Architecture of the Ancient Orient*, Harmondsworth.

Franz, Angelika 1998–9 'Thymiateria with Drooping Petalcapitals: Distribution and Function of an Early Iron Age Class of Objects', in *Talanta: Proceedings of the Dutch Archaeological and Historical Society* 30–1: 73–114.

Freitag, Klaus, Peter Funke and Matthias Haake 2006 *Kult – Politik – Ethnos: Überregionale Heiligtümer im Spannungsfeld von Kult und Politik*, con., Münster, 2001, Stuttgart.

Friese, Wiebke 2010 *Den Göttern so nah: Architektur und Topographie griechischer Orakelheiligtümer*, Stuttgart.

Froning, Heide 1971 *Dithyrambos und Vasenmalerei in Athen*, Würzburg.

Furtwängler, Adolf 1890 *Die Bronzen und die übrigen kleineren Funde* (Olympia IV), Berlin.

Furtwängler, Andreas, and Hermann J. Kienast 1989 *Der Nordbau im Heraion von Samos* (Samos III), Bonn.

Gadolou, Anastasia 2002 'The Pottery Fabrics and Workshops from Ano Mazaraki: The 1979 Excavation Season', in *Gli Achei e l'identità etnica degli Achei d'Occidente*, ed. Emanuele Greco, Athens: 165–204.

—— 2011 'A Late Geometric Architectural Model with Figure Decoration from Ancient Helike, Achaea', *BSA* 106: 247–73.

Gallet de Santerre, H., and J. Tréheux 1947–8 'Rapport sur le dépôt égéen et géométrique de l'Artémesion à Délos', *BCH* 71–2: 148–254.

Gardner, Ernest 1901 'The Greek House', *JHS* 21: 293–305.

Garland, Robert 1994 *Religion and the Greeks*, London.

Gartziou-Tatti, Ariadne 1990 'L'oracle de Dodone: Mythe et rituel', *Kernos* 3, 175–84.

Gauer, Werner 1968 *Weihgeschenke aus den Perserkriegen* (IstMitt, supp. 2), Tübingen.

Gebhard, Elizabeth R. 1993 'The Evolution of a pan-Hellenic Sanctuary, from Archaeology towards History at Isthmia', in AA.VV. 1993a: 154–77.

Gebhard, Elizabeth R. and Fritz P. Hemans 1992 'University of Chicago Excavations at Isthmia, 1989: I', *Hesperia* 61: 1–77.

Geertz, Clifford 1973 *The Interpretation of Cultures*, New York.

Genière, Juliette de la 1983   'À Propos des Métopes du monoptère de Sicyone à Delphes', *CRAI*: 158–71.

—— 1997   'Premiers Résultats des nouvelles fouilles de l'Héraion de Foce del Sele', in AA.VV. 1997d: 173–80.

Georgopoulou, Maria *et al.* 2007   *Following Pausanias: The Quest for Greek Antiquity*, New Castle, Del.

Gerhard, Eduard 1840–58   *Auserlesene griechische vasenbilder: hauptsächlich etruskischen Fundorts*, 4 vols, Berlin.

Gerkan, Armin von 1915   *Der Poseidonaltar bei Kap Monodendri* (Milet 1. Ergebnisse der Ausgrabungen und Untersuchungen seit dem Jahre 1899), Berlin.

—— 1946–7   'Betrachtungen zum ionischen Gebälk', *JdI* 61–2: 17–29.

—— 1948–9   'Die Herkunft des dorischen Gebälks', *JdI* 63–4: 1–13.

Germann, Georg 1991   *Vitruve et le Vitruvianisme*, Lausanne.

Giedion, Sigfrid 1941   *Space, Time and Architecture*, Cambridge, Mass.

Giuliani, Luca 1979   *Die archaischen Metopen von Selinunt*, Mainz.

—— 2005   'Der Koloss der Naxier', *Meisterwerke der antiken Kunst*, ed. L. Giuliani, Munich: 13–27.

Giuliano, Antonio 1994   'Vitruvio e l'acanto', *Palladio* 14: 29–36.

Gjerstad E. 1948   *The Swedish Cyprus Expedition*, IV, 2: *The Cypro-Geometric, the Cypro-Archaic and the Cypro-Classical Periods*, Stockholm.

Glowacki, Kevin T. 1998   'The Acropolis of Athens before 566 B.C.', in AA.VV. 1998b: 79–88.

Godelier, Maurice 1996   *L'Énigme du don*, Paris.

Goldberg, Marilyn Y. 1982   'Archaic Greek Acroteria', *AJA* 86: 193–217.

—— 1983   'Greek Temples and Chinese Roofs', *AJA* 87: 305–10.

Goldman, Bernard 1961   'The Asiatic Ancestry of the Greek Gorgon', *Berytus* 14: 1–23.

Goldstein, Michael S. 1978   'The Setting of the Ritual Meal in Greek Sanctuaries: 600–300 B.C.' (diss., University of California, Berkeley).

Gombrich, Ernst 1979   *The Sense of Order: A Study in the Psychology of Decorative Art*, London.

Goodyear, William H. 1891   *The Grammar of the Lotus*, London.

Gordon, R. L. 1979   'The Real and the Imaginary: Production and Religion in the Ancient World', *Art History* 2: 5–34.

Gordon Smith, Thomas 2003   *Vitruvius on Architecture*, New York.

Gould, Stephen Jay 1980   'The Episodic Nature of Evolutionary Change', in *The Panda's Thumb: More Reflections on Natural History*, New York: 179–85.

—— 1993   'Punctuated Equilibrium Comes of Age', *Nature* 366: 223–7.

Graf, Fritz 1991   'Prayer in Magical and Religious Ritual', in *Magika Hiera: Ancient Greek Magic and Religion*, ed. Christopher A. Faraone and Dirk Obbink, Oxford and New York: 188–213.

—— 1996a   'Gli dèi greci e i loro santuari', in Settis 1996, 2.1: 343–80.

1996b   'Pompai in Greece: Some Considerations about Space and Ritual in the Greek Polis', in AA.VV. 1996c: 55–65.

Greco, Emanuele, and Fausto Longo, eds. 2000   *Paestum, Scavi, studi, ricerche: Bilancio di un decennio, 1988–1998*, Paestum.

Greco, Giovanna 2000   'Nuove prospettive di ricerca nello studio delle terrecotte architettoniche magno greche di età tardo arcaica', in AA.VV. 2000b: 231–43.

Gropengießer, Hildegund 1961   *Die pflanzlichen Akrotere klassischer Tempel*, Mainz.

Gros, Pierre 1988   'Vitruve et les ordres', *Les Traités d'architecture de la Renaissance*, con., Tours, 1981, ed. Jean Guillaume, Paris: 49–59.

—— 1989   'Les Fondements philosophiques de l'harmonie architecturale selon Vitruve', *Aesthetics. Journal of the Faculty of Letters* (Tokyo University) 14: 13–22.

—— 1992   *Vitruve: De l'Architecture, Livre IV* (trans. with commentary), Paris.

—— 1993a   'Apollon, la ligue ionienne et les origines de l'ordre dorique selon Vitruve', in AA.VV. 1993c: 59–67.

—— 1993b   'Situation stylistique et chronologique du chapiteau corinthien de Vitruve', in AA.VV. 1993e: 27–37.

—— 1995   'La Sémantique des ordres à la fin de l'époque hellénistique et au début de l'empire: Remarques préliminaires', *Studi archeologici in onore di Antonio Frova: Studi e ricerche sulla Galla Cisalpina* 8, Rome: 23–32.

—— 1997   'Vitruvio e il suo tempo', in Corso and Romano 1997, 1: ix–lxxvii.

—— 2006   *Vitruve et la tradition des traités d'Architecture: Fabrica et Ratiocinatio: Receuil d'études*, Rome.

Gruben, Doris, and Gottfried Gruben 1997   'Die Türe des Pantheon', *RM* 104: 3–74.

Gruben, Gottfried 1957   'Die Südhalle', *AM* 72: 52–64.

—— 1960   'Die Kapitelle des Hera-Tempels auf Samos' (diss. University of Munich).

—— 1963   'Das archaische Didymaion', *JdI* 78: 78–177.

—— 1965   'Die Sphinx-Säule von Aigina', *AM* 80: 170–208.

—— 1972   'Kykladische Architektur', *MüJb* 23: 7–36.

—— 1989   'Das älteste marmorene Volutenkapitell', *IstMitt* 39: 161–72.

—— 1993 'Die inselionische Ordnung', in AA.VV. 1993c: 97–109.

—— 1996a 'Il tempio', in Settis 1996, 2.1: 381–434.

—— 1996b 'Griechische Un-Ordnungen', in AA.VV. 1996b: 61–77.

—— 1997 'Naxos und Delos: Studien zur archaischen Architektur der Kykladen', *JdI* 112: 261–416.

—— 2001 *Greichische Tempel und Heiligtümer*, Munich [1st ed. 1966].

—— 2007 *Klassische Bauforschung*, Munich.

Gruen, Erich S. 2011 *Rethinking the Other in Antiquity*, Princeton, N.J.

Grunauer, Peter 1981 'Zur Ostansicht des Zeustempels', *OlBericht* 10: 256–301.

Guadet, Julien 1909 *Éléments et théorie de l'architecture*, 4 vols, Paris 1909 [1st ed. 1892].

Guarducci, Margherita 1949 'L'iscrizione dell'Apollonion di Siracusa', *ArchCl* 1: 4–10.

—— 1987 'Il tempio arcaico di Apollo a Siracusa: Riflessioni nuove', in *Saggi in Onore di Guglielmo de Angelis d'Ossat*: 43–5.

Guillon, Pierre 1943 *Les Trépieds du Ptoion* (BEFAR 153), 2 vols, Paris.

Gullini, Giorgio 1974 *Sull'origine del fregio dorico* (Memorie dell'Accademia delle Scienze di Torino: Classe di scienze morali, storiche e filologiche 31), Turin.

—— 1980 'Il tempio E1 e l'architettura protoarcaica di Selinunte', in *Insediamenti coloniali greci in Sicilia nell'VIII e VII secolo a. C.*, con., Syracuse, 1977, Catania: 52–61

—— 1981 'Origini dell'architettura greca in Occidente', *AnnASAtene* 59: 97–126.

—— 1985 'L'architettura', in *Sikanie: Storia e civiltà della Sicilia greca*, ed. Giovanni Pugliese Carratelli, Milan: 415–91.

Gunter, Ann C. 2009 *Greek Art and the Orient*, Cambridge and New York.

Guralnick, Eleanor 1978 'The Proportions of Kouroi', *AJA* 82: 461–72.

—— 1981 'The Proportions of Korai', *AJA* 85: 269–80.

—— 1996 'The Monumental New Kouros from Samos: Measurements, Proportions and Profiles', *AA*: 505–26.

—— 1997 'The Egyptian–Greek Connection in the 8th to 6th Centuries BC: An Overview', in AA.VV. 1997f: 127–54.

—— 2004 'A Group of Near Eastern Bronzes from Olympia', *AJA* 108: 187–222.

Gwilt, Joseph 1825 *An Examination of the Elements of Beauty in Grecian Architecture, with a Brief Investigation of its Origin, Progress, and Perfection*, in Chambers 1825: 1–66.

—— 1891 *An Encyclopaedia of Architecture, Historical, Theoretical, and Practical*, London [1st ed. 1842]

Hägg, Robin 1987 'Gifts to the Heroes in Geometric and Archaic Greece', in AA.VV. 1987: 93–9.

——, and Dora Konsola, eds 1986 *Early Helladic Architecture and Urbanization*, con., Athens, 1985, Göteborg.

Hahn, Robert 2001 *Anaximander and the Architects: The Contributions of Egyptian and Greek Architectural Technologies to the Origins of Greek Philosophy*, Albany, N.Y.

—— 2010 *Archaeology and the Origins of Philosophy*, Albany, N.Y.

Haines, Richard C. 1971 *Excavations in the Plain of Antioch*, II: *The Structural Remains of the Later Phases, Chatal Hüyük, Tell-al-Judaidah, and Tell Tayinat*, Chicago, Ill.

Hall, Jonathan M. 1995 'How Argive Was the "Argive" Heraion? The Political and Cultic Geography of the Argive Plain, 900–400 B. C.', *AJA* 99: 577–613.

—— 1997 *Ethnic Identity in Greek Antiquity*, Cambridge.

—— 2002 *Hellenicity: Between Ethnicity and Culture*, Chicago, Ill.

Haller von Hallerstein, K. 1976 *Le Temple de Bassae publiés avec une biographie de l'auteur par G. Roux*, Strasbourg.

Hamilton, Richard 2000 *Treasure Map: A Guide to the Delian Inventories*, Ann Arbor, Mich.

Hampe, Roland 1938 'Ein bronzenes Beschlagblech aus Olympia', *AA*: 359–69.

——, and Ulf Jantzen 1937 'Die Grabung im Frühjahr 1937', *OlBericht* 1: 25–94

——, and Erika Simon 1981 *The Birth of Greek Art*, London.

Hanfmann, George M. A. 1975 *From Croesus to Constantine. The Cities of Western Asia Minor and their Arts in Greek and Roman Times*, Ann Arbor, Mich.

Hansen, Erik 1992 'Autour du Temple d'Apollon', in AA.VV. 1992g: 125–49.

—— 2009 'Trois Notes d'architecture delphique', *BCH* 133: 113–52.

Hansen, Mogens Herman 1993 'The Polis as a Citizen-State', in AA.VV. 1993f: 7–29.

——, ed. 1995 *Sources for the Ancient Greek City-State* (Acts of the Copenhagen Polis Centre, 2. *HfMedd* 72), con., 1994, Copenhagen.

—— 2006 *Polis: An Introduction to the Greek City-State*, Oxford.

Hardwick, Nicholas 1999 'A Triglyph Altar of Corinthian Type in a Scene of Medea on a Lucanian Calyx-krater in Cleveland', *QuadTic* 28: 179–201.

Harl-Schaller, F. 1975 'Die archaischen "Metopen" aus Mykene', *ÖJh* 50: 94–116.

Harris, Diane 1995 *The Treasures of the Parthenon and Erechtheion*, Oxford.

Harrison, Timothy P., and James F. Osborne 2012   'Building XVI and the Neo-Assyrian Sacred Precinct at Tell Tayinat', *Journal of Cuneiform Studies* 64: 125–143.

Haselberger, Lothar, ed. 1999   *Appearance and Essence: Refinements of Classical Architecture – Curvature*, Philadelphia, Pa.

Haspels, C. H. Émilie 1946   'Trépieds archaïques de Thasos', *BCH* 70: 233–7.

—— 1971   *The Highlands of Phrygia: Sites and Monuments*, I, Princeton, N.J.

Hasserodt, Monika 2009   *Griechische und orientalische Metallphialen des frühen ersten Jahrtausends v. Chr. in Griechenland*, Bonn.

Hauglid, Roar 1947   'The Greek Acanthus: Problems of Origin', *ActaArch* 18: 93–116.

Hayward, Chris 2003   'Geology of Corinth: The Study of a Basic Resource', in Williams and Bookidis 2003: 15–42.

Heberdey, Rudolf 1919   *Altattische Porosskulptur: Ein Beitrag zur Geschichte der archaischen griechischen Kunst*, Vienna.

Heiden, Joachim 1990   'Die archaischen Dächer von Olympia', in AA.VV. 1990a: 41–6.

—— 1995   *Die Tondächer von Olympia* (OlForsch 24), Berlin.

Heilmeyer, Wolf-Dieter 1969   'Giessereibetriebe in Olympia', *JdI* 84: 1–28

—— 1970   *Korinthische Normalkapitelle: Studien zur Geschichte der römischen Architekturdekoration* (*RM*, supp. 16), Heidelberg.

Hellmann, Marie-Christine 1992   *Recherches sur le vocabulaire de l'architecture grecque d'après les inscriptions de Délos* (BEFAR 278), Paris.

—— 2002   *L'Architecture grecque*, I: *Les Principes de la construction*, Paris.

—— 2006   *L'Architecture grecque*, II: *Architecture religieuse et funéraire*, Paris.

—— 2010   *L'Architecture grec*, III: *Habitat, urbanisme et fortifications*, Paris.

——, Philippe Fraisse and Annie Jacques 1983   *Paris – Rome – Athènes: Le Voyage en Grèce des architectes français aux xixe et xxe siècles*, cat. Paris, Athens, Houston, Tex., and New York [1984], Paris.

Hellner, Nils 2004   'Drehspuren am Säulenbauteil des archaischen Heraion von Argos?', *RA*: 69–78.

—— 2009   *Die Säulenbasen des zweiten Dipteros von Samos* (Samos 26), Bonn.

—— 2010   'Die Anfänge des griechischen Tempelbaus und die Gestaltungsidee der Säulenkannelur in Kalapodi/Phokis', in *Bericht über die 45. Tagung für Ausgrabungswissenschaft und Bauforschung*, con., Regensburg, 2008, Stuttgart: 153–60.

—— 2011   'Überlegungen zu achteckigen Stützen in der antiken griechischen Architektur', *RA*: 227–62.

—— forthcoming   'Räumliche Führung am Beispiel der spätgeometrischen und archaischen Süd-Tempel von Abai/Kalapodi', in *Architektur des Weges*, ed. U. Wulf-Rheidt and D. Kurapkat, con., Berlin 2012, Berlin.

Hellström, Pontus 1988   'Labraunda: Mixed Orders in Hecatomnid Architecture', in AA.VV. 1988d: 70–74.

—— 1994   'Columns, What are you up to?', *Opus mixtum: Essays in Ancient Art and History*, ed. E. Rystedt *et al.* Stockholm: 53–6.

Helm, Peyton Randlolph 1980   'Greeks in the Neo-Assyrian Levant and "Assyria" in Early Greek Writers' (diss., University of Pennsylvania).

Hemans, Fritz P. 1989   'The Archaic Roof Tiles at Isthmia: A Re-examination', *Hesperia* 58: 251–66.

Hendrich, Christof 2007   *Die Säulenordnung des ersten Dipteros von Samos* (Samos 25), Bonn.

Herdt, Georg 2013   'Votive Columns in Greek Sanctuaries of the Archaic Period' (diss., University of Bath).

——, and Mark Wilson Jones 2008   'Scanning Ancient Building Components', *Photogrammetrie Fernerkundung Geoinformation* 4: 245–51.

——, and Mark Wilson Jones 2010   'Neue Techniken zur Bauaufnahme', *Antike Welt*, 1: 78–83.

——, Aykut Erkal, Dina D'Ayala and Mark Wilson Jones, 2013   'Structural Assessment of Ancient Building Components: The Temple of Artemis at Corfu', in *Archaeology in the Digital Era: Computer Applications and Quantitative Methods in Archaeology*, con., Southampton, 2012, ed. Graeme Earl *et al.*, Amsterdam.

Herington, C. 1955   *Athena Parthenos and Athena Polias*, Manchester.

Hermary, Antoine 1993   'Les Colosses des Naxiens à Delos', *Revue des Études Anciennes* 95: 11–19.

—— 1996   'Chapiteaux à degrés d'Amathonte', *RDAC*: 89–94.

Herrmann, Georgina 1986   *Ivories from Room SW 37 Fort Shalmaneser: Ivories from Nimrud (1949–1963) IV*, 2 vols, London.

Herrmann, Hans-Volkmar 1966   'Urartu und Griechenland', *JdI* 81: 79–141.

—— 1972a   *Die Kessel der orientalisierenden Zeit*, II: *Kesselprotomen und Stabdreifüsse* (OlForsch 11).

—— 1972b   *Olympia: Heiligtum und Wettkampfstätte*, Munich.

Herrmann, Klaus 1976   'Beobachtungen zur Schatzhaus-Architektur Olympias', in Jantzen 1976: 321–50.

—— 1983   'Zum Dekor dorischer Kapitelle', *Architectura. Zeitschrift für Geschichte der Baukunst* 13: 1–12.

—— 1984 'Spätarchaische Votivsäulen in Olympia', *AM* 99: 121–43.

—— 1994 'Addenda zu den lakonischen Perirrhanterien' (OlBericht 9): 150–71.

—— 1996 'Anmerkungen zur ionischen Architektur in der Peloponnes', in AA.VV. 1996b: 124–32.

Herrmann, Wolfgang 1962 *Laugier and Eighteenth Century French Theory*, London.

—— 1973 *The Theory of Claude Perrault*, London.

—— 1984 *Gottfried Semper: In Search of Architecture*, Cambridge, Mass.

—— ed. 1992 *In What Syle Should We Build? The German Debate on Architectural Style*, Santa Monica, Calif.

Hersey, George L. 1988 *The Lost Meaning of Classical Architecture: Speculations on Ornament from Vitruvius to Venturi*, Cambridge, Mass.

Heston, Mary B. 1996 'The Nexus of Divine and Earthly Rule: Padmanabhapuram Palace and Traditions of Architecture and Kingship in South Asia', *Ars Orientalis* 26: 81–106.

Higbie, Carolyn 2003 *The Lindian Chronicle and the Greek Creation of their Past*, Oxford.

Hiller, Stefan 1986 'Early and Late Helladic Megara: Questions of Architectural Continuity in Bronze Age Greece', in Hägg and Konsola 1986: 85–9.

—— 1991 'The Greek Dark Ages: Helladic Traditions, Mycenaean Traditions in Culture and Art', in AA. VV. 1991c: 117–32.

—— 1996 'Apsidenbauten in griechischen Heiligtümern', in *Fremde Zeiten: Festschrift für Jürgen Borchhardt*, ed. Fritz Blakolmer *et al.*, Vienna, II: 27–53.

Himmelmann, Nikolaus 2002 'Frühe Weihgeschenke in Olympia', in Kyrieleis 2002: 91–107.

—— 2005 *Grundlagen der griechischen Pflanzendarstellung* (Nordrhein-Westfälische Akademie der Wissenschaften, Vorträge G 393), Paderborn.

Hirt, Alois 1821 *Die Geschichte der Baukunst bei den Alten*, Berlin.

—— 1823 *Heinrich Hübsch über griechische Baukunst*, Berlin.

Hittorff, Jacques-Ignaz 1851 *Restitution du temple d'Empédocle à Sélinonte, ou l'architecture polychrome chez les Grecs*, Paris.

——, and Ludwig Zanth 1870 *Recueil des monuments de Ségeste et de Sélinonte suivi de recherches sur l'origine et le développement de l'architecture religieuse chez les Grecs*, 2 vols, Paris.

Hodge, A. Trevor 1960 *The Woodwork of Greek Roofs*, Cambridge.

Höcker, Christoph 1996 'Architektur als Metapher: Überlegungen zur Bedeutung des dorischen Ringhallentempels', *Hephaistos* 14: 45–79.

Hoepfner, Wolfram 1989 'Zu dem grossen Altären von Magnesia und Pergamon', *AA*, 601–34.

—— 1991 'Zum Problem griechischer Holz- und Kassettendecken', *Bautechnik der Antike*, con., Berlin 1990, Berlin: 90–98.

—— 1994 'Stützentypen in Nordwestgriechenland', in *Mélanges S. Dakaris*, Joannina: 435–41.

——, and Ernst-Ludwig Schwandner 1986 *Haus und Stadt im klassischen Griechenland*, Munich.

Hoffelner, Klaus 1996 *Die Sphinx-Säule: Votivträger, Altäre, Steingeräte* (Alt-Ägina II, 4), Mainz: 7–58.

—— 1999 *Das Apollon–Heiligtum: Tempel, Altäre, Temenosmauer, Thearion* (Alt-Ägina I, 3).

Hoffman, Gail L. 1997 *Imports and Immigrants: Near Eastern Contacts with Iron Age Crete*, Ann Arbor, Mich.

Hogarth, David G. 1908 *British Museum Excavations at Ephesus: The Archaic Artemisia*, London.

Hölbl, Günther 1984 'Ägyptischer Einfluß in der griechischen Architektur', *ÖJh* 55: 1–18.

Holland, Leicester B. 1917 'The Origin of the Doric Entablature', *AJA* 21: 117–58.

—— 1939 'The Hall of the Athenian Kings', *AJA* 43: 289–98.

Hollinshead, Mary B. 1999 '"Adyton", "Opisthodomos" and the Inner Room of the Greek Temple', *Hesperia* 68: 189–218.

Holloway, Ross R. 1973 *A View of Greek Art*, Providence, R.I.

—— 1988 'Early Greek Architectural Decoration as Functional Art', *AJA* 92: 177–83.

Holmes, Alexandra M. 1995 'Regional Variations of Early Archaic Greek Doric Temples in the Peloponnese' (diss., Kings College, University of London).

Hölscher, Tonio 2001 'Schatzhäuser – Banketthäuser?', in Böhm and von Eickstedt 2001: 143–52.

—— 2002 'Rituelle Räume und politische Denkmäler im Heiligtum von Olympia', in Kyrieleis 2002: 331–45.

—— 2004 *The Language of Images in Roman Art*, Cambridge and New York [1st (German) ed. 1987].

—— 2009 'Architectural Sculpture: Messages? Programs? Towards Rehabilitating the Notion of "Decoration"', in AA.VV. 2009b: 54–67.

Homolle, Théophile 1908 'Monuments figurés de Delphes: La colonne d'acanthe', *BCH*: 205–35.

—— 1916 'L'Origine du chapiteau corinthien', *RA*: 17–60.

—— 1917 'L'Origine des caryatides, *RA* 5: 1–67.

Houser, Caroline 1987 *Greek Monumental Bronze Sculpture of the Fifth and Fourth Centuries B.C.*, New York.

Howe, Thomas Noble 1985 'The Invention of the Doric Order' (diss., Harvard University).

——, and Ingrid D. Rowland 1999   *Vitruvius: Ten Books on Architecture* (Cambridge and New York)

Howes Smith, P. H. G. 1984   'Bronze Ribbed Bowls from Central Italy and Etruria', *BABesch* 59: 73–112.

Hübsch, Heinrich 1824   *Über griechische Architektur: zweite mit einer Vertheidigung gegen Herrn A. Hirt vermehrte Ausgabe*, Heidelberg [1st ed. 1822].

—— 1828   *In welchem Style sollen wir bauen?*, Karlsruhe.

Hult, Gunnel 1983   *Bronze Age Ashlar Masonry in the Eastern Mediterranean. Cyprus, Ugarit and Neighbouring Regions* (SIMA 66), Gothenburg.

Humann, Carl 1904   *Magnesia am Maeander*, Berlin.

Hurwit, Jeffrey M. 1977   'Image and Frame in Greek Art', *AJA* 81: 1–30.

—— 1985   *The Art and Culture of Early Greece, 1100–480 BC*, Ithaca, N.Y.

—— 1993   'Art, Poetry and the Polis in the Age of Homer', in AA.VV. 1993b: 17–42.

—— 2000   *The Athenian Acropolis: History, Mythology, and Archaeology from the Neolithic Era to the Present*, Cambridge and New York.

—— 2005   'The Parthenon and the Temple of Zeus at Olympia', in AA.VV. 2005c: 135–45.

Hyde, Lewis 1979   *The Gift. Imagination and the Erotic Life of Property*, New York.

Iakovidis, Spyros E. 1983   *Late Helladic Citadels on Mainland Greece* (Monumenta Graeca et Romana 4), Leiden.

—— 1990   'Mycenaean Roofs: Form and Construction', in AA.VV. 1990b: 147–60.

—— 1999   Late Helladic Fortifications, *Aegaeum* 19: 199–204.

—— 2006   *The Mycenaean Acropolis of Athens*, Athens.

Intzesiloglou, Babis. G. 2002   'The Archaic Temple of Apollo at Ancient Metropolis (Thessaly)', in AA.VV. 2002: 109–15.

Işik, Cengiz 1986   'Tisch und Tischdarstellungen in der urartäischen Kunst', *Belleten. Türk Tarih Kurumu* 50: 413–45.

Işik, Fahri 2000   'Die Stilentwicklung der ionischen Vogelkoren aus Ton', in AA.VV. 2000b: 329–41.

Ito, Juko 2002   *Theory and Practice of Site Planning in Classical Sanctuaries*, Fukuoka.

Iversen, Erik 1975   *Canon and Proportion in Egyptian Art*, Warminster.

Iversen, Margaret 1993   *Alois Riegl: Art History and Theory*, Cambridge, Mass.

Jackson, A. H. 1991   'Hoplites and the Gods: The Dedication of Captured Arms and Armour', in *Hoplites: The Classical Battle Experience*, ed. V. D. Hanson, London 1991: 228–49.

Jacob-Felsch, Margrit 1969   *Die Entwicklung griechischer Statuenbasen und die Aufstellung der Statuen*, Waldsassen.

Jacobson, David M. 2000   'Decorative Drafted-margin Masonry in Jerusalem and Hebron and its Relations', *Levant* 32: 135–54.

——, and M. P. Weitzman 1992   'What was Corinthian Bronze?', *AJA* 96: 237–47.

Jacoby, Gustav, and Felix von Luschan 1911   *Ausgrabungen in Sendschirli IV*, Berlin.

Jacquemin, Anne 1999   *Offrandes monumentales à Delphes* (BEFAR 304), Paris.

James, Edwin O. 1966   *The Tree of Life: An Archaeological Study* (Studies in the History of Religions, supplements to *Numen: International Review for the History of Religions*) 11), Leiden.

Jameson, Michael H. 1988   'Sacrifice and Ritual: Greece', in *Civilization of the Ancient Mediterranean. Greece and Rome*, ed. Michael Grant and Rachel Kitzinger, New York, 2: 959–79.

Janson, H. W. 1977   *History of Art: A Survey of the Visual Arts from the Dawn of History to the Present Day*, London.

Jantzen, Ulf 1972   *Samos VIII: Ägyptische und orientalische Bronzen aus dem Heraion von Samos*, Bonn.

——, ed. 1976   *Neue Forschungen in griechischen Heiligtümern*, con., Olympia, 1974, Tübingen.

Jebb, R. C. 1886   'The Homeric House in Relation to the Remains at Tiryns', *JHS* 7: 170–88.

Jeffery, Lilian H. 1990   *The Local Scripts of Archaic Greece: A Study of the Origin of the Greek Alphabet and its Development from the Eighth to the Fifth Centuries B.C.*, Oxford.

Jenkins, Ian 2006   *Greek Architecture and its Sculpture in the British Museum*, London.

Jeppesen, Kristian 1957   *Paradeigmata: Three Mid-Fourth Century Main Works of Hellenic Architecture*, Aarhus.

Jéquier, Gustave 1924   *Manuel d'archéologie égyptienne: Les Éléments de l'architecture*, Paris.

Johannes, Heinz 1937   'Die Säulenbasen vom Heratempel des Rhoikos', *AM* 62: 13–37.

Johnson, Franklin P. 1936   'The Kardaki Temple', *AJA* 40: 46–54.

Jones, Owen 1856   *The Grammar of Ornament*, London.

Junker, Klaus 1993   *Der ältere Tempel im Heraion am Sele*, Cologne.

Kaasgaard Falb, Ditte Zink 2006   'Die Entstehung und Entwicklung des griechischen Monumentaltempels im 7 Jh. v. Chr. und seine möglichen Vorbilder' (diss., University of Aarhus).

—— 2009   'Das Artemis Orthia-Heiligtum in Sparta im 7. und 6. Jh. v. Chr.', in *From Artemis to Diana: The Goddess of Man and Beast* (Acta Hyperborea 12), ed. Tobias Fischer-Hansen and Birte Poulsen: 117–26.

Kähler, Heinz 1949   *Das griechische Metopenbild*, Munich.

Kalpaxis, Athanasios E. 1974   'Zum aussergewöhnlichen

Triglyphenfries vom Apollontempel C in Thermos: Ein Entgegnung,' *AA*: 105–114.

—— 1976 *Fr049charchaische Baukunst in Griechenland und Kleinasien*, Athens.

Kaminski, Gabriele 1991 'Thesauros: Untersuchungen zum antiken Opferstock', *JdI* 106: 63–181.

Kanellopoulos, Chrysanthos 2003 'The Classical and Hellenistic Building Phases of the Acropolis of Ancient Karthaia, Kea', *AM* 118: 211–38.

Karageorghis, Vassos 1973–4 *Excavations in the Necropolis of Salamis III* (Salamis 5, two parts), Nicosia and Haarlem.

—— 2000 *Ancient Art from Cyprus: The Cesnola Collection*, New York.

—— 2002 *Early Cyprus: Crossroads of the Mediterranean*, Los Angeles, Calif.

Karakasi, Katerina 2003 *Archaic Korai*, Los Angeles, Calif. [1st (German) ed. 2001].

Kawerau, G., and G. Soteriadis 1902–8 'Der Apollo-Tempel zu Thermos', *AntDenk* II.

Kearns, Emily 1992 'Between God and Man: Status and Functions of Heroes and their Sanctuaries', in AA.VV. 1992d: 65–107.

Keesling, Catherine M. 1995 'Monumental Private Votive Dedications on the Athenian Acropolis' (diss., University of Michigan).

—— 2003 *The Votive Statues of the Athenian Acropolis*, Cambridge.

Kendrick-Pritchett, William 1971 *Ancient Greek Military Practices*, Berkeley, Calif.

Kepenski, Christine 1982 *L'Arbre stylisé en Asie occidentale au 2e millénaire avant J.-C.*, 3 vols, Paris.

Kerschner, Michael 1996 *Perirrhanterien und Becken* (Alt-Ägina II, 4), Mainz: 59–132.

—— 2005 'Die Ionier und ihr Verhältnis zu den Phrygern und Lydern: Beobachtungen zur archäologischen Evidenz', *Neue Forschungen zu Ionien* (Asia Minor Studien 54), Bonn: 113–46.

Kiderlen, Moritz 2010 'Zur Chronologie griechischer Bronzedreifüße des geometrischen Typus und den Möglichkeiten einer politisch-historischen Interpretation der Fundverteilung', *AA*: 91–104.

Kienast, Hermann J. 1985 'Ausgrabungen im Heraion von Samos 1980/81: Der architektonische Befund', *AA*: 367–404.

—— 1991 'Neue Beobachtungen zum sog. Rhoikosaltar im Heraion von Samos', in AA.VV. 1991b: 99–102.

—— 1992 'Topographische Studien im Heraion von Samos', *AA*: 171–213.

—— 1996 'Die rechteckigen Peristasenstützen am samischen Hekatompedos', in AA.VV. 1996b: 16–24.

—— 1998 'Der Niedergang des Tempels des Theodoros', *AM* 113: 111–31.

—— 1999 'Das Ekkapitall am ersten Dipteros von Samos', in *Φως κυκλαδικόν: Τιμητικός τόμος στη μνήμη του Νίκου Ζαφειρόπουλου* (trans.: 'Cycladic Light: Essays in Honour of Nikos Sapheiropoulos'), ed. Nicholas C. Stampolidis, Athens: 140–47.

—— 2002a 'Topography and Architecture of the Archaic Heraion at Samos', in AA.VV. 2002: 317–25.

—— 2002b 'Zum dorischen Triglyphenfries', *AM* 117: 53–68.

Kiilerich, Bente 1989 'The Olive-Tree Pediment and the Daughters of Kekrops', *ActaAArtH* 7: 1–21.

Kilian, K. 1991 'La caduta dei palazzi Micenei continentali: aspetti archeologici', in AA.VV. *1991c*: 73–95.

Kilian-Dirlmeier, I. 1985 'Fremde Weihungen in griechischen Heiligtümern vom 8. bis zum Beginn des 7. Jahrhunderts v. Chr', *Jahrbuch des römisch/germanischen Zentralmuseums Mainz* 32: 215–54.

Kilinski, Karl 1990 *Boeotian Black Figure Vase Painting of the Archaic Period*, Mainz.

Kindt, Julia 2009 'Polis Religion – A Critical Appreciation', *Kernos* 22: 9–34.

King, Dorothy 1997 'Pergamene Palm Capitals and Other Foliate Fancies', *QuadTic* 26: 205–25.

—— 2000 'The Sculptural Decoration of the Doric Order ca. 375–31 BC' (diss., University of London).

Kirchhoff, Werner 1988 'Die Entwicklung des ionischen Volutenkapitells im 6. und 5. Jhd. und seine Entstehung' (diss., University of Bonn).

Kissas, Konstantin 2000 *Die attischen Statuen und Stelenbasen archaischer Zeit*, Bonn.

—— 2008 *Archaische Architektur der Athener Akropolis. Dachziegel-Metopen-Geisa-Akroterbasen* (Archäologische Forschungen 24), Wiesbaden.

Klebinder-Gauß, Gudrun 2007 *Bronzefunde aus dem Artemision von Ephesos* (FiE XII/3), Vienna.

Klein, Nancy L. 1991 'The Origin of the Doric Order on the Mainland of Greece: Form and Function of the Geison in the Archaic Period' (diss., Bryn Mawr College).

—— 1997 'Excavation of the Greek Temples at Mycenae by the British School at Athens', *BSA* 92: 247–332.

—— 1998 'Evidence for West Greek Influence on Mainland Greek Roof Construction and the Creation of the Truss in the Archaic Period', *Hesperia* 67: 335–74.

Kleiss, Wolfram 1989 'Zur Rekonstruktion des urartäischen Tempels', *IstMitt* 39: 265–71.

Klynne, A. 1998 'Reconstructions of Knossos: Artists' Impressions, Archaeological Evidence and Wishful Thinking', *JMA* 11: 206–29.

Knackfuss, H. 1941   *Didyma I*, Berlin.

Knell, Heiner 1980   *Grundzüge der griechischen Architektur*, Darmstadt.

—— 1985   *Vitruvs Architekturtheorie: Versuch einer Interpretation*, Darmstadt.

—— 1990   *Mythos und Polis: Bildprogramme griechischer Bauskulptur*, Darmstadt.

Koch, Herbert 1914   'Zu den Metopen von Thermos', *AM* 39: 237–55.

Koenigs, Wolf 1980   'Bauglieder aus Milet', *IstMitt* 30: 56–91.

—— 1996   'Rundaltäre aus Milet', *IstMitt* 46: 141–6.

—— 2007   'Archaische griechische Bauteile', *Archäologische Studien zu Naukratis II*, ed. Ursula Höckmann, Worms: 311–52.

——, and Hanna Philipp 1996   'Proportion und Grösse', in AA.VV. 1996b: 133–47.

Koldewey, Robert 1890   *Die antiken Baureste der Insel Lesbos*, Berlin.

—— 1891   *Neandria*, Berlin.

—— 1898   'Die Architektur von Sendschirli', *Ausgrabungen in Sendschirli* II, Berlin.

——, and Otto Puchstein 1899   *Die griechischen Tempel in Unteritalien und Sizilien*, Berlin.

Kolia, Erophile 2011   'A Sanctuary of the Geometric Period in Ancient Helike, Achaea', *BSA* 106: 201–246.

König, Jason ed. 2010   *Greek Athletics: Edinburgh Readings on the Ancient World*, Edinburgh.

Korres, Manolis 1994   'The Construction of Ancient Greek Temples' in *Acropolis Restoration: The CCAM Interventions*, ed. Richard Ekonomakis, London: 21–7.

—— 1995   *From Pentelicon to the Parthenon*, Athens.

—— 1996   'Ein Beitrag zur Kenntnis der attisch-ionischen Architektur', in AA.VV. 1996b: 90–113.

—— 1997a   'An Early Attic Ionic Capital and the Kekropion on the Athenian Acropolis', in Palagia 1997: 95–107.

1997b   'Die Athena-Tempel auf der Akropolis', in AA.VV. 1997b: 218–43.

—— 1999   'Bauforschung in Athen 1831–1841', in *Das neue Hellas: Griechen und Bayern zur Zeit Ludwigs I.*, ed. Reinhold Baumstark, Munich: 171–86.

—— 2002a   'Die klassische Architektur und der Parthenon', in *Die griechische Klassik: Idee oder Wirklichkeit*, cat., Bonn: 364–84.

—— 2002b   'Athenian Classical Architecture', in *Athens: From the Classical Period to the Present Day*, ed. Manolis Korres and Charalampos Bouras, New Castle, Del.: 3–45.

——, and Bouras, Charalampos 1983   Μελέτη αποκαταστάσεως του Παρθενώνος (trans.: Study for the Restoration of the Parthenon), 1, Athens.

Kostof, Spiro 1985   *A History of Architecture. Settings and Rituals*, New York and Oxford.

Kourou, Nota 2001   'The Sacred Tree in Greek Art: Mycenaean versus Near Eastern Traditions', in AA.VV. 2001c: 31–53.

Krause, Clemens 1981   'Eretria: Ausgrabungen 1979–1980', *Antk* 24: 50–87.

Krauss, Friedrich 1941   *Paestum: Die griechischen Tempel*, Berlin.

Krischen, Fritz 1938   *Die griechische Stadt*, Berlin.

—— 1956   *Weltwunder der Baukunst in Babylonien und Jonien*, Tübingen.

Krumeich, Ralf 1991   'Zu den goldenen Dreifüßen der Deinomeniden in Delphi', *JdI* 106: 37–62.

Küpper, Michael 1996   *Mykenische Architektur: Material Bearbeitungstechnik, Konstruktion und Erscheinungsbild* (Internationale Archäologie 25), Espelkamp.

Kuhn, Gerhard 1985   'Untersuchungen zur Funktion der Säulenhalle in archaischer und klassischer Zeit', *JdI* 100: 169–317.

—— 1986   'Der äolische Tempel in Alt-Smyrna', *MarburgWP*: 39–80.

—— 1993   'Bau B und Tempel C in Thermos', *AM* 108: 29–47.

Kunze, Emil 1931   *Kretische Bronzereliefs*, 2 vols, Stuttgart.

Kunze-Götte, Erika 1984   'Akanthussäule und Grabmonument in der Darstellung eines Lekythenmalers', *AM* 99: 185–97.

Kurtz, Donna C. 1975   *Athenian White Lekythoi: Patterns and Painters*, Oxford.

Kyrieleis, Helmut 1969   *Throne und Klinen. Studien zur formgeschichte altorientalischer und griechischer Sitz- und Liege möbel vorhellenistischer Zeit* (*JdI*, supp. 24), Berlin.

—— 1979   'Babylonische Bronzen im Heraion von Samos', *JdI* 94: 32–48.

—— 1988a   'Bronzener Bauschmuck', in Hermann Büsing and Friedrich Hiller ed., *Bathron. Beiträge zur Architektur und verwandten Künsten für Heinrich Drerup*, Saarbrücken: 279–86.

—— 1988b   'Offerings of "the Common Man" in the Heraion at Samos', in AA.VV. 1988a: 215–21.

—— 1993   'The Heraion at Samos', in AA.VV. 1993a: 125–53.

—— 1996   *Der grosse Kuros von Samos* (Samos X), Bonn.

—— ed. 2002   *Olympia 1875–2000, 125 Jahre Deutsche Ausgrabungen*, con., Berlin, 2000, Mainz.

—— 2006   'Anfänge und Frühzeit des Heiligtums von Olympia' (OlForsch 31), Berlin.

—— 2008   'Der dorisch Triglyphenfries und die mykenische Architektur', in AA.VV. 2008a: 199–212.

——, and W. Röllig 1988   'Ein altorientalischer Pferdeschmuck aus dem Heraion von Samos', *AM* 103: 37–45.

Lafitau, Jean-François 1724   *Moeurs des sauvages amériquains comparées aux moeurs des premiers temps*, Paris.

Lambrinoudakis, Vassilis 1991   'The Sanctuary of Iria on Naxos and the Birth of Monumental Greek Architecture', in AA.VV. 1991a: 173–88.

—— 1996   'Beobachtungen zur Genese der ionischen Gebälkformen', in AA.VV. 1996b: 55–60.

——, and Gottfried Gruben 1987   'Das neuentdeckte Heiligtum von Iria auf Naxos', *AA*: 569–621.

Lang, Franziska 1996   *Archaische Siedlungen in Griechenland: Struktur und Entwicklung*, Berlin.

Langdon, Merle 1976   *A Sanctuary of Zeus on Mount Hymettos* (*Hesperia*, supp. 16), Princeton, N.J.

—— 1997   'Cult in Iron Age Attica', in AA.VV. 1997e: 113–24.

Langdon, Susan 1987   'Gift Exchange in the Geometric Sanctuaries', in AA.VV. 1987: 107–13.

—— 1993   'Religion and the Rise of the Sanctuaries', in AA.VV. 1993b: 125–67.

Lapatin, Kenneth D. S. 2001   *Chryselephantine Statuary in the Ancient Mediterranean World*, Oxford.

Laroche, Didier 1989   'Nouvelles observations sur l'offrande de Platées', *BCH* 113: 183–98.

—— 2001   'Examen croisé de la maquette de l'Heraion d'Argos et de fragments d'architecture archaïque à Delphes', in Muller, ed. 2001: 321–9.

——, and Marie-Dominique Nenna 1990   'Le Trésor de Sicyone et ses fondations', *BCH* 114: 241–84.

—— 1993   'Études sur les trésors en poros à Delphes', in AA.VV. 1993c: 227–45.

Laroche-Traurecker, Françoise 1993   'Les Édifices d'époque archaïque et gréco-perse de Meydancikkale (Gülnar)', in AA.VV. 1993c: 13–28.

La Rosa, Vincenzo 1974   'Capitello arcaico da Festòs', *Antichità cretesi: Studi in onore di Doro Levi* (*Cronache di archeologia* 12), Catania 2: 136–52.

Laugier, Marc-Antoine, Abbé 1977   *An Essay on Architecture by Marc-Antonie Laugier*, Los Angeles, Calif. (trans. Wolfgang Herrman and Anni Herrman from *Essai sur l'architecture*, Paris (1st ed. 1753)).

Laum, Bernhard 1912   'Die Entwicklung der griechischen Metopenbilder', *Neue Jahrbücher für das klassische Altertum, Geschichte, deutsche Literatur und Pädagogik* 29, Part 1: 612–44; Part 2: 671–92.

Lauter, Hans 1975   'Die beiden älteren Tyrannenpaläste in Larisa am Hermos', *BJb* 175: 33–57.

—— 1976   *Die Koren des Erechtheion* (Antike Plastik 16), Berlin.

—— 1986   *Die Architektur des Hellenismus,* Darmstadt.

Lavin, Sylvia 1992   *Quatremère de Quincy and the Invention of a Modern Language of Architecture*, New Haven and London.

Lawrence, Arnold W. 1983   *Greek Architecture*, Harmondsworth [1st ed. 1957].

Layard, Austen Henry 1850   *Nineveh and its Remains*, 2 vols, London.

—— 1853   *Discoveries in the Ruins of Nineveh and Babylon*, London.

Lazzarini, Maria Letizia 1976   'Le Formule delle dediche votive nella Grecia arcaica', *Atti della Accademia nazionale dei Lincei: Classe di scienze morali. storiche e filologiche. Memorie 8*, 19: 47–354.

—— 1989–90   'Iscrizioni votive greche', *Scienze dell'antichità* 3–4: 845–59.

Lefkowitz, Mary R. and Guy M. Rogers 1996   *Black Athena Revisited,* Chapel Hill, N.C., and London.

Le Guen-Pollet, Brigitte 1991   'Éspace sacrificiel et corps des bêtes immolées', in AA.VV. 1991b: 13–23.

Leipen, Neda 1971   *Athena Parthenos, a Reconstruction*, Toronto.

Lemos, I. S. 2002   *The Protogeometric Aegean: The Archaeology of the Late Eleventh and Tenth Centuries BC*, Oxford.

Le Roy, Christian, 1962   *Les Terres cuites architecturales* (FdDelphes II), Paris.

Le Roy, Julien-David 2004   *The Ruins of the Most Beautiful Monuments of Greece*, Los Angeles, Calif. (trans. David Britt, from *Les Ruines des plus beaux monuments de la Grèce considerées du côté de l'histoire et de l'architecture*, Paris (1st ed. 1758)).

Lethaby, William R. 1891   *Architecture, Mysticism and Myth*, London.

—— 1917   'The Earlier Temple of Artemis at Ephesus', *JHS* 37: 1–16.

Levi, Doro 1927–9   *Arkades: Una città cretese all'alba della civiltà ellenica* (*AnnASAtene* 10–12), Bergamo.

Lévi-Strauss, Claude 1966   *The Savage Mind*, Chicago, Ill. [1st (French) ed. 1962]

—— 2005   *Myth and Meaning*, London [1st (French) ed. 1978]

Leypold, Christina 2008   *Bankettgebäude in griechischen Heiligtümern*, Wiesbaden.

Lichtenberg, Reinhold Freiherr von 1907   *Die ionische Säule als klassi-sches Bauglied rein hellenischem Geiste entwachsen*, Leipzig and New York.

Liebhart, Richard F. 1988   'Timber Roofing Spans in Greek and Near Eastern Monumental Architecture during the Early Iron Age' (diss., University of North Carolina, 2 vols).

Liljenstolpe, P. 1999   'The Roman Blattkelch Capital', *Opuscula Romana: Annual of the Swedish Institute in Rome* 22–3: 91–126.

Linders, Tullia 1987   'Gods, Gifts, Society', in AA.VV. 1987: 115–22.

—— 1989–90   'The Melting Down of Discarded Metal Offerings in Greek Sanctuaries', *Scienze dell' antichità* 3–4: 281–5.

Lippman, Mike, David Scahill and Peter Schultz 2006   'Knights 843–59: The Nike Temple Bastion and Cleon's Shields from Pylos', *AJA* 110: 551–63.

Lippolis, Enzo, Monica Livadiotti and Giorgio Rocco 2007   *Architettura greca: storia e monumenti del mondo della polis dalle origini al V secolo*, Milan.

Lissarrague, François 1995   'Women, Boxes, Containers: Some Signs and Metaphors', in *Pandora: Women in Classical Greece*, cat., Baltimore, ed. Ellen D. Reeder, Princeton, N.J.: 91–101.

Lloyd, Alan B. 2004   'Herodotus on Egypt and Ethiopia', in *The World of Herodotus*, con., Nicosia, 2003, ed. Vassos Karageorghis and Ioannis Taifacos, Nicosia: 43–52.

Lloyd, Seton, and Hans Wolfgang Müller 1986   *Ancient Architecture*, London [1st (Italian) ed. 1972].

Lorimer, Hilda L. 1950   *Homer and the Monuments*, London.

Louden, Bruce 2011   *Homer's Odyssey and the Near East*, Cambridge and New York.

Lovejoy, Alfred O., and George Boas 1935   *Primitivism and Related Ideas in Antiquity*, vol. 1 of *A Documentary History of Primitivism and Related Ideas*, Baltimore, Md.

Luce, Jean-Marc 2008   *L'Aire du pilier des Rhodiens (fouille 1990–1992) à la frontière du profane et du sacré* (FdDelphes II), Paris.

Luce, J. V. 1975   *Homer and the Heroic Age*, London.

Luke, Joanna 2003   *Ports of Trade, Al Mina and Greek Geometric Pottery in the Levant* (BAR 1100), Oxford.

Lupu, Eran 2005   *Greek Sacred Law: A Collection of New Documents* (Religions in the Graeco-Roman World 152), Leiden and Boston.

Luschan, Felix von 1912   *Entstehung und Herkunft der ionischen Säule*, Leipzig.

Luschey, Heinz 1939   *Die Phiale*, Bleicherode am Harz.

Maass, Michael 1977   'Kretische Votivdreifüße', *AM* 92: 33–59.

—— 1978   *Die geometrischen Dreifüsse von Olympia* (OlForsch 10), Berlin.

—— 1981   'Die geometrischen Dreifüsse von Olympia', *AntK* 24: 6–20

—— 1993   *Das antike Delphi, Orakel, Schätze und Monumente*, Darmstadt.

Mace, Hugh L. 1974   'The Archaic Ionic Capital: Studies in Formal and Stylistic Development' (diss., University of North Carolina).

Maier, Franz G., and Vassos Karageorghis 1984   *Paphos: History and Archaeology*, Nicosia.

Malkin, Irad 1987   *Religion and Colonization in Ancient Greece*, Leiden.

—— 1998   *The Returns of Odysseus: Colonization and Ethnicity*, Berkeley, Calif.

—— 2000   'La Fondation d'une colonie apolliene: Delphes et l'*hymne homérique à Apollon*', in AA.VV. 2000a: 69–77.

Mallgrave, Harry F. 1996   *Gottfried Semper: Architect of the Nineteenth Century*, New Haven and London.

Mallowan, Max E. L. 1966   *Nimrud and its Remains*, 2 vols, London.

——, and Herrmann, Georgina 1974   *Furniture from SW.7 Fort Shalmaneser: Ivories from Nimrud (1949–1963) III*, London.

Mallwitz, Alfred 1966   'Das Heraion von Olympia und seine Vorgänger', *JdI* 81: 310–76.

—— 1981a   *Ein Kapitell aus gebranntem Ton, oder zur Genesis des korinthischen Kapitells* (OlBericht 10), Berlin: 318–52.

—— 1981b   'Kritisches zur Architektur Griechenlands im 8. und 7. Jahrhundert', *AA*: 599–642 (Italian translation in *AnnASAtene* 59, 81–96).

—— 1982   'Ein hölzerner Untersatz aus Olympia', in *Praestant interna: Festschrift für Ulrich Hausmann*, ed. Bettina von Freytag, gen. Löringhoff *et al.*, Tübingen: 261–70.

Manakidou, Flora 1993   'Beschreibung von Kunstwerken in der hellenistischen Dichtung: ein Beitrag zur hellenistischen Poetik' (Beiträge zur Altertumskunde 36), Stuttgart.

Mansfield, John M. 1985   'The Robe of Athena and the Panathenaic "Peplos"' (diss., University of California, Berkeley).

Maran, Joseph 2000   'Das Megaron im Megaron: Zur Datierung und Funktion des Antenbaus im mykenischen Palast von Tiryns', *AA*, 2000: 1–16.

Marchand, Suzanne L. 1996   *Down from Olympus: Archaeology and Philhellenism in Germany, 1750–1970*, Princeton, N.J.

Marconi, Clemente 1997   'I Titani e Zeus Olimpio: Sugli Atlanti dell'Olympieion di Agrigento', *Prospettiva* 87–8: 2–13.

—— 2004   'Kosmos: The Imagery of the Archaic Greek Temple', *RES* 45: 209–24.

—— 2006   'Mito e autorappresentazione nella decorazione figurata dei *thesauroí* di età arcaica', in *Stranieri e non cittadini nei santuari greci*, ed. Alessandro Naso, Florence: 158–86.

—— 2007   *Temple Decoration and Cultural Identity in the Archaic Greek World: The Metopes of Selinus*, Cambridge and New York.

—— 2009a   'The Parthenon Frieze: Degrees of Visibility', *RES* 55–6: 155–73.

—— 2009b   'Early Greek Architectural Decoration in Function', in *Koine: Mediterranean Studies in Honor of R. Ross Holloway*, ed. Derek B. Counts and Anthony S. Tuck, Oxford: 4–17.

Marinatos, Nanno 1988 'The Imagery of Sacrifice: Minoan and Greek', in AA.VV. 1988a: 9–20.

—— 1993 *Minoan Religion: Ritual, Image and Symbol*, Columbia, S.C.

Marinatos, Spiridon 1936 'Le Temple geométrique de Dréros', *BCH* 60: 214–85.

Markle, Minor M. 1999 'A Shield Monument from Veria and the Chronology of Macedonian Shield Types', *Hesperia* 68: 219–54.

Markman, Sidney D. 1951 'Building Models and the Architecture of the Geometric Period', in *Studies presented to David M. Robinson*, ed. George E. Mylonas, St Louis, Mo.: 259–71.

Markoe, Glenn 1985 *Phoenician Bronze and Silver Bowls from Cyprus and the Mediterranean*, Berkeley, Calif.

—— 1996 'The Emergence of Orientalizing in Greek Art: Some Observations on the Interchange between Greeks and Phoenicians in the Eighth and Seventh Centuries B.C.', *BASOR* 301: 47–67.

—— 2000 *Phoenicians*, London.

—— 2003 'Phoenician Metalwork Abroad: A Question of Export or on-site Production?', in AA.VV. 2003: 209–16.

Marsden, E. W. 1971 *Greek and Roman Artillery*, Oxford.

Martienssen R. D. 1956 *The Idea of Space in Greek Architecture, with special Reference to the Doric Temple and its Setting*, Johannesburg.

Martin, Roland E. 1955–6 'Problème des origines des ordres à volutes', *Études d'archéologie classique*, 1: 117–32.

—— 1965 *Manuel d'architecture Grecque: Matériaux et techniques*, Paris.

—— 1967 *Living Architecture: Greek*, Fribourg and London.

—— 1973 'Compléments a l'étude des chapiteaux ioniques de Délos', *BCH*, supp. 1: 371–98.

Martinez, J. L. 1997 'La Colonne des danseuses de Delphes', *CRAI*: 35–45.

Martini, Wolfram 1986 'Vom Herdhaus zum Peripteros', *JdI* 101: 23–36.

Marx, Patricia A. 2011 'Athens NM Acropolis 923 and the Contest between Athena and Poseidon for the Land of Attica', *AK* 54: 21–40.

Masson, Olivier 1964 'Kypriaka. I. Recherches sur les Antiquités de Tamassos', *BCH* 88: 199–238.

Matthäus, Hartmut 1985 *Metallgefäße und Gefäßuntersätze der Bronzezeit, der geometrischen und archaischen Periode auf Cypern* (Prähistorische Bronzefunde Abteilung II, 8), Munich.

—— 1988 'Heirloom or Tradition? Bronze Stands of the Second and First Millennium B.C. in Cyprus, Greece and Italy', in *Problems in Greek Prehistory*, con., Manchester, 1986, ed. E. B. French and K. A. Wardle, Bristol: 285–93.

Mauss, Marcel 1990 *The Gift: The Form and Reason for Exchange in Archaic Societies*, London [1st (French) ed. 1950].

Mazar, Amihai 1992 'Temples of the Middle and Late Bronze Ages and the Iron Age', in *The Architecture of ancient Israel. From the prehistoric to the Persian Periods*, ed. Aharon Kempinski and Ronny Reich, Jerusalem, 161–87.

Mazarakis Ainian, Alexandre 1988 'Early Greek Temples: Their Origin and Function', in AA.VV. 1988a: 105–19.

—— 1997 *From Rulers' Dwellings to Temples: Architecture, Religion and Society in Early Iron Age Greece (1100–700 B.C.)* (SIMA 121), Jonsered.

—— 1999 'Reflections on Hero Cults in Early Iron Age Greece', in AA.VV. *1999c*: 9–36.

—— 2001 'From Huts to Houses in Early Iron Age Greece', in *From Huts to Houses: Transformations of Ancient Societies*, con., Rome, 1997, ed. J. Rasmus Brandt and Lars Karlsson, Stockholm 2001: 139–61.

—— 2005 'Inside the Adyton of a Greek Temple: Excavation on Kythnos (Cyclades)', in *Architecture and Archaeology in the Cyclades: Papers in Honour of J. J. Coulton*, ed. Maria Stampatopolou and Marina Yeroulanou, Oxford: 87–103.

McDonald, W., W. Coulson and J. Rosser 1983 *Excavations at Nichoria in Southwest Greece III: Dark Age and Byzantine Occupation*, Minneapolis, Minn.

McEwen, Indra 1993 *Socrates' Ancestor: An Essay on Architectural Beginnings*, Cambridge, Mass.

—— 2003 *Vitruvius: Writing the Body of Architecture*, Cambridge, Mass.

McGlew, J. F. 1993 *Tyranny and Political Culture in Ancient Greece*, Ithaca, N.Y.

McGowan, Elizabeth P. 1993 'Votive Columns of the Aegean Islands and the Athenian Acropolis in the Archaic Period' (diss., New York University).

—— 1995 'Tomb Marker or Turning Post: Funerary Columns in the Archaic Period', *AJA* 99: 615–32.

—— 1997 'The Origins of the Athenian Ionic Capital', *Hesperia* 66: 209–33.

Meiggs, Russell, and David Lewis 1988 *A Selection of Greek Historical Inscriptions to the End of the Fifth Century B.C.*, Oxford.

Memmo, Andrea 1953 *Elementi d'architettura lodoliana ossia l'arte del fabbricare con solidità scientifica e con eleganza non capricciosa*, 3 vols, Rome [1st ed. Milan 1786].

Menadier, Blanche 1995 'The Sixth Century BC Temple and the Sanctuary and Cult of Hera Akraia, Perachora' (diss., Rutgers University).

Merhav, Rivka ed. 1991 *Urartu: A Metalworking Center in the First Millennium B.C.E.*, cat. Israel Museum, Jerusalem.

Mertens, Dieter 1977   'Der ionische Tempel in Metapont', *Architectura: Zeitschrift für Geschichte der Baukunst* 7: 152–62.

—— 1989   'Note introduttiva per l'architettura', *Magna Grecia: Epiro e Macedonia* (CSMG 24), Taranto: 431–45.

—— 1990   'I templi greci di Paestum', in *Paestum*, ed. F. Zevi, Naples: 81–104.

—— 1991   'Bemerkungen zu Westgriechischen Monumentalaltären', in AA.VV. 1991b: 187–91.

—— 1993   *Der alte Heratempel in Paestum und die archaische Baukunst im Unteritalien*, Mainz.

—— 1996   'Die Entstehung des Steintempels in Sizilien', in AA.VV. 1996b: 25–38.

—— 2006   *Città e monumenti dei Greci d'Occidente: Dalla colonizzazione alla crisi di fine V secolo a.C.*, Rome.

Mertens-Horn, Madeleine 1978   'Beobachtungen an dädalischen Tondächern', *JdI* 93: 30–65.

—— 1992   'Die archaischen Baufriese aus Metapont', *RM* 99: 1–122.

—— 1996   'In der Obhut der Dioskuren: Zur Deutung des "Monopteros der Sikyonier" in Delphi', *IstMitt* 46: 123–30.

Meurer, M. 1896   'Das griechische Akanthusornament und seine natürlichen Vorbilder', *JdI* 11: 117–59.

—— 1909   *Vergleichende Formenlehre des Ornamentes und der Pflanze, mit besonderer Berücksichtigung der Entwicklungsgeschichte der architektonischen Kunstformen*, Dresden.

—— 1914   *Form und Herkunft der mykenischen Säule*, Berlin.

Michaud, Jean-Pierre 1973   *Le Trésor de Thèbes* (FdDelphes II), 2 vols, Paris.

Middleton, J. Henry 1886   'A Suggested Restoration of the Great Hall in the Palace of Tiryns', *JHS* 7: 161–9.

Middleton, Robin D., and David Watkin 1987   *Neoclassical and 19th Century Architecture*, I: *The Enlightenment in France and England*, New York.

Mieth, Katja 1993   'Bauten der Tyrannen in archaischer Zeit', in AA.VV. 1993d: 33–45.

Mikalson, Jon D. 2005   *Ancient Greek Religion*, Oxford and Malden, Mass.

Miles, Margaret M. 1998   *The City Eleusinion* (The Athenian Agora, Results of Excavations XXXI), Princeton, N.J.

—— 2008   *Art as Plunder: The Ancient Origins of Debate about Cultural Property*, Cambridge and New York.

Miller, J. C. Griffin 1996   'Temple and Statue: A Study of Practices in Ancient Greece' (diss., Bryn Mawr College).

Miller, Stella G. 1988   'Excavations at the Panhellenic Site of Nemea: Cults, Politics and Games', in AA.VV. 1988c: 141–51.

Miller, Stephen G. ed. 1990   *Nemea: A Guide to the Site and Museum*, Berkeley, Calif.

—— 1995   'Architecture as Evidence for the Identity of the Early Polis', in *Sources for the Ancient Greek City-State* (*HfMedd* 72), con., Copenhagen, 1994, ed. Mogens Herman Hansen, Copenhagen: 201–44.

—— 2004   *Ancient Greek Athletics*, New Haven and London.

Miroschedji, Pierre de 2001   'Les "maquettes architecturales" palestiniennes', in Muller 2001: 43–85.

Mordaunt Crook, J. 1995   *The Greek Revival: Neo-Classical Attitudes in British Architecture 1760–1870*, London [1st ed. 1972].

Moret, Jean-Marc 1984   *Oedipe, la Sphinx et les Thébains* (Bibliotheca Helvetica Romana 23), 2 vols, Rome.

Morgan, Catherine 1988   'Corinth, the Corinthian Gulf and Western Greece during the Eighth Century B.C.', *BSA* 83: 313–38.

—— 1990   *Athletes and Oracles: The Transformation of Olympia and Delphi in the eighth Century BC*, Cambridge.

—— 1993   'The Origins of pan-Hellenism', in AA.VV. 1993a: 18–44.

—— 1996   'From Palace to Polis? Religious Developments on the Greek Mainland during the Bronze Age/Iron Age Transition', in AA.VV. 1996a: 41–58.

—— 1997   'The Archaeology of Sanctuaries in Early Iron Age and Archaic *ethne*: A preliminary View', in AA.VV. 1997a: 168–98.

—— 1999   *Isthmia VIII: The Late Bronze Age Settlement and Early Iron Age Sanctuary*, Princeton, N.J., and Athens.

—— 2003   *Early Greek States beyond the Polis*, London.

—— 2009   'The Early Iron Age', in AA.VV. 2009c: 43–63.

——, and James J. Coulton 1997   'The *Polis* as a Physical Entity', in *The Polis as an Urban Centre and as a Political Community*, con., Copenhagen, 1996, ed. Mogens Herman Hansen (*HfMedd* 75), Copenhagen: 87–144.

Morgan, Lyvia 1988   *The Miniature Wall Paintings of Thera: A Study in the Aegean Culture and Iconography*, Cambridge.

Morolli, Gabriele 1985a   *'Vetus Etruria' il mito degli Etruschi nella letteratura architettonica nell'arte e nella cultura da Vitruvio a Wincklemann*, Florence.

—— 1985b   'Dal tempio etrusco all'ordine tuscanico: le origini mitiche dell'arte edificatoria nella trattatistica architettonica', in *Fortuna degli Etruschi*, ed. Franco Borsi, Milan: 82–101.

Morris, Ian 1987   *Burial and Ancient Society: The Rise of the Greek City-state*, Cambridge.

—— 1988   'Tomb Cult and the "Greek Renaissance": The Past in the Present in the 8th Century B.C.', *Antiquity* 62: 750–61.

—— 1993   'Poetics of Power: The Interpretation of Ritual Action in Archaic Greece', in AA.VV. 1993g: 15–45.

—— 1994   'Archaeologies of Greece', in *Classical Greece: Ancient Histories and Modern Ideologies*, Cambridge: 8–47.

—— 1997 'The Art of Citizenship', in AA.VV. 1997e: 9–43.

—— 2000 *Archaeology as Cultural History: Words and Things in Iron Age Greece*, Oxford and Malden, Mass.

—— 2009 'The Eighth-century Revolution', in AA.VV. 2009c: 64–80.

Morris, Sarah P. 1985 review of Akurgal E. 1981, *AJA* 89: 177–8.

—— 1992 *Daidalos and the Origins of Greek Art*, Princeton, N.J.

—— 1997 'Greek and Near Eastern Art in the Age of Homer', in AA.VV. 1997e: 56–71.

—— 2001 'The Prehistoric Background of Artemis Ephesia: A Solution to the Enigma of Her "Breasts"?', in Muss 2001: 135–51.

Moscati, Sabatino, ed. 1988 *The Phoenicians*, cat. Venice, Milan.

Mossé, Claude 1969 *La Tyrannie dans la Grèce antique*, Paris.

Moustaka, Aliki 2002 'On the Cult of Hera at Olympia', in AA.VV. 2002: 199–205.

Mühlbauer, Lore 2007 *Lykische Grabarchitektur vom Holz zum Stein* (Forschungen in Limyra 3), Vienna.

Müller, Kurt 1923 'Gebäudemodelle spätgeometrischer Zeit', *AM* 48: 52–68.

Müller-Wiener, Wolfgang 1988 *Griechisches Bauwesen in der Antike*, Munich.

Muller, Béatrice ed. 2001 'Maquettes architecturales' de l'antiquité. Regards croisés, con., Strasbourg, 1998, Paris.

—— 2002 *Les 'Maquettes architecturales' du Proche-Orient ancien*, 2 vols, Beirut.

Murray, Oswyn 1980 *Early Greece*, Glasgow.

—— 1988 'Greek Forms of Government', in *Civilization of the Ancient Mediterranean: Greece and Rome*, ed. Michael Grant and Rachel Kitzinger, New York: 439–86.

—— 1990 'The City of Reason', in Oswin Murray and Simon Price, *The Greek City from Homer to Alexander*, Oxford: 1–25.

—— 1991 'The Social Function of Art in Early Greece', in AA.VV. 1991a: 23–30.

Muscarella, Oscar W. 1962 'The Oriental Origin of Siren Cauldron Attachments', *Hesperia* 31: 317–29.

—— 1992 'Greek and Oriental Cauldron Attachments: A Review', in AA.VV. 1992c: 16–45.

Muss, Ulrike ed. 2001 *Der Kosmos der Artemis von Ephesos* (ÖJh Sonderschriften 37), Vienna.

—— ed. 2008 *Die Archäologie der ephesischen Artemis: Gestalt und Ritual eines Heiligtums*, Vienna.

Mussche, Herman 1997 'Quelques Considérations sur la genèse et l'évolution du temple grec', in *Marbres helléniques de la carrière au chef d'oeuvre*, ed. L. Demeyer, cat., Brussels: 46–55.

Musti, Domenico ed. 1985 *Le Origini dei Greci, Dori e mondo Egeo*, Rome and Bari.

Mylonas, George E. 1961 *Eleusis and the Eleusinian Mysteries*, Princeton, N.J.

—— 1977 *Mycenaean Religion: Temples, Altars and Temenea*, Athens.

Mylonopoulos, Joannis, ed. 2006 *Ritual and Communication in the Graeco-Roman World*, Liège.

——, ed. 2010 *Divine Images and Human Imaginations in Ancient Greece and Rome*, Leiden and Boston, Mass.

—— 2011 'Divine Images behind Bars: The Semantics of Barriers in Greek Temples', in *Current Approaches to Religion in Ancient Greece*, ed. Matthew Haysom, Stockholm: 269–91.

Nagy, Helen 1998 'Divinity, Exaltation and Heroization: Thoughts on the Seated Posture in Early Archaic Greek Sculpture', in AA.VV. 1998b: 181–91.

Nakayama, Norio 1982 'Untersuchung der auf weissgrundigen Lekythen dargestellten Grabmaeler' (diss., University of Freiburg).

Nassouhi, Essad 1925 'Les Autels trépieds assyriens', *Revue d'Assyrologie et d'archéologie orientale* 22: 85–90.

Naumann, Rudolf 1971 *Architektur Kleinasiens, von ihren Anfängen bis zum Ende der hethitischen Zeit*, Tübingen 1971 [1st ed. 1955].

Neils, Jenifer ed. 2005 *The Parthenon: From Antiquity to the Present*, Cambridge and New York.

Newberry, Percy E., and G. Willoughby Fraser 1893–1900 *Beni Hasan* (Archaeological Survey of Egypt), 4 vols, London.

Newcomb, Rexford 1921 *The Volute in Architecture and Architectural Decoration* (University of Illinois Bulletin 121), Urbana, Ill.

Nicholls, Richard V. 1991 'Early Monumental Religious Architecture at Old Smyrna', in AA.VV. 1991a: 151–71.

Nick, Gabriele 2002 *Die Athena Parthenos: Studien zum griechischen Kultbild und seiner Rezeption* (AM, supp. 19), Mainz.

Niemeyer, Hans Georg 1970 'Zum Thymiaterion vom Cerro del Peñón', *Madrider Mitteilungen* 11: 96–101.

—— 2004 'Phoenician or Greek: Is there a Reasonable Way out of the Al Mina Debate?', *Ancient West and East* 3, 1: 38–50.

—— 2007 'Jahresbericht 2006: Abteilung Athen', *AA*: 74–84.

Nilsson, Martin P. 1950 *The Minoan-Mycenaean Religion and its Survival in Greek Religion*, Lund [1st ed. 1927].

Noack, Ferdinand 1927 *Eleusis: die Baugeschichtliche Entwicklung des Heiligtumes*, Berlin.

Noegel, Scott B. 2007 'Greek Religion and the Ancient Near East', in Ogden 2007: 21–37.

Normann, Alexander von 1996 *Architekturtoreutik in der Antike* (Quellen und Forschungen zur antiken Welt 25), Munich.

Nylander, Carl 1970   *Ionians in Pasargadae*, Uppsala.

Oakley, John H. 2004   *Picturing Death in Classical Athens: The Evidence of the White Lekythoi*, Cambridge.

Odgers, Jo, Flora Samuel and Adam Sharr, eds 2006   *Primitive: Original Matters in Architecture*, London and New York.

Oechslin, Werner 2002   *Otto Wagner, Adolf Loos, and the Road to Modern Architecture*, Cambridge.

Oenbrink, Werner 1997   *Das Bild im Bilde: Zur Darstellung von Götterstatuen und Kultbildern auf griechischen Vasen* (EurHss 64), Frankfurt.

Ogden, Daniel 2007   *A Companion to Greek Religion*, Oxford.

Ohnefalsch-Richter, Magda H. 1913   *Griechische Sitten und Gebräuche auf Cypern*, Berlin.

Ohnesorg, Aenne 1993   'Parische Kapitelle', in AA.VV. 1993c: 111–18.

—— 1996   'Votiv-oder Architektursäulen?', in AA.VV. 1996b: 39–47.

—— 2001   'Ephesische Rosettenkapitelle', in Muss 2001: 185–98.

—— 2002   'Das Problem der Eckkapitelle: Neue Forschungen zum archaischen Artemistempel von Ephesos', in *Bericht über die 41. Tagung für Ausgrabungswissenschaft und Bauforschung*, con., Berlin, 2000: 48–56.

—— 2005   *Ionische Altäre: Formen und Varianten einer Architekturgattung aus Insel- und Ostionien* (Archäologische Forschungen 21), Berlin.

—— 2007   *Der Kroisos-Tempel: Neue Forschungen zum archaischen Dipteros der Artemis von Ephesos* (FiE 12/4), Vienna.

Oikonomos, Georgios P. 1931   'The Terracotta Model of a House from the Argive Heraion following a New Addition' (title translated from Greek), *ArchEph*: 1–53.

Oliver-Smith, Philip E. 1964   'Representations of Aeolic Capitals on Greek Vases before 400 B.C.', in *Essays in Memory of Karl Lehmann*, ed. Lucy F. Sandler, Locust Valley, N.Y.: 232–41.

—— 1969   'Architectural Elements on Greek Vases before 400 BC' (diss., New York University).

Onians, John B. 1988a   *Bearers of Meaning: The Classical Orders in Antiquity, the Middle Ages, and the Renaissance*, Princeton, N.J.

—— 1988b   'The Roots of the Normative Tradition in Greek Art, in Greek Trade and Greek Games', in AA.VV. 1988d, 1: 197–202.

—— 1989   'War, Mathematics and Art in Classical Greece', *Journal of the History of the Human Sciences* 2: 39–62.

—— 1999   *Classical Art and the Cultures of Greece and Rome*, New Haven and London.

Opitz, Dietrich, and Anton Moortgat 1955   *Tell Halaf* 3, Berlin.

Oppenheim, Max Freiherr von 1931   *Der Tell Halaf: Eine neue Kultur im ältesten Mesopotamien*, Leipzig.

Orchard, J. 1967   'Equestrian Bridle-harness Ornaments', in *Ivories from Nimrud (1949–1963)*, ed. Max Mallowan, London.

Orsi, Paolo 1919   'Gli scavi intorno a l'Athenaion di Siracusa negli anni 1912–1917', *MonAnt* 25: 353–762.

——, and F. S. Cavallari 1890   'Megara Hyblaea: Storia, Topografia, Necropoli e Anathemata', *MontAnt* 1: 689–950.

Ortolani, Giorgio 1997   'Tradizione e trasgressione nell'ordine dorico in età ellenistica e romana', *Palladio* 19: 19–38.

Osborne, Robin 1993   'Competitive Festivals and the Polis: A Context for Dramatic Festivals at Athens', in AA.VV. 1993a: 21–38.

—— 1996   *Greece in the Making, 1200–479 BC*, London.

—— 1998   *Archaic and Classical Greek Art*, Oxford.

—— 2009   'The Narratology and Theology of Architectural Sculpture, or What you can do with a Chariot but can't do with a Satyr on a Greek Temple', in AA.VV. 2009b: 2–12.

Østby, Erik 1978   'The Temple of Casa Marafioti at Locri and Some Related Buildings', *ActaAArtH* 8: 25–47.

—— 1991–2   'Templi di Pallantion e dell'Arcadia: Confronti e sviluppi', *AnnASAtene* 68–9: 285–391.

—— 1993   'Twenty-five Years of Research on Greek Sanctuaries: A Bibliography', in AA.VV. 1993a: 192–227.

—— 1994   'The Sanctuary of Athena Alea at Tegea: First Preliminary Report', *OpAth* 20: 89–141.

—— 1997   'Corinto e l'architettura dorica dell'Occidente', in *Corinto e l'Occidente* (CSMG 34), con., Taranto, 1994, Taranto: 211–27.

—— 2000   'Delphi and Archaic Doric Architecture in the Peloponnese', in AA.VV. 2000a: 239–62.

—— 2001   'Der Ursprung der griechischen Tempelarchitektur und ihre Beziehungen mit Aegypten', in AA.VV. 2001a: 17–33.

—— 2006a   'Continuatio, Renovatio and Innovatio: The Birth of the Doric Temple', *Acta ad Archaeologiam et Artium Historiam Pertinentia* 20: 9–38.

—— 2006b   'Recent Archaeological Investigations at Tegea', *Polis: Studi interdisciplinari sul mondo antico* 2: 111–26.

Osthues, Ernst-Wilhelm 2005   'Studien zum dorischen Eckkonflikt', *JdI* 120: 1–154.

Ottosson, Magnus, 1980   *Temples and Cult Places in Palestine* (Boreas 12), Uppsala.

Özgüç, Tahsin 1969   *Altintepe II: Tombs, Storehouse and Ivories*, Ankara.

Padel, Ruth 1992   *In and Out of the Mind: Greek Images of the tragic Self*, Princeton, N.J.

Padgett, Michael 1966   *Vase Painting in Italy: Red Figure and Related Works in the Museum of Fine Arts, Boston*, Boston, Mass.

—— 2003   *The Centaur's Smile: The Human Animal in Early Greek Art*, New Haven and London.

Pakkanen, Jari 2009   'A Tale of Three Drums: An Unfinished Archaic Votive Column in the Sanctuary of Poseidon in Kalaureia', *Opuscula: Annual of the Swedish Institutes at Athens and Rome* 2: 167–179.

——, and Petra Pakkanen 2000   'The Toumba Building at Lefkandi: Some Methodological Reflections on its Plan and Function', *BSA* 95: 239–52.

Palagia, Olga 1984   'A Niche for Kallimachos' Lamp?', *AJA* 88: 515–21.

——, ed. 1997   *Greek Offerings: Essays on Greek Art in Honour of John Boardman*, Oxford.

Palermo, Dario, *et al.* 2004   'Lo scavo del 2003 sulla Patela di Priniàs: Relazione preliminare', *Creta Antica* 5: 249–77.

Palyvou, Clairy 2005   *Akrotiri Thera: An Architecture of Affluence 3,500 Years Old*, Phildelphia, Pa.

Panofsky, E 1939   *Studies in Iconology: Humanistic Themes in the Art of the Renaissance*, Oxford.

Papadopoulos John K. 1993   'To Kill a Cemetery: The Athenian Kerameikos and the Early Ion Age in the Aegean', *JMA* 6: 175–206.

Papalexandrou, Nassos 2005   *The Visual Poetics of Power: Warriors, Youths and Tripods in Early Greece*, Lanham, Md.

—— 2008   'Boiotian Tripods: The Tenacity of a Panhellenic Symbol in a Regional Context', *Hesperia* 77: 251–82.

—— 2014   'Messenian Tripods: A Boiotian Contribution to the Symbolic Construction of the Messenian Past?', in *Attitudes towards the Past in Antiquity: Creating Identities. Proceedings of an International Conference held at Stockholm University, 15–17 May 2009*, ed. Charlotte Scheffer and Brita Alroth, Acta Universitatis Stockholmiensis, Stockholm: 127–37.

Papanikolaou, Alexandros 1998   'The Building Activity on the South Slope of the Akropolis at Karthea from the 6th to the 5th Centuries BC' (title translated from Greek), in *Kea-Kythnos: History and Archaeology*, con., Kea-Kythnos, 1994, ed. L. G. Mendoni and A. Mazarakis Ainian: 557–71.

—— 2012   *Η αποκατάσταση του Ερεχθείου (1979–1987)* (trans.: 'Restoration of the Erechtheion'), Athens

Papapostolou, Ioannes. A. 1994   *s.v.* Thermos, in *EAA*, 2nd supplement: 752–4.

—— 1995   'Excavations at Thermos' (title translated from Greek), *Praktika* 150: 87–107.

—— 2006   'Excavations at Thermos' (title translated from Greek), *Praktika* 158.2: 51–60.

—— 2010a   'Aspects of Cult in Early Thermos', *ArchEph* 149: 1–59.

—— 2010b   'Doch kein früher Ringhallen-Tempel in Thermos!', *Antike Welt*, 41.5: 49–60.

Papastamos, Dimitrios 1970   *Melische Amphoren*, Aschendorff.

Parke, Herbert W. 1967   *Greek Oracles*, London.

—— 1984   'Croesus and Delphi', *GRBS* 25: 209–323.

——, and Donald E. W. Wormell 1956   *The Delphic Oracle*, 2 vols, Oxford.

Parker, Robert 1983   *Miasma: Pollution and Purification in Early Greek Religion*, Oxford.

Partida, Elena C. 2000   *The Treasuries at Delphi: An Architectural Study* (SIMA 160), Jonsered.

Patera, Ioanna 2012   *Offrir en Grèce ancienne: Gestes et contetes* (Potsdamer Altertumswissenschaftliche Beiträge 41), Stuttgart.

Pauwels, Yves 1989   'Les Origines de l'ordre composite', *Annali di Architettura* 1: 29–46.

Payne, Alina 2000   'Ut poesis architectura: Tectonics and Poetics in Architectural Criticism circa 1570', in *Antiquity and its Interpreters*, ed. Alina Payne, Ann Kuttner and Rebekah Smick, New York: 145–58.

Payne, Humfry G. 1925–6   'On the Thermon Metopes', *BSA* 27: 124–32.

—— 1931   *Necrocorinthia: A Study of Corinthian Art in the Archaic Period*, Oxford.

—— 1940   *Perachora: The Sanctuaries of Hera Akraia and Limenia: Excavations of the British School of Archaeology at Athens 1930–1933.* I: *Architecture, Bronzes, Terracottas*, Oxford.

Pedersen, Poul 1989   *The Parthenon and the Origin of the Corinthian Capital*, Odense.

Pedley, John 2005   *Sanctuaries and the Sacred in the Ancient Greek World*, Cambridge.

Pemberton, E. 1989   *The Sanctuary of Demeter and Kore: The Greek Pottery* (Corinth XVIII, 1), Princeton, N.J.

Penglase, Charles 1994   *Greek Myths and Mesopotamia: Parallels and Influence in the Homeric Hymns and Hesiod*, London.

Pensabene, Patrizio 1993   *Elementi architettonici di Alessandria e di altri siti egiziani*, Rome.

—— 2010   'Canopo' di Villa Adriana: Programmi tematici, marmi e officine nell'aredo statuario', *AnnASAtene* 87 : 381–424.

Peponi, Anastasia-Erasmia 2012   *Frontiers of Pleasure: Models of Aesthetic Response in Archaic and Classical Greek Thought*, Oxford and New York.

Pernier, Luigi 1914   'Templi arcaici sulla Patela di Prinias: Contributo allo studio dell'arte dedalica', *AnnASAtene* 1: 19–111.

—— 1934   'New Elements for the Study of the Archaic Temple of Priniàs', *AJA* 38: 171–7.

Pernigotti, Sergio 1999   *I Greci nell'Egitto della XXVI Dinastia* (Piccola biblioteca di egittologia, 4), Imola.

Perrault, Claude 1993   *Ordonnance for the five Kinds of Columns after the Method of the Ancients*, Santa Monica, Calif. (trans. Indra K. McEwen from *Ordonnance des cinq Espèces de Colonnes selon la Méthode des Anciens*, Paris, 1683).

Perrot, Georges, and Charles J., Chipiez 1882–1914   *Histoire de l'Art dans l'Antiquité*, 10 vols, Paris

Perrot, Nell 1937   *Les Représentations de l'arbre sacré sur les monuments de Mésopotamie et d'Elam*, Paris.

Perouse de Montclos, Jean-Marie 1966   'Charles-François Viel, architecte de l'Hôpital général, et Jean-Louis de Saint-Maux, architecte, peintre et avocat au parlement de Paris', *Bulletin de la Société de l'Histoire de l'Art Française*: 257–69.

Persson, Axel 1942   *New Tombs at Dendra near Midea*, Lund.

Pesando, Fabrizio 1987   *La casa dei Greci*, Milan.

Peschken, Goerd 1988   'The Original Significance of the Model for the Doric Pteron and Triglyph', *Canon: The Princeton Journal for Thematic Studies in Architecture* 3: 11–33.

——— 1990   *Demokratie und Tempel: Die Bedeutung der dorischen Architektur*, Berlin.

Petrie, W. M. Flinders 1895   *Egyptian Decorative Art: A Course of Lectures delivered at the Royal Institution*, London.

——— 1930   *3000 Decorative Patterns of the Ancient World*, London.

Petrie, W. M. Flinders *et al.* 1896–8   *Naukratis*, 2 vols, London.

Petropoulos, Michales 2002   'The Geometric Temple of Ano Mazaraki (Rakita) in Achaia during the Period of Colonization', in *Gli Achei e l'identità etnica degli Achei d'occidente* (Tekmeria 3), con., Paestum, 2001, Paestum and Athens: 143–64.

Petropoulou, Angeliki 1984   'Studies in Greek Cult and Sacrifical Ritual' (diss., University of Colorado).

Pfaff, Christopher A. 1990   'Three-peaked Antefixes from the Argive Heraion', in AA.VV. 1990a: 149–56.

——— 2003   'Archaic Corinthian Architecture, ca. 600–480 BC', in Williams and Bookidis 2003: 95–140.

——— 2005   'Capital C from the Argive Heraion', *Hesperia* 74: 575–84.

——— 2007   'Geometric Graves in the Panayia Field', *Hesperia* 76: 443–537.

Philipp, Hanna 1968   *Tektonon Daidala: der bildende Künstler und sein Werk im vorplatonischen Schrifttum*, Berlin.

——— 1994   'ΧΑΛΚΕΟΙ ΤΟΙΧΟΙ – Eherne Wände', *AA*, 1994: 489–98.

Phillips, J. Peter 2002   *The Columns of Egypt*, Manchester.

Philpot, J. H. 1897   *The Sacred Tree or the Tree and Religion and Myth*, London.

Picard, Charles 1948   *Les Religions préhelléniques (Crète et Mycènes)*, Paris.

Pickard-Cambridge, Arthur 1968   *The Dramatic Festivals of Athens*, Oxford [1st ed. 1953].

Picon, Antoine 1992   *French Architects and Engineers in the Age of Enlightenment*, Cambridge [1st (French) ed. 1988].

Pimpl, Heidrun 1997   *Perirrhanteria und Louteria*, Berlin.

Piranesi, Giovanbattista 2002   *Observations on the Letter of Monsieur Mariette*, Los Angeles, Calif. (trans. Caroline Beamish and David Britt from *Osservazioni di Giovani Battista Piranesi sopra la lettera de M. Mariette . . .*, Rome, 1765).

Pirenne-Delforge, V. *et al.* 2005   'Personnel de culte: Monde grec', *ThesCRA* V (2005), 1–65.

Plommer, W. Hugh 1970   'Vitruvian Studies', *BSA* 65: 179–90.

——— 1977   'Shadowy Megara', *JHS* 97: 75–83.

——— 1979   'Vitruvius and the Origin of Caryatids', *JHS* 99: 97–102.

Pococke, Richard 1743–5   *A Description of the East and Some other Countries*, 2 vols, London.

Pollitt, Jerome J. 1974   *The Ancient View of Greek Art. Criticism, History and Terminology*, New Haven and London.

——— 1990   *The Art of Ancient Greece: Sources and Documents*, Cambridge and New York [1st ed. 1965].

Pomtow, Hans R. 1910   *Die alte Tholos und das Schatzhaus der Sikyonier zu Delphi*, Heidelberg.

Popham, Mervyn R. 1982   'The Hero of Lefkandi', *Antiquity* 61: 169–74.

Popham, Mervyn R., P. G. Calligas and L. H. Sackett, eds 1993   *Lefkandi II*, Part 2: *The Excavation, Architecture and Finds* (*BSA*, supp. 23), London and Athens.

Porphyrios, Demetri 2006   *Classical Architecture*, London [1st ed. 1991].

Potts, Alex 1994   *Flesh and the Ideal: Winckelmann and the Origins of Art History,* New Haven and London.

Poulsen, Frederik 1912   *Der Orient und die frühgriechische Kunst*, Leipzig.

Poursat, Jean-Claude 1977   *Catalogue des ivoires mycéniens du musée national d'Athènes*, Paris.

——— 2008   *L'Art Égéen*, I: *Grèce, Cyclades, Crète*, Paris.

Prado, Hieronymo, and Juan Bautista Villalpando 1596–1604   *In Ezechielem Explanationes et Apparatus Urbis ac Templi Hierosolymitani*, 3 vols, Rome.

Preisshofen, Felix 1984   'Zur Funktion des Parthenon nach den schriftlichen Quellen', in *Parthenon-Kongress: Referate und Berichte, c*on., Basel, 1982, ed. Ernst Berger, Mainz, 15–18.

Prent, Mieke 2003   'Glories of the Past in the Past: Ritual Activities at Palatial Ruins in Early Iron Age Greece', in *Archaeologies of Memory*, ed. Ruth M. Van Dyke and Susan E. Alcock, Oxford: 81–103.

——— 2005a   *Cretan Sanctuaries and Cults: Continuity and Change from Late Minoan IIIC to the Archaic Period* (Religions in the Graeco-Roman World 154), Leiden.

——— 2005b   Cult Activities at the Palace of Knossos from the End of the Bronze Age: Continuity and Change', in AA.VV. 2005a: 411–19.

Preziosi, Donald, and Louise A. Hitchcock 1999   *Aegean Art and Architecture*, Oxford.

Price, Simon 1985   'Delphi and Divination', in AA.VV. 1985: 128–54.

—— 1999   *Religions of the Ancient Greeks*, Cambridge.

Privitera, Santo 2003   'I tripodi dei Dinomeidi e la decima dei Siracusani', *AnnASAtene* 81: 391–424.

Prost, Francis 2009   'Norme et image divine: L'Example de la "statue d'or" de l'Acropole', *Kernos* 21: 243–60.

Przyluski, Jean 1936   'La Colonne ionique et le symbolisme oriental', *RA*: 3–15.

Puchstein, Otto 1887   *Das ionische Capitell*, Berlin.

—— 1907   *Die ionische Säule als klassisches Bauglied orientalischer Herkunft*, Leipzig.

Pugin, Augustus W. G. 1841   *True Principles of Pointed or Christian Architecture*, London.

Pugliese Carratelli, Giovannni, ed. 1996   *I Greci in Occidente*, cat. (Venice), Milan.

Pulleyn, Simon 1997   *Prayer in Greek Religion*, Oxford.

Pülz, Andrea M. 2009   *Goldfunde aus dem Artemision von Ephesos* (FiE XII/5), Vienna.

Quatremère de Quincy, Antoine Chrysostôme 1803   *De l'architecture égyptienne, considérée dans son origine, ses principes et son goût, et comparée sous les mêmes rapports à l'architecture grecque*, Paris (based on unpublished essay with same title of 1785).

—— 1832   *Dictionnaire historique d'architecture*, 2 vols, Paris

Quinn, Josephine Crawley 2013   'Monumental Power: "Numidian Royal Architecture" in Context', in *The Hellenistic West: Rethinking the Ancient Mediterranean*, ed. Jonathan R. W. Prag and Josephine Crawley Quinn, Cambridge: 179–215.

Quintavalle, Arturo C. 1981   'The Philosophical Context of Riegl's Stilfragen', *Architectural Design* 51, no. 6–7: 16–19.

Raglan, Fitzroy Richard Somerset, 4th Baron, 1964   *The Temple and the House*, London.

Ramirez, Juan Antonio 1991   *Dios Arquitecto: J. B. Villalpando y el Templo de Salomón*, Madrid.

Ransom, Caroline L. 1905   *Studies in Ancient Furniture. Couches and Beds of the Greeks, Etruscans and Romans*, Chicago, Ill.

Raspi-Serra, Joselita ed. 1986   *La Fortuna di Paestum e la memoria moderna del dorico 1750–1830*, 2 vols, Florence.

—— 1998   'La Grecia: un territorio da scoprire ed un' idea da trasmettere. L'opera di Michel Fourmont e di Julien-David Le Roy', *AnnASAtene* 70–71 (for 1992–3): 7–84.

Ratté, Christopher 1989   'Lydian Masonry and Monumental Architecture at Sardis' (diss., University of California, Berkeley).

—— 1993   'Lydian Contributions to Archaic East Greek Architecture', in AA.VV. 1993c: 1–12.

—— 2011   *Lydian Architecture: Ashlar Masonry Structures at Sardis*, Cambridge, Mass.

Raubitschek, Anthony E. 1943   'Early Attic Votive Monuments', *BSA* 40: 17–37.

—— 1949   *Dedications from the Athenian Acropolis: A Catalogue of the Inscriptions of the Sixth and Fifth Centuries*, Cambridge, Mass.

—— 1992   'The Tripods of Odysseus', in *Studia Aegaea et Balcanica in honorem Lodovicae Press*, ed. Anna Lipska, Ewa Niezgoda and Maria Zabacka, Warsaw: 99–102.

Raubitschek, Isabelle K. 1950   'Ionicizing-Doric Architecture: A Stylistic Study of Greek Doric Architecture of the Sixth and Fifth Centuries B.C.' (diss., University of Columbia).

Reade, J. E. 2002   'The Ziggurat and Temples of Nimrud', *Iraq* 64: 135–216.

Reber, Franz von 1866   *Geschichte der Baukunst im Alter-thum*, Leipzig.

—— 1883   *History of Ancient Art*, London.

—— 1898   'Über das Verhältnis des mykenischen zum dorischen Baustil', *Königlich Bayerische Akademie der Wissenschaften, 3: Classe, Abhandlungen* 21.3.

Reuther, Oscar 1957   *Der Heratempel von Samos: der Bau seit der Zeit des Polykrates*, Berlin.

Rhodes, Robin F. 1984   'The Beginnings of Monumental Architecture in the Corinthia' (diss., University of North Carolina).

—— 1987   'Early Corinthian Architecture and the Origins of the Doric Order', *AJA* 91: 477–80.

—— 2003   'The Earliest Greek Architecture in Corinth and the 7th-century Temple on Temple Hill', in Williams and Bookidis 2003: 85–94.

—— 2011   'The Woodwork of the Seventh Century Temple on Temple Hill in Corinth', *Holztragwerke der Antike*, ed. Alexander von Kienlin, Istanbul: 109–23.

Rhomaios, K. A. 1952   'The Sanctuary of Artemis Knakeatis at Tegea' (title translated from Greek), *ArchEph*: 1–31.

Richard, Heinrich 1970   *Vom Ursprung des dorischen Tempels*, Bonn.

Richter, Gisela M. A. 1960   *Kouroi: Archaic Greek Youths*, London.

—— 1966   *The Furniture of the Greeks, Etruscans and Romans*, London.

—— 1968   *Korai: Archaic Greek Maidens*, London.

Ridgway, Brunilde S. 1966   'Notes on the Development of the Greek Frieze', *Hesperia* 35: 188–204.

—— 1977   'The Plataian Tripod and the Serpentine Column', *AJA* 81: 374–9.

—— 1993   *The Archaic Style in Greek Sculpture*, Princeton, N.J. [1st ed. 1977].

—— 1999   *Prayers in Stone: Greek Architectural Sculpture (c. 600–100 B.C.E.)*, Berkeley, Calif.

—— 2005   '"Periklean" Cult Images and their Media', in AA.VV. 2005c: 111–18.

Riegl, Alois 1992   *Problems of Style. Foundations for a History of Ornament*, trans. Evelyn Kain (ed. David Castriota), Princeton, N.J. [1st (German) ed. 1893].

Riemann, Hans 1956a   *s.v.* Tripodes, in *RE*, supp. VIII: col. 861–88.

—— 1956b   *s.v.* Lysikratesmonument, in *RE*, supp. VIII: col. 266–347.

Riis, Poul J. 1998   *Vulcentia Vetustiora: A Study of Archaic Vulcan Bronzes* (Historisk-filosofiske Skrifter 19), Cophenhagen.

Ringgren, H. 1973, *Religions of the Ancient Near East*, London.

Riorden, Elizabeth 2009   'Wilhelm Dörpfeld's Theory of Wood and Mudbrick Architecture: Implications and a Reassessment', in *Bautechnik im antiken und vorantiken Kleinasien* (Byzas 9), ed. Martin Bachmann, Istanbul: 199–210.

Rizza, Giovanni 1996   'La scultura siceliota nell'età arcaica', in Pugliese Carratelli 1996: 399–412.

Roaf, Michael 1996   'Architecture and Furniture', in AA.VV. 1996d: 21–8.

Robertson, Noel 1998   'The City Center of Archaic Athens', *Hesperia* 67: 283–302.

Robinson, Henry S. 1976   'Temple Hill, Corinth', in Jantzen 1976: 239–60.

—— 1984   'Roof Tiles of the Early Seventh Century B.C.', *AM* 99: 55–66.

Rocco, Giorgio 1994a   *Guida alla lettura degli ordini architettonici*, I: *Il Dorico*, Naples.

—— 1994b   'Su di un fregio dorico da Villa Adriana: La soluzione vitruviana del conflitto angolare', *Palladio* 14: 37–44.

—— 2003   *Guida alla lettura degli ordini architettonici*, II: *Lo Ionico*, Naples.

Rodenwaldt, Gerhart 1938   *Altdorische Bildwerke in Korfu*, Berlin.

Rolley, Claude 1975   'Bronzes et Bronziers des Âges obscurs (XIIᵉ-VIIIᵉ siècle av. J.-C.)', *RA*: 155–60.

—— 1977   *Les Trépieds à cuve clouée* (FdDelphes V3), Paris.

—— 1983   'Les Grands Sanctuaires panhelléniques', in AA.VV. 1983: 109–14.

—— 1986   *Greek Bronzes*, London.

—— 1994   *La Sculpture grecque*, I: *Des Origines au milieu du Vᵉ Siècle*, Paris.

—— 2002   'Delphes de 1500 à 575 av. J.-C.: Nouvelles Données sur la problème "ruptures et continuité"', in Kyrieleis 2002: 273–9.

Romano, Elisa 1987   *La capanna e il tempio: Vitruvio o dell' architettura*, Palermo.

Romano, Irene B. 1980   'Early Greek Cult Images' (diss., University of Philadelphia).

—— 1988   'Early Greek Cult Images and Cult Practices', in AA.VV. 1988a: 127–34.

Rombos, Theodora 1988   *The Iconography of Attic Late Geometric II Pottery* (SIMA 68), Jonsered.

Romeo, I. 1989   'Sacelli arcaici senza peristasi nella Sicilia greca', *Xenia* 17: 5–54.

Rose, Brian C. 2000   'Post-Bronze Age Research at Troia, 1999', *Studia Troica* 10: 53–71.

—— 2008   'Separating Fact from Fiction in the Aiolian Migration', *Hesperia* 77: 399–430.

Rouse, William H. D. 1902   *Greek Votive Offerings: An Essay in the History of Greek Religion*, Cambridge.

Roux, Georges 1953a   'Autel *à triglyphes bas* trouvé sur l'agora d'Argos', *BCH* 77: 117–23.

—— 1953b   'Le Chapiteau corinthien de Bassae', *BCH* 77: 124–38.

—— 1961   *L'Architecture de l'Argolide aux IV et III siècles avant J.-C.*, Paris.

—— 1984   'Trésors, temples, tholos', in *Temples et sanctuaires: Séminaire de recherche 1981–1983*, ed. Georges Roux, Lyon: 153–71.

—— 1992   'La Tholos de Sicyone à Delphes et les origines de l'entablement dorique', in AA.VV. 1992g: 151–66.

Rowland, Benjamin 1935   'Notes on Ionic Architecture in the East', *AJA* 39: 489–96.

Rowland, Ingrid D. 1994   'Raphael, Angelo Colucci, and the Genesis of the Architectural Orders', *Art Bulletin* 76: 81–104.

——, and Thomas N. Howe 1999   *Vitruvius: Ten Books on Architecture*, Cambridge and New York.

Ruby, Pascal, ed. 1999   *Les Princes de la protohistoire et l'émergence de l'état* (Collection de l'École Française de Rome 252), con., 1994, Naples.

Rumscheid, Frank 1994   *Untersuchungen zur kleinasiatischen Bauornamentik des Hellenismus*, 2 vols, Mainz.

—— 1999   'Von Wachsen antiker Säulenwälder: Zu Projektierung und Finanzierung antiker Bauten in Westkleinasien und anderswo', *JdI* 114: 23–63.

Rupp, David W. 1974   'Greek Altars of the Northeastern Peloponnese c. 750–725 B.C. to c. 300–275 B.C.' (diss., Bryn Mawr College).

—— 1983   'Reflections on the Development of Altars in the Eighth Century B.C.', in AA.VV. 1983: 101–7.

—— 1991   'Blazing Altars: The Depiction of Altars in Attic Vase Painting', in AA.VV. 1991b: 56–62.

Rups, M. 1986   'Thesauros: A Study of the Treasury Building as Found in Greek Sanctuaries' (diss., Johns Hopkins University).

Ruskin, John 1849   *The Seven Lamps of Architecture*, London.

Rutherford, Ian 2001   *Pindar's Paeans*, Oxford.

Rutkowski, B. 1986 *The Cult Places of the Aegean*, New Haven and London.

Rykwert, Joseph 1972 *On Adam's House in Paradise: The Role of the Primitive Hut in Architectural History*, New York.

—— 1980 *The First Moderns: The Architects of the Eighteenth Century*, Cambridge, Mass.

—— 1994 'On the Palmette', *Res: Anthropology and Aesthetics* 26: 11–21.

1996 *The Dancing Column: On Order in Architecture*, Cambridge, Mass.

—— 2008 *The Judicious Eye: Architecture against the Other Arts*, London.

Şahin, M. C. 1972 *Die Entwicklung der griechischen Monumentalaltäre*, Bonn.

Sahlins, Marshall 1972 *Stone Age Economics*, Chicago, Ill.

Sakellarakis, Yannis 1988 'Some Geometric and Archaic Votives from the Idaian Cave', in AA.VV. 1988a: 173–93.

—— 1996 'Mycenaean Footstools', in AA.VV. 1996d: 105–10.

Sakellarakis, Yannis, and Efi Sapouna-Sakellaraki 1997 *Archanes: Minoan Crete in a New Light*, 2 vols, Athens.

Sakellariou, A. F. 1985 *Les Tombes à chambre de Mycènes: Fouilles de Chr. Tsountas (1887–1898)*, Paris and Athens.

Sakellariou, M. B. 1989 *The Polis-State: Definition and Origin*, Athens.

Sakowski, Anja 1997 *Darstellungen von Dreifusskesseln in der griechischen Kunst bis zum Beginn der klassischen Zeit* (EurHss 67), Frankfurt.

Salmon, John B. 1972 'The Heraeum at Perachora and the Early History of Corinth and Megara', *BSA* 67: 159–204.

—— 1984 *Wealthy Korinth: A History of the City to 388 B.C.*, Oxford.

Sandars, N. K. 1978 *The Sea Peoples: Warriors of the Ancient Mediterranean 1250–1150 BC*, London.

—— 1986 'Some Early Uses of Drafted Masonry around the East Mediterranean', in Φίλια έπη εις Γεώργιον Ε. Μυλωνάν δια τα 60 έτη του ανασκαφικού του έργου (trans.: 'Affectionate essays in honour of George E. Mylonas on his 60 years of excavation work'), Athens: 67–73.

Sapirstein, Philip 2008 'The Emergence of Ceramic Roof Tiles in Archaic Greek Architecture' (diss., Cornell University)

—— 2009 'How the Corinthians Manufactured Their First Roof Tiles', *Hesperia* 78: 195–229.

—— 2012 'The Monumental Archaic Roof of the Temple of Hera at Mon Repos, Corfu', *Hesperia* 81: 31–91.

Sapouna-Sakellaraki, Effie 1997 'A Geometric Electrum Band from a Tomb on Skyros', in Palagia 1997: 35–42.

Satlow, Michael L., ed. 2013 *The Gift in Antiquity*, Malden, Mass., and Oxford.

Scahill, David 2009 'The Origins of the Corinthian Capital', in AA.VV. 2009b: 40–53.

Schaber, Wilfried 1982 *Die archaischen Tempel der Artemis von Ephesos: Entwurfprinzipien und Rekonstruktion*, Waldassen.

Schattner, Thomas G. 1990 *Griechische Hausmodelle, Untersuchungen zur frühgriechischen Architektur* (AM, supp. 15), Berlin.

—— 1996 'Architrav und Fries des archaischen Apollontempels von Didyma', *JdI* 111: 1–23.

—— 2001 'Griechische und großgriechisch-sizilische Hausmodelle', in Muller 2001: 161–209.

Schefold, Karl 1938–9 'Das Äolische Kapitell', *ÖJh* 31: 42–52.

—— 1992 *Gods and Heroes in Late Archaic Greek Art*, Cambridge [1st (German) ed. 1978].

Scheibler, Ingeborg 1964 'Exaleiptra', *JdI* 79: 72–108.

—— 1988 'Dreifussträger', in *Kanon: Festschrift Ernst Berger*, ed. Margot Schmidt (AntK, supp. 15): 310–16.

Schleif, Hans 1933 'Der grosse Altar der Hera von Samos', *AM* 58: 174–210.

—— 1934 'Der Zeusaltar in Olympia', *JdI* 49: 139–156.

Schleif, Hans, Rhomaios, Konstantinos, and Günther Klaffenbach 1940 *Der Artemistempel: Architektur, Dachterrakotten, Inschriften* (Korkyra. Archaische Bauten und Bildwerke 1), ed. Gerhart Rodenwaldt, Berlin.

Schliemann, Heinrich 1878 *Mycenae: A Narrative of Researches and Discoveries at Mycenae and Tiryns*, London.

Schmaltz, Bernhard 1980 'Bemerkungen zu Thermos B', *AA* 1980: 318–36.

Schmidt, Evamaria 1982 *Geschichte der Karyatide: Funktion und Bedeutung der menschlichen Träger und Stützfigur in der Baukunst*, Würzburg.

Schmidt-Colinet, Andreas 1977 *Antike Stützfiguren: Untersuchungen zu Typus und Bedeutung der menschengestaltigen Architekturstütze in der griechischen und römischen Kunst*, Frankfurt.

Schmitt Pantel, Pauline 1992 *La cité au Banquet: Histoire des repas publics dans les cités grecques*, Rome.

Schnurr, C. 1995 'Zur Topographie der Theaterstätten und der Tripodenstrasse in Athen', *Zeitschrift für Papyrologie und Epigrafik* 105: 139–53.

Schofield, Richard, and Robert Tavernor 2009 *Vitruvius: On Architecture*, trans., with introduction, London.

Scholl, Andreas 1995 'Zur Deutung der Korenhalle des Erechtheion', *JdI* 110: 179–212.

Schuller, Manfred 1985 'Die dorische Architektur der Kykladen in spätarchaischer Zeit', *JdI* 100: 319–98.

—— 1991 *Der Artemistempel im Delion auf Paros* (Denkmäler antiker Architektur 18.1), Berlin.

Schultz, Peter 2001   'The Akroteria of the Temple of Athena Nike', *Hesperia* 70: 1–47.

Schwandner, Ernst-Ludwig 1985   *Der ältere Porostempel der Aphaia auf Ägina* (Denkmäler antiker Architektur 16), Berlin.

—— 1990   'Überlegungen zur technischen Struktur und Formentwicklung archaischer Dachterrakotten', in AA.VV. 1990a: 291–300.

—— 1996   'Spáthari: Tempel ohne Säulen und Gebälk?', in AA.VV. 1996b: 48–54.

Schweitzer, Bernhard 1971   *Greek Geometric Art,* London [1st (German) ed. 1967].

Schwendemann, Karl 1921   'Der Dreifuss: Ein formen- und religionsgeschichtlicher Versuch', *JdI* 36: 98–185.

Scott, Michael C. 2007   'Putting Architectural Sculpture into its Archaeological Context: The Case of the Siphnian Tresury at Delphi', *BABesch* 82: 321–31.

Scully, Vincent 1969   *The Earth, the Temple and the Gods: Greek Sacred Architecture*, New Haven, Conn.

Seaford, Richard 1994   *Reciprocity and Ritual: Homer and Tragedy in the Developing City-State*, Oxford.

Segal, Phoebe 2007   'Soaring Votives: Anathemata in Archaic Greek Sanctuaries' (diss., Columbia University, New York).

Segal, Robert A. 1999   *Theorizing about Myth*, Amherst, Mass.

Seidl, Ursula 1996   'Urartian Furniture', in AA.VV. 1996a: 181–6.

Seiler, Florian 1986   *Die griechische Tholos*, Mainz.

Semper, Gottfried 1989   *The Four Elements of Architecture and Other Writings*, Cambridge (trans. Harry F. Mallgrave and Wolfgang Hermann from *Die Vier Elemente der Baukunst*, Braunschweig 1851).

—— 2004   *Style in the Technical and Tectonic Arts*, Los Angeles, Calif. (trans. with commentary by Harry F. Mallgrave from *Der Stil in den technischen und tektonischen Künsten*, 2nd ed. Munich, 1878 (1st ed. published in two parts 1861–3)).

Sestieri, P. Claudio 1953   Anastilosi di una colonna votiva a Posidonia, *Bollettino d'Arte* 4: 317–20.

Settis, Salvatore, ed. 1996   *I Greci: Storia, cultura, arte, società* (4 vols, 1996–2002), 1: *I Greci e noi*; 2.1: *Formazione*, Turin.

Shapiro, H. Alan 1989   *Art and Cult under the Tyrants in Athens*, Mainz.

—— 1994   *Myth into Art: Poet and Painter in Classical Greece*, London.

Sharon, Ilan 1987   'Phoenician and Greek Ashlar Construction Techniques at Tel Dor', Israel, *BASOR* 267: 21–42.

Shaw, Joseph W. 2001   'The Mystery of the Pitsidian Slab', in Böhm and von Eickstedt 2001: 137–42.

——, and Shaw, Maria C., eds 2000   *Kommos IV: The Greek Sanctuary*, 2 vols, Princeton, N.J., and Oxford.

Shaw, Maria C. 1986   'The Lion Gate Relief of Mycenae Reconsidered', in *Φίλια έπη εις Γεώργιον Ε. Μυλωνάν δια τα 60 έτη του ανασκαφικού του έργου* (trans.: 'Affectionate essays in honour of George E. Mylonas on his 60 years of excavation work'), Athens: 108–23.

Shaya, J., 2005   'The Greek Temple as Museum: The Case of the Legendary Treasure of Athena from Lindos', *AJA* 109: 423–42

Shefton, Brian B. 1989   'The Paradise Flower: A "Court Style" Phoenician Ornament: Its History in Cyprus and the Central and Western Mediterranean', in *Cyprus and the East Mediterranean in the Iron Age*, con., London, 1988, ed. Veronica Tatton-Brown, London.

—— 2000   'The "Philistine" Graves at Gezer and the White Lotus Ornament', in *Periplous: Papers on Classical Art and Archaeology presented to Sir John Boardman*, ed. G. R. Tsetskhladze *et al.*, London: 276–83.

Shiloh, Yigal 1979   *The Proto-Aeolic Capital: Israelite Ashlar Masonry* (*Qedem* 11), Jerusalem.

Shoe Meritt, Lucy 1996   'Athenian Ionic Capitals from the Athenian Agora', *Hesperia* 65: 121–74.

Simantoni-Bournias, Eva 1990   'Chian Relief Pottery and its Relationship to Chian and East Greek Architectural Terracottas', in AA.VV. 1990a: 193–200.

Simon, Christopher E. 1986   'The Archaic Votive Offerings and Cults of Ionia' (diss., University of California, Berkeley).

—— 1997   'The Archaeology of Cult in Geometric Greece: Ionian Temples, Altars, and Dedications', in AA.VV. 1997e: 125–43.

Simon, Erika 1961   *s.v.* Kypselos, Arca di, in *EAA* IV: 427–32.

Simpson, Elizabeth 2010   *The Gordion Wooden Objects: The Furniture from Tumulus MM*, 2 vols, Leiden and Boston, Mass.

Sinn, Ulrich 1981   'Das Heiligtum der Artemis Limnatis bei Kombothekra', *AM* 96: 25–71.

—— 1993   'Greek Sanctuaries as Places of Refuge', in AA.VV. 1993a: 88–109.

—— 2001   'Die Stellung des Hera-Tempels im Kultbetrieb von Olympia', in AA.VV. 2001a: 63–70.

Smith, William Robertson 1889   *Lectures on the Religion of the Semites*, Edinburgh.

Smith, William Stevenson 1965   *Interconnections in the Ancient Near East: A Study of the Relationships between the Arts of Egypt, the Aegean and Western Asia*, New Haven and London.

Snodgrass, Anthony M. 1971   *The Dark Age of Greece: An Archaeological Survey of the Eleventh to Eighth Centuries B.C.*, London.

—— 1977   *Archaeology and the Rise of the Greek State*, Cambridge.

—— 1980   *Archaic Greece: The Age of Experiment*, London.

—— 1989–90   'The Economics of Dedication at Greek Sanctuaries', *Scienze dell'antichità* 3–4: 287–94.

—— 1993   'The Rise of the Polis: The Archaeological Evidence', in AA.VV. 1993f: 30–40.

—— 1998   *Homer and the Artists: Text and Picture in Early Greek Art*, Cambridge.

Soteriades, Georgias 1900   'Excavations at Thermon' (title translated from Greek), *ArchEph*: 171–211.

Sourvinou-Inwood, Christiane 1979   'The Myth of the First Temples at Delphi', *CQ* 73: 231–51.

—— 1990   'What is *polis* Religion?', in Murray and Price 1990: 295–322.

—— 1991   *'Reading' Greek Culture: Texts and Images, Rituals and Myths*, Oxford.

—— 1993   'Early Sanctuaries, the Eighth Century and Ritual Space, Fragments of a Discourse', in AA.VV. 1993a: 1–17.

Spawforth, Tony 2006   *The Complete Greek Temples*, London.

Spini, Gherardo 1568–9   *I tre primi libri sopra l'instituzioni de' greci et latini architettori intorno agl'ornamenti che convengono a tutte le fabbriche che l'architettura compone*, Florence (transcribed in F. Borsi *et al.* 1980, *Il disegno interrotto: trattati medicei d'architettura*, Florence).

Staccioli, R. A. 1989–90   'Case o templi nei modelli votivi di edifici etrusco-italici?', *Scienze dell'Antichità* 3–4: 89–98.

Stambaugh, John E. 1978   'The Functions of Roman Temples', in *Aufstieg und Niedergang der römischen Welt* II, 16.1: 554–608.

Stampolidis, Nicholas C., ed. 2003   *Sea Routes: From Sidon to Huelva. Interconnections in the Mediterranean 16th–6th c. BC*, cat., Athens.

Starr, Chester G. 1977   *The Economic and Social Growth of Early Greece 800–500 B.C.*, New York.

—— 1986   *Individual and Community: The Rise of the Polis, 800–500 B.C.*, New York and Oxford.

—— 1991   *The Origins of Greek Civilization, 1100–650 BC*, New York [1st ed. 1961].

Steinhart, Matthias 1997   'Bemerkungen zu Rekonstruktion: Ikonographie und Inschrift des platäischen Weihgeschenkes', *BCH* 121: 33–69.

Stevens, Gorham P. 1950   'Grilles of the Hephaisteion', *Hesperia* 19: 165–73.

—— 1951   'The Poros Tripods of the Acropolis of Athens', in *Studies presented to David M. Robinson*, ed. George E. Mylonas, St Louis, Mo.: 331–4.

Stewart, Andrew 1990   *Greek Sculpture: An Exploration*, 2 vols, New Haven and London.

——, and Manolis Korres 2004   *Attalos, Athens, and the Akropolis: The Pergamene 'Little Barbarians' and their Roman and Renaissance Legacy*, Cambridge and New York.

Stewart, Peter 2003   *Statues in Roman Society*, Oxford.

Stibbe, Conrad M. 1997   'Archaic Greek Bronze Palmettes', *BABesch* 72: 37–64.

—— 2000   *The Sons of Hephaistos: Aspects of the Archaic Greek Bronze Industry*, Rome.

Stieber, Mary 2004   *The Poetics of Appearance in the Attic Korai*, Austin, Tex.

Strathmann, Cordelia 2002   *Grabkultur im antiken Lykien des 6. bis 4. Jahrhunderts v. Chr.* (EurHss 75), Frankfurt.

Strøm, Ingrid 1988   'The Early Sanctuary of the Argive Heraion and its External Relations (8th - 6th Cent. B.C.): The Monumental Architecture, *ActaArch* 59: 173–203.

—— 1992   'Evidence from the Sanctuaries', in AA.VV. 1992c: 46–60.

—— 1995   'The Early Sanctuary of the Argive Heraion and its External Relations (8th.–Early 6th. Cent. BC.): The Greek Geometric Bronzes', *Proceedings of the Danish Insitute at Athens* 1: 37–127.

—— 1998   'The Early Sanctuary of the Argive Heraion and its External Relations (8th.–Early 6th. Cent. BC.): Bronze imports and Archaic Greek Bronzes', *Proceedings of the Danish Insitute at Athens* 2: 37–126.

Strong, Donald S. 1960   'Some Early Examples of the Composite Capital', *Journal of Roman Studies* 50: 119–28.

Stuart, James, and Nicholas Revett 1762–94   *The Antiquities of Athens Measured and Delineated*, 3 vols, London.

Stucchi, Sandro 1974   'Questioni relative al tempio A di Prinias ed il formarsi degli ordini dorico e ionico', *Antichità cretesi: Studi in onore di Doro Levi* (Cronache di archeologia 12), Catania, II: 89–119.

Stucky, Rolf A. 1988   'Die Tonmetope mit den drei sitzenden Frauen von Thermos: Ein Dokument hellenistischer Denkmalpflege', *AntK* 31: 71–8.

Sulze, Heinrich 1936   'Das dorische Kapitell der Burg von Tiryns', *AA*: 14–36.

Summerson, John 1980   *The Classical Language of Architecture*, London [1st ed. 1963].

Summitt, J. B. 2000   'Greek Architectural Polychromy from the Seventh to Second Centuries B.C.: History and Significance' (diss., University of Michigan).

Svenson-Evers, Hendrik 1996   *Die griechischen Architekten archaischer und klassischer Zeit*, Frankfurt.

—— 1997   ΙΕΡΟΣ ΟΙΚΟΣ: zum Ursprung des griechischen Tempels', in AA.VV. 1997b: 132–51.

Sybel, Ludwig von 1888   *Weltgeschichte der Kunst bis zur Erbauung der Sophienkirche*, Marburg.

Tadgell, Christopher 2007   *Antiquity. Origins, Classicism and the New Rome*, Abingdon and New York.

Tanner, Jeremy 2003   'Finding the Egyptian in Early Greek Art', in *Ancient Perspectives on Egypt*, ed. Roger Matthews and Cornelia Roemer, London: 115–43.

——, and Robin Osborne 2007   *Art's Agency and Art History*, Malden, Mass., Oxford and Carlton, Victoria.

Thalmann, Susan K. 1976   'The Adyton in the Greek Temples of South Italy and Sicily' (diss., University of California, Berkeley).

Theodorescu, Dinu 1974   *Chapiteaux ioniques de la Sicile méridionale* (Cahiers du Centre Jean Bérard 1), Naples.

—— 1980   *Le Chapiteau ionique grec: Essai monographique*, Geneva.

Thiersch, Friedrich 1879   'Die Tholos des Atreus zu Mykenae', *AM* 4: 177–82.

Thompson, Homer A. 1980   'The Tomb of Clytemnestra Revisited', in *From Athens to Gordion: Papers of a Memorial Symposium for Rodney S. Young*, con., Philadephia, 1975, ed. Keith DeVries, Philadelphia, Pa.: 3–15.

Thureau-Dangin, F. *et al.* 1931   *Arslan-Tash*, Paris.

Tiverios, M. A., and D. S. Tsiaphake, 2002   *Color in Ancient Greece: The Role of Color in Ancient Greek Art and Architecture 700–31 B.C.*, Thessalonika.

Tocco, G. 2000   'Nuove ricerche nel sanctuario di Hera al Sele', in Greco and Longo 2000: 85–90.

Toker, Ayşe 1992   *Museum of Anatolian Civilizations: Metal Vessels*, Ankara.

Tölle-Kastenbein, Renate 1974   *Samos XIV: Das kastro Tigani. Die Bauten und Funde griechischer, römischer und byzantinischer Zeit*, Bonn.

—— 1993   'Das Hekatompedon auf der Athener Akropolis', *JdI* 108: 43–75.

—— 1994   *Das Olympieion in Athen*, Cologne.

Tomlinson, Richard A. 1963   'The Doric Order: Hellenistic Critics and Criticism', *JHS* 83: 133–45.

—— 1976   *Greek Sanctuaries*, London.

—— 1992   'The Menelaion and Spartan Architecture', in *ΦΙΛΟΛΑΚΩΝ: Lakonian Studies in Honour of Hector Catling*, ed. J. M. Sanders, Athens.

Touloupa, Evi 1969   'Une Gorgone en bronze de l'Acropole', *BCH* 93: 862–84.

—— 1972   'Bronzebleche von der Akropolis in Athen: Gehämmerte geometrische Dreifüße', *AM* 87: 57–76.

—— 1991   'Early Bronze Sheets with Figured Scenes from the Acropolis', in *New Perspectives in Early Greek Art* (Studies in the History of Art 32), con., Washington, 1988, ed. Diane Buitron-Oliver, Hanover and London: 241–71.

Tournavitou, Iphiyenia 1995   *The 'Ivory Houses' at Mycenae* (*BSA*, supp. 24), London and Athens.

Travlos, John 1971   *Pictorial Dictionary of Ancient Athens*, New York.

—— 1988   *Bildlexicon zur Topographie des antiken Attika*, Tübingen.

Treadwell, Lawrence 1970   'Dodona: an Oracle of Zeus' (diss,. University of Michigan).

Tsigakou, Fani-Maria 1981   *The Rediscovery of Greece: Travellers and Painters of the Romantic Era*, London.

Tuchelt, Klaus 1991   'Branchidai-Didyma: Geschichte, Ausgrabung und Wiederentdeckung eines antiken Heiligtums', *Antike Welt: Sondernummer*: 1–54.

—— 2007   'Überlegungen zum archaischen Didyma', *Frühes Ionien: Eine Bestandsaufnahme* (Milesische Forschungen 5), con., Güzelçamli, 1999, ed. Justus Cobet *et. al.*, Mainz: 393–412.

Turfa, Jean M., and Alwyn G. Steinmayer 1996   'The Comparative Structure of Greek and Etruscan Monumental Buildings', *Papers of the British School at Rome* 64: 1–39.

Tusa, Vincenzo 1969   'Due nuove metope archaiche da Selinunte', *ArchCl* 21: 153–71.

Tuzi, Stefania 2002   *Le Colonne e il Tempio di Salomone: la storia, la leggenda, la fortuna*, Rome.

Ulf, Christoph 2009   'The World of Homer and Hesiod', in AA.VV. 2009c: 81–99.

Vallois, René 1944–78   *L'Architecture hellénique et hellénistique à Délos jusqu'à l'éviction des Déliens (166 av. J.-C.)* (BEFAR 157), Paris (I: *Les Monuments* 1944; II: *Grammaire historique de l'architecture délienne,* part 1, 1966; part 2, 1978).

—— 1953   *Les Constructions antiques de Délos: Documents* (BEFAR 157), Paris.

van Baal, J. 1976   'Offering, Sacrifice and Gift', *Numen: International Review for the History of Religions* 23, Leiden: 161–78.

Vanden Berghe, Louis, and Leon De Meyer 1982   *Urartu: Een vergeten Cultuur uit het Bergland Armenië*, cat., Ghent.

Vandier J. 1955   *Manuel d'archéologie égyptienne II.2: L'Architecture religieuse et civile*, Paris.

Van Dyke, Ruth M., and Susan E. Alcock 2003   'Archaeologies of Memory: An Introduction', in *Archaeologies of Memory*, ed. Ruth M. Van Dyke and Susan E. Alcock, Oxford: 1–13.

Van Keuren, F. 1989   *The Frieze from the Hera I Temple at Foce del Sele*, Rome.

van Straten, Folkert T. 1981   'Gifts for the Gods', in AA.VV. 1981a: 65–151.

—— 1988   'The God's Portion in Greek Sacrificial Representations: Is the Tail doing Nicely?', in AA.VV. 1988a: 51–68.

—— 1992   'Votives and Votaries in Greek Sanctuaries', in AA.VV. 1992d: 247–90.

—— 1995   *Hierà Kalá: Images of Animal Sacrifice in Archaic and Classical Greece*, Leiden.

Venturi, Robert 1966   *Complexity and Contradiction in Architecture*, New York.

Verdan, Samuel 2000   'Fouilles dans le sanctuaire d'Apollon Daphnéphoros', *AntK* 43: 128–30.

Vernant, Jean-Pierre 1981   'Théorie générale du sacrifice et mise à mort dans Θυσία grecque', in AA.VV. 1981b: 1–39.

—— 1982   *The Origins of Greek Thought*, Ithaca [1st (French) ed. 1962].

Versnel, H. S. 1981   *Faith, Religious Mentality in Ancient Prayer*, in AA.VV. 1981b: 1–64

—— 2011   *Coping with the Gods: Wayward Readings in Greek Theology*, Leiden and Boston, Mass.

Verzone, Paolo 1951   'Il bronzo nella genesi del tempio greco', in *Studies presented to David M. Robinson*, ed. George E. Mylonas, St Louis, Mo.: 272–94.

Vickers, Michael 1999   *Skeumorphismus oder die Kunst, aus wenig viel zu machen*, Mainz.

Vickers, Michael, and David Gill 1994   *Artful Crafts: Ancient Greek Silverware and Pottery*, Oxford.

Vidal-Naquet, Pierre 1986   *The Black Hunter: Forms of Thought and Forms of Society in the Greek World*, Baltimore, Md. [1st (French) ed. 1981].

Vidler, Anthony 1987   *The Writing of the Walls: Architectural Theory in the Late Enlightenment*, New York.

Viel de Saint-Maux, Jean-Louis 1787   *Lettres sur l'architecture des anciens, et celle des modernes, dans lesquelles se trouve développé le génie symbolique qui présida aux monumens de l'Antiquité*, Paris.

Viollet-le-Duc, Eugène E. 1858   *Entretiens sur l'architecture*, 2 vols, Paris.

—— 1990   *The Architectural Theory of Viollet-le-Duc: Readings and Commentary, Selected Texts 1843–1879*, ed. Millard F. Hearn, Cambridge, Mass.

Vokotopoulou, Julie 1995   'Dodone et les villes de la Grande-Grèce et de la Sicile', in AA.VV. 1995b: 63–90.

Vonderstein, Mirko 2000   'Das Olympieion von Akragas: Orientalische Bauformen an einem griechischen Siegestempel?', *Jdl* 115: 37–77.

Voyatzis, Mary E. 1990   *The Early Sanctuary of Athena Alea at Tegea and Other Archaic Sanctuaries in Arcadia* (SIMA 97), Göteborg.

—— 1999   'The Role of Temple Building in Consolidating Arkadian Communities', in *Defining Ancient Arkadia* (*HfMedd* 78), con., Copenhagen, 1998, ed. Thomas H. Nielsen and James Roy, Copenhagen: 130–68.

Wace, Alan J. B. 1923   *Mycenae: Report of the Excavations of the British School at Athens, 1921–1923*, London and Athens.

—— 1932   *Chamber Tombs at Mycenae*, Oxford.

—— 1949   *Mycenae: An Archaeological History and Guide*, Princeton, N.J.

Wagner, Otto 1988   *Modern Architecture*, Santa Monica, Calif. [1st (German) ed. 1902].

Waldstein, Charles 1902–5   *The Argive Heraeum*, 2 vols., Boston, Mass.

Walter, Gabriel 1938   'Das choregische Denkmal des Thrasyllos', *JdI* 53: 34–67.

Walter, Hans 1968   *Frühe Samische Gefässe* (Samos V), Bonn.

—— 1976   *Das Heraion von Samos: Ursprung und Wandel eines griechischen Heligtums*, Munich.

—— 1990   *Das griechische Heiligtum, dargestellt am Heraion von Samos*, Stuttgart.

Walter-Karydi, Eleni 1994   'Das Thearion von Ägina: Zum Apollonkult auf Ägina', *AA*: 125–48.

Warren, Herbert L. 1919   *The Foundations of Classic Architecture*, New York.

Washburn, Oliver M. 1918   'Iphigenia Taurica 113 as a Document in the History of Architecture', *AJA* 22: 434–7.

—— 1919   'The Origin of the Triglyph Frieze', *AJA* 23: 33–49.

Watkin, David 1996   *Sir John Soane. Enlightenment Thought and the Royal Academy Lectures*, Cambridge.

—— 2000   *A History of Western Architecture*, London [1st ed. 1986].

—— 2001   *Morality and Architecture Revisited*, London [revised ed.; first published 1977 as *Morality and Architecture*].

Watrous, L. Vance 1998–9   'Crete and Egypt in the Seventh Century BC: Temple A at Prinias', in *Post-Minoan Crete.*, con., London, 1995, ed. W. G. Cavanagh *et al.*, Athens and London: 75–9.

Webb, Pamela A. 1996   *Hellenistic Architectural Sculpture: Figural Motifs in Western Anatolia and the Aegean Islands*, Madison, Wis.

Weber, Berthold F. 2002   'Die Säulenordnung des archaischen Dionysostempels von Myus', *IstMitt* 52: 221–71.

Weber, Hans 1965   'Myus. Grabung 1964', *IstMitt* 15: 43–64.

Weber, Marga 1990   *Baldachine und Statuenschreine*, Rome.

Weber, Martha 1971   'Die geometrischen Dreifußkessel: Fragen zur Chronologie der Gattungen und deren Herstellungszentren', *AM* 86: 13–30.

—— 1998   'Ein Tempelabbild in Perachora für Hera Akraia', *AA*: 365–71.

Weickenmeier, Norbert 1985   *Theorienbildung zur Genese des Triglyphon, Versuch einer Bestandsaufnahme*, Darmstadt.

Weickert, Carl 1929   *Typen der archaischen Architektur in Griechenland und Kleinasien*, Augsburg.

Weissl, Michael 2002   'Grundzüge der Bau- und Schichtenfolge im Artemision von Ephesos', *ÖJh* 71: 313–46.

Welter, Gabriel 1938   'Das choregische Denkmal des Thrasyllos', *AA* 53: 34–67.

Werner, Kjell 1993　　*The Megaron during the Aegean and Anatolian Bronze Age: A Study of Occurrence, Shape, Architectural Adaption, and Function* (SIMA 108), Jonsered.

Werner, Peter 1994　　*Die Entwicklung der Sakralarchitektur in Nordsyrien und Südostkleinasien*, Munich.

Wescoat, Bonna D. 2005　　'Buildings for Votive Ships on Delos and Samothrace', in *Architecture and Archaeology in the Cyclades: Papers in Honour of J. J. Coulton*, ed. Maria Stampatopolou and Marina Yeroulanou, Oxford: 153–72.

—— 2012　　*The Temple of Athena at Assos*, Oxford.

Wesenberg, Burkhardt 1971　　*Kapitelle und Basen: Beobachtungen zur Entstehung der griechischen Säulenform* (*Bonner Jahrbücher* 32), Düsseldorf.

—— 1982　　'Thermos B1', *AA*: 149–57.

—— 1983　　*Beiträge zur Rekonstruktion griechischer Architektur nach literarischen Quellen* (*AM* Beiheft 9), Berlin.

—— 1986　　'Vitruvs Vorstellung von der Entstehung des dorischen Triglyphenfrieses', in *Studien zur klassischen Archäologie: F. Hiller zu seinem 60. Geburtstag*, Saarbrücken: 143–57.

—— 1994　　*s.v.* 'Capitello', in *EAA*, 2nd supplement, I, 852–8.

—— 1996　　'Die Entstehung der griechischen Säulen- und Gebälkformen in der literarischen Überlieferung der Antike', in AA.VV. 1996b: 1–15.

—— 2001　　'B. M. 1206 und die Rekonstruktion der *columnae caelatae* des jüngeren Artemision', in Muss 2001: 297–314.

—— 2008　　'Pro Vitruvio – iterum: zur mimetischen Formengenese in der griechischen Architektur', in AA.VV. 2008a: 185–97.

West, Martin L. 1971　　*Early Greek Philosophy and the Orient*, Oxford.

—— 1997　　*The East Face of Helicon: West Asiatic Elements in Greek Poetry and Myth*, Oxford.

—— 2011　　*The Making of The Iliad*, Oxford.

White, Donald 1971　　'The Cyrene Sphinx, its Capital and its Column', *AJA* 75: 47–55.

Whitley, James 1991a　　*Style and Society in Dark Age Greece: The changing Face of a Pre-literate Society 1100–700 BC*, Cambridge.

—— 1991b　　'Social Diversity in Dark Age Greece', *BSA* 86: 341–65.

—— 2001　　*The Archaeology of Ancient Greece*, Cambridge and New York.

Whittaker, Hélène 1997　　*Mycenaean Cult Buildings: A Study of their Architecture and Function in the Context of the Aegean and the Eastern Mediterranean*, Bergen.

Whyte, William 2006　　'How do Buildings mean? Some Issues of Interpretation in the History of Architecture', *History and Theory* 45: 153–77.

Wiebenson, Dora 1969　　*Sources of Greek Revival Architecture*, London.

Wiegand, Theodor 1904　　*Die archaische Poros-Architektur der Akropolis zu Athen*, Cassel and Leipzig.

—— 1915　　*Der Poseidonaltar bei Kap Monodendri* (Milet I, 4), Berlin.

—— 1941　　*Didyma*, Berlin.

Wiegartz, Hans 1994　　'Äolische Kapitelle: Neufunde 1992 und ihr Verhältnis zu den bekannten Stücken', in *Neue Forschungen zu Neandria und Alexandria Troas* (Asia Minor Studien 11), ed. E. Schwertheim and H. Wiegartz, Bonn: 117–32.

Wiencke, Martha H. 2000　　*Lerna IV.1: The Architecture, Stratification, and Pottery of Lerna III*, Princeton, N.J.

Wigand, Karl 1912　　'Thymiateria', *Bonner Jahrbücher* 122: 1–97.

Wightman, G. J. 2007　　*Sacred Spaces. Religious Architecture in the Ancient World*, Leuven.

Wikander, Örjan 1988　　'Ancient Roof-tiles: Use and Function', *OpAth* 17: 203–16.

—— 1990　　'Archaic Roof Tiles: The First Generations', in AA.VV. 1990a: 285–90.

—— 1992　　'Archaic Roof Tiles: The First Generation?', *OpAth*: 151–61.

Will, Édouard 1956　　*Doriens et Ioniens*, Paris and Strasbourg.

Willemsen, Franz 1955　　'Der Delphische Dreifuss', *JdI* 70: 85–104.

—— 1957　　*Dreifusskessel von Olympia: Alte und neue Funde* (OlForsch 3), Berlin.

Williams, Charles K. 1984　　'Doric Architecture and Early Capitals in Corinth', *AM* 99: 67–75.

—— 1988　　'Corinthian Trade in Roof Tiles', in AA.VV. 1988d: 227–30.

Williams, Charles K., and Nancy Bookidis, eds 2003　　*Corinth, the Centenary 1896–1996* (Corinth 20), Athens.

Williams, Dyfri 1982　　'Aegina, Aphaia-Tempel. IV: The Inscription Commemorating the Construction of the First Limestone Temple and Other Features of the Sixth Century Temenos', *AA* 1982: 55–68.

Wilson, Peter 2000　　*The Athenian Institution of the Khoregia. The Chorus, the City and the State*, Cambridge and New York.

Wilson Jones, Mark 2000a　　*Principles of Roman Architecture*, New Haven and London.

—— 2000b　　'Doric Measure and Architectural Design, I: The Evidence of the Relief from Salamis', *AJA* 104: 73–93.

—— 2001　　'Doric Measure and Architectural Design, II: A Modular Reading of the Classical Temple', *AJA* 105: 675–713.

—— 2002a　　'Tripods, Triglyphs and the Origin of the Doric Frieze', *AJA* 106: 353–90.

—— 2002b 'Doric Figuration', in *Body and Building: Essays on the Changing Relation of Body and Architecture*, ed. Robert Tavernor and George Dodds, Cambridge, Mass.: 64–77.

2006 'Ancient Architecture and Mathematics: Methodology and the Doric Temple', *Nexus: Architecture and Mathematics* 6: 1–20.

—— 2014 'The Origins of the Orders: Unity in Multiplicity', in *Tributes to Pierre du Prey: Architecture and the Classical Tradition, from Pliny to Posterity*, ed. Matthew M. Reeve, Tournhout and New York.

Winckelmann, Johann J. 1762 *Anmerkungen über die Baukunst der Alten*, Leipzig.

—— 2006 *History of the Art of Antiquity* (trans. Harry F. Mallgrave), Los Angeles [*Geschichte der Kunst des Alterthums*, Dresden 1764].

Winter, Nancy A. 1990 'Defining Regional Styles in Archaic Greek Architectural Terracottas', in AA.VV. 1990a, 13–32

—— 1993 *Greek Architectural Terracottas from the Prehistoric to the End of the Archaic Period*, Oxford.

—— 2000 'The Early Roofs of Etruria and Greece', in AA.VV. 2000b: 251–6.

Wood, John 1741 *The Origin of Building; or, the Plagiarism of the Heathens Detected*, Bath [reprinted 1968].

Wotschnitzky, Alfons 1948 'Zum korinthischen Kapitell im Apollontempel zu Bassae', *ÖJh* 37: 53–80.

Wright, George R. H. 2000 *Ancient Building Technology*, Leiden.

Wright, James C. 1982 'The Old Temple Terrace at the Argive Heraeum and the Early Cult of Hera in the Argolid', *JHS* 102: 186–201.

Wurz, Erwin 1913 *Der Ursprung der kretisch-mykenischen Säulen*, Munich.

——, and Reinhold Wurz 1925 *Die Entstehung der Säulenbasen des Altertums unter Berücksichtigung verwandter Kapitelle*, Heidelberg.

Wurz, Reinhold 1914 *Spirale und Volute: Von der Vorgeschichtlichen Zeit bis zum Ausgang des Altertums*, Munich.

Yalouris, Nicholas 1995 'Fondements communs des sanctuaires panhelléniques', in AA.VV. 1995b: 11–26.

Yavis, Constantine G. 1949 *Greek Altars: Origins and Typology*, St. Louis, Mo.

Younés, Samir 1999 *The True, the Fictive and the Real: The Historical Dictionary of Architecture of Quatremère de Quincy*, London.

Young, Philip H. 1980 'Building Projects and Archaic Greek Tyrants' (diss., University of Pennsylvania).

Young, Rodney S. 1956 'The Campaign of 1955 at Gordion: Preliminary Report', *AJA* 60: 249–66.

—— 1962 'Gordion: Phrygian Construction and Architecture' (*Expedition* IV, 4), Philadelphia: 2–12.

Zaccagnini, Carlo 1988 'Divisione della carne a Nuzi', in AA.VV. 1988b: 87–96.

Zaccagnini, Cristiana 1998 *Il thymiaterion nel mondo greco. Analisi delle fonti, tipologia, impieghi*, Rome.

Zambas, K. 2002 *Οι Εκλεπτύνσεις των Κιόνων του Παρθενώνος* (trans.: 'The Refinements of the Columns of the Parthenon'), Athens.

Zancani Montuoro, Paola 1940 'La Struttura del Fregio Dorico', *Palladio* 4: 49–64.

——, Ugo Zanotti-Bianco and Friedrich Krauss 1954 *Heraion alla Foce del Sele*, II: *Il primo Thesauros: L'architettura*, Rome.

Zimansky, Paul E. 1998 *Ancient Ararat: A Handbook of Urartian Studies*, Delmar, N.Y.

Zwickel, Wolfgang 1986 'Die Kesselwagen im Salomonischen Tempel', *Ugarit-Forschungen* 18: 459–61.

—— 1999 *Der Salomonische Tempel*, Mainz am Rhein.

ILLUSTRATION CREDITS

FREQUENTLY USED SOURCES

AUTHOR: endpapers; p. xiii; 0.1; 1.9; 1.16; 2.1; 2.2; 2.30; 2.36; 3.5; 3.7; 3.14; 4.7 left; 4.20; 5.4; 5.5; 5.8; 5.20; 6.6; 6.7; 7.21; 8.6: Wilson Jones 2002b, fig. 4.4; 8.7: Wilson Jones 2002a, fig. 16; 8.11; 8.14 bottom: Wilson Jones 2002a, fig. 12; 9.1; 10.4.

GEORG HERDT: 1.11: after Walter 1965, Abb. 33, 47, 86; 2.8: after publications in the notes to Table 2; 2.25: after publications in the notes to Table 3; 2.26: after publications in the notes to Table 5; 2.32; 3.19: after publications in the notes to Table 3; 3.20a and b: after Schleif et al. 1940, Abb. 70, 60; 3.20c: after Demangel 1923, pl. 13; 3.20d: after Degrassi 1981; 3.20e and f: after Mertens 1993, Abb. 13; 3.21a: after Nils Hellner; 3.21b: after Wesenberg 1971, Abb.104; 3.21c: after Mertens 2006, fig. 164; 3.21d: after Mertens 2006, fig. 152; 3.21e: after Rhomaios 1952, p. 10; 3.21f: after Mertens 1993, Abb. 63; 3.25: after publications in the notes to Table 3; 3.30; 4.18: after Akurgal 1968, fig. 43; Wesenberg 1971, Abb. 211, 191; 229; 4.22 and 4.27: after publications in the notes to Table 4.2; 4.28a: after British Museum website; 4.28b: after Akurgal 2001, fig. 209; 4.28c: after Herrmann, H.-V. 1972a, Taf. 65.1; 4.28d: after Niemeyer 1970, Taf. 21; 4.28e: after Barnett 1957, Pl. 74, s 210; 4.28f: after Akurgal 2001, fig. 195; 4.28g: after Akurgal 1968, fig. 44; 4.28h: after Barnett 1957, pl. 77, s 236; 5.9: after Gruben 1997, Abb.40; Mertens 2006, fig. 35, 533; 5.12a: after Gruben 1996, Abb. 4; 5.12b: after Gruben 1993, Abb. 3; 5.12c: after Ohnesorg 1996, Abb. 1; 5.12d: after Martin 1973, fig. 3; 5.12e: after Ohnesorg 1996, Abb. 5; 5.12f: after Herrmann, K. 1996, Abb. 1; 5.17; 5.18; 5.19; 5.21; 5.22: Aigina: own reconstruction using Hoffelner 1996, Abb. 1; Naxos: own reconstruction; Corfu: own reconstruction using Rodenwaldt 1938, Taf. 1; Aigina, column: Gruben 1965, Abb. 79; Aigina, temple, after Hoffelner 1996, Taf. 60, with modified height; Delphi: Gruben 1996, Abb. 18; Naxos, temple: after Gruben 1996, Abb. 18 and Gruben 1997, Abb. 2b; Samos, temple: Hendrich 2007, Abb. 19; Samos: own reconstruction using Kienast 1985, Abb. 15; Cyrene: White 1971; Ephesos, temple: Gruben 1996, Abb. 17; Ugento: Degrassi 1981, fig. 10 with modified height; Athens: own reconstruction using Korres 1997, fig. 2; Samos, temple: Gruben 1996: Abb. 17; Olympia: Herrmann, K. 1984, Abb. 3; Kalaureia: Pakkanen 2010, Fig. 7; Priene: Gruben 1996, Abb. 17; 9.9a: after Durm 1881, pl. opposite p. 118; 9.9b: after DAI, Athens, neg. Mykenai 37; 9.9c: after von Filseck 1986; 9.9d and e: after Cambitoglou 1988 (see here Fig. 2.10); 9.9f: after Wilson Jones 2002a; 9.9g: after Kähler 1949, fig. on p.42; 9.9h: after DAI Athens, neg. Samos 852; 9.12: after Korres and Bouras 1983, fig. on p. 23.

MAXIM ATAYANTS: pp. ii, viii, xii; 0.9; 1.1; 1.12; 1.24; 3.27; 5.1; 5.2; 5.26; 6.2; 6.5; 6.11; 6.15; 6.25; 6.26; 7.15; 7.18; 7.19; 8.20; 9.7; 9.11; 9.13.

MANOLIS KORRES: 1.3; 1.22; 2.33 top (Gruben 1997, Abb. 2a); 3.15; 3.16; 5.6; 7.11; 7.20; 8.16 (Touloupa 1993); 9.8 (Korres 1993, fig 22).

ÉCOLE NATIONALE SUPÉRIEURE DES BEAUX-ARTS, PARIS: pp. iv–v, x; 2.35; 6.13; 7.2; 7.14; 10.1.

DIETER MERTENS AND MARGARETA SCHUTZENBERGER: 1.2 (Mertens 2006, fig. 269); 3.23 (Mertens 1993, Abb. 54b, 56b); 3.30 (Mertens 1993, Taf. 45); 3.31.

DAI, ATHENS: 1.4: neg. Hege 526; 3.12; 4.5: neg. Mykenai 37; 4.12: neg. 69/627; 5.10; 6.21: neg. Elefsis 338; 8.4 left: neg. 74/115; 8.4 right: inv. B 1730, neg. OL 2032; 8.9 left: neg. 72/3751: 8.9 centre: inv. B 1421, neg. OL 1929; 8.9 right: inv. B 5768, neg. 72/3727; 8.12 (Samos 852); 9.5: Hege 1554.

AMERICAN SCHOOL OF CLASSICAL STUDIES, ATHENS, ALISON FRANTZ COLLECTION: 1.6; 2.16 bottom; 4.3 centre; 4.8; 6.4.

NATIONAL MUSEUM, ATHENS: 2.22 bottom; 4.7 right; 4.31; 5.14; 5.15; 6.18 (inv. 2308); 6.22 (inv. 1052); 8.14a (inv. 17874).

BRITISH MUSEUM: 4.21 (inv. 1856,0512.10, also B 49); 4.30 top (inv. 1848, 0720.13); 6.20 (inv. 1837,0609.85, also 558); 7.7: (inv. 1860,0404.1); 7.9 (inv. ME 124920); 7.10 (inv. GR 1920.5-29.2); 8.3 (inv. 1843,1103.76, also E 163); 9.6 (inv. 1994,0127.1).

REMAINING ILLUSTRATIONS SEQUENTIALLY

Half-title: FRGV, Taf. 140; p. xi: Collection of Sue Ann Kahn (from Eugene J. Johnson and Michael, J. Lewis, *Drawn from the Source: The Travel Sketches of Louis I. Kahn* (Cambridge, Mass., 1996), pl. 9, cat. no. 59); 0.2: Départment des Arts Graphiques, Louvre, Paris (inv. 3460); 0.3: Perrault 1683, pl. 1; 0.4: Laugier 1955 (2nd edition), frontispiece of the second edition [1755]; 0.5: Soane Museum, London (inv. 13/7/10); 0.6: Semper 1861-3 (separate illustrations compiled by Georg Herdt); 0.7: Riegl 1893, figs 31 and 32; 0.8: Codex Magliabechiano, National Library, Florence, II.I. 141, fol. 33v; 0.10: Royal Academy, London (inv. 03/4195).

CHAPTER 1 1.5: David Scahill; 1.7: Marinatos, N. 1988, fig. 2; 1.8: Museo Nazionale Etrusco di Villa Giulia, Rome; 1.10 top: Schleif

1933, Abb. 33; **1.10 bottom:** Walter 1965, Abb. 65; **1.13:** Furtwängler 1890, Tafelband IV.1, Taf. 115; IV.2, Taf. 47 (composed by Georg Herdt); **1.14:** Medelhavsmuseet, Stockholm (photo: Ove Kaneberg); **1.15:** Museo Nazionale Etrusco di Villa Giulia, Rome; **1.17:** Stewart 1990, fig. 60, drawn by Candace Smith; **1.19:** David Scahill; **1.20:** Gruben 1997, Abb. 3; **1.21:** Leipen 1971, fig. 60; **1.23:** Papanikolaou 2012, II, fig. 46; **1.25:** Krischen 1938, Taf. 39; **1.26:** Sarah Walker.

CHAPTER 2   **2.3:** Durm 1910, Abb. 13 (Lion Gate); **2.4:** Durm 1910 (Tiryns plan), Abb. 20; **2.5:** Maran 2000, Abb. 1; **2.6:** Popham et al 1993, Pl. 28, fig. 1; **2.7a:** Krause 1981, fig. 7; **2.7b and c:** Auberson 1968, Pls IV and V; **2.9:** compiled by Georg Herdt: 2.9 (1): Athens, NM (inv. 16684), Payne 1940, pl. 9b; 2.9 (2): Athens, NM (inv. 15131), Oikonomos 1931, fig. 15; 2.9 (3): Vathy Museum (inv. C 25), Schattner 1990, cat. 26; 2.9 (4): Vathy Museum (inv. C 8), Schattner 1990, cat. 38; 2.9 (5): Schattner 1990, Taf. 24; 2.9 (6): Catling, R. 1994; 2.9 (7): Georg Herdt (cf. Gadolou 2011); 2.9 (8): Schattner 1990, Abb. 38; 2.9 (9): Ferri 1948; **2.10:** Cambitoglou 1988 (a: pl. 205b, b: pl. 199b, c: pl. 233b, d: pl. 265b); **2.11:** Mertens 2006, fig. 126 (with addition by Georg Herdt); **2.12:** Stewart 1990, fig. 15, drawn by Candace Smith; **2.13:** Nils Hellner; **2.14:** Kolia 2011, fig. 46; **2.15:** Beyer 1976, Taf. 44.2; **2.16a:** Lawrence 1967, fig. 50; **2.17:** Winter 1990; fig. 4 and fig. 2; **2.18:** Robin Rhodes and Philip Saperstein; **2.19:** Kawerau and Soteriadis, 1902–8, Taf. 49; **2.20:** Mallwitz 1981, p. 84; **2.21:** Greco 2000, figs 144, 146; **2.22 top:** Hampe and Jantzen 1937, Taf. 34; **2.22 centre:** Furtwängler 1890, IV.1, Taf. 40; **2.23:** Broneer 1971, fig. 54 (drawn by W. B. Dinsmoor, Jnr.); **2.24:** Broneer 1971, figs 41 and 42; **2.27:** Mallwitz 1982, Abb.1; **2.28:** Hoffelner 1996, Abb. 1; **2.29:** Hoffelner 1999, Abb. 23, Taf. 59; **2.31:** Rodenwaldt 1938, Abb. 37; **2.33** (except top): Gruben 1997, Abb. 2a; **2.34:** Ohnesorg 2007, Taf. 38 (Aenne Ohnesorg and Irene Ring, emending Krischen 1938, Taf. 33, drawn by Walter Karnapp).

CHAPTER 3   **3.1:** Soane Museum, London (inv. P74.); **3.2:** Soane Museum, London (inv. 23/4/8); **3.3:** Durm 1910, Abb. 233; **3.4:** Viollet-le-Duc 1864, Pl. 1; **3.6:** FRGV, Taf. 3-5; **3.8:** Hirt 1809, Pl. II,4; **3.9:** Viollet-le-Duc 1864, Pl. 2; **3.10 top:** Hoepfner 1991, Abb. 2; **3.10 bottom:** Hodge 1960, fig. 4; **3.11:** Travlos 1971, fig. 645; **3.13 top left:** Schleif et al. 1940, Abb. 49; **3.13 top right, bottom left** and **bottom right:** Orsi 1919, figs 255, 250, 261 (compiled by Georg Herdt); **3.17:** Museo Nazionale Etrusco di Villa Giulia, Rome; **3.18:** Mertens 1993, 125, Abb. 74; **3.22:** DAI, Rome (cf. Mertens 1993, Taf. 28.2); **3.24:** Schwandner 1985, frontispiece; **3.26 top:** Herrmann 1976, Abb. 1 and 4; **3.26 bottom:** Durm 1910; **3.28:** Hittorff 1870, Pl. 82 (courtesy of the Canadian Centre for Architecture); **3.29:** Gruben 1996, Abb. 5.

CHAPTER 4   **4.1:** Marvin Trachtenberg; **4.2:** Jones 1856, Pl. VI (composed by Georg Herdt); **4.3a:** Metropolitan Museum, New York (inv. 17.10.1a); **4.4 top:** Wace 1923, fig. 51; **4.4 bottom:** Durm 1910, Abb. 47; **4.6 left:** Erik Østby; **4.6 right:** Marvin Trachtenberg; **4.9:** P&C VI (1894), figs 315 (drawn C. Chipiez) and 316 (drawn H. Durm); **4.10:** Oriental Institute of the University of Chicago (inv. E14089);

4.11: Durm 1910, Abb. 4; **4.13:** Furtwängler 1890 (composed by Georg Herdt); **4.14:** Markoe 1985, G3, p. 316; **4.15:** Barnett 1957, Pl. 34; **4.16:** Karageorghis, 1973-1974, Plate B; **4.17:** Krischen 1956, Taf. 14; **4.19:** Harrison and Osborne 2012, fig. 3; **4.23:** Akurgal 1981, Abb. 6-9; **4.24:** Wesenberg 1971, Abb. 160, 161; **4.25:** Betancourt 1977, fig. 42; **4.26:** P&C VII (1898) (a, e and f: Pl. 52; b, c and d: Pl. 53) (composed by Georg Herdt); **4.29a:** Haines 1971, Pl. 118; **4.29b and c:** Andrae 1943, Abb. 182-3; **4.30 bottom:** Israel Museum, Jerusalem; **4.32:** Sakellarakis and Sapouna-Sakellaraki 1997, vol. 2, fig. 841; **4.33:** University of Munich, photographic collection; **4.34:** Doumas 1992, fig. 55, 56, 50.

CHAPTER 5   **5.3:** Mertens 2006, fig. 244; **5.7:** Wescoat 2010, fig. 13; **5.11:** Haines 1971; **5.13:** Matthäus 1985, Taf. 90, 92, 96, 97, 100; **5.16:** Gruben 1960; **5.23:** Gruben 1996, Abb. 29; **5.24:** Gruben 1997, Abb. 40; **5.25:** Mertens 1977, Abb. 9.

CHAPTER 6   **6.1:** Museum of Fine Arts, Boston (inv. 03.804); **6.3:** Dimopoulou-Rethemiotaki 2005; **6.8:** Krischen 1938, Taf. 40; **6.9:** Cooper 1996, IV, pl. 49; **6.10:** Mallwitz 1981a, Abb. 109, Taf. 37; **6.12:** Mertens 1993, Taf. 71,6; **6.14:** Chrysanthos Kanellopoulos; **6.16:** Fréart de Chambray 1650, 63; **6.17:** Billot 1993, fig. 9 and 11; **6.19 right:** Amy, Seyrig and Will 1975, fig. 42; **6.19 (except right):** David Scahill; **6.23:** Homolle 1917 (composed by Georg Herdt); **6.24:** Wilson Jones 2000, fig. 7.15.

CHAPTER 7   **7.1:** Seipel 2008 (1-9: figures on pages 148, 145, 148, 149, 175, 146, 151, 164, 184 (courtesy of Ulrike Muss, composed by Georg Herdt)); **7.3:** Metropolitan Museum, New York (inv. 24.97.25); **7.4:** Brock 1957, Pl. 117; **7.5a:** Museum of Fine Arts, Boston (inv. 08.281); **7.5b:** Hoffelner 1996, Abb. 4; **7.5c:** Hoffelner 1999, Taf. 58; **7.5d:** Mertens 2006, fig. 125; **7.6 top:** P&C IX (1912), fig. 233 (drawn Conze); **7.6 bottom:** Papastamos 1971 (composed Georg Herdt); **7.8:** Barker 1966, fig. 422 (after Monumenti inediti 1829-1833, I, pl. 52); **7.12:** École Française, Athens, neg. 22.351; **7.13:** Merhav 1991, fig. on p. 203; **7.16:** Kienast 1985, Abb. 15, 16; **7.17:** Walter 1965, Abb. 72; **7.22:** Hittorff 1870, Pl. 74 (courtesy of the Canadian Centre for Architecture).

CHAPTER 8   **8.1:** Museo Archeologico Regionale, Agrigento (inv. 4668); **8.2:** Museum of Art, Toledo, Ohio (inv. 72.54; cf. CVA, USA 17, Toledo 1); **8.5:** Schwendermann 1921 (composed Georg Herdt); **8.8:** Schofield 2007, fig. 89; **8.10:** Mertens 1993, Taf. 73,2; **8.13:** CVA France 16 (Paris 1945), fig. on p.11; **8.15:** Louvre, Paris (inv. MNB 579, photo by M. and P. Chuzeville); **8.17:** FRGV, pl. 144; **8.18:** Papalexandrou 2008, fig. 13; **8.19:** Soprintendenza Archeologica per la Toscana (Florence; inv. 1413), Gabinetto Fotografico, neg. 28868.

CHAPTER 9   **9.2:** Museum of Fine Arts, Boston (inv. 61.195); **9.3:** Blondel 1675–83, frontispiece to Part 2; **9.4:** Koenigs 1996, Abb. 1, 2, 4; **9.10:** P&C VI (1894), fig. 309.

CHAPTER 10   **10.2:** Allard Peirson Museum, Amsterdam (inv. 25790); **10.3:** Blondel 1675–83, frontispiece to part 2.

INDEX